PUBLIC UTILITY ECONOMICS

PRENTICE-HALL INTERNATIONAL, INC., *London*
PRENTICE-HALL OF AUSTRALIA, PTY., *Sydney*
PRENTICE-HALL OF CANADA, LTD., *Toronto*
PRENTICE-HALL FRANCE, S.A.R.L., *Paris*
PRENTICE-HALL OF INDIA (PRIVATE) LIMITED, *New Delhi*
PRENTICE-HALL OF JAPAN, INC., *Tokyo*
PRENTICE-HALL DE MEXICO, S.A., *Mexico City*

PUBLIC UTILITY ECONOMICS

PAUL J. GARFIELD, Ph.D.

Economist, Foster Associates, Inc.
Washington, D.C.

WALLACE F. LOVEJOY, Ph.D.

Associate Professor of Economics,
Southern Methodist University
Dallas, Texas

PRENTICE-HALL, INC., *Englewood Cliffs, New Jersey*

Library of Congress Catalog Card Number: 64–10255

Printed in the United States of America: C–73936

To Professor Martin G. Glaeser

PREFACE

This book reflects the combined efforts of a practicing economist, formerly a university teacher, and a professor of economics currently engaged in university teaching and research. The textbook resulting from this joint effort is intended for use by students in universities and in the training programs of commissions and utilities. Its basic approach is institutional; its emphasis is upon problems and an economic analysis of public policy in problem areas.

Each chapter has been organized on the basis of separate sections and subsections, each bearing its own topic heading. The topic headings and subheadings provide a natural outline of the substantive material. The categorizing of the individual topics and subtopics in each chapter is intended to assist the instructor in assigning specific portions of any given chapter while excluding others. Subdividing the material in this way is intended to facilitate the organization of course work to suit the particular needs of individual instructors. At a few places in the text, some duplication may be observed. This reflects the objective of making each chapter stand on its own feet to the extent reasonably possible.

Predecessor authors of textbooks in this field have done their work well. Thus, no particularly useful function would be served if this volume merely updated by a few years and replowed the same ground. Whatever merit this book may have lies in its use of some new, or heretofore unused, materials and concepts in the exposition of traditional subjects and in its development of newer problem areas in this field of study.

The authors believe that some new light may be cast usefully on such diverse, but established, areas of study as the public utility concept, the economics of natural monopoly, the regulation of hydroelectric projects, the problems and economics of municipal water utilities and urban mass transportation systems, among others. Because pricing is the central problem in economics, this subject has been given a prominent place and expanded treatment in the discussion. A primary emphasis has been placed upon newer problem areas, particularly the diverse relationships between utilities and regulatory policy, on one hand, and the fuel, energy and technology sectors of the U.S. economy, on the other.

In this respect, the postwar emergence of natural gas as a national fuel has been made a focal point of major interest, with particular attention devoted to the economic and rate making problems affecting the three regulated industries comprising the overall natural gas industry. First, the natural gas pipeline industry is now the sixth largest in the United States, having grown enormously since World War II. The economic development, regulation and rate problems of this industry comprise a study area of major importance, heretofore generally unavailable to the reader in this field. Second, the general availability of natural gas, made possible by the new pipeline network, has done much to restore to health the once declining gas distribution industry. This segment of the natural gas industry has achieved new vigor by becoming the premier fuel supplier for space heating and an important supplier of industrial fuel. Third, since 1954, the Federal Power Commission has been contending with the problems of regulating the prices charged by producers of natural gas for sales to interstate pipelines. Because natural gas producers are also oil producers, this area of regulation presents new problems that are unique and particularly challenging. An effort has been made, overall, to link the postwar emergence of natural gas to the energy economy in general and to interfuel competition in particular.

Other areas of instructional interest include: a thorough review of administrative procedure and review, which we have found to be an indispensable foundation block in teaching a course in this subject; an analysis of the problems in public utility labor relations, a matter of greater than average importance in the utility industries because of the public necessity of a continuous flow of utility services; a survey of the developing problems in the areas where utility regulatory policies and antitrust policies overlap; an exposition of the problems in the dual regulation of telephone rates; and the regulatory policies of the Atomic Energy Commission, which directly affect some public utilities and large segments of the general public. In the interest of the beginning reader, the coverage of rates and rate making is concluded with a case study, selected on the basis of the breadth of the topics reviewed and the opportunity for classroom discussion it provides with respect to the operation of the regulatory process.

Two traditionally important areas of study have been treated somewhat differently than in earlier works in this field. These are the history of the respective utility industries and public ownership. Instead of developing these subjects separately, their coverage has been woven into the overall discussion of particular topics. Thus, historical matter has been employed as a foundation for the discussion of the public utility concept, natural monopoly, present day concepts of the rate base and rate of return, pricing practices, the growing importance of energy in the economy, and the regulation of corporate concentration as well as other topics. To the extent that public ownership creates special situations, it is discussed as part of such general topics as the appropriate pricing, taxing and financing techniques, the scope of state regulatory authority, and the unique problems in labor relations. In particular, attention has been devoted to the role of public ownership in the water and urban transit utility industries. In addition, there is public ownership of public utility functions which are subordinate to regional planning and resource development objectives. A discussion of this rests upon the theories of economic growth and development which are clearly beyond the scope of this study.

The authors acknowledge with gratitude the generous assistance of many others. In addition to those who responded to our requests for information, some three dozen or more busy people took the time to honor our requests for critical analysis of different parts of the manuscript in its various stages of preparation. They include our present and former university colleagues, professional associates in the fields of law, accounting, engineering and economics, and staff specialists in some of the regulatory commissions. In all, however, the authors must, and do, accept full responsibility for any errors. The views expressed, of course, are our own. The librarians and those in charge of public records were particularly helpful. Their kind cooperation was indispensable. Those who helped to produce this manuscript were unfailingly attentive to detail, for which we are most grateful.

Professor Martin G. Glaeser, ever generous with his students and in countless ways, has us lastingly in his debt. Although the weekends, evenings and "vacations" that went into this book were ours, the guiding principles essentially are his. For reasons only suggested here we respectfully dedicate this work to Professor Glaeser. His concepts of constructive public utility regulation, on behalf of all sectors of the public interest, we believe to be the best guide to effective public policy.

We are indebted to Professor Martin T. Farris of Arizona State University for his constructive comments and criticisms in his review of the draft of the manuscript. As was noted above, the facts and views presented are the responsibility of the authors. Our families and our editor, Alfred W. Goodyear, did much to make this book possible by their patience and understanding.

Paul J. Garfield
Washington, D.C.

Wallace F. Lovejoy
Dallas, Texas

TABLE OF CONTENTS

Part I INTRODUCTION AND BACKGROUND

1. The Public Utility Concept 1

Public Utilities: A Separate Business Category, 1; Public Utilities Defined and Enumerated, 2; Development of the Public Utility Concept, 3: *Early origins,* 3; *Munn v. Illinois,* 5; *Subsequent court decisions,* 8; The Paths to Public Utility Status, 11; Rights and Duties of Public Utilities, 12; The Significance of Public Utilities in the American Economy, 13.

2. Economic Characteristics of Public Utilities 15

Natural Monopoly, 15; The Economics of Supply Under Natural Monopoly, 16; The Demand for Public Utility Services, 19; Public Utility Pricing Policy, 22; Large Capital Investment Required, 22; The Operating Ratio, 24; Debt Ratio, 25; Dividend-Payout Ratios, 26; Comparative Profitability, 26.

3. The Development and Scope of Utility Regulation 27

Judicial Regulation, 27; Direct Legislative Regulation, 27; Local Regulation by Franchise, 28: *The duration of franchises,* 29; *Franchise terms,* 30; *Weaknesses of franchise regulation,* 31; *The present extent of franchise regulation,* 31; State Commission Regulation, 32: *An introduction to the state commissions,* 32; *Development of state utility commissions,* 32; *Current status of state regulation,* 34; Federal Regulation, 34: *Electricity and natural gas,* 35; *Telephone and telegraph,* 35; *Holding companies,* 35.

4. Administrative Procedure and Review 36

Rule Making, 37; Adjudication of Contested Cases, 38: *Starting a case,* 38; *Notice,* 38; *Hearing,* 38; *Decision,* 39; Judicial Review, 40: *Scope of review,* 41; *The Ben Avon rule,* 42.

Part II THE ESSENTIALS OF RATE REGULATION

5. The Regulation of Operating Expenses 44

The Cost of Service Concept, 44; The Bases of Operating Expense Regulation, 46; Measures of Reasonable Expenses, 48; Policies Toward Specific Operating Expenses, 50: *Allowance for future increases in expenses,* 50; *Atomic power research and development expenses,* 50; *Salary and wage costs,* 51; *Pension costs,* 51; *Payments to affiliates for services and supplies,* 51; *Sales promotion and advertising expenses,* 53; *Rate case expenses,* 53; *Expenses of adjusting customers' gas appliances,* 54; *Political and lobbying expenses,* 54; *Uncollectible bills,* 54; *Charitable contributions,* 55; *Public utility merchandising expenses,* 55.

6. The Rate Base 56

Introduction, 56; Rate-Base Methods, 58: *Actual cost methods,* 60; *Reproduction cost new,* 62; *Fair value,* 65; The Supreme Court and Rate Base, 65: *The judicial phase,* 66; *The beginning of the administrative phase,* 69; The Allowance for Working Capital, 71; Some Rate-Base Exclusions, 71; State Commission Valuation Policies After the Hope Case, 73: *Actual-cost states,* 74; *Fair-value states,* 75; Rate-Base Policies of Federal Agencies, 78; When Is a Rate Base Required? 79: *Economic characteristics determine regulatory method,* 79; *Traditional utilities: rate base required,* 81; *Urban transit, an important exception,* 82.

7. Valuation Procedures 83

The Appraisal Process, 83: *The inventory of physical property,* 83; *Costing the inventory,* 84; *Overhead construction costs,* 85; *Depreciation,* 85; *Land values,* 85; *The valuation of intangibles,* 85; *Working capital,* 86; *Summary,* 86; Original Cost, 86: *Background,* 87; *The determination of original cost,* 89; *Disposition of account 100.5,* 91; *Disposition of account 107,* 94.

8. Depreciation 94

The Nature and Purpose of Depreciation, 94; The Depreciation Base, 97; The Principal Depreciation Methods, 98: *The straight-line method,* 98; *The sinking fund method,* 99; *Retirement reserve accounting,* 99; Annual Depreciation Expense, 100: *Estimated service life,* 100; *Group basis of cost amortization,* 101; *The calculating of depreciation expense,* 101; Accrued Depreciation and the Rate Base, 102: *Should there be a deduction?,* 102; *Measuring the depreciation deduction,* 104; Economic Depreciation, 106; Accelerated Depreciation in Rate Making, 109: *The depreciation methods authorized,* 110; *The economic effects,* 111; *Rate-making effects,* 112.

9. Rate of Return **114**

Profits and Public Utilities, 115; Rate of Return and the Rate Base, 116; Legal Guideposts to a Fair Rate of Return, 116; Analysis of Legal Guideposts, 119: *Comparable earnings and the competitive standard,* 119; *Financial integrity and attraction of new capital,* 123; The Current Status of Rate of Return, 133.

10. Pricing Policies **134**

Underlying Principles of Rate Making, 135: *Differential pricing,* 135; *General objectives of utility pricing policies,* 137; *The range of rates,* 138; *Cost analysis,* 140; *Value of service,* 142; *Rate schedules and legal requirements,* 145; *Theoretical economics and public utility rates,* 147; Electric Utility Rates, 148: *Development and characteristics of electric utilities,* 148; *Some basic terms and concepts,* 152; *Types of rate schedules,* 154; *Costing procedure,* 158; *Allocation of demand costs,* 159; *Some tests of demand-cost allocation methods,* 163; Gas Distribution Utilities and Rates, 164: *Development of manufactured gas utilities,* 165; *The transition to natural gas,* 167; *Market characteristics,* 170; *Rates and rate schedule types,* 172; Natural Gas Pipeline Rates, 173: *Economic factors affecting pipeline rate making,* 174; *Gas tariffs,* 178; *Pipeline rate forms,* 180; *Rate-design procedure—the Atlantic Seaboard formula,* 181; *Some effects of Atlantic Seaboard,* 184; *Rate differentials reflect distance,* 185; *The "rolled-in" rate principle,* 188.

11. Pricing Policies (Continued) **189**

Telephone Rates, 189: *Introduction to the telephone industry,* 189; *Introduction to telephone rates,* 193; *Rates for exchange telephone service,* 196; *Toll rates,* 206; *Toll-rate disparity,* 210; *The separations of interstate and intrastate plant and expenses,* 215; Water Supply and Rates, 220: *Development of water service,* 220; *Economic characteristics,* 222; *Revenue requirements,* 227; *Water rates,* 228; *A costing method to aid in making rates,* 231; Urban Transit Fares and Problems, 233: *The development and decline of urban transit,* 235; *Economic characteristics,* 239; *Urban transit fares,* 242; *Policies during the decline of urban transit,* 245; *Federal assistance,* 247.

12. The Application of Rate-Making Essentials—A Case Study **249**

Background Facts, 249; The Questioned Rate, 250: *The capacity charge,* 250; *The automatic rate adjustments,* 251; Cost of Service, 252: *The test period,* 252; *Rate of return,* 252; *The allowance for income taxes,* 254; *Working capital,* 257; *Depreciation,* 257; *Interest during construction,* 257; *Cost and rate determination,* 258; Summary, 259.

Part III THE REGULATORY AGENCIES

13. The Regulatory Agencies 260

The State Commissions, 260: *Jurisdiction of state commissions,* 261; *The commissioners,* 262; *Organization and staff,* 263; *Financing of commissions,* 264; *Statutory provisions affecting rate changes,* 265; *Processing time of rate cases,* 266; *Compensating for regulatory lag,* 268; Federal Power Commission, 269: *History and development,* 269; *Hydroelectric power regulation,* 271; Federal Communications Commission, 278; Securities and Exchange Commission, 281; Appraisals of Regulatory Agencies, 282; The Atomic Energy Commission, 287: *Introduction to atomic energy program,* 287; *Regulatory program,* 288; *Power Reactor Development Company case,* 292.

Part IV THE EMERGING NATURAL GAS INDUSTRY AND THE ENERGY ECONOMY

14. Natural Gas Pipeline Development and Regulation 294

The Growth of Reserves and Production of Natural Gas, 294: *Oil and gas—joint products from one industry,* 294; *Natural gas reserves and production,* 295; *Consumption of gas,* 296; The Development of Natural Gas Transmission Systems, 296: *The gas supply situation,* 297; *Technology creates a market,* 297; *Postwar pipeline expansion,* 299; Regulation of Interstate Gas-Transmission Lines, 301: *The Federal Trade Commission Report on utility corporations,* 301; *The Natural Gas Act of 1938,* 301; Aspects of Regulatory Policy, 303: *Rate-making treatment of pipeline-produced gas,* 303; *Divestments and purchases of producing properties,* 311; *Interstate direct sales,* 312; *Pipeline certificates,* 312.

15. Regulation of Independent Natural Gas Producers 317

The Structure of the Gas-Producing Industry, 317: *The relationship of gas to oil,* 317; *Who looks for and produces gas?* 320; *Competition in the production of gas,* 321; *Economic rent and institutional barriers,* 323; Federal Regulatory Jurisdiction Over Gas Producers, 325: *The issue of jurisdiction,* 326; *The evolution of regulatory control,* 326; Background to Regulation, 329: *Implementation of regulation,* 329; *Gas sales contracts,* 330; Economic Characteristics of the Gas-Producing Industry, 332: *General characteristics,* 332; *Cost characteristics of gas supplies in the field,* 335; *Revenues and profits in gas production,* 337; Methods of Regulation, 337: *Methods proposed in individual-company cases,* 338; *Area pricing as a standard for regulation,* 340; Regulatory Policy and Problems, 343: *Rate-regulation policy,* 343; *Certificate-regulation policy,* 348.

16. Energy Supply and Demand—Past, Present, and Future **350**

Energy, Growth, and Public Utilities, 350; Past and Present Supplies and Consumption of Energy, 351: *Consumption of energy by types,* 351; *The location of fuel production and reserves,* 352; *Fuel and water power consumption by use and by area,* 354; Competition Among Energy Supplies for Various Markets, 359: *The importance of location,* 359; *The markets for energy,* 360; Energy Supplies and Consumption in the Future, 374: *Estimates of future energy supplies,* 375; *Estimates of future energy consumption,* 379; A National Fuels Policy, 383.

Part V **SPECIAL MANAGERIAL PROBLEMS**

17. The Economics of Taxation **385**

The Burden of Utility Taxation, 386: *The first proposition,* 387; *The second and third propositions,* 387; *The fourth proposition,* 388; *The tax burden of investors,* 390; *Tax burdens and utility rates,* 391; The Incidence of Public Utility Taxation, 391: *The general incidence,* 392; *The specific incidence,* 393; The Effects of Utility Taxation, 394.

18. The Labor Force and Labor Relations **396**

The Nature of the Utility Work Force, 396; Labor-Management Relations in Public Utilities, 402: *The public-interest concept as applied to labor relations,* 403; *Mediation and arbitration,* 403; *Attempts to prevent or halt work stoppages in public utilities,* 405; *Labor problems in government-owned utilities,* 409; *Proposed solutions to utility labor disputes,* 410.

Part VI **SPECIAL REGULATORY PROBLEMS**

19. Utility Financing and Financial Regulation **412**

The Needs for Capital, 412; Methods of Financing Capital Needs, 414: *Types of securities,* 414; *Internal financing,* 419; Capital Structure, 420; The Problem of Bigness, 421; Who Holds Utility Securities? 422; The Evolution of Financial Regulation, 424: *State regulation,* 425; *Federal regulation,* 426; Financing Publicly-Owned Utilities, 430: *Municipal ownership,* 430; *State and federal ownership,* 432.

20. The Structure and Organization of Utility Industries **434**

The Evolution of Gas and Electric Holding Companies and Their Regulation, 435: *Early public utility holding-company development,* 436; *The appearance of holding-company abuses,* 438; *Advantages of holding-company structures,* 439; *The Public Utility Holding Company Act of 1935,* 440; *Evaluation of the Public Utility Holding Company Act,* 442. The Bell System,

446: *The development of the Bell System,* 446; *Intercorporate relations within the Bell System,* 450; *Acquisition policies of A. T. & T.,* 459; Antitrust Problems in Public Utility Industries, 463: *The doctrine of primary jurisdiction,* 464; *Public interest,* 466.

Part VII **ENERGY, TECHNOLOGY, AND THE FUTURE**

21. Technology and Public Utilities 470

Electric Utilities, 470: *Improvements in conventional methods and equipment,* 470; *New methods of power generation,* 471; *New uses for electricity,* 473; Gas Utilities, 474: *Improvements in transmission and distribution,* 474; *Gas manufacturing and processing,* 475; Communications Utilities, 476: *New and improved communication equipment,* 476; *New markets for communication utilities,* 477; Technology in Water Utilities, 478; Fuels in the Future, 481: *Atomic energy,* 481; *Oil shale and tar sands,* 484; *Energy sources on the horizon,* 486.

Table of Cases 487

Index 493

PUBLIC UTILITY ECONOMICS

PART I

INTRODUCTION AND BACKGROUND

1 The Public Utility Concept

American business is largely conducted by stockholder-owned corporations which operate for profit. These business corporations may be divided into three major categories: (a) private corporations, which engage in manufacturing and mercantile activities; (b) financial or moneyed corporations, such as banking and insurance companies; and (c) public service corporations or public utilities, such as electric and telephone companies, which supply an indispensable service under monopoly conditions with governmental regulation of prices, profits, and service quality.[1] American laws have singled out each of these three types of business corporations for different treatment. Our concern here will be the economics of the public utility sector of the American economy and the legal institutions which determine economic policy in it.

1. PUBLIC UTILITIES: A SEPARATE BUSINESS CATEGORY

Unlike other stock corporations, public utilities operate with government approval as monopolies and supply a service which is indispensable to modern living. These two unique characteristics make inevitable a third distinguishing feature—public regulation of prices and profits—which sets public utilities further apart from the general run of American business. It is important to note that the workably competitive market place, which is relied on to set the terms of trade in other businesses, is absent in the case of public utilities. Consequently, government regulation has been adopted as a substitute for competition in the market for public utility services. The essential purpose of such regulation is to achieve the results of competition in the form of (a) reasonable prices, or rates, and reasonable profits; and (b) adequate service quality.

Public utilities are further distinguished from other sectors of business by the legal requirement to serve every financially responsible customer in their service areas, at reasonable rates, and without unjust discrimination. Further, public utilities generally are granted by law the power of eminent domain. By this authority a public utility can force, through court action, the sale of private property which it may need to serve the public. Finally, a public utility may not

[1] Common carriers in the transportation industry, some of which operate under competitive conditions, are public utilities; however, they are not within the scope of this book.

enter a new market, supply a new service, or abandon an existing market without the consent of public authority. From the foregoing it is apparent that public utilities comprise a distinctly separate category of business whose economics may be expected to differ accordingly.

2. PUBLIC UTILITIES DEFINED AND ENUMERATED

Public utilities comprise one part of a general class of businesses which are designated by our laws and courts as "business affected with a public interest." While not all the businesses in this group are public utilities, each one is regulated in some way by public authority because it has been legislatively determined (and upheld in the courts, if tested) to bear a particularly close relationship to the public as a whole. Seventeen states, for example, regulate milk prices on a "public-interest" basis, although milk producers are not public utilities. Nonetheless, in order to guarantee the public an adequate supply of pure and wholesome milk, extensive regulation of milk pricing and marketing has been undertaken. Other non-public utilities which have been regulated on a public-interest basis include insurance companies, employment agencies, and real estate rental property. The public interest has required substantial federal regulation of radio and television broadcasters; however, such regulation does not control the profits of broadcasting companies, and the quality of their service offering is subject to relatively little regulation. The principal function of broadcasting regulation is to control entry into the industry and, thus, the amount of competition.

Public utilities are distinguished from the other businesses affected with a public interest because they are:

(a) free from business competition to a substantial degree, and are often pure monopolies;

(b) required to charge only reasonable rates that are not unjustly discriminatory;

(c) allowed to earn but are not guaranteed a reasonable profit;

(d) obligated to provide adequate service to the entire public on demand; and

(e) closely associated with the processes of transportation and distribution.

In the development of the body of law governing the English-speaking peoples, the concept of the public utility first emerged in connection with transportation and the warehouses, docks, wharves, and cranes necessary to transportation. The term "common carrier" was applied to all those engaged in serving the public with commercial transportation and the associated services. As common carriers, they held themselves out to serve the public on demand and were allowed to charge no more than a reasonable price. By analogy, the concept of the regulated common carrier was extended to modern public utilities as technology advanced, since they, too, are transporters, although of gas, electricity, water, telephone messages, and urban passengers. It is important to note that present-day, for-hire carriers, such as railroads, trucking companies, and airlines, are also public utilities. However, these essentially intercity carriers, because of distinctive characteristics of their own, are covered separately under the general heading of *transportation*. Therefore, this study of public utilities will concentrate on those industries which supply electricity, natural and manufactured gas, water, telephone and telegraph communication, and urban mass transportation.

While these particular public utility industries transact the bulk of all utility business, a number of other businesses also fall within the public utility classification. Commonly designated by law as public utilities are warehouses, docks, wharves, toll bridges, sewerage companies, and stockyards. Regional and local circumstances have led to public utility status in some places for ice producers, steam heating companies, cotton gins, irrigation and canal companies, grist mills, and grain elevators. Ohio has included a coal pipeline company among its regulated utilities, while Wyoming accorded public utility status to a television antenna company which constructed a large antenna on a high point in order to receive and transmit television signals to subscribers over the lines of other utilities. Serious consideration has been given to the possibility of public utility status for retail milk distribution and automobile parking facilities.

3. DEVELOPMENT OF THE PUBLIC UTILITY CONCEPT

The public utility concept is a product of the legal mind responding to economic, social, and technological conditions. Its origins date back to early English commercial practices. The concept of a public utility first took form in English judicial decisions. Taken together, these and other decisions comprise the common law, which has served as the basis for subsequent judicial decisions and statutory law in all the English-speaking nations of the world. As part of the American legal heritage from England, the legal concept of a public utility was implemented in the post-Civil War years as part of the transition from an agricultural to an industrial economy.

A. *Early Origins.* During the Middle Ages, before the formation of the nations of Europe, production was carried on by manorial estates and associations of producing craftsmen called *guilds*. Near-universal regulation of prices prevailed under the "just price" doctrine which had been originated by the early churchmen and carried on in modified form by their successors during the Middle Ages. The just price was the equivalent of the customary price. It was not competitively determined. Instead, it was a regulated price which permitted the seller to recover production costs plus a margin of profit sufficient only to maintain himself at the customary living standard of his class.[2] Enforcement of the just price was the responsibility of town authorities, manorial courts, and, later, the guilds themselves. Such comprehensive regulation of market prices became embedded in European trade practices and institutions and provided precedent and example for the judicial decisions of a subsequent period which established the basis for the concept of business affected with the public interest.

With the formation of the nation-states of Europe, there emerged an economic policy known as *mercantilism*. Beginning about the sixteenth century, the newly formed national governments exerted dominating control over economic affairs within their boundaries. Control over prices was part of the system, along with controls over wages and the quality and quantity of production. By these devices, it was believed that the national economies could be made to promote most effectively the power and wealth of the monarchical state itself. In addition to its use of price and other types of regulation, mercantilist economic policy also favored the granting of monopoly rights by royal charters to trading and plantation companies. Such organizations were to serve national economic aims through their own commercial ventures and by discoveries of new

---

[2] Joseph Mayer, *Social Science Principles in the Light of Scientific Method* (Durham, N.C.: Duke University Press, 1941), pp. 361–363.

territory and colonization as well. Operating under monopoly franchises, these private enterprises performed certain governmental functions which the royal governments did not choose to administer. In this development, Professor Martin G. Glaeser has noted the origin of our modern concept of a public service corporation.[3]

The English common law developed with England's emergence as a unified nation. Under the common law then, as well as today, a judicial decision stands as a precedent, or a rule, by which future cases of the same kind may be decided. Of course, judge-made law may be changed by later court decisions or by the enactment of legislation.

By far the most significant impact of the common law upon the modern public utility concept resulted from a learned commentary on the common law by Sir Matthew Hale (1609–1676), Lord Chief Justice of the King's Bench. In his treatises *De Portibus Maris* and *De Jure Maris,* completed around 1670, Lord Hale summarized the law of businesses "affected with a publick interest." He singled out ferry boats, as well as wharves and cranes in port towns. Lord Hale concluded that, under common law, when these facilities were the only ones chartered or when there was only one to serve the entire public, they ceased to be entirely private because they were affected with a public interest. As a consequence, the owners of these facilities could not charge arbitrary or excessive duties or tolls, but only reasonable and moderate amounts. Referring to ferry boat service, Lord Hale went further in specifying that the law required, in addition to a reasonable toll, adequate service and proper maintenance of the facilities used. For failing in these duties, the operator was subject to fine. These ideas, distilled from the common law, were to become of living consequence in the United States in 1877, when the Supreme Court relied upon them in its historic decision in *Munn* v. *Illinois,*[4] wherein Lord Hale's conclusions were applied to present-day facilities bearing similar economic characteristics.

Mercantilism in Western Europe gave way to newer economic policies toward the end of the eighteenth century. A movement, already underway, to eliminate government regulation of much of the economy was accelerated by the publication in 1776 of Adam Smith's *An Inquiry Into the Wealth of Nations.* Smith criticized mercantilist restrictions upon private enterprise and argued for freedom for individual initiative. His principal contention was that the free and competitive market would best serve both the public and business, since the greatest profit would go to those who were most efficient in satisfying the needs of the public. Although Smith's ideas met with favorable response, businesses affected with a public interest remained a class apart. In 1820, for example, Congress authorized Washington, D.C., to regulate rates at private wharves, the price of chimney sweeping, and the weight and quality of bread. In 1841 the regulation of bread prices and weights by the city of Mobile was upheld as constitutional by the Alabama Supreme Court. Congress expanded the regulatory jurisdiction of Washington, D.C., in 1848 to cover the rates charged for horse-drawn transportation of passengers and property. While the development of the free market economy did not eliminate the regulation of business affected with a public interest, such regulation in the United States was small in scope and relatively unimportant until after the Civil War. This is explainable by the fact that the economy was essen-

3 Martin G. Glaeser, *Outlines of Public Utility Economics* (New York: The Macmillan Company, 1927), p. 159.

4 94 U.S. 113 (1877).

tially agricultural and rural and not industrial and urban in nature.

B. *Munn v. Illinois.* Rapid expansion took place in the manufacturing and railroad industries in the years that immediately followed Appomattox. Technological advancement made steel abundant and cheap, the railroads conquered the frontier, and technology in agriculture freed labor to work in industrial pursuits in urban centers. Almost everywhere but in the South, smelting, meatpacking, oil refining, milling, lumbering, and other manufacturing and extractive activities surged ahead, capitalizing on the new inventions and the vastly improved transportation. Despite this, there was deep discontent among the market-oriented farmers of the Midwest. This widespread unrest stemmed chiefly, but not solely, from the near collapse in the prices of agricultural commodities in both the domestic and world markets. From 1866 to 1870 the average decline in farm commodity prices was about 30 per cent. By 1873 the average of farm prices had fallen by 35 per cent from the 1866 level.[5] Reasons for this price behavior are not hard to find. A wave of post-Civil War homesteading on the fertile Midwestern plains followed the opening of the frontier by the railroads. This vast increase in total acreage under cultivation was coupled with an ever-rising productivity per acre as a result of important technical improvements in farm equipment and advancements in horticulture and breeding. To make matters worse for the prairie farmer, these same developments were taking place elsewhere in the world. Consequently, the amounts supplied far exceeded the amounts demanded at 1866 prices in both the domestic and world markets. Under these conditions, commodity prices were forced downward from past levels and stayed there. Farm grievances were compounded by the fact that the prices of necessary equipment and supplies continued to rise in the inflationary period following the Civil War. Moreover, many farm mortgages had been contracted at interest rates of 15 to 20 per cent. Accordingly, a price-cost squeeze threatened foreclosure and the loss of the fruits of pioneering effort over a wide area.

Much of the resentment stemming from this farm depression was focused on the rates and practices of the railroads and the grain elevators often associated with them. The railroads operated as monopolies in the farm lands and many of the communities served by their lines. Their rates were thought to be high in light of the fact that it often cost the equivalent of one bushel of wheat to ship another one to a principal Midwestern market. This charge sometimes exceeded the cost of transportation from the Midwestern market to England. Railroad rates in many instances were unjustly discriminatory, favoring the large shipper against the small. Farmers resented the fact that rates were higher west of the Mississippi River than east of it. Revelations of financial mismanagement and bribery on the part of the railroads acted to solidify agrarian resentment against what was commonly denounced as a monopoly profit situation.

Grain farmers had little bargaining power against railroad-owned grain elevators. They paid high rates for storage, and sometimes, if they had used an independent elevator, they paid the railroad's elevation charge anyway in order to get transportation. When Midwestern corn was marketed in the form of livestock, railroad handling of such live cargo was frequently careless. This reduced both the quantity and the grade at the final market.

The growing conviction in the farm states that competition was not working

[5] Bureau of the Census, *Historical Statistics of the United States, 1789–1945,* p. 234.

well in the railroad and grain elevator industries led to increased interest in regulatory legislation which would guarantee what seemed to them a greater measure of fairness. In the early 1870's a farmers' organization known as the Patrons of Husbandry, or the "Grange," began to serve as the focus for the agrarian uprising known as the Granger movement. By winning control of their state legislatures, the Grangers sought to remedy the railroad and grain elevator problems through legislative control of rates and practices. In these pioneer regulatory laws of the 1870's, the modern public utility concept was ultimately established in the United States.

It was a Granger regulatory law, enacted by the Illinois legislature, which resulted in the memorable opinion by the Supreme Court of the United States in the case of *Munn* v. *Illinois*.[6] Handed down in 1877, this decision constitutes the bedrock foundation of the modern public utility concept. Further, this case demonstrates beyond doubt the continuing importance of the Supreme Court in determining the nature and content of public utility economics.

As a result of Granger pressure, the new Illinois constitution of 1870 designated grain elevators as public warehouses. The Illinois legislature in 1871 passed a regulatory statute which prescribed the maximum rates which could be charged by operators of grain storage facilities. In 1874 there were 14 elevators of this kind in Chicago which were controlled by nine firms. Rates were fixed by agreement among them.

Munn and Scott, operators of grain elevators, charged higher rates than the Illinois statute permitted. They were found guilty in the state courts and fined. Their case was appealed to the Supreme Court of the United States with the claim that the due process clause of the Fourteenth Amendment denied Illinois the right to set maximum rates for grain storage.[7] The Supreme Court met the issue squarely in the *Munn* v. *Illinois* decision. The question was whether or not the Illinois legislature was empowered to fix by law the maximum rate for grain storage, in view of the constitutional limitation upon state legislative power.

The decision in *Munn* v. *Illinois* clearly upheld the constitutionality of the Illinois law. It turned on two characteristics of public utilities described above, necessity and monopoly. These two tests were used in later cases to support or disprove the contention that a particular activity was a public utility.

In considering the first test, necessity, the Court found grain elevators to be affected with a public interest and, therefore, legitimately subject to state regulation. Munn's contention that this constituted an unlawful deprivation of property was held invalid. Citing precedents from the history of regulation in this country, the Court said, ". . . it was not supposed that statutes regulating the use, or even the price of use, of private property necessarily deprived an owner of his property without due process of law."[8]

The Court next inquired into the legal principles which support the power to regulate. Lord Hale, whose common law treatises were discussed earlier, was cited as the authority in this issue. In one of the most significant paragraphs in the annals of the Supreme Court, it quoted from Lord Hale in ruling:

---

[6] 94 U.S. 113 (1877).

[7] By this Amendment no state may deprive any person of life, liberty, or property without due process of law. Counsel for the operators argued that the statutory limitation on rates constituted, in effect, a deprivation of property in the sense of property value, since rate regulation reduced the yield from such property. Of course, property value is a function of yield.

[8] 94 U.S. 113, 125.

. . . We find that when private property is "affected with a public interest, it ceases to be *juris privati* only." This was said by Lord Chief Justice Hale more than two hundred years ago, in his treatise *De Portibus Maris*, . . . and has been accepted without objection as an essential element in the law of property ever since. Property does become clothed with a public interest when used in a manner to make it of public consequence, and affect the community at large. When, therefore, one devotes his property to a use in which the public has an interest, he, in effect grants to the public an interest in that use, and must submit to be controlled by the public for the common good, to the extent of the interest he has thus created. He may withdraw his grant by discontinuing the use; but so long as he maintains the use, he must submit to the control.[9]

Having established the "necessity" test, the Court turned to a consideration of monopoly. The Court noted that nine companies controlled all Chicago grain elevators, and that prices had been determined by agreement. Observing that this "may be a 'virtual' monopoly," the Court again quoted from Lord Hale in saying of Munn and Scott:

They stand, to use again the language of this counsel, in the very "gateway of commerce," and take toll from all who pass. Their business most certainly "tends to a common charge, and is become a thing of public interest and use." Every bushel of grain for its passage "pays a toll, which is a common charge," and, therefore, according to Lord Hale, every such warehouseman "ought to be under public regulation, viz.: that he . . . take but a reasonable toll." Certainly, if any business can be clothed "with a public interest, and cease to be *juris privati* only," this has been. It may not be made so by the operation of the Constitution of Illinois or this statute, but it is by the facts.[10]

Commenting on the Illinois constitution, which made it the duty of the legislature to protect producers, shippers, and receivers of grain, the Court pointed out that: "This indicates very clearly that during the twenty years in which this peculiar business had been assuming its present 'immense proportions,' something had occurred which led the whole body of the people to suppose that remedies such as are usually employed to prevent abuses by virtual monopolies might not be inappropriate here. For our purposes we must assume that, if a state of facts could exist that would justify such legislation, it actually did exist when the statute now under consideration was passed."[11] Monopoly was thereby joined with necessity as a test of public utility status.

Although the *Munn* decision did not specifically categorize those activities which fall within the scope of regulation, it laid the foundation for both the utility and non-utility types of public regulation of business.

Coming as it did in 1877, the *Munn* decision was most timely, for it just preceded the development of our modern public utility systems. Thomas A. Edison patented his incandescent lamp in 1879, and commercial generation of electricity began in 1882. Alexander Graham Bell and Thomas A. Watson, his assistant, succeeded in perfecting the telephone in 1876 and demonstrated it at the Philadelphia Exposition of that year. Gas was beginning to be widely used for commercial and domestic cooking and lighting. The first modern electric street railway was operated in 1888 in Richmond, Virginia. It is significant that the *Munn* v. *Illinois* decision was handed down on the very eve of these technological developments which produced the public utilities we depend on today. Here, surely, is one area where basic law did not lag behind the needs of the times. The legal basis for state regula-

[9] 94 U.S. 113, 126.

[10] 94 U.S. 113, 131–132.

[11] 94 U.S. 113, 132.

tion of public utilities was in fact established before many of the utilities themselves. When these industries matured to a stage where their importance to the economy was recognized and had developed the distinguishing characteristics of utilities, the legal precedent which permitted their regulation was already available. Shortly after the turn of the twentieth century, state legislatures across the nation began to create the permanent utility regulatory commissions we know today. It was the *Munn* decision which had established beyond question the right of the states to regulate as public utilities these lineal descendants of the simpler technology of Lord Hale's era.

The lasting effect of the *Munn* v. *Illinois* decision certainly confirms the observation by Professor John R. Commons, who wrote that the Supreme Court ". . . occupies the unique position of the first authoritative faculty of political economy in the world's history."[12]

C. *Subsequent Court Decisions.* The category of business that is affected with a public interest is relatively broad in scope and includes many industries besides public utilities. A legislative act that is signed into law may designate an industry as one affected with a public interest or, more narrowly, as a public utility. Such laws, of course, are subject to judicial review. The present discussion undertakes to survey the court decisions in the years following *Munn* v. *Illinois* with respect to laws regulating public utilities and non-utility industries declared by law to be affected with public interest.

Two distinct trends may be identified. (1) The courts have generally upheld statutes imposing regulation upon what we now regard as conventional public utilities. (2) With respect to non-utilities that have been declared by law to be affected with a public interest, the trend of court decisions has not been entirely consistent, for: (a) in the years directly following *Munn,* such laws were generally upheld; but (b) during the 1920's and early 1930's, the Supreme Court was prone to find that such laws were unconstitutional and hence invalid; however, (c) beginning in 1934, the Supreme Court changed its position and began to uphold state laws regulating business affected with a public interest. Throughout this period, and until relatively recent times, the courts did little to distinguish public utilities from other business affected with a public interest. Ultimately, however, this necessary distinction was made. As a result there is now a clear judicial statement setting forth the tests of public utility status as well as a tested principle underlying the regulation of non-utilities that may be declared to be affected with a public interest.[13]

First, with respect to conventional public utilities, it should be noted that numerous regulatory agencies were permanently established after 1907 at both the state and federal levels of government. These agencies were modeled upon the Interstate Commerce Commission, which had been created by Congress in 1887. Many business activities had already met the tests of public utility status and were regulated by statutes which were tested and upheld. Included among these in some of the early cases were electric companies,[14] manufactured and natural gas distributors,[15] telephone

[12] John R. Commons, *Legal Foundations of Capitalism* (New York: The Macmillan Company, 1924), p. 7.

[13] Professors Horace M. Gray and Wallace F. Lovejoy develop different points of view in 16 *The Journal of Land and Public Utility Economics* 8 (1940) and 3 *South Texas Law Journal* 292 (1958), respectively.

[14] *Gainesville* v. *Gainesville Gas and Electric Power Co.,* 62 So. 919 (1913).

[15] *Gibbs* v. *Consolidated Gas Co.,* 130 U.S. 396 (1889); *Indiana Natural and Illuminating Gas Co.* v. *State,* 63 N.E. 220 (1902).

companies,[16] water companies,[17] urban transit companies,[18] and sewer companies.[19] It is interesting to observe that, although each of these activities was held to be a public utility and subject to regulation, the courts did not set forth a general definition of a public utility.

Second, with respect to non-utility industries declared by law to be affected with a public interest, the policy of the Supreme Court has passed through three stages. Following the *Munn* decision, the majority of the Court upheld the extension of state government regulation to industries not necessarily characterized by the tests of necessity and monopoly developed in the *Munn* case. In 1894, for example, the Supreme Court decided *Brass* v. *North Dakota ex rel. Stoesser*[20] and upheld, in a 5–4 decision, a state law regulating grain elevator operations in North Dakota. The decision was based essentially on the precedent of *Munn* v. *Illinois*. However, the North Dakota situation differed from that in *Munn* v. *Illinois* because there were about 600 grain elevators in the state and, therefore, considerable competition in the industry. The *Brass* decision apparently discarded the monopoly test and thereby broadened the category of business which could be regulated. The majority upheld the state law essentially on the ground that the grain elevator industry in North Dakota was sufficiently affected with a public interest. The minority argued that the industry did not meet the test of a public utility and, therefore, should not be regulated. Justice Brewer, dissenting, said, "If this be a monopoly, justifying public control of prices for service, I am at a loss to perceive at what point the fact of monopoly will cease and freedom of business commence."[21] There was a similar expression of divergent views when the Court upheld a state statute regulating fire insurance rates.[22]

During the 1920's and into the early 1930's, the Supreme Court took a position opposed to the regulation of business declared to be affected with a public interest. Essentially the same divergence of views, noted above, prevailed during this period. However, a majority of the Court as it was then comprised held the view that the Constitution allowed utilities alone to be regulated.[23]

This position was reversed in the famous *Nebbia* decision of 1934, which established the law as it now stands.[24] There, the Court in effect upheld the regulation of any business that a state legislature may, with adequate cause, declare to be affected with a public interest.

The *Nebbia* case grew out of the emergency economic controls that were legislated during the severe depression of the 1930's. When excessive competition and declining markets disrupted the milk industry in the State of New York to such an extent that the quality and adequacy of the supply were threatened, the state established by statute a milk control board, empowered to fix the minimum wholesale and retail prices of fluid milk. A conviction for violating this statute ultimately was appealed to the Supreme Court. The question presented asked whether these price controls, imposed by a state government, constituted

---

[16] *Wolverton* v. *Mountain States Telephone and Telegraph Co.*, 142 P. 165 (1914).

[17] *Omaha Water Co.* v. *Omaha*, 162 F. 225 (1908); affmd. 218 U.S. 180 (1910).

[18] *Platt* v. *San Francisco*, 110 P. 304 (1910).

[19] *State ex rel. Edwards* v. *Millar*, 96 P. 747 (1908).

[20] 153 U.S. 391.

[21] 153 U.S. 391, 410.

[22] *German Alliance Insurance Co.* v. *Lewis*, 233 U.S. 389 (1914).

[23] *Charles Wolff Packing Co.* v. *Court of Industrial Relations*, 262 U.S. 522 (1923); *Tyson & Brother* v. *Banton*, 273 U.S. 418 (1927); *Williams* v. *Standard Oil Co.*, 278 U.S. 235 (1929); *Frost* v. *Corp. Commission*, 278 U.S. 515 (1929); *New State Ice Co.* v. *Liebmann*, 285 U.S. 262 (1932).

[24] *Nebbia* v. *New York*, 291 U.S. 502.

a violation of the Fourteenth Amendment or a valid use of state police power.[25] The law was upheld in a 5–4 decision. The Supreme Court majority stated:

> The argument runs that the public control of rates or prices is *per se* unreasonable and unconstitutional, save as applied to business affected with a public interest; that a business so affected is one in which property is devoted to an enterprise of a sort which the public itself might appropriately undertake, or one whose owner relies on a public grant or franchise for the right to conduct the business, or in which he is bound to serve all who apply; in short, such as is commonly called a public utility; or a business in its nature a monopoly. . . .
>
> We may as well say at once that the dairy industry is not, in the accepted sense of the phrase, a public utility. . . .
>
> . . . "affected with the public interest" is the equivalent of "subject to the exercise of the police power;" and it is plain that nothing more was intended by the expression. . . .
>
> It is clear that there is no closed class or category of business affected with a public interest . . .
>
> The phrase "affected with a public interest" can, in the nature of things, mean no more than that an industry, for adequate reason, is subject to control for the public good. . . .[26]

The Court went on to state that, if a law of this kind is reasonable, then the courts have no right to substitute their judgment for that of the legislature on questions of the wisdom of such regulation.

A workable judicial definition of a public utility was set forth in 1943 in a case arising under the Emergency Price Control Act, one of a number of wartime laws designed to stabilize the economy. Among other things, this law exempted public utilities from the price control regulations imposed elsewhere in the economy. The rationale behind this exemption was that regulatory commissions would have control of utility rates, thus making further regulation unnecessary. A public warehouse company in California claimed it was a public utility under California law and thereby exempt from the Price Control Act.

The United States Emergency Court of Appeals held that the warehouse company was not a public utility and, thus, was subject to the federal law.[27] Chief Judge Vinson dissented in a separate opinion which contained what may be the most complete statement of the public utility concept ever to come from the bench. On appeal, the United States Supreme Court reversed the appellate court and held the warehouse company to be a public utility.[28] In its reversal, the Supreme Court called attention to Judge Vinson's "indicia" of public utility status.[29]

Judge Vinson's opinion in the lower court identified as the key characteristic of public utility status the close association of a business with transportation and distribution. He stated:

> The participation by a business in activities intimately connected with the processes of transportation and distribution, therefore, was the characteristic which caused it to be subjected to the impositions implicit in public utility regulations. A somewhat exhaustive enumeration of the businesses which frequently have been designated, operated, and regulated as public utilities illustrates that the gradual growth of the family has involved no departure from the initial concept, but merely reflected scientific progress in the facilities, auxiliaries, and varieties of transportation and distribution. . . .

[25] The police power is derived by the states from the Tenth Amendment. Under the police power, states may pass laws concerning the public health, welfare, safety, and morals.

[26] 291 U.S. 502, 531, 533, 536.

[27] *Davies Warehouse Co.* v. *Brown,* 137 F. 2d 201 (1943).

[28] *Davies Warehouse Co.* v. *Bowles,* 321 U.S. 144 (1944).

[29] 321 U.S. 144, 148.

An examination of numerous decisions wherein Federal and State Courts have had occasion to consider the nature and characteristics of public utility enterprises reveals that a distinguishing feature of that class of business is considered to be the presence of an obligation to serve public demand at reasonable and non-discriminatory rates.[30]

He then summarized what he considered to be the essential elements of the public utility concept:

If a business is (1) affected with a public interest, and (2) bears an intimate connection with the processes of transportation and distribution, and (3) is under obligation to afford its facilities to the public generally, upon demand, at fair and non-discriminatory rates, and (4) enjoys in a large measure an independence and freedom from business competition brought about either (a) by its acquirement of a monopolistic status, or (b) by the grant of a franchise or certificate from the State placing it in this position, it is . . . a public utility. . . .[31]

Judge Vinson pointed out that these four characteristics amounted to an affirmative test only, and that there may be other industries falling outside his definition which also could be public utilities:

It is these four attributes which make up the bundle or the public utility formula to the extent which I have promulgated it. The formula is a limited one. It is designed only to provide an absolute test or standard by which one may affirmatively determine that a particular business is a public utility. I do not wish to be misunderstood as indicating that a business possessed of or operating under less than the total of these features may not be considered a public utility. My formula has no negative or exclusive implications. What I do say is that, at least, any business which does possess and practice and operate under each and all of these features, is by a preponderance of considered judicial opinion a business in the public utility class.[32]

This opinion crystallizes the difference between public interest and public utility status. The latter concept is narrower than the former and is included in it. Regulation in the public interest apparently can encompass virtually any type of business activity if there is adequate reason. In cases of other than utility industries, a prime consideration is the adequacy or inadequacy of competition in a broad sense. Too much or too little competition may generate the need for some controls. In contrast, a utility has some rather definite characteristics that make extensive regulation a necessity.

4. THE PATHS TO PUBLIC UTILITY STATUS

Our economic history shows that unregulated businesses became public utilities as a result of legislation enacted by state legislatures or the Congress, depending on whether the business they transacted was intrastate or interstate in nature. Regulatory legislation of this kind has been passed for one of two reasons. The first, and by far the more important, has been widespread public dissatisfaction with the prices, quality of service, or terms of trade in the supply of some basically important service required in everyday living and commerce. The second and more recent cause for regulatory legislation has been the desire of a few industries to achieve particular business advantages by virtue of public utility status.

In the first case, regulatory legislation stemming from public dissatisfaction, such conditions as undependable service or prices deemed excessively high or unduly discriminatory have been an important cause of legislative action. In the

[30] 137 F. 2d 201, 212, 213, 214. Citations omitted.

[31] 137 F. 2d 201, 217.

[32] *Ibid.*

second case, where public utility status is actively sought by an industry hoping to benefit thereby, the motives may include: (a) protection from excessive competition by establishing a degree of regulated monopoly and (b) the achievement of the right of eminent domain. Motor carrier regulation, for example, is often cited as an example of public utility status sought for the purpose of restricting entry into the field.[33] Public utility status was sought and achieved, largely to gain the right of eminent domain, by an Ohio pipeline company which transports pulverized coal mixed with water. The same objective has been unsuccessfully pursued by a long-distance belt conveyor company in Ohio, which proposed to link Lake Erie and the Ohio River in order to ship iron ore southward and coal northward.[34]

The law which establishes a business as a public utility always designates a regulatory agency to administer and enforce the terms of the regulatory statute. If no agency exists, one is usually created as part of the same law. However, the passage of regulatory legislation is only part of the process through which public utility status is established. Interested parties which oppose regulation have the right to test the validity of the regulatory law in a court of law. The Supreme Court has held in cases of this kind that the judiciary has the power to decide whether or not the business is sufficiently affected with the public interest to justify regulation as a public utility.[35]

[33] Russel E. Westmeyer, *Economics of Transportation* (Englewood Cliffs, N.J.: Prentice-Hall, Inc., 1952), p. 394; Horace M. Gray, "The Passing of the Public Utility Concept," 16 *The Journal of Land and Public Utility Economics* 8 (1940).

[34] Paul J. Garfield and George W. Thatcher, "A Rubber Railroad in Ohio," 28 *Land Economics* 160 (1952).

[35] *Charles Wolff Packing Co.* v. *Court of Industrial Relations,* 262 U.S. 522, 536 (1923).

One important exception to the process of establishing public utility status, described above, should be mentioned here. In 1954 the Supreme Court upheld an interpretation of the Natural Gas Act of 1938, by which the independent producers of natural gas were held to be "natural gas companies" and, as such, within the regulatory jurisdiction of the Federal Power Commission.[36] This is by far the most prominent example of the establishment of regulatory control through judicial interpretation of a current statute. Heretofore, this method has been confined to relatively rare cases involving possible regulation of municipal utilities and REA cooperatives.

5. RIGHTS AND DUTIES OF PUBLIC UTILITIES

The rights and duties of public utilities are spelled out in laws and court decisions. The rights include the following: (a) A public utility is entitled to charge a "reasonable rate" for its services which, under prudent and economical management, will afford it an opportunity to collect revenues sufficient to cover: all proper operating expenses; taxes; depreciation expense; and a return on the net valuation of its property, adequate to provide debt interest, dividends on its capital stock, and a contribution to earned surplus. (b) A public utility is entitled to a grant, by public authority, of a franchise in some form which provides it with an exclusive right to serve a specific service area free of competition from another seller of the same service. The purpose of this grant extends beyond protection of the utility alone. It also protects the public from the comparatively high rates which would prevail if there were competition, since utility

[36] *Phillips Petroleum Co.* v. *State of Wisconsin et al.,* 347 U.S. 672 (1954).

services are most cheaply supplied by a monopolist—an important point which will be explained shortly. (c) A right inherent in public utility status is that of eminent domain. This is a governmental power delegated to public utilities for the limited purpose of acquiring private property or rights to some specific use of private property which is required to serve the public. Court action can compel a sale of private property for public use, in exchange for just compensation. (d) Public utilities have the right to operate under reasonable rules and regulations. Consequently, the utility is protected in such matters as office hours, service deposits, discounts for timely payment, and service cut-offs, to name a few.

Accompanying these rights is a substantial array of duties which utilities are obliged to assume: (a) A utility is required to supply all reasonable demands for service by those who can pay for it. (b) It is obliged to provide service adequate to the needs of its customers. Under this responsibility, utilities must serve to the limit of capacity, maintain reserve equipment, keep all facilities in good repair, and expand capacity as demand grows. (c) Utility service must be priced at reasonable rates and without unjust discrimination. (d) Public utilities cannot change their service or expand into a new market without the prior finding by a regulatory agency that such is in the public interest. (e) Public utilities must exercise care to protect the safety of the public. Laws and regulations, for example, specify such technical characteristics as the voltage of electricity and the pressure of gas to minimize the possibility of accident. (f) Utilities are required to secure approval from public authority before terminating a service or abandoning a market. Requirements of this kind are necessary when the public has no alternate source of supply of a vital service. They represent an attempt to assure an even exchange of adequate service for reasonable rates.

6. THE SIGNIFICANCE OF PUBLIC UTILITIES IN THE AMERICAN ECONOMY

Public utility services are fundamental to the existence of an industrial economy. Life as we know it in an urbanized society would not be possible without an abundant, reasonably priced supply of public utility services. This was vividly expressed in front-page headlines in *The New York Times,* which described the impact of a shutdown of public utility services in France. The headlines read, "France Crippled By Utility Strike, 12-Hour Stoppage Hits All Activities."[37]

Viewed as part of the entire American business economy, the public utility industry is second only to manufacturing in size, as indicated by the value of total assets of non-financial corporations. Table 1.1 shows total assets by major category of business. Although public

Table 1.1

Total Assets of Nonfinancial Corporations, 1960
(in billions of dollars)

Industrial Groups	*Total Assets*
Manufacturing	$252.0
Public utilities (privately owned)	89.9
Wholesale and retail trade	87.6
Transportation	47.2
Services	18.4
Mining and quarrying	15.8
Construction	14.2
Agriculture, forestry, fisheries	3.6
Other	.6
Total	$529.3

Source: U.S. Treasury Department, *Corporation Income Tax Returns, Statistics of Income* (preliminary), Internal Revenue Service Publication No. 159 (1962).

[37] *The New York Times,* October 17, 1957.

utilities are shown to rank second among nonfinancial corporate categories, it should be noted that the data do not include the substantial asset value of public-ownership utility systems, which include almost all water utilities, many of the largest urban transit systems, and some important electric utility operations. Total assets of the publicly owned and investor-owned public utilities approximate at least 20 per cent of the total asset value of nonfinancial corporations in the entire economy.

Public utilities influence the level of business activity in the economy as a whole through their sizable investment expenditures for new fixed assets. During the five-year period ending in 1954, for example, public utilities accounted for more than 20 per cent of the total investment expenditure by business for plant and equipment.[38] These investment outlays by utility companies were approximately one-half as large as the total recorded for all manufacturing industries. In order to finance their plant and equipment expansion, public utilities make heavy demands on the capital markets of the nation. In fact, financing the capital requirements of the utility industry is one of the major functions of the underwriters and distributors of new security issues. In the five years ending in 1954, for example, the total value of capital flotations by public utilities approximated 45 per cent of the total for the United States as a whole. In subsequent years, public utilities raised more capital by external financing than the manufacturing and mining industries combined.

Public utility securities are generally regarded as desirable by investors interested in less-than-average risk and stable income. Many state laws, for example, authorize savings banks to invest in public utility common stock. Insurance companies and other institutional investors have found the characteristics of public utility securities to their liking. During the 1950's, public utility securities comprised one-third or more of the total stock and bond assets of the nation's life insurance companies.

Finally, it should be noted that the public utility industry contributes much toward scientific research and development. The Bell Telephone Laboratories, for example, stand foremost among the research centers of the nation and have done much to reduce costs and improve efficiency in both communications and electronics. Bell scientists were the first to devise a practical amplifier tube which, when placed at intervals in long-distance lines, restored the energy of weakening voice currents, thus making coast-to-coast telephone service possible. The Laboratories also pioneered the development of coaxial cable and microwave radio-relay systems. Both can be used to transmit television programs and hundreds of telephone conversations. Important progress has been made in the perfection of electronic equipment that can remember and compute. One of the most important of recent discoveries is the transistor. This tiny, simple device performs most of the functions of the vacuum tube and performs other functions besides. The vacuum tube, which is basic in electronic devices, requires more space, power, and maintenance than the transistor and, apparently, is far shorter-lived. The transistor promises to be as revolutionary an innovation as the vacuum tube was a half-century ago. Recently, the Echo and Telstar satellites have signified breakthroughs in long-distance communication.

The electric utility industry has been among the leaders in adapting atomic energy to peaceful uses. Groups of utili-

[38] Derived from a requested breakdown of data in the series "Business Expenditures for New Plant and Equipment," prepared by the U.S. Department of Commerce and the Securities and Exchange Commission.

ties, sometimes joined by industrial firms, have formed to finance and promote research and development of pilot atomic power plants. However, of greater present importance is the successful effort of electric utilities and equipment manufacturers to improve efficiency and reduce the cost of conventional power generation. The general subject of technological change as it affects the utility industries is covered in the final chapter of this book.

2 Economic Characteristics of Public Utilities

1. NATURAL MONOPOLY

The outstanding economic characteristic of public utilities is that they operate at greatest efficiency as monopolies. It has long been recognized that it is in the public interest to authorize only one public utility the exclusive right to supply one or more services to a particular market.[1] Compelling economic and physical factors rule out all but the monopolistic form of market organization in the supply of local public utility services. As a result, public utilities are termed "natural monopolies." As such they are the outstanding exception to the generally competitive nature of our economy.

The principle of natural monopoly was originally noted by John Stuart Mill, after London became the world's first city to have gas service. Writing in 1848, Mill observed that: (a) gas and water service in London could be supplied at lower cost if the duplication of facilities by competitive firms were avoided; and that (b) in such circumstances, competition was unstable and inevitably was replaced by monopoly.[2]

The accuracy of Mill's observation was confirmed by the utility history of almost all the cities in the United States and Europe. Before and around 1900 it was common to find more than one utility company selling the same service in a particular city. The situation invariably resulted in price wars between the utilities in a drive to get or keep customers. The quality of service provided by utilities thus engaged was ordinarily inferior and sometimes irregular. In addition, wasteful and costly dupli-

---

[1] Most natural gas distributors are supplied by one natural gas pipeline company, although a relatively few distributors are served by more than one. In general, the achievement of maximum efficiency in pipeline operations is a function of the level of system-wide operations and is not dependent necessarily upon monopoly control of a particular market. Nevertheless, a situation that bears watching has developed from the fact that pipelines are not exclusive suppliers of the respective gas distributors in some cities. For example, the Federal Power Commission has noted, without particular comment on the matter at hand, that the Tennessee Gas Transmission Co. contract demand rate in the New York zone is 49.7 cents per Mcf and that the corresponding rate of another pipeline supplier to that same market, Transcontinental Gas Pipe Line Corp., is 37.7 cents per Mcf (both rates as averaged and stated on a 100 per cent load factor basis). Federal Power Commission, *Re Texaco Inc., et al.* (G-18078, *et al.*), November 22, 1960, p. 10 (mimeo.).

[2] As quoted from Mill's *Principles of Political Economy* in George T. Brown, *The Gas Light Company of Baltimore* (Baltimore: The Johns Hopkins Press, 1936), pp. 63–64.

cation of facilities usually resulted. The outcome of price wars among the first utilities, it is important to note, usually was an agreement to end the ruinous competition and to join forces in a combination of the companies.

The explanation is not hard to find. In the face of unstable and ruinous competition, the early public utilities found it far preferable to combine and to achieve thereby both monopoly control over prices and substantial operating economies in the form of lower costs. The latter point is the one which deserves special attention here. The dominant reason for the failure of competition to survive in the utility industry is the fact that utilities operate at or near lowest average cost, in supplying a particular market, when free from the competition of other sellers of the same service. Thus, utilities are inherently monopolistic. Viewed in this light, natural monopoly is both inevitable and desirable.

Once public utilities came to be recognized as natural monopolies, a genuine dilemma presented itself. How could the public achieve the benefits of lower-average-cost monopoly production of utility services without being forced to pay the prices that these monopolies could command for their indispensable services? At about the turn of the century this was an important public question. The choice lay between public ownership and public regulation of investor-owned public utilities. *Munn* v. *Illinois* had established clearly the right of a state to impose regulation on "virtual monopolies" which provided a service especially vital to the public. This, and our general disposition toward private ownership, resolved the dilemma largely in favor of public regulation. In fact, regulation was regarded as the substitute for competition when it became apparent that competition was not effective as a technique of market control. Public policy, through regulation, thus provided an avenue for the achievement of least-cost production of utility services and public protection from monopolistic prices.

Before considering further the economics of natural monopoly, it is important to observe that there are undeniable physical limitations which argue against allowing more than one supplier of each utility service to operate in any city. Electric and telephone company poles and underground conduits and cables occupy choice and strategic land sites in metropolitan areas and along our highways. Gas and water mains run under our streets. It is not hard to imagine the obstructions which would be presented by a duplication of utility company facilities—along and beneath our streets. Under regulated monopoly, only one supplier is authorized for each service. The same, of course, holds true for gas and water companies, which occasionally dig up city streets to repair or enlarge their mains. In light of the automobile traffic situation, it is apparent that more than one bus or streetcar line on a street is disadvantageous. Competition imposes another, special handicap on telephone companies. The value of their service is directly related to the number of telephones any subscriber can contact (without toll charge) through his own telephone. With more than one telephone utility, subscribers are faced with the dilemma of choosing between telephone service which will not reach everyone and subscribing for more than one telephone. Consequently, physical limitations alone indicate that public utilities are naturally monopolistic.

2. THE ECONOMICS OF SUPPLY UNDER NATURAL MONOPOLY

Early in the development of the modern public utilities, it became apparent that competition as a form of market organization was both undesirable and incapable of enduring. At the same time, it also became apparent that it was desirable and, indeed, inevitable to have a single seller supply one or more utility services in a city or area. In short, monopoly was recognized as "natural" on the supply side of the market for public utility services.

A chief cause of this may be found in the fact that the unit cost of supplying utility service is lower when monopoly exists than when competition is attempted. This factor provided a powerful motivation to the combination of would-be competitors into monopolies. The opposite side of the coin in this situation was that competition tended to be unstable and could not endure when significant economies could be achieved through combination.

What reasons explain the fact that public utilities operate at lower unit costs under monopoly than under competition?

a. One reason, already suggested, is that the combination of utilities into monopolies made possible the elimination of costly duplication of facilities.

b. The most important reason, however, is that public utilities achieve decreasing average unit costs as output increases. In this respect, it is important to note that the benefits of decreasing costs are greater when a monopolistic public utility serves an entire market than when a number of competitive public utilities serve portions of that same market. Decreasing average unit costs accompany increasing output (assuming that plant capacity is not fully utilized) when an increase in output results in a less-than-proportionate increase in total costs. This is not to suggest that decreasing unit costs will necessarily continue to be achieved until plant capacity is fully utilized; rather, decreasing unit costs are characteristic of a substantial portion of the output that a plant or system is capable of producing. An exception to the decreasing-cost tendency of the public utility industries is local telephone service, which is discussed in Chapter 11.

Part of the explanation of this decreasing-cost tendency is found in the fact that public utilities require a relatively greater investment in plant and equipment than other principal industries. In order to make sales of, say, $1,000,000, a public utility requires several times more investment in plant and equipment than a manufacturing, mining, or merchandising business. Because public utilities must have greater investment in plant and equipment than other industries, their cost structure is dominated by the costs related to that fixed investment. It is most important to note that plant-related costs are constant in amount and do not fluctuate with variations in production, assuming constant plant size. Such costs include depreciation, interest, amortization, property taxes, insurance, and, unique in the case of public utilities, dividends on the capital stock, among others.

To summarize to this point:

a. Public utilities require proportionately heavier investment in fixed assets than do other businesses.

b. Fixed assets are accompanied by substantial constant costs which are a function of plant size and not of the quantity of production. In this respect, public utilities differ considerably from industrial firms, whose costs are dominated by payroll and raw material costs, which are subject to virtually automatic variation when production varies.

In the operation of a utility plant of a given size, decreasing costs per unit of service result as production approaches ultimate capacity. This occurs because the heavy constant costs are distributed more thinly to each unit of output as production rises. Decreasing average costs with fixed plant size can be expected when there is an increase in the number of units of service sharing the constant costs, which are characteristically high in a public utility because of its disproportionately high capital requirements. Regulated monopoly makes possible a fuller realization of the benefits of decreasing costs than could be achieved when more than one utility strives to serve the same market.

Thus, public utilities are the classic example of businesses that are characterized by decreasing average cost. In addition to the comparatively high ratio of constant to total costs, utilities have a continuous process of production and a highly standardized product, in a technological but not an economic sense.

c. A third reason explaining why public utilities achieve lower average costs under monopoly than under competition is found in the factor of plant size. Once public utilities were able to serve an entire market under the protection of monopoly, it became feasible for many utilities to concentrate their production in the larger and more efficient plant and equipment units made possible by technological advancement. The larger facilities produce service at lower operating expenses and less plant investment per unit of output than do smaller facilities. Thus, regulated monopoly permitted the achievement of lower costs than would have been possible under competition, because utilities could take full advantage of the economies of large-scale production.

d. A fourth reason for lower average costs under monopoly arises from the more diversified demand that usually results from serving an entire market instead of a portion of that market. The more diverse the demand for utility service in a particular market, the greater is the tendency for the maximum demand of each customer or customer class to occur at different times. That is, the greater the diversity, the less the customers' maximum demands tend to coincide. The economy of greater diversity, in short, is that less plant capacity is needed to serve the system's peak demand than if diversity were less. More specifically, diversity is measured as the ratio of: (1) the total of the maximum demands of individual customers, occurring at any time within a stated period, to (2) the maximum total demand at any particular time during the same period. The higher the ratio, the greater is the diversity.

e. A final principal reason for lower costs under monopoly in this industry is one not necessarily related solely to public utilities. A business enterprise that is relatively large can realize economies from buying in large quantities. The overhead costs of purchasing are subject to decreasing average charges as the size and volume of purchases increase. Further, large buyers receive economies of quantity and volume discounts given by the seller filling large orders.

Around the beginning of the present century, numerous state courts and commissions issued decisions which gave formal and official recognition to the economics of natural monopoly in the public utility industries. The general conclusion of these decisions was that monopoly, suitably regulated, was in the public interest. One of these decisions was written in 1908 by Commissioner Milo R. Maltbie, of the New York commission, in the *Long Acre* case.[3]

Long Acre Electric Light and Power Company had applied to the New York Commission for authority to issue securities in order to finance prospective electric utility operations in New York City. At the time, two suppliers of electricity (each one the result of several previous corporate consolidations) were

[3] *In the Matter of the Application of the Long Acre Electric Light and Power Company*, 1 PSCR (1st Dist. N.Y.) 226 (1908).

providing service in the market Long Acre proposed to enter. The Long Acre application was denied on the grounds that regulated monopoly was more beneficial to the public than any additional competition that might be provided by Long Acre.

Speaking for the division of the New York commission which heard the case Commissioner Maltbie stated, "The whole electric history of New York City points the futility of competition."[4] He termed this experience a recurring cycle of numerous corporations that were absorbed by others, followed by still other new companies with the same procedure repeated. "The new companies," he said, "were merged or swallowed up, until at the present time there are but two electric supply companies operating in Manhattan, and these two companies, although nominally independent, are owned and controlled by the Consolidated Gas Company."[5] Commissioner Maltbie went on to observe that this history had been duplicated in nearly every large city in the United States and in most of those in Europe. Where there might be the appearance of competition, he pointed out, either the suppliers were affiliated or the market territory had been apportioned among them. Accordingly, he said, public measures to maintain competition were then being abandoned, not only as futile, but as detrimental to the best interests of the public.

> "It is coming to be generally recognized that monopoly control of electric light, heat and power may be very beneficial to the public if the one company or the few non-competing companies can be placed under such public regulation and control as will secure for the public a fair share in the many benefits arising from unified management. That competition cannot be relied upon to protect the consumer from high prices and poor service has been fully demonstrated."[6]

Turning to a consideration of the advantages of monopoly, Commissioner Maltbie cited, first, the avoidance of duplication of connection facilities and the public inconvenience related to such duplication. Second, he said that a single company would require less investment in total generating-plant capacity and substations than several companies serving the same market, because each of the nominally competing companies would have to install its own reserve capacity. Third, distribution losses are greater when there are several systems serving one market. As a result of the latter two factors, Commissioner Maltbie concluded, the cost of electricity is greater under competition than under efficient monopoly. Further, it was his view that the then present electric rates in Manhattan would be lower if it were not for the fact that the two suppliers were "overloaded with an inheritance from the period of competition."

3. THE DEMAND FOR PUBLIC UTILITY SERVICES

Public utilities in general are required to stand ready to serve whatever reasonable demands the consuming public may place upon them. This at once distinguishes public utilities from monopolies in the more conventional sense of the term, for public utilities are not able to withhold their services from the market. In fact, as a matter of general practice, public utilities devote considerable effort to studies of their markets and to the direction and character of expected market growth. Planning to meet future demands requires forecasts of the nature

[4] *Ibid.*, p. 249.

[5] *Ibid.*, pp. 249–250.

[6] *Ibid.*, p. 250.

of the market development that is expected to take place, so that the appropriate facilities can be ready when needed.

In surveying the demand for public utility services, it is necessary first to consider the *timing* of that demand and its related economic consequences. As viewed from this standpoint, the most prominent characteristic of the demand for public utility services is its wide periodic fluctuations, which follow daily, weekly, and seasonal patterns throughout the year. The significance of these regular fluctuations in the timing of demand lies in the fact that, in general, public utility services are non-storable. Therefore, service must be produced and delivered as it is demanded by consumers. In order to meet this fluctuating but largely predictable demand, public utilities are required to invest in sufficient plant capacity to enable them to serve the maximum or peak demand anticipated in any year. In addition, they must provide reserve plant capacity in order to assure the continuity of service in the event of a breakdown or some other outage. The size of utility plant is therefore dictated by the maximum demand anticipated in each year. This follows, of course, as a consequence of the non-storability of utility services and the widely fluctuating demand for utility services that is experienced during each year.

A significant economic consequence of the factors discussed above is that a portion of public utility plant capacity will be idle a large part of the time in each year, while the entire plant capacity will be used for only a relatively short period of time during the year. However, it should be noted carefully that the constant costs of operating a public utility continue to be incurred regardless of the level of plant utilization, because the total of such costs is a function of plant size rather than of the volume of production. The size of plant, in turn, is a function of the annual peak demand. Thus, a problem common to all utilities is that of supplying a peak annual demand for a relatively short period in each year, which leaves a substantial amount of unused plant capacity during the remainder of the year. This problem is of primary concern in pricing public utility services, and in some instances price policy is effective in influencing the timing of demand.

Public utilities of a particular kind are faced with essentially similar time patterns of consumer demand, although differences in market characteristics due to local or regional circumstances necessarily have an impact. Water utilities, for example, anticipate a summer-long daytime peak period due to the lawn-sprinkling and other seasonal uses made of water. Local distributors of natural gas, and the pipelines supplying them, expect and experience their annual maximum or peak demand for firm (non-interruptible) service to coincide with the coldest winter weather, when the demand for space-heating fuel is greatest. Urban transit utilities expect twice-daily peaks on working days during the time their patrons are traveling to and from their jobs. They may experience an annual peak sometime during the Christmas shopping season, when home-bound shoppers increase the usual volume of evening rush-hour patrons. Electric utilities may experience an annual peak in demand during the summer, when the air-conditioning demand is greatest, or during a winter day during the period when the number of daylight hours is at or near its annual minimum. Telephone utilities experience daytime peaks in business calls and evening peaks principally comprised of social and personal calls.

Telephone, electric, and urban transit utilities supply completely non-storable services. In the case of electric utilities, interconnection with other electric utilities enables them to assist one another in serving peak demands when their respective peaks are not coincidental. Exchange agreements of this kind, of course, have the beneficial effect of reducing the size of electric plant required to serve a particular peak load. On the other hand, gas and water utilities supply a commodity in addition to a service; therefore, some use of storage facilities is feasible and can serve to reduce the size of some, but not all, types of plant required to serve the annual peak-demand period. Some natural gas pipelines and a few gas distributors have developed underground gas storage facilities. However, the benefits of storage to most gas and water distributors —in terms of plant size—are somewhat limited at present. In general, their situation differs only in degree from that of other types of utilities. With the exceptions noted, utility services are properly regarded as essentially non-storable and subject to production as demanded.

Second, it is necessary to consider the *price elasticity* of the demand for public utility services. For the present purpose, price elasticity of demand may be regarded as a measure of the change in the amount of a commodity or service that will be demanded as a result of a change in price. Alternately, price elasticity of demand may be viewed as a measure of the change in the buyers' total expenditure for a commodity or service that results from a change in price. If a price change is followed by no change in the amount demanded by buyers, or by a less-than-proportionate change, then the commodity or service is said to have an "inelastic" demand. On the other hand, if a price change is followed by a more-than-proportionate change in the amount of the product demanded, then the demand is said to be "elastic." In short, price elasticity is a measure of buyer response or sensitivity to price changes. This sensitivity varies among different commodities and services and is directly influenced by such factors, among others, as: (a) the price and availability of substitutes; (b) the degree of necessity attached to the particular commodity or service; and (c) the proportion of the household budget that is devoted to the particular commodity or service.

Applying the concept of price elasticity to the demand for public utility services, it may be said, in general, that greater amounts of public utility services will be demanded at relatively lower prices than at relatively higher prices. However, it is not very meaningful to speak in terms of the elasticity of the aggregate demand for utility services. Instead, it is much more useful to relate elasticity of demand to separate market components of the aggregate demand. This is necessary because of the great diversity in the uses made of utility services, the relative size of the customers, the timing of their demands, and the availability of substitutes, among other factors.

Accordingly, it may be said that the demand for utility services is extremely elastic for some uses and relatively inelastic for some other uses. For example, the demand for natural gas for residential cooking is relatively inelastic by comparison with the demand for natural gas as an industrial fuel, which is highly elastic. Whereas the residential cooking customer consumes a very small amount of gas, the usefulness of it to him is great and its cost is not relatively important as a budget item. Although the adoption of a substitute is possible (electricity, for example), he is not in a ready position to switch once he has made his investment in a gas range. On the other hand, the industrial customer to whom fuel is a principal cost item is often equipped to burn gas, oil, or coal —and therefore is in a position to take advantage of the rigorous price competition in the market for industrial fuel. This type of gas consumer is concerned primarily with achieving the lowest fuel cost per million Btu of heat, allowing for possible differences in the efficiency of utilization, and he is prone to switch from one fuel to another to take advantage of the opportunities in the market. This comparison, although perhaps oversimplified, certainly suggests the differences among various classes of consumers or service insofar as the respective price elasticities of demand are concerned. The relatively inelastic demand of the residential consumer of gas for cooking and the highly elastic demand of the industrial consumer of gas as a fuel present a contrast that, in varying degrees, is illustrative of the demand situation throughout the market for public utility services.

4. PUBLIC UTILITY PRICING POLICY

The pricing of public utility services is a matter which arises in the course of regulation after determination of the total revenues that the utility will be allowed to earn from consumers for a stated or estimated quantity of service. In most but not all instances, the utility is required by the regulatory commission to submit proposed schedules of rates that will produce revenues closely approximating the amount approved. The commission, after scrutiny, may order the proposed rates into effect with or without modification or may schedule a hearing on the proposed rates before deciding upon the rates it will authorize to be charged.

Although the units of service supplied by a public utility are standardized in a technological sense, they are by no means standardized in an economic sense. Thus, such matters as: (a) the demand characteristics of different kinds of customers; (b) the different uses made of the service; and (c) the time at which service is demanded, among other factors, serve as a basis for making valid economic distinctions among the separate components of the total supply being sold. These economic distinctions are reflected in the pricing of public utility services. Accordingly, public utilities follow a policy of differential pricing rather than a policy of uniform pricing. Differential pricing involves: (a) classifying customers into groups; and (b) charging different prices to each group. The same schedule or schedules of rates are available to all customers within each group.

Differential pricing enables a public utility to maintain and to promote sales in each segment of its market. The objectives of this pricing policy are: (1) to earn the revenue total authorized by the regulatory commission; (2) to promote sales so as to maximize the utilization of plant capacity and thereby to reduce the average unit costs of supplying all service; (3) to charge more heavily those who create the peak demands, or alternatively, to encourage a shift in the timing of demand to an "off-peak" period. The foregoing is a very general introduction to differential pricing by public utilities. The subject will be covered more fully in Chapters 10 and 11

5. LARGE CAPITAL INVESTMENT REQUIRED

One of the most important economic characteristics of public utilities is their comparatively large investment in fixed capital. This characteristic alone determines numerous other economic characteristics. An important example of this was noted earlier, when it was pointed out that public utilities have comparatively high constant costs (comprised of such items as interest and property taxes) whose annual total is determined by plant size rather than by the quantity of annual production. Plant size, in turn, is determined by the annual maximum demand for service. Because of this heavy investment characteristic, public utility services are much more the product of plant and equipment than of labor.

In financial analysis, a convenient measure of the relative importance of fixed capital investment is the annual rate of capital turnover, which is expressed by the *capital turnover ratio.* The capital turnover ratio is defined as the relationship of gross revenues to capital investment.

$$\text{Capital Turnover Ratio} = \frac{\text{Gross Revenues}}{\text{Capital Investment}}$$

The capital turnover ratio shows the gross revenues earned per dollar of book cost of assets or capital liabilities. Stated differently, the capital turnover ratio reflects the capital requirements of a company or an industry relative to the dollar volume of business done in a stated time period, ordinarily taken as one year. A relatively low capital turnover ratio would be less than 1.0, such as 0.3, while a relatively high capital turnover ratio would be at least about 2.0. Through the use of this ratio, public utilities and other industries can be compared from the standpoint of their respective capital investment requirements.

Public utilities have low capital turnover ratios relative to practically all other industries. This is suggested by the following representative capital turnover ratios for selected industries:

Electric utilities	0.30
Natural gas utilities	0.60
Natural gas pipelines	0.40
Bell Telephone System	0.40
Water utilities	0.20
Total manufacturing	2.00

The lowest capital turnover ratio among the utilities is that of the water utilities. This ratio is affected by factors tending to restrict water utility revenues, which are discussed in Chapter 11. On the other hand, the capital turnover ratio of natural gas distribution utilities—somewhat higher than that of other utility industries—reflects the more intensive use of existing facilities as a result of greater volumes of gas supplied and the abandonment of plant formerly used to manufacture gas. An exception among the relatively low capital turnover ratios of public utilities is found in the case of those urban transit systems which have substituted bus fleets for electric streetcars. A bus transit system does not require the investment in way and structures (and, sometimes, power plant) that is required by an electric street railway system. Accordingly, while an electric street railway system has a characteristically low utility-type capital turnover ratio, a bus system by contrast ordinarily has a capital turnover ratio in excess of 1.0.

Among the respective non-utility industries, there are, of course, variations in capital turnover ratios which are not expressed by the 2.0 ratio for total manufacturing shown above. For example, the food and kindred products industry and the leather and leather products industry have capital turnover ratios of about 4.0. The capital turnover ratios of wholesale and retail trade operations ordinarily are much higher than those of manufacturers, typically ranging from 4.0 to 6.0.

The representative industry ratios shown above indicate that electric utilities, for example, require over three years of operations to earn revenues equivalent to their capital investment, while the total manufacturing group typically earns annual revenues that are twice the amount of its capital investment. The utilities thus have a relatively slow rate of annual capital turnover, while the rate for the manufacturing (and mercantile) industries is comparatively rapid. As more capital is required in a business or industry relative to the dollar volume of sales, the rate of capital turnover tends to slow down.

The low capital turnover ratios of public utilities also demonstrate their comparatively greater requirements for capital investment in plant and equipment. The 0.30 capital turnover ratio of the electric utility industry, for example, indicates that over three dollars of capital must be employed in order to produce one dollar in revenue. (This may be calculated by taking the reciprocal of the capital turnover ratio, that is, dividing it into 1.0.) Conversely, the typical capital turnover ratio of 2.0 for total manufacturing indicates that only about 50 cents in capital investment is required to produce one dollar in sales revenue. Thus, in terms of the foregoing comparison, an electric utility would require about six times the capital investment of a representative manufacturer doing the same volume of business. This comparison, in varying degrees, applies generally among the public utility industries and other industries and confirms the fact that public utilities have relatively greater capital requirements than other industries.

6. THE OPERATING RATIO

The *operating ratio* is defined as the ratio of operating expenses, including depreciation expense and taxes, to gross revenues.

$$\text{Operating Ratio} = \frac{\text{Operating Expenses plus Depreciation Expense and Taxes}}{\text{Gross Revenues}}$$

Expressed as a percentage, the operating ratio shows the proportion of annual gross revenues which is required to meet the costs of doing business before compensation of capital. The complement of the operating ratio (the difference between total expenses as defined and gross revenues) is termed the *return margin.* The return margin is the amount remaining for the payment of a return on the investments of security holders after expenses (as defined) have been met. Thus, if the operating ratio is 90 per cent, the return margin is 10 per cent. Consequently, the lower the operating ratio, the higher the return margin.

The operating ratio is related to the capital turnover ratio, because there is a strong tendency for the operating ratio to be relatively lower as the amount of capital required increases. This is to be expected, particularly where public utilities are concerned. The large capital requirement of public utilities makes essential an operating ratio that is low enough to result in a return margin sufficient to provide a reasonable return to the investors who finance public utility plant and equipment. Thus, industries such as public utilities whose capital turnover ratios are relatively low (or whose capital requirements are relatively great) are apt to have relatively low operating ratios. Conversely, industries with relatively high capital turnover ratios (and whose capital requirements are relatively lower) generally have relatively high operating ratios. This is illustrated by the following representative operating ratios for selected industries:

Electric utilities	80%
Natural gas utilities	88
Natural gas pipelines	82
Bell Telephone System	86
Water utilities	75
Total manufacturing	94

As among different manufacturing industries, the same tendency is borne out; those industries with the relatively higher capital turnover ratios, say 4.0, tend to have operating ratios in excess of 95 per cent.

The contrast among the utility and manufacturing industry operating ratios (and, therefore, return margins) provides one measure of the investment risks in the respective enterprises. The high operating ratio-narrow return margin of the manufacturers indicates that their return margins are vulnerable in the face of either declining revenues or increasing costs, or both, other things remaining equal. Each of these factors, when present, narrows further the already narrow return margin. Consequently, industrials are thought to bear comparatively greater investment risks, by this standard, than do public utilities. Investments in the latter are accompanied by comparatively less risk because their wider return margins are better able to withstand erosion and still meet the return requirements on fixed-income securities.

This risk difference, and others, are reflected in the way utilities and industrials are financed. Prudent financing of an industrial firm, characterized by rapid capital turnover and a narrow return margin, permits only a small proportion of total capitalization to be comprised of fixed-income debt financing. Conversely, the proportion of debt which a public utility may safely assume is apt to be much greater. To summarize: public utilities require proportionately more capital investment than do industrial firms; high capital requirements tend to be accompanied by lower operating ratios and higher return margins; investment risk is reduced as return margins widen; this and other risk factors influence the amount of debt financing which can be undertaken with prudence.

7. DEBT RATIO

The *debt ratio* is the percentage relationship of long-term debt to total capitalization.

$$\text{Debt Ratio} = \frac{\text{Long-Term Debt}}{\text{Total Capitalization}}$$

Public utilities have made extensive use of long-term debt to finance their sizable plant and equipment requirements. The reasons are not difficult to find. Lenders have been willing to buy public utility bonds in large quantity because these securities have exhibited attractive investment characteristics. One contributing factor—the relatively high return margin in utility operations—has been discussed previously. In addition, public utilities are judged to be relatively low-risk enterprises because they sell indispensable services under monopoly conditions. In general, the demand for public utility services has shown unusual stability during recession and depression. One study, for example, showed that median earnings of a group of 40 large industrials fell from 11.6 per cent in 1928 to 2.6 per cent in 1932, the worst year of the great depression. By contrast, median earnings of a group of nine large public utilities fell from 7.9 per cent to 6.2 per cent during the same period.[7]

Public utility debt ratios ordinarily range between about one-third and two-thirds of total capitalization, with many utilities tending toward debt ratios of about 50 per cent. In contrast, industrials commonly show debt ratios of approximately 10 to 15 per cent. The relatively high utility debt ratios indicate that the issuance of bonds is a principal means employed to finance the large capital requirements and that the rela-

[7] *How Profitable Is Big Business?* (New York: Twentieth Century Fund, 1937), p. 117.

tively stable earnings which characterize public utility operations make debt financing feasible.

8. DIVIDEND-PAYOUT RATIOS

The *common stock dividend-payout ratio* is the percentage relationship between cash dividends paid to common stockholders and net income.

$$\text{Common Stock Dividend-Payout Ratio} = \frac{\text{Cash Dividends}}{\text{Net Income}}$$

Public utilities have comparatively high dividend-payout ratios by contrast with industrial corporations. Over the period 1947–1961, the payout ratio for Moody's 24 electric utilities group ranged between 64.9 and 77.0 per cent and averaged 70.2 per cent. During the same period, the payout ratio for Moody's 125 industrials ranged between 39.5 and 63.2 per cent and averaged 54.6 per cent.

The comparatively high dividend-payout ratios that are characteristic of public utilities reflect the fact that public utility earnings under regulation are generally confined to a level that permits relatively little of net income to be carried to earned surplus. Because their retained earnings generally are not a significant proportion of total earnings, public utilities usually do not place great reliance upon the reinvestment of retained earnings to finance growth and expansion. Instead, public utilities rely more heavily on the capital markets, private placements, and subscriptions as sources of new financing. Industrial firms, because of their lower dividend-payout ratios, are able to finance an important share of their needs for new capital from the reinvestment of retained earnings. Both utilities and industrials also depend upon depreciation for significant amounts of corporate funds.

9. COMPARATIVE PROFITABILITY

It has been indicated that public utilities in general bear comparatively less risk than industrial corporations. Because profit is, in important part, a function of risk, public utilities earn lower rates of profit than industrials. Table 2.1 shows a comparison of annual profit rates for utilities and industrials during the postwar period. The average annual return on book net assets for the period 1947–1961 was 13.5 per cent for total manufacturing and 9.3 per cent for total public utilities. The average profit rate for the manufacturing group fluctu-

Table 2.1

Average Annual Return on Book Net Assets, 1947–1961[1]

(in per cent)

Year	*Total Manufacturing*	*Total Public Utilities*
1947	17.0%	8.0%
1948	18.9	8.4
1949	13.8	8.7
1950	17.1	9.8
1951	14.4	9.0
1952	12.3	9.0
1953	12.5	9.2
1954	12.3	9.3
1955	14.9	9.7
1956	13.9	9.8
1957	12.8	9.6
1958	9.8	9.7
1959	11.6	10.1
1960	10.6	9.9
1961	10.1	9.9
Average . . .	13.5	9.3

[1] The data represent the relation of reported net income after taxes in each year to book net assets at the beginning of each year, calculated as the excess of total balance sheet assets over liabilities. Owing to the relatively large proportion of public utility capitalization in the form of funded debt, the rate of return on total utility property would be lower than that shown on net assets only.

Source: First National City Bank Monthly Letter, "Business and Economic Conditions," figures published annually for each industry group.

ates within a wider range than that of the public utility group. Relative instability of earnings is an important measure of risk. The range for manufacturing was between 18.9 and 9.8 per cent, while the public utility average profit rate varied within a much narrower range: from 8.0 to 10.1 per cent. Nevertheless, over the entire period the average return of the total manufacturing group was 45.2 per cent greater than that of the total public utility group.

3 The Development and Scope of Utility Regulation

Public utility regulation in its present form is the end-product of considerable experimentation and adjustment. Experimentation in the techniques of regulation has resulted in the expert administrative commission, a distinctly American contribution to the science of government. Adjustment has taken place as the local, state, and federal governments, in essentially that order, have undertaken public utility regulation in response to changing economic conditions and advancing technology in the utility industries. The regulatory system that has evolved is a workable one, although not beyond improvement. From present indications, it has reached a form that seems likely to remain unchanged for some time. This chapter surveys that development to the present. The institution of commission regulation is discussed in greater detail in Chapter 13.

1. JUDICIAL REGULATION

The earliest form of regulation in this country was processed through the courts. Enforcement of the common law right of consumers to adequate utility service at reasonable rates was attempted through lawsuits, which were initiated to achieve some measure of public utility regulation. Judicial regulation, as this approach has been termed, proved to be wholly unsatisfactory. The cost and delay inherent in such proceedings served to thwart the effective achievement of common law rights. The judges sometimes were not sufficiently informed to deal competently with the technical problems of utility regulation. Further, courts could not provide continuing regulation or take preventive measures. Above all, the courts were unsuited to perform the most important function of regulation, that of determining the level of just and reasonable rates. Although a court might find an existing rate to be unreasonable (and, hence, unlawful), it could not prescribe a reasonable rate for the future, because such action is legislative in nature. Consequently, other methods of regulation were sought.

2. DIRECT LEGISLATIVE REGULATION

The early public utilities were incorporated through the passage of special acts by the state legislatures. The charters thus granted contained both the usual corporate rights and a number of special privileges besides. These privileges were promotional in nature and often included tax exemption, the power of eminent domain, the right to use the public streets, and others. Monopoly rights to a particular service area were not usually granted, because competition was then thought to be suitable to public utilities. Rate regulation through the provisions of a corporate charter took the form of a ceiling or maximum limit on the rate which could be charged. In some cases a specific schedule of maximum rates was set forth. In other cases the yield or return on the common stock was limited to stated percentages. Toward the end of the nineteenth century, the states began to enact general incorporation laws under which the organization of a corporation became a routine matter of filing the necessary application with an officer of the state government. The charters granted to public utilities under the general incorporation laws contained broadly worded clauses relating to rates, service, and security issues. There was little difference in the effectiveness of regulation by corporate charter as between the special and general incorporation laws. Neither one was effective.

Direct legislative regulation through corporate charters failed for many reasons. The charter laws were general in nature and were not well adapted to specific situations which varied from place to place within a particular state. Legislators were not informed sufficiently on the technical aspects of utility operation, so that charter terms were often inadequate to serve the purposes intended. Charter terms were also rigid and inflexible in the face of changing circumstances in a growing industry, which encouraged violation. When violations occurred, whether defensive or offensive, enforcement could be obtained only through court action. Hence, enforcement was sporadic and ineffective. Charter regulation could not provide the continuous and informed regulation which experience soon showed was necessary. As a result of the ineffectiveness of both judicial and legislative regulation, a new approach was taken. Late in the nineteenth century, utility regulation came under the control of the local governments. This was the first important form of regulation.

3. LOCAL REGULATION BY FRANCHISE

From the late nineteenth century to about 1920, public utilities were regulated principally by local governments through franchise contracts. In a few states, this form of regulation continues in use. The *franchise* may be defined as a grant of special privileges by a city to a public utility which permits the company: (a) to occupy the streets with its poles, mains, underground conduits, pipes, tracks, and so forth; and (b) to supply stated public utility services, usually as a monopoly. Without authority to occupy the streets to conduct business, the utility would be trespassing. Municipal authority in this area is derived from the state. After franchise terms have been negotiated by representatives of the city and the company, the agreement is enacted into law through the passage of a municipal ordinance. When accepted by the company, the franchise becomes a contract between the city and the company. In return for the privileges conferred by the franchise, there are also obligations imposed on the utility which govern maximum rates, adequate and safe service, taxes, and facilities and their extensions. Local regulation by franchise contract, it should be noted, was a logical development in a time when technical and market factors confined the service areas of public utilities largely within the city limits of the communities served.

Before continuing this survey of regulation by franchise, it would be useful to define the current importance and function of the franchise in public utility regulation. The franchise served as the most important method of regulation through much of the latter half of the nineteenth century and into the period which ended with World War I. Inherent weaknesses in the franchise method and technological change in the utility industries caused local franchise regulation to be almost completely superseded in importance by state commission regulation. In a few states franchise regulation continues to be important. For the most part, however, local franchises still exist but are limited in function, often dealing largely with the character and use of the streets by the physical facilities of the utilities, while economic regulation is carried out by the state commissions.

Of greater present importance than the franchise is the *certificate of public convenience and necessity,* which is the basic authority required from the state government in order to do business as a local public utility in a specified service area. The state utility commissions in most states have the authority to issue these certificates. In a few states certificates are not required; there, the local franchise is usually the basic operating authority.

The public policy governing the issuance of certificates operates consistently with the public policy clearly favoring monopoly in the supply of local public utility services. As a practical matter, the monopoly status of local public utilities is established and maintained by the refusal of state commissions to authorize competition in individual markets. This holds true regardless of the provisions of the certificates issued, for many states do not issue certificates that confer monopoly rights upon the certificate holders. For example, a study of the certificates issued in each state to privately owned electric and gas distribution utilities shows that, although most states issue certificates which confer monopoly rights ("exclusive" certificates), a sizable minority issues certificates that specifically refrain from granting monopoly rights ("nonexclusive" certificates).[1] In states where the certificates are nonexclusive, the franchises issued locally usually are also nonexclusive. Thus, the monopoly status of local public utilities is primarily a function of public policy favoring that objective rather than a consequence of the terms and provisions of certificates. It should be added that the certificate, unlike the franchise, is not a contract. Ideally, franchise and certificate terms should complement one another in placing regulatory authority where it is best carried out. This discussion now returns to an examination of franchise regulation.

A. *The Duration of Franchises.* Public utility franchises are classified on the basis of the time periods over which they extend. The duration of the franchise is important because it can influence both the effectiveness of regulation and the financing of the utility to which it applies. On the basis of duration, franchises are classified as *perpetual, limited-term,* and *indeterminate.*

Perpetual franchises are those which have no date of expiration, or which have such long terms (999 years) as to amount to the same thing. Such franchises date from the earliest years of the industry and are not issued any longer. Those still in force are largely held by urban transit companies. Some franchises have been held to be perpetual in circumstances where both the state law and the franchise itself placed no limits on the duration of a franchise.[2] The perpetual franchise is thought to be advantageous in that it attracts capital investment. The disadvantages include the fact that the city gives up substantial bargaining power in negotiating with the

---

[1] *Moody's Public Utility Manual 1960,* pp. a153–154.

[2] *Owensboro* v. *Cumberland Telephone and Telegraph Co.,* 230 U.S. 58 (1913).

utility, since the perpetual franchise can only be terminated by condemnation through the city's power of eminent domain.

Limited-term franchises have a duration of about 50 years or less. Franchises of longer duration take on the character of perpetual franchises. The limited-term franchise developed out of the need for periodic adjustments in franchise terms due to changing economic and technological conditions. This, in fact, is the principal advantage of franchises of this type. Disadvantages, however, also accompanied such franchises. When the limited-term franchise was confined to a relatively short period, say ten years, the utility company often faced difficulty and high costs in financing permanent improvements. In addition, long-range planning was not encouraged. As the franchise neared its end, the uncertainty of renewal terms or renewal itself sometimes led utilities to hold back on both service extensions and general and street maintenance, where the latter was required. However, the chief disadvantage lay in the fact that rates set by contract for a fixed time period could be rendered either too high or too low by changed technical and economic conditions subsequent to the negotiation of the franchise. Modification usually could not be obtained without the consent of both parties, which sometimes proved difficult to arrange if one party or the other sought to retain what had turned out to be an advantage. It should also be noted that the limited-term franchise ordinarily was supposed to provide conditions for the transfer of the company's assets to the city or to another company at the end of the franchise term. This condition was intended to assure good performance by the utility. In practice, this provision commonly proved to be unworkable. Franchise terms sometimes were inadequate in defining the method whereby the value of the property could be determined; or the city was in no position to make the purchase regardless of whether or not it desired to do so.

A third type of franchise is the *indeterminate term,* or *terminable, franchise.* It is ordinarily referred to as an *indeterminate permit* and is more closely associated with the era of state commission regulation than with municipal regulation. The principal feature of the indeterminate permit is that it has no expiration date; instead, it remains in effect until terminated by public authority. If terminated, the city ordinarily has an option to acquire the property, and the utility is assured of just compensation as determined by the state commission. The indeterminate permit is intended to encourage the utility to perform its duties faithfully. In this respect it reflects a past era when service quality was not of the generally satisfactory kind expected and received today. The indeterminate permit has the advantage of enabling the utility to continue to expand as required by the public, knowing that it will be fairly compensated for its property in the event that the permit is terminated. In its modern form, the indeterminate permit ordinarily has these characteristics: (a) it constitutes a franchise authorizing local operations through the use of streets and alleyways, with the city retaining relatively few regulatory powers; (b) principal regulatory authority is removed from city jurisdiction and conveyed to the state commission; and (c) the utility gains exclusive control of its market, provided that it renders adequate service. It is provided, further, that the permit may be terminated by municipal acquisition upon payment of just compensation.

B. *Franchise Terms.* When franchises were the chief means of exercising public regulation, they tended to become elaborate documents. Because franchises were an attempt to regulate by contract, their terms spelled out in detail the specific points of agreement which had been negotiated. The matter of franchise duration has been surveyed above. In addition, franchises covered numerous other matters. Service quality was defined in terms which covered adequacy, dependability, extensions, speed of streetcars, the purity of water, the heating value of gas, and so on. Other provisions governed safety and facilities and their inspection. The franchise also contained rate provisions, often rigidly defining the amounts which would be charged for the duration of the franchise. Where no provision permitted the periodic readjustment of rates, changing economic conditions often rendered the rates unreasonably high or low. The inflation of the World War I period, for example, dealt ruinously with the urban transit industry—bound by franchise to the five-cent fare. The best rates are not necessarily the lowest. More desirable by far is a policy which promotes a good quality of utility service and then prices that service so as to cover costs plus a fair return or profit. Other franchise terms covered accounts and reporting, monopoly rights, the arbitration of labor disputes, taxes, free and special services for the city, and franchise acquisition and transfer to another company. The foregoing only outlines the nature of franchise terms and provisions, which in their actual statement became exceedingly complex.

C. Weaknesses of Franchise Regulation. Franchise regulation in almost all states was replaced in the years following 1907 by the state regulatory commissions. The transition changed the franchise into little more than a permit to use the streets. The reasons for this transition are not hard to find. First of all, franchise regulation was largely ineffective. This was largely due to the fact that it was impossible to regulate a dynamic industry in a rapidly growing economy by rigid franchise terms that were not readily capable of adjustment to changing circumstances. In addition, the drafting of franchise terms often left much to be desired. Second, franchise regulation encountered the problem of inadequate jurisdiction. Effective regulation requires the jurisdiction of the regulatory authority to be coextensive with the area served by the utilities regulated. This was made increasingly difficult under franchise regulation as cities grew beyond their defined limits and, more important, as advancing public utility technology made it more economical for one utility to serve a number of cities within an area instead of only one city, as had been the case earlier. Accordingly, regulation by state commissions came to be regarded generally as a more practical alternative. A third weakness of franchise regulation was that city governments generally failed to equip themselves to undertake the conduct of effective regulation. Even if cities were to do so, it would be unnecessarily duplicative. A single state commission could ordinarily administer the regulatory function at lower cost and with greater efficiency.

D. The Present Extent of Franchise Regulation. Franchise regulation at present is important in only a few states. Among these states there is considerable variation in procedure and regulatory jurisdiction. In Louisiana, for example, the state commission has no jurisdiction over New Orleans Public Service, Inc.; the city of New Orleans regulates the company's electric, gas, and transit rates. Minnesota and South Dakota are both prominent franchise-regulation states. However, the state commissions in South Dakota and Minnesota regulate telephone rates and, in Minnesota, transit rates as well. A somewhat similar situation prevails in Ohio, where the state commission regulates telephone rates directly and serves as an appellate body to decide disputes over rates set at the local level for other utilities. Texas cities of over 2,000 population have the power to regulate public utility rates; the rates thus determined may be appealed to the state commission in gas utility cases only. In Kansas, the primary power to regulate utilities operating entirely within the confines of a single city rests with the city council; rate ordinances may be appealed to the state commission. In Arkansas, the cities and the state commission have concurrent jurisdiction over rate making; however, any rate making by cities may be appealed to the state commission.

4. STATE COMMISSION REGULATION

A. An Introduction to the State Commissions. The principal powers of the state commissions cover: rate, service, and financial regulation; the prescription of accounting systems; and the issuance of certificates and permits authorizing various services and the extension, expansion and abandonment of facilities. The extent of commission authority in each field varies somewhat from state to state, depending on statutory language and judicial interpretation.

The authority to regulate intrastate public utility business rests with each of the state legislatures. This power to regulate, however, has been delegated to state commissions by the state legislatures which created them. The state commissions receive their delegated powers in the form of broadly worded but limited statutory authority over specifically designated public utility industries. Once created, empowered, and organized, a state commission operates as the expert arm of the state legislature and performs the regulatory functions which the legislature is not well qualified or equipped to undertake. In exercising its delegated authority, the commission establishes specific standards and requirements in the form of rules and regulations in order to implement and give meaning to its broadly worded statutory powers.

A typical state utility commission consists of three elected or appointed commissioners and a technical staff composed of engineers, accountants, economists, and lawyers. The commissions in most states are called either the *public service commission* or the *public utilities commission*. In some states the agency is called the *railroad commission* and, in a few, the *corporation commission, commerce commission,* or *warehouse commission*.

Regulatory commissions perform legislative, judicial, and administrative functions. The commission acts in a legislative capacity when, by a majority vote of the commissioners, it authorizes the rates which a public utility may charge the public for its service. It also acts in a legislative capacity when it prescribes rules and regulations which give specific meaning to statutory provisions. Commissions act judicially when they decide that the existing rates of a public utility are unlawful, as they would have to do in the course of a decision prescribing different rates for the future. They also have a judicial role in hearing service complaints from customers. In addition, the commissions use an essentially judicial procedure in holding hearings to take evidence in formal cases. This is discussed more fully in Chapter 4. Finally, commissions act in an administrative capacity in seeing that their decisions and orders are carried out and in receiving and studying regular reports from the utilities under their jurisdiction.

B. Development of State Utility Commissions. Public utility regulation by state commissions became important when the ineffectiveness of franchise regulation came to be recognized. The state commissions in their modern form date from 1907, when New York, Wisconsin, and Georgia enacted effective permanent regulatory legislation. Within the first ten years after 1907, 24 states had established commissions along the lines of the Wisconsin and New York commissions, although not all had the same broad jurisdiction and powers. By 1930 every state except Delaware, together with the District of Columbia, Hawaii, the Philippines (which became independent in 1946), and Puerto Rico, had organized regulatory commissions. Delaware later created a state commission, and Alaska established a commission in 1960.

This widespread reliance upon the state utility commission as a permanent regulatory instrument came long after the first use of the commission for this purpose. The development passed through three stages, which included: (a) the "weak," or advisory, commissions; (b) the short-lived Granger commissions; and (c) the modern commissions of today. The first stage saw the formation of so-called "weak" commissions for the purpose of regulating railroads. These initial commissions were organized in Rhode Island in 1839, in New Hampshire in 1844, in Connecticut in 1853, in Vermont in 1855, in Maine in 1858, in Ohio in 1867, and in Massachusetts in 1869. These commissions had no power over rates. They appraised the property taken by the railroads under the right of eminent domain, enforced railroad safety statutes, investigated to determine whether the railroads complied with the terms of their corporate charters, collected and reported data, and made recommendations to the state legislatures. Competition was relied upon to assure proper rates and service.

The second stage in state commission development resulted from the Granger movement, which was mentioned earlier in connection with *Munn* v. *Illinois*. The Granger regulatory laws were designed to place a ceiling on railroad rates. The maximum rates were either prescribed by law and administered by a commission or were left to the determination of the commission. Between 1871 and 1874 the Grange-dominated legislatures of Illinois, Iowa, Minnesota, and Wisconsin passed such maximum rate statutes. Iowa, however, did not establish a commission. In 1879 Georgia established a state commission for this purpose and, in the same year, the new California constitution directed the establishment of a similar commission.

The Granger commissions did not last long. Between 1875 and 1876, for example, Minnesota, Iowa, and Wisconsin substituted weak advisory commissions in place of Granger regulation. The rapid decline of this phase of regulation has been attributed to the Panic of 1873, which was associated with a decline in railroad construction and also seemed to bear out charges that Granger legislation discouraged investment in the regulated enterprises. It should be noted, too, that Granger regulation was not particularly well-conceived. It was characterized by the rigidity which necessarily accompanies legislative rate making and by the pitfalls inherent in setting a uniform rate level for companies operating under varying conditions and in different markets.

The third or modern phase in the development of the state commissions, as mentioned earlier, began with the enactment of thoroughgoing regulatory statutes in New York, Wisconsin, and Georgia in 1907. Although this date is commonly acknowledged as the start of the state commission movement, Massachusetts in 1885 had established state regulation of gas utilities. This step, however, was not prompted by an interest in rate regulation so much as by the desire of the suppliers of coal gas for market protection from prospective competitors using the water gas-manufacturing process.

The pioneer regulatory statutes of 1907 were largely the result of the leadership of Governor Charles Evans Hughes of New York and Governor Robert M. LaFollette of Wisconsin. Hughes was later a candidate for the Presidency and a Chief Justice of the United States Supreme Court. LaFollette was later a distinguished member of the United States Senate. Both these reform governors saw the need for continuous utility regulation by competent state authority.

The Wisconsin statute, which served as a model for many other states, granted the existing state railroad commission jurisdiction over companies furnishing the public with light, power, heat, water, gas, telephone, and telegraph services. Street railways were defined as railroads and regulated with the other transportation public utilities. The law required the commission: (a) to determine the valuation (for rate-making purposes) of the property of each utility; (b) to be informed of all utility construction; (c) to prescribe mandatory uniform systems of accounts; (d) to determine annual rates of depreciation; (e) to provide for examinations and audits; and (f) to keep itself informed of the conduct of utility management. Each utility was required to post its rates with the commission and charge only these rates. The commission was authorized to investigate, on its own motion or on the motions of others, the rates or service of a utility. If, after proper investigation, the commission found the service in question to be substandard or the rates in question to be unreasonable or unjustly discriminatory, it could prescribe reasonable rates or adequate standards of service which would be mandatory upon the utility. Appeal to the courts for review of commission orders was provided, with the burden of proof on the party contesting the commission's order. This, then, was the nature of the powers conferred on the Wisconsin commission in the 1907 act, which set the pattern followed in varying degrees throughout the country.

C. Current Status of State Regulation. Commissions with power to regulate one or more of the public utility industries (including transportation utilities) now exist in all of the 50 states, the District of Columbia, and Puerto Rico. Commissions with some powers to regulate gas and electric rates of privately owned utilities exist in all but a few of the states. Only two state commissions do not regulate telephone rates. As of 1960, 15 states did not regulate urban transit companies and 11 did not regulate privately owned water supply utilities.[3]

5. FEDERAL REGULATION

The Constitution delegates to Congress an unrestricted power to regulate interstate and foreign commerce. Through the use of this authority, the Congress has undertaken the regulation of some of the public utilities which are the concern of this book. For this purpose, Congress has delegated limited regulatory authority to three administrative commissions of its own creation. These include the Federal Power Commission (FPC), the Federal Communications Commission (FCC), and the Securities and Exchange Commission (SEC). Taken together, these commissions regulate the development of jurisdictional hydroelectric power sites, the interstate transmission and sales at wholesale of electricity and natural gas, interstate communication via telephone, telegraph, and cable, and public utility holding companies.

---

[3] Federal Power Commission, *State Commission Jurisdiction and Regulation of Electric and Gas Utilities* (Washington, D.C.: Government Printing Office, 1960), pp. 2–3 and 36–39.

A. *Electricity and Natural Gas.* The Federal Power Commission was created by the Federal Water Power Act of 1920.[4] Its jurisdiction at that time covered only the licensing of applicants seeking to construct hydroelectric power projects on the navigable waters of the United States. Subsequently, the jurisdiction of the FPC was extended by Congress to include: (a) the transmission and sale at wholesale of electric energy in interstate commerce; and (b) the transportation and sale for resale of natural gas in interstate commerce. This expansion of FPC jurisdiction was accomplished by the passage of the Federal Power Act of 1935[5] and the Natural Gas Act of 1938.[6]

Before the passage of these acts, the interstate transportation and wholesale prices of electricity and natural gas were not subject to government regulation. Supreme Court decisions during the 1920's barred state commissions from regulating the wholesale rates of gas and electricity sold in interstate commerce.[7] The expansion of the electric and natural gas industries into interstate commerce gave rise to a new problem, sometimes referred to as a "regulatory gap," for these cases demonstrated the fact that public utility technology and markets had outgrown the jurisdiction of the state commissions. This was another case of a need for regulatory authority of the same scope as the service area of the utilities involved. The problem was significant because the wholesale cost of the natural gas or electricity imported from another state may be an important component of the costs of retail service supplied in the importing states. The effect of the electric and natural gas legislation of 1935 and 1938, respectively, was to give jurisdiction to the FPC to regulate the wholesale prices at which retail gas and electric distributors purchased natural gas and electricity produced outside the consuming state. It has been noted previously that in 1954 the Natural Gas Act was held to be applicable to independent producers of natural gas.

B. *Telephone and Telegraph.* The interstate telephone, telegraph, and cable industries were brought under Federal regulation in 1910 and placed under the jurisdiction of the Interstate Commerce Commission. The passage of the Communications Act of 1934[8] transferred to the newly created Federal Communications Commission the powers of the ICC over telephones, telegraphs, and cables and the powers of the Federal Radio Commission over radio and broadcasting.

C. *Holding Companies.* Gas and electric utility holding companies during the 1920's grew to be large and complex. There was unmistakable evidence of financial mismanagement in this part of the public utility industry. The Public Utility Holding Company Act of 1935[9] was enacted in order to achieve geographic and corporate simplification and a fair distribution of voting power among the security holders in the companies under jurisdiction. The Securities and Exchange Commission was designated by the Congress to administer the Holding Company Act.

---

[4] 41 Stat. L. 1063.

[5] Title II of the Public Utility Act of 1935 (49 Stat. L. 838).

[6] 52 Stat. L. 821.

[7] *Missouri* v. *Kansas Natural Gas Co.*, 265 U.S. 298 (1924); *Public Utilities Commission of Rhode Island* v. *Attelboro Steam and Electric Co.*, 273 U.S. 83 (1927).

[8] 48 Stat. L. 1064.

[9] Title I of the Public Utility Act of 1935 (49 Stat. L. 803).

4 Administrative Procedure and Review

This chapter mainly concerns: (a) the administrative procedure by which public utility commissions reach decisions and (b) the right to test those decisions in the courts, which is called *judicial review*.

Administrative procedure, first, must accord with certain "rules of fair play," formally designated as *procedural due process of law*. The essence of procedural due process in utility regulation comprises: (a) adequate notice to the utility company and others who may be interested that at a certain time, date, and place a specified matter involving the regulated company will be the subject of a public hearing to be held by the regulatory agency, and (b) opportunity for a public hearing on that particular matter, for the purpose of presenting evidence and rebutting opposition evidence. With respect to the Federal Administrative Procedure Act,[1] for example, it has been stated authoritatively that the law was designed to ". . . afford parties affected by administrative powers a means of knowing what their rights are and how they may be protected. By the same token administrators are provided with a simple course to follow in making administrative determinations."[2]

Second, the substance of the decisions issued by regulatory commissions must accord with the constitutional protections against confiscation of property. This requirement is designated as *substantive due process of law*.

A public utility, under regulation by government, has a right to both procedural and substantive due process. These rights are enforced and protected by a further right—judicial review—which permits the appeal of commission decisions to the courts. For example, if a commission rate order were to authorize a utility to earn an amount clearly insufficient to compensate its investors reasonably, to maintain its credit, and to attract capital, the utility would have grounds to take an appeal to the proper court and to claim there that the commission order should be reversed as confiscatory. Taken together, these rights incorporate in public utility regulation the protections guaranteed in applicable parts of the Fifth and Fourteenth Amendments of the Constitution.

As noted earlier, this chapter is concerned mainly with the procedural aspects of utility regulation and with judicial review. The substantive elements of the decisions issued by regulatory commissions are discussed in the chapters on rate making, which follow. Administrative procedure and review are a part of administrative law and not a part of the study of economics. However, the making and reviewing of regulatory decisions has undeniable economic significance in that those decisions determine economic rights and duties. Accordingly, the entire process of making and reviewing regulatory decisions assumes an economic importance and requires understanding. As a final introductory note, it should be pointed out

---

1 60 Stat. 237 (1946).

2 *Administrative Procedure Act, Legislative History,* Sen. Doc. No. 248, 79th Cong., 2nd sess., 1946, p. 193.

that, although regulatory commissions act in a legislative capacity when prescribing rates for the future, the process by which the decision and its implementing order are determined is judicial in nature. In fact, the administrative procedure followed in public utility regulation was adapted to commission use from the procedure of the courts.

Administrative procedure in all federal commissions is governed by the Administrative Procedure Act of 1946. In the respective states, a variety of circumstances prevail. At least seven have enacted comprehensive administrative procedure statutes; some, such as the Wisconsin and North Dakota laws, predated that of the federal government. By 1953 about half the states had enacted laws dealing with important segments of administrative procedure. States without general legislation of this kind are not without procedural safeguards, however. It has been a general practice to include provisions prescribing administrative procedure in the initial legislation establishing the regulatory agencies themselves.

Utility commissions handle both informal matters and formal cases. Informal matters are relatively numerous at the state commission level. They arise largely from consumer grievances concerning various aspects of the quality of utility service. After investigation by a commission staff member, the matter is usually adjusted or otherwise terminated with relatively little cost or time involved. However, the major concern here is with the formal cases decided by regulatory commissions, both state and federal. Formal cases include two types: (a) those which are initiated for the purpose of rule making and (b) those which require a decision on a contested issue (adjudication), such as an application by a utility for a change in rates or for authority to provide service in a new area.

1. RULE MAKING

A very important power of regulatory commissions is their statutory authority to adopt rules and regulations. The terms "rule" and "rule making," as used in the present context, include both rules and regulations. *Rule making* may be described as legislation at the administrative level within standards set by the statutes granting the agency authority to act.[3] A *rule* is a statement by a commission which applies generally and serves to implement a law or to prescribe a policy. When properly made, rules have the force of law. The authority of an agency to prescribe rules is circumscribed by the underlying statute.

The two types of rules are: (a) rules of practice and procedure and (b) substantive rules. *Rules of practice and procedure* set forth for the practicing lawyer the details relating to the filing of various documents with the commission and the conduct of formal hearings. *Rules of a substantive nature* serve to give specific meaning to the general language in the governing statutes. For example, the rule-making power has been used to prescribe uniform systems of accounts for the various types of utilities, to establish service standards, to require utilities to qualify for certificates of authorization before constructing and installing additional facilities, to establish safety standards, and to accomplish numerous other regulatory objectives.

The procedure by which rules are adopted varies in different statutes. The commission may or may not be required to hold a public hearing before it adopts a rule, depending upon the statute. Even when not required to do so, commissions considering the adoption or amendment of a rule may: (a) inform interested parties of the matter under consideration; (b) invite the filing of written

[3] *Willapoint Oysters, Inc.* v. *Ewing,* 174 F. 2d 676, 693 (1949); *cert.* den. 338 U.S. 860 (1949).

comments; and (c) provide for a public hearing. This is especially the case where important matters are concerned. When the matter is of lesser importance and there is no requirement of a hearing, the commission may simply adopt the rule and serve it upon the parties affected. New or amended rules are usually published upon adoption. The federal agencies, for example, utilize the *Federal Register* for this purpose. Finally, an order implementing a new or amended rule is subject to court review if a person claiming to be aggrieved by it institutes a suit.

2. ADJUDICATION OF CONTESTED CASES

Adjudication is the process whereby a commission arrives at a decision and issues an order disposing of a formal case involving a contested issue. For the most part, adjudicated cases involve: (1) proposed changes in rates; (2) applications for authority to change the scope and nature of the utility company's business activities, such as plant expansions, service to a new area, acquisition of the facilities of another utility, abandonment of an existing service, or the issuance of securities; and (3) service complaints, which occur primarily among state commissions.

A. *Starting a Case.* A formal case may be instituted by a utility, by one or more customers, or by the commission acting on its own motion. The cases which are started by utilities or their customers result from the filing of a motion, petition, application, or complaint with the commission. If the commission acts on its own motion to institute a case, it will issue an order to that effect. After a formal case is initiated, the commission by notice will set a date for a public hearing which will provide interested parties an opportunity to present evidence, cross-examine opposition evidence, and present rebuttal evidence. A verbatim record of what is said at the hearing serves as the basis for the decision of the commission.

B. *Notice.* Proper procedure requires that all parties receive full and adequate notice before a public hearing is held in which their interests are involved. The primary object of this requirement is to provide the parties the opportunity to prepare adequately to defend or represent their interests during the hearing. Accordingly, adequate notice requires the commission to inform the parties, sufficiently in advance, of the time, date, and place of the hearing and of the legal authority and jurisdiction under which the hearing is to be held. More important, however, is the fact that notice of hearing must also include a statement of the matters of fact and law asserted, so as to inform all concerned of the subject matter and the issues involved. The rules of the Federal Power Commission, for example, provide for the publication of notice in the *Federal Register* at least 15 days in advance of the hearing, and for the mailing of copies of the notice to interested parties and to states or other government authorities deemed to have an official interest in the case.[4]

C. *Hearing.* The hearing provides each party with the opportunity to present evidence in the form of testimony and exhibits in order to make a record supporting its position. Witnesses are sworn before testifying and may be subjected to cross-examination afterward. A verbatim record of the proceedings is made by a reporter, and copies of the transcript may be obtained by anyone concerned with the case.

The hearing sometimes takes place before the commissioners; however, many cases are heard before a hearing examiner, an official whose function and responsibilities are similar to those of a

[4] Federal Power Commission, *Rules of Practice and Procedure,* Section 1.19 (b).

trial judge. He serves as the representative of the commission and is its agent. Ordinarily, he is empowered to make an initial decision or a recommended decision on the case, which he passes up to the commissioners themselves for final decision. Examiners serving in federal commissions are by law independent of agency control insofar as decision-making is concerned. In the state commissions, examiners are not always independent to the same extent.

It is sometimes written that the evidence presented during a commission hearing is not bound by the same strict rules of evidence that prevail in the courts. In fact, this is provided for officially in some jurisdictions. However, some experienced lawyers in this field think that as a matter of practice there is now little, if any, difference between the courts and the commissions in this respect. During the hearing, the presiding officer rules on the admissibility to the record of evidence offered. The Wisconsin law, for example, provides for the admission of ". . . all testimony having reasonable probative value," while requiring the exclusion of ". . . immaterial, irrelevant or unduly repetitious testimony."[5] Examiners' rulings on admissibility of evidence can be appealed to the commission by any of the parties to the case. The weight accorded to the evidence admitted to the record is determined by the examiner in preparing the initial decision and by the commission in reaching its final decision. The Federal Power Commission has held that the evidence and contentions presented by its staff are not entitled to preferred consideration ". . . when our staff assumes an adversary position in a formal proceeding. . . ."[6]

Thus, the hearing is an opportunity for all interested parties: (a) to present evidence in support of their positions; (b) to cross-examine the testimony of opposition witnesses; and, if desired, (c) to present rebuttal testimony designed to invalidate specific parts of opposition testimony. When the hearing has been carried through these phases, it is adjourned.

D. *Decision.* There are several principal routes which may be taken toward a final commission decision once the public hearing has been concluded. (1) If the commission hears the case, it may receive *briefs* (summaries of the evidence and arguments) from the parties at some time after the hearing and later issue its decision and serve copies on all parties. (2) If an examiner hears the case, the commission upon request may decide to dispense with his decision and may direct him to certify the entire record to the commission for final decision. The purpose of this is to speed the decision-making process when the public interest requires it. If the commission decides to adopt this method, the same procedure is followed as in (1) above. (3) If the examiner hears the case, he usually writes an initial or recommended decision or report, after receiving briefs from the parties. The examiner's decision may be served on the parties and passed up to the commission for final decision. If this method is followed, the parties may file exceptions to the examiner's decision which advance specific objections to one or more parts of that decision. (4) In some commissions the examiner's decision is sent directly to the commission for final decision and is not served on the parties. Regardless of the procedure followed to arrive at a final decision, the party or parties aggrieved by that decision may file an application for rehearing for the purpose of persuading the commission that it has decided incorrectly.

Under Federal Power Commission procedure, for example, the parties may

[5] *Wisconsin Statutes,* Sec. 227–10 (1953).

[6] *In re Colorado Interstate Gas Co.,* 10 FPC 105, 106 (1951).

file briefs with the examiner prior to his decision; at the examiner's discretion, he may hear oral argument in addition, although this seldom occurs. The function of the brief is to argue the essentials of the case made by each party or participant during the hearing, with appropriate references to the places in the record where substantiation may be found.

After the Federal Power Commission examiner files his initial or recommended decision, copies are served on all parties. If, within the following thirty days, none of the parties or the Commission raises any objection to the examiner's decision, it becomes the final decision of the Commission. If, more likely, exceptions (objections) are filed, the Commission makes a final decision, giving due consideration to the exceptions and, sometimes, after hearing oral argument in cases deemed important.[7]

The decisions issued by examiners and commissioners must set forth *findings of facts,* which are the conclusions reached on all disputed factual issues. Findings of fact are required to be based upon substantial evidence of record. If the case involves disputed issues of law, it is necessary for the decision to set forth conclusions of law as well as findings of fact. The basic reason for the requirement of findings is to assure a reasoned decision rather than an arbitrary one. The findings also provide a reviewing court and the parties with a basis for understanding how the commission arrived at its decision. Thus, findings permit review to be undertaken on a more informed basis. The Federal Administrative Procedure Act goes beyond a requirement of findings of fact based upon substantial evidence. It requires federal commission actions to be supported by substantial evidence upon consideration of the *whole* record, as distinguished from substantial evidence to support only one side of the case. The Supreme Court on this point has said, "The substantiality of evidence must take into account whatever in the record fairly detracts from its weight."[8]

When making decisions, the examiners and commissions are required to rely upon the record in deciding questions involving disputed facts. Aside from matters of fact, it is permissible to rely upon court and commission precedents and expertise in the technical subject matter involved in the case. However, expertise cannot be substituted for evidence. It has been held that ". . . the expertise of a commission usefully serves it in evaluating the evidence but that expertise cannot supply evidence and cannot without findings made upon the critical issues before it, guide a commission to a rational and lawful decision."[9]

The commission's decision, once made and ordered into effect, may be the subject of an application for rehearing filed by a dissatisfied party. The Natural Gas Act, for example, allows 30 days after issuance of a final decision or order for the filing of applications for rehearing. Such requests must be accompanied by a showing of alleged error in the decision or order, or it may be advanced that events subsequent to the final order have changed the situation. If the commission rejects this application, the aggrieved party has no further remedy available through the commission. The next possible step is to seek judicial review.

3. JUDICIAL REVIEW

Judicial review of commission decisions and orders is available to those parties to a commission case who are

[7] Federal Power Commission, *Rules of Practice and Procedure,* Sections 1.30 and 1.31.

[8] *Universal Camera Co.* v. *NLRB,* 340 U.S. 474, 487–488 (1951).

[9] *Capital Transit Co.* v. *Public Utilities Commission,* 213 F. 2d 176, 187 (1953).

aggrieved as a result of the commission's action. Review can be initiated only after all remedies available at the commission have been exhausted. Upon review, the commission's decision and order may be reversed, modified, or upheld. The party who seeks to have the commission's order overturned ordinarily bears the burden of proof in the proceedings before the reviewing court, for the commission's order usually carries a presumption of validity. If the commission is upheld in the reviewing court, the aggrieved party can appeal that decision to a higher court. Similarly, if the commission is reversed upon review, it can appeal that decision to a higher court.

Regulatory statutes almost always designate the court to which appeals from commission decisions may be taken. The decisions of the federal commissions may be reviewed initially in the United States Court of Appeals. The decisions of the state commissions are reviewed in the state court systems, with ultimate appeal to the United States Supreme Court possible if a constitutional issue is raised. In most jurisdictions, the reviewing court bases its decision upon the record made during the hearing at the commission (appellate review), while in three states the court may rehear the whole case (*de novo* review).[10]

The Johnson Act, passed by Congress in 1934, caused a substantial change in approach with respect to the review of state and local rate case decisions. The effect of the Johnson Act was to confine to the state court systems the review of state and local decisions and orders in public utility rate cases. Stated differently, the Johnson Act prohibits the initial review of state and local rate orders by the United States District Courts. Prior to the Johnson Act, state and local rate orders frequently were appealed to Federal District Courts on constitutional grounds. Owing to the nature of the then existing law applicable to such cases, the state and local rate orders often were reversed in the federal courts. Resentment in the states, caused by these reversals, led to the enactment of the Johnson Act.[11]

More specifically, the Johnson Act excludes from the original jurisdiction of the United States District Courts any suit seeking to restrain the enforcement of a rate order issued by a state commission or a rate-making body of a political subdivision of a state.[12] The Act provides that Federal District Courts cannot restrain state or local rate orders where the jurisdiction of the court is based solely upon (a) diversity of citizenship[13] or (b) constitutional grounds —if the order in question:

(1) affects rates chargeable by a public utility;

(2) does not interfere with interstate commerce; and

(3) has been made after reasonable notice and hearing, and where a plain, speedy, and efficient remedy may be had at law or in equity in the courts of the state.

A. *Scope of Review.* Commission decisions and the orders implementing them may be appealed to the courts on a number of grounds. Some of the principal grounds for review are listed below.

(1) The statute relied upon by the commission is unconstitutional.

(2) The commission exceeded its statutory authority or jurisdiction.

(3) The commission's order was not supported by findings.

[10] Federal Power Commission, *State Commission Jurisdiction and Regulation of Electric and Gas Utilities* (Washington, D.C.: Government Printing Office, 1960), p. 15.

[11] 32 *Mich. L. Rev.* 1154 (1934).

[12] 48 Stat. 775 (1934).

[13] A basis for federal jurisdiction when the parties on each side of a suit are citizens of different states.

(4) The findings were not supported by substantial evidence.

(5) The order violates specific constitutional guarantees.

(6) The order resulted from unlawful procedure or some other error of law.

(7) The order was based upon a misinterpretation of the law administered by the commission.

As a general rule, the courts will accept the commission's findings of fact as conclusive if based upon substantial evidence. This is known as the *substantial evidence rule*. It was established by the Supreme Court early in the history of the Interstate Commerce Commission.[14] As a result, review is ordinarily based upon legal and constitutional grounds. The Supreme Court has stated:

> Once a fair hearing has been given, proper findings made and other statutory requirements satisfied, the courts cannot intervene in the absence of a clear showing that the limits of due process have been overstepped. If the Commission's order as applied to the facts before it and viewed in its entirety, produces no arbitrary result, our inquiry is at an end.[15]

One qualification to the substantial-evidence rule merits noting. In cases where a constitutional issue is involved, the reviewing court may make an independent judgment of both the law and the facts, if it adheres to the *Ben Avon* rule or some variation of it.

B. *The Ben Avon Rule.* The *Ben Avon* case, decided by the Supreme Court in 1920, grew out of a state commission rate order that was challenged by a utility on constitutional grounds.[16] The company claimed that its rates had been set so low that its property had been confiscated and therefore taken without due process of law, in violation of the Fourteenth Amendment. The company contended that the state court should review both the law and the facts determined by the state commission and make an "independent judgment" on the constitutional question. The state commission, on the other hand, claimed that there was substantial evidence to support its factual findings and decision. Thus, this case involved a test of the claim for independent judgment where a constitutional issue was raised, as against reliance upon the substantial-evidence rule.

The Supreme Court ruled that, when a property owner claimed confiscation as the result of an administrative order, the due process clause of the Fourteenth Amendment required an independent judicial review of both the law and the facts in the case. The Court also held that a review limited to an inquiry of whether there was substantial evidence to support the commission's findings was insufficient to protect the constitutional rights of the complainant. The effect of this decision was to expand the scope of review to include the facts bearing upon any constitutional issue.

In 1936 the Supreme Court handed down a decision in the *St. Joseph Stock Yards* case which reaffirmed *Ben Avon* but modified it.[17] The Court held that the findings of fact determined by the agency should be accorded considerable weight. In effect, this meant that commission findings of fact were presumed to be valid until the contrary was shown. Nevertheless, the independent-judgment rule was reaffirmed. Chief Justice Hughes, for the majority, stated:

> . . . Legislative agencies, with varying qualifications, work in a field peculiarly

[14] *Interstate Commerce Commission* v. *Illinois Central Railroad Co.,* 215 U.S. 452, 470 (1910); *Interstate Commerce Commission* v. *Union Pacific Railroad Co.,* 222 U.S. 541 (1912).

[15] *FPC* v. *Natural Gas Pipeline Co.,* 62 S.Ct. 736, 742 (1942).

[16] *Ohio Valley Water Co.* v. *Ben Avon Borough,* 253 U.S. 287 (1920).

[17] *St. Joseph Stock Yards Co.* v. *U.S.,* 298 U.S. 38 (1936).

exposed to political demands. Some may be expert and impartial, others subservient. It is not difficult for them to observe the requirements of law in giving a hearing and receiving evidence. But to say that their findings of fact may be made conclusive where constitutional rights of liberty and property are involved, although the evidence clearly established that the findings are wrong and constitutional rights have been invaded, is to place those rights at the mercy of administrative officials and seriously to impair the security inherent in our judicial safeguards.[18]

What is the present status of the *Ben Avon* doctrine? Although it has never been expressly overruled, it is no longer important in the federal courts. This has come to pass because of: (a) the decline in the number of federal cases that might involve *Ben Avon,* resulting from enactment of the Johnson Act; (b) the emphasis of the courts and the Administrative Procedure Act upon proper agency procedure; and (c) the general retreat of the courts from their former position, in cases involving complex technical questions of fact and in which the commission's ruling was made pursuant to statutory authority and on the basis of findings supported by substantial evidence.[19]

In the state courts, the experience has been mixed. *Ben Avon,* or *Ben Avon* as modified by *St. Joseph Stock Yards,* prevails in some states while in others this doctrine has been rejected.[20] The wide range of current views on this subject was indicated by the Supreme Judicial Court of Massachusetts, when it was confronted with the conclusion of one authority to the effect that the *Ben Avon* rule had "gradually died." The Court responded, "Perhaps so, but we would like to see the death certificate."[21]

---

18 *Ibid.,* p. 52.

19 *Railroad Commission* v. *Rowan and Nichols Oil Co.,* 310 U.S. 573, 581–582 (1940).

20 43 *Va. L. Rev.* 1027 (1957); 102 *U. Pa. L. Rev.* 108 (1953).

21 *Opinion of the Justices,* 106 N.E. 2d 259, 262 (1952).

PART II

THE ESSENTIALS OF RATE REGULATION

5 The Regulation of Operating Expenses

This chapter begins a survey of the economics of public utility rate making, which extends through Chapter 12—a case study that is intended to illustrate an application of rate-making principles.

The present chapter is primarily concerned with the regulation of public utility operating expenses as part of the process of rate making. However, before beginning an examination of that subject, it is necessary to present a capsule summary of the rate-making process as a whole. The beginning student is urged to master the terms and concepts set forth immediately below, because they provide a foundation for much that lies ahead.

1. THE COST OF SERVICE CONCEPT

The chief problem in public utility economics and regulation is that of rate making. Rates are made on an individual company basis, which is appropriate in light of the fact that each utility has a monopoly or near-monopoly position in the supply of one or more services to the public in a prescribed area. By contrast, a different rate-making approach is employed in the regulation of industries where there is intra-industry competition, such as the railroad and motor carrier industries. There, rates are made on an industry basis or an industry-area basis. This matter will be developed further in the next chapter.

The basic question involved in rate making is this: what is the utility company's total *cost of service?* Stated another way, this question asks: how much in *total revenue* should the public utility be authorized to collect through the rates charged for its sales of service? While not an answer to the question, it is a fundamental truism that the public utility under regulation should be authorized to collect, if possible, total revenues equal to its cost of service. For this reason, the revenue total that the utility is authorized to collect for sales of an estimated volume of service is usually called the *revenue requirement.*

The cost of service of a public utility is defined as the sum total of: (a) proper operating expenses; (b) depreciation expense; (c) taxes; and (d) a reasonable return on the net valuation of property. This is summarized in the following simple equations.

(1) Revenue Requirement = Cost of Service

(2) $RR = E + d + T + (V - D)R$

The symbols in the second equation represent the following factors:

RR = Revenue requirement
E = Operating expenses
d = Depreciation expense
T = Taxes
V = Gross valuation of the property serving the public
D = Accrued depreciation
R = Rate of return (a percentage)
$(V-D)$ = Rate base (net valuation)
$(V-D)R$ = Return amount, or earnings allowed on the rate base

The second equation above is the public utility rate-making formula. It says that a public utility, under efficient and economical management, requires revenues sufficient: (a) to cover proper operating expenses, depreciation expense, and the taxes that would be payable if the authorized rate of return were earned; and (b) to provide a reasonable return on the net valuation of the property used and useful in serving the public. As the formula indicates, the return amount is found by multiplying the net or depreciated valuation of utility property, called the *rate base* $(V-D)$, by the allowed rate of return thereon, R.

After the cost of service and revenue requirement have been determined by decision of the regulatory commission, the next and final step in the rate-making process involves pricing the service, or designing schedules of rates that are intended to produce the total revenue that the utility is authorized to collect from the public. Two aspects of the pricing of utility services merit noting. First, the formulation of schedules of rates, in most instances, is undertaken by the management of the utility, subject to commission review and possible modification. Second, individual rates for particular public utility services necessarily reflect many other factors besides costs. This will be discussed further in due course.

The public utility rate-making formula discussed above may indicate to the beginning reader that rate making is a relatively simple process. It is not. In actual practice, the determination of each of the components of the cost of service requires the exercise of informed and seasoned judgment with respect to a host of economic, financial, accounting, engineering, and other considerations. For this reason, "instant" rate making in contested proceedings is not ordinarily obtainable. A word of caution also should be expressed with respect to rate of return. A regulatory commission is powerless to "guarantee" a specified rate of return. All it can do is determine the rate of return that may be earned by the utility. It is up to the utility to earn it. Thus, the authorized rate of return is in the nature of an "opportunity" rather than a "guarantee." Some utilities in the urban transit and manufactured gas industries, among others on occasion, have found it impossible to convert this opportunity into realized earnings.

The present chapter and those that follow will consider in order each component in the cost of service as well as the pricing of each of the public utility services, except that public utility taxation will be taken up in Chapter 17.

In a public utility rate case, the regulatory commission will determine the cost of service of the utility company involved. The commission, in making rates, presumably does so for an indefinite period into the future. However, in order to do so, the commission must rely upon the record of costs of service in a "test period," or test year, which is usually the latest 12 months for which there are complete data. Consequently, future rates are made on the basis of past costs. Of course, "known changes" —occurring after the test period—usually are taken into consideration by commissions in order to make the test-year data as representative as possible of the cost situation that is apt to prevail in the future. Recognition is also sometimes given to expected near-future costs and to increasing cost trends. This adjustment of test-period data is particularly important when new financing for expansion is already in the process of arrangement but will not be reflected in test-year figures. A similar problem with respect to known changes arises in connection with operating expenses, which will be discussed later in this chapter. In conclusion, it may be noted that, although it is theoretically sound to make public utility rates on the basis of costs in a test period considered to be representative of the future, the test periods used in the post-World War II years generally have not remained representative for very long. This is to be expected, for the postwar years have been characterized by rapid expansion of plant and markets and inflationary increases in the costs of construction, equipment, supplies, and labor. Important technological advancements also occurred in this period. In addition, part of the decade of the 1950's and the early 1960's were characterized by higher costs of debt capital than had been experienced for some time previously, as well as by increased competition in the market for equity capital as a result of growth in other segments of the economy.

2. THE BASES OF OPERATING EXPENSE REGULATION

In most of the uniform systems of accounts prescribed for public utilities, the operating expense accounts are designed to show in detail the costs—except depreciation, amortization, certain property losses, taxes, and return to investors—incurred in supplying utility service. Thus operating expenses mainly include the costs of labor, maintenance, materials and supplies, and various services during the accounting period when the benefits of those costs are realized. Since operating expenses, by this approach, do not include depreciation expense or taxes, another term—*operating revenue deductions*—is used to refer to the aggregate of the amounts which must be deducted from gross operating revenues to determine net operating revenues for an accounting period. Included in operating revenue deductions are the operating expenses, depreciation expense, and taxes. However, in the uniform system of accounts for telephone utilities prescribed by the Federal Communications Commission, operating expenses include depreciation expense.

The regulation of operating expenses is an important part of public utility rate regulation; its purpose is to prevent the inclusion of improper operating expenses in the cost of service. On the other hand, commissions frequently treat as pro forma expense amounts that are charged under accounting regulations to income or otherwise. A common example of this is the treatment of charitable contributions in many jurisdictions. The importance of operating expense regulation becomes apparent when it is considered that annual operating expenses ordinarily amount to at least one-half of the annual gross operating revenues of a public utility. Nevertheless, far more regulatory attention has been directed toward other cost of service factors, particularly the rate base and the rate of return. This is largely the result of court decisions which, although not encouraging any hands-off policy with respect to regulation of operating expenses, have suggested a presumption of good faith on the part of management and which have recognized a latitude of proper managerial discretion.

The Supreme Court, as early as 1892, recognized the importance of regulatory review of utility operating expenses.[1] On that occasion, the Court observed that the rate-making power included the authority to disallow improper expenses. It was thought that to deny to regulatory authority the jurisdiction over operating expenses would render the legislative power to regulate rates subservient to the discretion of the regulated company. This refers to the fact that, under the cost-of-service method of regulation, the incurrence and allowance of improper operating expenses would result in a reduction of the return earned on rate base during a given test period and therefore might provide some basis for a claim for higher rates. However, on this point it has been ruled that operating expenses, to be allowable as part of the cost of service, must be limited to the reasonable costs of efficient operation.[2] In the determination of what is reasonable, managerial judgment is accorded considerable, but not limitless, latitude. The Supreme Court has held the following statement to comprise the "applicable general rule":

> The Commission is not the financial manager of the corporation and it is not empowered to substitute its judgment for that of the directors of the corporation; nor can it ignore items charged by the utility as operating expenses unless there is an abuse of discretion in that regard by the corporate officers.[3]

This matter also was ruled on in a case involving the regulation of Chicago stockyard charges by the Secretary of Agriculture. There, it had been contended that the incurrence of expenses was solely a matter of managerial discretion. The Court took an opposite view and upheld the regulatory policy of disallowing improper expenses, with this statement:

> The contention is that the amount to be expended for these purposes is purely a question of managerial judgment. But this overlooks the consideration that the charge is for a public service, and regulation cannot be frustrated by a requirement that the rate be made to compensate extravagant or unnecessary costs for these or any purposes.[4]

Commissions generally control operating expenses by excluding improper expenses from the cost of service. The effect of this policy of "disallowance" is to charge the expense in question to the stockholders instead of to the ratepayers. However, this policy is not without hazard, for to the extent that the return is diminished by disallowed expenses, the credit standing of the utility may be weakened, a fact which would be reflected in terms of the ease and cost of selling either refunding or new security issues. An alternative to the policy of disallowance would be one requiring utilities to submit for commission approval a budget of proposed expenses. Thus far, this approach has been little used.

In determining the operating expenses allowable in the cost of service, the expenses incurred are presumed to be reasonable and necessary for efficient operation until proved otherwise. In making rates for the future, commissions have included in the expenses allowed amounts which have not been incurred but which can be anticipated with some degree of certainty. Nonrecurring ex-

[1] *Chicago & Grand Trunk Railway* v. *Wellman,* 143 U.S. 339, 345–346 (1892).

[2] *Reno Power, Light & Water Co.* v. *Nevada Public Service Commission,* 298 F. 790 (1923).

[3] *Southwestern Bell Telephone Co.* v. *PSC of Missouri,* 262 U.S. 276, 289 (1923).

[4] *Acker* v. *U.S.,* 298 U.S. 426, 430–431 (1936).

penses, if allowed at all for rate-making purposes, are commonly amortized over a reasonable period of years.

3. MEASURES OF REASONABLE EXPENSES

Although regulatory commissions can, with cause, exclude improper operating expenses from the cost of service, managerial judgment in incurring costs is ordinarily given considerable weight. Assuming that the expense in question has been or will be incurred, and that it is necessary in order to serve the public, the only question remaining is one of reasonableness of amount. To this end, comparative *expense ratios* have been developed which provide a point of departure for further inquiry. Expense-ratio analysis involves a determination of the relationship between a particular expense category (such as electric distribution expenses) and some measure relating to total operations (such as gross operating revenues, total customers, or total output of service). Ratios thus construed permit one utility to be compared with others individually, or with a group of comparable utilities in a given year or over a period of time. Ratios of this kind can indicate that one utility has incurred relatively greater or lesser expenses of a particular type than some other individual utilities or group of comparable utilities. Alternately, expense ratios for one company, taken over time, can reflect the effect of a change in managerial policy in the incurrence of expenses or a change in market characteristics. Ratios at best serve only to call attention to the need for deeper inquiry into the facts. Of themselves, the ratios may be relatively meaningless without a determination of the cause for any particular expense ratio which may appear to be out of line. Differences in the composition of demand, density of the markets served, or the nature of the equipment employed, to cite only a few examples, can explain differences in expense ratios among utilities comparable in size.

Expense ratios can be calculated on a number of bases, but those in common use include ratios of: (a) expenses per dollar of operating revenue; (b) expenses per average customer; and (c) expenses per unit of output. Examples of such ratios for privately owned electric utilities in Wisconsin are shown in Table 5.1.

The regulation of operating expenses and the determination of reasonable standards have been greatly assisted by the establishment of uniform systems of accounts. All the federal commissions have prescribed uniform accounting systems for jurisdictional companies. Except for the commissions in Delaware, Mississippi, Tennessee, and Wyoming, all the state commissions regulating gas and electric utilities have prescribed a uniform system of accounts and an annual financial report form for privately owned gas and electric utilities.[5]

The principal groups of operating expense accounts in the uniform systems of accounts for electric and gas utilities include: (a) production; (b) transmission; (c) distribution; (d) customers' accounting and collecting; (e) sales promotion; and (f) administrative and general. The principal groups of operating expense accounts for telephone utilities are: (a) maintenance; (b) depreciation and amortization; (c) traffic; (d) commercial; (e) general office salaries and expenses; and (f) other operating expenses.

The outline below indicates the typical organization of operating expense accounts for an electric utility.

---

[5] Federal Power Commission, *State Commission Jurisdiction and Regulation of Electric and Gas Utilities* (Washington, D.C.: Government Printing Office, 1960), p. 4.

Table 5.1

Expense Ratios
Wisconsin Electric Utilities
1958

Expense	*Per Dollar of Revenue*	*Per Average Customer*	*Per KWH Sold*
Production and transmission	30.70¢	$ 62.35	.59¢
Distribution	8.94	18.16	.17
Customers accounting and collecting	2.57	5.22	.05
Sales promotion	2.07	4.20	.04
Administrative and general	6.44	13.08	.13
Total operating expenses	50.72¢	$103.01	.98¢
Depreciation	10.66	21.65	.21
Taxes other than income taxes	7.39	15.02	.14
Income taxes	13.23	26.87	.26
Total operating revenue deductions	82.00¢	$166.55	1.59¢

Source: Statistics of Wisconsin Public Utilities, Bulletin No. 8, Rates and Research Department, Public Service Commission of Wisconsin, 1958.

Operating Expense Accounts

I. Production Expenses
- A. Electric Generation—Steam Power
  - Operation
  - Maintenance
  - Miscellaneous
- B. Electric Generation—Hydraulic Power
  - Operation
  - Maintenance
  - Miscellaneous
- C. Electric Generation—Internal Combustion Engine Power
  - Operation
  - Maintenance
  - Miscellaneous
- D. Other Production Expenses and Credits

II. Transmission Expenses
- Operation
- Maintenance
- Miscellaneous

III. Distribution Expenses
- Operation
- Maintenance
- Miscellaneous

IV. Customers' Accounting and Collecting Expenses

V. Sales Promotion Expenses

VI. Administrative and General Expenses

To illustrate further, the detailed accounts under "Operation" are shown for Electric Generation—Steam Power, in I-A above.

I. Production Expenses

A. Electric Generation—Steam Power

Operation

701 Operating Supervision and Engineering
702 Station Labor
702-1 Boiler Labor
702-2 Prime mover and Generator Labor
702-3 Electric Labor
702-4 Miscellaneous Station Labor
703 Fuel
704 Water
705 Supplies and Expenses

705-1 Lubricants
705-2 Station Supplies
705-3 Station Expenses

4. POLICIES TOWARD SPECIFIC OPERATING EXPENSES

This section surveys regulatory policy toward specific expenses, particularly those which have been the subject of rulings in more than one jurisdiction.

A. *Allowance for Future Increases in Expenses.* Rate making on a test-period basis encounters a problem when there are changes in individual expenses which take place at some time within the test period or at some point in time shortly after the test period ends. This factor, of course, is apt to complicate the determination of proper operating expenses more often in a period of continued price inflation, such as that which followed World War II, than in a period of relative price stability.

With respect to known expense changes which are not fully reflected in the test period, commission policy generally provides that such changes will be fully recognized in rate making provided that they are definite. When an increase in wages, for example, occurs in the middle of the test period, the commission is faced with the question of whether to fix proper operating expenses for the future as if that change had taken place on the first day of the test period. The problem also arises when such changes occur after the end of the test period.

The Maine Supreme Court, for example, has required the state commission to recognize for rate-making purposes a negotiated wage increase which became effective after the close of the test period.[6] In so ruling, the Court said that it was known with certainty that the higher wage scale would increase total expenses. It held that to ignore this definite change was contrary to the idea of making rates for the future on the basis of the latest data available. On the other hand, the Court upheld the disallowance of claimed additional fuel costs. The important distinction between the two was that the wage increase, although effective after the test year, was based on a contract, while the claimed adjustment for increased fuel costs was based only on an estimate of future costs. Similar rulings in other states have required known expense changes to be included in the cost of service on an annualized basis when the increase occurred before the end of the test year.

B. *Atomic Power Research and Development Expenses.* Some electric utilities incur research and development expenses leading toward the commercial use of nuclear power to generate electricity. The state commissions have approved the inclusion of these expenses in the cost of service. The Michigan commission, for example, has held such expenses to be desirable and in the public interest in the case of a utility which joined with others to finance a nonprofit corporation established to develop, construct, and operate a developmental atomic power reactor under the federal atomic energy program.[7] The California commission has adopted a similar policy, holding that the development of the skills and technology capable of utilizing nuclear power sources would be important in providing efficient electric service in the future.[8] Other jurisdictions also have held that, after a proper showing, the costs of atomic power development and research were properly allowable in the cost of service.

---

[6] *Central Maine Power Co.* v. *Maine Public Utilities Commission,* 136 A. 2d 726 (1957).

[7] *Re Consumers Power Co.,* 15 PUR 3d 471 (1956).

[8] *Re Pacific Gas & Electric Co.,* 21 PUR 3d 48, 58 (1957).

C. *Salary and Wage Costs.* The salaries of directors and officers and the wages of the work force are subject to commission review insofar as their inclusion in the cost of service for rate making is concerned. The commission decisions on this subject indicate that in relatively numerous cases commissions have disallowed for cost-of-service purposes part of the total compensation paid by very small, family-owned and -operated utilities (mostly telephone companies) where the proportion of such salaries to total revenues was found to be unreasonable or where the commission was not convinced that the salaries were reasonable for the services performed. In addition to this type of ruling, practically the only others of any current interest relate to the annualization of contract wage increases occurring within the test year or to the recognition of such wage-level increases when they are known to have occurred after the test year. Issues involving wage and salary levels almost never arise, outside the category of family-owned utility operations mentioned above. Chapter 18 discusses a question of public policy arising in connection with the apparent willingness of commissions to accept as reasonable the wage-level agreements reached by methods other than collective bargaining.

D. *Pension Costs.* Retirement pension costs are regarded as an ordinary cost of doing business, in the nature of compensation for services rendered. Where "pay as you go" plans are employed, the pension payments are charged to operating expenses for the accounting period in which they are paid. This approach has the merit of simplicity, but it fails to distribute the burden of such costs equitably among consumers in different time periods. Far more often, utilities adopt actuarial pension systems in which the estimated costs of pension payments are spread evenly over future accounting periods. Such plans require the establishment of a fund into which irretrievable accruals or contributions are deposited as services are performed.

With the establishment of an actuarial pension system, a problem arises involving unfunded actuarial liability, if the plan covers existing and retired employees and not just new ones. The unfunded liability problems exist because the retirement fund is deficient, at the time it is established, in the amount of the accruals due on past services performed by all but new employees. Policies differ with respect to the amortization of this unfunded actuarial liability. The New York commission and a number of others have held that the amortization should be charged to current operating expenses, even though such payments relate to past service. The New York commission, in taking this position, said that this policy contributed to the total benefits provided by a pension system, and cited improved employee morale and greater operating efficiency as possible benefits.[9] The opposite position, held in a very minor number of instances, declines to recognize these intangibles and holds that it is improper to charge to present and future consumers the costs associated with past services. When this position is taken, the costs of amortizing the actuarial deficiency cannot be included in the cost of service and must be provided by stockholders through surplus or income deductions.

E. *Payments to Affiliates for Services and Supplies.* Public utilities which are part of holding company systems often receive important services from affiliated companies. These services may include accounting, purchasing, engineering, sales promotion, billing, and others. Payments to affiliates for services re-

---

[9] *Re Uniform Systems of Accounts for Electric Corporations, et al.,* 82 PUR (NS) 161 (1950).

ceived may be included in operating expenses for rate-making purposes, but usually after careful commission scrutiny. Commissions have been particularly prone to question such expenses because of the presumed absence of arm's-length bargaining between the parties. In justifying an expense for services received from an affiliate, the utility may be required to show that the services were proper and that the amounts paid were not greater than the reasonable costs of performing the services. Where the amount allowed is limited to the actual cost of furnishing the service, an amount may be included for a reasonable return on the investment involved.[10] Contracts between the utility and an affiliate, covering the provision of services, are not necessarily binding on the regulatory commission insofar as allowance of the fees paid is concerned. The general rule applying holds that only reasonable expenses are allowable. On occasion commissions have disallowed management fees paid by utilities to parent companies when the charges were based on a fixed percentage of gross revenues. In these cases, the absence of any demonstrated relationship between the worth of the services received and the fees payable has been cited. When costs incurred on behalf of the entire utility system are distributed to individual companies, the basis for the distribution is subject to question and must pass the test of reasonableness.[11]

In addition to services, affiliated companies sometimes supply public utilities with materials and supplies (charged to expense). This is particularly important in the telephone industry, where the Western Electric Company is the manufacturing and purchasing affiliate of the Bell System. General Telephone, the nation's second largest system, is organized along similar lines. Expenses incurred for materials and supplies purchased from an affiliated company are subject to regulatory scrutiny and are ordinarily allowed upon a showing of reasonableness, often based on the comparative prices of other suppliers. Thus, the Massachusetts Department of Public Utilities approved the prices paid by New England Telephone and Telegraph Company to Western Electric where there was evidence showing that the prices of competitive suppliers ranged from 112 per cent to 177 per cent of Western's prices, and where the profits earned by the supplier and its parent did not appear to be excessive.[12] In so ruling, the Department considered the "exhaustive" annual report on Western's activities and earnings, prepared by a committee of the National Association of Railroad and Utilities Commissioners.

Only a few commissions have taken the opposite position. In a Michigan case, for example, the staff of the commission proposed a reduction in the Michigan Bell Telephone Company test-period expenses for materials and supplies, on the ground that the profit rate of Western Electric exceeded the rate of return authorized for Michigan Bell in the latest rate order issued. The staff contended that, since the companies are affiliated and since Western's prices are not regulated, Western's profit rate on the sale of materials and supplies to Michigan Bell should be reduced to a level comparable to that authorized for Michigan Bell. The latter argued, among other points, that Western's prices were reasonable by comparison with prices of other suppliers and that its risks compare with those of manufacturers, not public utilities. The posi-

[10] *Smith* v. *Illinois Bell Telephone Co.,* 282 U.S. 133, 157 (1930).

[11] *Re Interstate Power Company of Wisconsin,* 93 PUR (NS) 33 (1952); *Re New York State Electric & Gas Corp., et al.,* 20 PUR (NS) 388 (1937).

[12] *Re New England Telephone & Telegraph Co.,* 2 PUR 3d 464 (1953).

tion of the staff was approved, and test-period expenses were reduced in the amount the staff had recommended.[13] However, the same approach was not taken with respect to capital items similarly supplied; where the latter are concerned, California alone holds that the affiliated supplier is entitled to no greater return than the purchasing utility is allowed to earn. The prices and profits of Western Electric are discussed in some detail in Chapter 20.

F. Sales Promotion and Advertising Expenses. Commissions generally approve as proper operating expenses the costs of sales promotion and advertising intended to increase sales. Managerial judgment has been accorded considerable discretion in this area. Commissions have rejected protests against the allowance of such expenses, when the claims made were not based upon proof of either extravagance or excessiveness.[14]

Commission actions in specific cases further illustrate policy making with respect to sales promotion and advertising expenses. The Arkansas commission reduced the allowable sales promotion expense incurred by an electric utility after making a comparative study of the ratios of such expenses to total expenses for a number of companies.[15] The Pennsylvania commission held that disputed promotional expenses were not excessive where it appeared that the costs involved had increased both the number of customers and the average consumption of services, and where the total expenditure had remained unchanged for 14 years.[16]

The California commission approved a telephone company's advertising expenses, which had been protested as unnecessary because the company was a monopoly, on the ground that the advertising had permitted the company to hire additional employees in a tight labor market, thus avoiding payment for overtime. The commission also concluded that the advertising had resulted in greater revenues, from directory advertising and long-distance service, and in reducing the cost of answering inquiries from the public. The total expense involved—less than one per cent of revenues—was not regarded as excessive.[17] The California commission also approved comparatively large expenses for traffic promotion by transit utilities attempting to gain additional riders and to stop the loss of patronage.[18] Several states have disallowed the expenses of institutional advertising for goodwill purposes and advertising aimed at winning public approval of proposed rate increases.

G. Rate Case Expenses. As a general rule, reasonable rate case expenses incurred by utility companies are allowed as proper operating expenses. When allowed, rate case expenses are usually amortized over periods ranging from two to ten years. When a rate increase proposal is found to be largely justified, commissions regularly allow the company to include the amortization costs of reasonable rate case expenses in the cost of service, although the amount deemed reasonable may not necessarily equal actual expenses. The New Jersey commission has ruled that rate case expenses could be recognized only when the company was reasonably justified in initiating the case.[19] Commissions

13 *Re Michigan Bell Telephone Co.,* 32 PUR 3d 395 (1960).

14 *Illinois Commerce Commission* v. *Peoples Gas Light & Coke Co.,* 99 PUR (NS) 361 (1953); *Re Ohio Bell Telephone Co.,* 82 PUR (NS) 341 (1949).

15 *Re Arkansas Power & Light Co.,* 13 PUR 3d 1 (1956).

16 *Pennsylvania Public Utility Commission* v. *Pennsylvania Power & Light Co.,* 14 PUR 3d 438 (1956).

17 *Re Pacific Telephone & Telegraph Co.,* 5 PUR 3d 396 (1954).

18 *Re San Jose City Lines, Inc.,* 7 PUR 3d 80 (1954); *Re Pacific Electric Railway Co. et al.,* 96 PUR (NS) 105 (1952).

19 *Re New Jersey Natural Gas Co.,* 6 PUR 3d 249 (1954).

tend to be more liberal in accepting rate case expenses when the company appears in defense of rates which are challenged.

In the event that a rate case consumes an undue amount of time, and a rate increase is allowed to go into effect subject to possible refund pending an ultimate decision, the general policy is to disallow the costs of making refunds should the utility lose the case. It is thought that, in the absence of such a policy, management would feel less responsibility for the establishment of reasonable rates, and customers would be required to pay for possible errors in managerial judgment as to revenue requirements.[20] The costs of an appeal for judicial review of a commission order may be recognized as proper operating expenses, particularly if the company is successful on appeal. The California commission has shown a tendency, particularly where the appeal is unsuccessful, to disallow such costs.[21] On the other hand, the Ohio commission had held that the costs of an appeal, incurred to protect the interests of the company, must be recognized when the appeal is justified.[22]

H. *Expenses of Adjusting Customers' Gas Appliances.* Expenses are necessarily incurred by gas distribution companies in adjusting consumers' gas appliances whenever the heating value of gas is changed. In recent years this has occurred with the introduction of natural gas into areas formerly served by manufactured gas. Natural gas has a relatively higher thermal content. Appliance adjustments may also be necessary with a change in the heating value of mixed gas.

Commission policies have differed in the treatment of these expenses. In a number of cases, commissions have held that the costs of appliance adjustments were proper operating expenses, and the utilities involved have been authorized to amortize the costs incurred over a period of five years and sometimes ten. In another case, the amortization period was limited to the life of the securities issued to finance the changeover. The California commission in one case disallowed the inclusion of certain changeover costs on the ground that they had not imposed an excessive burden upon the revenues of a utility earning a seven per cent rate of return.[23]

I. *Political and Lobbying Expenses.* Under federal law, corporations are prohibited from making political contributions where the election of federal officeholders is involved. Some states have similar statutes. In addition, Section 12 (h) of the Holding Company Act prohibits political contributions by registered gas and electric holding companies and their subsidiaries. The standard regulatory policy is to exclude political and lobbying expenses from the cost of service, as well as expenditures deemed to relate to such activities. For example, the expenses of public utility advertising on the question of private versus public power have been disallowed as operating expenses in the cost of service.[24]

J. *Uncollectible Bills.* Public utilities incur losses due to uncollectible bills. In determining the proper operating expenses for rate-making purposes, questions sometimes arise as to whether

---

[20] *Re Southwestern Bell Telephone Co.*, 2 PUR 3d 1 (1953); *Re Mountain States Telephone & Telegraph Co.*, 8 PUR 3d 176 (1954).

[21] *Re Citizens Utilities Company of California*, 4 PUR 3d 97 (1954).

[22] *Cleveland Electric Illuminating Co.* v. *City of Cleveland*, 67 PUR (NS) 65 (1947).

[23] *City of San Diego* v. *San Diego Consolidated Gas & Electric Co.*, 7 PUR (NS) 443 (1935).

[24] *Re Consumers Power Co.*, 29 PUR 3d 36 (1959); *Re Pacific Power & Light Co.*, 34 PUR 3d 36 (1960).

losses of this kind should be recognized and, if so, in what amount. Most commissions allow some amount for uncollectibles, so that the regulatory question generally becomes one of the amount to be allowed. This amount may be based upon some representative loss over a period of time or upon the test-year experience. The California commission, for example, found in one case that a reasonable allowance for uncollectibles could be determined by applying a percentage factor of 0.42 per cent to the estimated firm gas service revenues in the test year.[25] In another case, the Pennsylvania commission agreed with a telephone utility that the uncollectible portion of a proposed revenue increase could be properly determined on the basis of the ratio of net uncollectibles to total operating revenues in the test year.[26] Other commissions, in a relatively few cases, have refused to approve an allowance for uncollectibles. In one case, for example, the Wisconsin commission adopted this policy on the principal grounds that uncollectibles should be negligible where customer deposits may be demanded by the utility and where service can be disconnected to prevent loss.[27]

K. *Charitable Contributions.* Charitable contributions by public utilities, although recognized as deductible for tax purposes, may or may not be allowed as a proper operating expense for rate-making purposes. An increasing number of commissions—now about half of them—recognize reasonable contributions as proper operating expenses.[28] Where this position is adopted, it is based on the view that the utility is no less a citizen of the community than others, and that it therefore has community responsibilities which it cannot decline to accept. The Supreme Court has held that it would not disallow charitable expenses approved by a state commission.[29] It is not unusual, among the commissions which recognize charitable contributions as proper expenses, to include in the cost of service the amount of such contributions less the tax savings resulting from the related income tax deduction.

On the other hand, there is also a sizable number of commissions which do not recognize charitable contributions as proper operating expenses, on the ground that the consumers of utility services should not, in effect, be made involuntary donors to charities, when the amount given and the choice of charity are not within their control.[30]

L. *Public Utility Merchandising Expenses.* The gas and electric utilities engage in the marketing of home appliances and other equipment which consume their services, such as ranges, refrigerators, hot water heaters, and others. Most commissions hold that both the expenses and revenues of utility merchandising activities are not to be considered in rate making. However, some commissions have made exceptions to this general rule on the ground that appliance merchandising tends to promote sales of utility services. The Maryland commission, for example, has taken this position on the ground that merchandising activities were load (demand) -building in character.[31] New Hampshire has permitted the recovery of losses from appliance sales in the

[25] *Re Southern California Gas Co.,* 35 PUR 3d 300 (1960).

[26] *Pennsylvania Public Utility Commission* v. *General Telephone Co.,* 28 PUR 3d 413 (1959).

[27] *Re Central Wisconsin Gas Co.,* 3 PUR 3d 65 (1954).

[28] *United Gas Corp.* v. *Mississippi PSC,* 38 PUR 3d 252 (1961); *Re Consumers Power Co.,* 38 PUR 3d 355 (1961).

[29] *West Ohio Gas Co.* v. *Public Utilities Commission of Ohio,* 294 U.S. 63 (1935).

[30] *Op. cit.,* Note 6.

[31] *Re Consolidated Gas, Electric Light & Power Company of Baltimore,* 67 PUR (NS) 144 (1946).

utility cost of service because such activities were deemed promotional in nature.[32]

Taxes and annual depreciation expenses are important operating revenue deductions which utility companies are allowed to include in the cost of service and to recover through rates charged consumers. Both will be treated in separate chapters (17 and 8, respectively).

[32] *Re Exeter & Hampton Electric Co.*, 94 PUR (NS) 124 (1952).

6 The Rate Base

This chapter and the one that follows concern the public utility rate base. Although this survey is intended primarily to develop the economic factors which bear upon rate base determination, the relevant legal precedents and accounting practices are also brought out.

1. INTRODUCTION

Public utility rate making under regulation follows two basic steps: first, the utility's cost of service under prudent management is determined; second, the utility is authorized to charge for its services under schedules of rates which, on an anticipated volume of business, will produce total revenues about equal to the cost of service. As stated earlier, the cost of service is the sum of: (a) operating expenses; (b) depreciation expense; (c) taxes; and (d) a reasonable return on the net valuation of the property devoted to the public service. The total net value of the company's tangible and intangible capital is called the "rate base" or the valuation for rate-making purposes.

The rate base is composed principally of the net (or depreciated) valuation of the public utility's tangible property, comprising the plant and equipment used and useful in serving the public. (Such tangible property is called "plant in service" in the uniform systems of accounts prescribed for public utilities.) In addition, the rate base includes an allowance for working capital and, depending on the circumstances, may also include amounts for the overhead costs of organizing the business, intangibles, and going-concern value. Each of these rate-base components will be examined separately in the course of this discussion.

At this point, however, it should be noted that the key issue in the determination of the rate base is the valuation of the public utility's plant and equipment. This is emphasized for two reasons: (a) the valuation of plant and equipment is the largest component part of the rate base; and (b) the particular valuation method employed can affect the size of this principal component. Further, and as the above might indicate, the valuation of plant and equipment has long been an issue in controversy. At the heart of this controversy is the fact that the total valuation of plant and equipment may vary with the particular method of valuation applied. Implicit in this controversy is the fact that the greater the valuation of public utility tangible property, the greater will be the rate base and, therefore, the total cost of service, other things remaining equal.

And the lower the valuation of public utility tangible property, the lower the rate base and total cost of service, other things remaining equal. Of course, as the cost of service goes, so goes the level of rates that will be charged. Standing over this entire problem and complicating it further is the factor of long-term price inflation which has characterized our economy.

What are the principal valuation methods which may be applied to a public utility's tangible property in order to measure that component of the rate base? Essentially, there are three valuation methods: (a) actual cost less depreciation; (b) reproduction cost new less depreciation; and (c) "fair value." Variations in each of these approaches are found. For the present, however, the principal valuation methods and some of their variations will be described only briefly, with fuller discussion to be taken up shortly.

Actual cost methods include: (a) historical cost; (b) prudent investment; and (c) original cost. Generally speaking, *historical cost* includes both the construction and acquisition costs of the properties serving the public, including additions and betterments, less depreciation. Where accounting records have been inadequate, historical cost has been found by estimating the cost of the present plant on the basis of costs of materials and labor at the time each property unit was constructed or acquired, less depreciation. A second actual cost method, called *prudent investment,* may be taken as historical cost, as defined, less any amounts found to be dishonest or obviously wasteful. Under the prudent investment standard, every investment is assumed to be prudent unless the contrary is shown. A third measure of actual cost, called *original cost,* has acquired a specialized accounting definition since the 1930's. This definition holds that original cost is the total investment cost of constructed and acquired property when first devoted to public service, less depreciation.

Reproduction cost new is the cost of duplicating the existing plant and equipment at recent average prices, less depreciation. Sometimes used as a substitute for reproduction cost is an approach called "trended original cost" or, more precisely, *net trended original cost.* Valuation by this method, briefly stated, is found by multiplying the actual cost of each property unit or class of units by the ratio of (a) the cost index number for the present year to (b) the cost index number for the year the property was installed, less depreciation.

Another approach to valuation, which originated in the important case of *Smyth* v. *Ames,* is called the *fair value method.* Fair value is a composite method which considers both depreciated actual cost and reproduction cost new less depreciation, and other factors affecting value, with each factor given the weight judged appropriate to the individual case.

Relating these valuation methods to the matter of price inflation, it can be said as a general proposition that if prices were historically stable, other things remaining equal, each valuation method would tend to yield about the same result. Price stability, however, has been a largely unobtainable goal during most of the present century. This fact alone may be said to account for a major share of the controversy as to the method used to measure the valuation of tangible property for rate making. Table 6.1 shows a series of index numbers measuring certain relative average public utility construction costs in the period from 1915 to our own time. It can be seen in each column that the respective construction costs rose through time at approximately the same rate. Second, it appears that one of the economic aftermaths of war was an additional upward spurt in public utility construction costs, with the greatest increases recorded in the years following World War II. Finally, it can be observed that the over-all change in such costs was great, and that they more than doubled in the decade following the end of World War II in 1945. Moreover, there has been no abundant evidence that this upward trend in prices and costs was tending to stabilize or decline. It has been argued that these indexes tend toward overstatement to the extent that increases in productivity, due to technological advancement, are not reflected.

2. RATE-BASE METHODS

In *Munn* v. *Illinois,* as we have seen, the United States Supreme Court upheld as constitutional the right of a state to regulate the prices charged by business affected with a public interest. The matter could not end there. Standards of reasonableness in regulation had to be developed.

The Supreme Court asserted its interest in the reasonableness of regulatory policy in deciding *Chicago, Milwaukee and St. Paul Railway* v. *Minnesota* in 1890.[1] There, the Court found a state law unconstitutional because it imposed rate regulation while denying the regulated utility judicial review to test the reasonableness of the rates it was required to charge. Thus, the Court established that the reasonableness of regulated rates was subject to judicial review. The Court held that this particular state law, which denied a court test of the reasonableness of the rate fixed, violated the due process clause of the Fourteenth Amendment. This clause provides, in part, that a state shall not deprive any person of property without due process of law. Ruling on the constitutionality of the state law, the Court held that, if the utility were deprived of the power to charge reasonable rates for the use of its property, and if it were denied judicial review, then the company

1 134 U.S. 418.

Table 6.1

Public Utility Construction Cost Indexes[1]

(1947–1949 = 100)

Year	*Buildings*[2]	*Gas Plant*[2]	*Electric Plant*[2]	*Tel. and Tel.*[3] *Lines*
1915	34	27	29	42
1920	68	61	59	78
1925	55	53	53	66
1930	50	50	52	61
1935	48	50	55	52
1940	53	58	62	54
1945	66	66	69	70
1950	112	111	113	109
1955	141	142	146	131
1956	154	155	159	167
1957	165	165	169	162
1958	169	172	173	162
1959	174	178	177	167
1960	175	181	175	162

1 Index numbers rounded.

2 Handy-Whitman Public Utility Construction Cost Indexes; U.S. Department of Commerce, Office of Business Economics.

3 Interstate Commerce Commission, Bureau of Valuation.

would be deprived of the lawful use of its property and, in effect, of the property itself. This was held to be unlawful as a denial of the protection assured in the Constitution. In other words, a regulated rate that is less than reasonable would be unlawful, because such would constitute a deprivation or confiscation of property in violation of the Constitution. Further, the courts would have the final word on the reasonableness of the rates determined directly by the legislature or by its regulatory agency. However, what was meant by the "reasonableness" of a regulated rate had to await clarification in the Supreme Court's famous decision in *Smyth* v. *Ames* in 1898.[2]

This case is one of the most significant ever decided by the Supreme Court, because of its sustained effect on public utility rate regulation for nearly half a century and its continuing importance, particularly in rate regulation at the state level. The case of *Smyth* v. *Ames* arose out of a Nebraska state law which reduced the maximum freight rates that the railroads could charge in that state. A successful suit was brought by railroad stockholders, preventing the application of the lowered schedule of rates. The state appealed to the United States Supreme Court.

Counsel for the state, among whom was William Jennings Bryan, maintained that the adequacy of the rates in question should be tested by reference to the return they would provide on the then present value, or reproduction cost, of railroad property. This position was advantageous to its proponent because the price level of the 1890's, after the Panic of 1893, was the lowest since the Civil War. The railroad opposed this standard, pointing out that it had been built during the Civil War period, which was marked by substantial price inflation. Accordingly, the railroad contended that its past costs and securities outstanding merited recognition in any test of the reasonableness and constitutionality of the rates in question.

The Supreme Court decided that the Nebraska freight rates were unconstitutionally low by any standard of reasonableness. However, the most important result of its decision was the formulation of the "fair value" doctrine, which prescribed a test of the reasonableness and constitutionality of regulated rates. Essentially, the fair value rule constitutes a compromise between the diverse positions that had been urged before the Court by the state and the railroad. In so ruling, the Court took "into consideration the interests both of the public and of the owner of the property," holding that

> . . . the basis of all calculations as to the reasonableness of rates . . . must be the fair value of the property being used . . . for the convenience of the public.[3]

"Fair value" was to be determined by considering essentially these three factors: (a) the actual cost of the property; (b) the present cost of construction, which is generally termed *reproduction cost new;* and (c) other matters, generally taken to represent various intangibles. Each of these elements was to be given such weight as may be just and reasonable in each case. Thus, the "fair value" standard for testing the reasonableness of regulated rates represents a composite of different valuation methods, each of which was to receive appropriate weight in light of the circumstances in the individual case. Any regulated rate which failed to provide a "fair return" on the fair value of utility property used and useful in serving the public would constitute a deprivation of utility property in violation of the Fourteenth

[2] 169 U.S. 466.

[3] 169 U.S. 466, 546.

Amendment. Fair return on fair value was the law of the land for decades thereafter. At this point, and before tracing the development of Supreme Court policy, the principal rate-base methods will be discussed.

A. *Actual Cost Methods.* Actual cost determinations of public utility tangible property, as noted earlier, may employ either the historical cost, prudent investment, or original cost method. Historical cost usually can be found by consulting the books and records of the company. In that event, the property element in the rate base is the sum of the amounts actually spent for initial construction, acquisitions, and additions and betterments less depreciation. In the past, the utility companies' books and records were sometimes inadequate to permit a determination of historical cost. In such cases, the historical cost of the existing plant was estimated by making an inventory of the physical property and pricing each of the items at actual cost at the time of construction or installation. The historical cost, thus found, plus an allowance for the overhead charges incurred during construction and less depreciation would provide a valuation of the tangible property.

The prudent investment method of determining actual cost would subtract from depreciated historical cost any amounts found to be dishonest or obviously wasteful. However, every investment is assumed to be reasonable until the contrary is shown.

A third actual cost method is the "original cost" approach. In its specialized accounting meaning, *original cost* is the cost of the property in its first use as public utility plant, less depreciation. The Federal Power Commission definition, with respect to electric plant, states that

> "Original cost," as applied to electric plant, means the cost of such property to the person first devoting it to public service.[4]

The same FPC definition applies to gas plant. The definition used by the Federal Communications Commission spells out the original cost concept in greater detail.

> "Original cost" or "cost," as applied to telephone plant, franchises, patent rights, and right-of-way, means the actual money cost of (or the current money value of any consideration other than money exchanged for) property at the time when it was first dedicated to the public use, whether by the accounting company or by predecessors.[5]

Original cost differs from the other actual cost methods above in the fact that historical cost and prudent investment use the term "cost" as cost to the *owner* of the property. Original cost, by contrast, means "first" original cost of the property as a public utility. For example, if an industrial power plant costing $200,000 (ignoring depreciation) were sold to a public utility for $250,000, the original cost would be $250,000. However, if the seller in this case were a public utility, the original cost would be $200,000, and the $50,000 difference would be disposed of. This subject will be examined in detail later. For now our purpose is to analyze the general concept of actual cost.

The principal advantages of actual cost are administrative simplicity and stability. Administrative simplicity has been made possible in large part by the fact that uniform systems of accounts

---

[4] Federal Power Commission, *Uniform System of Accounts Prescribed for Public Utilities and Licensees,* effective January 1, 1957, definition 29, p. 6.

[5] Federal Communications Commission, *Uniform System of Accounts, Class A and Class B Telephone Companies,* effective January 1, 1936, Section 31.01–3(x).

have been put into effect which provide a verified source of data on the costs of property construction and acquisition as well as depreciation. As a result, actual cost determinations can be made with ease, speed, and definiteness. In addition, they can be kept continuously up to date. The second principal advantage of actual cost is its stability. The costs of tangible property units, when properly recorded in the company's plant accounts, have not been subject to unpredictable fluctuation. In fact, once the actual-cost rate base is established, it is essentially insulated from subsequent fluctuations in the economy at large.

On the other hand, an actual-cost rate base is open to valid criticism on economic grounds because, as conventionally administered, it disregards changes in the value of money. A change in the value of money is a change in the quantity of goods and services that a dollar can buy. Stated another way, a change in the value of money is a change in its purchasing power. Changes in the value of money are caused by price changes. A basic principle of economics provides that changes in the value of money will vary inversely with changes in prices. American economic history shows that prices have tended more to fluctuate than to be stable through time. Thus, the value of money also has fluctuated by declining when prices rose and by increasing when prices fell.

Importantly related to the historic variation in the value of money is the fact that the present plants of a good many public utility systems have been assembled on a piecemeal basis. That is, the present plants in service are composed of initial construction, plus additional facilities added from time to time as growth demanded, plus acquired properties which, themselves, were as often as not assembled through piecemeal construction and acquisition. The significance of this in the present discussion is that each property addition, in the case of numerous companies, was paid for with dollars of dissimilar purchasing power.

Thus, the first criticism of the actual cost approach is that it produces a result which, for all of its definiteness, can be seriously misleading if considered from an economic point of view. This criticism of actual cost rests on the fact that it is a sum of dollars which may represent several different values of money. Because it is composed of dollars of dissimilar purchasing power, the actual-cost rate base does not succeed perfectly in its principal purpose, which is to determine a meaningful cost of tangible property for rate-making purposes. What explanation is there for this? The explanation is that the actual cost approach implicitly assumes that the dollar is a unit of measure of constant economic size, when it is not. Owing to the variations in the value of money brought on by price changes, the unadjusted dollar as a unit of measure is comparable to a yardstick whose length changes periodically. Thus, an actual-cost rate base composed, for example, of the sum of 1916 dollars, 1920 dollars, 1932 dollars, and 1958 dollars can produce a result which is misleading and of doubtful economic validity. It should be added at this point that the above criticism of actual cost is not at the same time a criticism of the uniform systems of accounts prescribed for public utilities. There is no necessity to use the actual costs of plant, as carried in such systems, as the rate base for rate-making purposes. Such is a policy decision of the regulatory authorities and not a requirement of the uniform systems of accounts.

Justice Jackson has suggested that the apparent certainty of actual cost determinations, based as they are upon accounting records, may be delusory. In his dissenting opinion in the *Hope* case, he stated:

> To make a fetish of mere accounting is to shield from examination the deeper causes, forces, movements, and conditions which should govern rates. Even as a recording of current transactions, bookkeeping is hardly an exact science. As a representation of the condition and trend of a business, it uses symbols of certainty to express values that actually are in constant flux. It may be said that in commercial or investment banking or any business extending credit success depends on knowing what not to believe in accounting. . . . If one cannot rely on accountancy accuracy to disclose past or current conditions of a business, the fallacy of using it as a sole guide to future price policy ought to be apparent. However, our quest for certitude is so ardent that we pay an irrational reverence to a technique which uses symbols of certainty, even though experience again and again warns us that they are delusive. . . .[6]

A second criticism of the actual-cost rate base is that during a period of price inflation, other things remaining equal, it results in a declining rate of return—as measured in terms of the value of money. This would come about because, for example, a return that remains constant in dollar amount as inflation progresses represents a lesser quantity of purchasing power than it did prior to the increase in the level of prices. Both common stockholders and bondholders are affected. The common stockholder, who invested at a lower price level than that prevailing at the time an actual cost valuation is used in rate making, may suffer an erosion in the real value of his investment, for dividends will be paid in dollars whose purchasing power is less than that of the dollars invested. With an actual-cost rate base, other things remaining equal, the common stockholder would not receive an increase in dividends to offset the decline in the real value of the dividends received. The result of such shrinkage in the real value of the dividends received on past common stock investments is an erosion of the real value of the original common stock investment, which follows from the fact that value is largely a function of annual yield. Bondholders, under the above circumstances, would be affected because bond coverage would not rise as it would in non-public utility industries. It may be noted that the foregoing economic effects of the use of an actual-cost rate base during inflation are not required in the interest of effective regulation of natural monopoly.

Numerous proponents of the actual-cost rate base have long since acknowledged the problem, discussed above, arising from its use during a period of price inflation. They also have recommended a remedy, which is to adjust the rate of return allowed on the actual-cost rate base so as to offset the effects of inflation. Professor Martin G. Glaeser recommended this policy in 1927. Among others who subsequently endorsed this view are: Professors William E. Mosher and Finla G. Crawford, co-authors, who attribute it (erroneously) to Justice Brandeis; Professors Eliot Jones and Truman C. Bigham, co-authors, who suggest that one remedy for the "unjust" effect of inflation upon the common stockholder would be the allowance of a "generous" rate of return; Dr. John Bauer, who prefers an additional rate-of-return increment as against trending original cost by the use of index numbers; and Professor Eli W. Clemens, who leaves open the question of maintaining the purchasing power of the return on an actual-cost rate base while approving a rate-of-return adjustment if that objective were to be obtained.[7]

B. *Reproduction Cost New.* Another

[6] *FPC* v. *Hope Natural Gas Co.,* 320 U.S. 591, 643–644 (1944).

[7] Martin G. Glaeser, *Outlines of Public Utility Economics* (New York: The Macmillan Co., 1927), pp. 479–480.

William E. Mosher and Finla G. Crawford,

method of determining the rate base is known as *reproduction cost new less depreciation,* or *RCND.* The RCND valuation is a measure of the cost of duplicating the existing plant at recent or present prices, less depreciation. How this is done will be discussed in some detail later. For the present, however, it is sufficient to note that RNCD requires the following steps: (a) taking an inventory of all the company's property units that are used and useful in serving the public; (b) computing construction costs and equipment prices at the level of recent average prices or current prices; (c) ascertaining and deducting accrued depreciation; and (d) adding amounts for working capital and various intangible elements of value, if any.

A second and simpler approach to an RCND valuation is called *trended original cost.* This method employs various index numbers of prices in order to convert the actual investment cost experienced by the company into the equivalent value as expressed in current dollars. This is done by multiplying the recorded actual cost of each property unit or class by the ratio of the appropriate index number of prices for the current year to that of the year in which the property unit was installed, as follows:

$$\text{Trended original cost of property unit in current year} = \text{Actual recorded cost of the property unit in year of installation} \times \frac{\text{Index number of current year}}{\text{Index number of year of installation}}$$

This method provides a cost- and time-saving substitute for the more involved inventory-pricing method of determining an RCND valuation. An application of one form of this method by the Maryland commission was rejected by the Supreme Court in 1935.[8] The commission had applied a composite "fair value index" of prices to the 1923 value of the property and the annual additions in order to determine a gross valuation as of the end of 1932. From this gross valuation were deducted the 1923 depreciation reserve and the subsequent annual provisions for depreciation, with all figures converted into 1932 values. By adding an allowance for working capital to the net amount thus found, the rate base was determined. In rejecting this valuation, the Court objected primarily to the manner in which the Commission applied the method rather than to the method itself. In recent years other variations of this method have come to be used by some of the state commissions in developing a fair-value rate base.

The RCND rate base takes into account changes in the value of money. As a result it is capable of stabilizing the real income of common stockholders in utility enterprises. The use of RCND also can result in flexible consumer rates which are higher when prices and disposable income are high and lower when prices and disposable income decline. There is an important but little recognized economic result stemming from the fact that RCND leads to higher rates in times of comparatively high or rising prices. Higher rates tend to prevent possible artificial stimulation of the demand for utility services which otherwise

Public Utility Regulation (New York: Harper & Row, 1933), pp. 215–216.

Eliot Jones and Truman C. Bigham, *Principles of Public Utilities* (New York: The Macmillan Co., 1937), pp. 242–243.

John Bauer, *Transforming Public Utility Regulation* (New York: Harper & Row, 1950), pp. 168–169.

Eli W. Clemens, *Economics and Public Utilities* (New York: Appleton-Century-Crofts, Inc., 1950), p. 153.

[8] *West et al.* v. *Chesapeake & Potomac Telephone Co. of Baltimore,* 295 U.S. 662 (1935).

might occur if such service were underpriced in terms of the real value of money. The effect of this is twofold. The utility company is protected from overbuilding its plant in service, which, in turn, averts the utilization of economic resources (human, natural, and capital) that could be more productively employed elsewhere in the economy. Finally, RCND provides a means of recognizing the impact of a new price-level plateau in cases where the rate of return is related to the market cost of raising capital, a factor which does not necessarily reflect price changes occurring elsewhere in the economy.

Critics of RCND point out that physical appraisal of a utility's property by the inventory-pricing approach may be time-consuming, expensive, and possibly out of date when completed, owing to a subsequent change in prices. Perhaps the most important criticism, however, is that an RCND valuation is apt to be inexact. This criticism has reference to the fact that the RCND valuation process requires many assumptions to be made, for example, as to the profit margins of construction contractors, the present cost of a type of property unit no longer being made, and others. Reasonable and equally qualified valuation engineers may differ in this respect and reach dissimilar conclusions. When differing RCND valuations of the same company are advanced as evidence in a given case, doubt as to the validity of the method naturally arises. RCND is also subject to criticism in view of the typical capital structure of a public utility, which ordinarily is substantially composed of fixed-income senior securities and a comparatively thin equity. In times of rising prices, the increased return on the RCND rate base would accrue entirely to common stockholders. However, it is not likely that the return on an RCND rate base during a period of depressed prices would be so low as to impair the financial integrity or credit standing of the utility. The reproduction cost of utility properities does not fluctuate in the same degree as commodity prices in general. In addition, an insufficient return is unlikely, regardless of the rate-base method employed, because the Supreme Court has held that:

> The return should be reasonably sufficient to assure confidence in the financial soundness of the utility and should be adequate . . . to maintain and support its credit. . . .[9]

Effective criticism has been directed toward RCND on the ground that it measures the cost of duplicating a partially obsolete plant which would not be built again, because of technological advancement and because past mistakes, if any, would not be repeated. However, this criticism applies to any rate-base method which looks to the costs, however measured, of the existing plant.

A simplified method of determining RCND has been put into use by the Public Utilities Commission of Ohio. The regulatory law administered by the Commission has been held to require exclusive reliance upon RCND in determining the valuation for rate making.[10] The simplified method of RCND determination was developed by the Commission after World War II in order to speed the processing of an increased volume of applications for changes in rates. In essence, the Ohio method determines an RCND valuation as of a given date by updating the RCND valuation found for the particular company in its last previous rate case. The previous RCND determination is made current by deducting the plant retirements and adding the gross additions to plant which oc-

[9] *Bluefield Water Works & Improvement Co.* v. *Public Service Commission,* 262 U.S. 679, 693 (1923).

[10] *City of Marietta* v. *Public Utilities Commission,* 74 N.E. 2d 74 (1948).

curred since the previous determination. The value of retirements and additions is found by multiplying their book costs by index numbers reflecting the difference between such book costs and reproduction costs. The previous RCND determination is similarly adjusted. This approach permits the staff of the Commission to substitute a desk method for a detailed field investigation of the property included in the RCND determination. The Ohio method has been used principally in telephone company rate cases, because the Commission has direct jurisdiction over telephone rates but serves only as an appellate body in the case of disputed rates for other utilities, whose rates are made by local rate ordinances.

C. *Fair Value* The fair-value rate base originated in the *Smyth* v. *Ames* case discussed previously. The fair-value rate base is a composite which gives weight to both depreciated actual cost and RCND. The amount of weight given to each of these indications of value may vary from case to case. It will be recalled that in *Smyth* v. *Ames* it was stated that such weight should be given each measure of valuation, and other factors, as the facts of the case warranted. Thus, in one of the cases to be referred to shortly, it will be seen that the Iowa Supreme Court found fair value to be a weighted average composed 70 per cent of RCND and 30 per cent of depreciated actual cost, while the Minnesota commission found a 50-50 weighting to be appropriate. Thus, the fair-value rate base is essentially a short-run compromise between consumer and investor interests which are identical in the long run. This is at once a source of strength and weakness.

As we have seen, neither the actual cost nor reproduction cost methods are perfect. The strength of the fair value approach is that it lies somewhere between the lowest and highest possible valuations. It represents a determination based upon judgment. The commissions using the fair value approach are mediating between diverse interests in a manner consistent with the way we resolve most issues in a democratic society. On the other hand, there is often little to guide policy-makers in establishing where the balance really lies. Thus, the fair value method has been characterized critically as the "huddle" method, because it lacks certainty and is subject to variation that is often unexplainable in precise economic terms. This indefiniteness, in part, is explainable in the fact situation presented to the Supreme Court in *Smyth* v. *Ames*. The Interstate Commerce Commission has noted, "The Supreme Court was called upon to consider a schedule of rates which was clearly unlawful, and was not therefor embarrassed by the indefiniteness of the standard which it proposed."[11]

3. THE SUPREME COURT AND RATE BASE

This section surveys the important decisions of the United States Supreme Court relating to rate-base methods in the period following *Smyth* v. *Ames*. There, it will be recalled, the Court set forth the fair value doctrine requiring that consideration be given to actual cost, reproduction cost, and other factors in determining the rate base. A study of these decisions permits at least four broad generalizations of a summarizing nature. First, for over forty years after *Smyth* v. *Ames* (1898), the Supreme Court exercised considerable control over the rate-base policies of regulatory commissions. Second, during this period the Court required regulatory commissions to give substantial weight to RCND in

---

[11] *Re Proposed Advances in Freight Rates*, 9 I.C.C. 382, 404 (1903).

determining the fair-value rate base. Third, in two cases, *Natural Gas Pipeline Co.* (1942) and *Hope Natural Gas Co.* (1944), the Supreme Court reversed its long-standing position by holding that: (a) regulatory commissions were not required to use any single valuation method or combination of methods; and (b) the end result of the rate-making process was what really counted, not the method employed to reach that result. Fourth, as a result of these decisions, the state and federal commissions attained greater independence in the selection of regulatory methods. In fact, it may be said that after 1944 (with respect to the federal courts) the judicial phase in rate-base policy making was at an end and that the administrative phase had begun.

A. *The Judicial Phase.* In deciding *Knoxville* v. *Knoxville Water Co.* in 1909, the Supreme Court recognized the importance of depreciation in determining the rate base of a public utility for rate-making purposes. Thereby the Court also remedied an important omission from *Smyth* v. *Ames,* for the matter of depreciation had been overlooked there. In *Knoxville,* the lower court had in effect approved the use of an undepreciated RCND rate base. This was reversed by the Supreme Court, which held that it was necessary to deduct accumulated depreciation from the gross valuation of utility property when determining the rate base.[12] The purpose of using the net valuation after depreciation is to reflect the fact that the existing plant is not entirely new and that a part of the investment cost has been amortized through charges to expenses which are borne by the rate-payer. Although the Court in the *Knoxville* case was concerned with the deduction of accrued depreciation from reproduction cost, such a deduction also is made when other rate-base methods are used. In addition, the Court also recognized that current depreciation expense must be considered in order to determine whether or not earnings are excessive. The Court regarded the charging of current depreciation both as a right of the utility and as a duty to the investors and public.

In the year following *Smyth* v. *Ames,* the Supreme Court decided the *San Diego Land & Town Co.* case, in which it held, "What the company is entitled to demand, in order that it may have just compensation, is a fair return upon the reasonable value of the property at the time it is being used for the public."[13] In holding, in effect, that the present value of public utility property had to be reflected in the rate base, the Court took a position it was to maintain for over forty years. Of some interest, too, is the fact that this decision was handed down at a time when prices had risen very little from the lowest prices of the nineteenth century, which had been recorded in the years immediately following the Panic of 1893. Subsequently, as prices rose considerably, RCND was used to measure the then present value of public utility property.

In *Willcox* v. *Consolidated Gas Co.,* decided in 1909, the Court took a strong position favoring the recognition of higher price levels in fair value determinations. The Court set forth the "general rule" that, ". . . If the property, which legally enters into the consideration of the question of rates, has increased in value since it was acquired, the company is entitled to the benefit of such increase."[14]

In 1913 the Court decided the *Minnesota Rate Cases* and reaffirmed its position favoring reproduction cost as a significant element in valuation. The

12 212 U.S. 1, 10.

13 *San Diego Land & Town Co.* v. *National City,* 174 U.S. 739, 757 (1899).

14 *Willcox* v. *Consolidated Gas Co.,* 212 U.S. 19, 52 (1909).

Court said, ". . . The making of a just return for the use of the property involves the recognition of its fair value, if it is more than cost. The property is held in private ownership and it is that property and not the original cost of it which the owner may not be deprived without due process of law."[15] With respect to the determination of fair value, the Court held:

> The ascertainment of that value is not controlled by artificial rules. It is not a matter of formulas, but there must be a reasonable judgment having its basis in a proper consideration of all relevant facts.[16]

During and after World War I, prices rose sharply. The wholesale commodity price index (1926 = 100) for all commodities, for example, stood at 69.5 in 1915 and rose to 154.4 in 1920. Thereafter, from 1921 to 1929, this index fluctuated between 95.3 and 103.5. Subsequently, during the great depression a low of 64.8 was reached in 1932 before prices started to rise once again.[17] As a result of the higher level of prices in the 1920's, by comparison with those of the previous decade, the courts and commissions were increasingly asked to approve fair value determinations reflecting the new price level.

In *Galveston Electric Co.* v. *Galveston,* decided in 1922,[18] the Supreme Court upheld a lower court's finding that an historical cost valuation, adjusted upward by 33.33 per cent in recognition of the new level of prices, was proper.

In its 1923 *Southwestern Bell Telephone* decision, the Supreme Court reversed an order of the Public Service Commission of Missouri which provided for a reduction in telephone rates. The Supreme Court's decision was based largely upon the fact that the Commission had given no weight to the greatly enhanced costs of material, labor, and supplies over those prevailing in the 1913–1916 period.

In proceedings before the Missouri commission, the company had presented evidence to show an RCND rate base of $31.4 million and an actual cost (undepreciated) of $22.9 million. The opposition evidence of the Commission's staff related to three telephone exchanges rather than to the company as a whole. This evidence consisted of pre-World War I RCND valuations and data on the actual costs of additions since these valuations were made. The Commission combined these data for the three telephone exchanges and compared the total to the company's RCND valuation of the three exchanges. The latter was 153.7 per cent of the total calculated by the Commission. The 153.7 per cent figure then was divided into the company-wide RCND of $31.4 million, which resulted in the rate base of $20.4 million adopted by the Commission.

In reversing this determination, the United States Supreme Court found that a rate base of at least $25 million was required. The Court took notice of the evidence of the higher level of prices prevailing at the time of the Commission's decision as against the level of prices prevailing when the Commission's basic valuation studies were made. The Court cited the *Willcox* decision and the *Minnesota Rate Cases* in holding that it was impossible to determine a fair return on public utility properties without considering present costs. In making rates to be charged in the future, the Court said, it was also essential to make a forecast of probable future values. If present costs are ignored, such a fore-

---

15 230 U.S. 352, 454 (1913).

16 230 U.S. 352, 434.

17 The Bureau of Labor Statistics has revised this index several times with the most recent base period being 1957–59. Each revision has involved changes in commodity classifications as well as index weights.

18 258 U.S. 388.

cast becomes impossible, the Court concluded.[19]

In a separate opinion Justice Brandeis concurred in the judgment of reversal, but on the ground that the Commission's order prevented the utility from earning a fair return on the amount prudently invested. The opinion was highly critical of the fair value rule of *Smyth* v. *Ames,* particularly on the grounds that the valuation for rate-making purposes found under it lacked certainty. Justice Brandeis urged, in the alternative, that definiteness could be achieved by "The adoption of the amount prudently invested as the rate base and the amount of the capital charge as the measure of the rate of return. . . ."[20] If prudent investment were rejected as the measure of valuation, Justice Brandeis maintained that the maximum rate base should be the cost of establishing a plant capable of rendering the same service. This refers to the criticism of the reproduction cost standard, on the grounds that it determines the cost of duplicating a plant that would not be rebuilt because technological advancements have provided alternatives that would be logically preferable. Thus, Justice Brandeis in effect recommended the cost of reproducing the service as a substitute for the cost of reproducing the existing plant. Although the *Southwestern Bell* decision was regarded as highly significant because it explicitly required the recognition of price-level changes in rate-base determinations, the recommendations of Justice Brandeis also must be regarded as important because of their subsequent impact on regulatory practices.

In the *Bluefield* case (1923), the Court held that the West Virginia commission had acted erroneously in failing to recognize the higher post-World War I construction costs and in disregarding the company's evidence of reproduction cost new. In so ruling, the Supreme Court overturned a decision of the West Virginia Supreme Court upholding the commission. The United States Supreme Court through Justice Butler said:

> It is clear that the court also failed to give proper consideration to the higher cost of construction in 1920 over that in 1915 and before the war, and failed to give weight to cost of reproduction less depreciation on the basis of 1920 prices, or to the testimony of the company's valuation engineer, based on present and past costs of construction, that the property in his opinion was worth $900,000. The final figure, $460,000, was arrived at substantially on the basis of actual cost less depreciation plus ten per cent for going value and $10,000 for working capital. This resulted in a valuation considerably . . . less than would have been reached by a fair and just consideration of all the facts. The valuation cannot be sustained.[21]

The 1926 decision of the Court in *McCardle* v. *Indianapolis Water Co.*[22] has been regarded as the high-water mark in gauging the level of importance of reproduction-cost evidence in rate-base determinations. There, the Court reaffirmed its *Bluefield* and *Southwestern Bell* decisions and appeared to insist on reproduction cost new at spot or current prices as the principal, if not the sole, evidence of value. The difference in prices between the time the plant was built and the time of the decision was regarded as so great that the actual cost of the company's plant did not constitute any real indication of its value at the then present time. The Court also restated its position in *Southwestern*

[19] *State ex rel. Southwestern Bell Telephone Co.* v. *Public Service Commission of Missouri,* 262 U.S. 276, 287–288 (1923).

[20] 262 U.S. 276, 306.

[21] *Bluefield Waterworks & Improvement Co.* v. *Public Service Commission of West Virginia,* 262 U.S. 679, 692 (1923).

[22] 272 U.S. 400.

Bell requiring that the valuation reflect a forecast of probable price levels during the immediate future.

A change in the Court's position may be noted as beginning with its 1933 decision in the *Los Angeles Gas & Electric* case.[23] First, the Court was explicit in pointing out the distinction between the functions of the legislative and judicial branches of government, with respect to rate making. "We do not sit as a board of revision, but to enforce constitutional rights . . . ,"Chief Justice Hughes stated in his majority opinion.[24] The Court added that the legislative discretion, implied in the rate-making power, necessarily extended to the entire legislative process, including both the method used and the result found. It was stated that the function of the Court is to determine whether the rates fixed are confiscatory. Unless confiscation is clearly established by the complainant, the Court may not interfere with the exercise of state authority. Thus, the Court gave some indication of a position it was to take at a later date, when, in the *Hope Natural Gas Co.* decision (1944), it held that federal judicial interest extended to the end result of the rate-making process rather than to the methods employed in reaching the end result. However, during the period under discussion, the mid-1930's, the Court showed continuing concern with valuation methods as well as with the results of the rate-making process. In *West* v. *Chesapeake & Potomac Telephone Co.*, as noted previously in this chapter, the Court rejected as inappropriate a rate base found by the Maryland commission through the use of index numbers.[25]

A second important aspect of the *Los Angeles* decision was that it upheld the California commission's use of an essentially historical-cost rate base. It was noted that in the *Minnesota Rate Cases* and others the Court had stated that the judicial ascertainment of value, for the purpose of deciding whether rates are confiscatory, is not a matter of formulas but of reasonable judgment based upon proper consideration of all relevant facts. The Court did not think that historical cost underestimated the value of the company's plant, in that the greater part of it had been added at price levels higher than those prevailing in the period in which the prescribed rates applied.

B. *The Beginning of the Administrative Phase.* The administrative phase in the development of regulation began with the Supreme Court's 1942 decision in *Federal Power Commission* v. *Natural Gas Pipeline Co.*[26] There, the Court held that the Constitution did not require regulatory commissions to use any one formula or combination of formulas in the rate-making process. The Court did not go so far as to authorize commission action without any formula at all. If the commission observed the requirements of procedural due process and issued an order that was not arbitrary, the inquiry of the courts was at an end. The Court's statement follows.

> The Constitution does not bind rate-making bodies to the service of any single formula or combination of formulas. Agencies to whom this legislative power has been delegated are free, within the ambit of their statutory authority, to make the pragmatic adjustments which may be called for by particular circumstances. Once a fair hearing has been given, proper findings made, and other statutory requirements satisfied, the courts cannot intervene in the absence of a clear showing that the limits of due process have been overstepped. If the Commission's order, as applied to the facts before it and viewed in its entirety,

---

23 *Los Angeles Gas & Electric Corp.* v. *Railroad Commission of California*, 289 U.S. 287 (1933).

24 *Ibid.*, p. 304.

25 295 U.S. 662 (1935).

26 315 U.S. 575.

produces no arbitrary result, our inquiry is at an end.[27]

The *Natural Gas Pipeline* decision marked a substantial change in the Court's policy. First, in effect, it withdrew the requirements set forth in previous cases with respect to the methods that commissions were required to follow in determining the valuation of utility property for rate-making purposes. Second, this decision marked the closing of an era in which the federal judiciary had exercised substantial authority in the area of rate-base policy-making and the beginning of a period of increased authority on the part of the administrative agencies. Finally, this decision proved to be the precursor of the *Hope Natural Gas Co.* case, which set forth the "end-result doctrine."

In *Federal Power Commission* v. *Hope Natural Gas Co.*,[28] a majority of the Court held that it was the result reached and not the method employed which was controlling. In other words, the Court held that it was not the theory but the impact of the rate order that counted. If the total effect of the rate order cannot be said to be unreasonable, the Court held, judicial inquiry is at an end. The fact that the method employed to reach that result may contain infirmities was not then to be regarded as important. This has been termed the "end-result doctrine."

What is the nature of the *end-result* standard? Assuming that procedural due process had been accorded by the commission issuing a rate order, then the reasonableness of the end result of that order would be measurable by whether it permitted the company to earn revenues sufficient to cover its expenses and the capital costs of the business. The capital costs would include service on the debt and dividends on the stock sufficient: (a) to provide a return to the equity owner commensurate with returns earned on investments in other enterprises having corresponding risks; and (b) to assure confidence in the financial integrity of the enterprise, so as to maintain its credit and to attract capital.[29] As noted above, an end result found to be satisfactory would be approved by the Court, regardless of "infirmities" in the methods used by the regulatory commission. In so ruling, Justice Jackson subsequently stated, the Court ". . . introduced into judicial review of administrative action the philosophy that the end justifies the means," a philosophy he regarded as questionable.[30]

In approving the end result of the FPC rate order in the *Hope* case, the Court held, ". . . Rates which enable the company to operate successfully, to maintain its financial integrity, to attract capital, and to compensate its investors for the risks assumed certainly cannot be condemned as invalid, even though they might produce only a meager return on the so-called 'fair value' rate base."[31]

The rates thus upheld had been made by the FPC on the basis of a net "actual legitimate cost" rate base. This is not to say that the Court either approved or required the use of some form of actual cost. The "end result doctrine" looked to the results of the rate-making process, not the methods employed. The Court made specific reference to its *Natural Gas Pipeline* decision, handed down two years earlier, and its statement there that no single formula or combination of formulas was required.

In conclusion, it should be noted that the Court has not ruled on a rate-base question since 1945. Thus, there has

[27] *Ibid.*, p. 586.

[28] 320 U.S. 591 (1944).

[29] *Ibid.*, p. 603.

[30] *Colorado Interstate Gas Co.* v. *FPC*, 324 U.S. 581, 609 (1945).

[31] *Op. cit.*, p. 605.

been no opportunity to ascertain what effect, if any, the higher postwar price levels may have exerted upon the Court's position.

4. THE ALLOWANCE FOR WORKING CAPITAL

The rate base includes an allowance for working capital in addition to the net valuation of the utility's tangible property, however measured. Working capital represents an investment in cash, supplies, and other assets that are required to enable the utility to meet current obligations as they arise and to operate economically and efficiently. The amount of working capital required is affected by the average period of time between the provision of service and the receipt of cash in payment for such service. These time periods are sometimes subject to analysis and determination in the course of arriving at a proper allowance for working capital.

Various methods have been employed to determine the working capital allowance. One of these will be illustrated by the Federal Power Commission's traditional method. First, gross working capital is determined by totaling the following: (a) for cash working capital, the FPC allows 12.5 per cent of the company's annual (test-year) operating expenses, which is the equivalent of 45 days' average expenses; (b) an amount representing average materials and supplies inventories; and (c) prepaid expenses, for such items as insurance premiums, lease rentals, and others. Second, from the total of these amounts, the FPC deducts the average annual amount of cash accrued in advance for income tax payments. The average tax accrual balance is credited to the gross working capital because the cash thus generated and available for working capital purposes is not provided by the investors. The average tax accrual credited to gross working capital by the FPC usually amounts to about 65 per cent of the annual income tax accruals. With reference to the gross working capital computation, outlined above, it should be noted that the Commission excludes amounts for purchased gas and materials and supplies inventories used in construction.

The Commission's calculation of the credit to gross working capital for the average income tax accrual was challenged successfully in 1957. In a rate proceeding involving Trunkline Gas Co., an interstate gas pipeline, the initial decision of the presiding examiner held that 33.34 per cent of the annual tax accrual was to be offset against gross working capital. The Commission reversed the examiner and found that a credit of 65.5 per cent was necessary. The United States Court of Appeals for the Fifth Circuit reversed the Commission and held that the credit could not exceed 33.34 per cent.[32] In claiming that the credit should not exceed 33.34 per cent, Trunkline took the position that the Commission had erred in using the annual average tax accrual available to the company as the measure of the credit. A more realistic amount, the company contended, was the maximum amount of such accruals constantly in the custody of the company and available at all times for its use. The Court of Appeals agreed. The Commission has not generally implemented this ruling, on the ground that it is applicable only to the specific fact situation presented in the above case.

5. SOME RATE-BASE EXCLUSIONS

Customers' contributions of capital are usually excluded from the rate base.

[32] *Trunkline Gas Co.* v. *Federal Power Commission,* 247 F. 2d 159 (1957).

Under some circumstances, plant under construction also is excluded. Customers' contributions of capital arise when members of the consuming public, who benefit directly from an extension of utility service, bear part of the capital cost of undertaking such expansion. Thus, utility customers may make contributions of property or money which aid in the construction of the facilities required to supply the additional service. Customers' contributions, as they are called, and also customers' deposits and noninterest-bearing advances, are generally excluded from the rate base. The guiding principle here is that customers should not be required both to provide the utility with capital and to pay a return on the net value of such amounts. Alternatively, the public utility property that originates from customers' contributions is regarded as having no cost to the company for rate-base purposes. The fact that the utility may have title to such property is generally not controlling. Very few cases have held to the contrary.

The general background of plant under construction is explainable by the fact that our national economy has experienced a long-run growth in population, productivity, and living standards which has required a continuous expansion in public utility services. Hence, it is quite common for public utilities to have construction work in progress almost continuously. As a result, many public utility rate cases have been concerned, in part, with the question of whether or not to include plant under construction in the rate base. In most jurisdictions, plant under construction is not included in the rate base when interest on construction is capitalized. This is subject to numerous exceptions for property that is soon to go into operation. As in so many rate-making matters, this is more a question of judgment than a hard-and-fast rule. Thus, for example, the New York commission held in an early case that an allowance should be made in the rate base for plant under construction when such plant will actually be used in the public service during the period when the rates will be in force, and especially so if in considering future revenues the estimates are based upon increased business and consequently the use of the additional property.[33]

The investment in plant under construction merits a return. This is conventionally recognized, at least in part, by capitalizing as a cost of construction an amount for interest during construction. The latter is determined by three factors: (a) the rate of interest during construction; (b) the amount of investment in construction in progress; and (c) the time factor. The effect of capitalizing interest during construction is to recognize that the company has sacrificed an alternative use of the money invested in plant under construction, and that a return on the money tied up in construction represents a part of the cost of the completed plant.

An exception to the somewhat general policy of excluding plant under construction from the rate base, when interest during construction is capitalized, arises where the Bell System's method of crediting such interest is approved. The Bell System uses a rate of interest during construction which is below the rate of return ordinarily allowed on rate base. It then includes plant under construction in the rate base but eliminates the possibility of a duplication of return by crediting interest during construction against income in the determination of revenue requirements.

This serves to bring out some of the considerations involved in determining the interest to be allowed during construction. In a sense, the term "interest"

33 *Re New York Telephone Co.*, PUR 1923B, 545.

is a misnomer, for the money invested in plant under construction, like that invested in plant in service, is not necessarily debt money alone. In many cases, construction is financed by general corporate funds, derived from all the types of securities which finance the company's operations. In such instances, interest during construction is measurable by the company's current cost of total capital, for the alternatives foregone by investing in construction are of the present. As a practical expedient, the experienced cost of capital is an alternative measure. In instances where debt is marketed to finance specific construction, some of the uniform systems of accounts limit interest during construction to the net interest payments. This policy, it has been argued, does not recognize the full cost of the borrowed capital, in that a part of the cost thereof is borne by the equity investors who absorb the risk incurred in employing borrowed capital.[34]

6. STATE COMMISSION VALUATION POLICIES AFTER THE HOPE CASE

The *Hope* case was very important in terms of its impact on the rate-base policies of the state commissions. As a consequence of the *Hope* decision, the rate-base methods used by the state utility commissions were no longer subject to judicial review on federal constitutional grounds, provided that procedural due process had been accorded and the end result was reasonable. Thus, the state commissions gained new and greater power and responsibility in the selection of regulatory methods. However, it is important to note that the rate-base policies of the state commissions must comply with the state laws and state court decisions on the subject. Consequently, the *Hope* case permitted the state commissions to adopt any rate-base method their state courts would approve as consistent with state law.

The *Hope* decision in 1944 was followed by a period of general price inflation; this affected the manner in which the *Hope* decision influenced state commission policies on the question of rate-base method. Two summarizing generalizations may be advanced to cover state commission experience since the *Hope* case. First, after *Hope,* a majority of states abandoned fair value in favor of of some form of actual-cost rate base. Second, as the postwar inflation continued, a trend developed toward the fair value standard once again. A decade after the *Hope* decision, a study of the decisions of the state commissions and courts showed that nine states were using some form of fair value in rate-base determinations.[35] As of 1961, the number had increased considerably, as will be shown shortly. The following is a summary of state commission rate-base policies since the *Hope* case.

A classification of state commission rate-base policies cannot be perfectly precise or divorced from judgment. Some examples will suggest the problem. The Maryland commission, in rate cases involving the Chesapeake and Potomac Telephone Company, has used a net original-cost rate base. However, the governing state law requires a fair-value rate base. Consequently, the Commission in several cases added $3,060,000 as an adjustment to bring the net original cost up to the figure the commission regarded as fair value. This was done, for example, in a case where the original-cost rate base was $327 million.[36] The Mary-

---

[34] J. Rhoads Foster and Bernard S. Rodey, Jr., *Public Utility Accounting* (Englewood Cliffs, N.J.: Prentice-Hall, Inc., 1951), pp. 274–275.

[35] 54 *Col. L. Rev.* 188, 212 (1954).

[36] *Re Chesapeake & Potomac Telephone Co.,* 22 PUR 3d 321, 329 (1958).

land Court of Appeals has upheld the use of a net original-cost rate base where inflation was given recognition through adoption of a year-end rather than an average test-year rate base and allowance of an additional rate-of-return increment.[37] Under the circumstances, Maryland is classified here as an original-cost state. On the other hand, Kentucky is also a statutory fair-value state, but one where an initially computed actual-cost rate base is usually increased by about ten per cent to allow for the effects of inflation.[38] Under these circumstances, Kentucky would be classified here as a fair-value state.

A. *Actual-Cost States.* A few states used some form of actual-cost rate base before the *Hope* case. California, as pointed out earlier in connection with the *Los Angeles* case, long has used historical cost. Massachusetts was using prudent investment before Justice Brandeis discussed this concept favorably in the *Southwestern Bell* case. As early as 1914 the Massachusetts commission ruled that reproduction cost was not to be taken as the basis for determining rates; instead, it held that the capital honestly and prudently invested must be taken as the controlling factor.[39] The Washington state commission was upheld by the state supreme court, before the *Hope* case, in its use of actual cost as a measure of fair value.[40] The question naturally arises as to how these states stayed outside the fair-value orbit during its period of approval by the United States Supreme Court. The answer lies in the fact that the state supreme courts upheld the commissions in the actions taken, apparently finding no necessity to require the application of the fair value doctrine as then interpreted by the United States Supreme Court. Second, where these state supreme court rulings were not appealed to the United States Supreme Court, there was no specific ruling requiring the use of fair value in these states. In the case of California, as noted, the state commission was upheld in the *Los Angeles* case. A situation of the opposite kind illustrates this point. The Wisconsin commission was upheld by the state supreme court in 1923, which ruled that controlling weight should be given to actual investment cost when prudently made.[41] However, in a subsequent case in 1927, the same court reversed itself, holding that it was bound by the *McCardle* decision of the United States Supreme Court. Therefore, the commission was required to use fair value.[42] If the state court had ruled to the contrary, and if it was not reversed by the United States Supreme Court, a situation comparable to that in Massachusetts or Washington would have prevailed.

Second, there is a group of states whose statutes require a fair-value rate base but whose state commissions have modified the fair-value concept by either relying entirely on original cost or by giving it very substantial weight in their rate-base determinations. This is the case in Maryland, West Virginia, Rhode Island, Georgia, and Kansas.

Third, there is a group of states which appear to have adopted original-cost or prudent investment as the rate-base method since the *Hope* case. Not all of these commission actions have been tested by judicial review, and in some states the case material is limited. The

[37] *Baltimore Gas & Electric Co.* v. *People's Counsel,* 152 A. 2d 825 (1959).

[38] *Re Kentucky Utilities Company,* 22 PUR 3d 113 (1958).

[39] *Middlesex & Boston Rate Case,* 2 Ann. Rep. Mass. PSC 99, 111–112 (1914).

[40] *State ex rel. Pacific Tel. & Tel. Co.* v. *Department of Pub. Serv.,* 142 P. 2d 498, 520 (1943).

[41] *Waukesha Gas & Elec. Co.* v. *Railroad Comm.,* 194 N.W. 846, 854 (1923).

[42] *Waukesha Gas & Elec. Co.* v. *Railroad Comm.,* 211 N.W. 760 (1927).

courts have approved the use of original cost or prudent investment in Utah, Florida, Arkansas, Oklahoma, Louisiana, and the District of Columbia. Other states which have turned to actual cost since the *Hope* case include Wisconsin, New Hampshire, Vermont, Connecticut, Maine, Virginia, Michigan, Wyoming, Colorado, Oregon, South Dakota,[43] North Dakota (by statute), Tennessee, Mississippi, Hawaii, and Idaho. New York State adopted original cost as its basis for rate making after the *Hope* case. At present, this does not apply strictly in the case of telephone and railroad companies. This will be discussed in greater detail shortly.

B. *Fair-Value States.* The fair-value states do not necessarily determine the valuation for rate-making purposes in precisely the same way. However, these states do have in common the important fact that, in their rate-base determinations, substantial recognition is accorded to cost of reproduction or current costs. The fair-value states can be divided into two categories. First, there is the group of states in which the fair-value method has been firmly established for some time. Second, there is another group of states which has turned to fair value in recent times.

The states where fair value is more or less traditional include Ohio, Pennsylvania, Illinois, Delaware, Indiana, Arizona, Montana, and New Mexico. Of these, Ohio is unique in that the governing statute has been interpreted by the Ohio Supreme Court to require the Ohio commission to use RCND exclusively in determining the public utility rate base.[44] Pennsylvania has consistently employed fair value. The recent policy has been to rely on trended original cost less depreciation; the latter has been calculated on the basis of depreciation reserve requirement studies based on current annual depreciation rates. In Illinois, adherence to fair value has been confirmed by the reversal of the state commission in a case in which it relied on the *Hope* decision in using an original-cost rate base. Although the statute does not explicitly require fair value, the Illinois Supreme Court has interpreted the act to require it.[45] The commission has tended to give approximately equal weight to RCND and to depreciated original cost. The New Mexico Public Utility Act calls for consideration of elements of value other than original cost. Neither the State Corporation Commission (with jurisdiction over telephone and transportation companies) nor the State Public Service Commission (with jurisdiction over electric, gas, and water utilities) has followed identical methods in determining the fair-value rate base from case to case.

In addition to the traditional fair-value states, there is a second group of fair-value states comprised of those adopting this approach more recently. These include New York (in part), Minnesota, Iowa, Missouri, North Carolina, Texas, Alabama, and apparently New Jersey and Kentucky. With the addition of this latter group to the list of fair-value states, it can be observed that this rate-base method is now employed in a majority of the industrial states where the bulk of public utility property is located. The experience in

---

43 The South Dakota Supreme Court has held that fair value was required in *Farmers' Educ. & Coop. Union* v. *Circuit Court,* 85 PUR (NS) 362, 364 (1950); however, the Court upheld the Commission's use of original cost after the latter gave consideration to reproduction cost in *Re Northwestern Bell Telephone Co.,* 92 PUR (NS) 65, 68 (1952).

44 *City of Marietta* v. *Public Utilities Commission of Ohio,* 148 Ohio St. 173 (1947); *City of Cleveland* v. *Ohio Public Utilities Commission,* 164 Ohio St. 442 (1956).

45 *Illinois Bell Telephone Co.* v. *Illinois Commerce Commission,* 98 PUR (NS) 379 (1953).

the recent fair-value states is summarized below.

Perhaps the most famous fair-value decision since World War II was that which the highest court in New York State handed down in the 1956 *New York Telephone Co.* case. The New York commission regulates telephone utilities under a different statute from that applicable to other public utilities. The law dealing with all utilities except telephone companies and railroads calls for a reasonable average return upon capital actually expended. This has been taken to mean net original cost. However, the law governing telephone companies and railroads requires a reasonable average return upon the value of property actually used in the public service. In interpreting the latter language, a lower state court concluded that the fair-value concept of *Smyth* v. *Ames* was required in the regulation of telephone and railroad companies, and that this expression of legislative intent was not altered by the *Hope* case. It was held that the state commission had erred in excluding evidence of reproduction cost. However, the consideration this factor receives was held to be a matter for the commission to decide. This lower court ruling was upheld on appeal to the highest state court.[46]

After this case was remanded to the state commission for application of the principles decided, the commission considered the company's evidence as to reproduction cost but found that it was not feasible to rely upon such evidence in making rates. Instead, the commission followed the direction of the court by making an adjustment for the factor of inflation in the rate of return allowed. Thus, the commission departed from its rigid 6 per cent rate-of-return policy, and found a rate of return of 6.5 per cent on a net-property-account rate base (plus working capital) to be reasonable. In effect, this was equivalent to an increase of 8.33 per cent in the rate base, assuming the 6 per cent rate of return formerly applied.[47]

The Minnesota commission has rate jurisdiction over telephone and urban transit utilities. By virtue of a 1957 amendment to the statute governing rate making for telephone utilities, this commission is now required to consider the current values of telephone utility property, along with original cost and prudent investment, in determining the valuation for rate making.[48] The Minnesota commission has put this policy into effect by giving about equal weight to the principal alternative methods.[49] A comparable situation exists in Minnesota with respect to urban transit utilities. The Minnesota Supreme Court has recognized the impact of inflation upon rate-making policy in ruling against strict adherence to the prudent investment standard in a case involving the Minneapolis Street Railway Co.[50]

Public utilities in Iowa are regulated at the local level of government, through the enactment of rate ordinances by each city council. In a 1957 case involving gas rates in Fort Dodge, the Iowa Supreme Court held that a fair-value rate base was required. In light of the fact that the last valuation of the company's property had been made in 1939, and that the prices of most property and services had doubled since that date, the Court concluded that fair value was to be calculated by giving 70 per cent

---

[46] *New York Telephone Co.* v. *New York Public Service Commission,* 8 PUR 3d 299 (1955); 12 PUR 3d 399 (1956).

[47] *Re New York Telephone Co.,* 20 PUR 3d 129 (1957).

[48] Chapter 917—S.F. No. 1470, amending *Minnesota Statutes 1953,* Section 237.08 (1957).

[49] *Re Northwestern Bell Telephone Co.,* 23 PUR 3d 267 (1958).

[50] *Minneapolis Street Railway Co.* v. *Minneapolis,* 86 NW 2d 657, 22 PUR 3d 223, 243 (1957).

weight to RCND and 30 per cent weight to net original cost. It was also found that the accumulated depreciation should be computed at the same straight-line rate for both the original cost and the reproduction cost valuations. A six per cent rate of return, uncontested by the parties, was found not to be confiscatory.[51]

In a unanimous 1957 decision, the Missouri Supreme Court overturned the state commission's exclusive reliance upon original cost. A proper determination of rates, it was held, should be based on all relevant factors, including fair value. The Court declared that the *Hope* decision was no authority for abandoning a present-value rate base, since that case was decided on facts arising in the year 1939, near the end of a 20-year period of level or declining values. At that time, it was concluded, original cost and reproduction cost, or any other valuation approach, would have been essentially fair value. With reference to the state commission's contention that the reproduction-cost method was speculative and cumbersome, the Court stated that modern accounting methods, together with recognized cost-trending percentage tables and price indexes, could be applied to original cost to determine reproduction cost and depreciation with reasonable accuracy.[52]

The North Carolina Supreme Court has held that the state law, which incorporates almost verbatim some of the language in *Smyth* v. *Ames,* requires consideration of both original cost and replacement value. Therefore, a net actual-cost rate base was held to be in error.[53] This decision was then implemented by the state commission, which fixed a fair-value rate base of $89 million in considering various valuation measures which ranged from $78.1 to $98.6 million.[54]

Rate regulation in Texas is administered at the local level, with the state commission acting as an appellate body in cases involving gas rates. In a case where the state commission had found a rate base that was approximately equal to depreciated book cost, the Texas Supreme Court overturned the commission's finding and interpreted the governing statute to require a fair-value rate base.[55] A similar ruling in Alabama has led to the implementation of a fair-value policy by the state commission, which formerly had relied upon net original cost.[56]

The New Jersey Supreme Court held in the *New Jersey Bell Telephone Co.* case that inflation has had such an impact that original cost does not reflect accurately the fair value of the company's property. On remand, the state commission set forth findings to support as fair value a year-end rate base increased by about five per cent as an "inflation allowance."[57] In conclusion, it may be noted that there is an apparent trend toward inflation recognition in the rate-base policies of the state commissions. Second, this tendency has resulted far more as a result of directives from the state courts than from voluntary action by state commissions. Third, it appears that a relatively large proportion of the states adhering to actual cost are

---

[51] *Iowa-Illinois Gas & Electric Co.* v. *City of Fort Dodge et al.,* 85 NW 2d 28, 47 (1957).

[52] *Missouri ex rel. Missouri Water Co.* v. *Missouri Public Service Commission et al.,* 308 SW 2d 704 (1957).

[53] *State of North Carolina ex rel. Utilities Commission* v. *State of North Carolina et al.,* 3 PUR 3d 307 (1954).

[54] *Re Southern Bell Telephone & Telegraph Co.,* 7 PUR 3d 43 (1954).

[55] *Texas Railroad Commission* v. *Houston Natural Gas Corp.,* 289 S.W. 2d 559 (1956).

[56] *Re Alabama Gas Corp.,* 25 PUR 3d 257 (1958); *Re Southern Bell Tel. & Tel. Co.,* 31 PUR 3d 254 (1959).

[57] *State of New Jersey* v. *New Jersey Bell Telephone Co.,* 152 A. 2d 35 (1959); *Re New Jersey Bell Telephone Co.,* 31 PUR 3d 453 (1959).

those which are below average in industrialization or relative growth or per capita income, or some combination of these factors.

7. RATE-BASE POLICIES OF FEDERAL AGENCIES

Federal regulatory agencies, like the state commissions, use either net actual cost or fair value where the rate-base method of rate making is employed. The Federal Power Commission traditionally uses an average net original-cost rate base in regulating the interstate wholesale rates charged by electric utilities and natural gas pipelines.[58] The Federal Communications Commission has jurisdiction over the rates charged by common carriers of communications in interstate and foreign commerce; these include telephone, domestic telegraph, and international telegraph and cable companies. Although the body of decided cases in this area is relatively small, the Federal Communications Commission to date has relied upon a net original-cost rate base.[59]

For purposes of comparison, the rate-base policies of the federal commissions which regulate the transportation utilities may be noted. The Civil Aeronautics Board has adopted a net actual-cost rate base for the regulation of the domestic trunkline air carriers.[60] On the other hand, a fair-value rate base is the policy of the Federal Maritime Board in regulating the rates of the ocean carriers under its jurisdiction; fair value is also employed by the Interstate Commerce Commission to regulate the earnings of the interstate oil pipelines. The Federal Maritime Board regulates the rates charged by ocean carriers operating between continental United States and ports in "offshore" possessions and territories such as Puerto Rico. The Board applies a fair-return-on-fair-value standard to the dominant carrier in a particular trade in determining the general rate level for all the carriers serving that trade route.[61] The practice of the Board is to test the reasonableness of the rates proposed to be charged by determining whether the rate of return that such rates would yield on a number of different rate bases will fall "within the zone of reasonableness." To this end, the Board has considered together the respective rate-base computations representing net book value, reproduction cost, domestic market value of the ships, and various measures of fair value found by combining net book value and RCND. The Board makes its decision as to whether the proposed rates are just and reasonable without selecting any particular rate-base calculation as controlling. However, the Board has held that sole reliance upon the net book value of vessels is unrealistic, and has given substantial weight to domestic market values (adjusted for short-run variations) in evaluating vessels for rate-making purposes.[62]

The Interstate Commerce Commission determines a "final value" rate base by the fair-value approach in its regulation of pipelines transporting crude oil and its products. The final value is determined after consideration of the reproduction cost and original cost of the property, appreciation, depreciation, the values of land and rights-of-way, working capital, going-concern value, and all other matters which appear to have a bearing upon the values reported. "Re-

58 *In the Matter of South Carolina Generating Co.*, 16 FPC 52 (1956).

59 *Re Western Union Telegraph Co.*, 25 FCC 532 (1958).

60 *General Passenger Fare Investigation*, Docket No. 8008, November 25, 1960 (mimeo.).

61 *General Increase in Alaska Rates and Charges*, 5 FMB 486 (1958).

62 *General Increases in Hawaiian Rates*, 5 FMB 347 (1957); *Atlantic-Gulf/Puerto Rico General Rate Increases*, 6 FMB 14 (1960).

production cost" for this purpose is computed by the trended original cost method, whereby: (a) the 1947 year-end inventory is adjusted for capital additions and retirements subsequent to that date, as measured in 1947 prices; and (b) the present reproduction cost is found by applying to the 1947 value thus found for the present plant a multiplier reflecting the price relationship between 1947 and the present.[63] The rate-base method is not employed in the regulation of transportation utilities other than those mentioned above.

8. WHEN IS A RATE BASE REQUIRED?

This section is intended to compare in broad scope the regulatory methods employed with respect to the utilities under consideration here as well as to the transportation utilities.

A. Economic Characteristics Determine Regulatory Method. It is fundamental that the regulation of rates requires the use of some standard or method to determine when rates are within a zone of reasonableness and when they are not. Otherwise, the courts would have no basis to review the reasonableness of the rates authorized by state and federal regulatory commissions. Granting that some standard of reasonableness must be used in rate regulation, the present discussion of the rate base can be put into proper economic perspective by considering this question: is the rate-base method the only one which provides a proper basis for the determination of just and reasonable rates under regulation? Inspection of the practices of the state and federal regulatory commissions reveals that the answer to that question is decidedly negative. On one hand, it is true that the rate-base approach is used, and properly, to regulate utilities supplying electricity, water, telephone and other communication services, gas distribution and transmission, and, in some cases, urban transit. On the other hand, the rate-base method is not always used in the regulation of the public utilities supplying freight and passenger transportation services.

The rate-base standard is appropriate for the regulation of the traditional public utilities we are concerned with in this book. This holds true because the rate-base method is directly related to the outstanding economic characteristics of such public utilities. In every case, the appropriate regulatory method is the one which is best adapted to the economic characteristics of the industry involved. The principal economic characteristics of the traditional public utilities are: (a) monopoly status, and (b) low capital turnover ratios. The individual-company rate-base method is appropriate for the regulation of the traditional public utilities because: (a) regulation on a company-by-company basis is practical and realistic where monopolies are involved; and (b) the use of the individual-company rate base recognizes that the business risk of the traditional utilities is a function of investment in fixed plant.

However, the individual-company rate-base approach is not appropriate where: (a) elements of competition exist in the industry under regulation; and/or (b) the risk element is not principally a function of investment. Where elements of competition prevail in a regulated industry, an individual-company approach is invalid because it would likely result in a variety of rates, owing to individual differences among the companies. It is apparent that dissimilar rates for competitors, such as intercity motor carriers serving the same points, would tend to channel business toward those charging the comparatively lower rates and away from those charging the relatively higher

[63] *Ajax Pipe Line Corp.* (Appendix 4), 50 Val. Rep. 1 (1949); *Service Pipe Line Co.*, 56 Val. Rep. 369 (1958).

rates. Hence, in a case of this kind, the general regulatory practice is to make rates for *groups* of regulated companies rather than for individual members of the group. Such is the case in the regulation of motor carriers, railroads, freight forwarders, international telegraph and cable companies, ocean carriers, and airlines. This applies whether or not the companies involved have low capital turnover ratios.

There is intra-industry competition in the international telegraph and cable communications industry and the ocean carrier industry, which are regulated by the Federal Communications Commission and the Federal Maritime Board, respectively. Because of the element of competition, rates are made on a group basis. Uniform rates are prescribed for each company within the group on the basis of the rate of return on rate base requirement of the "dominant" or "bellwether" company in the group. This was done, for example, by the Federal Communications Commission in setting the rates for the international telegraph and cable companies in the 1958 *Western Union* case; of course, appropriate adjustments were made in the rate structures of the respective companies to compensate for special circumstances in both the operations carried on by and the areas served by specific carriers.[64] Similarly, the Federal Maritime Board looks to the rate of return on rate base for the dominant ocean carrier in each noncontiguous domestic trade route, and deems this carrier the "rate-making line" for the determination of rates applicable to all carriers within the group.[65] A somewhat similar approach was adopted by the Civil Aeronautics Board in the General Passenger Fare Investigation.[66] There, the Board approved an over-all rate of return on rate base for the domestic trunkline air carrier industry, based upon a somewhat lower rate of return for the Big Four carriers and a higher rate of return for the then remaining eight intermediate-size trunkline carriers.

Interstate motor carriers of freight and passengers are regulated by the Interstate Commerce Commission on the basis of the average conditions confronted by the companies in each industry, and sometimes for the industry in prescribed areas. These companies are characterized by relatively rapid capital turnover. Because there is a competitive element in these industries, regulation is applied to groups of companies rather than to individual companies. The rate-base method is not employed at all, because the business risk of high capital-turnover companies is not related to investment in fixed plant so much as to operating expenses. Thus, the Interstate Commerce Commission uses the group operating ratio as the principal standard for the regulation of motor carrier rates.[67] The operating-ratio standard is being applied with increasing frequency to individual urban transit utilities, as discussed shortly.

The rate-base method of regulation is no longer applied to the railroads. Instead, the Interstate Commerce Commission makes rates on a group basis, sometimes by individual areas, on the basis of average conditions confronted by the companies as a group. In this respect, the Commission has looked to increased operating expenses and other general economic factors as a measure of the required general level of revenues.[68]

[64] *Op. cit.*, Note 59.

[65] *General Increases in Hawaiian Rates*, 5 FMB 347 (1957).

[66] *Op. cit.*, Note 60.

[67] *Middle West General Increases*, 48 MCC 541 (1948); *Increases, Calif., Ariz., Colo., N. Mex., and Tex., 1949*, 51 MCC 747 (1950).

[68] *Increased Freight Rates, 1947*, 270 ICC 403 (1948); *Increased Freight Rates, 1951*, 291 ICC 589 (1952).

B. ***Traditional Utilities: Rate Base Required.*** The end-result doctrine of the *Hope* case gave rise to the question of whether it was necessary to determine a rate base in making rates for the traditional public utilities such as electric and water companies. This question originated in the post-*Hope* shift in emphasis from rate-base methods to the end result of the entire rate-making process. Specifically, there was some uncertainty as to whether a rate-base determination could be avoided altogether in favor of a direct determination of the revenue requirement of the utility company. This matter was settled relatively soon after the *Hope* decision. The general rule is that a rate base is required where the traditional public utilities are concerned. Exceptions will be noted subsequently.

One year after the *Hope* decision, the Supreme Court set aside a Federal Power Commission rate order on the ground that the Commission had not furnished sufficient evidence to support its rate findings. Speaking through Justice Douglas, who had written the *Hope* decision, the Court said that it could not understand the method used by the Commission and insisted on more clarity and completeness in the basic findings on which administrative orders rest.[69] In reversing the Commission, the Court raised another important point, namely, that effective judicial review required the regulatory commission to provide clear findings of fact by a well-defined method of analysis. The Federal Power Commission has taken this decision to mean that clear findings of fact with respect to the rate base are necessary in its electric and natural gas pipeline rate cases.

A similar decision was handed down by the Wisconsin Supreme Court in a case in which the state commission directly fixed telephone rates without determining either a rate base or a rate of return. There, the commission reached its conclusion as to the revenue requirement which would yield a reasonable profit by considering three factors. These were the estimated future costs of furnishing proper service, the value of the service, and the reasonable profit for an operation of this kind.[70] The Wisconsin Supreme Court found the commission's action to be arbitrary and unlawful.[71] The court ruled that the commission was required in a case of this kind to accompany its decision with findings of fact and conclusions of law. The findings of fact were to consist of the commission's ultimate conclusions on each contested issue. The court inquired as to how the commission itself or the reviewing court could determine whether a reasonable profit had been authorized in the absence of specific findings of fact in the case. It may be noted that the courts in both of the foregoing cases insisted that commission rate orders set forth clearly the basis for the decision reached. Regardless of the type of rate base employed, there remains the need for some means of testing the end result of commission actions. For purposes of this test, properly drawn findings as to the rate base and the rate of return seem indispensable in conventional public utility rate cases. Further support for the necessity of a rate base in traditional utility rate making has come from the New Hampshire Supreme Court in a case closely similar to the Wisconsin case above and from the Florida commission.[72] In the Florida case, the utility had expressed willingness to accept a proposed rate decrease

---

69 *Colorado-Wyoming Gas Co.* v. *FPC,* 324 U.S. 626, 634 (1945).

70 *City of Two Rivers* v. *Commonwealth Telephone Co.,* 32 PSCW 120, 70 PUR (NS) 5 (1947).

71 *Commonwealth Telephone Co.* v. *PSCW,* 32 N.W. 2d 247 (1948).

72 *New England Telephone & Telegraph Co.* v. *State,* 64 A. 2d 9 (1949); *Re Florida Power & Light Co.,* 19 PUR 3d 417 (1957).

without a formal proceeding; however, the state commission held that the fixing of rates would be an arbitrary exercise of statutory authority without rate-base and rate-of-return findings.

In a somewhat different type of case, a United States Court of Appeals reversed a Federal Power Commission decision which set aside the rate-base method and adopted an alternative method to evaluate pipeline-produced gas for rate-making purposes. The court made clear that the rate-base method was not the only one that could be used for this purpose. However, if the Commission were to adopt an alternative to the rate-base method, it was held necessary to use the rate-base method as a basis of comparison.[73] This is considered further in Chapter 14.

C. *Urban Transit, an Important Exception.* Even among the traditional public utilities, the rate-base method may be omitted in certain rate-making situations. The most prominent example is found in the regulation of the urban transit industry, where the operating-ratio method is replacing the rate-base approach. Under the operating-ratio method, the need for additional revenues is determined by the size of the return margin available for the payment of a return on investment. The return margin is the difference between 100 per cent of revenues and the operating ratio, which expresses as a percentage the relationship of operating and other expenses to operating revenues. As the operating ratio aproaches 100 per cent, the smaller is the return margin, or the revenue remainder after expenses, available to meet the return requirements. Regulatory commissions judge a transit company's need for additional revenues by comparing the operating ratio resulting from actual operations with the operating ratio found necessary to provide a reasonable return. The Interstate Commerce Commission, for example, concluded that an operating ratio, before federal income taxes, of 85 per cent, or about 93 per cent after such taxes, would be a reasonable standard. This conclusion was drawn after conducting a comprehensive investigation of over 200 passenger carriers, which included companies providing both intercity and local passenger service by motor carrier.[74]

In numerous jurisdictions the operating-ratio method has been replacing the rate-base approach in the regulation of urban transit companies. The principal reason for this is that the conversion from streetcar to bus transportation has been accompanied by changing economic characteristics in that industry. Many urban transit operations are now characterized by a relatively quick capital turnover ratio. Hence, the level of expenses provides a standard for regulation which is more meaningful economically than the amount of property invested. The operating ratio also is more appropriate owing to the rapid fluctuation in the rate base due to the relatively short service lives of operating properties, the greater competitive risks than those of other public utilities, the absence of a minimum service charge, and declining traffic in some cities. The principal reason, however, is that cited earlier, namely, the quicker rate of capital turnover, which signifies that plant investment is smaller in relation to a given volume of business than in the case of the other traditional utilities.

This principle has been recognized by both the Interstate Commerce Commission and numerous state commissions. The Utah Public Service Commission has stated:

[73] *City of Detroit* v. *FPC,* 230 F. 2d 810 (1955); *cert.* denied, 352 U.S. 829 (1956); but see also *Minneapolis Gas Co.* v. *FPC,* 278 F. 2d 870 (1960), *cert.* denied, 81 S. Ct. 220 (1960).

[74] *Investigation of Bus Fares,* 52 MCC 332, 336 (1950).

The Commission is cognizant of the fact that the ordinary rate base-rate of return approach to allowable earnings is not as reliable a gauge in the case of bus transit utilities as it is in the case of electric, gas, and telephone utilities for the reason that the revenues and expenses are both relatively high in the bus transportation field as measured against the plant accounts of the companies concerned.[75]

With respect to the difficulty of applying the rate-base approach to urban transit utilities, the Massachusetts commission has said:

The investment of respondent (the transit company) or, for that matter, of any motor carrier is in short-lived property requiring a very substantial annual depreciation charge. . . . Hence, respondent's net investment might vary sharply from year to year, making the rate base as understood in the traditional concept unstable and unsatisfactory for use in rate-making proceedings which should have as nearly permanent results as possible.[76]

In addition to the urban transit industry, the rate base sometimes is not used in cases involving temporary or emergency rate increases and deficit operations. In some cases commissions have found it unnecessary to determine a rate base when gas and electric distribution utilities have sought rate increases solely to offset higher costs of purchased gas and boiler fuel, respectively, and studies of the company's earnings by the staff of the commission have been taken into consideration.

[75] *Re Salt Lake City Lines, Inc.*, 78 PUR (NS) 1, 6 (1949).

[76] *Re Eastern Massachusetts Street Railway Co.*, 95 PUR (NS) 33 (1952).

7 Valuation Procedures

This chapter is concerned with the two principal procedures used to determine the valuation of public utility property for rate-making purposes: (a) the appraisal process, by which the reproduction cost new less depreciation is found; and (b) original cost, a specialized accounting concept which ascertains the cost of the operating property to the person first devoting it to public service.

1. THE APPRAISAL PROCESS

Reproduction cost new less depreciation is found through an appraisal of the tangible assets of a public utility, to which is added an allowance for working capital and certain intangible elements of value. *Reproduction cost,* with which we are concerned here, is not the same as *replacement cost. Reproduction cost* of an operating property is the estimated cost of duplicating essentially the identical property at the price level of a specified date or the average price of a stated time period. The *replacement cost* of property is the estimated cost of providing the same service through the most efficient substitute property, at the price level of a stated date or time period. It has been little used in public utility cases. The principal steps in the development of a reproduction cost valuation are discussed below.

A. The Inventory of Physical Property. The first major objective in the appraisal process is the development of a complete and correct list of all the units of property owned by the company, which is called the *inventory*. Before the inventory work begins, however, the valuation engineer may conduct a preliminary examination of the company covering its life history and periodic financial reports. In addition, he ordinarily will examine the property ledger and also attempt to determine whether any of the property is not used or useful in service to the public. At this point it should be noted that the maintenance of continuing property records (CPR) provides a useful property inventory as well as other assistance in the appraisal process. The CPR consist of a current, detailed, and descriptive inventory of the physical property plus data as to its installed original cost. Not all utilities are required to maintain continuing property records. In 1960 twenty-four states provided for their establishment.[1] However, some utilities maintain CPR voluntarily although not required to do so. Accurate CPR provide a reasonable, inexpensive basis for reproduction cost appraisals of utility plant. Accuracy can be verified by spot checks. When taking a complete field inventory by actual examination of the property being appraised, it is necessary to classify the units of property into groups and subgroups which can be identified, enumerated, and valued. The inventory field parties which examine the property furnish the data needed. Where accurate continuing property records are maintained, this is provided automatically, thus reducing costs while speeding the appraisal process.

The inventory should include only the property necessary to prudent operation of the utility business. For example, a commercial parking lot operating on land owned by the company, where its employees and the general public are served on the same basis, would be excluded as non-utility property. The only property included in the inventory for rate-making purposes is that which is *used or useful* in serving the public. Property need not be used to be useful. It may be largely idle, standing in reserve in the event of equipment failure. Such property, although not used, is highly useful because it helps to assure uninterrupted public service. Needless to say, there are many occasions when the question of the usefulness of a particular property unit is not a simple matter to decide. Another question often arising involves property held for future use. Generally, such property will be included in the inventory when it is related to the company's expected growth and will be used within a reasonable period of time.

B. *Costing the Inventory.* After the property inventory has been completed, whether derived from the continuing property records or from a field study, the next step is to apply unit costs to each of the individual classes of property, however grouped. The unit cost times the number of units in each subgroup in the classification equals its direct construction cost. This cost, when found for each group of property units, will then be totaled.

The unit costs applied to the inventory property classes may not be defined by all appraisers in the same way. This may result from differences in the assumptions made as to whether the plant was built by the owner or by a contractor. Nonetheless, the unit costs typically will include: (a) actual or average list prices of materials and equipment as of some date or time period; (b) freight, storage, and handling charges; (c) labor costs; and (d) an allowance, sometimes called a "labor loading," which may re-

---

[1] Federal Power Commission, *State Commission Jurisdiction and Regulation of Electric and Gas Utilities* (Washington: Government Printing Office, 1960), p. 27.

flect such items as plant supervision, small-tool expense, workmen's compensation insurance, social security taxes, and others. This allowance may be allocated or assigned on a unit basis or may be calculated directly as a specified percentage of labor costs.

C. *Overhead Construction Costs.* Overhead construction costs are added to the direct construction costs in order to measure the total reproduction cost of the property under appraisal. Overhead construction costs include those for engineering services and supervision, general office salaries and expense, law expenses, insurance, injuries and damages, taxes on the property, interest during construction, and others. These costs will be incurred by the utility when it serves as its own contractor. If, however, the project is constructed by a contractor, many of the items above will be included in "contract work" and made a part of direct construction costs. Sometimes overhead construction costs will include an allowance for omissions and contingencies and the cost of organizing and promoting the company.

The largest of the overhead construction costs are the items for engineering and interest during construction. The latter is included whether the construction of property is financed by borrowed funds or by the utility's own funds. It represents the return foregone on the investment in property under construction. The total overhead construction costs, if expressed in dollars, may be allocated to property units on the basis of direct construction costs. Sometimes, however, the amount for construction overhead is expressed instead as a percentage of direct costs.

D. *Depreciation.* The reproduction cost of the physical property in new condition is found by totaling the inventory valuation and the overhead construction costs. The next step in the appraisal process calls for deducting some measure of the accumulated depreciation from the "reproduction cost new" figure. The basic purpose of this deduction is to reflect the fact that the property is not in new condition. The various methods of calculating the accumulated depreciation will be covered in Chapter 8.

E. *Land Values.* The value of land must be added to the net or depreciated value of the physical property. Land values are added at this point in the valuation process because, unlike the tangible property and capitalized overhead costs, land is not depreciable. The basis of land valuation in the appraisal process is the fair market value of abutting and adjacent lands of similar character. However, this is not necessarily the case where an original-cost rate base is used. The Federal Power Commission, for example, requires the accounts for land and land rights to include "the first cost, including the amounts of mortgages or other liens assumed. . . ."[2]

F. *The Valuation of Intangibles.* The value of a public utility, operating as a going concern, is greater than the value of its tangible property alone. Therefore, the reproduction cost may include elements of intangible value over and above the net valuation of the physical property:

(1) *Franchise value,* or the value of the utility's right to serve a particular service area, ordinarily as a monopoly, is not included in the rate base. Although there is no dispute that the monopoly franchise is valuable, it is recognized as having originated in a grant by the public. Accordingly, it would be illogical to include the value of the franchise in the rate base and require the public to pay a return on it. Of course, where proper costs have been sustained

---

[2] Federal Power Commission, *Uniform System Accounts Prescribed for Natural Gas Companies,* Effective January 1, 1940, Instruction 9, p. 46.

in securing the franchise, they may be included in the rate base.

(2) *Good will,* the value built up over time which causes customers to return to a given product or seller, is not recognized as a rate-base element. Although good will is indispensable to a competitive business, it can hardly be viewed in the same light for a monopoly seller of a necessity.

(3) *Going-concern value* is an element of value which reflects the fact that a utility company is an operational and functioning enterprise which had to incur costs, and possibly deficits, in order to develop a market and establish its business organization. Recognition of going-concern value may be accorded in the utility rate base, with the showing required to substantiate the allowance for this purpose tending to vary in different jurisdictions. Conventionally, the burden is upon the company to make a showing that such an allowance is proper.

G. Working Capital. A final step in determining the reproduction cost valuation is to add an allowance for working capital. This matter was discussed in the previous chapter.

H. Summary. The determination of public utility valuation for rate-making purposes, by the appraisal process, generally involves the following:

(1) Taking an inventory of the physical property by reference to continuing property records or by an actual field inventory.

(2) Costing the inventory thus determined.

(3) Adding an amount for overhead construction costs.

(4) Deducting from the gross valuation of the physical property, as found in the foregoing, an amount for accumulated depreciation.

(5) Adding an amount for the value of land.

(6) Adding an amount for intangible values as the facts and commission policy may warrant.

(7) Adding an allowance for working capital.

2. ORIGINAL COST

One of the most significant developments in utility regulation has been the adoption by practically all commissions of uniform systems of accounts which require public utilities to state their fixed asset or plant accounts on the basis of first original cost. The Federal Power Commission, for example, defines *original cost* as ". . . the cost of such property to the person first devoting it to the public service."[3] The requirement that a utility company shall state its plant accounts on the basis of original cost is equally applicable to: (a) plant constructed by the utility; and (b) plant acquired from others. The cost of plant constructed by the utility conventionally is carried on the books at original cost. Where property is acquired, it would be conventional to record the acquisition price as the book cost. However, under original-cost accounting, now required by the uniform systems of accounts, acquired property would be recorded at the cost to the predecessor owner who first devoted the particular property to public utility service. Original cost is determined by studies of available books and records. If the original cost of plant cannot be determined, it may be estimated.

Because public utility plant accounts did not reflect original cost until required to do so by the uniform systems of accounts, it became necessary to segregate original cost from book cost and to dispose of the resulting difference

[3] Federal Power Commission, *Uniform System of Accounts Prescribed for Public Utilities and Licensees,* effective January 1, 1937, definition 29, p. 6.

as each commission ordered. This required restatement of public utility plant accounts on a first-original-cost basis is sometimes referred to as "retroactive accounting." This subdivision of book cost to the accounting company is a marked departure from conventional private business accounting, which ordinarily looks only to the affairs of the accounting company and no other. When it is considered that present-day utility systems invariably are the product of numerous combinations of property, the impact of original cost accounting can be properly termed most significant. The historical background of this accounting distinction between book cost and original cost will be covered shortly. However, a brief summary of the rate-making effects of original-cost accounting is in order first.

The federal and state commissions, which follow an actual-cost rate-base policy, have found in net original cost a measure of the rate base which can be read directly from the accounts. It also merits noting that those jurisdictions recognizing fair value sometimes use original-cost data as a point of reference in their rate-base determinations. Second, the uniform systems of accounts have required the adoption of depreciation accounting, which previously had not been employed by all utilities. Depreciation expense and accrued depreciation, as noted earlier, are factors which bear upon the determination of a cost of service for rate-making purposes.

A. *Background.* During the first three decades of this century, there were numerous transactions involving public utility properties in mergers, consolidations, and other forms of combination. These transactions often represented steps aimed at realizing the savings inherent in natural monopoly and in large-scale production as well as those made possible by constantly improving technology. However, not all combinations in public utility properties were solely of this kind. Particularly during the 1920's, with the growth of the public utility holding company systems, the buying and selling of utility operating properties was often motivated by prospects of financial gain not necessarily related to achieving increases in efficiency or reductions in the costs of providing service. In addition, and of particular importance, there was the fact that many acquisitions of utility property were at a price in excess of book cost to the seller. Consequently, there resulted an increase in the cost of utility plant, as recorded on the books of the buyer.

Why were the acquisition prices of public utility properties ordinarily higher than the book costs of the seller? The reasons are diverse, and some reflect reasonable business practices while others do not. This last point should be emphasized, because much of the writing on this subject is inclined to oversimplify. First, a factor affecting acquisition prices was the generally higher level of prices and construction costs at the time of acquisition, as compared to those prevailing when the property was constructed. Second, acquisition prices sometimes reflected a capitalization of economies and savings in operating expenses and capital costs made possible by operating the acquired properties as part of an integrated utility system. Third, acquisition prices reflected in part a capitalization of increased earnings expectations from future operations in growing markets. Finally, where transactions involved affiliated interests, acquisition prices in many cases reflected the absence of arm's-length bargaining. This will be discussed shortly.

These acquisitions of public utility operating properties, for the most part, involved electric, gas, and transit companies. The nature of the acquisitions and the circumstances under which they took place were highly diverse and cannot be described as all of one kind or of another. Some transactions were negotiated at arm's length between wholly unaffiliated parties. Others, however, involved holding company affiliates. Some of the transactions involving an affiliated buyer and seller were at prices determined by "outside," that is, independent, appraisers or at prices approved by state regulatory agencies. Some of the transactions involving affiliates were subject to state agency approval insofar as the securities issued against the sale price were concerned, and were consistent with the uniform systems of accounts then in effect. Some of the transactions between affiliates, it was later maintained, reflected the then going value of the properties, which could not have been sold for less without damaging the interests of bondholders and minority stockholders.

On the other hand, some of the transactions among affiliates provided opportunity to take advantage of the absence of arm's-length bargaining and resulted in speculative write-ups of plant accounts. The principal means of accomplishing a write-up, through the affiliated company structure of utility organization, was by the issuance of additional securities. Thus, a transfer, merger, or consolidation of public utility properties could be made the occasion for: (1) the issuance of additional securities to stockholders and the public; and (2) a write-up of the plant accounts of the affiliated buyer of the properties to reflect the securities then newly issued. In addition, plant accounts in some cases were made to reflect bonus stock issued to promoters, bond discount and expense, capital stock discount and expense, duplication of organization expenses, and finders' fees.

The foregoing practices could not long endure, and in 1928 Congress ordered the Federal Trade Commission to conduct an investigation of these and related matters. The findings of this investigation documented the existence of a host of financial and accounting abuses, which led to the enactment of much of the regulatory legislation of the 1930's. Chief among these was the Public Utility Holding Company Act of 1935, which brought the electric and gas utility holding companies under federal control. This important phase of regulation is examined in Chapter 20. However, for purposes of the present discussion, the important regulatory statutes of the 1930's were the Federal Communications Act of 1934, the Federal Power Act of 1935, and the Natural Gas Act of 1938. These statutes not only vested substantial authority to regulate interstate public utility rates in the Federal Communications Commission and the Federal Power Commission but also gave them broad authority to prescribe the present uniform systems of accounts. The establishment of these systems of accounts and the restatement of public utility plant accounts on a first original-cost basis were given top priority by these federal commissions.

Prior to the enactment of the federal legislation referred to above, some of the state commissions had come to doubt the usefulness of public utility book costs which showed for acquired property only the cost of such property to the current owner. Inflated property accounts were of little use to the state commissions in rate making as either a measure of actual cost or as a check on the estimates of reproduction cost submitted in rate proceedings. On the other hand, write-ups in the book cost of acquired property could be used to support claims for a larger rate base. In addition, public utility plant accounts often were not classified in detail, that is, many of the purchased properties were recorded in one lump sum in the Cost of Purchased Plant and Equipment or some other mass property account. This absence of an itemized breakdown of the lump-sum balances made it most difficult to determine how much of the plant account should be written off when the purchased properties were retired or became obsolete.

In an effort to find a uniform basis of accounting, one unaffected by property transfers, some state commissions during the 1920's required utilities in individual cases to show separately on their books the difference between the acquisition price and the fair value or rate-making value. However, in 1931 the Wisconsin commission adopted a uniform system of accounts which provided an account to include ". . . the difference between (a) the amount approved for the purchase of any utility plant or . . . system and (b) the actual original cost of constructing and installing such plant less . . . depreciation."[4] In the opinion accompanying this new classification of plant accounts, Commissioner David E. Lilienthal stated that the purposes of this account were to perpetuate records of original cost of the property and to minimize variations in cost records merely by reason of changes in ownership of the plant.

Subsequently, the original cost principle, as embodied in uniform systems of accounts, was put into effect by: (a) the Federal Communications Commission for interstate telephone companies, effective January 1, 1936; (b) the Federal Power Commission for interstate electric utilities and hydroelectric power licensees, effective January 1, 1937, and for natural gas pipeline companies transporting or selling for resale in interstate commerce, effective January 1, 1940. In addition, almost all the state commissions ultimately adopted the same or closely similar accounting systems for the utilities under their jurisdiction doing intrastate business. It should be noted at this point that the development of uniform systems of accounts, embodying the original-cost principle, occurred shortly before the *Hope* decision and, therefore, speeded the adoption of an original-cost rate base by many commissions.

[4] *Re Uniform System of Accounts for Class A Electric Utilities,* PUR 1932A, 423.

B. *The Determination of Original Cost.* As an initial step in establishing its plant accounts on an original-cost basis, each utility was required to prepare and file a reclassification and original-cost study with the commission within a stated period of time after the uniform system of accounts became effective for that company. The Federal Power Commission, for example, allowed a period of two years to the electric utilities under its jurisdiction, and thereafter granted extensions of time as required. A reclassification and original-cost study constitutes a breakdown of the primary plant accounts as carried on the company books into new accounts. Each of the new accounts is stated on the basis of original cost less depreciation to the person first devoting the property involved to public utility service. This breakdown of costs as booked is known as *cost reclassification.* A utility making such a study would ordinarily be referred to as the accounting company or the accounting utility. The Federal Power Commission provides, for example, for the reclassification of the electric utility plant account into the following subaccounts:

Account 100. Electric Plant
- Account 100.1 Electric Plant in Service
- Account 100.2 Electric Plant Leased to Others
- Account 100.3 Construction Work in Progress
- Account 100.4 Electric Plant Held for Future Use
- Account 100.5 Electric Plant Acquisition Adjustments

Account 100.6 Electric Plant in Process of Reclassification
Account 107. Electric Plant Adjustments

The primary plants accounts, 100.1 through 100.4, inclusive, are required to be stated on the basis of net original cost, which is defined in terms of the cost to the person who first employed the property in the public service. Any amounts in the plant accounts of the accounting company which may exceed net original cost must be recorded in either of two accounts, Account 100.5 or Account 107. The Acquisition Adjustment Account 100.5 contains the difference between what the accounting company actually paid to acquire property purchased from others and the net original cost of that property, that is, the excess of acquisition cost over net original cost. The balance in Account 100.5 is subject to disposition, as discussed shortly. The purpose of Account 107, Electric Plan Adjustments, is to record the difference, if any, between bona fide cost to the accounting utility and book cost, that is, the excess of book cost over cost to the utility. Amounts classified to Account 107 may have arisen through write-ups or by other means not approved. The balance in Account 107, like that in Account 100.5, must be disposed of as set forth by the Commission in ruling on the reclassification plan submitted by the company. The foregoing, which relates to the Federal Power Commission system of accounts for electric utilities, is illustrative of the systems of accounts adopted by other commissions. Although the account numbers may differ, their nature and function are either identical or closely similar.

To illustrate these concepts in a simple example (excluding depreciation): assume that a paper products manufacturer built an electric generating plant in 1899 at a cost of $50,000, sold it to electric utility A in 1916 at $60,000, who sold it to utility B at arm's length in 1920 for $70,000, and that the latter revalued the property in 1928 at $75,000. The cost to the person first devoting the property to the public service—original cost as defined—would be the $60,000 acquisition price paid by utility A in 1916. The excess of utility B's actual acquisition cost ($70,000) over original cost ($60,000) would be classified to Account 100.5, and the excess of book cost in 1928 ($75,000) over utility B's acquisition cost ($70,000) would go into Account 107.

Before turning to the matter of disposing of the balances in Accounts 100.5 and 107 or similar adjustment accounts, further consideration of reclassification procedure may be helpful. Original cost is determined through a study of the records of the accounting utility plus those of predecessor companies. A study of the company's history with respect to its acquisitions of property is the first step. Next, total plant is classified by nature of its origin, as follows: (a) plant constructed by the company; (b) acquired plant previously devoted to public service; (c) acquired plant not previously so devoted (for example, an acquired industrial power plant); and (d) plant whose book cost differs from construction or acquisition cost. Problems necessarily arise where complete accounting records are not available. In such cases, it is necessary to use engineering estimates based upon a prepared property inventory and appropriate unit prices.

Upon completion of its reclassification study, the accounting utility would file it with the commission and request approval. The commission's accounting staff would then conduct an examination and review. In the interest of prompt settlement, the conference method ordinarily would be used, whereby company representatives and commission staff members confer informally during the course of investigations and upon their completion. If the staff of the commission and representatives of the utility could not reach agreement, a hearing would be held. Subsequently, the commission would issue an order setting forth the accounting procedures approved for the company. Because of the diversity of circumstances in each instance, settlements or decisions would be made on a case by case basis rather than by general rule.

The Federal Power Commission, the most important single agency in the matter of the reclassification of plant accounts, administered this program in a most rigorous manner. Hearings held on the matter of plant account reclassification were the scene of procedures which would not now be possible under the Administrative Procedure Act of 1946. The Final Report of the Attorney General's Committee on Administrative Procedure noted instances where the Commission's procedures were deemed to fall short of conventional standards of fairness.[5]

The uniform system of accounts prescribed by the Federal Communications Commission for telephone companies was upheld as constitutional by the Supreme Court in 1936. This was the *American Telephone* case.[6] Because of the close similarity of the uniform systems of accounts of the various commissions, that decision is generally considered to apply to them as well. This case will be discussed shortly.

C. Disposition of Account 100.5. The various uniform systems of accounts provide that Account 100.5 (or equivalent accounts bearing different numbers) shall be depreciated, amortized, or otherwise disposed of as the commission may direct. In disposing of the balances in Account 100.5 and equivalent accounts, different policies may be followed. These may include: (a) annual amortization by charges to operating expense ("above the line" and in the nature of the annual depreciation expense), thus placing the charge on consumers; (b) annual amortization by charges to income ("below the line"), which places the burden on the common stockholders; or (c) charges to surplus, which also places the burden on the stockholders.

Included in the various uniform systems of accounts are two income accounts which provide alternative means for amortizing the balances in Account 100.5 or equivalent plant acquisition adjustment accounts: (1) Account 505 in many of the systems of accounts contains the amounts includible in operating revenue deductions for amortization of the amount in Account 100.5 or similar acquisition adjustment accounts. Charges to Account 505 therefore are in the nature of depreciation charges and are included in the operating revenue deductions that are made in order to determine utility operating income. Stated differently, charges to Account 505 become part of the cost of service determined for rate-making purposes, and thus are charged to consumers. (2) Account 537, in many of the systems of accounts, is included among the income deductions. Charges to this account are deducted from the income of the stockholders. Finally, in the event the balance in Account 100.5 or like accounts is charged against surplus, the burden also is upon stockholders but is immediate rather than extended over a stated period of amortization. Thus, the effect, except for the time factor, is the same when charges to Account 537 or to surplus are directed.

The fact that provision is made, alternatively, for charges to operations or to income reflects an important aspect of

---

[5] 14 *The George Washington Law Review* 174, 186 (1945).

[6] *American Telephone & Telegraph Co.* v. *United States,* 299 U.S. 232 (1936).

the Supreme Court's ruling in the *American Telephone* case, mentioned previously, wherein the system of accounts prescribed by the FCC was upheld. There, the Court indicated concern as to the policy the FCC would follow in disposing of amounts classified to an account similar to 100.5 (designated Account 100.4). The Court requested the Assistant Attorney General to submit a written statement clarifying the policy that would be followed. This was done, and the statement was in large part incorporated in the opinion of the Court. The Attorney General's statement made clear that, upon determination of the character of the items comprising the acquisition adjustment account, the amounts therein would be disposed of to operating expenses, income, or surplus. Further, it was held that, when amounts classified to the acquisition adjustment account were found definitely to represent payment for depreciable plant (as opposed to "intangibles," such as capitalized earnings expectations), provision would be made for amortization of such amounts through operating expenses.[7] The ruling of the Court has generally been considered to apply to the other systems of accounts as well as to the particular accounting system involved in that case. Thus, in disposing of Account 100.5, or its equivalent, it is clear that state and federal commissions may look to the nature and origin of the amounts included in this balance and order their disposition by charges to be borne by consumers or stockholders as a study of the circumstances warrants.

What has been the policy followed by various commissions in this matter? Generally speaking, it is to inquire into the character of the amounts comprising the acquisition adjustment account, with the ordered disposition being governed by the character of the items within it. Thus, some commissions have charged the amortization to consumers where the utility showed that it paid an amount in excess of original cost to acquire operating plant whose addition to its system promoted operating economies or an improvement in service. Similar recognition also has been given in cases where the difference between book cost and original cost is explainable in terms of price-level differentials. On the other hand, acquisition adjustment amounts reflecting intangibles such as higher earnings prospects or good will, with no improvement in efficiency or service, have been subject to amortization below the line from income. Some commissions have taken the position that the entire acquisition adjustment account reflects intangible elements and that the entire amount should be written off against stockholders of the utility company. It is thus apparent that there is a wide range of policies on this matter among the various commissions.

Some of the state commissions and the Federal Power Commission have followed a policy of requiring the entire balance in Account 100.5 or its equivalent to be charged to stockholders, by charges either to income or to surplus. The Federal Power Commission, for example, held in 1942 that the entire Account 100.5 balance represents amounts paid for intangibles that are rooted in and associated with prospective earning power.[8] In another case, the FPC was faced with a contention, based upon the *American Telephone* decision, to the effect that it was required to classify the amounts contained in Account 100.5 so as to distinguish between amounts relating to depreciable plant and those relating to intangibles. The Commission held that: (1) it was not required to make any finding with respect to the

7 299 U.S. 232, 240 ff.

8 *Re Pacific Power & Light Co.*, 3 FPC 329 (1942).

character of the amounts contained in Account 100.5; and (2), if it were so required, it would find that the entire balance in that account represented payments for intangibles.[9] Thus, the FPC has maintained a consistent policy of disallowing any part of Account 100.5 to be charged to expenses to be borne by consumers. Where the utility has not elected to charge off Account 100.5 immediately to surplus, the FPC has required this account to be amortized by charges to income over periods not exceeding 15 years. This inflexible FPC position, which charges all acquisition adjustments to stockholders, is indeed curious in that its own systems of accounts provide a separate account for the amortization of such amounts to operating expense, Account 505, which can serve no other purpose. No less curious is the fact that not one dollar of the more than $500,000,000 classified by the FPC to electric utility Account 100.5 was found to have sufficient substance to merit its being charged to expenses, even though many of the acquisitions represented bona fide purchases approved by the state commissions.

The state commissions have followed differing policies with respect to the amortization of acquisition adjustment accounts. States requiring that the amortization be charged to stockholders include New York, Illinois, Colorado, Connecticut, Florida, Indiana, Kansas, New Jersey, New Mexico, North Carolina, Oklahoma, Rhode Island, West Virginia, and Wyoming. Other states, however, will recognize as proper charges to operations the amortization of acquisition adjustments arising from arm's-length transactions which can be shown to provide benefits through increased efficiency, improved service, or lower rates, among other things. States taking this position include Louisiana, Missouri, Arkansas, Alabama, Georgia, Michigan, New Hampshire, Utah, Wisconsin, Idaho, Kentucky, Washington, and California.

What is the regulatory treatment of acquisition adjustment accounts insofar as rate making is concerned? Some jurisdictions permit the unamortized balance of the acquisition adjustment account to be included in a determination of an actual-cost rate base and some do not. A general rule is that: (1) where the acquisition adjustment account is included in the rate base, the amortization is treated as a charge to operating expenses; and (2) where the acquisition adjustment account is not included in the rate base, the amortization is a charge to income. There are some exceptions to these general rules, as might be expected. Wisconsin, for example, excludes from the rate base but permits amortization to be charged to expense. There also have been compromise rulings in California, Pennsylvania, Washington State, and New York.[10]

In conclusion, it is necessary to consider an important consequence of a policy requiring stockholders to bear the entire burden of the disposition of the acquisition adjustment account. It is that such a policy can prevent desirable and economic combinations of operating properties because of lack of incentive, since any purchase price greater than net original cost will have to be charged to stockholders. This has become a current problem that has nothing to do with the accounting treatment of past acquisitions. Affected by the above policy are the utilities whose plant accounts long since have been restated on an original-cost basis. If nothing more, the inflation of the postwar period has rendered un-

[9] *Re St. Croix Falls Minnesota Improvement Co., et al.,* 3 FPC 148 (1942).

[10] Samuel M. Koenigsberg, "Acquisition Adjustments In Rate Cases," 64 *Public Utilities Fortnightly* 344 (1959).

attractive the sale of many properties on a net original-cost basis. A question of public interest would apear to be involved where, as here, useful combinations of properties in the present are prevented by policies adopted in the 1930's to remedy conditions of the 1920's.

D. Disposition of Account 107. The FPC uniform system of accounts for electric utilities includes Account 107, Electric Plant Adjustments, which contains any difference between book cost and cost to the present owner. Other accounting systems contain similar accounts which in some cases bear different designations. The amounts classified to Account 107 or equivalent accounts may represent unrecorded retirements, items improperly capitalized, profit from transactions with affiliates, or write-ups of plant accounts. The state and federal commissions have generally required that such amounts be charged to earned or capital surplus. This policy has been implemented without regard for historic circumstances, discussed previously, such as state approval of acquisitions or security issues. For example, the federal commissions and some of the state commissions have adopted a "no profits to affiliates" rule. This has been applied so as to eliminate the profit earned by an affiliated construction company where the price charged was shown to have been less than what an independent contractor would have charged.

In 1950 the Federal Power Commission announced the completion of the reclassification and original cost program insofar as it related to the electric utilities and water power licensees under its jurisdiction. The Commission reported total adjustments, as recorded in Accounts 100.5 and 107, of $1.6 billion; this total was said to equal about 25 per cent of original cost. Of the total adjustments of $1.6 billion, about 32 per cent related to Account 100.5 and 68 per cent related to Account 107.[11]

[11] Federal Power Commission, *Report On the Reclassification and Original Cost of Electric Plant of Public Utilities and Licensees* (Washington: 1950).

8 Depreciation

This chapter is concerned with the concept of depreciation as it is employed in the generally prevailing practices of the state and federal regulatory commissions. Broadly speaking, the depreciation of a capital asset is the loss, not restored by current maintenance, which is due to all the factors causing its ultimate retirement. Depreciable assets include long-lived plant and equipment used and useful in the public service. Land is not considered a depreciable asset.

1. THE NATURE AND PURPOSE OF DEPRECIATION

In public utility regulation, the dominant concept of depreciation has been developed largely by members of the accounting profession on the staffs of the state and federal commissions. Accordingly, depreciation is defined in terms of "cost" rather than the economists' concept of "value" or the engineers' concept of present as against new physical "condition" of the depreciable assets. The prevailing and applied definition of depreciation may be found in the various uniform systems of accounts. For example, the Federal Power Commission's uniform system of accounts for natural gas companies provides that: "'Depreciation,' as applied to depreciable gas plant, means the loss in service value not restored by current maintenance, incurred in connection with the consumption or prospective retirement of gas plant in the course of service from causes which are known to be in current operation and against which the utility is not protected by insurance." Among the causes of depreciation which are to be given consideration are "wear and tear, decay, action of the elements, inadequacy, obsolescence, changes in the art, changes in demand and requirements of public authorities, and, in the case of natural gas companies, the exhaustion of natural resources." To implement the definition of depreciation, the system of accounts state that "'Service value' means the difference between original cost and the net salvage value of gas plant." Another definition provides that "'Salvage value' means the amount received for property retired, less any expenses incurred in connection with the sale. . . ."[1] These definitions are closely similar to those found in other uniform systems of accounts.

Under the various uniform accounting systems, depreciation is directly related to the cost of depreciable assets and to the amortization of such cost (less net salvage value) over the time period through which benefits are received from the property involved. Thus, depreciation accounting distributes the prepaid investment cost of depreciable assets to the production expense of each accounting period and serves the purposes of: (1) securing proper periodic income determinations; and (2) recovering gradually the utility's investment in depreciable assets. In light of its apparent nature under prevailing practices, depreciation could be called "cost amortization" with equal or greater appropriateness.

The purposes of depreciation are accomplished by the adoption of some reasonable method whereby an annual charge for depreciation is determined (referred to as the *depreciation accrual* or *depreciation expense*). The method selected, and thus applied, conventionally will spread the annual depreciation charges over the estimated service life of the depreciable assets involved. The annual depreciation expense, technically speaking, is not an operating expense. However, it is an operating revenue deduction and a true element of cost. Annual depreciation expense is accepted under the uniform systems of accounts as the measure of the portion of total service value of depreciable assets which is used up in a year.

The annual depreciation charges are accumulated in the depreciation reserve, which is generally taken as the measure of the total accrued depreciation of a property on a given date. It is important to note that, under the uniform accounting systems, the annual charges for depreciation and the accrued depreciation are consistently related to one another. That is, the depreciation reserve is intended to reflect the total of the annual depreciation charges accumulated through time. The United States Supreme Court in 1934 set forth this requirement in the *Lindheimer* case.[2]

Next, the way depreciation figures in public utility rate making should be reviewed. First, it has been pointed out previously that the annual depreciation expense is treated as a proper expense

[1] Federal Power Commission, *Uniform System of Accounts Prescribed for Natural Gas Companies,* effective January 1, 1954, pp. 4–5.

[2] *Lindheimer* v. *Illinois Bell Telephone Co.,* 292 U.S. 151 (1934).

for rate-making purposes. Second, accrued depreciation is deducted from the gross measure of depreciable property in determining the rate base.

Finally, a comparatively wide range of causes of depreciation are recognized. These may be physical as well as functional in nature. The physical causes of depreciation are the result of use, decay, and the action of time and the elements. Functional depreciation occurs because property is no longer adapted to use. It results from such causes as obsolescence, inadequacy, and action by public authority. Obsolescence occurs when existing plant and equipment, although not worn out, is made uneconomic by the availability of newer equipment of sufficiently greater efficiency as to require the retirement of existing property units. Inadequacy has reference to the fact that certain units of property may have to be replaced with larger facilities as the demand for service increases. Action of public authority may require that public utilities make changes in serviceable property in the interest of public safety, convenience, or the appearance of the city. The required placement of electric and telephone lines underground instead of overhead and property relocations due to highway construction are examples of this. Casual causes such as breakage and accidents add to depreciation. In recognition of these causes of depreciation, particularly as they affect the estimated service life of property, it is possible to revise the annual depreciation charge as changing circumstances require. A study of the causes of retirements by gas and electric utilities showed that 72.2 per cent of retirements were due to inadequacy and obsolescence; 18.1 per cent were due to physical causes, and 9.7 per cent to other causes.[3] This is hardly surprising in light of technological advances and the growth in demand.

To summarize: (1) the principal purpose of depreciation is to distribute the costs of plant and equipment to accounting periods so as to assist in determining periodic income; (2) this is accomplished by adopting a method to determine the depreciation expenses assignable to each accounting period, which expenses become an operating revenue deduction; (3) the annual depreciation charges and the book reserve for depreciation are consistently related to one another, with the depreciation reserve serving in many cases as a deduction from the gross measure of depreciable assets in calculating the rate base; and (4) a number of causes of depreciation are recognized which may affect estimates of service life, and therefore, the annual depreciation expense. Although the Supreme Court did not discuss depreciation in its historic *Smyth* v. *Ames* decision, it recognized the relation of depreciation to rate making in its 1909 *Knoxville* decision.[4]

Although depreciation is important generally, it is of special importance where public utilities are concerned. Public utilities differ from other enterprises because they require proportionately greater investment in plant and equipment. It will be recalled from the earlier discussion of the capital turnover ratio (Chapter 2) that public utilities characteristically must have several dollars in plant investment to produce a dollar in annual operating revenue, whereas manufacturing and mercantile operations ordinarily produce a dollar of annual revenue with less than a dollar in fixed investment. Thus, the annual charge for depreciation will be proportionately greater for utility companies than for other companies doing the same

[3] American Gas Association and Edison Electric Institute, Report of Committee on Depreciation, 1941 (based on retirements 1928–1937).

[4] *Knoxville Water Co.* v. *Knoxville,* 212 U.S. 1 (1909).

annual volume of business because utilities have a relatively greater investment in depreciable assets. This is illustrated in the following ratios of depreciation expense to gross sales in 1960 for some representative utility and industrial groups:[5]

Electric and gas utilities	11.0%
Water and sewer utilities	10.0
Communications utilities	7.0
Primary metals	3.4
Motor vehicles and equipment	2.8
Electrical machinery and equipment	1.9
Apparel and fabric products	0.7

Second, depreciation is of greater importance for utility companies than for others because the regulation of depreciation policy directly affects the prices at which utility services are sold. Depreciation policy does not have the same direct price-determining effect in the non-regulated segment of business. Third, since depreciation accruals represent cost amortization, price inflation will have a more adverse effect on public utilities than upon non-regulated businesses because of the utilities' proportionately greater investment in fixed assets of long service life. As in the case of the actual-cost rate base, depreciation in the nature of cost amortization follows the nominal dollar approach which regards a dollar as a dollar, regardless of its purchasing power. This matter will be considered in further detail.

2. THE DEPRECIATION BASE

The depreciation base is the dollar amount subject to depreciation which serves as the basis for calculating the annual charge for depreciation. Under the uniform accounting systems, the depreciation base is the properly recorded cost of depreciable assets in use. Various alternatives have been suggested and, in some cases, adopted. These include replacement cost, reproduction cost, and fair value. In 1930 the Supreme Court, for example, held in the *United Railways* case that present value was the depreciation base to be used in calculating the annual depreciation charge.[6] The majority opinion took the position that the annual depreciation charge should be the amount necessary to restore property worn out so as to maintain the plant at a continuous level of efficiency. The annual depreciation charge, the Court stated, cannot be limited by original cost, because, if values have increased, the annual allowance based on cost would not be sufficient to maintain the required level of efficiency.

The minority opinion in *United Railways* held for cost as the proper depreciation base, stating that any other approach invited indefiniteness and frequent revision in annual depreciation charges. This view subsequently came to prevail generally in regulatory practice after the 1944 *Hope* case, previously mentioned. There, the Court specifically reversed its position in *United Railways* on the question of the proper depreciation base. Under the end-result doctrine, commissions are allowed to adopt any reasonable depreciation method. Accordingly, *Hope* removed any federal judicial barrier to the use of cost as the depreciation base as contemplated by the uniform systems of accounts.

A period of relatively stable prices would not raise the economic problem with respect to the amortization of long-lived assets that is presented during price inflation. Public utility operating expenses for labor or supplies generally

[5] U.S. Treasury Department, Internal Revenue Service, *Statistics of Income—1959–1960, Corporation Income Tax Returns* (Washington: Government Printing Office, 1962), pp. 59–61.

[6] *United Railways & Electric Co.* v. *West*, 280 U.S. 234, 253, 254 (1930).

raise no major problem, regardless of the behavior of prices, because there is so short a time between the incurrence of expenses and collection of revenues. On the other hand, where the depreciation base of long-lived assets is actual cost, depreciation expense alone among the operating revenue deductions will be recovered during inflation on the basis of dollars of a purchasing-power value below that of the original outlay. The general effect of this is that depreciation accruals recover less in purchasing power than was originally invested. This result would be avoidable, however, if changing price levels were considered in the determination of the allowance for depreciation.

A matter unique to public utilities arises under the uniform system of accounts and their use of original cost as the depreciation base. Where acquired properties are involved, there is a question as to which owner's cost should be taken as the depreciation base. Some commissions employ as a depreciation base the cost to the first person devoting the property to the public service, and any amount paid in excess thereof by the present owner either may or may not be amortized in the nature of depreciation depending upon commission policy. In this respect, depreciation accounting for public utilities differs from the conventional accounting practice for unregulated businesses, which employs the present owner's cost of acquired assets as the depreciation base.

3. THE PRINCIPAL DEPRECIATION METHODS

Although the straight-line method of depreciation accounting is predominant among public utilities, the sinking fund method merits attention as well as the now little-used retirement reserve method. Each of these is surveyed in the following discussion.

A study comparing the depreciation practices followed by electric utilities in 1937 and 1951 showed that the number of companies using the straight-line method increased from 15 per cent to 89 per cent of the total. In 1951 only 3 per cent still employed retirement reserve accounting. The remainder used sinking fund depreciation and various other methods.[7] In 1958, 92 per cent of these companies employed straight-line depreciation; their depreciation reserves amounted to 20.9 per cent of plant.[8]

A. *The Straight-Line Method.* The straight-line depreciation method distributes the depreciation base uniformly and in equal amounts to the expenses of each accounting period throughout the estimated service life of depreciable property, except when the service life estimate is changed. However, the depreciation accruals are not intended to recover estimated net salvage value, referred to previously. The following simplified illustration of the operation of straight-line depreciation will be supplemented shortly by a more detailed example.

Estimated life of plant	20 years
Original cost	$330,000
Estimated net salvage value	10,000
Total to be distributed	$320,000
Annual depreciation expense ($320,000 ÷ 20)	$ 16,000

Rate-base determination ordinarily requires the deduction of some measure of accrued depreciation from the gross measure of depreciable assets when straight-line depreciation is used. Accrued depreciation in most cases is

[7] NARUC, *Proceedings,* 1952 Annual Convention, pp. 286–287.

[8] Federal Power Commission, *Electric Utility Depreciation Practices, 1958* (Washington: Government Printing Office, 1960), pp. 1–2.

measured by the book reserve for depreciation. Under the straight-line method, the depreciation reserve will tend to equal one-half of the depreciation base where the size of the utility becomes relatively stable.[9] One authority has expressed the view that it is doubtful whether reserves exceeding about 30 per cent should be accrued.[10] On the other hand, if depreciation accruals recover the original cost of the property, the resulting reserve will be proper regardless of its size in relation to the original cost.

B. *The Sinking Fund Method.* The sinking fund method of depreciation differs substantially from the straight-line method. Under the sinking fund approach, the annual uniform depreciation charge is a calculated amount which, at compound interest, will accrue a total equal to the cost of the property less net salvage over the estimated service life. More specifically, the depreciation reserve is credited with: (a) equal annual amounts charged to depreciation expense, called the *annuity;* and (b) interest at a specified rate, which is charged to income. The year-end deposit to what is only a hypothetical sinking fund is the total of the annuity component and the interest component, with the latter calculated as the reserve account balance times the specified interest rate. Unlike the situation where straight-line depreciation is concerned, standard regulatory policy under the sinking fund method calls for the use of an undepreciated rate base. This proceeds on the theory that the reserve is invested (presumably in the utility itself) and that the interest earned thereby will accrue to the reserve and not be available for distribution to investors. Thus, because the interest on the reserve balance is an income deduction, there is no need to deduct the accrued depreciation from the rate base.

The sinking fund method accumulates larger amounts during the later years of estimated service life than does the straight-line method. This reflects a comparative disadvantage of the sinking fund method because, when retirements due to obsolescence and inadequacy occur, there is likely to be a larger unamortized balance than under the straight-line method. The large late accruals to the reserve under the sinking fund method also may present a problem when events prove that service life has been overestimated. Of course, the lower the interest rate employed, the more closely the sinking fund accruals will approximate those of the straight-line method.

C. *Retirement Reserve Accounting.* Retirement reserve accounting was used by most utilities prior to the general adoption of depreciation accounting in the mid-1930's. The major exception was the Bell System, whose interest in depreciation accounting dates back to 1884. The utilities employing retirement reserve accounting did so, in large part, in accordance with the uniform systems of accounts prescribed by the National Association of Railroad and Utilities Commissioners (NARUC) and issued subsequent to 1922.

Under the retirement reserve method, it is anticipated that the annual retirements by a mature company will tend to stabilize. Therefore, retirements for a given year are charged to the operating expenses for the same period, with a small retirement reserve established for the purpose of equalizing any variations in the annual retirement expense. The retirement reserve is not construed as a measure of the loss in service value.

---

[9] L. B. Nash, *The Economics of Public Utilities* (New York: McGraw-Hill Book Co., Inc., 1931), p. 212.

[10] Eli W. Clemens, *Economics and Public Utilities* (New York: Appleton-Century-Crofts, Inc., 1950), p. 214.

Its sole purpose is to equalize the effects of property retirements. In addition, the charges for major retirements at a particular time could be evened out over a period of years before and after the date of retirement, or such charges could be made in part to expense and in part to the reserve.

Sometimes the charging of retirement expenses tended to be irregular and was subject to deferral or acceleration. As a result, the provision for retirement could be varied so as to affect the financial results of the operations in a given year. The departure from retirement reserve accounting for depreciation accounting has simplified public utility regulation and has been regarded generally as a constructive development because the orderly assignment of capital costs to operating periods has resulted in more meaningful accounts and periodic reports of income. This has assisted regulators in the performance of their duties and has enhanced the status of public utilities with the financial community, thus assisting them in raising capital at lower costs. Retirement reserves in the past tended to be low by present depreciation accounting standards. For example, following the general change from retirement to depreciation accounting in 1937, there was a 100 per cent increase in electric plant, 1937–1951, which was accompanied by an increase of 160 per cent in the aggregate depreciation reserve balance.[11] Prior to the adoption of the uniform accounting systems, it was not unusual to find that depreciation reserves, where maintained, were also sometimes low or haphazardly accrued and in some cases quite high. The retirement and depreciation reserves accrued before the uniform systems of accounts were adopted were a source of problems, as we shall see, when the transition to depreciation accounting was required in practically all jurisdictions.

[11] *Op. cit.*, Note 7, p. 288.

4. ANNUAL DEPRECIATION EXPENSE

The annual depreciation expense or accrual is calculated by applying a composite annual percentage rate of depreciation to the original cost of depreciable assets in service, ordinarily taken on a group basis. Broadly speaking, the composite annual percentage rates of depreciation express the relationship of book cost and some measure of estimated service life. Under the straight-line method, these percentage rates are calculated so as to distribute book cost less net salvage value in equal amounts to each accounting period during the service life of the property.

A. Estimated Service Life. Estimates of the average service life of the property units within each property group established for the purpose of calculating depreciation expense are developed through studies of average age, the company's retirement experience, and information relating to probable future conditions. The estimates of service life cannot be precise. The causes of depreciation, discussed earlier, are so diverse as to make impossible entirely accurate service-life estimates. Although detailed records of past retirement experience and continued engineering studies may be helpful, such data do not necessarily furnish accurate guides to the future. This is particularly the case where functional causes of depreciation are predominant. Periodic reviews and reappraisals of estimates of service lives and net salvage are important.

Service life can be measured in terms of average property life through actuarial methods or turnover methods. Actuarial methods determine survivor curves and annual retirement frequency curves, which lead to estimates of average service life. Detailed property records are required where actuarial methods are employed, because such methods are similar in nature to the life insurance methods of estimating human mortality. Turnover methods require less detailed data and are based on annual additions and retirements. Turnover methods are designed to measure the average time period between installation and retirement for various property groups—in short, the life cycle.

B. *Group Basis of Cost Amortization.* Depreciation expenses and reserves may be accounted for by groups of property or by a company's entire property. The particular property grouping established for this purpose is directed by the applicable system of accounts and may constitute the plant as a whole, respective primary plant accounts, or functional classes of property. Accordingly, composite percentage rates of depreciation are determined for each group as defined. For example, the Federal Power Commission's accounting systems for electric and natural gas companies provide for the classification of property into a relatively few functional groups. The system of accounts for natural gas companies provides for the subdivision of depreciation expense applicable to gas plant in service as follows:

- Depreciation of Production Plant
  - Manufactured Gas
  - Production and Gathering
  - Products Extraction, Natural Gas
- Depreciation of Storage Plant
  - Underground Gas Storage
  - Local Storage
- Depreciation of Transmission Plant
- Depreciation of Distribution Plant
- Depreciation of General Plant

C. *The Calculating of Depreciation Expense.* The calculation of depreciation expense under the straight-line method ordinarily employs annual rates of depreciation which are based upon estimated average service life. The annual depreciation expense is found by multiplying the original cost of the property by the annual depreciation rate calculated for that property. The annual depreciation rate is found for a particular property group by dividing the estimated service life into the cost (taken as 100 per cent) less estimated net salvage (expressed as a percentage of cost). Thus, where estimated service life is 20 years and net salvage is estimated at 10 per cent, the annual depreciation rate is calculated as 90 per cent divided by 20, or 4.50 per cent per year. This is illustrated in the following example:

Original Cost	$200,000
Net Salvage	$ 20,000
Average Service Life	20 years

$$\text{Salvage per cent} = \frac{\$20{,}000}{\$200{,}000} = 10\%$$

$$\text{Depreciation rate} = \frac{100\% - \%\ \text{Net Salvage}}{\text{Average service life}}$$

$$= \frac{100\% - 10\%}{20}$$

$$= 4.5\%$$

$$\underset{(4.5\% \times \$200{,}000)}{\text{Annual depreciation expense}} = \$9{,}000$$

A somewhat different approach, called the *remaining-life method,* is employed by the California PUC. This method places primary emphasis upon the estimated service life remaining rather than the estimated average total life. The annual depreciation accrual is caculated as follows for each plant account under the remaining-life method:

$$\text{Annual Depreciation Accrual} = \frac{\text{Gross Plant (less) Net Salvage (less) Depreciation Reserve}}{\text{Remaining Life (years)}}$$

The gross plant account and depreciation reserve figures are taken as at the beginning of the year. Net salvage is an estimate. Remaining life is calculated as the total estimated service life of the surviving property units represented in the account, less the average age. The California PUC favors the remaining-life approach on the ground that it is more adaptable in adjusting to the depreciation-causing factors which cannot be foreseen with exactness at the time of installation of plant.

5. ACCRUED DEPRECIATION AND THE RATE BASE

The general practice of deducting for accrued depreciation in determining the rate base raises two questions: (a) Should there be such a deduction? If so, (b) how shall the deduction be measured?

A. *Should There Be a Deduction?* In considering the question of whether accrued depreciation should be deducted from the rate base, it is important to bear in mind the essential nature of the deduction and what it is intended to achieve. The use of a net actual cost rate base, for example, in which accrued depreciation has been deducted from the gross actual cost of depreciable assets, is the equivalent of using an undepreciated rate base and charging the income of the utility with annual interest on the accrued depreciation. Essentially the same result would be achieved if a utility were: (a) allowed a rate of return annually on a net rate base; or (b) allowed a rate of return on an undepreciated rate base and its income charged annually with interest (at the over-all level of the allowed rate of return) on the accrued depreciation.

With this in mind, we may next inquire into the reasoning behind the general policy of deducting for accrued depreciation. The depreciation deduction is based on the premise that consumers, through the payment of rates covering depreciation expenses, have returned to the utility the capital consumed in producing service. This premise leads to the conclusion that the use of an undepreciated rate base (making no other adjustment) would require consumers to pay a return upon capital which has been recovered by the utility. This would not be fair; therefore, it is appropriate to deduct accrued depreciation in determining the rate base.

Before considering the countervailing equities, it should be pointed out that the assets reflected by the accrued depreciation are the property of the utility and cannot be returned to investors except in the event of liquidation. Thus, the assets reflected by the accrued depreciation are a permanent part of the enterprise.

The first countervailing equity arises from the fact that the depreciation funds may not be fully reinvested in the utility. The possible size of the reserve has been indicated previously. It should be recognized that implicit in the full deduction of the accrued depreciation is the assumption that the cash generated by depreciation will be fully reinvested. (This follows from the fact that the deduction of accrued depreciation is the equivalent of using an undepreciated rate base and charging to utility income an amount for interest on the entire accrued depreciation at a rate equal to the allowed rate of return.) This assumption holds true only during periods of expansion. The assumed full investment of depreciation funds does not hold true during *status quo* or slow-growth periods or where declining industries are involved. In such cases, depreciation funds will accumulate, because reinvestment will lag behind accrual. In such instances, deducting the entire amount of accrued depreciation would penalize the utility —unless it can invest the recovered capital elsewhere and earn the allowed rate of return—because the effect of the full deduction is to charge the utility a higher rate for the use of the funds than it earns through their use. If there is no reinvestment, net working capital will increase; however, actual working capital is not included in the rate base —only an amount calculated as proper and necessary. The use of depreciation funds for the retirement of debt will in effect earn the utility the interest saved. However, the rate of interest on debt is below the over-all rate of return which the utility is charged for the use of the depreciation funds. This also applies to investments in government bonds, other senior securities, and bank accounts. The remaining alternatives are to invest the funds in securities which prospectively can earn as much as the utility's over-all rate of return or to branch out into other lines of business.

A second countervailing equity arises from the fact that the utility is not compensated for performing the entrepreneurial functions of management and risk taking in connection with the assets reflected by the accrued depreciation. The deduction of the full depreciation reserve in effect channels to consumers the full return earned on such assets, including the compensation for the entrepreneurial functions performed by the utility. In recognition of this factor, the Missouri PSC at one time adopted for all utilities under its jurisdiction an undepreciated rate base coupled with a credit to the cost of service equal to three per cent of the accrued book depreciation.[12] The effect of this general policy was to divide between the utility and its customers the earnings of the assets reflected by the accrued depreciation. The credit to the cost of service was determined in consideration of evidence as to the cost of borrowed money, the right of utilities to just compensation for managing and operating property and assuming the related risks, and varying economic conditions when depreciation funds could not be invested in income-producing assets. Referring to the assets reflected by the accrued depreciation, the Commission stated:

> The utilities assume all of the hazards and risks associated with the ownership, management, and operation of such property, including any losses or reductions of earnings below a fair or compensatory return, whereas the customers assume no responsibilities or risks whatever, with respect to the property. And the utilities are justly entitled to receive proper compensation for assuming those responsibilities and risks. To deprive the utilities of the full amount of the income from such property, as interest on depreciation funds, would be grossly unfair, and would be equivalent to confiscating the property for the exclusive benefit of the customers, and at the same time requiring the utilities to gratuitously operate the property and assume all of the risks as to the property and its operation. However, the customers are entitled to share in such income at least to the extent of the value of depreciation funds, just as any lender of funds is paid from the income of a corporation for the value of his funds.[13]

The adoption of a flat percentage in this decision was qualified to the extent that modification could be made where the circumstances in a particular case indicated that the 3 per cent rate was not fairly and equitably applicable. Other-

[12] *Re General Order No. 38-A,* 62 PUR (NS) 129 (1945).

[13] *Ibid.,* pp. 135–136.

wise, the same percentage was to apply to all utilities under the Commission's jurisdiction. The flat-percentage policy has administrative simplicity to recommend it. However, it would be more precise if, along with an undepreciated rate base, the cost of service were credited with amounts reflecting the actual use made of the depreciation funds.

These are the principal countervailing equities opposing the general practice of deducting the full measure of accrued depreciation in determining the rate base. They are seldom stated. On the other hand, it is generally acknowledged that the full deduction is not proper when a utility fails to recover the total of allowed depreciation charges. In a related situation, where a utility is earning less than the allowed rate of return, consumers may not be providing the full depreciation accrual to the extent that the allowed return is not earned. In such instances, the portion of the depreciation accrual equal to the return deficiency is in effect furnished by stockholders.

B. Measuring the Depreciation Deduction. In most cases, the rate-base deduction for accrued depreciation is either the book depreciation reserve or a theoretical reserve, sometimes called the "reserve requirement." The latter is an estimate that is intended to reflect the depreciation that would have accrued if straight-line depreciation accounting had been in effect prior to the time it became a requirement and had been continued into the present. The calculation of a theoretical reserve is no simple matter, and the results of any such determination are not necessarily agreed to by all parties to a case. The term "reserve requirement" is a misnomer to some extent, because it is not a legal requirement and in many instances it is not an administrative requirement. Because present depreciation policies for the most part were instituted in the late 1930's, the book reserve and the theoretical reserve are not apt to be the same. It goes without saying that, in choosing between the book reserve and the theoretical reserve as a measure of the rate-base deduction, commissions can exert a substantial impact on both the rate base and the total cost of service. Regulatory authorities have had to choose between the book reserve and the theoretical reserve for reasons which will now be considered.

It was noted previously that, except for the Bell System, many utilities used retirement reserve accounting in the years before present depreciation policies were required. The effect of the adoption of depreciation accounting was to leave many utilities with reserves for depreciation which were deficient by comparison with the theoretical reserve, although the existing reserves had been accrued properly under the previous uniform accounting systems. Second, the book reserve and the theoretical reserve are likely to differ when an unregulated industry is brought under regulation for the first time. A case in point is the natural gas pipeline industry, which was placed under Federal Power Commission regulation by the Natural Gas Act of 1938. Further, the book reserve may be greater or less than the theoretical reserve, owing to haphazard or unsatisfactory or highly conservative accounting practices in the past or failure of the books to reflect accurately the total of past depreciation expenses, or where service life estimates proved to be incorrect.

In light of these diverse situations, a question arises as to the proper regulatory policy to be followed in selecting the measure of the deduction for accrued depreciation. A general policy was set forth in the report of the Committee on Depreciation of the NARUC as part of the 1943 *Proceedings*. There, it was noted that in some cases equity required the deduction of the book reserve rather than the theoretical reserve. The determination of when it is proper to deduct the lesser of the two, the report said, involves among other things consideration of the history of regulatory requirements in the particular jurisdiction and the experience and practices of the company. A general policy was recommended which called for recognition of the problems set forth above.

What policies have been followed in measuring accrued depreciation for the purpose of rate-base determination? The Federal Power Commission, for example, has stated consistently that, where reasonable and proper depreciation (and depletion) accounting policies have been observed by a company, the resulting book reserves are the best measure of the depreciation (and depletion, if wasting assets are involved) in the property, and for this reason should be deducted from gross original cost in the rate-base determination. However, the Commission has been faced with varying fact situations which have led it to adopt pragmatic policies as each case demanded, rather than follow its preferred policy in all cases.

In the now famous *Hope* case, the FPC was faced with a choice between a book reserve of $38.4 million, which had been accrued before federal regulation, and a retroactively calculated theoretical reserve of $22.3 million. The difference of about $16 million—in terms of its rate-base impact—meant a net rate base of either $17.7 or $33.7 million.[14] The FPC used as a deduction the lesser alternative, the theoretical reserve, stating that, under the existing circumstances, where a large part of the company's business was brought under regulation for the first time and where incorrect depreciation and depletion practices have prevailed, the best procedure was to deduct the "reserve requirement" in computing the rate base. The Commission also followed this policy in the *Canadian River Gas Co.* case, where it pointed out, "The reserve requirement deducted herein is far less than that actually accrued."[15]

In the illustrative cases above, the theoretical reserve was less than the book depreciation reserve. The companies involved had been newly brought under the Natural Gas Act, and the book reserves reflected management policies and not the past requirements of a uniform system of accounts.

In a situation where the theoretical reserve exceeded the book reserve that had been accumulated under regulatory direction, the District of Columbia commission followed a policy similar to that in the cases above, for it also deducted the lesser alternative amount—the book reserve rather than the straight-line theoretical reserve. In so ruling, the commission gave weight to testimony by Charles W. Smith, a leading expert then on the FPC staff, ". . . that where a utility has been restricted as to the amount of depreciation expense by a regulatory Commission . . . it is not proper, nor is it equitable, to adopt a higher reserve requirement than that developed under regulatory authority. . . . "[16] The FPC ordered a similar policy in the 1946 *Safe Harbor* case, where the existing book reserve was less than the straight-line theoretical reserve. There, the FPC took notice of the fact that the existing reserve had been accumulated out of specific payments made by customers, and that the company had not collected the larger amounts it would have collected if it had followed the straight-line method.[17]

[14] *Re Hope Natural Gas Co.*, 44 PUR (NS) 1, 24 (1942).

[15] *Re Canadian River Gas Co., et al.*, 3 FPC 32, 48 (1942).

[16] *Re Potomac Electric Power Co.*, 55 PUR (NS) 65, 85 (1944).

[17] *Re Safe Harbor Water Power Corp.*, 66 PUR (NS) 212, 244 (1946).

A study of state and federal commission policies on the deduction for accrued depreciation was made by Henry F. Lippitt II, a practicing attorney in the field of public utility law.[18] His study of FPC actions led him to conclude generally that the FPC policy was to deduct the lesser of the two alternative measures of accrued depreciation. It was also observed, however, that the Commission would adopt the theoretical reserve where past accounting practices were deemed haphazard or unsatisfactory. In a case where the service life of property had been underestimated, which resulted in an excessive book reserve, the Commission refused to use the lesser theoretical reserve on the ground that such would unfairly require consumers to contribute to a reserve that had already been built up out of past rates.[19]

State commissions, as shown in the Lippitt study, have deducted the book depreciation reserve in most instances. This also applies to those states which nominally favor deduction of the full theoretical reserve. It is understandable that the state commissions generally deduct the lesser book reserve rather than the theoretical reserve, because the states have had jurisdiction in this matter for a relatively long period of time. Thus, book reserves which may be deficient relative to the theoretical reserve in many cases have been accrued in accord with whatever the respective state commissions have required or permitted in the past.

The most notable of the few exceptions to the above summary of state policies is that of the New York PSC. Since 1935 it has followed the policy of adopting the straight-line theoretical reserve in determining the rate base. It also has required reserve deficiencies to be made up through appropriations from surplus or by reducing the stated value of the company's common stock.

6. ECONOMIC DEPRECIATION

This section is concerned with the concept of economic depreciation, or price-level depreciation, as it is sometimes called. Simply defined, *economic depreciation* is the cost of depreciable assets consumed during a year, expressed in terms of the purchasing power of the original investment. Economic depreciation can be calculated by adjusting either the actual-cost depreciation base or the actual-cost depreciation accrual so as to produce an annual depreciation accrual reflecting changes in the value of money brought about by price-level changes.

Standard accounting practices for purposes of income taxation, financial reporting, and public utility regulation provide for the use of an actual-cost depreciation base in the calculation of annual depreciation expense. The use of an actual-cost depreciation base and conventional methods of depreciation accounting results in the ultimate recovery of the actual number of dollars invested in depreciable property. However, in an inflationary period such as that experienced since the end of World War II, these conventional accounting practices fail to permit the recovery of the same amount of purchasing power originally invested. This comes about because the annual depreciation accruals, once prices have risen, recover dollars of lesser purchasing power than those originally invested. It has been noted previously that the purchasing-power value of money varies inversely with changes in the general level of prices.

The problem thus presented is one which affects all industries. However, its effect upon the public utility industries is comparatively greater because they

[18] 62 *Harvard Law Review* 1155 (1949).

[19] *Re New York State Natural Gas Corp.*, 5 FPC 184, 191 (1946).

employ larger quantities of depreciable assets than other industries. Industry in general has been interested in finding a means of maintaining the real value of depreciation accruals during the postwar period. The method generally favored involved one application or another of the concept of economic depreciation. Testimony along these lines also has been offered in public utility rate cases—thus far, with relatively little effect.

As defined more precisely, *economic depreciation* is a current depreciation accrual whose purchasing power is equivalent to that which depreciation calculated on an actual-cost basis had at the time the property was acquired or constructed. In other words, economic depreciation is the depreciation accrual for a given year, calculated by a conventional method on an actual-cost depreciation base, adjusted to the purchasing power of the dollar in that year. Thus, economic depreciation could be calculated by converting each year's actual-cost depreciation accrual to its purchasing-power equivalent by the use of an appropriate price index number, or the annual depreciation rate could be applied to an actual-cost depreciation base that had been adjusted by the use of a price index number. This is not to say that economic depreciation is intended to permit the replacement of retired property units. (Some units of property, as a result of technological, market, and other changes, never will be replaced.) Rather, its purposes are to achieve more meaningful determinations of income and to permit the recovery of the purchasing power originally invested in long-lived assets.

Those who urge the recognition of economic depreciation in income taxation, accounting, and public utility regulation base their position on some of the following consequences of actual-cost depreciation during an inflationary period. It is maintained that present depreciation practices impede the achievement of the primary objectives of depreciation accounting, namely, a sound determination of net income and the recovery of capital consumed in the course of production. Where depreciation accruals are understated in purchasing-power terms, net income is overstated. In addition, an erosion of capital occurs because the purchasing power recovered by current depreciation accruals is less than that originally invested. A further and related consequence is that the overstatement of income in effect includes a return of capital in income, and any tax paid on such income, in part, constitutes a levy upon capital rather than income. Finally, the purchasing-power deficiency in present depreciation accruals in many cases must be offset through the issuance of new securities, which may have the effect of diluting the equity.

A study of the experienced loss attributable to deficient purchasing-power recovery under present depreciation practices was reported to the 1960 National Conference of Electric and Gas Utility Accountants.[20] That study, based upon 1959 data, concluded that the electric and gas distribution industries would have to increase their annual depreciation charges by about one-third in order to restore the purchasing-power loss in that year. If economic depreciation were charged and allowed for tax purposes, it was estimated that industry-wide gas rates would increase two per cent and electric rates four per cent. If economic depreciation were not recognized for tax purposes, the effect of adopting it was estimated to be a four per cent increase in gas rates and an eight per cent increase in electric rates. The relatively

[20] John F. Fant, Jr., "Economic Effect of Price Level Depreciation On Regulated Utilities," an address before the National Conference of Electric and Gas Utility Accountants, New York, April 26, 1960.

higher percentages for electric utilities reflect their comparatively greater plant requirements per dollar of revenue, and thus their higher depreciation expenses. The total accumulated deficiency in purchasing-power recovery was calculated at $4 billion for electric utilities and $1 billion for gas distributing companies. These amounts were stated to approximate the entire retained earnings of the two industries.

Formidable barriers to the recognition of economic depreciation exist at present. First, a change in existing income tax laws would be required. Until this comes about, economic depreciation is not likely to be recognized as a generally accepted accounting practice. Finally, economic depreciation probably will not be acceptable for public utility rate making and prescribed accounting purposes until it is accepted for both the other purposes.

Since the *Hope* case, there has been little recognition of inflation in depreciation allowances. The leading case is the 1957 fair-value decision of the Iowa Supreme Court. There, it was held that the annual depreciation allowance should be based on present value rather than original cost.[21] The opinion of the Court quoted from a Texas decision which had held that current depreciation expenses for rate purposes should be closely correlated with the fair-value appraisal of the same piece of property.[22] Accordingly, it was found that the company's composite annual cost depreciation rate of 2.0 per cent should be applied to its present fair value to determine the annual depreciation allowance.

In this regard, it is interesting to compare the treatment of the problem of economic depreciation in Great Britain in the case of the nationalized electric power industry. In 1954 the Minister of Fuel and Power appointed a committee to inquire into the organization and efficiency of the electric power industry in England and Wales and to make recommendations. The committee's report was presented to Parliament in 1956. On the subject of depreciation, the report concluded that, in recognition of inflation, it was necessary to provide annual depreciation accruals consistent with the prevailing level of prices. It was noted with approval that in the 1954–1955 fiscal year the industry had provided for depreciation on the basis of then current price levels rather than on the basis of book cost alone. In the industry's accounting for 1954–1955, the provision for original cost depreciation was supplemented by an appropriation of over one-half the annual profit (called "surplus") to a supplementary depreciation reserve. In doing so, the industry was said to have followed the recommendations of the Institute of Chartered Accountants in England and Wales.[23]

What is said against the recognition of economic depreciation? First, it is pointed out that allowing for economic depreciation would not be so easily administered as the present system of cost depreciation, and that recognizing economic depreciation would not necessarily result in the accrual of replacement cost by the time retirement occurs, except by chance. Further, to the extent that utilities have fixed dollar obligations, they redeem and refund in inflated dollars, which is an offset to the economic depreciation sustained. In addition, technological improvements in some installation methods and types of equipment have resulted in longer service lives and higher efficiency in current replacements. Thus, proponents of cost depreciation conclude that, from the standpoint of

---

[21] *Iowa-Illinois Gas & Electric Co.* v. *Fort Dodge,* 85 N.W. 2d 20 (1957).

[22] *Texas R. Commission* v. *Houston Natural Gas Corp.,* 289 S.W. 2d 559 (1956).

[23] *Report of the Committee of Inquiry into the Electricity Supply Industry* (London: Her Majesty's Stationery Office, 1956), pp. 87–89.

maintaining the service capacity of plant, current depreciation allowances tend to be adequate.

Opponents of economic depreciation also state that, owing to the fact that income taxes only permit depreciation recovery of actual cost, the allowance of any amount in excess of cost depreciation would require rate-payers to pay several dollars in revenues in order to net the utility an additional dollar of depreciation accrual after taxes. Further, in the event that price levels decline, utilities may recover depreciation funds reflecting economic appreciation rather than depreciation. Finally, opponents of economic depreciation take the position that the size of the problem is not great in light of the fact that many utilities have installed and constructed the bulk of present plant since World War II and at costs reflecting inflated prices.

7. ACCELERATED DEPRECIATION IN RATE MAKING

The 1954 Internal Revenue Code, Section 167, permitted industry to elect to use for income tax purposes one of the accelerated or liberalized methods of depreciating new property acquired, constructed, or reconditioned on or after January 1, 1954. Construction undertaken before that date also may come under accelerated depreciation to the extent that costs are incurred after that date. This is a permanent part of the law, as such things go. It is not dependent upon the amortization of defense facilities; rather, accelerated depreciation for tax purposes may be applied to all classes of property additions. Section 167 permits industry to depreciate new property for tax purposes at a more rapid rate than under the straight-line method, previously the one most frequently used for tax purposes. Whereas the straight-line method charges off the original property cost uniformly over the estimated service life, the various accelerated methods depreciate two-thirds to almost three-quarters of original cost over the first half of the service life. Compared with the straight-line method, accelerated depreciation results in: (a) larger depreciation deductions for tax purposes during the earlier years of property life; and (b) smaller depreciation deductions during the later years. However, regardless of the depreciation method the taxpayer may elect, the total of the depreciation deductions for tax purposes will not exceed the actual cost of the property less net salvage value. Accelerated depreciation methods are intended to permit taxpayers to accumulate depreciation funds more quickly, thus providing additional working capital and allowing plant expansion or modernization to occur sooner or in larger amount. This is made possible because of the temporary tax benefit, due to larger-than-straight-line deductions for tax purposes in the earlier years of the service life of property, which are offset by an equal tax liability in the later years, if tax rates remain unchanged and there is net income in each year.

In authorizing accelerated depreciation, Congress expected "far-reaching economic effects" by assisting the maintenance of a high level of investment, increasing working capital, and aiding the expansion of growing businesses. Such a policy shows that Congress is well aware that fluctuations in real investment have been the major cause of economic recessions. It also is an example of public economic policy of a preventive nature with respect to the problems of periodic economic recessions. The reports filed by the respective committees of the House and Senate contained identical language as to the effects expected of the provisions for accelerated depreciation in what became Section 167 of the 1954 Code:

> More liberal depreciation allowances are anticipated to have far-reaching economic effects. The incentives resulting from the changes are well timed to help maintain the present high level of investment in plant and equipment. The acceleration in the speed of tax-free recovery of costs is of critical importance in the decision of management to incur risk. The faster tax write-off would increase available working capital and materially aid growing businesses in the financing of their expansion. For all segments of the American economy, liberalized depreciation policies should assist modernization and expansion of industrial capacity, with resulting economic growth, increased production, and a higher standard of living.[24]

The new alternatives for computing the depreciation deduction for tax purposes have caused some important regulatory and accounting problems for public utilities which will be discussed in the following sections.

A. *The Depreciation Methods Authorized.* Property used in a trade or business or held for the production of income may be depreciated for federal income tax purposes by the straight-line method, the "declining-balance" method, the "sum of the years' digits" method, or any other method, subject to certain limitations.

The declining-balance method was made part of the Regulations in 1939; until 1954 the annual depreciation rate allowed was 150 per cent of the straight-line depreciation allowance. The law now allows a write-off of 200 per cent of the straight-line rate annually, applied to the undepreciated balance at the end of each year. In recognition of the fact that this method will not depreciate the entire original cost, the Code permits a taxpayer to change from the declining-balance method to the straight-line method at any time during the useful life of the asset.

The sum of the years' digits method computes annual depreciation by applying a constantly declining fraction to the unvarying original cost less salvage. It operates through: (a) the addition of each year in the series of years in the expected life of the property (so that, for a five-year life, this sum would be 5 plus 4, plus 3, plus 2, plus 1, equals 15); (b) the division of this total into the number of years of remaining life expectancy, including the current year, in order to find the percentage of original cost less salvage that is to be written off in that year. Assuming an original cost of $1,000, estimated salvage value of $100, and a life expectancy of five years, the first year's depreciation charge would be $300 (5/15 times $900), and in the second year, $240 (4/15 times $900), and so on. Any other method selected by the taxpayer may be used, provided that the total of the deductions at the end of any given year, during the first two-thirds of life expectancy, shall not exceed the total deductions under the declining-balance method.

The sum of the years' digits method provides a longer deferral of taxes; the declining-balance method provides greater immediate assistance to the financing of expansion, because the earlier deductions accumulate depreciation funds more rapidly. The election of accelerated depreciation methods applies to the additions in each year. Thus, if a taxpayer does not adopt accelerated depreciation with respect to a particular property in its initial year, the taxpayer may not elect to do so in a subsequent year. The taxpayer may not switch methods without approval, with the single exception noted above for which

---

[24] House Committee on Ways and Means, *Internal Revenue Code of 1954,* House Report No. 1337, 83rd Cong., 2d sess., 1954 (Washington, D.C.: Government Printing Office, 1954), p. 24.

no approval is needed. However, the taxpayer is free to elect any method in any year for the additions of that year, and may select different methods for different properties acquired in a given year. The elections for a given year's additions are made in the tax returns for that year. Adoption of accelerated methods requires utilities to establish a second set of property records for tax purposes; because this is a cause of expense, it is a factor tending to limit the application of accelerated methods to larger property items.

B. *The Economic Effects.* The use of accelerated depreciation permits depreciation deductions for tax purposes in the early years of the service life of new property which exceed the deductions provided by the straight-line method. During subsequent years, the deductions under the accelerated methods are smaller than under the straight-line method. Accordingly, as applied to a given property, the larger depreciation deductions will result in lower income taxes during the early years and higher income taxes later on, all other things remaining equal. Thus, a benefit to the taxpayer arises because the adoption of accelerated depreciation defers to later years the payment of income taxes otherwise payable during the earlier years under the straight-line method. The deferred taxes constitute interest-free funds, in the nature of an interest-free loan. The additional funds resulting from the use of accelerated depreciation for tax purposes are available to finance plant expansion or to provide additional working capital. The availability of such funds has the effect of reducing both the over-all cost of capital to the taxpayer and the amount of new equity financing that would be required otherwise. A possible adverse effect of the adoption of accelerated depreciation may result in the event that an excess profits tax is imposed at some later date. The previous excess profits taxes have measured the taxable excess by reference to earnings in some past base period. To the extent that the accelerated depreciation deductions for tax purposes have the effect of either depressing base-period income or augmenting income during a period of excess profits taxation, the adoption of accelerated methods may be disadvantageous.

A question arises as to whether accelerated depreciation results in a tax deferral or in a tax saving. This question has become particularly important to regulatory commissions in deciding whether public utilities should be permitted to retain the benefits of accelerated depreciation in rate making. Aside from the possibility of a change in income tax rates one way or another, this question must be viewed from the respective standpoints of one property unit and of the company as a whole. Taking first the situation with respect to a single unit of property, there seems to be no doubt that accelerated depreciation results in a tax deferral and not a tax saving. In this case, less tax is paid during the early years of service life than would be payable under the straight-line method, and a greater tax would be payable in the later years. The total depreciation deductions for tax purposes equal the original cost of the property, and, assuming constant tax rates, the total tax effect is unchanged and equal regardless of the method of depreciation employed.

It is possible, under some assumptions, to take the position that a tax saving results from accelerated depreciation where the entire company is considered and not just a single property unit. The assumptions are, first, that corporate tax rates remain unchanged and that Section 167 remains in the law. A second and rather extreme assumption contemplates that the company experiences ever-continuous growth, and that the taxpayer's total outlays for new plant and equipment are the same or larger in each subsequent year and that the new property has the same life expectancy. Then, the total deductions for tax purposes under accelerated depreciation in any subsequent year would not be less than the total of such deductions under the straight-line method. Under such circumstances, the tax reductions obtainable through the use of accelerated depreciation would never be offset by future tax increases. Accordingly, it is possible to conclude that a tax saving would result. However, what the tax laws may provide and what the annual future additions to plant may be after one decade, or two or three, are plainly anyone's guess. The Federal Power Commission argued successfully in the Supreme Court that the foregoing assumptions, leading to the conclusion that a tax saving would result, ". . . are at best largely speculative and conjectural." The Commission also maintained, successfully, that "It was within the Commission's discretion to decline to make these assumptions."[25]

C. *Rate-Making Effects.* The fact that public utilities may elect to adopt accelerated depreciation for tax purposes raises a question as to the related accounting and rate-making treatment of accelerated depreciation by the regulatory commissions. In deciding upon the treatment of accelerated depreciation, commissions generally rule on the underlying question of whether accelerated depreciation results in a tax saving or in a tax deferral. In some cases, the commission also will rule on the intent of Congress in authorizing accelerated depreciation.

One approach to the regulatory treatment of accelerated depreciation is called "normalization." It assumes that the result of accelerated depreciation is a tax deferral. Under this approach, the commission will "normalize" the item, covering federal income tax expense in the cost of service used for the purpose of making rates. *Normalization* is the adjustment of the tax expense for rate-making purposes so that it reflects the amount which would have been payable if the straight-line method had been used to compute the depreciation expense deduction in the company's tax return. In other words, the commission allows the utility to use an accelerated method to calculate the depreciation deduction for tax purposes, but calculates the tax expense for rate-making purposes by using a depreciation deduction based upon the straight-line method. Thus, the income tax expense for rate-making purposes is calculated without giving effect to the statutory provisions for accelerated depreciation which the taxpayer may have elected for tax purposes. The excess of this normalized tax allowance over the actual tax is charged to tax expense and credited to a reserve for deferred taxes or to a restricted surplus account not distributable as dividends. Subsequently, in later years, when the actual tax expense exceeds that calculated under the straight-line method, the excess of the actual tax over the normalized tax is credited to tax expense, and the reserve for deferred taxes or the restricted surplus will be written off by equivalent debits. In this manner, the federal income tax expense for a given period reflects the full tax attributable to the income for that period. The process of normalization provides equal treatment for successive generations of customers and avoids giving present customers a windfall at the possible expense of future rate-payers or, possibly, stockholders.

Approval of normalization is not the

---

[25] Solicitor General's brief for the FPC, at p. 15, arguing for denial of *certiorari* in *People of the State of California et al.* v. *FPC et al.* (No. 599, October Term, 1960); *certiorari* denied, May 1, 1961.

same as allowing the utility to retain the benefits of accelerated depreciation. Once normalization is approved, it is then necessary for the commission to decide upon the rate-making treatment to be accorded the reserve for deferred taxes or the restricted surplus that arises under normalization. Commissions have followed a variety of policies in this respect. In general, however, commissions have adopted one of two alternatives. (1) If the commission decides that all the benefits of accelerated depreciation should be passed on to consumers, it will direct that the reserve for deferred taxes or the restricted surplus be deducted in determining the rate base (in the same manner as the deduction for accrued depreciation). Rate-payers thus are given the free use of the plant and equipment financed from the interest-free fund of capital arising from the use of accelerated depreciation. Alternatively, the same result is obtained where the allowed rate of return is reduced by including the accumulated deferred tax funds as part of the capital structure of the company at a zero rate of return. (2) Some commissions have adopted the opposite policy and have neither deducted the reserve for deferred taxes in determining the rate base nor considered the reserve in determining the rate of return. This policy allows the utility to retain the full benefits of accelerated depreciation. In addition to the two policies noted above, a few commissions have found that the interest-free funds provided by normalization should be considered in determining working capital requirements. Finally, at least one commisison, the FPC, has attempted to divide the benefits of accelerated depreciation and normalization by including the deferred tax funds as part of the capital structure of the company at 1.5 per cent rate of return.[26]

[26] *Re Northern Natural Gas Co. et al.*, Docket No. G-19040 *et al.*, March 7, 1961.

A second approach to the treatment of accelerated depreciation is called "flow-through." This approach assumes that the larger depreciation deductions for tax purposes, available under accelerated methods during the early years of property life, result in a permanent tax saving rather than a deferral. Where state commissions adopt flow-through, they also may conclude that Congress in enacting a tax statute did not intend to affect the regulation of intrastate utility rates. In such cases, utilities adopting accelerated depreciation for tax purposes are not allowed to provide for either a reserve for deferred taxes or a restricted surplus to meet the deferred income taxes which may become payable in the later years of the service life of the property being depreciated by an accelerated method.

Thus, under flow-through, the cost of service for rate-making purposes includes an amount for income taxes which reflects the tax deduction provided by use of an accelerated method. In short, actual taxes are included in the cost of service. Since the income tax expense thus calculated for rate-making purposes is less than the amount calculated under straight-line depreciation in the early years, the benefit of the current reduction in taxes resulting from the use of accelerated methods is allowed to flow through to the consumer in the form of a lower cost of service. Under this method, consumers receive the benefits of accelerated depreciation through the reduced tax expense for rate-making purposes, where the deductions for accelerated depreciation are given effect. The possibility exists, however, that the payment of the taxes deferred to later years will require a different generation of rate-payers to pay rates reflecting such costs, or that the burden will be imposed upon stockholders.

Where commissions have adopted policies denying the benefits of accelerated depreciation to utility companies, there is no incentive to use it; many utilities have ceased to use accelerated depreciation for this reason and have returned to the straight-line method. The Federal Power Commission has observed that "Many, probably a majority of the companies regulated by commissions which have required that the benefits accruing as a result of the use of liberalized depreciation be passed on to the ratepayer, either by adoption of the flow-through method, or by requiring that the accrued deferred taxes be deducted from the rate base, have ceased to take advantage of Section 167 of the Internal Revenue Act and have returned to straight-line depreciation in the computation of their income taxes."[27]

Normalization was adopted as the official position of the accounting profession in 1958, and the Securities and Exchange Commission in 1960 required the use of deferred tax accounting in financial statements filed with it under the Securities Act, Securities and Exchange Act, Public Utility Holding Company Act, and Investment Company Act. Both of the above authorities agreed that recognition of deferred income taxes is necessary in order to obtain an equitable matching of costs and revenues and to avoid income distortion.[28]

The endorsement of normalization by the accounting profession also set forth an exception in the case of public utilities. That exception provides that, where charges for deferred income taxes are not allowed for rate-making purposes, accounting recognition need not be given to the deferment of taxes "if it may reasonably be expected" that increased future income taxes will be allowed in future rate determinations. This exception is of limited significance, because it applies to circumstances which may be impossible of achievement. It is highly doubtful that any present commission or court could provide assurance that increased future taxes will be allowed in rate determinations made in future decades. Rate making, as a legislative function, is not readily subject to such restraint.

In conclusion, it may be noted that normalization has been adopted by the Federal Power Commission, the Civil Aeronautics Board, and the Securities and Exchange Commission; 22 state commissions require or permit the normalization of taxes. The Interstate Commerce Commission and 18 states subscribe to the flow-through theory.[29]

27 *Ibid.*, p. 10.

28 Committee on Accounting Procedure, American Institute of Certified Public Accountants. "Accounting Research Bulletin No. 44 (Revised)," Paragraphs 7 and 8, 1958; Securities and Exchange Commission, "Accounting Series Release No. 85," 1960.

29 *Op. cit.*, Note 25, pp. 9–11.

9 Rate of Return

Under capitalism as we know it in the United States, one of the keys explaining rapid economic development and technological advance is profit. Under a system where competition, in one degree or another, holds sway, the "profit motive" cannot be denied an important place. It is the prospect of profit which gives business the incentive to work harder, to produce more efficiently, and to experiment with new ideas which will give a competitive advantage.

It is not to be inferred here that the classroom model of "perfect competition" is the dominant form of market structure in the American economy. We can, however, make the generalization that competition in some degree or form is a hallmark of our system. The significance of profits in this system cannot be overemphasized. Through the competitive pricing system, profits perform the function of allocating human, capital, and natural resources among the numerous types of economic activities. Resources are attracted to those activities having the greatest expected profits relative to the risks incurred. Those activities with low expected profits are in a less advantageous position to attract resources. In a dynamic economy, risks, profits, and profit expectations vary greatly over time, with some industries becoming more profitable and others less so. As these changes occur, resources shift into or out of the various affected industries. Although this system is far from perfect, it does seem to bring about in a general way the most efficient resource allocation consistent with the basic economic freedoms that our society demands. Although some waste is perhaps inevitable in such a system, the costs have been willingly incurred as the price of these freedoms. The alternative method of resource allocation, that is, allocation by a central planning organization, has been rejected by our society.

1. PROFITS AND PUBLIC UTILITIES

The generalization is frequently made, and rightly so, that firms tend to set output and prices in such a way as to maximize profits.[1] This is frequently done through what economists call "marginal-cost pricing," whereby output is expanded to the point where the cost of adding the last unit of output is exactly offset by the additional revenue brought in by this last unit produced. Because of regulation, public utilities are unable to maximize profits in the usual sense of the term. What they seek to do is to set consumer rates at levels which will provide revenues to cover the economic costs of doing business, which includes the whole gamut of operating expenses, depreciation, taxes, and a fair rate of return that will attract capital into the business. The rate of return approved for a utility, of course, includes the element of profit. A utility must satisfy a commission that its "costs" are necessary to provide service of adequate quality and quantity. Thus, one thing that a utility maximizes is the "necessary" cost of attracting and keeping capital. If in pleading for a rate increase, a utility can convince a commission that a rate of return on rate base of 7 per cent rather than 6 per cent is needed to attract and hold capital, the company has gone about as far as it can toward "maximizing" profits via the commission route. It should be noted that this maximization occurs not through pricing policy but rather through rational argument, based on evidence, in commission rate proceedings. In many instances, prices come after the fact. They are set to provide revenues which will cover total costs.

The fact that profit maximization in the usual sense does not occur in public utility industries has nothing to do with the resource-allocating effects of profits. Every utility must compete with regulated and non-regulated industries alike

[1] Although there are exceptions to this generalization, it stands as the basic rationale for most firms.

for factors of production—land, labor, and capital. The amount of money in earnings allowed by a commission to attract capital sets a limit on what utilities can bid for the services of capital. If the rates they can pay do not meet the competitive rate, then resources will seek employment in alternative activities. A regulatory commission, therefore, has a tremendous influence on resource allocation because it does, in effect, help to establish profit levels for utilities.

The subject of this chapter is profits in the popular sense—public utility profits: how large or how small they should be, by what standards their adequacies or inadequacies are measured, and what legal and economic concepts apply. In addition, we shall be dealing with the rate of profit, or *rate of return,* as it is called in public utility economics.[2]

The *rate of return* is the amount of money a utility earns, over and above operating expenses, depreciation expense, and taxes, expressed as a percentage of the legally established net valuation of utility property, the rate base. Included in the "return" are interest on long-term debt, dividends on preferred stock, and earnings on common stock equity. In other words, the return is that money earned from operations which is available for distribution among the various classes of contributors of money capital. In the case of common stockholders, part of their share may be retained as surplus. The rate-of-return concept merely converts the dollars earned on the rate base into a percentage figure, thus making the item more easily comparable with that in other companies or industries.

[2] In a technical accounting sense, rate of return and rate of profit are different concepts. The rate of return includes profits as well as interest on debt capital, which is usually considered a cost of doing business and thus excluded from profits.

2. RATE OF RETURN AND THE RATE BASE

It should be reiterated at this point that there is a close and critical relationship between the rate of return allowed a utility and the net valuation of the utility's property, or rate base. The return amount available for distribution to bond- and stockholders is a function of two things: the size of the rate base and the specific rate of return. A regulatory commission can achieve a higher or lower level of allowed return for a utility by changing either of these two variables. For example, a 6 per cent rate of return on a rate base of $140,000,000 yields the same dollar return as a 7 per cent rate of return on a rate base of $120,000,000. For a commission to spend much time and effort determining the proper rate base while at the same time paying scant attention to the determination of the rate of return is nonsensical and wasteful. The converse is also true. Only if careful consideration is given to both of the elements or, more precisely, to the product of these two factors, will the outcome be truly reasonable and equitable to all the parties concerned.[3] The rate base has already been discussed, and what was said there should be kept in mind when analyzing problems of the rate of return.

3. LEGAL GUIDEPOSTS TO A FAIR RATE OF RETURN

It has only been in the past several years that regulatory commissions have turned their primary attention from valuation procedures to questions of a "fair" rate of return. This change of emphasis occurred partly because of the "end result" doctrine suggested in the

[3] *Re Chesapeake & Potomac Teleph. Co. of Virginia,* 85 PUR (NS) 435, 494 (1950).

Natural Gas Pipeline Co. case and spelled out in the *Hope Natural Gas Co.* case.[4] These cases have already been discussed in the chapters on valuation. Basically, they held that the regulatory methods employed were immaterial so long as the end result was reasonable to the consumer and investor. Many state commissions and courts, as well as most federal regulatory agencies, viewed this as permitting the adoption of some form of actual-cost rate base.[5] As inflation occurred in post-World War II years and an actual-cost rate base became a burden on some utilities because of its unresponsiveness to price-level changes and of the fact that depreciation reserves were not adequate to maintain real capital, relief in some cases was sought through changes in the rate of return rather than through the rate base. Thus, because of two factors—(1) the end-result doctrine, which paved the way for use of the actual-cost rate base, and (2) inflation in postwar years—recent rate cases have dealt largely with determining the proper rate of return on a rate base which, in many instances, was undisputed. There has also been, of course, a concerted effort by utilities in many states to have a "fair value" rate base used.

Some earlier legal guideposts should be examined in order to have a proper understanding of the evolution of the "fair rate of return" concept. The fundamental basis for allowing a utility to earn a reasonable rate of return is found in the Constitution of the United States. The Fifth and Fourteenth Amendments, which provide for limitations on the federal and state governments respectively, state, in part, that a person, including a corporation which is a legal entity, cannot be deprived of property without "due process of law." In the famous *Smyth* v. *Ames* case, which established the rate-base concept, it was also pointed out that "What the company is entitled to ask is a fair return upon the value of that which it employs for the public convenience."[6] This interpretation of the Constitution, in effect, stated that a regulatory commission must allow a person an opportunity to earn a reasonable return on his property. Earnings are property and they affect the market value of property; an unreasonable restriction of earnings through regulation would be a deprivation of property without "due process of law." Undue restriction of earnings can also be regarded as a violation of the constitutional guarantee of equal protection of the law, under the argument that if other companies of a similar nature are allowed to earn larger returns than the utility company, then there has been discrimination against the utility and unequal protection of the laws. The role of the "due process" and "equal protection" clauses in rate cases is well illustrated in an early railroad case in which the Supreme Court held:

> If the company is deprived of the power of charging reasonable rates for the use of its property, and such deprivation takes place in the absence of an investigation by judicial machinery, it is deprived of the lawful use of its property, and thus, in substance and effect, of the property itself, without due process of law and in violation of the Constitution of the United States; and in so far as it is thus deprived, while

[4] *FPC* v. *Natural Gas Pipeline Co.,* 315 U.S. 575 (1942), and *FPC* v. *Hope Natural Gas Co.,* 320 U.S. 591 (1944).

[5] These cases did not approve or disapprove specific rate-base methods but merely said that any method was adequate if the end result of the rate order was reasonable. A majority of state and federal commissions have adopted some form of net actual-cost rate base under the *Hope* doctrine unless there is a legislative or judicial mandate to the contrary. Reasonableness was taken to apply both to consumer and to investor.

[6] *Smyth* v. *Ames,* 169 U.S. 466, 547 (1898).

other persons are permitted to receive reasonable profits upon their invested capital, the company is deprived of the equal protection of the laws.[7]

The question arises at this point whether any given rate of return which is "non-confiscatory" is also reasonable; or, conversely, whether it is possible to have a non-confiscatory rate which is unreasonable. The issue is important because the constitutional limitation applies to the *confiscation* of property without due process of law, and not to the question of reasonableness. Court and commission decisions are far from unanimous in their answers to this question. However, at present it appears that there is much legal precedent upholding the view that there is a zone of reasonableness above the point of confiscation. The zone-of-reasonableness concept is clearly spelled out in a Wisconsin telephone rate case. In this case the Wisconsin Supreme Court stated that there is a zone of reasonableness within which acceptable rates of return can be found. This zone lies ". . . somewhere between the lowest rate that is not confiscatory and the highest rate that is not excessive or extortionate."[8] This seems to be the most sensible approach, since it enables a commission to vary the rate of return and thus take cognizance of such things as efficiency of management, special local or regional problems, general business conditions, and other similar factors which might be peculiar to a given situation. In general, the courts have held that it is not necessary for rates of return to be pushed down to the level of confiscation, and also that a rate (price of service) may become unreasonable before it becomes confiscatory.[9]

How does a commission determine the return (a dollar amount) or rate of return (a percentage) which is "fair" or "reasonable"? There is no hard-and-fast rule, nor are there formulas which can be applied. The courts have often pointed out that what is fair or reasonable is subject to a myriad of factors and requires the enlightened judgment of commissions and courts.[10] The *Consolidated Gas Company* case in 1909 begins to outline some of the factors which the courts have said must be considered in arriving at a reasonable return:

> There is no particular rate of compensation which must in all cases and in all parts of the country be regarded as sufficient for capital invested in business enterprises. Such compensation must depend greatly upon circumstances and locality; among other things, the amount of risk in the business is a most important factor, as well as the locality where the business is conducted and the rate expected and usually realized there upon investments of a somewhat similar nature with regard to the risk attending them.[11]

The landmark case which sets forth the criteria for a fair rate of return is the *Bluefield Water Works* case. Although decided in 1923, it is still relied on heavily in cases dealing with rate of return. The court stated:

> A public utility is entitled to such rates as will permit it to earn a return on the value of the property which it employs for the convenience of the public equal to that generally being made at the same time and in the same general part of the country on investments in other business undertakings

[7] *Chicago, M. & St. P. Ry. Co.* v. *Minnesota,* 134 U.S. 418, 458 (1899).

[8] *Wisconsin Telephone Co.* v. *PSCW,* 323 Wis. 274, 329 (1939).

[9] See Ellsworth Nichols, *Ruling Principles of Utility Regulation: Rate of Return* (Washington: Public Utilities Reports, Inc., 1955), pp. 48 ff., for an extended discussion of the legal arguments over confiscation and reasonableness.

[10] See, for example, *United Railways & Elec. Co. of Baltimore* v. *West,* 280 U.S. 234 (1930).

[11] *Willcox* v. *Consolidated Gas Company,* 212 U.S. 19, 48 (1909).

which are attended by corresponding risks and uncertainties; but it has no constitutional right to profits such as are realized or anticipated in highly profitable enterprises or speculative ventures. The return should be reasonably sufficient to assure confidence in the financial soundness of the utility and should be adequate, under efficient and economical management, to maintain and support its credit and enable it to raise the money necessary for the proper discharge of its public duties. A rate of return may be reasonable at one time and become too high or too low by changes affecting opportunities for investment, the money market and business conditions generally.[12]

In 1944, the *Hope* case elaborated on the guides to be used to judge reasonableness of return.

. . . it is important that there be enough revenue not only for operating expenses but also for the capital costs of the business. These include service on the debt and dividends on the stock. . . . By that standard the return to the equity owner should be commensurate with risks on investments in other enterprises having corresponding risks. That return, moreover, should be sufficient to assure confidence in the financial integrity of the enterprise, so as to maintain its credit and to attract capital.[13]

The *Bluefield* and *Hope* cases provide the foundation for virtually all later cases dealing with this problem. Since they are so important, it is appropriate to summarize the prevailing legal tests of fairness or reasonableness of the allowed rate of return for a public utility as found in them:

1. The rate of return (accruing ultimately to the investor) should be similar to the return in businesses having *similar or comparable risks*.

2. The rate of return is partly a function of local conditions and should be commensurate with the return being earned by comparable companies at the same *time* and in the same general *part of the country*.

3. The return ought to be sufficiently great to assure *confidence in the financial condition* of the utility.

4. The return should also be sufficient to allow the utility to *maintain and support its credit* and should enable it to *attract the capital* necessary for the proper discharge of its duties.

5. The return should *not be as high as* that earned in highly profitable or speculative ventures.

6. The proper level of the rate of return may vary with changes in investment opportunities, money market conditions, and general business conditions.

7. *Efficient and economical management* is a necessary prerequisite for profitable operations.

Most of the arguments currently used in rate-of-return cases are based on one or more of these points, despite the substantial inflation experience and despite the major strides in technology. New interpretations are often added and new techniques are developed to reveal the "basic truths," but for the most part the foundation has remained firm.

4. ANALYSIS OF LEGAL GUIDEPOSTS

Although the courts and commissions have set out the general framework for considering what constitutes a fair rate of return, closer economic analysis reveals a number of problem areas. The following discussion will consider, from an economic standpoint, the legal criteria set down in the *Bluefield, Hope,* and other cases.

A. *Comparable Earnings and the*

---

[12] *Bluefield Water Works & Improvement Co.* v. *Public Service Com. of West Virginia,* 262 U.S. 679, 692–93 (1923).

[13] *FPC* v. *Hope Natural Gas Co.,* 320 U.S. 591, 603 (1944).

Competitive Standard. It is frequently stated that public utility regulation attempts to approximate in its results the financial conditions which would exist under competitive conditions, particularly the profits that would be earned if the industry were competitive.

> "Reasonable profits" refers to the level of profits at which, under competition, there will be enough suppliers to equate the demand and supply for particular commodities in a given market. . . . Regulation was developed to do the job competition could not do with respect to public utilities.[14]

To induce investment in any industry, there must be an anticipated rate of return (or "profit," in the popular sense) sufficient to lead investors to undertake the risks (uncertainties) inherent in the particular line of business. If there were such a thing as a riskless business investment, as commonly assumed in the theory of a "perfectly competitive" market, this anticipated return would need be no more than a "pure rate of interest" comparable, say, to the yield on government bonds. Any profit or loss, deviating from this norm, would be the result of a temporary disequilibrium in the competitive market. Since no actual business is riskless, the chances of gain must be balanced against the chances of loss. Before risk is assumed, a decision must be reached that there is a chance of gain of some attractive size over and above pure interest. What is "necessary"—or, in other words, what must be anticipated to attract capital into a particular industry and firm—is related to the degree of uncertainty involved when considered in the light of alternative opportunities. Actual profit doubtless never exactly matches anticipations except by accident. Nevertheless, it is the expectations thus considered which furnish the motivation to go ahead with a plan.

Where an industry is regulated, the regulators are under the necessity of determining some "reasonable rate of profit" sufficient to induce the desired capital investment. With this type of broad standard of reasonableness in mind, regulators commonly try to evaluate the relative risks and uncertainties involved in a given utility operation and to estimate the earnings requirement related thereto. In general, the level of the "reasonable profit rate" is directly correlated with the hazards and uncertainties of the business in question.

A fair return to a public utility corresponds to what is being earned from other investments of similar risk. A common approach to the profit-risk relationship is to examine comparatively the earnings experience of other public utilities and unregulated industries, respectively. The first approach compares the earnings experience of a particular utility with other utilities which are similar in some important characteristics, such as size, general location, bond rating, type of service, market composition, and capital structure. The rationale of this type of comparison is to show the regulatory commission that other similar companies have been treated in a particular manner, presumably because of similar risks, thus indicating that the utility company in question should receive similar treatment. This approach has the advantage of being able to indicate to the commission the returns alternatively available to investors in other regulated companies, so that it may have some measure of the kind of competition that the particular utility faces in seeking funds in the capital market. This approach is not without limitations. First, there is a degree of circularity of analysis in looking to the earnings of other regulated utilities as an indication

---

[14] Civil Aeronautics Board, *General Passenger Fare Investigation,* Initial Decision of Examiner Ralph L. Wiser, Docket Nos. 8008, *et al.,* May 27, 1959, pp. 15 and 17, mimeo.

of what a fair return to a particular regulated utility may be. Second, the earnings of companies in the test group may have lagged adjustment to changed conditions, so that they either understate or overstate typical average earnings for such companies. Third, there is the question of whether the utilities in the test group are regulated by the same methods as the utility in question. Despite these limitations, the earnings experience of generally comparable utilities furnishes one helpful test of the reasonableness of the rate of return proposed by a particular utility.

The second approach compares the earnings experience of unregulated firms or industries with a given utility, allowing for differences in risk. This approach, in brief, operates from the premise that regulation is supposed to bring about the conditions which would exist under competition. Stated in greater detail, this approach maintains that, since unregulated firms operate in a relatively free market under competitive conditions, their rate of return approximates the competitive norm and, thus, is what should be used, among other things, for a guide to set utility rates of return. This line of reasoning makes some basic assumptions about the nature of competition and about normal profits. It is difficult to find an unregulated firm or industry that is directly comparable with a utility in economic characteristics, market, capital structure, and so on. The fact that one is unregulated and the other regulated adds to the difficulties of risk and earnings comparisons. Despite these limitations, it does seem useful to compare a utility's earnings over an extended period of time with an appropriate sample of earnings of unregulated firms. At least a bench mark is found. In addition, it serves to furnish the commission with information as to alternative earnings opportunities available to investors in unregulated industries. Because the regulated and unregulated industries both rely importantly upon the capital market, the difference in the earnings experience of the two and the variations therein merit analysis as a guide to decision-making.

Finally, it should be noted that the measurement of differences in risk or uncertainty is an extremely difficult assignment. A myriad of factors tend to increase or decrease risk. In a dynamic economy, the risk picture is kaleidoscopic and everchanging. Nevertheless, it is important to keep searching for ways to pinpoint and define kinds and degrees of risk.

The foregoing discussion suggests that a utility company faces risks, but what is included in this term has not been spelled out.[15] One set of risks has to do with the susceptibility of the utility's business to fluctuations in the general level of business activity. We usually think of the consumption of utility service (other than transportation) as being fairly stable over the business cycle, thus indicating relatively lower risks of the cyclical type than in many other industries. In competition with other goods and services for the consumer's dollar, utilities fare quite well; consumption of utility services by residential users is usually less sensitive to personal income

[15] The term "risk" is subject to several different interpretations. Technically, there is a difference between "risk" and "uncertainty," as pointed out by Professor Knight. Risk is susceptible to measurement and thus to predictability within the limits of probability analysis. Risks such as death, fire, illness, and so forth are readily insured against when large numbers are used. Uncertainty is not susceptible of measurement and thus cannot be predicted and insured against. It is uncertainty, in this sense, which is the basis for competitive profits. We bow to usage, however, and substitute the word *risk* for *uncertainty*. Risk in most public utility economics is of the "nonquantitative" type. See Frank H. Knight, *Risk, Uncertainty and Profit* (Boston: Houghton Mifflin Company, 1921), pp. 19 ff. and Chapter VII.

changes.[16] Some specific utilities are more susceptible to economic fluctuations than others because of the characteristics of the markets served and other factors. To the extent that this is true, these utilities should be accorded the opportunity to earn profits compensating for these risks.

Another type of risk facing every firm in any industry is competitive risk, or the risk of loss of business to other firms offering the same or substitute products or services. The over-all competitive risk of public utilities is less than that of unregulated firms. Where utilities are concerned, this factor is difficult to assess on a general basis, because: (a) local and regional market characteristics differ widely; and (b) the competitive element, where present, ordinarily affects portions of a market rather than the entire market served by a utility. Given these basic qualifications, it may be noted that gas and electricity compete in certain important residential and commercial uses, that gas also competes with coal or oil in the fuel markets, and that the telephone competes with private radio or telegraph in some important services. Electric, water, and transit utilities in differing degrees face a variant of the traditional competitive risk in the form of possible customer self-supply of the service offered by the utility. In addition, electric utilities in some instances face competition from government-owned or -sponsored electric operations. On the other hand, substitutes for many particular types of utility service are quite poor. The foregoing suggests that a question of competitive risk involving utilities can only be analyzed in the context of a given market situation.

Changing technology creates another type of risk which must be considered in the rate of return. These risks may arise on either the demand side or the supply side, that is, consumer preferences or requirements may change or existing plant may become outmoded by new innovations. Any industry faced with sudden and frequent technological changes of major magnitude is confronted with serious risk. Industries, such as utilities, which have tremendous fixed investment, can be particularly hard hit. Such risks must be accompanied by returns high enough to compensate for early obsolescence. While this technological type of risk may not be as great among utilities as it is in some manufacturing industries, it certainly is present. To the degree that utilities are not faced with direct competition of the price-cutting type, and to the degree that they control major inventions, it is possible for them to affect the rate of technological innovation. On balance, technological risks seem to have been less in the past in the utility industries than in many unregulated industries. What the future will reveal is difficult to foresee. Changes in technology are exceedingly difficult to forecast. Chapter 21 gives a glimpse of what innovations may be in store for utilities. Conceivably, such things as atomic power, liquid methane, fuel cells, and mobile radio could revolutionize current utility technology.

Regulation itself, in conjunction with long-term inflation, may create a risk. The regulatory process is slow and meticulous. If a utility is faced with rapidly rising operating costs, it ordinarily cannot without commission approval increase rates to provide additional revenues to meet the rising costs. Rates usually cannot be set in anticipation of rising costs, except where their future incurrence is definite; thus a utility always may be somewhat behind if there is a steady, general inflation. Should

[16] For a study of this, see Clement Winston and Mabel A. Smith, "Income Sensitivity of Consumption Expenditures," *Survey of Current Business,* January, 1950, pp. 17–20.

the reverse situation of secular deflation occur, and this seems improbable in today's world, the regulatory lag would benefit the utility. If a utility can cut costs through efficiency, the introduction of new equipment, or otherwise, it may be able to enjoy a return greater than that set by a commission. The longer the lag, in this instance, the greater the benefit to the utility.

This discussion does not exhaust the numerous types of risks that beset business in the United States economy, but it does point up a few of the major types that regulatory commissions must include in their deliberations. Any assistance that commissions can get in clarifying the kinds and degrees of relative risks should benefit consumers and investors alike.

B. *Financial Integrity and Attraction of New Capital.* Courts and commissions, perhaps sensing the difficulties inherent in the comparable earnings standard, have resorted to a more empirical or quantifiable test of reasonable return. They have said, in effect, that if a utility is able to compete successfully in the markets for capital and can do so without impairing its financial integrity, then a return based on the "cost of capital" to the firm is adequate. Unfortunately, the cost-of-capital approach has serious limitations also. However, it, along with other considerations, can contribute to the deliberative process of determining a fair rate of return if used properly. The following discussion will outline the mechanics of computing the cost of capital and will point out areas where critical problems lie.

The *cost of capital* is the composite, weighted cost of the various classes of capital (debt, preferred stock, common stock, and surplus) used by a company. The weighting is done according to the proportion which each class of capital is of total capital. The reasoning behind the calculation of the cost of capital is that it will provide a return sufficiently large to maintain the financial integrity of the company and to allow the company to attract new capital when necessary.[17]

The theory underlying the cost-of-capital approach was well stated in a recent decision:

> Thus, while utilities enjoy varying degrees of monopoly in the sale of their services, they enter the capital markets as competitors for investment funds, and out of this competition the price of money, i.e., the required earnings rate, is set by the relative uncertainties of the different businesses which seek capital. . . . Competition among commodities does not bring the same price if there are differences among the products, and competition among companies for capital does not bring the same price if there are differences in the quality of the investment. Such differences in hazard will be equated by the capital markets into differences in price. . . . In summary, the cost of capital is determined by the relative security of a particular investment, in light of alternative opportunities.[18]

Superficially, it would appear that the cost of capital is easily computed and enables a regulatory body to determine the return a utility needs in order to continue giving adequate service to the public. In actuality, results are not obtained until a host of problems are solved. Before delving into some of these problems, however, let us examine a simple numerical example of how the cost of capital is determined for a utility. Table 9.1 presents the dollar amounts of the various types of capital for a hypothetical utility. Also given are

---

[17] For an expanded discussion see J. Rhoads Foster, "Capital Cost and Fair Return," reprinted by *Public Utilities Fortnightly,* from its March 4, March 18, and April 1 issues of 1954; Lionel W. Thatcher, "Cost-of-Capital Techniques Employed in Determining the Rate of Return for Public Utilities," 30 *Land Economics* 85 (1954).

[18] *Op. cit.,* Note 14, pp. 18–19.

Table 9.1
Example Computation of the Cost of Capital

Type of Capital	*Amount of Capital*	*Per Cent of Total Capital*	*Cost of Each Type of Capital*	*Composite Cost*
Long-term debt	$20,000,000	40%	4.5%	1.8%
Preferred stock	5,000,000	10%	6.0%	0.6%
Common stock and surplus	25,000,000	50%	10.0%	5.0%
			Composite cost of capital	7.4%

illustrative "costs" of each type of capital and the composite cost of capital weighted by the percentage of each type of capital.

This method of determining the cost of capital seems to be straightforward. However, the problems that arise, even in this simple example, are numerous. Among the determinations which must be made are:

1. The cost of debt capital.
2. The cost of preferred stock capital.
3. The cost of equity capital.
4. The costs of flotation of and underpricing for new capital.
5. The capitalization ratios.
6. The payout ratio.
7. The level of surplus.
8. An allowance which is just sufficient to induce the proper growth rate of the utility.
9. Adjustment for possible changes in the value of money.
10. An allowance sufficient to bring forth the most efficiency from management.

It is clear that there is overlapping in these problem areas; but, generally speaking, a commission must resolve all problems if it is to arrive at a fair estimate of the over-all cost of capital. We shall deal with each in order to point out the types of decisions which must be made.

(1) *Cost of Debt and Preferred Stock Capital.* In utility rate cases, much time is spent on the determination of the cost of each category of capital. The estimation of long-term debt costs is relatively simple, provided the actual capital structure is used. The usual starting point is the actual historical cost of any debt capital that the company has outstanding, regardless of the time issued. Frequently, evidence on the current cost of debt capital of similar companies is introduced to indicate what investors would require if they bought today. It should be noted that the interest rate stated on the face of the bond is not usually the actual cost to the company of obtaining the money. In addition to the interest, such factors as cost of flotation, premiums and discounts on the sale, and call premiums, if exercised, must also be considered.[19] After certain judgment factors have been resolved, the process involves fairly simple arithmetic to discover the *historical* cost of bonded indebtedness and the *current* cost of debt to other utilities which are similar to the company under consideration.

The determination of the cost of preferred stock is carried out in much the same manner as for debt. Commissions look upon the percentage dividend as being almost as much a contractual obligation as interest on bonds. The actual historical cost of preferred stock is computed by taking the fixed dividend rate and adjusting for costs of flo-

[19] The inclusion of other than interest costs is by no means a settled issue. See Thatcher, *op. cit.*, for a discussion of the pros and cons on this point.

tation and any other unamortized expenses. Current cost of preferred stock is often estimated by seeking the costs incurred by similar firms issuing such stock.

The use of historical cost or current cost of debt and preferred stock capital is not usually hotly contended. Commissions frequently adopt an historical-cost approach unless the company is actually contemplating the issuance of debt or preferred stock. A number of commissions have declared that, when an original-cost rate base is used, it is logical to use the historical cost of senior capital.[20] Rarely will a commission use only the current cost of senior capital in its determinations.

(2) *Cost of Common Stock Capital.* By far the most difficult and controversial part of determining the cost of capital is the estimation of the cost of common stock capital. Since there is no contractual interest rate or fixed-dividend rate, such as is found on long-term debt or preferred stock, some other method or approach must be used. From an economic standpoint, it is quite obvious that the "necessary profit" to attract equity capital is as much a cost of doing business as wages, rent, supplies, and the like. No business can continue as a going concern in the long run and not earn some profits for its equity owners. The big problem is how to estimate accurately the amount of return just large enough "to assure confidence in the financial soundness of the utility . . ., to maintain and support its credit and enable it to raise the money necessary for the proper discharge of its public duties," while still allowing no more than is "necessary."

The method frequently used to find the cost of equity capital is to compute earnings-price and/or dividend-price ratios based on current information or based on data from a relevant period of years. Usually the ratios of the company under consideration are compared with those of "similar" companies. Those who advocate using these ratios consider them to be the best starting point to measure the "costs" of equity capital. An earnings-price ratio expresses the relationship of earnings per share in a given period of time (usually a year) stated as a percentage of some average of the market price for the stock. For example, if a share of common stock earned $12 per year and this same stock sold on the open market for an average price of $100 per share, the earnings-price ratio would be $\frac{E}{P} = \frac{\$12}{\$100} = 12$ per cent. Similarly, the dividend-price ratio is the current annualized dividend in dollars stated as a percentage of the average market price of the stock. Using the above example, if the annual dividend per share were $10, the dividend-price ratio would be $\frac{D}{P} = \frac{\$10}{\$100} = 10$ per cent. Given this much information, it is also possible to compute the dividend-payout ratio; $\frac{D}{E} = \frac{\$10}{\$12} = 83.33$ per cent. This means that 83.33 per cent of current earnings are paid out in dividends.

Potential investors are motivated to purchase a given stock by one or more of a number of factors. Certainly one important factor is past, current, and expected dividend income. Therefore, knowledge of the price that investors are willing to pay for an asset that will yield a given amount of dividend dollar income introduces *one* measure of the cost of equity capital. Since almost all firms withhold some earnings from dividend recipients and reinvest these earnings, other things being equal, the book value per share of stock tends to rise. This

[20] See J. R. Rose, "Cost of Capital in Public Utility Rate Regulation," 73 *Virginia Law Review* 1079 (1957), for citations on this point.

growth of a company from internal sources is another motive for the purchase of stock by investors. If, when buying stock, an investor takes into consideration earnings, which include both dividends and appreciation in the book value of the stock, the earnings-price ratio is a better measure of how much equity capital will cost than is the dividend-price ratio.

Economists do not agree on the relative roles of current, past, and expected dividend income, or current, past, and expected asset appreciation in the determination of the prices of utility common stocks. Certainly all these things have a place in price determination. However, their relative importance is still an unsettled question. This disagreement on emphasis will be more fully discussed below.

In addition to the conflicting views over the impact of the payout ratio on stock prices, there is much disagreement over what periods should be used to compute earnings, dividends, and prices; the length of periods that should be used to compute earnings, dividends, and prices; and the date picked for the number of shares of stock outstanding. It is possible to come up with entirely different ratios by merely selecting certain periods of time to measure prices or earnings. Efforts have been made to "lag" prices behind earnings so as to take into account the fact that today's market prices reflect tomorrow's anticipated earnings. No agreement has been reached on the length of the lag. In this and other matters outlined above, a substantial element of judgment enters into the cost-of-capital computation.

(3) *Limitations of the Earnings-Price Ratio Approach.* Critics claim that the use of earnings-price ratios has a number of limitations which, if not remedied, render the cost-of-capital approach inaccurate and misleading. These criticisms are as follows:

a. The use of earnings-price ratios, E/P, assumes that investors are interested in no more than the current or past earnings. The justification for use of this ratio is that it measures the capitalization rate implied by a perpetuity income of E purchased at P. To the extent that investors consider that they are buying something other than a perpetuity of E, the ratio does not measure the capitalization rate and therefore does not measure the cost of equity capital.

b. The rate base of a utility reflects, in some jurisdictions, the book value of the net assets of the company. On the other hand, the cost of equity capital, as found by the use of earnings-price ratios, reflects primarily market-value data. Therefore, it is inconsistent to apply a cost of equity capital based on market values to a rate base reflecting book values. More logically consistent would be a measurement based upon returns on book equity.

c. The earnings-price ratio approach is valid only if book value and market value coincide. If market value exceeds book value, as it very well may and should do for a number of reasons,[21] the earnings-price ratio on common stock would be less than the return on book value per share. Where an actual-cost rate base is adopted, the use of earnings-price ratios during a period of stock market optimism would penalize the utility. This would result because the cost of equity thus found would be applied to the rate base (on a weighted basis), while the relevant portion of the rate base is apt to be smaller than the market value of the equity capital. A

[21] If there is inflation or real growth in the economy, the market value is apt to exceed the book value. This would also occur if the particular company were in an expanding market or if, for any other reason, investors anticipate future appreciation of the company's stock or earning power or both. Market values above book values ease the placement of new capital issues.

very simple example suggests the problem. Let us assume that the company earns $1.00 per share and that the book value per share of its stock is $10.00. Assume further that the 10 per cent thus earned on book value is consistent with the allowed rate of return previously authorized, and that the market price is at or about the book value. Under these circumstances, the subsequent development of a stock market boom which raised the market price of this stock to $20 also would reduce the earnings-price ratio to five per cent. Use of earnings-price ratio as a measure of the cost of equity capital then would require a reduction in the return on equity by one-half, when the only changed factor was the behavior of stock market prices.

d. In one sense it is circular to use earnings-price ratios to determine the cost of equity. The earnings-price ratio is influenced by the earnings allowed under regulation. Therefore, an element of circularity arises in regulating the rate of return on the basis of a factor which in turn is at least partially determined by regulation.

e. The use of earnings-price ratios to measure the cost of equity capital has the problem of incorporating in one ratio "earnings," which are of historical and factual nature, and "price," which is a function of a myriad of things, including prospects of future earnings, estimated future regulatory action, anticipated behavior of the general economy, and expected price movements. In addition to these economic factors, a number of political or noneconomic factors influence stock prices. Under such circumstances, the proper measure of the cost of equity capital would be the ratio of *expected* earnings to price. Investors' evaluations of expected earnings are, however, difficult to gauge. It would be accidental if expected earnings were to equal exactly the actual earnings.

f. If a company is efficiently managed and investors recognize this by bidding up the market price of the stock in anticipation of greater future earnings, the earnings-price ratio would decline, and the company therefore would be penalized. In the case of the inefficient company, the reverse would be true; it would be rewarded.

g. The use of current or spot earnings-price ratios is particularly meaningless. This is exemplified in a recent report of the Committee on Corporate Finance of the NARUC. The report states:

> The drop in current earnings-price and dividend-price ratios to levels below debt costs and even Government debt costs, highlights even more than in previous years the need for the careful use and interpretation of these ratios in determining equity costs. . . . The fact that current . . . ratios have been trending downward since 1950 in the face of rising interest rates made this Committee sound notes of caution on the use of these ratios in previous reports. With these ratios now below bond costs, your Committee's prior warnings have indeed been justified. It is clear that equity investors are not buying stocks for current yields but rather in anticipation of future increases in earnings, dividends, and prices. . . .[22]

Some critics of the earnings-price ratio do not oppose the entire cost-of-capital approach, but propose to estimate the cost of equity capital by use of an "earnings-investment" ratio, which is the ratio of earnings per share related to the book value per share of common stock. This method compares comparables, that is, past earnings with past book value of stock. On the other hand, it contains an element of circularity, akin to that noted in d, above. Other alternatives have been suggested and offered for commission consideration. One of these is the "coverage test" of

[22] NARUC, *Report of the Committee on Corporate Finance* (Washington: 1959), p. 10.

the reasonableness of proposed common stock equity return, which analyzes the relation between the average coverage of senior security requirements for a test group and that resulting for a given utility of comparable bond rating after allowing for the proposed return on equity. Another alternative is to adjust earnings-price ratios by "investors' experienced returns" over a test period. The experienced return for purposes of this analysis reflects not only the returns realized by investors from dividends and other valuable distributions but also those from realized or realizable net appreciation of their holdings in the market. The foregoing suggests that the determination of the cost of equity capital is far from a settled matter, particularly in jurisdictions which place important emphasis upon earnings-price ratios in a period of stock market optimism.

(4) *Allowance for Costs of Flotation.* It has already been noted that, in determining the costs of each component of capital, some expenses are incurred over and above the interest or owner yield. This is merely to say that a company cannot float either stocks or bonds without some necessary administrative expense, which is a legitimate expense the utility is entitled to recover, just as it recovers operating expenses such as wages, cost of supplies, and so forth. Flotation costs include security registration and other fees at the state and federal levels, underwriting commissions paid to the company or group of companies marketing the securities, and fees for accounting and legal services needed to draw up and authenticate the various documents used in the flotation. There may be, in addition to these costs, allowances for market declines, adjustments for "underpricing" caused by market pressure or by the desire to assure sale, certain call premiums on debt or preferred stock, or possibly discounts necessary to secure the money at the time of issuance. Such costs are customarily amortized by a utility and considered a necessary part of the cost of raising new money from external sources. It is difficult to state an average cost of flotation. Studies by the Securities and Exchange Commission seem to indicate that for publicly placed debt issues during the 1945–1949 period, electric, gas, and water utilities paid about 1.25 per cent of the proceeds of the average issue.[23] The study further shows that flotation costs for privately placed securities are somewhat less than for publicly placed issues, although over the life of the security the cost saving may be more than offset by such disadvantages as limited distribution, and thus a limited market for the securities, or stricter terms of indenture than would be required in a publicly placed issue.

(5) *Capital Structure.* The problem of determining the capital structure for a particular utility is an especially thorny one, and one on which there is much disagreement among financial experts, lawyers, and economists.[24] The basic problem lies in the fact that cost-of-

---

[23] Securities and Exchange Commission, "Privately-Placed Securities—Cost of Flotation" (Washington: 1952), p. 10. See also Securities and Exchange Commission, "Cost of Flotation of Issues Effectively Registered with the Securities and Exchange Commission" (Washington: 1951).

[24] Recent theoretical discussions in the literature cast serious doubt on the claim that the capital structure influences the over-all cost of capital except (1) for the cost-reducing effect of income tax laws which allow interest as a tax deduction, and (2) for extreme situations in which an attempt is made by a company to push its debt ratio up beyond what the market might reasonably be expected to take. Attempts at empirical verification are underway. See Franco Modigliani and M. H. Miller, "The Cost of Capital, Corporation Finance and the Theory of Investment," 48 *American Economic Review* 261 (June 1958); David Durand, "The Cost of Capital and the Theory of Investment: Comment," 49 *American Economic Review* 639

capital computations utilize the per cent of capital falling into the debt, preferred stock, and equity categories to multiply by the cost of each of these portions of total capital. The difference in total cost of capital caused by different capital structures is illustrated in the following example:

	Case A			Case B		
	Per Cent of Total Capital	*Cost*	*Wtd. Cost*	*Per Cent of Total Capital*	*Cost*	*Wtd. Cost*
Long-term debt	45	4.5%	2.025%	50	4.5%	2.250%
Preferred stock	15	5.0	0.750	20	5.0	1.000
Equity	40	9.5	3.800	30	9.5	2.850
Total cost of capital			6.575%			6.100%

In Case A, the 45–15–40 debt, preferred, and equity relationship, yields a total cost of capital of 6.575 per cent, given the costs shown. In Case B, the capital structure is 50–20–30 and the total cost of capital is 6.100 per cent, a difference of almost one-half of one per cent. On a rate base of $20,000,000, this means a difference of $1,315,000, compared with $1,220,000 in the allowed return. However, this example contains some very basic assumptions, some of which are open to considerable question. Does the cost of a type of capital remain the same, even though the relative proportions have been changed? Or would a more accurate assumption be that capital costs change to offset the changing proportions of capital? Is there some "ideal" capital structure? Should regulatory commissions have a voice in establishing the capital structure of a company? The following discussion will explore these questions.

In general, if a company has 100 per cent of its capital in equity form and wishes to increase its capital, the issuance of debt will probably lower the total cost (in percentage terms) of capital. No doubt there are exceptions to this generalization. If this hypothetical company continues to expand capital by issuing more and more debt, the cost of capital would probably drift down and then begin to rise. As the company approaches 100 per cent debt, it will find it virtually impossible to sell more debt, and the cost of capital would be extremely high. The reasons for this fall and subsequent rise in the cost of capital are extremely complex and can only be outlined here. In the initial situation, in which the company is moving away from 100 per cent equity, the total cost of capital is reduced because, in general, a dollar of capital can be raised for less by the debt route than by the equity route. For example, the addition of some 4.5 per cent debt to 10 per cent equity lowers the over-all cost of capital. As debt increases, however, the fixed interest charge grows. The risk to the investor who owns the company's common stock also increases, for he faces two dangers. First, revenues of the company are subject to the prior claim of interest payments, and his earnings may suffer, particularly if there is a decline in revenues. Second, while a company may be able to meet its interest payments, it may be unable to make payments on the principal of the debt outstanding. Such default could result in bankruptcy of the business and substantial losses for the equity-holder.

At any given instant in time, there is

(Sept. 1959); Modigliani and Miller, "The Cost of Capital, Corporation Finance and the Theory of Investment: Reply," *Ibid.*, p. 655; Miller and Modigliani, "Dividend Policy, Growth, and the Valuation of Shares," 34 *Journal of Business* 411 (October 1961); Modigliani and Miller, "Corporate Income Taxes and the Cost of Capital: A Correction," 53 *American Economic Review* 433 (June 1963).

a *theoretical* capital structure which will minimize the cost of capital for a particular company. However, it can only be theoretical, and it can only be instantaneous. While it is perhaps possible to compute a cost of capital with an actual capital structure and given prices, earnings, book values, and similar information, it is impossible to compute a cost of capital, other than some theoretical cost, if some structure other than the actual is used. To do so necessitates assuming what happens to prices, earnings, interest rates, investor expectations, credit ratings, book values, and the like, if the capital structure is something hypothetical, that is, different from what it actually is. The computation must be instantaneous because all these factors change over time, owing to both endogenous and exogenous factors. The "ideal" capital structure today would likely be somewhat different tomorrow, since literally hundreds of controllable and uncontrollable factors are constantly at work. Thus, if a utility strives for and achieves the ideal structure at a given point in time, it is unlikely that exactly the same structure will be ideal again. Finally, it should be noted that, at any given instant in time, the theoretical ideal capital structure differs from company to company. Such considerations complicate the regulatory process.

We might pull together some of the thoughts in the preceding discussion: (1) The over-all cost of capital is influenced somewhat by the capital structure, although there certainly are other influences; (2) the precise measurement of the effects of changes in capital structure is difficult to make; (3) an ideal, hypothetical capital structure has serious shortcomings in precise calculations because of the very basic, major assumptions that have to be made; (4) capital structures are largely built into companies in pieces.

A question frequently argued is whether or not regulatory commissions should determine what a capital structure of a utility should be, for purposes of establishing a cost of capital and rate of return. Since most regulatory commissions have jurisdiction over the issuance of securities, it would appear that the existing capital structure has already been approved. To the extent that a commission cannot control capital structure through its power to authorize new securities, there is no question that capital structure is a relevant factor in commission deliberations. The *right* of commissions to consider this area in setting rates cannot be questioned, since a commission has an obligation to protect the consumer from excessive wages, excessive pension provisions, excessive prices for purchased materials and supplies, and other such things, including excessive costs of capital. On the other hand, the right, while always there, should be exercised sparingly, since the problems of corporate finance are extremely intricate and complex, and are best known to the utility which lives with these problems from day to day.

The ideal situation would seem to be one in which a commission sets a range in which the capital structure may fall, thus leaving it up to the particular company to decide where, within the range, the actual structure will be. It appears that there is a fairly broad range for most companies in which the cost of capital does not vary appreciably.[25] In one case it was noted that: "It is the

[25] See Joseph R. Rose, "'Cost of Capital' in Public Utility Regulation," 43 *Virginia Law Review* 1079 (1957), and *Public Utilities Fortnightly,* Sept. 29, 1955, p. 503 and Sept. 24, 1959, p. 525, for a discussion of the states which have adopted the hypothetical capital structure in cost of capital determination and those which use actual capital structures. See also the Staff Report to the Federal Communications Commission, "The Problem of the 'Rate of Return' in Public Utility Regulation," Washington, 1938, for discussion of the "optimum" capital structure.

duty of the company to adopt the most economical methods of financing consistent with maintaining that degree of flexibility in capital structure necessary to assure its future ability to sell any securities that may be desirable."[26] The commission, in turn, has an obligation to allow efficient management to work, while it sets up broad boundaries of restraint as guide lines for management.

(6) *The Dividend-Payout Ratio and Retained Earnings.* It was noted earlier that both dividends and growth or appreciation are among the factors inducing investors to purchase the securities of a company. *If* dividends are the primary concern of investors, then a high payout ratio will cause the price of common stock to be bid up, (or to remain up), thus lowering (or keeping low) the cost of equity capital from this source. This, of course, assumes the use of earnings-price ratios to determine the cost of equity capital, which, as we have already seen, has major flaws. There is really no way to break out the various factors in stock pricing, but one recent study seems to indicate a growing investor concern with earnings rather than dividends.[27] This view is by no means accepted universally.[28] If the earnings-price ratio approach is utilized, then payout ratios must be considered.

The problem of retained earnings is basically the same as the payout ratio problem. If a utility is allowed to earn 6.5 per cent on its rate base and does so, it would appear to be a matter of indifference whether 10 per cent or 50 per cent of the earnings available to the common stockholder were retained and not paid in dividends. Presumably, the retained earnings would mean an appreciation in the value of the stock. However, *if* earnings-price ratios are used, and *if* investors place a higher value on dividends than on "growth," the 50 per cent retention of earnings is apt to bring about (in the future) a higher cost of equity capital than the 10 per cent would. The commission, of necessity, must try to gauge investors' motivations and expectations and to urge payout ratios that coincide with these expectations.

(7) *Growth and the Role of Surplus.* One of the most difficult aspects of rate-of-return regulation is that of surplus and the proper rate of growth. In cost of capital analysis, some increment of earnings is usually urged by the company for surplus. The surplus performs several functions. It enables the company to have greater continuity in its dividends than would otherwise be possible over the business cycle. To the extent that this boosts investors' confidence in the company, it lowers the cost of capital.[29] Thus, a portion of surplus becomes an "insurance fund" from which dividends are paid in bad times, and which would be expected to average out to zero over a complete business cycle or over several cycles. On this aspect of surplus there is little or no disagreement.

Quite apart from the dividend stability argument, it is often urged that an increment be allowed over and above the cost of capital already established (which is partly a function of dividends

---

[26] Nichols, *op. cit.*, p. 264, citing *Re: New England Teleph. & Teleg. Co.*, 83 PUR (NS) 414 (1950).

[27] Fred P. Morrissey, "Current Aspects of the Cost of Capital to Utilities," 62 *Public Utilities Fortnightly* 217 (1958).

[28] For the opposite view, see, for example, E. W. Clemens, "Some Aspects of the Rate-of-Return Problem," 30 *Land Economics* 32 (1954).

[29] Some interesting liquidity problems arise in this situation. Surplus is rarely kept in liquid form. It is ploughed back into plant and equipment. Therefore, this surplus represents fixed assets which could not be liquidated to pay dividends should current earnings be inadequate. Only insofar as there is a cash flow from depreciation will liquid funds be available for dividend payments.

and growth itself) for growth. The implication is that this increment will be returned and ploughed back into the company to meet the long-term increase in the demand for utility services. Ideally the growth in output of a utility should parallel the growth in demand for the utility's service at some price or range of prices. Problems are encountered when an attempt is made to measure the demand for a service. A firm may know how many unfilled orders it has at the current price, but it can only estimate what quantity would be sold at different prices or at different consumer income levels.

Commissions can, in several ways, influence the rate at which a utility grows. Growth can be too rapid as well as too slow. Commissions should and do take into consideration the growth needs of a particular utility, but not to the extent that present-day consumers bear an unreasonable portion of that expansion which ultimately will benefit future consumers.

(8) *Inflation.* One of the most controversial problems in public utility economics today is caused by inflation.[30] Some of the discussion of inflation was presented in Chapter 6 and will not be gone into again in detail. The basic controversy evolves from the fact that in many jurisdictions a utility is allowed to earn a fair return only on its depreciated actual-cost rate base. Under such jurisdictions and during periods of rising prices, it is impossible to keep the *plant* "whole," that is, to replace through depreciation that part of capital used up by consumers; in addition, the purchasing power of the return declines. Unless technological improvements can offset the "erosion" caused by inflation, it is necessary to obtain new capital from some other source.

One proposed solution to the inflation problem is to use a fair-value method of rate-base determination or some variant of this approach. Another possible solution is to adjust the rate of return upward so as to provide the common stockholder with an additional increment of income which offsets the inflation effect, that is, the fact that an original-cost rate base does not reflect inflation. Several states have taken the rate-base rather than the rate-of-return approach to adjust for inflation. A number of states use a "fair value" rate base, which in effect provides an adjustment for the portion of the rate base represented by the common stockholders' interest.[31] Other states have allowed some adjustment in depreciation accruals.[32] Still other states have allowed higher rates of return while retaining an original-cost rate base. Whether the adjustments for inflation in these states

[30] The most comprehensive analysis of the inflation problem can be found in a series of articles appearing in *Land Economics.* These are: James C. Bonbright, "Public Utility Rate Control in a Period of Price Inflation," Vol. 27, p. 16, February, 1951; Walter A. Morton, "Rate of Return and the Value of Money in Public Utilities," Vol. 28, p. 91, May, 1952; E. W. Clemens, "Some Aspects of the Rate-of-Return Problem," Vol. 30, p. 32, February, 1954; Lionel W. Thatcher, "Cost-of-Capital Techniques Employed in Determining the Rate of Return for Public Utilities," Vol. 30, p. 85, May, 1954; Fred C. Morrissey, "A Reconsideration of Cost of Capital and a Reasonable Rate of Return," Vol. 31, p. 299, August, 1955. In addition to the above articles, there is one by Harold M. Somers, "Cost of Money as the Determinant of Public-Utility Rates," 4 *Buffalo Law Review,* Spring, 1955, which deals with the inflation problem. Numerous articles in the *Public Utilities Fortnightly* also discuss inflation.

[31] There is no justification for granting an inflationary adjustment for that portion of the rate base represented by debt and preferred stockholders. These individuals cannot benefit. The additional income will accrue, through leverage, to the equity owners.

[32] See Fred P. Morrissey, "Inflation and Public Utility Regulation," *California Management Review,* Vol. 1, No. 4, Summer 1959, pp. 74 ff., for a discussion of depreciation adjustment.

have been adequate is a matter debated by experts in many cases. There are some states which make little or no adjustment for inflation. The rationale behind this type of regulation is that equity capital devoted to utility enterprises is not entitled to protection against a loss which general economic conditions threaten. Finally, some states try to "split the difference" by allowing a return which gives the equity-holder more than he would receive if inflation were completely ignored but not allowing a return so high as to completely preserve "real" income.

(9) *Efficiency of Management.* The final problem which a commission must resolve in establishing a fair rate of return or an over-all cost of capital is the one of efficiency. Perhaps an example would best illustrate this problem. Assume that we have at a given time two firms with identical operating costs, plant and equipment investment, capital structures, markets, and so forth. Assume also that both firms are granted permission to charge identical rates, high enough to earn 6.5 per cent on their identical rate bases. Firm A is efficiently managed by a group of men who are anxious to lower costs in any way possible. Firm B has a management whose attitude is complacent. At the end of a given period of time, the commission examines the financial statements of each firm and finds that Firm A is earning 8 per cent while Firm B is just earning 6.5 per cent, even though consumer rates are the same. In view of this situation, should the commission seek to reduce the rates charged by Firm A so as to push its rate of return back down to 6.5 per cent? To do so would be to penalize efficiency and reward inefficiency.

This problem is inherent whenever there is price regulation on a cost-plus basis, but it still must be dealt with by the commission. In some states the commissions seem to feel that companies will continue to strive for greater efficiency and lower costs despite the eventual removal of the rewards for such efforts. There is always the regulatory lag which allows the company to enjoy these returns, if present, for some period of time. Other states attempt to recognize efficiency by allowing a slightly higher return, although the benefits are most generally shared with the public through lower rates. In such situations the judgment factor of the commission must play a very important role.

5. THE CURRENT STATUS OF RATE OF RETURN

This chapter has stressed the difficulties encountered in devising an equitable and workable approach to determining the rate of return for public utilities. However, despite these numerous problems, state and federal regulatory agencies must determine some rate of return in each case they hear. Table 9.2 summarizes a study made by Arthur Andersen & Company of rates of return at the state level in 1957, 1958, 1959, and through mid-1960. A total of 202 cases were used, and these were broken down according to the type of rate base used. The range of rates of return is reported as well as the median (midpoint) figure for original cost, fair value, and investment rate bases by type of utility. The median rates of return appear to be highest under the original-cost rate base and lowest under the fair-value rate base. This would perhaps indicate the recognition of inflation by state commissions generally. The rather wide ranges make it apparent that specific circumstances surrounding given situations play a major role in the ultimate determination of the rate of return.

Having pursued some of the details of how commissions determine a fair rate of return, it is useful, perhaps, to step

Table 9.2

Rates of Return for Intrastate Utilities, 1957–Mid-1960

Type of Utility	No. of Cases	Type of Rate Base					
		Original Cost		Fair Value		Investment	
		Range	Median	Range	Median	Range	Median
Telephone.	71	6.03-7.24	6.44	4.74-6.25	6.00	5.02-6.80	6.20
Electric	47	5.59-6.50	6.00	5.25-6.25	5.87	4.61-6.98	6.02
Gas distribution. . .	41	4.50-6.90	6.30	5.45-6.40	6.00	4.10-6.73	6.29
Gas transmission. .	9	5.50-6.90	NC	5.75	NC	6.00-6.35	NC
Water.	34	4.60-6.50	6.00	4.34-6.10	5.77	4.02-6.50	5.90

NC—Not computed because of fewness of numbers.

Source: Arthur Andersen & Co., *Return Allowed in Public Utility Rate Cases,* 1960 Edition.

back and once again look at the broad requisite:

> . . . The fixing of a fair rate of return involves a consideration of the interests of both investors and the consuming public. The rate of return should not be so high as to place an unnecessary burden on consumers, or give rise to unusual or speculative profits. But it must be high enough to insure investor confidence in the financial soundness of the enterprise, and sufficient to maintain its credit standing so that it may be able to raise any funds which may be needed to permit the carrying out of its public duties and responsibilities. The determination of a fair rate of return in accordance with these criteria necessarily requires the use of judgment and the consideration of all facts which are relevant to the subject.[33]

The statement succinctly sums up what a commission must try to do: (1) It must treat *both* consumer and investor equitably, insofar as this is possible. (2) It must consider all facts relevant to the subject. (3) It must exercise its expertise and apply the best *judgment* possible.

[33] From proposed testimony of FPC Staff Witness F. I. Shaffner in Docket No. G–9385, *et al.,* Amerada Petroleum Co., 1960, p. 5.

10 Pricing Policies

The central problem in the study of economics concerns the pricing of goods and services. This is also true of public utility economics, as the preceding chapters indicate. The present chapter and the one that follows survey the pricing policies of the various public utility industries. This chapter begins with a summary of the general principles underlying the pricing of public utility services and then discusses pricing by electric utilities, gas distribution utilities, and interstate natural gas pipelines. The next chapter covers the pricing of telephone, water, and urban transit services.

Pricing is the final step in the over-all rate-making process. Under the conventional practice, pricing becomes a matter of regulatory concern after commission determination of the utility's approved cost of service, including a fair return. At that point, the commission ordinarily orders the utility to prepare schedules of proposed rates that are designed to provide total revenues equivalent to the approved cost of service. These proposed rate schedules are then submitted to the commission for review. The commission may accept or reject them or require modification before approval is granted. Public utility commissions use their delegated authority to legislate when they approve schedules of rates and authorize them to be applied to sales of service to the public. In this phase of the regulatory process, the commission makes effective one of the principal objectives of public utility regulation—that all rates shall be just and reasonable. However, it is most important to note that the approval of just and reasonable rates cannot guarantee that the utility will actually earn adequate revenues. All the utility is guaranteed is the opportunity to do so.

Public utility rates are intended to accomplish much more than produce revenues equivalent to the approved cost of service. They are also intended to apportion the company-wide cost of service among consumers in a reasonable manner and to provide an effective instrument for the marketing of public utility services. This last objective has received insufficient recognition, or none at all, from many of the commentators on public utility rates. The proper design of public utility rates is fundamentally important to the successful marketing of public utility services. It is for this reason that commissions generally allow utility management considerable latitude in the design of rate schedules, within the limitation that total revenues are not to exceed the approved cost of service. This follows from the fact that utility management, which bears the entire marketing responsibility, also is in the best position to achieve detailed knowledge of market characteristics.

1. UNDERLYING PRINCIPLES OF RATE MAKING

Unlike some of the matters considered up to this point, such as rate base, depreciation, and rate of return, there has been relatively little controversy in the area of rate structures. The following discussion sets forth the basic rate-making principles and practices which have become generally accepted through the years.

A. *Differential Pricing.* The pricing of public utility services differs from the pricing of most of the goods and services that consumers are accustomed to buying. The prices of the groceries on display in a supermarket or the prices of dry-cleaning services are ordinarily the same to all customers. This uniformity does not prevail in public utility pricing. Instead, (1) relatively homogeneous groups of customers, called *customer classes,* are established; (2) a different schedule of rates is applied to each class; and (3) each rate schedule ordinarily offers the individual customers within each class a graduated, descending scale of rates for incremental blocks (additional, successive quantities) of service taken. The classification and pricing process also often makes distinctions for the different types of services as well. Accordingly, public utilities engage in "differential pricing," rather than uniform or "supermarket" pricing, primarily because different schedules of rates apply to different classes of customers and services. It should be made clear that public utility rates generally are not made for individual customers but for different classes of customers and services. All customers within a particular class are charged under the same schedule of rates for each service. Differential pricing in this context has reference solely to different schedules of rates for different classes of customers and services.

An electric utility, for example, may have its customers grouped for rate-making purposes into these classes: residential, commercial, industrial, urban transit, street lighting, rural, and others. Further, subgroups are sometimes provided for the different types of service available to each customer class. For example, a residential electric consumer may be charged under a "residential service" rate schedule which covers all residential uses, including lighting, refrigeration, cooking, water heating, and other domestic electric appliances. On the other hand, the family in the next house may be charged under a "residential lighting service" rate schedule. That rate schedule may be applicable solely to residential customers who do not have electric ranges, water heaters, or other major domestic electric appliances over a specified kilowatt rating; such customers probably have gas ranges, gas hot-water heaters, and other large gas appliances.

Differential pricing is an entirely lawful and economically desirable form of price discrimination, insofar as regulated public utilities are concerned. Three conditions are necessary in order for differential pricing to be possible: (1) monopoly or near-monopoly on the supply side of the market; (2) a total demand that can be subdivided into separate markets, each with different price elasticities of demand; (3) some means of insulating each market from the others, so that those who buy at the lower prices cannot resell to those who would have to pay higher prices.[1]

[1] George J. Stigler, *The Theory of Price* (New York: The Macmillan Company, 1947), p. 223.

Public utilities fit into this pattern very well. Although public utilities ordinarily do not compete with one another in selling the same service, they do face competition from other public utility services that can perform the same function (such as gas versus electric cooking) and from other fuels (coal and oil). In addition, industrial customers of electric service, if large enough, can generate their own power as an alternative to the purchase of electric service. Generally speaking, there is no problem in insulating one market from another so as to prevent resales among customers. It is ordinarily unlawful for anyone other than the authorized utility to sell utility service for public consumption. Price elasticity of demand, referred to above, is one among a number of factors considered in classifying customers and services for pricing purposes. Price elasticity of demand is a measure of the *change* in the quantity of a commodity or service that will be bought as a consequence of a change in price. Knowledge of price elasticity of demand helps to predict the effect of price changes upon the total expenditure for a commodity or service. If the demand for a service is relatively inelastic, the total consumer expenditures on it will change in the same direction as a change in price. That is, a price increase will result in increased gross revenues. If demand is relatively elastic total expenditures will change in the opposite direction from a change in price. Thus, a price increase will lead to a reduction in gross revenues. Because public utilities sell a wide variety of services, many of which are in competition with substitutes that can perform the same function, market studies and an awareness of market characteristics must be given consideration in the pricing of public utility services. This will be discussed further in connection with the "value of service" principle.

The classification of customers is

based upon two principal factors: (1) the "size" of the consumer—as measured, for example, in the case of electric service, by the number of kilowatt-hours consumed per month or the maximum demand or both; and (2) the purpose to which the public utility service is devoted. The related factors of value of the service to the customer class and elasticity of demand are inherent in the classification process when the factors of customer size and purpose of use are under consideration. Other factors taken into account may be the quality of service required, any hazards that may be involved, the time at which the service is required, and the stability of demand from year to year. It is apparent that a number of these factors reflect cost differences. Each schedule of rates states in detail the class of customers to which it applies, the nature of the service to be provided, the method of calculating the bill, and other terms and conditions affecting the sale.

The following quotation is from a decision of the Public Service Commission of Wisconsin in a case involving a question of the proper classification of the space heating service offered by gas utilities. It illustrates the application of classification principles in a specific case:

> To justify the separate classification of any utility service there must be something about that particular service which makes it different from any other service which that utility furnishes to the public.
>
> The essential fact which makes the respondents' space-heating service different . . . , and thus justifies the separate classification . . . , is the simple fact that gas used for space heating is not worth as much to the consumer as gas which is used for the other purposes for which respondents' other consumers make use of gas.
>
> The difference in value between gas for space heating and the same gas for other uses furnishes the logical basis for the separate classification for respondents' space-heating services because of the fundamental principle of rate making that reasonable utility rates cannot result in charges for any utility service which are more than such service is worth to the customer. This principle was established in *Smyth* v. *Ames* (1898). . . .[2]

Why is there not a uniform or "supermarket" price for all classes of service or to all classes of consumers? A preliminary answer, in essence, is that demand and supply factors differ among the different classes. Recognition of both these factors in the pricing of public utility services results in fuller utilization of plant than would be the case if prices were uniform. Where, as among public utilities, constant or fixed costs comprise a major share of total costs, it is readily seen that full utilization of plant leads to economies which are reflected in lower average unit costs. Such economies are unobtainable to the extent that facilities are idle all or some of the time. This matter will be discussed more fully in the following section.

B. *General Objectives of Utility Pricing Policies.* A public utility's structure of rates should be designed to accomplish the following *general objectives:* (1) produce revenues equivalent to the approved cost of service determined by the commission; (2) maximize utilization of fixed plant; (3) assure maximum stability of revenues; (4) distribute the total cost of service reasonably among the different classes of customers; and (5) promote and retain the maximum economic development of its market. Except for the first of these objectives, practical necessity often requires a balancing of objectives when the fullest achievement of one conflicts with the fullest achievement of another.

To accomplish these ends, the *guiding principle* in the design of rates calls for

---

[2] *Re Milwaukee Gas Light Co. et al.,* 51 PUR (NS) 299, 306, 307 (1943).

consideration of both: (1) the costs, or relative cost differences, of supplying each class of customers or service; and (2) the value of the service or, in other words, the demand characteristics of the different segments of the total market served by the utility. Thus, in public utility pricing, as in the pricing of other goods and services, both the market demand and cost of supply factors must be recognized to the extent feasible. A useful statement on the objectives of utility pricing policy, and the factors requiring consideration in setting rates, has been set forth by an authoritative rate-study group, as follows:

> Rates should be designed to hold existing business, promote new business, be just and equitable to the customer, promote good public relations and provide a fair return to the utility thereby making it possible to attract new capital to meet the industry's growth. No formula can be designed to attain these ends, but two basic factors must be constantly kept in mind—cost of service and value of service.[3]

However, analyses of costs and studies of market-demand characteristics can take one just so far; ultimately, the setting of rates requires the exercise of experienced judgment. Rate making is an art and not an exact science. It is for this reason that most commissions, once they have fixed the over-all revenue requirement, generally give substantial weight to managerial judgment in reviewing proposed schedules of rates. This approach recognizes that the management knows the market through experience and is responsible for merchandising the utility's services. The following quotation, from a 1958 decision of the Massachusetts Department of Public Utilities, illustrates the general approach of most commissions toward the function of management in rate making:

> Normally this department leaves to the discretion of management the task of establishing the rate structure, as distinct from the rate level unless it determines that an unreasonable discrimination exists. The theory behind this position is clear. On the question of what a utility is entitled to earn, its interests and the interests of customers are divergent. . . . Once this issue has been determined, however, this divergence of interests is no longer necessarily present.
>
> . . . Through its intimate knowledge of its own business, a company can be reasonably expected to establish a rate structure which will achieve the level of earnings to which it is entitled, and promote a steady growth of the type which will in the long run benefit its customers.
>
> An additional reason is that rate making is still far from being a science. Although cost studies may be useful, and in some instances necessary, they contain no magic formula. . . .[4]

C. The Range of Rates. Public utility rates must fall within a prescribed range or zone of reasonableness. The upper limit is a rate which reflects the value of the service to the representative consumer; the lower limit is a rate which is at least compensatory to the utility. A compensatory rate both covers the out-of-pocket cost associated with the service and makes some contribution to the fixed costs of the enterprise. Where the actual rate falls within this range is a matter of experienced judgment in the light of the general objectives and the guiding principle discussed above.

Out-of-pocket costs, for the purpose of considering the minimum compensatory rate, consist of the variable costs which are incurred in providing a particular service; that is, they are the costs which could have been avoided by not selling the service. For a natural gas pipeline, for example, the out-of-pocket costs would be the cost of the gas supply

---

[3] American Gas Association, *Report of Rate Committee* (New York: American Gas Association, 1953), p. 3.

[4] *Re Boston Edison Company,* 24 PUR 3d 153, 159 (1958).

provided in connection with a particular service plus the variable transportation expense incurred in its transmission. The fixed or constant costs of the utility are those which continue to be incurred regardless of the volume of service supplied the public. Such costs are made up of certain maintenance and other operating expenses which, in whole or in part, do not vary with changes in the quantity of service sold, as well as taxes, insurance, depreciation, amortization, and return on investment. Thus, the lower limit of the possible range within which a rate may fall—the sum of out-of-pocket costs plus some contribution to fixed costs—is an indication of the minimum price that will make it worthwhile for the utility to take on a class of service, bearing in mind that the utility's obligation to serve does not extend to customers who will not or cannot pay reasonable charges. Sales of service at this price level, it should be emphasized, are unquestionably desirable, if the utility has idle capacity at the time of the additional demand. The reason is that whatever revenue such sales contribute toward the fixed costs of the enterprise automatically reduces the fixed costs that other customers must bear.

It is important to take into account the fact that this traditional minimum level in the permissible range of rates may prove to be uneconomically low, if in all cases it is confined to out-of-pocket costs plus some contribution to fixed costs. Where service is priced at or about this level, the effect may be to attract a volume of additional business so large as to require an expansion of plant and equipment. If that is likely to occur, the economic minimum rate would be one which also reflects the incremental fixed costs associated with the additional plant.

The upper limit of the range of rates is a price which reflects the value of the service, that is, the conditions of demand which characterize each segment in the total market of a utility. The maximum price possible, by reference to value of service, is a price beyond which a satisfactory volume of the service cannot be sold. The term *value of service,* while assisting in describing the upper limit of utility rates, also is used in another important sense. In this latter respect, the term *value of service,* when used in connection with the setting of utility rates, means giving due weight to conditions of demand under circumstances where the allowable revenue total has been determined previously. Used in this sense, "value of service" reflects such factors as the valuation of money by consumers in respective classes, as well as the necessity, usefulness, profitability, or convenience of the utility service; it also is affected by the price elasticity of the demand in various sectors of the market. One of the major influences upon demand elasticity that is particularly important here is the price and availability of substitutes. The Supreme Court recognized value of service as the upper limit of rates in *Smyth* v. *Ames,* when it held that ". . . what the public is entitled to demand is that no more be exacted from it for the use of a public highway than the services rendered by it are reasonably worth."[5] The term "public highway" refers in this case to a railroad, which, of course, is also a public utility.

The Wisconsin commission, in spelling out the range within which a gas rate for space-heating service would fall, stated as follows:

> It is clear that the rates . . . permit a recovery not only of the incremental expense incident to respondents' space-heating services, but also some portion of the remainder of the total operating and other expenses comprising the total costs of fur-

[5] *Smyth* v. *Ames,* 169 U.S. 466, 547 (1898).

nishing respondents' services in their entirety. We think this is not only proper, but that the rates for such . . . service should be designed to recover as much of such remainder of costs as is possible within the limitation of the value of such services.

Just as the incremental cost of the space-heating services of respondents serves as a criterion (although not the measure) of the minimum level of rates that could lawfully be prescribed for such services, so their value is both a criterion and a measure of the maximum level of rates that can reasonably be prescribed for the same services. . . .[6]

Similarly, the New York commission, in ruling on the question of proper telephone rates, stated:

. . . In making rates, consideration must be given to both the cost of the service and its value. . . . As a measure of rates, value of service alone is an elusive standard and not satisfactory as a yardstick. . . . Neither is cost of the service a proper measure standing alone. . . .[7]

Cost analysis and value of service, respectively, are discussed in the following sections. It is necessary to emphasize that neither of these guides to the establishment of specific rates is sufficiently precise to preclude the exercise of experienced judgment.

D. *Cost Analysis.* Various types of cost analysis serve usefully in utility management and regulation. Some studies of costs can be used as a guide to the design of public utility rates. Cost analyses of this kind provide a measure of the average unit cost of supplying service to the various classes of customers. These cost studies ordinarily show that unit costs are different for each class of customer or service. This is one basis for differential pricing. In order to make an analysis of costs, it is necessary to apportion or to allocate property and expenses among the respective customer classes. Either a company-wide basis or some territorial subdivision may be used for the calculation of costs. Such studies can also be made on a more specialized basis in order to provide cost information relating to specific types of appliances or equipment. Another purpose of cost analysis is to find a measure of the incremental costs, or additional costs, of serving additional customers or providing additional service to present customers.

Analyzing costs is not the same thing as making rates; the two processes are quite distinct. First, cost analysis is concerned solely with the supply side of the market for public utility services, while rate making (or any other pricing practice) requires consideration of both the supply and the demand factors. Second, an analysis of public utility costs cannot produce definitive results. This follows from the fact that cost analyses unavoidably involve the difficult problem of allocating to each class of service a share of the joint costs that are incurred in the production of all classes of service.

Public utilities operate under joint-cost conditions because a substantial proportion of their facilities are used jointly to supply service to most or all classes of service. Under such circumstances, only a part of total cost can be separated by identification with particular classes of customers or services. There remains, however, a sizable proportion of total cost that is associated with all or much of the service supplied and which is not identifiable with any specific service or customer class. Broadly speaking, these are the joint costs.

In a conventional analysis of public utility costs, the most difficult problem encountered is the allocation of joint costs to customer classes or classes of service. This problem has no universal

---

[6] *Re Milwaukee Gas Light Co. et al.*, 51 PUR (NS) 299, 310 (1943).

[7] *Re New York Telephone Co.*, PUR 1930C, 325, 367.

or even generally satisfactory solution, because joint costs are incapable of "accurate" or "certain" allocation among the respective types of service. This follows from the fact that the allocation of joint costs among the different services produced by a public utility is dependent upon methods or formulas, each containing elements of arbitrariness which can produce widely varying average unit costs. Consequently, the results obtained from an analysis of costs are materially affected by the particular allocation methods employed. For this reason, there is a quality of uncertainty in any cost analysis. Thus, there is no "royal road" leading from costs to rates.

For the benefit of the beginning reader, it is necessary to make clear at this point that analyses of costs for rate-design purposes are rarely presented as evidence in public utility rate cases. Rather, their principal function is as an aid to managerial decision-making on the design of proposed rate schedules that are submitted to the commission for review. However, if a substantial rate-design issue arises in a public utility rate case, cost analyses may be presented in evidence. When this occurs, the results may be less than satisfactory because of the wide range of average costs that are obtainable through the use of different costing techniques. Thus, for example, the California Public Utilities Commission in a 1960 decision stated:

> A major issue in this proceeding is the spread of rates among the various classes of customers. . . . In this connection five cost-allocation studies reflecting various hypotheses and philosophies were introduced. . . . The results of these studies vary widely.[8]

The foregoing general discussion permits identification of the principal, specific problem area in joint-cost allocation. In an analysis of costs, the major difficulty arises in the allocation of a cost category designated the "demand costs" or "capacity costs." This cost category includes all or much of the fixed costs associated with plant and equipment, such as return-on-rate base, depreciation and amortization, the principal taxes, and certain non-variable operating and maintenance expenses. The demand or capacity costs are largely joint costs. Their allocation to customer classes has been a subject of study since before the turn of the twentieth century. Many capable analysts have contributed to a sizable international literature on the subject. In all, at least twenty methods or formulas have been developed for the allocation of demand costs to customer classes. None has emerged as paramount, although some have more merit than others. Some of the principal allocation methods will be discussed in connection with electric rates. The remainder of the present section presents a survey of authoritative views on the general matter of joint-cost allocation.

Professor Glaeser has stated that ". . . joint costs cannot be traced to specific joint products. . . ."[9] An expert cost accountant has written that, under joint cost conditions, separate true costs cannot be found for the respective joint products. He adds that, although total joint costs for all joint products can be compiled, this total cannot be divided accurately among the several products.[10] The Cost Finding Section of the Interstate Commerce Commission has concluded that: "The expenses for the joint operation are obviously not capable of separation between the jointly produced

[8] *Re Southern California Gas Co.*, 35 PUR 3d 300, 318 (1960).

[9] Martin G. Glaeser, *Public Utilities in American Capitalism* (New York: The Macmillan Company, 1957), p. 424.

[10] Charles F. Schlatter, *Cost Accounting* (New York: John Wiley & Sons, Inc., 1948), p. 652.

products on a cost-of-service basis."[11] In this same respect, former Chairman Maltbie of the New York commission once observed that pricing, whether for utilities or for competitive business, is never a mathematical application of a theoretical principle.[12] The Federal Power Commission has pointed out that "When an unrealistic result is reached, the formulae for allocations must be changed in order to bring about a reasonable result. The allocation methods then become a means of supporting a result already arrived at, rather than a means of arriving at a result which was previously unknown."[13]

The problem of allocating joint costs also has been recognized by the Supreme Court in many cases. In 1919, for example, the Court considered a question of joint-cost allocation between railroad passenger and freight services. Justice Brandeis, speaking for the Court, stated:

> What method should be pursued in making such division is a very difficult problem to which railroad accountants, the Interstate Commerce Commission and State Railroad Commissions have for years given serious attention. [Footnote omitted] Despite such patient study and the exhibition of great ingenuity no wholly satisfactory method has yet been devised. The variables due to local conditions are numerous; and experience teaches us that it is much easier to reject [allocation] formulas presented as being misleading than to find one apparently adequate. The science of railroad accounting is in this respect in process of development; and it may be long before a formula is devised which can be accepted as satisfactory.[14]

A quarter of a century later, the Supreme Court in an opinion by Justice Douglas apparently found little change, for it stated that the "Allocation of costs is not a matter for the slide-rule. It involves judgment of a myriad of facts. It has no claim to an exact science. . . ."[15]

E. *Value of Service.* The term *value of service,* as used in this discussion of public utility pricing principles, refers to the conditions of demand which characterize the different segments of a utility's market. Whereas cost analyses look to conditions on the supply side of the market, consideration of value-of-service factors gives recognition to the demand side of market. Value of service is not subject to precise measurement. The market-demand studies that well-managed utilities regularly undertake are an important aid in this respect. Ultimately, however, experienced judgment on the part of those in management who know the market best must be brought to bear in any ascertainment of the conditions of demand.

Public utility services are produced because they are valuable. However, utility services are not valuable because companies incur costs in producing them. Rather, their value derives primarily from the fact that they can satisfy consumers' needs and wants so effectively that consumers are willing to pay a price to acquire them. It is this want-satisfy-

[11] Interstate Commerce Commission, Cost Finding Section of the Bureau of Accounts, Cost Finding and Valuation, "Explanation of the Development of Motor Carrier Costs With Statement As to Their Meaning and Significance," Statement No. 4–59, 1959, p. 5. See also: Irston R. Barnes, *Economics of Public Utility Regulation* (New York: Appleton-Century-Crofts, Inc., 1947), p. 325; Emery Troxel, *Economics of Public Utilities* (New York: Holt, Rinehart & Winston, Inc., 1947), p. 576.

[12] *Re Rates and Rate Structures of Corporations Supplying Electricity in City of New York and Suburban Territory,* PUR 1931C, 337, 347.

[13] *Re Phillips Petroleum Co.,* 24 FPC 537, 544 (1960).

[14] *Groesbeck* v. *Duluth, S.S. & A. Ry. Co.,* 250 U.S. 607, 614–615 (1919).

[15] *Colorado Interstate Gas Co.* v. *Federal Power Commission,* 324 U.S. 581, 589 (1945).

ing or value-giving characteristic which provides economic justification for incurring the costs of supply. Accordingly, in the matter of pricing utility services, it would be erroneous to look solely to the results of cost analyses, for they cannot provide useful information with respect to the value of such services or what the public may be willing to pay for them.

It is a generally accepted principle of public utility rate making that differences in the conditions of demand, as among the respective customer classes, indicate that each class has a different capacity and willingness to bear charges. Accordingly, with reference to value-of-service factors, rates are made so as to distribute the approved company-wide cost of service in relation to the capacity and willingness of the customer groups to bear such costs. More specifically, each class bears the identifiable costs that can be associated with its service plus the portion of the joint costs that its demand characteristics indicate it can bear, while continuing to consume a satisfactory quantity of service. In addition, the operation of the value-of-service principle in utility rate making extends to the earning of different rates of profit from different classes of customers or service, within the framework of the over-all return approved under regulation.

The purposes of this approach to the differential pricing of utility services are: (1) to enable the utility to sell a volume of service which will maximize the utilization of its plant and equipment; (2) to achieve thereby the lowest average unit costs of operation; and (3) to afford the utility the best possible opportunity of earning the allowed rate of return. As discussed in Chapter 2, every utility experiences periodic peaks and valleys in the amount of service demanded. Sufficient plant must be installed to supply the annual peak demand.[16] The charging of differential rates, giving proper weight to the conditions of demand in each segment of the market, is intended to increase the utilization of otherwise idle plant capacity and, in some cases, to affect the timing of that utilization. One authority, Dr. G. P. Watkins, has written, "The economic foundation for differential rates is the desirability of more fully utilizing a fixed-capital investment through the granting of specially low rates to business that can only be so obtained."[17] Professor Glaeser has pointed out the experimental nature of public utility pricing policy, under which rates equal the costs identified with each class of service plus the differential portion of joint costs that relative demand conditions allow to be charged. He has noted that market responses to prices thus set are watched carefully, and has concluded that the initiative in pricing should rest with utility management because of its close contact with its market.[18]

---

[16] Although the size of plant generally is determined by the peak annual demand on the utility system, it is also important to note that pricing policy is influential in determining the magnitude of the annual peak. Thus, an interrelationship exists wherein: (a) peak demand determines plant size and, therefore, to a considerable extent, the total of plant-related costs whose recovery from sales revenues is an important consideration in pricing policy; while (b) at the same time, pricing policy directly influences the size of the annual peak, particularly where industrial customers are concerned. This suggests that public utility pricing policy involves, in effect, the simultaneous solution of questions relating both to plant size and to price level for different classes of service. Regulation does not determine these questions, at least not directly; in general these are matters of managerial responsibility ultimately subject to commission review.

[17] G. P. Watkins, *Electrical Rates* (New York: D. Van Nostrand Company, 1921), p. 191.

[18] Martin G. Glaeser, *Outlines of Public Utility Economics* (New York: The Macmillan Company, 1927), pp. 625–627; *Public Utilities in American Capitalism* (New York: The Macmillan Company, 1957), p. 411.

In a study by the Cost Finding Section of the Interstate Commerce Commission, it was stated:

> It is this buyer's demand which ultimately determines the apportionment of the constant and joint costs, i.e., the distribution of the "burden." Stated differently, the distribution of the constant and joint costs must take into consideration the value of the service or conditions of demand. An evaluation of these non-cost factors is essential whenever constant or joint costs are present. . . .
>
> When brought within proper bounds the "value of the service" (i.e., conditions of demand) plays as indispensable function in the apportionment of constant and joint costs. It is not just a substitute for inadequate cost data. It means, in effect, taking advantage of conditions of expansible traffic volume where the traffic will respond to reductions, the results being the encouragement of the maximum utilization of the carrier's plant and equipment, the distribution of the constant costs over a larger volume of tonnage, and the attainment of a lower level of rates on all traffic . . . than could be realized if differences in rates were limited solely to the differences in the cost of service. [Footnotes omitted.][19]

A consistent view has been expressed by Dr. John Bauer, who maintains that rates should be based upon costs—but that the joint costs should be allocated on the basis of the relative value of service of each customer class. He identifies the promotion of consumption as the primary objective of joint-cost allocation and the pricing of utility services. To this end, he indicates that the rates charged those customer classes whose demand is relatively inelastic should include a greater proportion of joint costs than the rates charged customer classes characterized by a comparatively elastic demand. The extent of such justifiable differentiation, he writes, is determined by the effects upon the volume of service consumed. Throughout, Dr. Bauer emphasizes the importance of the variation of rates in relation to the value of service as a means by which: (a) the utility may earn its revenue requirement; and (b) constructive utilization of service may be promoted.[20] Dr. G. P. Watkins, writing in 1921, also looks to an unequal "loading" of the joint costs among the respective customer classes as a means of increasing the volume of business transacted.[21]

The leading Supreme Court decision on this subject is *Northern Pacific Railway Company* v. *North Dakota*.[22] There, in an opinion by Justice Hughes, it was held that: (a) rates may be made for individual classes of service; (b) uniform rates are not required for all classes of service; (c) the same percentage of profit need not be secured from each type of service; and (d) value of service is to be included among the factors considered in setting rates. In a later Supreme Court decision, differential pricing involving differing rates of profit on respective classes of service was again approved. There, the Court held that the public utility involved had "no constitutional right to the same rate or percentage of return on all of its business."[23] H. E. Eisenmenger has noted that differential pricing, with due regard to value of service, results in the utility earning different rates of profit for sales to different classes of customers.[24]

Thus, rates for public utilities are designed with reference to cost of service and value of service factors. Costing is not to be confused with pricing, be-

---

[19] Interstate Commerce Commission, *op. cit.*, pp. 14, 16.

[20] John Bauer, *Transforming Public Utility Regulation* (New York: Harper & Row, 1950), pp. 280–281.

[21] Watkins, *op. cit.*, p. 105.

[22] *Northern Pacific Railway Company* v. *North Dakota,* 236 U.S. 585, 598–599 (1915).

[23] *Banton* v. *Belt Line Railway,* 268 U.S. 413, 421 (1925).

[24] H. E. Eisenmenger, *Central Station Rates in Theory and Practice* (Chicago: Frederick J. Drake & Co., 1921), pp. 54–55, 80–81.

cause costing serves only to analyze the conditions of supply. Pricing also requires proper consideration of demand conditions, for utility service must be sold and in quantities sufficient to achieve the economies of decreasing costs to the greatest extent possible. As one state commission has observed:

> . . . Cost is only one of the many elements to be considered in determining the appropriateness of particular rates. The value of service is a matter of great importance in the establishment of individual rates.[25]

F. *Rate Schedules and Legal Requirements.* A utility's rates are available for public inspection at all times in a tariff, which is a compilation of the schedules of rates applicable to each of the services supplied the public and the rules and regulations governing other aspects of the sale of service. Each rate schedule states the nature of the service and the class of customers to which it applies. In addition, the rate schedule sets out the availability of the service, the territory served, the minimum charge, the measurement of the service provided, and how the periodic charges to consumers are to be computed.

In most jurisdictions, the applicable statutes provide that all rates shall be "just and reasonable" and that utilities may not discriminate unreasonably in rates or conditions of service among individuals, communities, or classes of service.

Utilities may not charge any rates other than those which have been published and made effective under provisions of the governing statute and the regulations prescribed by the commission. Ordinarily, utilities may not change their rates without giving 30 days' notice. After a utility files an application for authority to change its rates, the commission may: (1) permit the proposed changes to go into effect in less than 30 days in special circumstances or at the end of the 30-day notice period; or (2) as is more likely, "suspend" the proposed rates, that is, delay their going into effect for a number of months while it either studies the proposal or holds a hearing in a formal rate case so that a decision may be reached. If a decision is not reached by the end of the period of suspension, the proposed rates may be allowed to go into effect subject to possible refund of any amounts later found not justified. (This matter is discussed further, in Chapter 13, in connection with the powers of the state commissions in the area of rates.) Finally, it should be pointed out that rate-change proceedings may be initiated by interested parties other than utilities. Thus, governmental units, such as cities, as well as consumer groups and the commissions themselves, may institute proceedings to inquire into the reasonableness of a public utility's rates.

Most commissions have jurisdiction over public utility rate schedules. The procedure for putting new rate schedules into effect, after a commission decision has determined the revenue requirement and cost of service, runs more or less as follows: (1) The commission orders the utility to file proposed schedules of rates, which are intended to produce revenues equal to the approved cost of service. (2) After filing, the proposed rate schedules are reviewed by the staff of the commission and may be made public for a period of time so that interested parties may examine them. (3) If there is no opposition, the commission may order the proposed rates into effect; however, the commission's staff or consumer groups may have questions or objections. (4) If the latter is the case, there may be informal negotiation, or the matter may be set for formal hearing, or both. (5) The commission thereafter

---

[25] *Re Virginia Electric & Power Co.*, 9 PUR 3d 225, 239 (1953).

issues its decision and orders the rates it approves into effect.

During a period of changing prices, the costs of providing public utility services also change. In many cases, where electric utilities and gas distribution utilities are involved, the changed cost of service is due to causes which are measurable and not controversial. In such cases, the time, expense, and strain upon public relations which may accompany a formal rate case can be avoided if the utility's rate schedules provide for adjustments in the rates paid by the public which more or less automatically reflect changes in specific costs incurred by the utility and which are beyond its control.

For some two decades the general price level has been rising. Electric and gas distribution utilities have been affected, in part, through increases in the fuel costs of electric utilities and increases in the gas-purchase costs of the natural gas distributors, along with increases in materials costs to those distributors which manufacture gas. Both gas and electric utilities have experienced increased taxes. Cost increases of this kind can be calculated with some definiteness and are beyond dispute as a proper component of a utility's cost of service. Accordingly, some rate schedules of gas and electric utilities include rate-adjustment clauses which change the rates charged consumers up or down as certain specific costs to the utilities vary with time. In the case of natural gas distributors, the cost of purchased gas is about 50 per cent or more of total operating revenue deductions. An increase in this important component of total cost, unless promptly recovered in increased rates, could have the effect of reducing the utility's earned rate of return below that allowed. Although rate-adjustment clauses are intended only to offset cost changes, and not to change the rate of return, their effect is to protect the authorized rate of return during a period of cost increases.

As of the beginning of 1956, 179 gas distributors had rate-adjustment clauses in effect; this was about 20 per cent of the 860 gas distributors listed in the American Gas Association Rate Service. The most frequently found rate-adjustment clauses among electric utilities are those linked to fuel costs. Among gas distributors selling natural gas, the principal form of rate adjustment is related to the cost of purchased gas. For utilities distributing liquefied petroleum gas, manufactured gas, or mixed gas, the rate adjustment most often depends upon changes in the price of the fuel used for producing gas. Rate-adjustment clauses reflecting tax changes are less frequently found. A few adjustment clauses cover all operating expenses.

Some adjustment clauses are automatic, while others require a presentation of data in support of a proposed rate adjustment. However, this involves far less than a formal rate case. The South Jersey Gas Company general service rate schedule, for example, provides that the company's rate shall be either increased or decreased .01 cents per therm (a measurement of the heat content of the gas delivered) for each .081 cents per Mcf of increase or decrease in the cost of purchased gas from a base rate of 32.51 cents per Mcf. The adjustment is not automatic and must be supported with extensive financial information accompanying the rate-change filing. Full-fledged rate cases have not resulted from such filings, although hearings have been held. The adjustments have been allowed. In conclusion, it may be noted that the operation of rate-adjustment clauses is intended to offset essentially short-run cost changes; longer-term factors affecting costs—such as technological advances or changing market structures—would ordinarily be the subject of formal rate proceedings.

G. Theoretical Economics and Public Utility Rates. The present development of an economic theory of public utility rates leaves much to be desired. This incomplete state of the art is regrettable but perhaps inevitable. It is due in part to the fact that engineers, far more than economists, have concerned themselves with the problems in this area. According to Professor James C. Bonbright, a critic of present rate-making practices, the problems encountered in rate making are: (1) complexity due to the mass of technical detail which must be considered in designing and administering rate schedules; (2) "ignorance" on the part of rate makers of demand and supply functions; and (3) the need to consider "numerous conflicting standards of fairness and functional efficiency. . . ." He views the last of these as the cause of the "most serious theoretical difficulty."[26]

The economist dealing with utility rate problems at the theoretical level must, of necessity, make *normative* judgments—decisions on what is "fair" or "unfair," "reasonable" or "unreasonable," "good" or "bad." Economists' analytical tools are not designed to make these value judgments by themselves, although an economist working in any applied field where policy matters are concerned must, of course, have some system of values and standards to provide a framework in which to use the tools he is trained to use. In this respect, Professor Bonbright lists three primary objectives of a sound rate structure as: (1) a fair return and adequate revenues to operate the firm; (2) a fair distribution of costs among consumers; and (3) rates that discourage waste and promote all justified uses of public utility services.[27] While theoretical economic analysis can be highly useful in assisting policy makers who must decide what is "fair" or "justified," it cannot do so alone because ethical, strategic, and public policy considerations also bear upon such decisions. This suggests that the application of theoretical economics to public utility rate making, while useful, also has important limitations.

A number of economic theorists have thought that current rate-making practices create unnecessary social costs or wastes. The problems seen to exist in this area have disturbed academic economists, interested in public utility rate making, but thus far there has been little or no discussion on the subject of a proper rationale for rate making between this group and the policy makers who design rates. Economists in this group have indicated considerable interest in "marginal cost pricing." Under this approach, the utility would expand its output until the marginal cost (incremental variable cost) of the last unit of service offered was equal to the demand price that would be paid for it. All of the output would then to sold at this marginal cost price. It is recognized that, under decreasing-cost conditions, this type of pricing very likely would result in a deficit, which would have to be offset by a subsidy financed through taxation of utility service or the general public. Proponents of marginal cost pricing justify it on the ground that the benefit to society from the larger output would exceed the cost of the subsidy.[28] While it is true that

[26] James C. Bonbright, *Principles of Public Utility Rates* (New York: Columbia University Press, 1961), pp. 288–289.

[27] *Ibid.*, p. 292.

[28] This proposal was set forth by Professor Harold Hotelling in "The General Welfare in Relation to Problems of Taxation and of Railway and Utility Rates," 6 *Econometrica* 242–269 (1942). Since that time there has been a great deal written on this problem. See W. S. Vickery, "Some Implications of Marginal Cost Pricing for Public Utilities," 45 *American Economic Review, Proceedings* 605–620 (1955); *ibid.*, "Some Objections to Marginal Cost Pricing," 56 *Journal of Political Economy* 218

optimum resource allocation theoretically can be achieved with marginal-cost pricing, the income-distribution effects caused by the subsidy and tax aspects are not neutral. Thus, it is impossible to solve the problem raised by the application of theoretical economics to utility rates without a greater amount of information on what norms society has and what form and shape consumption and production functions take.[29]

Although American and British utilities have not indicated an interest in applying marginal-cost pricing principles to rate structures, utilities in some continental European nations (notably France) have experienced some success in specialized applications.[30] This, however, occurred in publicly owned enterprises where profit and loss considerations are not necessarily paramount.

The theoretical economist asks the question—can public utility rates be so designed that they cover costs including a fair return, are not unduly discriminatory among classes of customers and within classes of customers, and achieve "optimum" utilization of resources? The pragmatic rate maker can answer that these factors are given consideration, and that the final result comes as close as is practical to achieving these goals.

2. ELECTRIC UTILITY RATES

Rate making in the electric utility industry has been the subject of much study since practically the beginning of the industry. As a result, the pricing principles and practices developed in this industry have been adopted in the pricing of most other public utility services in greater or lesser degree, depending upon their respective characteristics and markets. Much of the following discussion of electric rates is applicable to the pricing of other public utility services, particularly those of the gas distribution utilities and the natural gas pipelines, which are also discussed in this chapter.

A. Development and Characteristics of Electric Utilities. Electricity was first generated in 1831 by a dynamo developed by Michael Faraday, but the electric light and power industry did not begin until the incandescent light bulb was perfected by Thomas A. Edison in 1879. The great inventor participated in the organization in 1880 of the Edison Electric Illuminating Co. of New York, which had an initial capital of one million dollars. The company's pioneer Pearl Street station began operation in 1882. Other electric generating stations were established rapidly in the United States. By 1902 the industry had total invested capital of about $500 million and annual gross revenues of over $85 million. In 1959 the total investment in stockholder-owned electric utilities was about $47 billion, and gross revenues exceeded $11.1 billion. The annual energy generated by electric utilities has in-

---

(1948); R. H. Coarse, "The Marginal Cost Controversy," 13 N. S. *Economica* 169 (1946); B. P. Beckwith, *Marginal-Cost, Price Output Control* (New York: Columbia University Press, 1955); R. W. Harbeson, "A Critique of Marginal Cost Pricing," 31 *Land Economics* 54 (1955). See also Bonbright, *op. cit.*, Chapter 20, for a discussion of the application of marginal cost pricing.

[29] This area of welfare economics has received little attention in connection with public utility problems except in the area of cost-benefit comparisons in multipurpose hydroelectric projects. For a survey and discussion see C. J. Oort, *Decreasing Costs as a Problem of Welfare Economics* (Amsterdam: Drukkerij Holland N. V., 1959). Note, too, the extensive bibliography on this topic.

[30] Organization for European Economic Co-Operation, *The Theory of Marginal Cost and Electricity Rates* (Paris: 1958). For a comprehensive theoretical discussion, see Ralph Kirby Davidson, *Price Discrimination in Selling Gas and Electricity* (Baltimore: The Johns Hopkins Press, 1955).

creased from about 2.5 billion kilowatt-hours in 1902 to over 683 billion in 1960. Total customers increased from about 600,000 in 1902 to about 59 million in 1960.

Initially, electric utilities were quite small, and their service areas were confined to a relatively few city blocks surrounding the generating station. The Edison plants distributed direct current. The distribution radius had to be small because of the power losses that occurred when transmission over a greater distance was attempted. George Westinghouse developed a competitive alternative to direct current. This was alternating current, which is in general use today. Alternating current permitted solution of the problem of excessive power losses in transmission. This was due to the invention of the transformer in 1898, which works only with alternating current. The transformer enabled the generated energy to be stepped up to a relatively high voltage for transmission purposes and then transformed to low voltage for distribution and customer use. Transmission at high voltage results in low power losses. Accordingly, the use of alternating current, high transmission voltage, and transformers enabled a particular generating station to serve a larger area more economically than was possible with lower-voltage direct current. Other major technical problems were solved before the turn of the century. However, technological advancement by electric utilities has never ended. Thus, the consumption of coal to produce steam for electric generation has steadily decreased on a per-kilowatt-hour basis as a result of increasing technological efficiency. While an average of about 6.7 pounds of coal was required per kilowatt-hour generated in 1902, modern plants require less than one pound. In 1960 the national average was 0.88 pound per kilowatt-hour.

With advancing technology, small electric systems were combined into larger and more economical units. Before World War I and then into the 1920's, the industry experienced a high tide in the consolidation of operating properties. Under the direction of major public utility holding companies, operating properties were physically interconnected and consolidated, and large numbers of them were integrated financially as well. The results were desirable from the standpoint of promoting an economical supply of electricity produced under conditions of near-maximum engineering efficiency. On the other hand, the holding companies were often associated with financial abuses, which ultimately gave rise to regulatory legislation designed to protect consumers and investors alike. The net effect of the holding company legislation, it is broadly agreed, has been beneficial. This topic will be covered separately in a later chapter.

Because of the economies arising from consolidated and interconnected systems, the combination of markets with diverse demand characteristics, and technological advancement, electric rates have declined through time despite a sharply rising general price level and increasing costs in the economy as a whole. For example, as of January 1, 1960 the weighted-average bill for 500 kilowatt-hours of residential service per month was \$10.62, whereas the same service had cost \$13.87 in 1935. This comparison is all the more impressive in light of the doubling of the general price level during this period. However, inflation belatedly has made an impact on electric rates. After reaching an historic low average level following World War II, average electric bills have begun to edge upward slightly, while remaining substantially below the levels of previous years. For example, the average residential bill for 500 kilowatt-hours, quoted above as \$10.62 in 1960, was recorded at an all-time low of $10.02 in 1951. The experience shown in data covering the average bills for commercial and industrial electric service is closely similar. While in 1931 the average residential consumer used 583 kilowatt-hours at an average rate of 5.78 cents per kilowatt-hour, the average consumption in 1960 was 3,827 kilowatt-hours and the average rate was 2.47 cents per kilowatt-hour.

In 1960 electric utilities in the United States had a total year-end capacity of 168.6 million kilowatts. In 1920, by comparison, when the industry was beginning its greatest expansion, total capacity was 12.7 million kilowatts. The Federal Power Commission estimates that electric utilities will require 329 million kilowatts of capacity in 1970 and 597 million kilowatts in 1980.[31] Returning to the 1960 situation, it should be noted that, in addition to public utility electric generating capacity, industrial establishments owned 18.2 million kilowatts of installed capacity.

Of the 168.6 million kilowatts of utility capacity in 1960, the principle method of generating electricity was steam power (133.3 million kilowatts). Although gas and oil also are used for fuel to manufacture steam for this purpose, the principal fuel is coal. In addition, the total of installed utility capacity included 32.4 million kilowatts of hydroelectric capacity, which generates electricity by releasing the power of falling water previously accumulated in reservoirs behind dams. In addition, there were 2.9 million kilowatts of generating capacity which employed internal-combustion engines, principally diesel units.

Viewing the industry from the standpoint of ownership of generating plant capacity, two generalizations may be made: (1) the industry is substantially owned by private investors; and (2) there is also a diverse range of government ownership arrangements. In 1960, for example, investor-owned electric utilities had about 76.5 per cent of total generating capacity, and federal agencies held about 13 per cent of the total. The remainder was distributed among municipally owned utilities (about 7 per cent), state and public utility district ownership (about 2.5 per cent), and cooperatives (less than one per cent).[32]

Data for 1960 on the consumption of electric energy by class of customers showed that industrial service provided the largest market for electricity, but that sales to residential customers were the principal source of revenue to the electric utility industry. For example, residential sales of electric energy accounted for 27.8 per cent of the total sales volume and 40.7 per cent of the electric utility industry's total revenues. Industrial customers, on the other hand, purchased 49.8 per cent of the total energy output and provided electric utilities with 28.4 per cent of their revenues. Commercial sales accounted for 16.6 per cent of the energy total and 24.3 per cent of electric utility revenues. Sales to other classes of customers were comparatively small.[33]

These figures reflect the comparatively low average rate charged for the large volume and, in effect, wholesale purchases by industrial consumers, as well as the relatively higher average rate charged the small-quantity residential customer. The latter, by comparison, are served by electric utilities in a true retail sense, which causes the incurrence of higher unit costs. As a class, residential customers also place a higher value on the service than do industrial customers. Not to be overlooked in this respect is the fact that the largest industrial customers can and do place a definite

---

[31] Federal Power Commission, Release No. 11829, January 30, 1962.

[32] *Moody's Public Utility Manual,* 1961 Edition, p. a12.

[33] *Ibid.,* p. a13.

ceiling on the value of electric service purchased from utilities, which is measurable by the alternative cost of generating their own electric supplies.

Turning next to the characteristics of electric utilities, it is apparent from their slow rates of annual capital turnover that they require a comparatively greater investment in fixed assets per dollar of revenue per year than do commercial and industrial corporations. This necessarily high investment arises from the fact that electric and other utilities primarily provide services, or services in combination with a commodity, which are predominantly the product of capital equipment. The high capital-investment requirement is also due to the fact that public utilities must provide facilities to transport and deliver their services to whatever sites customers choose. Electric utilities supply a predominantly retail market made up of numerous small customers, each of which must be connected to a source of supply. This is in contrast, for example, to natural gas pipelines, which are wholesalers of gas for retail sale by local gas distributors.

The chief result of the comparatively great investment in fixed capital assets is the fact that the total fixed costs associated with such investment are relatively greater in the utility industries than in others. These fixed costs, comprising return, taxes on income and property, depreciation expense, and some of the expenses of operation and maintenance, often exceed one-half the total company cost of service in the electric and other utility industries. One of the economic effects of the inflationary trend in prices since World War II has been to bring about, temporarily, some degree of understatement of the proportion of fixed costs to the total annual cost of service for some utilities. This has occurred because the effect of higher prices does not appear at once in fixed costs, which reflect in part the lower price levels of past time periods. A study of electric utilities in England showed that, for the period 1935–1948, fixed costs declined as a proportion of total cost from seven-eighths to less than two-thirds.[34] However, with the addition of new equipment at postwar prices and the retirement of older equipment, it was expected that something like the earlier relation of fixed costs to total costs would again prevail in the future.

The total fixed costs, other things equal, are independent of the volume of service provided. That is, their total is a function of the size of total plant and does not fluctuate in accord with variations in output from a plant of a given size. This characteristic permits utilities other than telephone companies (Chapter 11) to achieve decreasing average unit costs as total plant capacity becomes more fully used.

As with other utilities, an important influence in electric utility rate making is the fact that total fixed plant generally is used in no more than 55 per cent of the total hours available in a year. The presence of substantial amounts of unused capacity at some time is not difficult to explain: (1) Customer demands for service must be supplied instantaneously. (2) The pattern of hourly, daily, seasonal, or annual use of facilities, called the *load curve,* is characterized by considerable variation taking the form of peaks and valleys. (3) Electricity, like some other public utility services, cannot be stored or produced in anticipation of demand. (4) Accordingly, electric utilities must invest in sufficient plant capacity to serve the peak or maximum annual demand, and must also provide reserve capacity to guarantee continuous service in the

---

[34] D. J. Bolton, *Electrical Engineering Economics, Volume 2: Costs and Tariffs in Electricity Supply,* 2nd ed. rev. (London: Chapman & Hall Ltd., 1951), p. 75.

event of breakdown or other developments which take production equipment out of service. (This may be somewhat modified by interconnections with other electric utilities.) Electric and other local public utilities must serve all customers. Almost all customers for electricity require "firm" service—that is, service which has assured availability throughout each hour of the year and in whatever quantity the customer desires. Electric utilities do not have the large market that gas utilities have for "interruptible" service, which can be sold subject to curtailment at the seller's option in the interest of guaranteeing service to firm customers. Accordingly, electric utilities have both high fixed costs and periodically unused capacity; these factors raise a major problem that must be dealt with in the design of rates.

B. *Some Basic Terms and Concepts.* It would be useful to introduce some basic terms, before going further. First, it is important to distinguish between electric energy and electric power. Electric energy is the same thing as work received by the customer. A measure of electric energy is the kilowatt-hour (Kwh). Electric power, on the other hand, is the rate of doing work. Power is measured in kilowatts (Kw) or other units. One kilowatt of power (1,000 watts) is 1.34 horsepower; one horsepower is equivalent to lifting one pound 33,000 feet in one minute. One kilowatt-hour of energy is the result of one kilowatt of power operated for one hour. The kilowatt is also a measure of the capacity of electrical equipment and the "load" or demand for power by a customer, a customer class, or the system as a whole. Thus, a 150-watt light can cause a load or demand of 150 watts or 0.15 kilowatt. If operated for ten hours, 1.5 kilowatt-hours of energy would be consumed ($10 \times 0.15 = 1.5$). The relation between power and energy, therefore, is one of time. Power equals energy divided by time; and energy equals power multiplied by time.

The distinction between power and energy also has significance in terms of the nature and incurrence of costs. In the operation of a steam electric generating station, generally speaking, the amount of coal or other fuel consumed is determined by the total kilowatt-hours supplied to consumers, whereas the amount of plant capacity employed is determined by the maximum total power requirement on the system or the maximum rate at which energy is taken by consumers. Accordingly, the costs of electric supply and most other utility services have an essentially dual nature; some are related to the plant or capacity, while others are related to energy output. (Where gas and water utilities and gas pipelines are concerned, the term "commodity" is substituted for "energy.") The costs related to capacity and to energy, respectively, have different characteristics, behavior, and origins.

The maximum load, or the maximum power requirement, upon a machine, plant, or system is called the *peak load* or the *peak demand*. The peak demand must be stated in terms of the time period within which it occurs, such as the day, month, or year. Thus, there are daily peaks, monthly peaks, and the annual peak. Because electricity cannot be stored, the annual system peak load dictates the size of plant required by an electric utility, except to the extent that interconnections with other utilities may be depended upon for assistance in meeting peak demands. The peak demand must be further defined so as to state the period of time the peak is averaged. Thus, the peak might be stated as the highest demand averaged over thirty minutes within a day. The day on which the annual peak demand occurs is called the peak day. Traditionally, the annual peak demand on an electric utility system has been expected to occur late in the afternoon some day late in December, around the time of the shortest and darkest day in the year. However, this traditional winter peak may not continue to be expected in markets where important growth in the summer air-conditioning load, together with the industrial load, has provided the basis for an annual peak that rivals or exceeds the winter peak.

The *load factor* shows the average use of facilities as a percentage of the maximum use. It is defined as the ratio of the average load over a designated period of time to the peak load occurring in that period. Alternatively, the load factor could be stated as the ratio of average power to peak power. The load factor is always stated in terms of some period of time, such as a year or month, and may apply to a machine, plant, system, group of consumers, or one consumer. The load factor is usually stated as a percentage. If, for example, a generating station on a given day supplied consumers with a total of 432,000 kilowatt-hours and had a peak load of 36,000 kilowatts, the load factor on this day would be 50 per cent, calculated as follows: (a) average load equals total kilowatt-hours (432,000) divided by 24 hours, or 18,000 kilowatts; (b) the ratio of average load (18,000 kilowatts) to peak load (36,000 kilowatts) equals 50 per cent. The load factor shows how steadily the maximum power requirement has been employed—in this case, one-half the day. In a public utility enterprise characterized by high fixed costs, the importance of the load factor may be assessed in cost terms. The higher the system load factor, the lower the average unit of cost of service. The achievement of economies through load-factor improvement follows from the acquisition of new loads in off-peak hours or new loads that are predominantly off-peak.

In considering the annual peak load, it is important to bear in mind that the peak demands of the respective classes of service do not necessarily coincide with the annual peak demand. The fact that these class peaks do not occur simultaneously is referred to as the *diversity* among the classes of service. The concept of diversity may be illustrated by assuming two classes of customers, A and B, each using 1,000 kilowatts throughout the day, but raising their respective demands to 3,000 kilowatts each for one hour per day. If the two 3,000-kilowatt-class peak loads coincide, a plant of 6,000-kilowatt capacity would be required. However, if the two class peaks occur successively instead of simultaneously, a plant of only 4,000-kilowatt capacity will be needed—1,000 kilowatts to serve one class plus 3,000 kilowatts to serve the other. In effect, 2,000 kilowatts can be used twice, because of the diversity, or non-coincidence, of the two demands. The degree of diversity is measured by the *diversity factor,* which is defined as the ratio of the sum of the class peak demands to the system maximum demand. In the example above, the diversity factor (if the class peaks follow one another) is 1.5, found by dividing the sum of the class peaks (6,000 kilowatts) by the peak load (4,000 kilowatts). The diversity factor cannot be less than 1.0, or unity.

The higher the diversity factor, the less the total plant capacity required to serve a particular market or service area. In addition, a high diversity factor helps to offset the economic consequences of the low load-factor customers which form an important part of the market for electric service. Improved diversity is one of the principal economic benefits of the consolidation of a number of electric utilities, each formerly serving one community, into one large system serving an area. A customer class cannot at the same time have a high load factor and a high diversity factor. (For a class of customers, the diversity factor would be the ratio of class peak demand to the demand of that class at the time of the system peak.) High load-factor usage means relatively continuous use, which is apt to contribute both to the peak and the off-peak demands alike. Low load-factor use, on the other hand, can have a high diversity factor because the time of nonuse may free capacity to supply the needs of other customers. A high load-factor customer necessarily has a low diversity, while the lower the load factor, the higher the diversity factor.

When the costs of electric and most other utilities are analyzed, it is found that: (a) some costs are a function of the total number of customers; (b) some costs are a function of the volume of service supplied; and (c) some costs are a function of the service capacity of plant and equipment in terms of capability of carrying hourly or daily peak loads. Accordingly, an established procedure for analyzing public utility costs provides for the assignment or distribution of total costs among three categories on the basis of the characteristics suggested above. These cost categories are: customer costs, energy costs, and demand or capacity costs. As noted earlier, the term *commodity costs* would be substituted for *energy costs* if gas or water untility costs were under consideration. *Customer costs* include the expenses of meter reading, billing, collecting and accounting, and the costs associated with such company property as metering equipment and service connections. *Energy costs* include, for the most part, the expenses for fuel, fuel handling, and part of power plant operating and maintenance expenses. *Demand* or *capacity costs* consist of all or most of the plant-related costs, such as return on rate base, principal taxes, the annual depreciation accrual, and certain expenses of operation and maintenance.

C. Types of Rate Schedules. Public utilities are required to maintain published tariffs which contain schedules of rates and the rules and regulations under which different types of service are available. Tariffs are open to public inspection and cannot be changed without public notice and submission of proposed rate or rule changes to the regulatory commission for review as to justness and reasonableness. The rate schedules contained in public utility tariffs set forth the basis for pricing different quantities of each service offered the public as well as information specifying the applicability of the rate schedule, the nature of the service to be provided, and the minimum charge for each billing period. The following discussion surveys the principal types of rate schedules used in the past or currently by electric and most other utilities.

(1) *Flat-Rate Schedules.* The first rate schedules were in the form of the flat rate, which charged the customer a lump sum for a given time period, such as $4.00 per month, regardless of the quantity or time of use. Another type of flat rate, called a "fixture rate," charged a flat amount per specified time period, based upon the number and size of the electric lamps and appliances serving a customer. In either form, a flat rate would not reflect the actual amount of service used. Flat rates were largely abandoned with the development of inexpensive and effective meters which would permit billing on the basis of actual use. The flat rate is now little used by electric utilities except for street lighting, where it is possible to estimate the amount of use with reasonable accuracy. Under the flat-rate type of rate schedule, the net bill remains the same regardless of the kilowatt-hours consumed, while the average effective rate per kilowatt-hour of electric energy used declines with increased use. Flat rates are used by telephone companies for

local exchange service and by urban transit utilities. Their services are supplied under circumstances which make this the most feasible form of pricing.

(2) *Straight-Line Meter-Rate Schedules*. Straight-line meter-rate schedules provide service at a constant charge per metered unit of energy, regardless of the quantity of energy used. For example, the rate schedule might provide for a charge of 4 cents per kilowatt-hour. Under this type of rate schedule, the average rate per kilowatt-hour remains the same regardless of the amount consumed, but the customer's bill increases proportionately with the increase in energy used. This type of rate schedule is used in some cases for off-peak water heating and special services; however, it has been largely abandoned for general use. The advantage of this type of rate schedule is its simplicity. The principal weakness is that it does not provide any rate reduction or incentive for larger volume use.

(3) *Block Meter-Rate Schedules*. The block meter-rate schedule is now the type most widely used for residential and other small-volume consumers. This type of rate schedule offers a decreasing price per unit of energy for successive blocks (quantities) of consumption. More specifically, this type of rate schedule offers successively lower rates per kilowatt-hour for all or part of each block of energy consumed. The customer's bill is calculated by cumulating the charges incurred for each successive block of energy taken or fraction thereof. This example illustrates a block meter-rate schedule for monthly billing; the minimum charge is $1.05.

First 10 Kwh or less	$1.05
Next 30 Kwh	4.5 cents per Kwh
Next 60 Kwh	3.9 cents per Kwh
Next 100 Kwh	2.7 cents per Kwh
201 Kwh or more	2.0 cents per Kwh

Minimum charge, $1.05 per month

The block meter-rate schedule is simple and easily understood by consumers. The average over-all rate charged per kilowatt-hour declines with increased use, thus promoting sales. The bill increases more or less proportionately to energy used within each block but less than proportionately when all consumption beyond the first block is considered.

The block meter-rate schedule, and others, may include either a "service charge" or a "minimum charge." There is an important difference between the two. The *service charge* is a fixed amount per month, say 75 cents, that a customer must pay, regardless of the consumption of energy, and for which he can use no energy. The *minimum charge,* on the other hand, is based upon a minimum amount of consumption which the customer will have to pay for—whether or not that amount is actually used. Thus, the minimum charge permits the utility to collect some amount from the convenience user without increasing the bill of the average customer. In the above illustration of a block meter-rate schedule, for example, a minimum charge of $1.05 per month is related to the first block of 10 kilowatt-hours. Any monthly total consumption of less than that amount would be billed at $1.05 nonetheless. In summary: (a) the service charge is a fixed monthly sum that is unrelated to any specified quantity of consumption; while (b) the minimum charge is a fixed monthly sum that is related to a specified minimum monthly consumption of energy which the customer must pay for whether it is used or not. Where the rate schedule calls for a service charge, the block charges are ordinarily lower than in rate schedules providing a minimum charge.

The purpose of both the service charge and the minimum charge is to cover at least some of the costs incurred by the utility whether or not the customer uses energy in a particular month. For small customers under the block meter-rate schedule, a charge of this kind is intended to cover the expenses relating to meter service and maintenance, meter reading, accounting and collecting, return on the investment in meters and the service lines connecting the customer's premises to the distribution system, and others. Such expenses as these represent as a minimum the "readiness-to-serve" expenses incurred by the utility on behalf of each customer. In the absence of a service charge or minimum charge, these expenses would be avoided by the convenience user and transferred unfairly to those consuming service.

In some states there has been public protest against the service charge, largely on the ground that it permitted the utility to receive "something for nothing." This type of public opinion has arisen because no energy use is related to the service charge. Accordingly, some state commissions have prohibited the service charge in favor of the minimum charge. The New York commission, for example, has recognized that the basis of the public opposition to the service charge ". . . is not so much economic or accounting as it is psychological." A different attitude was found to exist with respect to the minimum charge.[35]

A predecessor of the block meter-rate schedule, called the *step meter-rate schedule,* is now almost never used. Under this type of rate schedule one price was charged per unit of energy for the entire amount of service consumed. That unit price was determined by the price attaching to the particular block in which the total consumption happened to fall; prices decreased with each successive block. Because of this feature it was sometimes possible to reduce the over-all bill by wasting service so as to cause total consumption to come within the next, lower-priced energy block. The block meter-rate schedule, which cumulates block charges, was a substantial improvement.

(4) *Hopkinson Demand Rate Schedules.* The Hopkinson-type rate schedule is widely used for medium and large commercial and industrial customers. It was devised by Dr. John Hopkinson in 1892. The Hopkinson rate schedule provides for a two-part rate, consisting of separate charges for maximum demand and energy consumption. The customer's bill under this type of rate schedule, therefore, is the sum of the two components—the demand charge and the energy charge. As the Hopkinson-type rate schedule has been adapted for present-day use, either the demand charge or the energy charge or both may be graduated by blocks so as to provide lower charges for larger volumes of consumption. The Hopkinson-type rate schedule requires a measurement of kilowatts of demand and kilowatt-hours of energy. The rate schedule may provide that the customer's maximum demand be either measured or estimated. For larger customers, the maximum demand for billing purposes is generally obtained through measurement by use of a demand meter or demand indicator. The billing demand may be the maximum 15-minute or 30-minute demand measured in kilowatts as recorded in the billing month, or some similar measure of demand. The following is an illustration of a Hopkinson rate schedule for monthly billing.

Demand Charge:

$2.25 per Kw .... first 2 Kw of demand
$2.00 per Kw .... next 18 Kw of demand
$1.50 per Kw .... next 80 Kw of demand
$1.25 per Kw .... all over 100 Kw of demand

[35] *Re Rates and Rate Schedules of Corporations Supplying Electricity,* PUR 1931 C, 337, 347.

Energy Charge:

2.50¢ per Kwh....	first 1,000 Kwh
2.00¢ per Kwh...	next 4,000 Kwh
1.60¢ per Kwh....	next 5,000 Kwh
1.40¢ per Kwh....	next 10,000 Kwh
1.20¢ per Kwh....	next 15,000 Kwh
0.90¢ per Kwh....	next 20,000 Kwh
0.75¢ per Kwh....	next 150,000 Kwh
0.70¢ per Kwh....	all additional Kwh

There is ordinarily a minimum bill provided in Hopkinson rate schedules, which may cover not only a portion of customer costs, but also part of demand costs. The minimum charge may take the form of a demand "ratchet." A ratchet provision serves to put a floor under the maximum demand for billing purposes, and may hold the billing demand to no less than the highest demand recorded in some stated past period or some percentage thereof.

Because the Hopkinson rate schedule contains a demand element, it is sometimes termed a "load factor" rate. The load factor, which relates average load to peak load during a specified time period, is automatically a consideration in the Hopkinson rate schedule. This necessarily follows from the fact that it is based upon maximum demand and kilowatt-hours of energy. (Kilowatt-hours divided by the period of time equals average load.) Studies of Hopkinson rate schedules show that, as the customer increases his use without any increase in maximum demand, or with a less than proportionate increase in maximum demand, his load factor will increase and his average rate will decrease. If a customer decreases his use without any decrease in maximum demand, or with a less than proportional decrease in his maximum demand, his load factor will decrease and his average rate will increase.

(5) *Wright Demand Rate Schedules.* This type of demand rate schedule was proposed by Arthur Wright in 1896. Like the Hopkinson-type rate schedule, the Wright type is applied to medium and large commercial and industrial customers. Whereas the Hopkinson type provides for separate demand and energy charges, the Wright type combines the two into a blocked energy charge based on the number of hours that the maximum demand is used each month. As first proposed, the Wright-type rate schedule consisted of two blocks. The energy rate of the first of these blocks was designed to cover the demand, energy, and customer cost. The rate for the second block was to be largely an energy charge.

As later developed, the Wright-type rate schedule has been modified to include a number of energy blocks. Succeeding blocks have decreasing rates and increasing size corresponding to increasing loads. An illustrative Wright-type rate schedule follows:

5.0¢ per Kwh for the first 30 hours' use of demand per month;
2.0¢ per Kwh for the next 60 hours' use of demand per month;
1.0¢ per Kwh for the next 60 hours' use of demand per month;
0.8¢ per Kwh for all energy in excess of 150 hours' use of demand per month;
Minimum bill, 75¢ per Kw of demand per month.

The computation of a customer's monthly bill under this rate schedule is illustrated below. It is assumed that the customer has a demand of 6 kilowatts and uses 750 kilowatt-hours per month.

6 Kw/30 hours = 180 Kwh at 5¢ each ..	$ 9.00
6 Kw/60 hours = 360 Kwh at 2¢ each ..	7.20
6 Kw/35 hours = 210 Kwh at 1¢ each ..	2.10
Total bill, 750 Kwh	$18.30

Like the Hopkinson-type rate schedule, the Wright type also reflects load-factor differences. Thus, as a customer increases his use without increasing his maximum demand, or with a less than proportionate increase in maximum demand, his load factor will increase and his average rate will decrease. The reverse of this is also true.

(6) *Doherty Three-Part Rate Schedules.* This type of rate schedule was developed by Henry L. Doherty in 1900, before he became aware of Hopkinson's two-part demand-type rate schedule. Essentially, the Doherty-type rate schedule is a Hopkinson type plus a separate customer charge in the form of a service charge. The Doherty-type rate schedule is not widely used. The Hopkinson and Wright-type rate schedules accomplish the same objective and somewhat more simply. The Hopkinson rate schedule, for example, includes the customer charge in the first block of the demand charge.

D. *Costing Procedure.* The analysis of costs as an aid to the design of rates has been the subject of serious study in the electric utility industry for a long period of time. In fact, most of the professional literature in this field has been concerned with electric utilities rather than other utility industries. As a result, the costing techniques developed for electric utilities generally serve as a basis for such cost studies as other utilities may undertake. The following discussion of the costing of electric utility service by classes of customers is intended primarily as a brief introduction to this area of study.[36]

The costs of electric generation, transmission, and distribution are maintained in the uniform system of accounts prescribed by each commission for the utilities under its jurisdiction. In addition, each utility files a detailed annual report with the commission, with all data stated on the basis of the accounts and subaccounts of the prescribed accounting system. Cost data in this form are not directly usable in cost analyses developed to aid in the design of rates. Accordingly, it is necessary to undertake these basic procedures: (1) classification of the total cost of service into three basic categories, called *customer costs, energy costs,* and *demand* or *capacity costs;* (2) allocation and distribution of the classified costs to customer classes or types of load; and (3) totaling the customer, energy, and capacity costs thus assigned to each customer class or type of load to provide a basis for determining the average costs of supplying the respective classes of service.

The classification of costs to the customer, energy, and demand or capacity categories was first proposed by W. J. Greene in 1896. This approach is now regarded as conventional. The components of the three cost classifications and the behavior of such costs are summarized below:

(1) The total of customer costs varies directly with the number of customers served. Customer costs include the expenses of meter reading, billing, collecting, and accounting. Also included are the expenses associated with the capital investment in metering equipment, customers' service connections, and part of the investment in the general distribution system. If administrative and general expenses are spread on the basis of investment, part of that expense total may be included in customer costs.

(2) Energy costs vary in total with the quantity of kilowatt-hours produced. Energy costs are largely made up of the cost of fuel and fuel handling, water, and part of power plant operating and maintenance expenses. Costs in this category would be called *commodity costs,* instead of *energy costs,* if gas or water utility costs were under consideration.

(3) Demand or capacity costs vary in total with the quantity of plant and equipment. Such costs consist of return on rate base, taxes, and depreciation ex-

---

[36] For comprehensive analysis see D. J. Bolton, *op. cit.,* the premier study now in print. See also Russell E. Caywood, *Electric Utility Rate Economics* (New York: McGraw-Hill Book Company, Inc., 1956), Chapter 11; and *Gas Rate Fundamentals* (New York: American Gas Association, 1960), Chapters 12, 13.

pense, with the exception of that part thereof which is assigned to customer costs. Capacity costs also include part of administrative and general expenses and those operating and maintenance expenses which do not vary with the quantity of service supplied. Finally, some portion of the fuel expense of electric utilities may be included in demand costs, in recognition of the fact that part of the fuel consumed, perhaps 20 per cent, may be required to keep the plant in readiness to serve.

In classifying the basic cost data to the three cost categories, it is necessary to consider the characteristics of the particular utility system and to exercise judgment. No hard-and-fast rules apply. It is also necessary to examine the various cost items from the standpoint of the cause or causes of their incurrence. The first step in establishing the three-category grouping of costs is to segregate the costs that can be assigned directly to individual customer classes. Thereafter, the analysis proceeds on an account-by-account basis which covers each of the property and plant accounts and the various expense accounts. Once the property and plant accounts have been assigned to or among cost categories, the related fixed costs can be assigned on the same basis.

After the classification of costs to the customer, energy, and demand categories, each such classification will be distributed or allocated to the various customer classes: (a) Customer costs may be distributed to respective groups in proportion to the number of customers in each one. Alternatively, a more detailed study may be made whereby certain components of the customer cost total may be distributed on a per-customer basis and others on a weighted per-customer basis. The latter permits recognition of known or ascertainable customer cost differences. (b) Energy costs may be distributed to customer groups on the basis of kilowatt-hours of energy consumed in the test period or kilowatt-hours plus energy losses. (c) Demand or capacity costs require an allocation to classes on the basis of one of the many formulas available for this purpose. These are discussed in the following section.

The cost study will be completed by totaling the customer, energy, and capacity costs for each class of customer or service so that average unit costs may be calculated. In addition, the cost data thus derived also may be used to determine rates of return earned from respective classes of business.

E. *Allocation of Demand Costs.* The annual peak demand on the system determines the size of plant; the latter essentially determines the total of demand or capacity costs. Such costs, as noted previously, are relatively fixed in total amount for a system of a given size and, for the most part, are in the nature of joint costs. The joint-cost characteristic arises from the fact that the same facilities simultaneously serve more than one class of customers. A further element of jointness arises from the fact that one kilowatt of capacity can serve both to help meet the annual peak demand and to provide service throughout the remainder of the year as called upon. Thus, joint products also result in the form of peak and off-peak service. Viewed in this way, a kilowatt of capacity is seen to be able to serve both a peak demand and an annual energy function.

The general problem inherent in allocating joint costs has been discussed previously. In the allocation of joint demand or capacity costs to classes of service, that problem is posed in its largest dimension. The following summary considers briefly six of the 20 or more allocation methods that have been developed through the years.

(1) The Peak Responsibility Method

was the first to be employed. It is sometimes credited to Arthur Wright, one of the earliest important students of the problem. This method allocates demand costs among customer classes in proportion to the respective class loads at the time of the annual peak demand on the system. The underlying hypothesis of this method is that the size of plant is determined by the annual peak, which is built up by those customer classes requiring service at that time. Accordingly, the demand costs associated with that maximum annual load are allocated among the classes in proportion to their contribution to that peak demand, regardless of how long they may use the demands they create. Thus, with a system peak load of 1,000 kilowatts, the allocation would be determined as follows:

Class Load	*Peak Responsibility*	*Allocation Percentages*	*Capacity Allocated*
A	400 Kw	40%	400 Kw
B	0	0	0
C	600	60	600
	1,000 Kw	100%	1,000 Kw

It is apparent from the above that one of the failings of the peak responsibility method is that a class or load whose demand is entirely off peak would not be allocated any share in the total demand cost of the system. This method depends on a single, stable peak; in the past, the very opposite has been the case. Hence, there was considerable instability in the resulting allocation of costs. Originally, when the electric utility industry was quite young, the lighting load was by far the largest one served, and this method could serve usefully. However, the development of an important industrial power load was soon forthcoming. The peak responsibility method was then found inadequate, because the industrial load changed the timing and composition of the annual peak. Owing to the industrial load, the annual peak sometimes changed from the December peak —identified with the lighting load—to a morning in summer. Further, such changes were not necessarily permanent, largely owing to such factors as irregular rates of load growth and fluctuations in industrial production. Accordingly, the annual peak in some cases changed back and forth between industrial power and lighting peaks. If rates had been based upon costs to any extent, it is apparent that major rate schedule revisions would have been necessitated with each change in the annual peak. This problem can be encountered in any developing market. Where there are two peaks of almost equal size, at different times, a small increase in one of them can also change the annual system peak and cause a major change in the allocation of costs. This method considers demand and time of use only at the time of the system peak; it does not take into account the quantity of energy consumed. It was to be expected that the Peak Responsibility Method would be superseded; one authority, L. R. Nash, writing in 1933, described it as "abandoned."[37]

(2) The Non-Coincident Demand Method, or Maximum Demand Method, was discussed in the writings of Dr. John Hopkinson in 1892 and by Wright a few years later. The theoretical basis of this method provides that the joint-demand costs incurred in serving a number of customer groups should be allocated in proportion to the facilities necessary to serve each customer group separately. Accordingly, this method looks to class peak demands, regardless of the time of occurrence. These steps are required: (a) the peak demands of each class, regardless of time of occurrence, are added to find the sum of the maximum class demands; and (b) allocation of system demand costs to each class is calculated

[37] L. R. Nash, *Public Utility Rate Structures* (New York: McGraw-Hill Book Company, Inc., 1933), p. 231.

on the basis of the ratio of each class peak to the sum of the maximum demands. In the following illustration it is assumed that the peak load is 2,000 kilowatts.

Class Load	*Class Peaks*	*Allocation Percentages*	*Capacity Allocated*
A	1,500 Kw	50.00%	1,000 Kw
B	500	16.67	334
C	1,000	33.33	666
	3,000 Kw	100.00%	2,000 Kw

The Maximum Demand Method recognizes as important only the peak demand of each class, but not the amount or time of use. Thus, a class whose peak occurred at the time of the system peak would be allocated the same proportion of demand costs as another class of equal peak demand occurring clearly off peak. This method is not affected drastically by small shifts in loads. However, it does not recognize diversity differences between classes. A 100 per cent load-factor class would share in the benefits of diversity on an equal basis with the other classes while contributing nothing to diversity. In fact, any class whose load factor exceeded the average would receive unearned benefits from diversity, while any class with a lower-than-average load factor would not receive all the benefits it merited. Nevertheless, the Maximum Demand Method represents a distinct improvement over the Peak Responsibility Method, because every class of service would be charged with some part of the total demand costs.

(3) The Phantom Customer Method developed by H. W. Hills is one of a number of methods that looks to "used" and "unused" capacity. This method proceeds on the hypothesis that, if a combination of loads resulted in a 100 per cent load factor, demand costs could be distributed equally to all kilowatt-hours. Accordingly, a phantom customer is assumed, whose load characteristics are such that a 100 per cent load factor would result. The demand costs are then assigned to all customer classes, including the phantom customer, in proportion to the kilowatt-hours taken by each. The phantom, of course, cannot pay. Therefore, the phantom's share of demand costs would be divided among customer classes on the basis of the excess over average demand of each class at the time of the annual peak demand on the system.

The Phantom Customer Method recognizes demand and quantity of use but not time of use of energy. Because it relies on an element of peak responsibility, it is subject, to some extent, to the limitations of that method. A class load that was below its average at time of system annual peak would be treated as an off-peak load.

(4) The Complete Peak Method proposed by John Oram and H. H. Robison does not rely on the system annual peak demand; instead, it looks to the "complete system peak," which includes all time periods in which the system load exceeds the average. For practical purposes, the complete peak is taken as the excess of demand over average annual demand on the peak day of the year. Oram and Robison reasoned that, whenever the system load exceeds the annual average load, the cause lies in the fact that some customer classes have demands which sometimes exceed their average annual demands. Accordingly, the total demand costs are first spread equally over the entire output at an assumed 100 per cent load factor, as in the Phantom Customer Method. However, the demand costs associated with the unused capacity are allocated to those customer classes demanding service at some time during the complete peak, on the basis of their excess demands over their average demands during each hourly or other time segment comprising the complete peak.

This method recognizes the factors of

demand, kilowatt-hours of use, and time of use. A class load that is less than its annual average during the period of the complete peak would be treated as if it were an off-peak load. The Complete Peak Method provides a practicable approach to the problem of allocating demand costs, so long as the peak day may be depended upon to occur on a weekday. Otherwise, the commercial and industrial loads would be regarded as off peak for allocation purposes.

(5) W. J. Greene's Consumption and Demand Method does not rely on peak responsibility in any form. Rather, it combines the factors of use in kilowatt-hours with the theory underlying the Maximum Demand Method: that demand costs should be allocated on the basis of serving customer classes separately. Thus, part of the total demand cost is allocated to classes on the basis of class peak demands, regardless of time of occurrence; the remainder is allocated on the basis of the total kilowatt-hours of energy consumed by each class. The first of two basic equations used to determine the allocation of demand costs is $C = Kx + Dy$, where:

C = Total annual demand cost of the system;

K = Total kilowatt-hours of energy consumed in the year;

D = Sum of the annual class peak demands.

The coefficients, x and y, are unknown relative values which must be calculated. The x coefficient represents the per-kilowatt-hour share of that part of total demand cost which is allocated on the basis of the total kilowatt-hours consumed in a year. The y coefficient represents the per-kilowatt share of that part of total demand cost which is allocated on the basis of class peak demands.

The assumption is maintained that a 100 per cent load factor class will be assigned its exact proportion of the total demand costs. That is, a 100 per cent load-factor class that monopolizes, say, 20 per cent of system capacity would be allocated 20 per cent of total demand costs. This is an important test of the reasonableness of any allocation method.

Greene's second basic equation is $C/P = 8{,}760x + y$, where:

P = Annual peak demand on the system;

C/P = Average demand cost per kilowatt; and

8,760 = 24×365, or the total kilowatt-hours consumed in one year by a load of one kilowatt at 100 per cent load factor and 100 per cent power factor. (The latter is defined as the ratio of kilowatts to kilovolt amperes.)

Combining the two equations will give specific values for x and y. Once these have been calculated, the first equation, $C = Kx + Dy$, is applied successively to each customer class to determine the respective demand-cost allocations.

Demand and use are recognized in this method but not time of use. The reliance on class peak demand, regardless of time of use, results in an effect similar to that under the Maximum Demand Method, in that no distinction is made between peak and off-peak loads.

(6) The "E.R.A. Method for Allocating Demand-Related Cost," as developed by the British Electrical and Allied Industries Research Association, is an adaptation of Greene's Consumption and Demand Method. However, the E.R.A. Method applies only to those hours of the year when a system peak could occur as the result of a normally possible increase in demand by a class of customers. Thus, the E.R.A. Method may be regarded as a "potential" peak responsibility method, because it is concerned solely with the hours of prospective system peak demand. It excludes from direct consideration all the periods of time when there is no likelihood that

a system peak will develop, even if the rates charged during such times include nothing for demand costs. Thus, as the Association states, this method ". . . allocates the cost to all customers whose decisions to consume more or less are liable to affect the undertaking's expenses, and only to such consumers."[38] Accordingly, no demand costs would be allocated to off-potential peak periods, although the E.R.A. Method provides that any amount could be allocated to such periods as judgment might indicate. Proponents of this method have suggested that it could be refined by zoning the potential peak periods to reflect differing degrees of peak potentiality.

More specifically, the E.R.A. Method is based upon consumption and the highest thirty-minute peak demand during potential peak periods. The symbols and equations employed are similar to those in Greene's Consumption and Demand Method, except that they apply only to the potential peak period. Like Greene's method, the E.R.A. Method takes into consideration the factors of demand and use. By largely excluding from consideration all periods in which no peak potentiality is judged to exist, the E.R.A. Method is superior to the Consumption and Demand Method from the standpoint of the time-of-use factor.

F. *Some Tests of Demand-Cost Allocation Methods.* Standards for testing the reasonableness of methods of allocating demand costs have been developed by Dr. Henry Herz, consulting economist. These standards are intended to apply generally, rather than to any one of the public utility industries. Dr. Herz would judge the reasonableness of an allocation method in terms of its capacity to meet the following principles:

(1) All utility customers should contribute to capacity costs.

(2) The longer the period of time that a particular service pre-empts the use of capacity, the greater should be the amount of capacity costs allocated to that service.

(3) Any service which makes exclusive use of a portion of capacity should bear all the demand costs assignable to that portion of capacity. Thus, a 100 per cent load-factor service should be allocated the entire demand costs associated with the portion of capacity pre-empted, but no more.

(4) The allocation of capacity costs should change gradually with changes in the pattern of sales as the market develops. As noted previously, the original Peak Responsibility Method is prone to produce erratic results with changes in the timing of systems peaks.

(5) The capacity costs allocated to one class of service should not be affected by the way in which the remaining capacity costs are allocated to other classes.

(6) More demand costs should be allocated to a unit of capacity pre-empted during a peak period than to one pre-empted off peak.

(7) Service that can be restricted by the utility should be allocated less in demand costs as the degree of restriction increases. This principle goes to the difference between firm service (assured availability) and interruptible and other forms of restricted-availability service. Interruptible service is supplied under agreements which permit curtailment or cessation of delivery by the supplier. There are differing priorities of possible curtailment of deliveries. This seventh principle states, in effect, that a unit of firm demand for service should be allocated a greater share of capacity costs than a unit of demand which cannot

[38] As quoted in: Cost Allocation Committee of the Engineering Committee of the National Association of Railroad and Utilities Commissioners, "Comparison of Methods of Allocating Demand Costs (Electric Utilities)" June, 1955, p. 47.

pre-empt system capacity on an equal basis with firm service.[39]

A set of standards for use in selecting a demand-cost allocation method for electric utilities has been set forth by a committee of the National Association of Railroad and Utilities Commissioners. Those standards are reviewed below:

(1) The method should be based on some basic philosophy.

(2) The method should be judged on its recognition of the following three factors: (a) demand in kilowatts; (b) use in kilowatt-hours; and (c) time of use of energy.

(3) The method should recognize the characteristics of various loads.

(4) The method should result in a relatively stable cost assignment which would not change radically with a shift in loads.

(5) The method should require a minimum of measurements before and after allocation.

(6) The method should permit allocation to a load which is completely under utility control, such as off-peak water heating.

(7) The method should permit an estimate of the capacity cost that would be assigned to prospective loads.

(8) The method should establish a minimum demand-cost allocation to off-peak customers.

(9) The method should not be dependent upon judgments introduced in the allocation process.[40]

3. GAS DISTRIBUTION UTILITIES AND RATES

Local gas distribution utilities supply gas to metropolitan area customers. Since the mid-1950's, these utilities have supplied their customers almost entirely with natural gas brought by pipelines. Previously, however, most of them distributed synthetic gas manufactured by themselves and others. At present, manufactured gas comprises a negligible portion of the total supply. With the almost total transition to natural gas, the gas industry essentially has become three rather separate industries, which serve the respective functions of: (a) exploring and producing; (b) transporting and wholesaling; and (c) distributing at retail.

First, the primary producers of natural gas are oil companies, which produce oil and natural gas largely as joint products. Second, the natural gas pipelines: (a) provide long-distance transmission service, connecting the gas-producing fields to the ultimate markets; and (b) sell natural gas at wholesale to gas distributors for resale to the public and directly to industrial customers for ultimate consumption. The pipeline industry includes some companies which produce substantial amounts of gas and others which produce none. Taken as a whole, pipelines produce about one-fifth of the natural gas which they transport in interstate commerce. Third, local gas distribution utilities supply gas at retail to residential, commercial, and industrial customers. Although gas distributors for the most part sell natural gas, a few supply manufactured gas in various forms as well as gas mixtures. Some distributors are affiliates of their pipeline suppliers. Others own relatively short pipeline systems or are affiliated with companies that perform that function. This occurs in cases where the long-distance pipeline makes delivery at the state line, or where a distributor makes a direct connection with natural gas fields in the area. For the most part, however, the long-distance transmission function and the distribution function are performed by separate, unaffiliated companies.

---

39 Henry Herz, "Impact of Cost Allocation on Gas Pricing," 58 *Public Utilities Fortnightly* 685, 692–694 (1956).

40 Cost Allocation Committee, *op. cit.*, p. 13.

This section is concerned with the gas distribution utilities and their rates. Much of the preceding section on electric utility rates is equally applicable here and will not be repeated. Natural gas pipeline rates are discussed in the next section of this chapter; the development of the pipeline industry and its regulation are discussed in Chapter 14. The gas producing industry and its regulation are covered in Chapter 15.

A. Development of Manufactured Gas Utilities. Throughout most of their long history, gas distributors dealt in manufactured gas unless located relatively close to natural gas fields. Beginning about 1930, with the first construction of major pipelines, and particularly after World War II, gas distributors have changed increasingly to natural gas. As a result, the basic nature of the gas distribution industry has changed drastically, for it has become an important supplier of fuel for both space-heating and industrial uses. Local distributors of manufactured gas once provided lighting service, as indicated by the names of some present companies—such as Washington Gas Light Co. in the District of Columbia, Milwaukee Gas Light Co., and others. Gas distributors were superseded in the lighting market by the electric utilities, which also competed aggressively for the remainder of the market served by manufactured gas. This was mainly comprised of the cooking-range and water-heating loads. However, with the introduction of natural gas, local gas companies were able to enter the space-heating and industrial fuels markets in competition with coal and oil. This had not been feasible on a large scale during the manufactured-gas era, because of the relatively high cost of producing such gas relative to the prices of competitive fuels. However, the delivered price of natural gas at the city gate, in most areas, is well below the cost of manufactured gas and is competitive with or priced below substitute fuels. Natural gas has other characteristics which make it an ideal fuel. It requires no storage on the consumers' premises; it burns cleanly and with no fumes or residue. It provides controllable heat, which is particularly important in certain industrial processes. In addition, processed natural gas is non-toxic, is virtually odorless (although an odor is added for safety), and has about twice the Btu or thermal content of conventional manufactured gas (about 1,050 Btu per cubic foot for natural gas as compared to about 540 Btu for manufactured gas).

Manufactured gas is a combustible gas produced from coal, coke, or oil. It can be produced in a number of ways. The first principal type developed was coal gas, made by heating bituminous coal so as to drive off the gas. This process leaves salable by-products such as coke, tar, ammonia, and others. Second, lower-cost production was achieved with the patenting of the Lowe process, in 1873, for the manufacture of water gas. Under this process, anthracite coal or coke is raised to high temperature in a furnace, called a *generator,* and to a state of incandescence by being blown with air. After the air stream is stopped, steam under pressure is blown through the bed of coal; this produces a mixture of hydrogen and carbon monoxide. The mixture is enriched by an oil spray which vaporizes in the heat and mixes with the gas. Enriched water gas was the principal manufactured gas before the transition to natural gas. Third, coke-oven gas is coal gas that is produced as a by-product in the manufacture of coke for use by steel producers. Fourth, oil gas can be manufactured in areas such as the Pacific Coast and others where coal is unavailable on economic terms, and oil is relatively inexpensive. Fifth, some gas distributors furnish their customers with liquefied petroleum gas (LPG), which is comprised mostly of butane and propane gas. LPG is transported under pressure in a liquid state and is transformed into the vapor stage by distributors after being mixed with air. Finally, there is mixed gas, which is manufactured gas commingled with natural gas or LPG in order to increase the Btu content of the gas. Experiments continue to be made in an effort to find an economical method of producing gas from coal.

The first gas company in the United States was established in Baltimore in 1816. A few years earlier a similar company had been established in London. The organization of gas companies in other American cities followed that in Baltimore in due course—in Boston in 1822, in New York in 1823, in New Orleans in 1835, in Pittsburgh and Philadelphia in 1836, and so on. These companies represented the culmination in practical use of the original discovery of manufactured gas by the Belgian chemist Van Helmont in 1609, who found that the combustion and treatment of fuels produced an inflammable gaseous substance. Van Helmont was the first in a long series of experimenters who sought to manufacture gas and to develop facilities for its use.

The principal use of manufactured gas at first was for street lighting. Gas cooking equipment was invented in 1840 in England, but it was not until the invention of the blue-flame burner by Von Bunsen in 1855 that gas was well adapted to cooking use. Large-scale use of gas for cooking did not take place until much later in the nineteenth century. In fact, the whole industry did not experience sizable growth until after 1865. Development of the lighting market was hampered for a long time by the high cost of gas relative to average consumer incomes, although it was agreed that gas was superior as a lighting agent to candles, whale-oil lamps, and the like. Accordingly, during much of the industry's early history gas lighting was limited to the illumination of streets, some businesses, and the homes of above-average-income families. It was not until the late nineteenth century, when the cost of gas manufacturing was reduced, that lower rates were charged and gas came into relatively wide use.

In 1826 the price of gas in New York was $10 per Mcf (thousand cubic feet), largely owing to the high cost of basic fuels for the manufacture of gas, the high cost of their transportation, and the inefficient early production methods. For example, the long-distance shipment of supplies for gas making resulted in a gas rate of $15 per Mcf in San Francisco in 1855. With improving technology, manufactured gas prices declined sharply. For example, the price of gas in New York City declined from $10 per Mcf in 1826 to $1.25 in 1900. The average industry price of gas of $1.04 per Mcf in 1899 declined to 92 cents in 1919 and stood at $1.02 in 1938. Thereafter, the substantial increase in the general price level and the large-scale change to natural gas make later data much less comparable. However, for rough comparison purposes, it may be noted that the national average unit revenues from natural gas sales by distributors in 1960 (for gas of about twice the Btu content of manufactured gas) were as follows: (a) 97.2¢ per Mcf for residential customers; (b) 76.8¢ for commercial customers; and (c) 32.76¢ for sales to industrial customers.[41]

The early gas industry was confronted with competition during the very time it began to gain widespread public acceptance. Oil was discovered in Pennsylvania in 1859, and thereafter comparatively cheap kerosene and improved lamps for its use restrained the fullest development of the lighting market. Competition for

[41] Calculated from American Gas Association, *Gas Facts,* 1961 ed., pp. 98, 116.

the street-lighting market, beginning in 1878, came from electric arc lights. Not much later, central electric generating stations were developed, and electricity began to compete for the entire lighting market. However, gas lamps were improved substantially by the development of the Wellsbach mantle in 1885, which replaced the open-flame burners in use previously. The Wellsbach mantle makes gas a more effective illuminant; it also diffuses the gas light and produces a very agreeable quality of softness in gas lighting. Although this development enabled gas to hold out somewhat longer in the lighting field, electric lighting ultimately won out because it was less expensive, safer, and more convenient. A gas refrigerator was invented in 1915. However, in the 1920's the electric appliance industry began large-scale production of a wide range of appliances that could substitute for gas appliances in many functions. The gas utilities encouraged the development of improved gas appliances and began to seek space-heating and industrial customers. Nonetheless, once the competitive situation stabilized, the manufactured gas industry was primarily in the business of supplying gas for cooking and water heating.

During the first four decades of this century, distributors of manufactured gas did not experience the same great rate of growth achieved by electric utilities. From a total of 4.2 million gas customers in 1901, the industry grew to 10.6 million customers in 1925. A peak of over 11.0 million customers for manufactured and mixed gas was recorded in 1946. Thereafter, the accelerated construction of pipelines enabled most gas distributors to change over to natural gas and to begin a new era as effective competitors in the space-heating and industrial fuels markets. By 1955, natural gas had almost completely replaced manufactured gas, and by 1960 there were only 176,200 manufactured gas customers, 2.2 million mixed gas customers, and 125,400 liquefied petroleum gas customers. At the same time there were over 30.5 million natural gas customers served by utilities.

B. *The Transition to Natural Gas.* Natural gas has long been distributed by utilities in and near the areas where it is produced. However, natural gas was essentially a local fuel until long-distance pipelines were constructed to transport it to major metropolitan markets. The earliest pipelines, built between 1891 and the mid-1920's, were seldom more than 150 miles in length. The first long-distance pipelines were constructed during the period from the late 1920's to World War II. The largest of the first long-distance pipelines were those of Natural Gas Pipeline Company of America (to Chicago, 1931), Northern Natural Gas Co. (to Minneapolis, 1932), and Panhandle Eastern Pipe Line Co. (to Muncie, Ind., 1931, and to Detroit, 1936). These pipelines served gas distributors in cities along and near their routes as well as those in the principal cities in which they terminated. During the war and afterward began the greatest period of pipeline construction, which was still in progress 15 years after the war ended. This expansion phase has included growth by the older long-distance pipelines as well as the creation of major new pipelines. The pipeline network now connects the gas-producing areas of the Southwest, mid-continent, and Appalachian areas to all the metropolitan centers in the country and to many points between.

The transition to natural gas was motivated by a number of factors. First of all, many gas distributors were not faring very well in competition with electric utilities; some were not capable of earning the fair rate of return authorized by regulatory agencies. The prospect of changing over to natural gas held out the promise of a new era of financial success in the highly competitive fuel markets. A second and related factor causing the change to natural gas was composed of the need for and prospect of lower costs of gas supply. This was made urgent by the sharp increase in manufactured gas production costs beginning with World War II. The American Gas Association cites the case of a representative Eastern gas distributor whose gas production costs per Mcf tripled from 1939 to 1948.[42] As a result of increasing manufacturing costs, rate increases were sought; the higher rates often priced manufactured gas well above competitive fuels and also weakened its position as a competitor with electricity. The way out of this situation lay in the transition to natural gas. Conditions were favorable: large reserves of natural gas had been discovered; improvements in pipeline technology made long-distance transportation feasible from an economic standpoint; and the pipeline industry and the financial community were interested in expansion. Furthermore, advances in the prices of other fuels made additionally attractive the prospect of entering that area of competition.

Expectations have been realized. Gas sales by distributors have grown substantially with the availability of natural gas. In the period 1945–1960, utility sales of natural gas in the United States increased by 300 per cent. A brief analysis of the transition to natural gas is presented in the following table, which compares sales of gas by types in the periods 1932–1945 and 1945–1960. Among other things, the table shows that manufactured gas sales declined 92 per cent in the postwar period and that the volume of natural gas sold by utilities has reached a level that makes all previous sales figures seem insignificant. It may also be noted in the following table that natural gas sales greatly exceeded manufactured gas sales in 1932. This merits a word of explanation. The natural gas sold in that year was marketed largely in and near the natural gas-producing areas, with well over half the total consumed by large-volume industrial consumers and electric utilities. In effect, natural gas was serving the markets served elsewhere by coal. At the same time, the bulk of manufactured gas was consumed in residential and commercial uses.

The transition to natural gas changed the basic nature of the gas distribution industry from primarily a supplier of gas for residential cooking and water heating to a major supplier of fuel for space-heating and industrial uses. Thus, in 1960, 52 per cent of the natural gas sold by utilities was consumed in industrial uses and 33 per cent was consumed by residential customers, most of which was for space heating. As an example of the growth in space-heating sales, the experience of the Wisconsin gas utilities may be noted. There, in the first decade of natural gas development (1949–1958), the volume of space-heating sales increased from 22.5 million therms to 371.5 million therms, or an increase of over 1,500 per cent.[43] It is important to observe that much more gas is sold in total than the amount distributed by gas utilities. A large volume of gas is also sold directly by producers and by pipelines to ultimate consumers. Of the total marketed production of natural gas in 1960, 67.0 per cent was consumed by industrial customers, 24.8 per cent by residential customers, and 8.2 per cent by commercial customers.[44]

42 American Gas Association, *Gas Rate Fundamentals* (New York: 1960), p. 11.

43 Public Service Commission of Wisconsin, *Statistics of Wisconsin Public Utilities,* 1952 and 1959 Editions.

44 American Gas Association, *Gas Facts,* 1961 ed., p. 98; U.S. Bureau of Mines, *Mineral Market Report MMS No. 3298* (1961).

Table 10.1

Sales by Gas Distributors
1932–1960
(millions of therms)[1]

Types of Gas	1932	1945	1960	Percentage Change	
				1932-1945	1945-1960
Natural	8,190.0	22,562.8	90,545.5	+175	+301
Manufactured[2]	1,731.1	2,110.7	175.9	+ 22	− 92
Mixed	520.2	1,194.2	2,155.0	+130	+ 80
Total	10,441.3	25,867.7	92,876.4	+148	+259

[1] One therm equals 100,000 Btu.

[2] Includes liquefied petroleum gas.

Sources: American Gas Association, *Historical Statistics of the Gas Industry,* p. 157; *Gas Facts,* 1961 Edition, p. 98.

The transition to natural gas and the growth in its sales were stimulated by the comparatively greater increases in the retail prices of competitive fuels during the past inflationary period. To be sure, the relation of gas prices to prices of other fuels varies regionally and from city to city. However, in some areas the greater price rises of other fuels left natural gas comparatively underpriced, which stimulated sales. In others, natural gas was priced so little above other fuels that its superior qualities made the price nonetheless attractive. Average retail prices are compared in the price indexes shown in the following table, which summarizes the pricing experience in the postwar period. There, it may be seen that natural gas has been priced substantially below competitive fuels, even though its average price rose at a comparatively more rapid rate during the period 1955–1960.

The problems encountered in the transition to natural gas were substantial but manageable. Plans had to be developed for the construction of facilities to receive and transport the gas from the point of pipeline delivery to the distribution system. Ordinarily these plans for construction required approval of the regulatory commission. It was also necessary to initiate a program to inform the consuming public of the transition so as to secure cooperation. This was required because natural gas has characteristics different from those of manufactured gas, and the necessary adaptation of customers' appliances had to be completed before natural gas could be supplied. The utilities also reconditioned their distribution systems so as to prevent leakage of the drier natural gas. Facilities were installed to humidify the gas (to prevent the drying out of pipe-joint packings and meter diaphragms) and to odorize it in the interest of safety.

The transition had the effect of making obsolete some of the plant and equipment formerly used to manufacture gas. The net book cost of the property sub-

Table 10.2

Indexes of Retail Fuel Prices
United States
(1945 = 100)

Fuels	1950	1955	1960
Natural gas	92.7	106.8	133.5
Anthracite coal	150.0	168.9	185.3
Bituminous coal	159.2	171.0	191.9
No. 2 Fuel oil	146.6	173.5	179.6

Source: U.S. Bureau of Labor Statistics, *Retail Price Indexes of Fuels and Electricity.*

ject to retirement, as well as the expenses incurred in accomplishing the transition, generally were allowed to be amortized over periods ranging from five to ten years. The new facilities installed to receive, transport, and treat the natural gas were included in the rate base. For the most part, the gas-manufacturing facilities retained and not retired were those which produced or could be converted to produce high-Btu-content gas such as oil gas and liquefied petroleum gas. These facilities serve as stand-by equipment in the event of an emergency and as an aid in peak-shaving. This refers to the use of gas-manufacturing facilities to produce gas on the coldest days of the year to supplement the deliveries of natural gas received from the pipeline. The effect of holding down the takes of pipeline gas on peak days is to reduce the distributor's peak demand. The latter is an important factor in determining pipeline charges for gas service as well as the pipeline's minimum bill. Peak-shaving reduces the distributor's peak demand upon the pipeline and results in a higher load factor for pipeline deliveries. Nearly all major utilities have some peak-shaving capacity. Aside from providing stand-by protection, the value of peak-shaving facilities can be calculated by contrasting the annual cost of service of such facilities with the costs of the one or more winter supply services offered by pipelines.

The effect upon rates of the transition to natural gas was varied and depended upon such factors as the adequacy of the rate of return that had been earned previously, the way rates were redesigned (if such occurred), the nature of the interfuel competition in the local market, the extent of the promotional rate policy adopted by management, and other factors. The experience in one state, Wisconsin, shows that rate decreases resulted from the introduction of natural gas, which began in 1949. The total of the rate decreases ordered into effect by 1952 amounted to over 20 per cent of the gas companies' annual operating revenue prior to the transition.[45]

C. Market Characteristics. During the manufactured gas era, gas utilities primarily served a residential market whose annual peak load in many cases occurred on Thanksgiving Day. As noted earlier, the volume of gas sold then was much less than that marketed after the transition to natural gas and the entrance into the space-heating and industrial fuels markets on a large scale.

In order to summarize the characteristics of the retail natural gas market, it is necessary to distinguish the basic types and classes of gas service. First of all, "firm" service is intended to have assured availability to the customer to meet his load requirements. Firm service is ordinarily available to all classes of customers. Space heating, although required only in winter, is a firm service. Second, "interruptible" service is made available under agreements which permit the curtailment or cessation of deliveries. Interruptible customers are almost always large-volume industrial consumers of fuel or steam electric generating stations. Curtailment or cessation of deliveries to interruptible customers ordinarily occurs when the gas is needed for firm service. (Interruptible customers generally are equipped to use more than one type of fuel.) A distributor may provide more than one type of interruptible service—each with a different curtailment priority. Third, "off-peak" and "seasonal" services are firm, but only for intervals of time specified by the utility. These differences in the character of the service warrant recognition in rates, because of the variations in the obligation of the utility to serve. The rates for interruptible and off-peak gas: (a) should be some-

[45] Calculated from data on file at the Public Service Commission of Wisconsin.

thing more than the out-of-pocket or incremental cost of providing the service; and (b) cannot exceed the prices of competitive fuels, or the gas will not be sold.

The respective classes of gas service and their demand characteristics differ considerably. The classes of service and their annual load factors are outlined in the following discussion: (1) *Residential general service* includes the various domestic uses of gas, exclusive of space heating. This class is characterized by substantial regularity and a high load factor, ranging between 75 and 85 per cent in most localities. (2) *Commercial general service* has the same characteristics. (3) *Residential and commercial space heating* provides a relatively low load factor of 20 to 28 per cent, because the demand for such service is highly seasonal. Space heating is an increasingly important market for natural gas, but it also places maximum demand upon the system during peak periods. (4) *Firm industrial service,* both large and small, has a load factor of 60 to 75 per cent, which is relatively high but is characterized by sensitivity to business recessions. Ideally, industrial loads should be well diversified between industries, so that the utility's sales need not follow the cycle of any particular industrial activity. Aside from this factor, however, the greater the firm industrial load, the better the possibility of improving the system load factor and the less will be the relative effect of the seasonal demands for space heating. (5) *Interruptible sales,* generally considered to have no load factor, are made under the condition that service can be curtailed in any degree at any time. Interruptible sales are depended upon by many gas distributors to fill in the off-peak summer "valley" (or low point) in demand and, thereby, to maintain the system annual load factor at a high level. Such sales are made at relatively low rates to industrial and steam electric customers equipped to use whatever fuel (oil, gas, or coal) may be the cheapest at any given time on a thermal basis.

The growth in the space-heating load, following the transition to natural gas, has been accompanied by an annual winter peak demand of enormous proportions compared to the summertime base load. The daily peak load during severe winter weather may be as much as ten times the base load provided by other firm services. During the warmer months, of course, space-heating sales fall sharply, depending upon seasonal temperatures. Thus, the winter space-heating peak is associated with a low summer valley in gas sales. Accordingly, many gas distributors are compelled to secure off-peak, seasonal, and interruptible markets in order to dispose of substantial amounts of "valley" gas. For example, the affiliated gas companies serving the Los Angeles metropolitan area ordinarily sell about half their annual volume of gas to interruptible customers. This relatively high proprotion of interruptible sales is largely due to the fact that natural gas has obtained about a 99 per cent saturation of the space-heating market in the Los Angeles area.

In making interruptible sales to industrial and power-plant customers in competition with other fuels, the utilities are required by the market to sell gas at a much lower price than that charged to firm customers. Of course, firm service is premium-quality service because of its assured availablity and therefore is more valuable. In addition, the unit cost of serving numerous small customers exceeds the cost of serving the relatively few large buyers of interruptible gas. However, the important point here is the fact that interruptible sales build up the load factor, increase revenues, and decrease the average cost per unit of gas sold to the firm customers. The need to make off-peak interruptible sales can be mitigated to the extent that the supplying pipeline and/or the distributor develop underground gas storage. The availability of underground storage capacity serves as a substitute for interruptible sales; off-peak gas can be stored for firm use later during the peak demand period in the winter. Thus, as storage capacity increases, there is a strong tendency to sell more firm gas and less interruptible gas.

D. *Rates and Rate Schedule Types.* Gas rates are stated on the basis of either the number of cubic feet or the number of therms delivered to the customers. One *therm* is a quantity of gas which has a heat content of 100,000 Btu. Some gas utilities adopted therm billing when they began to distribute different types of gas and gas mixtures which differed from one another in Btu content. Therm billing is adaptable to any type of gas, because it employs as a unit of measure a common denominator that looks only to the quantity of heat in the gas delivered to the customer. However, some commissions are averse to therm rates because of the difficulty customers have in checking their bills against meter readings.

Unlike the electric utilities, relatively few gas distributors establish class rate schedules that apply individually to residential, commercial, and industrial customers or subdivisions of those customer classes. In general, the rate schedules of gas distributors are fewer and considerably simpler than those of electric utilities. Although some gas distributors do establish class rate schedules, the majority employ a "general service" rate schedule that is applicable to all or most classes of firm service. Demand rate schedules, such as the Hopkinson and Wright types, are relatively little used by gas distributors. The block meter-type rate schedule predominates, to the virtual exclusion of all others. Monthly minimum charges are a standard characteristic of gas distributors' rate schedules.

Space-heating service may be offered under the general-service rate schedule; where this is the case, the last blocks are designed to be competitive with other fuels. If space heating is not offered under the general-service rate schedule, it may either be offered under a separate rate schedule and metered separately, or it may be offered under a rate schedule which also includes service to the space-heating customer's other gas-using appliances. Gas distributors have recognized a need to keep space-heating rates attractively low. They have generally taken the approach that, unless gas-heating units are installed in new housing, it may be uneconomic to build gas-main extensions to newly developed areas. If the latter occurs, the gas utilities would stand to lose the entire market in new housing projects. Hence, relatively low space-heating rates, especially in areas where competition is vigorous, are sometimes employed as a means of entering the new-housing market and making possible the sale of gas for other residential appliances.

In addition to the rate schedules referred to above, the gas distributor also may have rate schedules for: (a) large-volume service; and (b) seasonal, off-peak, and interruptible large-volume service. Depending upon the market, there may be more than one interruptible-rate schedule, each with differing priorities for curtailment; in addition, lower interruptible rates may be made available to specified classes of industrial customers where price competition with other fuels so requires.

A general-service rate schedule available to any customer for any purpose is illustrated below. (The term "per C" is an abbreviation for "per hundred cubic feet.")

Rate—Per meter per month	
First 1,000 cu. ft.	$1.12
Next 1,000 cu. ft.	8.0¢ per C
Next 4,000 cu. ft.	7.5¢ per C
Next 44,000 cu. ft.	7.2¢ per C
Next 50,000 cu. ft.	6.7¢ per C
All additional	6.2¢ per C
Minimum monthly charge	$1.50

A rate schedule for large-volume service is illustrated by the following:

Rate—Per month	
First 1,060 therms	9.07¢ per therm
Next 1,590 therms	8.67¢ per therm
Next 7,950 therms	7.86¢ per therm
Next 15,900 therms	7.36¢ per therm
Next 26,500 therms	6.85¢ per therm
Next 53,000 therms	6.15¢ per therm
All additional therms	5.54¢ per therm
Minimum monthly charge	$115.00

A rate schedule for interruptible industrial large-volume service is illustrated below:

Rate—Per month	
First 10,000 therms or less	$510.00
Next 90,000 therms	4.64¢ per therm
All additional	4.18¢ per therm
Minimum monthly charge	$510.00

The illustrative rate schedule shown above for interruptible sales is representative of a large number of cases. However, it may be noted that, in the area of off-peak, seasonal, and interruptible sales, a variety of rate-schedule types have been used in order to adapt prices and pricing practices to competitive market conditions.

In conclusion, the problem of the "regulatory lag" as it affects gas distributors' rates should be noted. (This matter also is discussed in Chapter 13.) A major expense item for gas distributors is the cost of natural gas purchased from pipeline suppliers. For many gas distributors, for example, the cost of purchased gas amounts to about half of total operating revenue deductions. The rates paid by distributors to interstate pipelines for purchased gas are under Federal Power Commission jurisdiction. Pipelines in recent years have been compelled to apply to the FPC for rate increases more often than in the past, as a result of their rising costs of doing business. Under the Natural Gas Act, these rate increases (after a five-month suspension period) may be put into effect subject to possible refund when the case is ultimately decided. The FPC has not been able to decide these cases as fast as they have been arising. The result has been a regulatory lag, with 200 to 300 million dollars in pipeline rate increases (on an annual basis) pending ultimate decision during the late 1950's and early 1960's. In other words, distributors were paying pipelines large amounts annually due to undecided rate cases, an unknown portion of which was subject to possible refund by the pipelines. This has posed important problems for gas distributors: (a) uncertainty as to the ultimate cost of purchased gas, which has made planning very difficult; (b) the possibility that some state commissions may decline to recognize a pipeline rate increase until made final by the FPC; and (c) the amount of the pipeline's increase finally authorized may be less than the rates originally permitted to become effective subject to refund, thereby requiring refunds to distributors and by distributors to their customers—a costly procedure. Gas distributors have made an effort to offset pipeline rate increases by: (a) filing for conventional rate increases with their state commissions; (b) filing "keep-whole" rate-increase applications which involve no issue other than offsetting the higher cost of purchased gas; and (c) increasing retail rates by the use of adjustment clauses, discussed previously.

4. NATURAL GAS PIPELINE RATES

Pipeline companies transport great and growing volumes of natural gas long distances in the countries of the North

American continent. In the United States, natural gas production is centered in the Southwest, while some of the principal markets are in the cities on the coasts and in the industrial heartland. Similarly, Canada's gas reserves are principally in Alberta, whereas the major markets are on the Pacific Coast, the cities of Eastern Canada, and the upper Midwestern states of this country. North America is not the only place where long-distance pipelines have been constructed; however, this form of transportation has not been so extensively developed in other areas of the world. At the time of writing, pipelines were transporting natural gas in Argentina, France, Italy, India, Pakistan, and Russia. Although there has been a promising experiment in the long-distance ocean transportation of natural gas in liquid form by tanker, the most economical means of transporting gas is by pipeline.[46] The present section is concerned with rate making for interstate natural gas pipelines in the United States; other important aspects of natural gas pipeline regulation and economics are discussed in Chapter 14.

Under the Natural Gas Act of 1938, the Federal Power Commission regulates the rates charged by interstate natural gas transmission companies for sales to local gas distributors and to other interstate pipelines. These are interstate wholesale sales for resale to the public. The Commission does not have rate jurisdiction over "direct" sales by interstate pipelines to ultimate consumers. Thus, for example, the Commission cannot pass upon the justness and reasonableness of a pipeline's rate for sales made directly to a steel mill. This is explained by the fact that pipeline direct sales to ultimate consumers are predominantly to industrial customers, and the interfuel competition for the industrial market is so great that industrial buyers have no need for regulatory protection. However, the foregoing does not mean that the Commission is without any powers over the rates charged by pipelines making nonjurisdictional sales. This matter will be discussed in the present section in connection with cost allocations and in Chapter 14.

A. *Economic Factors Affecting Pipeline Rate Making.*[47] Natural gas transmission companies are characterized by large fixed capital investments. Plant investment averages about three times the annual gross operating revenues, thus indicating a slow rate of capital turnover. Second, pipelines are faced with sharp seasonal variations in demand, largely due to the winter space-heating load. The investment in the pipeline system is determined primarily by: (a) the volume of gas to be delivered on the peak day each year; (b) the distance the gas is transported; and (c) the nature of the areas traversed. Owing to the large fixed costs resulting from the heavy investment in plant, small volumes of gas cannot be transported economically over great distances. Thus, the problem in making rates is centered around the fact that high fixed costs and fluctuating seasonal demand characterize the economics of most pipeline operations.

Other important economic factors are these: (1) The bulk of the plant investment is in the form of mains and compressing equipment, with relatively small amounts in the form of measuring and regulating equipment, related structures,

[46] Henry F. Lippitt II, analyzes the regulatory jurisdiction over tanker shipments of natural gas in 39 *Texas Law Review* 601 (1961).

[47] The principal sources of this section are J. J. Hedrick, "Economics of Long-Distance Gas Supply," *Gas Age,* Sept. 6, 1956, pp. 37–42; and Federal Power Commission, Natural Gas Investigation, *Report of Commissioner Nelson Lee Smith and Commissioner Harrington Wimberly* (Washington, D.C.: Government Printing Office, 1948), pp. 252–294.

and land rights. (2) The delivery cost of natural gas increases in close proportion to the length of a transmission line of any given diameter operating at a given load factor. Accordingly, there is strong incentive to seek a high utilization of pipeline capacity in order to spread the heavy fixed costs over a large volume and to reduce the average unit cost of transportation. (3) The average book cost per mile of line generally increases somewhat more than proportionately as the diameter of the line increases. (4) The volume capacity rises more rapidly with increased diameter than the increased cost per mile. Therefore, the larger the line diameter, the lower the unit transportation cost at capacity volume. (5) Fixed costs, covering such items as depreciation, taxes, and return, account for 80 to 90 per cent of the total costs of transporting natural gas. (6) Accordingly, for a transmission line of any given length, diameter, and operating pressure, the cost of transportation per unit of volume varies inversely (although not necessarily proportionately) with the load factor. This statement simply expresses the mathematical fact that more complete utilization of capital facilities involving mostly fixed costs will result in declining unit costs. The annual load factor is the percentage relationship of the average daily demand to the maximum daily demand.

The effect of higher load factors in producing decreasing unit costs, while important, should not be overemphasized. First of all, the effect of load factor upon the transportation costs per unit (conventionally 1,000 cubic feet or an Mcf, at stated temperature and pressure) is quite pronounced in the lower range of load factors up to about 60 per cent, reflecting the influence of larger volumes over which to spread the fixed costs. However, as load factors rise above 60 per cent, further reductions of unit costs are progressively smaller, in part because variable costs are a greater percentage of total costs. There is thus a tendency toward a leveling off in the downward-sloping average unit-cost curve with increases in load factor. Second, the diminishing ability of successively higher load factors to yield further economies is also influenced by the diameter of the line. For any given length of line with a given load factor, the larger the line diameter, the lower the delivery cost of gas. Within broad limits, the diameter of the pipeline is a more important economic factor affecting transportation costs than the load factor. For example, at a given operating pressure, a 24-inch line operated at 60 per cent load factor will have about the same transportation cost per Mcf as a 16-inch line operated at 100 per cent load factor, if the two lines were built at about the same time. This reflects the fact that as the diameter increases, the capacity or volume increases by about the square of the increase in diameter. There is, of course, a practical upper limit to the diameter of the pipe. These factors lead to the conclusion that higher system load factors, while important, should not be regarded as an exclusive test of sound marketing policy by pipelines.

The demand upon a pipeline system for firm service is characterized by a maximum or peak demand in the winter and a minimum demand, or "valley," in the summer. ("Firm" service is that having assured availability to meet customer requirements.) This sharp seasonal difference in the demand for firm service is due almost entirely to space-heating requirements during the cold months of the year. The following diagram of the annual load curve of a major interstate gas pipeline system illustrates the seasonal character of the firm demand. In order to fill in the summer valley period, pipelines find it necessary to make some other disposition of the

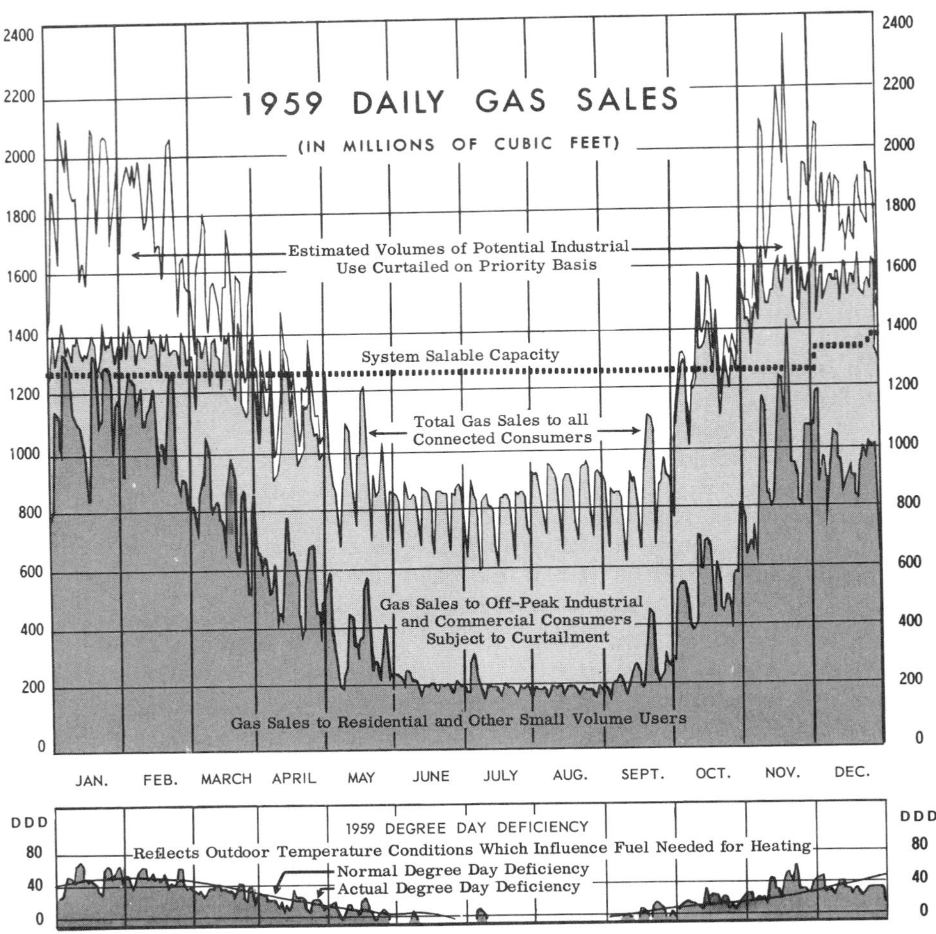

FIGURE 10-A. DIAGRAM ILLUSTRATING THE ANNUAL CYCLE OF NATURAL GAS DELIVERY AND USE.

From: Northern Natural Gas Company 1959 Annual Report to Stockholders, page 13.

gas they can deliver at that time. The principal off-peak market is provided by interruptible sales both to gas distributors for resale to industrial customers and to industrial customers directly served by the pipeline itself. (Interruptible service is made available under agreements which permit curtailment or cessation of deliveries by the supplier.) The diagram of the pipeline annual load curve also illustrates the time of occurrence of off-peak sales. Sales of this kind are of vital importance to the pipeline and its firm customers for two principal reasons: (1) They assist materially in maintaining the annual load factor at a level which permits attainment of the economies inherent in high fixed-cost operations. (2) They bear a portion of the fixed costs, which reduces the fixed-cost burden otherwise borne by firm customers. On the other hand, interruptible gas in many markets must be sold in rigorous price competition with oil or coal or both. Industrial customers whose fuel costs are a significant element in total costs ordinarily are prudently equipped to convert their fuel-consuming facilities on short notice to the use of the cheapest fuel that may be available from time to time. Thus, producers of cement, bricks, and steel, as well as steam electric utilities and others, will buy off-peak and interruptible gas only if the price is right. In short, the value of service as measured by the cost of alternative fuels sets a definite ceiling on the prices that can be charged for various types of off-peak service. This places a particular responsibility upon the Federal Power Commission, for it has chosen to exercise a far greater measure of control over the design of pipeline rates than is ordinarily the case in the other regulatory agencies. This is all the more important in light of the fact that FPC rate-design policies with respect to pipeline interruptible sales simultaneously affect the ability of the gas distributors to resell interruptible gas purchased from pipelines. This matter will be discussed in greater detail presently.

As an alternative to off-peak interruptible sales, some pipelines and distributors have developed underground gas-storage capacity in depleted natural gas reservoirs or other suitable geological structures near important markets. Where such is possible, summer and excess daily deliveries can be held in storage until needed in the winter heating season. The development of storage by a pipeline is ordinarily more feasible than for a distributor, because a storage field is usually not available close to the distributor's service area and, except for the largest service areas, would probably provide more capacity than needed. Although the pipeline industry traditionally has depended upon interruptible sales for load equation, the recent trend is toward the development of storage facilities by pipelines and, in some cases, by major distributors. The main reasons for the increased development of storage capacity are summarized below:

(1) The interruptible market, in this maturing stage of the pipeline industry's development, appears to hold considerably less prospect for growth than it did when the industry was younger.

(2) Rising costs and FPC pricing policies have tended to reduce the profit margin on interruptible sales in some areas and have limited the ability of natural gas to compete with other fuels for the industrial market.

(3) Residential service, especially space heating, appears to represent the principal source of potential growth in the demand for gas. Moreover, the value of gas in the residential market is greater than in the interruptible market. However, growth in the residential market will have the effect of increasing winter-peak demands.

(4) While pipelines without storage capacity must have pipeline capacity to meet peak demands, the use of storage reduces the amount of installed capacity, between the gas fields and the storage area, required to serve a given peak.

(5) The development of storage capacity to meet peak demands is sometimes more economical than providing the equivalent pipeline capacity. Furthermore, storage provides deliverability near the furthest points of pipeline delivery, where the cost of pipeline capacity exceeds the system average owing to the relatively higher costs of land rights and the need to cross a greater number of highways, railroad tracks, and similar installations.

Storage capacity has increased at a rapid rate. The number of storage pools increased from 50 in 1944 to 205 at the end of 1958, an increase of over 300 per cent. The growth in storage capacity, a more important measure, has increased even more. The total of storage capacity in the country has increased from 135 billion cubic feet in 1944 to 2.7 trillion cubic feet in 1958—an increase of twenty times in the 14-year period. The location of storage capacity is concentrated in a few states, but near major markets. The principal states, by far, are Pennsylvania, Ohio, West Virginia, and Michigan, which account for over 60 per cent of storage capacity and over 70 per cent of all the gas in storage. Also important, but considerably less so, are New York, California, Iowa, Illinois, and Missouri, among others.

It has been recognized in some quarters of the natural gas industry that the policy of seeking maximum load factor through off-peak interruptible sales may require reconsideration. Where there are markets for firm rather than interruptible industrial gas service, a pipeline or distributor may be better off with the selective development of such markets, even though the resultant load factor may be 60 to 70 per cent rather than 90 per cent through interruptible sales. A general shift from interruptible to firm industrial service, with appropriate repricing of the service, would make high system-load factors less important to successful operations. Another prospect for the solution of the summer valley problem is gas air conditioning.

B. *Gas Tariffs.* The rates charged by an interstate pipeline for jurisdictional service (sales for resale to the public) are shown in the rate schedules included in the pipeline's FPC Gas Tariff. Under these tariff rate schedules, a pipeline charges each customer on the same basis for each class of service provided. This pricing format is relatively simple and assures uniform rates throughout the pipeline's system or within each rate zone for each class of service sold. Standard rate schedules, set forth in tariffs, are a relatively recent development. Before the passage of the Natural Gas Act in 1938, pipelines made sales on an individual contract basis with each customer. In the absence of regulation, conducting business on the basis of private contracts, of course, is conventional practice. As might be expected, the terms contained in the contracts between a pipeline and its customers often varied from one to another. The Natural Gas Act authorized the Commission to prescribe rules whereby each company subject to the Act would file its schedules of rates, together with the classifications, practices, and regulations affecting such rates, and all related contracts. Accordingly, the Commission prescribed provisional rules allowing the companies to file their existing contracts as rate schedules. The bulk, complexity, and dissimilarity of the hundreds of contracts filed made it apparent that simplification was necessary.

As a first step in the simplification process, the Commission in 1940 released a draft of tentative instructions for preparing and filing pipeline rates in the form of system-wide tariffs under which each pipeline would charge each customer under the same rate schedule for each class of service. (This is not to say that the Commission intended rate uniformity as among pipelines; rather, the purpose was to have each pipeline charge under the same rate schedule for each class of service to each of its distributor customers within the same general area.) The work involved in reaching agreement on how to convert contractual rate schedules to the tariff form was delayed by World War II. However, a substantial number of pipeline companies voluntarily converted their rate forms from contracts to tariffs. By 1948, the Commission and the industry had worked out a plan for going forward with a general conversion to tariff rates. In that year the Commission issued Order No. 144, which prescribed rules for converting all pipeline rate contracts into the "tariff-and-service-agreement" form.[48] Additionally, Order No. 144 provided for special situations where it was preferable to permit the filing of contracts as rate schedules. By 1950 the conversion had been completed. The filed tariffs covered about 100 companies and consisted of about 1,860 pages in replacement of over 13,000

[48] 13 Fed. Reg. 6371 (1948).

pages contained in over 700 contracts which previously served as rate schedules.

A pipeline's tariff consists of three parts: (1) the schedules of rates; (2) the terms and conditions of service; and (3) the service agreement between the pipeline and its customers. The forms of the schedules of rates will be discussed shortly. The terms and conditions of service consist of definitions and provisions relating to the quality and measurement of the gas to be delivered, billing, payments, delivery pressures, and other similar matters. The service agreements are contracts which constitute acceptance by the customer of the service, terms, and rates offered in the tariff. Most important of all is the language in the service agreement describing what the parties have agreed to with respect to future changes in pipeline rates.

Service agreements in the form of contracts between a pipeline and its customers are definite over the long term as to quantities and conditions of service but indefinite as to price. By the terms of the service agreements, pipelines reserve the right to change their rates in accordance with the provisions of the Natural Gas Act. To explain this, it should be pointed out first that the rates authorized by the Commission to be charged by a pipeline at the commencement of service under uniform tariffs are called "initial rates." The initial rates would continue to be charged until: (a) the Commission, after an investigation, ordered a change; or (b) the pipeline's cost of service changed. In the latter event, the rate-changing procedure then and now is this: (1) if the company files a notice of a change in rates with the Commission, proposing to put such rates into effect at a particular date, and (2) if the Commission permits the changes in rates to become effective, then the pipeline's customers will be required to pay the new effective rates. It should be noted that, under law, the Commission may suspend, or delay, the effectiveness of the proposed new rates for up to five months in order to study the matter or to hold hearings and to reach a decision. Where this is not enough time to decide, the new rates may become effective "subject to refund"—that is, the pipeline is allowed to charge the new rates, but under an obligation to repay any amounts subsequently found to be unjustified, plus interest at seven per cent per annum.

The nature of the service agreement with respect to rates, therefore, is that future rates are indefinite; the customer companies agree to pay under the applicable rate schedules as they may be superseded or changed from time to time by order of the Commission. The pipeline customers retain the right to protest any proposed increase in rates and to file a petition to take part in the Commission's proceedings in order to oppose them. To illustrate the nature of the agreement between pipelines and their customers with respect to future changes in rates, the Tennessee Gas Transmission Co. service agreement provision on this point states: "Buyer agrees that Seller may seek authorization from duly constituted authorities for such adjustment of Seller's existing FPC Gas Tariff as may be found necessary to assure Seller just and reasonable rates." Similarly, United Gas Pipe Line Co. and its customers agree that "All gas delivered hereunder shall be paid for by Buyer under Seller's Rate Schedules . . . or any effective superseding rate schedules, on file with the Federal Power Commission." The key words here are "effective superseding."

The Commission has found the above procedure for charging and changing pipeline rates to be in the public interest.[49] The foregoing procedure was

[49] *Re El Paso Natural Gas Co.,* 19 FPC 154; 21 PUR 3d 453 (1958).

upheld by the United States Supreme Court in the now famous *Memphis* case.[50]

C. *Pipeline Rate Forms.* The principal rate form used by pipelines for sales of firm service is the two-part "demand-commodity" rate. Under the demand-commodity rate form, the customer's bill is the total of: (1) a demand charge, stated in terms of a specific dollar amount per Mcf of demand per month; and (2) a commodity charge, stated in terms of cents per Mcf of gas delivered. For example, the Lake Shore Pipe Line Co. G-1 General Service rate schedule for firm service to customers in its service area in northeastern Ohio and northwestern Pennsylvania sets forth the following charges:

Monthly Demand Charge—$4.57 per Mcf of daily demand
Commodity Charge—28.64¢ per Mcf

This rate schedule also provides for a minimum monthly bill equal to the demand charge. "Billing demand" is defined as the greatest day's delivery during the twelve-month period ending with the billing month.

Pipelines which transport gas over particularly great distances usually have their service areas divided into rate zones, with higher rates charged in the zones farthest from the sources of gas supply. This is illustrated by the Northern Natural Gas Co. Contract Demand, or CD, rate schedules:

Rate Schedule	Zone	Charge per Mcf: Monthly Demand	Commodity
CD–1	1	$2.87	21.9¢
CD–2	2	3.18	22.4
CD–3	3	3.50	22.9

The minimum monthly bill is the demand charge. For this purpose the billing demand is the "contract demand," which is the specified portion of the pipeline's installed capacity dedicated to the service of each gas distributor supplied under this series of rate schedules. Because the demand-commodity rate form is the principal method of charging for firm service to distributor customers, it will be discussed further at a later point in this section.

Second, there is the "volumetric" type of rate schedule, under which a stated rate in cents per Mcf is charged for the entire volume of gas delivered. The straight volumetric rate is seldom used for firm service except as noted below. However, it is sometimes required by the FPC for a new pipeline during its early years and until the pipeline has had some experience with its market. The Michigan Wisconsin Pipe Line Co., for example, commenced service late in 1949 under a straight volumetric rate, and was authorized to convert its rate schedules to the demand-commodity form in 1959. The volumetric rate is also used for non-firm services, as well as an optional rate form available to small distributors. The use of the volumetric rate for pipeline sales of firm service to small distributors, served under Small General Service rate schedules, permits such companies to avoid the complexities accompanying the use of the demand-commodity rate form, particularly the task of estimating demand.

Third, the "base load-excess" rate form is used in a few cases but has been almost entirely superseded by the demand-commodity rate. The base load-excess rate is sometimes called the "summer-winter" rate, for reasons which will be made clear. Texas Gas Transmission Corp. offers this form of rate in each service zone as an option to small distributors having daily contract demand of less that 5,000 Mcf for resale.

---

[50] *United Gas Pipe Line Co. et al.* v. *Memphis Light, Gas and Water Division,* 358 U.S. 103 (1958); rehearing denied, 358 U.S. 942 (1959).

The base load charge in Zone 1, for example, is 23.37 cents per Mcf. The *base load* is defined as the number of days in the month multiplied by the average daily delivery during the previous June, July, August, and September. All gas taken in excess of the base load in any month is charged for at the rate of 34.37 cents per Mcf. Fourth, some pipelines charge for their deliveries under a "cost-of-service" type of rate. This form of rate is used when the selling pipeline supplies gas to an affiliated company. The rate is determined entirely from the selling company's accounting records and is independent of any specific delivery volume.

Some further detail in the demand-commodity rate form merits noting. The illustrations of demand-commodity rates in the discussion above indicate different methods of determining the billing demand. Three bases are ordinarily used: (1) contract demand, which is the firm delivery obligation of a pipeline to a distributor customer; (2) the greatest day's delivery during the twelve months ending with the billing month, but not less than some stated percentage of contract demand nor more than contract demand; and (3) the same as (2) above, except that the greatest day's delivery during the billing month is used instead of the twelve-month period ending with the billing month. Among the demand-commodity rates charged by pipelines, the predominant measure of billing demand is contract demand. A second important function of contract demand, in addition to pricing, is defining the service that is to be supplied and received. Some companies, which do not use contract demand in pricing, place contract-demand limitations upon the service to be supplied.

Since the end of World War II, most pipelines at one time or another have been faced with demands for more gas during the winter than they had capacity to supply. The function of contract demand as a limitation upon service reflects this fact, because formerly, when pipelines had excess winter capacity, they ordinarily contracted to serve their customers' "entire requirements." With a reversed situation, contract-demand limitations provide distributors with a clear indication of the pipeline capacity available to them. Further, contract-demand limitations permit planned expansion and development of distributors' markets, balancing at all times distributor demand and pipeline supply. As pipelines expand, contract-demand changes enable distributors to share in the allocation of the additional pipeline capacity. An important benefit resulting from this approach is that distributors' estimates of their needs are under pressure to be accurate, because the distributor will pay the pipeline on the basis of the capacity dedicated to it. Careful estimates tend to prevent overexpansion of the pipeline's installed capacity, with the benefits shared by all parties. Further, with contract demand setting the billing demand, installation of peak-shaving capacity can be undertaken in light of the relative costs of either a higher contract demand or the installation of peak-shaving facilities. Above all, excessive capacity of either alternative tends to be avoided.

D. Rate-Design Procedure—The Atlantic Seaboard Formula. Pipeline rates, like public utility rates generally, are designed to produce revenues equivalent to the approved cost of service. However, the policy of the Federal Power Commission toward the design of pipeline rates differs from the practices generally followed in other jurisdictions. It has been pointed out previously that the prevailing regulatory practice is to allow utility management considerable latitude in proposing and designing the rates to be charged, and that the design of such rates may reflect consideration of cost analysis and value of service, together with the application of experienced judgment. Federal Power Commission policy in this area differs from the general practice elsewhere; the Commission ordinarily will approve only those rates which are based upon its Atlantic Seaboard formula, discussed below, for the allocation of system-wide costs. This is not to say that the element of judgment has no function in the design of pipeline rates, for it does. However, the judgment element enters in the treatment of costs in the Atlantic Seaboard formula rather than in the design of the rates themselves. On the other hand, managerial judgment and value of service, as a rule, are given little or no weight in the design of pipeline rates.

The Commission's formula for determining the rates it will approve was set forth at length in a 1952 decision involving the rates of the Altantic Seaboard Corporation.[51] Hence, it has come to be called the Atlantic Seaboard formula. The Commission has stated that this formula is a rule of general applicability in rate cases. The Atlantic Seaboard formula enters the rate-making picture after the total cost of service for the test year has been determined. In this respect it should be noted that, where a pipeline has nonjurisdictional business (such as firm and interruptible sales directly off the main line and not for resale), the Commission will consider the over-all cost of service for both jurisdictional and nonjurisdictional business. The Commission has received court approval of its right to consider the total operations of a pipeline as one step toward determining the costs of the regulated portion of the business.[52]

In applying the Atlantic Seaboard formula, the Commission generally requires a system-wide allocation of costs. Under this procedure, the first step is a functional segregation of total system costs into such categories as production, storage, transmission, distribution, and general costs. Second, these costs are classified between the demand (capacity) and commodity (volume) functions. Conventionally, demand costs are considered to be the fixed costs associated with the capacity of facilities, while commodity costs are taken to be the variable costs associated with the volume of service delivered. This distinction is not preserved in the Atlantic Seaboard formula, as discussed below. Third, the costs classified to the demand and commodity categories are allocated between jurisdictional and nonjurisdictional business. Fourth, rates are determined on the basis of the jurisdictional costs, which may apply on a system-wide basis or to individual rate zones reflecting distance differentials.

A principal feature of the Atlantic Seaboard formula arises in the classification of system-wide costs to the demand and commodity functions. Here the formula requires that the fixed-cost items be distributed equally, on a 50–50 basis, to the demand and commodity categories. Thus the costs comprising the commodity category include all the variable costs plus at least half the fixed costs, such as depreciation expense, return, property and income taxes, and those transmission expenses which are not a function of volume. The demand category of costs accordingly includes only half these fixed transmission costs. Another characteristic of the formula is that the costs of gas gathering, processing, and production, as well as the cost of gas purchases from independent producers, are all classified entirely to the commodity function, even though some of those costs are fixed and not variable.

[51] *Re Atlantic Seaboard Corp.*, 11 FPC 43; 94 PUR (NS) 235 (1952).

[52] *Colorado Interstate Gas Co.* v. *FPC*, 324 U.S. 581 (1945).

Similar treatment is accorded operating and maintenance expenses related to the volume of gas transported, such as compressor station fuel, supplies, and maintenance of equipment. In some cases, the Commission has treated the following as commodity costs: sales promotion, regulatory expenses, and portions of distribution and customers' accounting and collection costs. General and administrative expenses are classified on the basis of supervised expenditures.

After the classification of costs between the demand and commodity functions, the next step is the allocation of the classified costs among classes of jurisdictional service and the nonjurisdictional service. (1) The costs classified as commodity costs are allocated to jurisdictional and nonjurisdictional service in proportion to the test-year volumes of gas taken by each. (2) The costs classified as demand costs are allocated to classes of jurisdictional service and to nonjurisdictional sales on the basis of peak responsibility, using the three-day (average) sustained peak demand on the system for this purpose. Thus, annual volume and peak responsibility serve to allocate the classified costs both to classes of jurisdictional service and to nonjurisdictional sales.

As a final step, the jurisdictional rates are determined by relating allocated costs to demand and sales volumes. In the simple example shown below, the demand and commodity components of the two-part rate are calculated by: (1) dividing the total jurisdictional costs allocated to demand by the total demand billing units; and (2) dividing the total jurisdictional costs allocated to commodity by the annual volume of gas sold.[53]

In its *Atlantic Seaboard* decision, the Commission viewed a pipeline as serving a demand (capacity) function during peak periods as well as an annual commodity (volume) function wholly apart from consideration of peak demands. Accordingly, both the demand and the commodity functions were found to be responsible for portions of a pipeline's fixed costs. The Commission held that the relative importance of the demand and commodity functions could not be measured with scientific accuracy. Thus, the amount of fixed costs to be allocated to each function was concluded to be a matter of informed judgment. Neither the capacity nor the volume function was found to predominate. Therefore, the Commission decided to allocate the fixed costs equally between the demand and commodity functions. As a result, all gas transported by the pipeline bears a share of the fixed costs. This ruling thereby recognized the important principle that no type of service is entitled to a "free ride" on the line, because there had to be a line before there could be a ride. In this regard it can be seen that pipeline sales of interruptible gas, priced at the level of the commodity charge alone, will recover out-of-pocket costs and make some contribution toward fixed costs. This follows necessarily from the fact that the costs classified to commodity include at least one-half the fixed costs. The fact that the formula permits no free ride on the line is its greatest strength, wholly apart from the

[53] *Re Ohio Fuel Gas Co.*, 15 FPC 1623, 1634 (1956).

	Total	*Demand*	*Commodity*
Cost of service	$21,127,008	$5,967,176	$15,159,832
Demand billing units (Mcf)		3,816,887	—
Commodity volume (Mcf)		—	46,756,900
Unit costs		$1.56336	32.42266¢
Unit rates		$1.56	32.45¢

amount of the charge made for such use. However, the formula and the way it is administered also have been the subject of serious criticism, as discussed in the following section.[54]

E. *Some Effects of Atlantic Seaboard.* It has been noted that the Commission ordinarily uses the three-day sustained peak demand on the system in applying the peak-responsibility method of allocating the costs classified to demand among nonjurisdictional business and classes of jurisdictional business. However, the system peak, thus measured, does not necessarily occur during the coldest weather when the space-heating demands of firm customers are the greatest. During the coldest days of the winter, pipelines curtail or stop interruptible deliveries so as to assure an adequate supply of firm gas. At other times the interruptible service is again made available without endangering the supply to firm customers. The latter situation is more apt to result in a greater sustained peak demand on the system than the maximum demand recorded in coldest weather when caution requires the interruptible sales to be curtailed. In fact, some pipelines have experienced their annual peaks in spring or fall.

The Commission's use of the sustained peak demand on the system as an allocation basis, rather than the peak registered on the coldest days, has the effect of shifting some capacity costs from the pipeline's firm sales to its off-peak and interruptible business. The significance of this, apart from other considerations, is that the Commission's method of measuring peak demand increases the portion of total costs which must be recovered from sales of interruptible gas sold directly for ultimate consumption or for resale. Such gas can only be sold on a comparative price basis in rigorous competition with fuel oil and coal. Thus, the effect of the peak selected is to reduce the ability of gas to compete on a price basis in the market for industrial fuels. It has been noted that interruptible sales, for some pipelines, are necessary to maintain load factors at economical levels; the shifting of costs to these sales hampers the maintenance or achievement of such load factors.

The foregoing effect of the formula is further enlarged by the inflexible allocation of one-half the fixed costs to the commodity category without consideration of the conditions of demand in the markets where the gas must be sold. Since the resulting commodity charge is a basis for the pricing of interruptible sales, the formula in effect sets a price floor which limits the salability of this type of gas, while its competitor fuels are free to adjust prices to meet market conditions. To the extent that the sales of off-peak and interruptible gas are limited, the fixed costs which might have been recovered from such sales cannot be recovered, and the burden thus shifts to firm customers. The tendency of the formula to impede interruptible sales is borne out by the fact that the various coal interests are the staunchest supporters of the Atlantic Seaboard formula, in their numerous interventions in pipeline cases before the FPC. The purpose of their participation in such cases, of course, is to protect their markets from gas competition.

Second, the Atlantic Seaboard formula tends both to overcharge for service to high-load-factor customers and to undercharge for service to low-load-factor customers. This comes about as a result of the allocation of half the fixed costs to the commodity category for recovery in proportion to the volume of sales to

---

[54] Henry Herz, "Impact of Cost Allocation on Gas Pricing," 58 *Public Utilities Fortnightly* 685 (1956); Hans E. Nissel, "The Impact of Cost Allocations upon Future of the Natural Gas Industry," 66 *Public Utilities Fortnightly* 512 (1960).

the various pipeline customers. For example, if a high-load-factor firm customer and a low-load-factor firm customer have equal peak demands, they pre-empt the same amounts of peak capacity, and the pipeline therefore has incurred the same amount of fixed costs for each. However, although these two customers would pay the same demand charges under the formula, the high-load-factor customer would bear a greater share of the pipeline's fixed costs. More specifically, the high-load-factor customer will bear a greater share of the 50 per cent of fixed costs that are classified to the commodity category. This necessarily follows from the fact that the high-load-factor customer purchases a greater volume than the low-load-factor customer. Since each unit of volume, as priced under the formula, includes a share of the fixed costs, the large-volume customer accordingly bears considerably more in total fixed costs than the low-load-factor customer of equal peak responsibility.[55] The effects of this tendency appear to be undesirable. A low-load factor pipeline customer oftentimes is a gas distributor with a substantial space heating load, who has neither underground storage nor extensive peak-shaving facilities, while the high-load-factor customer ordinarily has achieved that condition by the development or installation of such facilities. The tendency to undercharge the low-load-factor customer tends also to underprice and hence to stimulate that customer's sales of peak-causing, low-load-factor space-heating service. This has the further effect of widening the gap between the summer valley and winter peak in demand. On the other hand, the pipeline's high-load-factor customers both incur the costs of the facilities which make the high load factor possible and pay more for gas as a result. This deters investment in peak-shaving and underground storage facilities, and thus works against the achievement of high-load-factor operations. It may be noted that the above effects combine to produce a particularly disadvantageous situation, in that peak-causing space-heating sales tend to be stimulated at the same that the off-peak and interruptible sales, needed to fill the valley period, are made more difficult to achieve.

Another effect of the Atlantic Seaboard formula is to increase the risk of the pipeline industry, which is characterized by a high debt ratio even by comparison with the electric and gas distribution utility industries. At the same time, the Atlantic Seaboard formula makes pipelines dependent for the recovery of at least half their fixed costs upon volumetric sales, whose quantity is sensitive to both warm winters and business recessions. In recognition of this risk element, some pipelines have instituted a minimum take-or-pay-for requirement in the commodity charge in their rate schedules. This would be unnecessary if the demand charge were calculated so as to better protect the pipelines' fixed-cost responsibilities.

F. ***Rate Differentials Reflect Distance.*** The Commission has held that "In the absence of compelling reasons to the contrary, it is good and desirable practice to fix rates that are uniform."[56] This

---

[55] A recognized rate-design principle requires charging the high-load-factor customer more per unit of capacity than the low-load-factor customer of equal peak demand, on the ground that the high-load-factor customer makes greater average use of a unit of capacity. However, a correlative rate-design principle requires that a customer using a portion of capacity exclusively should pay no more in demand costs than those associated with the capacity pre-empted. The Atlantic Seaboard formula is consistent with the first principle but incapable of observing the second principle. To the extent that the latter is not observed, the high-load-factor customer tends to be overcharged.

[56] *In the Matter of City of Cleveland* v. *Hope Natural Gas Co.*, 3 FPC 150, 190 (1942).

refers to system-wide rate schedules for each class of service offered by the pipeline. However, in the case of some pipelines, the Commission has found the distance separating different customers to be sufficiently important to compel a departure from uniform system-wide rate schedules. In such cases, the Commission has required the pipeline's service area to be divided into rate zones and has prescribed zone rate differentials which are intended to reflect the effect of distance upon the cost to serve. Where zone rates are substituted for system-wide rates, the rate level in each successive zone increases as the transmission distance from the source of gas supply increases.

The leading FPC case on the question of zone rate differentials, decided in 1955, involved Northern Natural Gas Co.[57] The Northern system runs in an essentially northeasterly direction. At the time of the case, it originated in the West Texas Panhandle and in the Hugoton Field in Kansas and Oklahoma and terminated near Minneapolis. Northern also supplies gas utilities at points in Kansas, Nebraska, Iowa, and South Dakota, as well as in Minnesota. The Commission found that Northern's system-wide rates to customers located as much as 600 miles apart were unlawful as unduly discriminatory and preferential. As a result, Northern was ordered: (1) to file revisions to its tariff reflecting the division of its system into three rate zones; and (2) to revise its rate schedules to provide an average rate differential of two cents per Mcf per zone as distance increased from the source of supply.

The claim that Northern's system-wide rates were unduly preferential and discriminatory was made by Northern's customers located relatively close to the sources of gas supply. They maintained that system-wide rates caused them to "subsidize" customers more distant from supply sources, and that this constituted the undue discrimination prohibited in the Natural Gas Act. Accordingly, these customers urged adoption of zone rates, contending that the distance gas is transported to points of delivery is a primary variable in the incurrence of transportation costs. The proponents of zoning took the position that Northern's markets closer to the source of gas supply involved less transportation expense than more remote markets and were entitled to a lower rate—unless factors other than distance counterbalanced the differences in transportation mileage and related costs. It was contended that no such offsetting factors were present.

In opposition, Northern and its Minnesota customers took the position that the large-volume sales made in the upper reaches of Northern's system benefited customers closer to the supply, because lower average transmission costs resulted. This argument in effect states that, for a given length of pipeline, with any given load factor, the average unit transmission cost declines as the diameter of the pipeline increases. This follows from that fact that, although costs increase approximately in proportion (or a little more) with increases in diameter, the capacity increases more than proportionately; thus, for example, the capacity of a 24-inch line is about three times that of a 16-inch line. Second, Northern argued that higher zone rates in the upper part of its service area would result in the loss of interruptible industrial sales, which would force higher demand charges to be borne by all of its customers. This argument turned on the fact that industrial gas sales in the Minneapolis–St. Paul area compete with low-priced coal transported by barge over waterways subsidized by

[57] *Re Northern Natural Gas Co.*, 9 PUR 3d 8 (1955).

the Government. In short, the value of service of industrial gas is less in the more distant reaches of the Northern system than in the area closer to the source of gas supply, where coal competition is not equally strong.

The commission decided in favor of zoning. It acknowledged that Northern's sales in Minnesota benefited customers elsewhere on the system by contributing to the large volume of gas handled and by reducing the unit cost of transmission. However, the fact that about 45 per cent of Northern's jurisdictional sales took place in Minnesota caused the Commission to conclude that jurisdictional sales in other states would make an equal or greater contribution to the reduced average cost of transmission. (Volumes of direct industrial sales were not considered.) The fact that over half of Northern's jurisdictional sales required less than 650 miles of transportation was regarded as significant. Accordingly, the Commission found that there was no concentration of sales in a single area of the system sufficient to prevail against the arguments of the proponents of zoning. In view of the fact that the delivery cost of natural gas increases in close proportion to the length of a pipeline of a given size, the Commission found that the distance factor was the prime determinant of the cost of rendering service, unless other circumstances outweighed the distance factor. No sufficiently counterbalancing factors were found to exist. Hence, distance was held to reflect with reasonable accuracy the relative cost of serving Northern's widely separated customers. Uniform system-wide rates in this case were found to be unlawful on the ground that such rates shifted transmission costs from Northern's more distant customers to others not responsible for such costs. The Commission ordered Northern's service area to be divided into three zones, each involving maximum transmission distances of 180 to 190 miles. The distances were calculated from the last northward point of supply input into the main line.

In order to give effect to its decision to reflect the distance factor through zone rate differentials, the Commission adopted the "Mcf-mile" method of allocating to each rate zone a share of the system-wide costs as classified in accordance with the Atlantic Seaboard formula. Costs thus allocated to zones, as a general rule, provide the principal or sole basis for the rates the Commission is willing to approve. Under the Mcf-mile method of allocating system-wide costs to rate zones, the first step is to determine total demand Mcf-miles and total commodity Mcf-miles for each rate zone. This is done by: (1) multiplying the average daily demand at each delivery point during the three-day system peak by the miles of haul to each point to obtain the total demand Mcf-miles for each zone; and (2) multiplying the annual delivery volume at each delivery point by the miles of haul to each point to obtain the total commodity Mcf-miles for each zone. In the second step of the Mcf-mile method, the costs classified to demand under the Atlantic Seaboard formula are divided by the total demand Mcf-miles in order to determine an average system-wide cost per demand Mcf-mile. This unit demand cost is then multiplied by the demand Mcf-miles for each zone to obtain the demand cost allocated to each zone or class of service therein. Third, the same procedure is followed with respect to the costs classified to the commodity function. The Mcf-mile method thus assigns the same cost to the transportation of an Mcf of gas per mile regardless of where within a pipeline's system the transportation takes place.

In the Northern case under discussion, the FPC employed the Mcf-mile method as a basis for ordering the company to file revised rate schedules which would produce an average revenue which increased two cents per zone as distance increased. This differential reflected the difference in average cost per Mcf purchased at a 70 per cent load factor.

It was noted previously that Northern and its Minnesota distributor customers opposed zoning, in part, on the ground that the resulting higher rates in the most distant zone would cause the loss of substantial industrial sales of gas. In recognition of the competitive market situation, the Commission authorized Northern to maintain a uniform commodity charge throughout its system and permitted the zone rate differential to be reflected solely in the demand charge. Thus, the rate impact of zoning would not affect off-peak and interruptible sales priced at or about the level of the commodity charge. If the FPC had not authorized this placement of the zone differential in the demand charge, the commodity charge in the most distant zone would have been 26 cents per Mcf. However, by permitting Northern to retain its prevailing system-wide commodity charge of 22.1 cents, industrial sales could continue to be made in competition with coal. Such sales could not have continued at the 26-cent level. Thus, the Commission departed from its formula so that the gas could be sold. This matter was to come up again in the "Black Dog" case, wherein the coal representatives opposed certification of a proposed direct sale of industrial gas by Northern on the ground that it was priced below the 26-cent commodity charge derived under a strict application of the Atlantic Seaboard and Mcf-mile methods. This will be discussed in Chapter 14.

G. The "Rolled-In" Rate Principle. The FPC has held consistently that it would be improper to base the allocation of costs and the determination of rates upon either the specific facilities or the specific gas supply sources serving a particular pipeline customer or group of customers. Thus, the costs associated with expanding the system physical plant or adding to the system gas supply are combined with past costs and taken as a whole for cost allocation and ratemaking purposes. This is called the "rolled-in" principle. It follows from the general view that a pipeline's facilities and gas supply constitute an integrated system serving all customers, rather than a specific customer or customer group.

Although rolling-in new costs with past costs is administratively feasible, it can be disadvantageous to the existing customers of an expanding pipeline if those customers do not receive or require additional service. The costs of new transmission facilities and new gas supplies historically have tended to increase. Under the rolled-in principle, the relatively higher costs of supplying expanded service are lumped together with the lower costs of the past. Thus, a rolled-in rate requires existing customers to pay a higher price and to bear part of the cost of an expansion from which they may receive little or no additional service. Conversely, use of the rolled-in principle ensures that two otherwise similar customers will not pay substantially different prices for commingled gas delivered by one pipeline system solely because one happens to have been receiving the service longer than the other. On balance, the rolled-in principle has been upheld upon review because it is considered to provide equal treatment for customers receiving equal service.[58] It may be noted that one reason why some pipelines have expanded through the incorporation of subsidiary pipeline companies is to avoid rolling-in the new,

[58] *Battle Creek Gas Co.* v. *FPC*, 281 F. 2d 42 (1960).

higher costs accompanying expansion. This is particularly the case where a pipeline, serving an area characterized by keen inter-fuel competition, cannot afford to roll-in the higher costs of later expansion without risking the possibility of pricing itself out of its industrial market.

11 Pricing Policies (Continued)

This chapter is concerned with the pricing policies of the telephone, water, and urban transit utility industries. It continues the survey of public utility pricing policies that was begun in the previous chapter.

The pricing of telephone, water, and urban transit services involves unique elements not encountered in the previous chapter. The telephone industry is regulated at the state and federal levels of government with respect to its intrastate and interstate services. No other utility industry is involved to the same extent in dual regulation of this kind. The water utility industry is predominantly government-owned and almost entirely free of rate regulation. As a result, the pricing of water service is based upon procedures and considerations which are quite different from those encountered up to this point. The urban transit industry is characterized by a long-run decline and relatively low earnings. Accordingly, it, too, provides a pricing situation involving a combination of factors not surveyed previously.

1. TELEPHONE RATES

This section examines telephone rates and their regulation. The development of this industry is covered in Chapter 20 in the discussion of the organization and structure of the utility industry.

A. *Introduction to the Telephone Industry.* Telephone services in the United States are provided by the American Telephone and Telegraph Co. (AT&T) and its associated operating companies, together with the 3,560 interconnecting independent (unaffiliated) telephone companies. AT&T is a holding company; through its Long Lines Department and associated operating companies, it provides practically all of the interstate long-distance telephone service supplied to consumers in this country. The Bell System, or the American Company, as AT&T is sometimes called, also provides local telephone service through the associated operating companies, which also supply intrastate long-distance service and assist in supplying interstate long-distance service. The operating telephone companies in the Bell System provide numerous types of telephone communication and facilities within their respective territories with the aid of services received from AT&T under license contracts. The Western Electric Co. is an AT&T subsidiary which manufactures, purchases, and distributes supplies, apparatus, and equipment throughout the Bell System; it also installs and maintains central office equipment for the Bell System. The Bell Telephone Laboratories, owned equally by Western Electric and AT&T, performs research, development, and design work for the Bell System. The general departments of the American Company provide services to each of the associated operating telephone companies under license contracts and similar services to the Long Lines Department.

The *license contract* is an agreement under which the American Company grants certain licenses to and performs certain services for the licensee operating company. The license contract sets forth the functions that can best be handled on a centralized basis. The most important services furnished under the license contracts come within the following four classes. First, the American Company agrees continuously to pursue fundamental research, investigation, and experimentation in the development of the art and science of telephony. This portion of the work is performed by the Bell Telephone Laboratories, the expense being borne by the American Company and Western Electric. Second, the American Company agrees to furnish advice and assistance in engineering, traffic, plant, commercial, accounting, legal, and other matters pertaining to the telephone business. Third, the American Company agrees to furnish financial advice and assistance. This includes not only technical advice on financial problems but active assistance in marketing the securities of the operating companies. The American Company also maintains a central pool of funds available to the operating companies on demand to meet their needs for temporary or permanent new capital or for operating purposes. Fourth, the American Company makes available for royalty-free use all apparatus and equipment covered by the many patents owned by it or which it has acquired the right to use or which it may acquire in the future. Further, it agrees to protect the companies from suits for infringement of patents arising from the use of apparatus and equipment which it recommends. Each operating company in the Bell System pays a fee for the services and rights which it receives under the license contract. The fee charged is one per cent of each operating company's local and long-distance revenues less uncollectibles. This method is simple to administer and gives recognition to differences in the value of the services to companies of different size. It also recognizes that those factors which influence the costs of an operating company also influence the cost of license-contract services. In a telephone rate case, the applicant company is required to substantiate by cost evidence the license-contract fee it pays, in order to qualify that item as a proper operating expense.

The independent telephone companies are those that are not affiliated with the Bell System. They comprise a very important part of the interconnected telephone network, as shown by these facts: (a) as of the end of 1959, 3,560 independents operated 10,560 local telephone exchanges; (b) the independents served about twice as many communities in the United States as the Bell System; (c) about one out of every seven telephones in the United States and possessions is owned and operated by an independent company; and (d) their service area comprises about one-half the United States. In addition, the independents provide a market for the equipment manufactured by firms other than Western Electric. Generally speaking, independent telephone companies serve in smaller communities and in outlying areas. Some of the latter have been the scene of substantial population growth as metropolitan areas have expanded in size. The quantity of service supplied by independents has been growing. However, the number of companies supplying such service has been diminishing, principally as the result of mergers with other independent telephone companies. (As a general rule, the Bell System does not acquire independent telephone companies; however, it has done so on relatively few occasions where the independent fits economically into nearby Bell System facilities and the acquisition is held to be in the public interest.) The number of independent telephone companies has declined from over 6,400 in the early 1930's to over 5,500 in 1950 to 3,560 in 1959.[1] The independent companies perform an invaluable service in bringing to a large number of communities both local communications and connection with Bell System long-distance facilities. The value of service provided through any one telephone is enhanced by the availability of interconnection anywhere in the country, in part through the facilities of the independents.

Much of the telephone service in rural areas has been provided by associations organized by farmers to provide themselves with such service. In recent years, the expansion of rural telephone service has been assisted by a low-cost loan program sponsored by the federal government acting through the Rural Electrification Administration. This governmental agency was established originally to make loans for the purpose of financing facilities to provide electricity in rural areas. In 1949 the Rural Electrification Act was amended to authorize the agency to make loans to improve and expand rural telephone service. Under this program, loans are made at a two per cent rate of interest for a maximum amortization period of 35 years. Eligible borrowers include private telephone companies and cooperative, non-profit, limited-dividend or mutual associations. Loans are not available to state and local governmental bodies for the expansion of telephone service, although these public bodies do qualify for electrification loans.

In the first decade of the telephone lending program, 1950–1959, loans totaling over $633 million were approved, which would provide service to 1,288,856 subscribers. Of the total of 686 loans approved, 475 were to independent telephone companies; the latter accounted for over $386 million of the total loans approved and for 875,336 of the total telephone subscribers benefited by this program.[2]

A statistical summary of the telephone industry, contrasting the independents and the Bell System, appears in Table 11.1. These statistics, relating to the independent telephone companies, require further explanation to account for the increasing importance of General Telephone & Electronics Corp. General is a diversified holding company, whose operating companies make it the largest independent telephone company in the country as well as a major manufacturer of telephone equipment, electronics systems, electric light bulbs, fluorescent lamps and lighting systems, radio and television receivers, and cameras. It is a leading defense contractor; moreover, it maintains a large-scale electronics and communications research program. Half or more of General's revenue is from non-public utility activities.

The present company began as General Telephone Corp. in 1935, emerging from the bankruptcy proceedings of a predecessor, Associated Telephone Utilities Co., which was organized in 1926. Beginning in 1951, under the leadership of Donald C. Power, General has grown rapidly in the telephone utility and manufacturing industries. In 1955 General acquired Theodore Gary & Co., the second largest independent telephone company, whose Automatic Electric Co. subsidiary was second only

---

[1] United States Independent Telephone Association, *1960 Annual Statistical Volume,* p. 1; *Hearings* on S. 2910, 73d Cong., 2d sess., p. 136, as quoted in James M. Herring and Gerald C. Gross, *Telecommunications* (New York: McGraw-Hill Book Company, Inc., 1936), pp. 61–62.

[2] *Ibid., 1960 Annual Statistical Volume,* p. 32.

Table 11.1

Statistical Summary of the Telephone Industry as of 1959

Line Item	Independent[1] Companies	Bell System
	(a)	(b)
1. Operating companies	3,560	23
2. Telephones (000)	10,785	60,110
3. Percentage dial operated	82.2%	95.7%
4. Exchanges	10,760	7,050
5. Average daily calls (000)	55,310	208,042
6. Employees	100,000	597,100
7. Gross plant investment ($000)	$3,580,369	$21,497,215
8. Total operating revenues ($000)	$915,189	$7,583,982
9. Ratio, net operating income to average net plant[2]	6.4%	7.51%
10. Per telephone:		
a. Net plant	$274	$286
b. Operating revenues	$93	$131
c. Expenses and taxes	$76	$109
d. Net operating income	$17	$22
11. Selected ratios:		
a. Capital turnover ratio	34.8%	45.7%
b. Operating ratio	69.9%	69.1%
c. Operating ratio (all expenses)	81.7%	83.2%

[1] Lines 1–2 and 4–8 of Column (a) relate to all independent telephone companies; Lines 3 and 9–11 relate to the 533 companies which reported to the United States Independent Telephone Association in 1959.

[2] These ratios do not measure rates of return earned in 1959. However, they do indicate in a general way the industry level of financial performance. Compared with rates of return, these ratios are overstated; this results from the fact that necessary rate-base components are not included in average net plant. The items omitted include plant under construction and working capital.

Sources: United States Independent Telephone Association, *1960 Annual Statistical Volume;* American Telephone and Telegraph Company, 1959 *Annual Report;* Federal Communications Commission data, relating to Bell System, prepared for NARUC, June 14, 1960.

to Western Electric as a manufacturer of telephone equipment in the United States. Prior to this merger, General had acquired in 1950 a relatively small equipment manufacturer, Leich Electric Co. After the Gary merger, General became practically self-sufficient with respect to its own telephone equipment needs and also supplied a substantial portion of the equipment purchased by other independent telephone companies. In 1959 General merged with Sylvania Electronics Products, Inc. and became General Telephone & Electronics Corp. As a result, it has become an integrated and diversified supplier of communications equipment and related products, with particular strength in electronics. The latter is especially important insofar as telephone service is concerned, because electronic switching is expected to be a major innovation in the near future.

General, since its beginning, has continuously absorbed and improved smaller telephone properties. This has been accelerated under Mr. Power. In 1959 the General operating companies in the United States provided service to about 5,500 communities in 31 states. Over 90 per cent of the telephones served were dial-operated. The 3,874,000 telephones served by General companies accounted for over one-third the total for all independent telephone companies in 1959. Similarly, the total telephone operating revenues of General companies ($375,-130,000) was more than one-third the total for all independents.

General's numerous acquisitions of other independent telephone companies have resulted from a combination of favorable factors. First, the Bell System policy against that type of geographic expansion left the field open for development by someone else. Second, the smaller independents, many of them family-owned, were not able to meet the postwar demands for expanded service and modernization of equipment, such as automatic dialing. Accordingly, many of them came to General with offers to sell. The management of General has been vigorous in reorganizing the internal structure of the company to promote efficiency and in raising capital to permit modernization.

B. ***Introduction to Telephone Rates.*** Telephone service is broadly classified between local and toll calls. This classification is essentially a distinction between service within a community and service between communities. The geographic unit for administration of local telephone service and the quoting of telephone rates is the "exchange" or "exchange area"; hence, local service is also referred to as "local exchange" or "exchange" service, and the rates charged are termed "exchange rates." The rates for most local exchange service are quoted in the form of: (a) flat rates for an unlimited quantity of service; or (b) message rates for a measured quantity of service. Under the latter, the customer pays a specified amount per month which entitles him to a fixed number of calls. Any calls in addition are charged at a stated amount, such as five cents each. The charge for most toll, or long-distance, service is made on a per-message basis; thus, it is referred to as "message toll service," and the rates charged are termed "toll rates." Various classes of local and toll service are established for rate-making purposes.

The need for classification of telephone service as between local exchange and toll for rate-making purposes became evident as soon as it was clear that telephonic communication could take place over more than very short distances. It is necessary to have some basic local rate covering the provision of the customer lines and stations and the local facilities required to give them access to the system. It is also desirable, in order to encourage use and increase the value of telephone service, to include at these basic charges sufficient scope of service to meet the day-to-day needs of the majority of customers. There is necessarily a limit to the area which can reasonably be covered at local rates; this is usually the area within which the majority of customers have the bulk of their communication requirements. Without such a limit, local service would be company-wide or state-wide, and the charges required would be so high that telephone service would become a luxury utilized only by those having special requirements and unusual means; the majority of present customers probably would have no service at all. Even those making considerable use of long-distance service, who might be expected to benefit from placing this business on a local basis, would find that many of the persons with whom they wished to talk were not connected to the system. Thus the value of the service even to the larger toll users would be greatly curtailed. It should be noted, however, that local-service areas have grown tremendously over the years, and that state-wide rates may become practicable in the foreseeable future at a reasonable level as technology develops.

Practically all interstate toll service is provided by the Long Lines Department of AT&T. The operating companies of the Bell System assist in providing interstate toll service and also supply intrastate toll service. Independent telephone companies connect with the long-distance network. The division of toll revenues between the Bell System and the connecting independent telephone companies is a matter of contract negotiation. The United States Independent Telephone Association has taken an active part in the matter of toll compensation for independents in the industry. It maintains studies of toll-compensation problems and negotiates with the Bell System for increased compensation for independent companies on interchanged business. The efforts of the Association are generally accorded considerable credit for the fact that, since 1936, toll compensation to independents has grown from $12 million to about $200 million in 1960.

Because of the dual nature of our system of government, the regulation of telephone rates is divided between the states and the federal government. Generally, the division of regulatory jurisdiction places intrastate rates and service, whether local or long-distance, under the state commissions, and interstate rates and service under the Federal Communications Commission. An important exception to the exclusive federal jurisdiction over interstate telephone operations and rates arises in the case of local exchange service which may partly overlap a state boundary, where such service is "subject to regulation by a state commission or by local governmental authority."[3] A situation of this kind arises, for example, in Kansas City, Missouri, and Kansas City, Kansas.

The Federal Communications Commission succeeded to its jurisdiction over interstate telephone and telegraph messages upon its establishment in 1934. Previously, from 1910 to that time, this regulatory authority had been vested in the Interstate Commerce Commission. Although the latter agency did bring about some decreases in interstate telephone rates, the principal result of its regulation was the development of a uniform accounting system, which also was adopted by many of the state commissions. In 1935 the new federal commission adopted its present Uniform System of Accounts for Telephone Companies, which the states also have adopted.

The regulation of intrastate telephone rates by the state commissions follows the conventional public utility ratemaking procedure that was discussed earlier. Accordingly, the state commissions hold formal hearings for the presentation of evidence, and on the basis of the record they determine the intrastate revenue requirement of the telephone utility as the equivalent of its cost of service.

Generally speaking, the regulation of interstate toll rates by the Federal Communications Commission follows a similar pattern, except that in almost all cases the proceedings are informal in the sense that they do not involve formal rate litigation. In practically all cases before the Communications Commission, the result has been a settlement whereby the company agreed to a "voluntary" reduction in annual revenues. The Commission in this respect follows the pattern of procedure established by its predecessor agency in this area of regulation. An expert staff is assigned by the Commission to make continuous studies of the earnings on interstate toll service. These staff studies ascertain a cost-of-service and revenue requirement, using various hypotheses. This is done because the Commission has not found it necessary to set forth a particular regulatory method. The results of these studies by the Commission's staff are used in negotiations leading to interstate toll-rate settlements. In the last 35 years, this

[3] Communications Act of 1934, Sec. 221 (b), 48 Stat. 1080.

informal method of regulation has resulted in many voluntary revenue reductions by the Bell System and in a few increases. Reductions in annual interstate toll revenues occurred in 1926, 1927, 1929, 1941, 1943, 1944, 1945, 1946, and 1959. The last of these was an annual revenue reduction of $50 million. Small increases were approved in 1952 and 1958. In 1953, an increase in toll revenues of about $73 million annually was authorized. In part, this was necessitated by the decline in interstate toll revenues brought on by the economic recession of that year. This suggests the highly "volatile" (literally, "prone to evaporate") character of the interstate toll revenues. That is, the business recession resulted in a sharp decline in the volume of interstate toll traffic generated by the principal customer group using the interstate toll system—business callers.

The design of telephone rate schedules is determined almost entirely by value-of-service considerations. In fact, there has been next to no interest shown by either regulatory commissions or telephone companies in basing the rates for different classes of telephone service, or the rate differentials among them, on the results of cost analyses. To be sure, the total revenues produced by a company's rate schedules must cover and must not exceed its approved total costs, including a reasonable rate of return, and broad recognition of cost differences among classes of service is also necessary. Nonetheless, the design of rate schedules for different classes of telephone service is substantially dependent upon value-of-service considerations (which are not purported to be precisely measurable) rather than upon a determination of the cost of providing the respective classes of service. The predominant reasons for this are discussed below.

Local exchanges of various sizes within one company are very different from one another with respect to the equipment employed, the character of the service provided, and the usefulness of such service to subscribers. In short, although the exchange is the basic geographic unit for administering exchange service and quoting local rates, it is not suitable for use as a costing unit because exchanges are not comparable. On the other hand, reliance upon value-of-service considerations allows telephone rates to reflect existing differences in the character of service provided by exchanges of different sizes as well as the relative usefulness of different classes of service to the public and the capacity of the different markets for telephone service to bear charges. Second, numerous allocations of joint costs would be required to calculate a cost for each class of service provided by a company in exchanges of different sizes. Owing to the numerous allocations required, the resulting cost calculations would be highly suspect and, very likely, meaningless. Moreover, for a company with hundreds of exchanges, the amount of work involved in making such cost studies would be prohibitive.

Finally, it would not be in the public interest to base rates for specific classes of service upon costs alone, even if costs were available, because such rates would interfere with maximum development of the market. For example, the value of exchange telephone service is, in general, much greater for business customers than for residence customers. Rates based upon costs would not necessarily reflect these differences adequately, but very likely would result in increased residential rates and decreased business rates. Such rates, together with the different value of service to each of these customer classes, could be expected to cause some of the residential customers to choose to do without telephone service, while few new business customers would be gained. On the other hand, recognition of value of service in telephone rates encourages maximum telephone development, because such rates are tailored to the demand characteristics of each segment of the market served.

C. *Rates for Exchange Telephone Service.* Local exchange telephone service is that which is provided without the application of a long-distance charge. The "exchange area" is the basic geographic unit for administering exchange service and quoting exchange rates in a city or village and its environs.

(1) *Classification of Service.* Basic exchange telephone service is classified, first of all, by type of use, that is, whether business or residence and whether available for subscriber's use only or for public or semipublic use. Second, service is classified by grade of line, that is, whether individual line (not shared with another subscriber) or party line (with varying numbers of sharing parties). Third, service is classified by whether it is unlimited or measured in amount. *Unlimited service* is provided under a monthly flat rate, such as $5.75 plus 10 per cent federal tax for individual-line residential service. *Measured service* is provided under a message rate, which entitles the customer to a specified number of outgoing messages per month at a stated charge, with all outgoing calls in excess of the specified amount billed on a per-message, or message-unit, basis. For example, an individual-line residential customer subscribing for measured service might pay $4.50 per month plus tax for 50 outgoing calls per month, with each additional call billed at five cents each.

The classification of telephone service between business and residential customers results in lower charges to residential customers; this difference in rate levels reflects value-of-service differentials. The business telephone clearly has monetary value because it facilitates business transactions. Further, the telephone bill to a business concern is a cost of doing business and presumably will be reflected with other costs in the prices of goods and services sold. The residence telephone, on the other hand, has no monetary value in the same sense; it is a part of the cost of living. For these reasons, the business customer is able and willing to pay more for service than the residential customer and is much less likely to refrain from subscribing to telephone service because of the level of rates. In addition, business customers have a higher calling frequency than do residential customers. This fact enhances the value of business telephone service and tends to make it more costly to furnish. The comparatively lower residential rates promote telephone development and increase the number of customers who can conveniently contact business firms.

In addition to serving their subscribers, telephone companies furnish public telephone facilities for the use of non-subscribers and the transient public. Semipublic service, on the other hand, is a classification of business service which combines features of public and subscriber use. Like public telephones, semipublic facilities have a coin box; they are intended to provide service in small retail stores, large rooming houses, gasoline stations, and so forth, where there is some public business. The amounts deposited by public use contribute toward the guarantee for the telephone, and provide a means by which a small business can achieve a very low rate.

With respect to grade of line, individual-line service provides the customer with exclusive use of a line to the central office. In the case of party-line service, the customer shares a line with others and thus receives a lower rate and a lesser immediate availability of service on some occasions, since only one party can use the line at a time. The chief purpose of party-line service is to provide a lower rate to customers who might not subscribe otherwise. By sharing a line, economies are achieved in those investment items which vary with the number of lines. Urban party-line service is usually limited to two and four parties. Rural lines may have a larger number.

Unlimited flat-rate service and measured service each have certain advantages in the telephone industry. Flat rates, which predominate, encourage customer use and thereby contribute to system growth. Customers generally prefer flat-rate service because of the freedom of use and the certainty of the bill. Flat rates are simple for the public to understand and for the company to administer. On the other hand, measured service at a stated rate per message over a fixed minimum permits more variation and spread in bills than is possible with flat rates. Message rates permit a low minimum charge which attracts customers who might not subscribe otherwise. This is very important, because the rate level for flat-rate service—particularly in the very large cities—would be too high for maximum development of the market. For the Bell System as a whole, two-thirds of all telephones are on flat rates, which includes about 80 per cent of residence telephones and about half of the business subscribers.

A class of business service not mentioned earlier is *private branch exchange* (PBX) service. This type of service is installed in large offices, hotels, and other businesses and institutions of substantial size. The private branch exchange provides a larger number of extension telephones within the subscriber's premises. The PBX equipment generally is operated by the subscriber's employees.

(2) *Local Service Areas.* A telephone company divides its territory into exchange service areas; within each exchange area, customers may call at exchange rates and without toll charges. The establishment of such local service areas is the means of making effective the classification of telephone service between exchange and toll. All telephone service rendered within an exchange is defined by law as "exchange service."[4] Each exchange area has specific boundaries. In establishing each exchange area, the basic objective is to include the primary social and economic interests of the people residing in and around a central community. Thus, the exchange area also ordinarily includes the outlying and rural areas surrounding the built-up central community.

There is at least one "toll rate center" within each exchange area, which serves as the measuring point for toll-rate distances. Most exchanges have one toll-rate center—usually the post office or some other centrally located point. Metropolitan exchanges usually have more than one toll-rate center.

Exchange service may include communications between exchanges. This "extended area" local service is furnished where there are two or more exchanges (each including a central community and its surrounding territory) with a substantial community of interest between them. It has been found that customers' requirements are best met by local service areas which include not only their own exchange but the other exchanges in which they are interested. In most cases local service is supplied under the same rate schedules throughout the local service area. This is true whether the local service area includes only the originating exchange or is an extended area including additional exchanges.

Extended-area service between contiguous exchanges avoids requiring toll charges of near neighbors. The advantages in this are: (a) the value of the service to customers is increased, be-

[4] Communications Act, *op. cit.,* Sec. 3(s) and Sec. 3(r).

cause a larger calling area is available to them; and (b) the telephone company avoids the ticketing, timing, collecting, and related costs required in connection with toll calls. Where, as here, the toll charges would be small, the costs of completing such calls would eat up most, if not all, of the toll revenue. If only a minority of customers desire extended-area service and a substantial difference in rates is involved, the extended-area service is made optional if the service is provided at all. Where a large majority of customers are interested in extended-area service, or where the difference in rate is small, the extended-area service may be non-optional.

In the built-up area within an exchange, local service is provided to all customers under approximately the same conditions. That is, cost differences resulting from locational differences within this central area tend to be small, because distances are relatively short and customer density tends to reduce line costs. On the other hand, providing exchange service in the remote locations within an exchange area involves substantial additional costs, largely for subscriber lines. Accordingly, special rate treatment is required for customers located in the outlying portions of exchange areas for grades of service better than rural multi-party.

In metropolitan exchange areas serving the largest cities, the local-service areas which will fully meet customers' requirements are often so large that it is necessary for rates to reflect the distance factor. Accordingly, the customer receives flat-rate service (or one-message unit if he has message-rate service) within only a portion of his local-service area. This portion is called the "primary calling area." Calls to points beyond this designated area, but within the exchange area, require payment of additional message-unit charges. For example, to call a point outside the primary calling area that is designated at three message units, the flat-rate caller might be billed five cents per message unit for calls of five minutes or less plus one message unit for each additional two minutes or fraction thereof in excess of five minutes. Message-rate customers would be billed similarly. Of course, calls to points beyond the exchange boundary require payment of toll charges. However, by requiring long-haul callers within metropolitan area exchanges to pay additional message unit charges, rates can be lower within the primary calling area than otherwise, and those requesting a long-haul exchange connection will bear the costs properly attributable to that service. In addition, the charging of additional message units outside the primary calling area provides a gradual transition in rates from local to toll.

The non-metropolitan exchanges, which are the most numerous, are faced with a somewhat similar problem. These exchanges usually have a "base rate area," which comprises the built-up area. The rural and other areas outside the base-rate area, but within the exchange, are thereby separated for rate-charging purposes on the basis of the density of market development. Within the base-rate area of an exchange, urban classes of service are offered at uniform rates regardless of customer locations. These urban customers either require individual-line service (not shared with another customer) or are willing to share a line with only one or at most three others. However, outside the base-rate area, rural multi-party service (six or more parties per line) is offered; these customers alternatively may obtain urban grades of service at base-area rates plus extra exchange-line mileage or zone incremental charges which vary with class of service and distance from the base-rate area. Zone rates gradually are replacing mileage charges.

(3) *The Variation of Costs with Size*

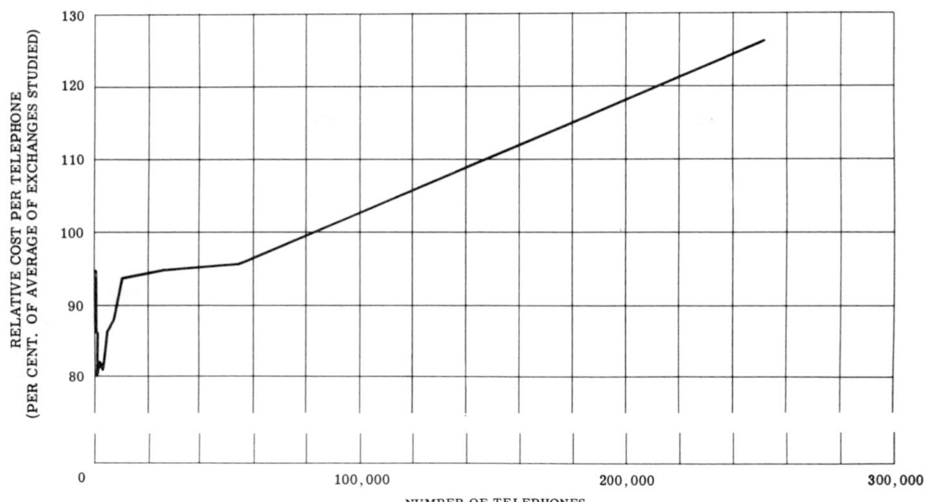

FIGURE 11-A. ILLUSTRATIVE TREND OF EXCHANGE COSTS WITH SIZE OF EXCHANGE. (ANNUAL COSTS INCLUDING EXPENSES AND 7% COST OF MONEY)

Source: American Telephone and Telegraph Co.

of Exchange. If the size of exchange areas is measured in terms of the number of telephones served, the average cost of serving each telephone tends to increase as the size of the exchange increases. (The costs referred to are all those assigned to exchange operations, including the cost of capital.) Apparent exceptions to this tendency include: (a) the relatively high average cost per telephone in the smallest exchanges; and (b) the lowest average cost per telephone in exchanges in the range of about 5,000 telephones.

The relatively high average cost per telephone indicated for the smallest exchanges reflects the fact that certain minimum amounts of equipment and personnel are required for satisfactory operation of any exchange. Thus, when relatively few telephones are served, the cost per telephone necessarily tends to be high, because there is idle capacity. In such cases, when some additional customers can be taken on without major additions to plant or personnel, the result is a reduction in cost per telephone. On the other hand, lowest unit costs appear to result in exchanges of about 5,000 telephones, where: (a) the exchange can be served from one building; (b) subscribers' lines are not unduly long; and (c) the exchange is not affected by large-city conditions which tend to increase costs.

As the size of exchange increases above about 5,000 telephones, average costs tend to increase. This is illustrated in Figure 11-A. Where the metropolitan-area exchanges are concerned, costs tend to be substantially higher than in exchanges in medium-size cities. This apparent tendency toward "increasing costs," not characteristic of public utility operations generally, is due to a number of conditions, many of which are peculiar to the telephone industry. First, it should be noted that the benefits of mass production of telephone equipment and standardization of operations are available to large and small exchanges alike. Standard unit prices apply for equipment, regardless of the amount used in a particular exchange. Second, there are a number of factors which tend to make the operation of practically any business more costly in a metropolitan area than in smaller communities. Generally, wage rates are higher in large metropolitan centers. The importance of the wage factor in telephone operations is indicated by the fact that wages and related personnel costs amount to over 70 per cent of total Bell System expenses before taxes. In addition, the largest cities almost always have higher local taxes and usually have more stringent requirements with respect to the use of underground rather than aerial construction. It goes without saying that land costs and the costs contingent upon delay and street congestion tend to be greater in metropolitan areas.

Third, a number of factors peculiar to the telephone industry also contribute to higher costs in large cities. Because of the necessity of providing for interconnection between any two customers, switching equipment and operations become more costly and complex as the number of customers increases. When a new customer is added in an exchange of 100 customers, it is necessary to arrange to connect the additional customer with each of the existing 100 customers. In an exchange of 100,000 customers, it is necessary to make provision for each new customer to reach each of the 100,000 existing customers. In an exchange of 100,000 terminals, for example, there are five billion possible channels of communication. Of course, many will never be used, but all must be provided for. This is not to suggest that each exchange is equipped to handle the theoretical maximum number of calls at any given moment, for the size of the exchange plant is determined by the safely expected peak load, as in the case of other utilities. Rather, the point here is that the exchange plant and equipment must be of a type which makes possible the connection of any one telephone with every other telephone in the exchange. Accordingly, as exchange size increases, additional and more complicated switching equipment must be employed. These comparatively greater requirements for interconnection in metropolitan area and large city exchanges are directly reflected in increased plant and equipment costs per subscriber line, as compared with the costs in the smaller exchanges. In addition, the greater complexity of the equipment required in the larger exchanges also causes increased maintenance and operation expenses, in part due to the fact that the services of the more experienced and highly skilled employees are needed. An important underlying factor which tends to compound these increasing cost effects is the fact that the average use per telephone increases substantially as the size of the exchange increases.

The growth of metropolitan areas requires longer lines from the newly built-up areas, and the average haul of a local message tends to increase, especially where several exchanges or zones are included in the local-service area. This factor also tends to cause higher average investment and maintenance costs per line. Other cost-increasing factors are related to the comparatively greater mobility of population in the larger cities. Among these is the unfortunate fact that many of the larger cities have blighted areas in which the density of telephone development is less than it was formerly. As a consequence, the existing plant installed to serve such areas is only partially used, while new plant is required in the suburban areas to accommodate the customers who have moved from the city.

(4) *The State-Wide Basis of Rate Making*. In the regulation of intrastate telephone rates, the state commissions employ some form of the "state-wide

basis" of rate making.[5] State-wide rate making treats all of a telephone company's properties and operations within a state as a single unit for purposes of rate making, whether or not the various exchanges are contiguous to each other or directly interconnected through the company's own facilities. Under this process, rate making begins with the determination of the revenue requirement, or cost of service, of the system as a whole within the state. The revenue requirement is established, as discussed previously, as the total of the proper operating expenses, depreciation expense, taxes, and return-on-rate base—each as related to the company's entire operations within the state subject to the jurisdiction of the state commission. The revenue requirement as thus determined is then distributed among subscribers in the form of rates which take into account primarily the relative value of service and, to a lesser extent, elements of cost attributable to the furnishing of particular types of service which are especially expensive to provide. No effort is made under this system-wide approach, however, to make any precise allocation of all costs to any geographical area smaller than the state as a whole or to any particular class of exchange service.

Implementing the state-wide basis in order to make exchange rates results in rate schedules that are applicable to groups of exchanges rather than to individual exchanges considered one at a time. More specifically, under the state-wide basis of rate making, all of a company's exchanges within a state are first classified into groups on the basis of size, as measured (in most instances) by the number of telephones available at local rates. In some instances, size is measured by the number of main stations plus private branch exchange trunks. Second, rate schedules are established for each group of exchanges; and every exchange within a particular group will quote the same rates to its customers. In most cases there are seven to eleven groups of exchanges established for this purpose, depending on the state. Thus, under the state-wide basis, different rates may be established for each group of exchanges, but the same rate schedules will apply to each exchange within a particular group.

The state-wide basis simplifies the problem of making rates, because it permits rates to be designed for a relatively few groups of exchanges rather than for the numerous individual exchanges operated by many companies. In a recent year, for example, The Ohio Bell Telephone Company had 185 exchanges, with additional exchanges being created each year. Anyone familiar with railroad class rates for freight transportation will see at once that class rates involve the same principle as that underlying the state-wide basis of telephone rate making. Railroad class rates are not established for individual commodities as such, but for classes or groups of commodities bearing similar characteristics; each commodity within a given class takes the same schedule of freight rates. Essentially, the state-wide basis provides that the total costs of furnishing telephone service and the resulting revenue requirements are to be considered for the state as a unit in recognition of the fact that the telephone service, both exchange and toll, furnished by a given company throughout a state is essentially an integrated whole, all portions of which are interdependent.

The fundamental basis for state-wide exchange rate schedules is the grouping of exchanges on the basis of the number

---

[5] *New York Tel. Co.* v. *Prendergast, et al.*, 36 F. 2d 54 (1929); *Michigan Bell Tel. Co.* v. *Odell, et al.*, 45 F. 2d 180 (1930); *Re Southern Bell Tel. & Tel. Co.*, 52 PUR (NS) 200–201 (1944); *Re Northwestern Bell Tel. Co.*, 66 PUR (NS) 148–150 (1946).

of telephones available to the customer at local rates. State-wide rate schedules provide uniform classes of service and rates applicable to the exchanges in each group. The level of rates generally rises with increases in the number of telephones in the local service area. This system recognizes that the value of local telephone service largely depends upon the number of telephones a customer can reach at local rates, and that the value of local exchange service increases as the scope of the service increases. The practice of charging relatively higher rates in the larger exchanges is consistent with the tendency toward higher costs per telephone in the larger exchanges.

The validity of the reliance upon value-of-service factors in designing exchange rates is demonstrated by the fact that the average number of calls per telephone increases substantially as the total telephones in the local-service area increase. For example, for all Bell System exchanges, the smallest exchanges average about four calls per telephone per day; in the largest exchanges, the average calling rate is about 7.5 calls per telephone per day. In addition, local service in larger cities covers a wider area and the average length of haul increases with size of exchange. Owing to these longer average distances, the telephone is a greater convenience and results in greater savings of time as against other methods of communication. Offsetting the higher rate levels in larger exchanges is the fact that, as the scope of local service increases, customers require less use of toll calls. For example, in the smallest exchanges in the Bell System, there are about 65 toll messages per telephone per year, whereas the largest exchanges average about 18 toll messages per telephone per year. For the smallest exchanges, toll messages comprise about 7 per cent of total messages, while in the largest exchanges they are less than one per cent of the total. Owing to these value-of-service considerations and the related fact that average incomes in larger communities exceed those in smaller communities, customers are generally able and willing to pay comparatively higher rates in the larger exchanges. This permits lower rates to be charged in smaller exchanges where the value of local exchange service tends to be less than in larger exchanges and where average incomes are generally lower. A related consideration is that the value of telephone service in urban areas, particularly to business customers, increases with the increase in the number of telephones in surrounding trade areas.

Illustrative state-wide flat rates for individual-line service to business and residential customers are shown in Table 11.2. Exchange groups ordinarily are accorded larger numerical designations as the size of the exchanges within each group increases. Thus, Group 1 might include exchanges with up to 299 telephones, while Group 2 might include exchanges with 300 to 599 telephones, and so on.

The number of exchange rate groups and size ranges varies with the individual company and the conditions in each state. The general objective in setting up the grouping of exchanges is to provide: (a) enough groups to permit a reasonable spread of rates; with (b) moderate increases in rate levels from one group to the next higher group; but (c) not so many groups as to result in insignificant differences in the rates of different groups. Regrouping of exchanges, ordinarily due to growth in the number of telephones in service, usually takes place in connection with general rate-change proceedings before the state commission.

It is clear from the foregoing that rate making on the state-wide basis makes unnecessary a separate revenue-requirement determination for each exchange or class of service. This is all to the good,

Table 11.2

Illustrative State-Wide Rates, Individual-Line Service

Exchange Group	*Monthly Flat Rates*		*Exchange Group*	*Monthly Flat Rates*	
	Residence	*Business*		*Residence*	*Business*
1.	$4.50	$ 7.25	7	$5.75	$11.75
2.	4.75	8.00	8	5.90	12.75
3.	5.00	8.50	9	6.00	13.25
4.	5.25	9.25	10	6.35	14.00
5.	5.50	10.25	11	6.50	15.25
6.	5.65	11.00	12	7.00	17.25

Source: Southwestern Bell Telephone Co., Kansas Exchange Rate Schedule, effective September 16, 1960 under bond.

for a likely result of making exchange rates on the basis of the allocated costs of each exchange would be to increase substantially the rates for small exchanges. Such rates would be apt to exceed the value of service to many customers, who may discontinue their telephone service.

To indicate the nature of individual exchange costs, we may look to a Wisconsin commission case where such costs were determined—although ultimately rates were made on the state-wide basis. The commission approved a company-wide rate of return of 6.52 per cent; however, under the approved exchange rates, the respective rates of return calculated for individual exchanges varied from 7.22 per cent to a negative 6.87 per cent.[6]

(5) *The Design of Exchange Rates.* The design of state-wide schedules of exchange rates requires careful weighing of the value of service and cost factors relating to the various classes of business and residence service provided by exchanges of different sizes. The following is a general survey intended only to suggest some of the considerations which bear upon the design of exchange rates and is not a detailed treatment of the subject.

As the size of exchange increases, business rates increase more than residence rates—both in absolute amount and on a percentage basis. This rule recognizes that the size and scope of family contacts in a community do not increase so rapidly as those of business firms, as exchange size increases. Thus, whereas the individual-line flat rate to business customers may be 50 per cent greater than that for similar service to residence customers in the smallest exchanges, the business rate is usually well over twice the residence rate for such service in the larger cities. Another general principle is that individual-line rates increase more than party-line rates, as the size of exchange increases, since the latter are kept to the lowest practicable level in all size groups in order to encourage maximum telephone development.

The vast majority of business customers (except in the largest cities) require individual-line service. Accordingly, the individual-line flat rate is the "key rate" in the business-rate schedules, because the offering of other classes of business service and their rate levels are related downward from the individual-line flat business rates. On the other hand, the key rate in residence-rate schedules is ordinarily the minimum rate offered, and the rate schedule is built upward from it. Both cost and value-

[6] *Application of North-West Telephone Company for Authority to Increase Rates,* 33 PSCW 347 (1948).

of-service factors indicate a greater differential between one-party and two-party flat-rate service than between two-party and four-party flat-rate service.

The design of state-wide rate schedules for medium and small exchanges is similar to that for large-city exchanges but not the same. This difference is essentially a matter of emphasis for the purpose of recognizing large-city conditions. These include: (a) the relatively high revenue requirements in the largest cities in view of the higher costs and value of telephone service in such exchanges; (b) large areas of dense development with widespread communities of interest; (c) a high proportion of business customers, including those of a size and type not usually found in small exchanges, whose communications requirements are large and specialized; and (d) a residence market covering a wider range of income groups than in most smaller communities, making desirable a wider spread of telephone charges. Further, the importance of special consideration in the design of large-city rate schedules is indicated by the fact that about one per cent of the Bell System exchanges serve over half of the System's telephones and produce over 60 per cent of the exchange revenue.

The design of business-rate schedules in the largest exchanges is affected by two other points of difference between large and small exchanges: (a) the large-city changes are dependent upon business rates to a greater extent than smaller exchanges where residence service predominates; (b) a much larger proportion of business service is private branch exchange (PBX) in large cities than in smaller and medium-size communities.

Individual-line flat-rate service is preferred by practically all business customers, except in the largest cities where PBX telephones comprise over half the total business telephones. There is little demand for party-line business service. In the smallest exchanges (the first two or three groups), an offering of one-party flat-rate service and one-party semipublic service usually meets business customers' needs. In these groups the flat rate is usually scaled so low as to be well within the means of most business customers. The small shopkeeper may take semipublic service so that the public will cover part of his telephone bill. In medium-size exchanges, the individual-line flat rate may reach a level where it becomes necessary to offer an additional class of service, such as two-party flat rate or individual-line message-rate service, to attract very small businesses requiring only a limited use of telephone service. In the larger exchanges, it is definitely necessary to offer a business rate below the individual-line flat rate. For the most part, in medium and large exchanges, the individual-line message rate has proved to be preferable to two-party flat-rate business service. The reasons for this are that a two-party flat rate that is only a little below the one-party rate would not be attractive to the small business customer, whereas a comparatively great differential between one- and two-party flat-rate service would attract such customers but would result in their being dissatisfied because the line would sometimes be in use by others. Accordingly, except at small dial offices where the provision of message-rate service involves additional expense, a general policy is to price the underlying business service on the basis of an individual-line message rate. This permits a fixed number of calls to be made under the monthly guarantee, with an additional charge per message for all calls in excess of the stated number.

Because two-party flat-rate service to business customers is not generally found to be entirely satisfactory when many customers use it, the differential in rate between this service and individual-line flat-rate service is ordinarily small, so as not to encourage this type of development. When one-party message-rate service is the underlying class, the differential below flat-rate service can be greater. Rates then are designed so as to provide an adequate flat rate for business consumers requiring complete freedom of telephone use, and at the same time message-rate guarantees that are low enough to attract the small business customer. In effect, the offering of individual-line message service provides a gradual upward gradation in rates, as between message and flat rates, in going from medium to the larger exchanges. The relationship of one-party semipublic rates to the balance of the business-rate structure is based on the principle that the rate treatment should not encourage subscribers to elect this class of service where there is no requirement for public or group use. An illustrative monthly business-rate schedule is shown below.

Class of Service	
Individual line:	
Flat	$14.00
Message	85—$ 6.50—5¢
Semipublic	110—$ 7.50—5¢
PBX Trunks:	
Flat	$21.00
Message	85—$ 6.50—5¢
Each Extension or PBX Telephone:	
Flat	$ 1.50
Message	$ 1.00

Residence customers, even more than business customers, prefer flat-rate service so long as quality of service is satisfactory and rates are reasonable. The residence schedule requires some degree of "spread," ranging from the best grade of service to a minimum class at the lowest practicable rate which is designed to attract the maximum number of customers. Accordingly, with flat-rate service, the only method of obtaining this spread is by offering at least one grade of party-line service. The basic residence offerings of most state-wide exchange rate schedules are individual-line and two- and four-party flat-rate service, except in the largest cities. Four-party offerings are gradually being withdrawn. In the smallest exchanges, however, only one class of party-line service is usually offered because the total party-line development may be too small to obtain a reasonable number of "fills" (the number of parties served by a party line). In medium-size exchanges, both two- and four-party-line service may be offered to adapt to the larger spread of incomes likely in such communities. Adequate rate differentials between these residence services are necessary in order to offer the lowest practicable minimum rate to encourage maximum development. On the other hand, in recognition of the relative value placed on different classes of service, rate differentials are intended to be low enough, in relation to value, to encourage upward regrading of service and to prevent undue concentration of customers on party lines.

Special factors affecting residence rates in the largest cities include the wider spread in charges necessary to meet the higher revenue requirements while maintaining minimum rates at levels which will attract the maximum number of customers. This wider spread of charges is also consistent with the greater range of family incomes and communications requirements in the largest cities. However, in the interest of avoiding substantial flat-rate differentials that might cause customers to choose the lower grades of service, it becomes practical to introduce message-rate service. Accordingly, in large exchanges maximum telephone development is achieved by offering two-party message service as the minimum rate—usually in place of four-party flat-rate service, combined with flat-rate classes for customers preferring unlimited service. In designing residence-rate schedules, the objectives are to provide: (a) the lowest practicable minimum rate; (b) liberal message allowances for message-rate classes; and (c) differentials as low as practicable in view of revenue requirements, in order to encourage the largest proportion of residence customers to take flat-rate service.

The rate-design factors discussed above, among others, are reflected in Table 11.3, which shows general state-wide rate relationships for different classes of business and residence service, illustrated on an index-number basis.

D. *Toll Rates.* Long-distance, or message-toll, telephone service is classified for pricing purposes on a number of bases: (1) the message basis; (2) distance; (3) whether completion is requested to a specific person or to anyone who answers; (4) period of day; and (5) length of conversation. These classifications are discussed below, as they apply to service between two telephones.

(1) *The Message Basis.* In the message toll rate schedule, a message, or conversation, has always been the basic unit for rate-charging purposes. Wide variations among customers as to the number of toll messages required and the variation of total costs of operation with number of messages have made this basis of classification essential.

However, the wide introduction of Direct Distance Dialing, the advent of automatic number identification, and the tremendous expansion of the switching network are bringing about some changes in the usage and cost patterns of long-distance service. As a result, various optional flat-rate toll plans have been studied by the Bell System. In 1960, it filed with the FCC a proposal to provide unlimited interstate calling within specified areas for a flat monthly rate. Approval of this plan has allowed wide-area long-distance service to be offered for the first time.

(2) *Distance.* The next important classification of message-toll service is by distance. Toll rates increase generally as distance increases, but less than pro-

Table 11.3

Illustrative State-Wide Rate Schedule

Classes of Service and Relative Levels of Rates

(Minimum Residence Rate in Lowest-Size Group = 100)

Exchange Group	*Business*[1]			*Residence*[1]		
	1FB	*1MB*	*1SP*	*1FR*	*2FR*	*4FR*
1	207	-	202	134	113	100
2	238	-	219	143	118	100
3	261	-	236	152	123	105
4	293	-	252	161	127	105
5	328	233	269	170	136	109
6	359	247	285	177	143	114
7	391	261	302	184	114	114
8	426	275	319	191	149	114
9	454	284	329	203	154	119
10	486	296	340	213	163	128
11	569	329	375	231	171	134
12	646	324	402	248	191	147

[1] The abbreviations in the column headings are standard in the Bell System. The number refers to the parties on the line; *F* is *flat; M* is *message* and *SP* is *semipublic; B* and *R* stand for *Business* and *Residence* customers, respectively.

Source: Supplied upon request by Southwestern Bell Telephone Co.; the figures represent a composite of Missouri and Kansas rate schedules.

portionately at the longer distances. Increases in toll rates with greater lengths of haul reflect the tendency of the cost per message to increase with distance as the result of the greater length of circuits, the additional facilities required to secure satisfactory transmission, the lower volumes of traffic over the average route, and, on operator-placed calls, the somewhat greater operating labor due to the higher proportion of switched traffic. Long-haul calls also tend, on the average, to have greater value to customers, since alternative means of communication involve greater expenditures of time or money or both.

Rate distances do not depend upon the actual routing of the call, since the route is determined automatically by whatever circuits are open rather than the shortest possible distance. For short hauls, toll distances are usually measured point-to-point between toll-rate centers, discussed previously. For longer hauls, the toll-rate distances are measured between the centers of specified "blocks"—which are seven square miles each as mapped throughout the nation. For the longest hauls, toll distances are measured between the centers of specified "sections"—which are 35 square miles each as mapped throughout the country. The location of each rate center is designated by two coordinates —Vertical and Horizontal—based on latitude and longitude adjusted for the earth's curvature. Using the differences between the Vertical and Horizontal coordinates of any two rate centers, the distance between them is determined mathematically. The mathematical solution results in a mileage which represents the distance from a rate center to the center of a square area encompassing the distant rate center. The square area increases in size as the length of haul increases. Accordingly, interstate toll rates are the same for different calls of equal distance, other things being equal. By this approach, rates do not have to be made for specific pairs of points.

(3) *Type of Completion Requested.* Toll messages are classified as "station" or "person," depending upon whether the customer requires the connection to be completed to a given telephone or to a specified person (or private branch exchange telephone). This classification recognizes: (a) that on certain calls the calling party desires to speak only with a particular person and may not be sure that this person can be readily reached at the called telephone; and (b) that more operating labor is required and circuits and equipment are used for a longer time when a person must be secured at the called telephone before conversation begins.

In determining the differentials between station and person rates, due weight has been given to keeping the station rate as low as practicable because it is the minimum and, therefore, the most effective development rate. On the other hand, person service is also an important factor in the development of toll business at the longer hauls. The most desirable differential is that which is low enough to permit the use of person service by those who actually need it but high enough so that person service will not be requested when it is not really required. Since the establishment of this classification in 1919, various differentials have been tried out. In the schedules most recently adopted, the differentials in initial-period day rates range as high as 100 per cent of the station rate. The fact that about 35 per cent of the traffic hauls of over 25 miles are on the person basis is an indication that the present differentials do not unduly limit the use of this service. The Bell System has not found thorough cost studies to be practicable in providing a basis for the rate differential between person and station service. Nonetheless, the general belief at present is that the costs of station service are declining relative to person service. Technological advancements, among them Direct Distance Dialing, have contributed to this trend. The result has been gradually widening rate differentials between person and station service.

At the request of the calling person, the charges for either a person or a station call will be reversed, that is, billed to the called telephone, provided that someone at the called telephone agrees to accept the charges. The regular rates apply for reversed charge ("collect") calls, except that for station calls at the shorter distances (and at all distances in some states) the reversed-charge rate is somewhat higher than the regular rate. For example, on interstate station calls where the regular rates for the initial calling period are 10¢, 15¢, 20¢, and 25¢, the "collect" charges are 15¢, 15¢, 10¢, and 5¢, respectively, in addition to the regular charges.

(4) *Period of Day*. Message-toll service is also classified on the basis of the time of day that the call is placed. The effect of this classification is to offer the public reduced rates, or a discount from the regular rates, on both person and station calls (except at the shorter hauls) between 6:00 P.M. and 4:30 A.M. daily, all day Sunday, Thanksgiving, Christmas, and New Year's Day. At these times the demand for toll service by the principal daytime toll customers —people transacting business—tends to be light.

There is a wide variation of toll use by hour of the day and day of the week. The main objective of classifying toll service by period of day through offering reduced rates is to attract, during hours which otherwise would have a comparatively light volume of traffic, business which would not be obtained at full rates. The discount periods and the amounts of the discount are adjusted to attract as much additional development as practicable while avoiding a shift of traffic from normal hours to discount hours which would build up undesirable traffic peaks at the beginning of the discount period.

Unfavorable effects on service may arise when the discounted traffic reaches such proportions that it cannot be handled without considerable delays except by the provision of additional facilities which would have little or no use outside the discount period. To add material amounts of plant solely to care for discounted traffic would defeat the main purpose of the discounts and place a burden on other users. On the other hand, if plant were engineered without regard to discount-period peaks, there would be a marked deterioration in speed of service in this period. While certain customers might countenance material delays in order to obtain lower-priced service, experience indicates that the majority of customers are not satisfied with service that consistently falls below current standards. Therefore, it has been found essential to adjust discount periods and amounts of discounts so as to avoid, so far as possible, traffic peaks in the discount periods. The load distributions of many individual routes are quite different from average conditions and for the same route may vary considerably at different times. However, for the convenience of customers and ease of administration, the classification is kept simple and is applied in a generally uniform manner. This makes it impracticable and undesirable, except under unusual circumstances, to attempt to fit discount periods to conditions on particular routes and necessitates wide periods based on average conditions.

Discounts of various amounts and applying at different periods have been tried out in the various toll-rate schedules applying from time to time. Changes have been made in an effort to adjust the discounted rates so that they will best fulfill their fundamental purpose of encouraging toll use while maintaining satisfactory service and avoiding, so far as practicable, the building up of traffic peaks in the discount periods. The present rate schedules have been evolved from this experience. They generally provide reduced rates at the times specified on all traffic for which the station day rate is more than about 45¢. The reductions on station calls average between 15 per cent and 20 per cent throughout the schedules.

(5) *Length of Conversation.* Finally, message-toll service is classified by length of conversation for purposes of pricing. Toll rates are quoted separately for "initial" and "overtime" periods of conversation, generally in multiples of 5¢. In most cases, initial periods are three minutes and overtime periods one minute for all calls except station calls at the shorter distance. On interstate station calls, where the initial rates are 10¢, 15¢, 20¢, and 25¢, the initial periods are four minutes and the overtime periods 2, 2, 1, and 1 minutes, respectively.

Variation of toll message charges with length of conversation is desirable chiefly because it permits lower basic, that is, initial-period, rates and thus helps to develop the service. This rate treatment puts the customer in a position to decide how long a conversation is really worthwhile. Conversations are not needlessly prolonged, tying up expensive toll circuits and unnecessarily increasing total costs. Yet the customer is able to use the service as long as he wishes on those calls where additional conversation time has real value. Thus, lower initial-period rates are made practicable by both the overtime revenues derived from the longer conversations and the economical use of the circuit.

Each toll call involves recording, line operating, billing and collection work, and so forth, and definite and considerable use of the facilities either by operators or by expensive automatic equipment in establishing the connection and holding the necessary circuits preparatory to communication between customers. Thus, a large proportion of the total costs and revenue requirements are fixed regardless of the length of conversation. Consequently, a reduction in the length of the initial conversation period would not make practicable anything like a proportionate reduction in the initial-period rates. Therefore, the initial period has been established largely on the basis of average needs. Too short an initial period would tend to restrict the usefulness of toll service by making customers unduly conscious of time limitations. Furthermore, if a very large proportion of calls had overtime charges, customers might feel dissatisfied because total charges so frequently and so materially exceeded the rates usually requested and quoted. On the other hand, if the initial period were lengthened, there would be so little revenue from overtime that, in order to meet over-all revenue requirements, initial-period rates would have to be raised, tending to restrict development of the service. Experience indicates that, while the average length of conversation is somewhat affected by the initial period, the difference is not at all proportionate. Therefore, the shorter the initial period, the larger the percentage of conversations bearing overtime charges, and vice versa.

Initial periods ranging from one to five minutes in length have been used at various times. With these different initial periods, average lengths of conversation for the traffic of various companies have tended to range from about two to six minutes. The present average length of conversation on Bell System toll calls is about 5.5 minutes. The general application of a three-minute initial period seems simple and satisfactory except at very short hauls, where there is considerable casual social use and where added use of the line on longer conversations involves relatively less additional expense. Present schedules generally provide a three-minute initial period except for station calls bearing charges at 25¢ or less, on which the initial period may be four or five minutes. With the three-minute initial period, the unit for overtime charges is one minute. The one-minute overtime period is simple and practical and seems satisfactory to the public. A longer period would result in relatively high charges for calls which only slightly exceed the initial period. A shorter period would unduly complicate the rate structure, making it harder for the customer to gauge the charges on a call and slowing down and increasing the costs of rate quoting, rating of toll tickets, billing, and so forth.

In concluding this discussion of toll rates, it may be noted that a study of the principles underlying toll-rate design, by the Toll Rate Subcommittee of the Joint NARUC–FCC Staff Committee on Telephone Regulatory Problems, concluded that the fundamental objectives of such rates are: to meet service requirements of the public; to produce adequate and stable revenue; to encourage use of the service; to provide an equitable distribution of service and charges; to permit economic operation; and to provide simplicity of administration and ease of understanding.[7]

Message-toll rate schedules, current at time of writing, are set forth in Tables 11.4 and 11.5. The two rate schedules shown cover interstate service and Kansas intrastate service.

E. ***Toll-Rate Disparity.*** The rates charged for interstate message-toll service generally are less than the intrastate toll rates for comparable calls. This differential, called the "toll-rate disparity," has been a cause of concern to some state commissions. The toll-rate disparity has been the subject of years of study by the Toll Rate Subcommittee of the Joint NARUC–FCC Staff Committee on Telephone Regulatory Problems, of which more will be said shortly. In part, the toll-rate disparity has been the cause of continuing efforts by the state commissions to bring about changes in the allocation of jointly used plant and joint operating expenses, as between interstate and intrastate operations, in the direction of increasing the amounts allocated to interstate operations. The matter of allocations will be discussed in the next section. The present section is intended to examine the nature of the toll-rate disparity and some of the reasons for it.

The size of the toll-rate disparity does not appear to be great on the basis of the rates for individual interstate and intrastate toll calls. For example, the rate schedules shown in Tables 11.4 and 11.5 indicate that the rates for both services are 30¢ for the initial period of day station calls up to 27 miles. This is particularly significant, because most intrastate long-distance calls are short-haul. At 28 miles, the intrastate rate schedule shown becomes 5¢ higher than the interstate. At 80 miles, the intrastate rate is 10¢ higher than the interstate rate. At 400 miles, the difference shown is 15¢. If the two rate schedules were graphed, it would be seen that the interstate and intrastate rates tend to be parallel, with the interstate rates generally about 15 per cent lower at each mileage step. On the other hand, the toll-rate disparity has been estimated at $125 million per year when measured in terms of charges for intrastate toll service above the charges which would result

[7] National Association of Railroad and Utilities Commissioners, 1951 *Proceedings*, pp. 128–129.

Table 11.4

Message Toll Telephone Service
Rates of American Telephone and Telegraph Company
For Interstate Service

Rate Mileage	*Initial Period*				*Overtime*	
	Station-to-Station		*Person-to-Person*		*Station and Person*	
	Day	*Night*	*Day*	*Night*	*Day*	*Night*
0-8	$ .10	$ .10	$ .25	$ .25	$ .05	$ .05
9-13	.15	.15	.30	.30	.05	.05
14-18	.20	.20	.35	.35	.05	.05
19-24	.25	.25	.40	.40	.05	.05
25-30	.30	.30	.45	.45	.10	.10
31-40	.35	.35	.50	.50	.10	.10
41-55	.40	.40	.55	.55	.10	.10
56-70	.45	.40	.65	.60	.15	.10
71-85	.50	.40	.70	.60	.15	.10
86-100	.55	.40	.75	.60	.15	.10
101-124	.60	.45	.85	.70	.15	.15
125-148	.65	.50	.90	.75	.20	.15
149-172	.70	.55	1.00	.85	.20	.15
173-196	.75	.55	1.05	.85	.20	.15
197-220	.80	.60	1.10	.90	.20	.15
221-244	.85	.65	1.20	1.00	.25	.20
245-268	.90	.70	1.25	1.05	.25	.20
269-292	.95	.70	1.35	1.10	.25	.20
293-316	1.00	.75	1.40	1.15	.25	.20
317-354	1.05	.80	1.45	1.20	.30	.20
355-392	1.10	.85	1.55	1.30	.30	.25
393-430	1.15	.85	1.30	1.30	.30	.25
431-468	1.20	.90	1.70	1.40	.30	.25
469-506	1.25	.95	1.75	1.45	.30	.25
507-544	1.30	1.00	1.80	1.50	.35	.25
545-600	1.35	1.05	1.90	1.60	.35	.30
601-675	1.40	1.10	1.95	1.65	.35	.30
676-800	1.45	1.15	2.10	1.80	.40	.30
801-925	1.50	1.20	2.25	1.95	.40	.30
926-1050.	1.55	1.20	2.40	2.05	.40	.30
1051-1175.	1.60	1.25	2.50	2.15	.40	.30
1176-1360.	1.70	1.30	2.65	2.25	.45	.35
1361-1605.	1.80	1.40	2.85	2.45	.45	.35
1606-1910.	1.95	1.50	3.10	2.65	.50	.40
1911-2300.	2.10	1.65	3.30	2.85	.55	.45
2301-3000.	2.25	1.75	3.50	3.00	.60	.45

Effective September 19, 1959

if the interstate toll-rate schedule were applied.[8] This is not due wholly to the fact that interstate initial-period rates are generally below intrastate rates throughout the country; for in addition, the interstate rate schedule in many instances provides for longer initial periods, lower overtime charges, and greater rate reductions when time of day and person-station differentials are concerned.

The toll-rate disparity results from two basic causes: (a) interstate message-toll service is nationwide in scope, and hence has different characteristics from intrastate message-toll service that is confined within boundaries of a par-

[8] *Ibid.*, p. 130.

Table 11.5

Message Toll Telephone Service
Rates of Southwestern Bell Telephone Company
For Kansas Intrastate Service

RATE MILEAGE	DAY, NIGHT AND SUNDAY					
	STATION TO STATION			PERSON TO PERSON		
	PAID		COLLECT	PAID AND COLLECT		
	INITIAL 3 MIN.	EA. ADD'L MIN.	AMOUNT TO BE ADDED TO CHARGES COMPUTED ON "PAID" BASIS	INITIAL 3 MIN.	EACH ADD'L MINUTE FIRST 3	EACH ADD'L MINUTE AFTER FIRST 3
0- 8	10	03	15	30	10	03
9- 12	15	05	15	35	12	05
13- 17	20	07	10	40	13	07
18- 22	25	08	05	45	15	08
23- 27	30	10	—	50	17	10
28- 32	35	12	—	60	20	12
33- 38	40	13	—	70	23	13
39- 44	45	15	—	75	25	15
45- 52	50	17	—	85	28	17

RATE MILEAGE	PAID AND COLLECT									
	DAY (EXCEPT SUNDAY)					NIGHT AND SUNDAY				
	STATION TO STATION		PERSON TO PERSON			STATION TO STATION		PERSON TO PERSON		
	INITIAL 3 MIN.	EA. ADD'L MIN.	INITIAL 3 MIN.	EA. ADD'L MINUTE FIRST 3	EA. ADD'L MINUTE AFTER FIRST 3	INITIAL 3 MIN.	EA. ADD'L MIN.	INITIAL 3 MIN.	EA. ADD'L MINUTE FIRST 3	EA. ADD'L MINUTE AFTER FIRST 3
53- 66	55	18	95	32	18	50	17	90	30	17
67- 80	60	20	100	33	20	50	17	90	30	17
81- 96	65	22	110	37	22	55	18	100	33	18
97-114	70	23	120	40	23	60	20	110	37	20
115-132	75	25	130	43	25	65	22	120	40	22
133-150	80	27	135	45	27	70	23	125	42	23
151-174	85	28	145	48	28	70	23	130	43	23
175-198	90	30	155	52	30	75	25	140	47	25
199-222	95	32	160	53	32	80	27	145	48	27
223-246	100	33	170	57	33	85	28	155	52	28
247-270	105	35	180	60	35	90	30	165	55	30
271-294	110	37	185	62	37	95	32	170	57	32
295-318	115	38	195	65	38	100	33	180	60	33
319-342	120	40	205	68	40	100	33	185	62	33
343-372	125	42	215	72	42	105	35	195	65	35
373-402	130	43	220	73	43	110	37	200	67	37
403-432	135	45	230	77	45	115	38	210	70	38
433-462	140	47	240	80	47	120	40	220	73	40
463-492	145	48	245	82	48	125	42	225	75	42

EFFECTIVE DECEMBER 1, 1958

ticular state; and (b) the fact that telephone toll-rate regulation is divided between federal and state authority.

Let us first consider two important differences between interstate and intrastate toll service: (a) length of haul, and (b) volume of traffic. In general, the length of haul, or the distance covered by the average interstate message, is much greater than the distance covered by the average intrastate message. A study of 29 states by the Toll Rate Subcommittee of the Joint NARUC–FCC Staff Committee, for example, showed that the average length of haul per intrastate toll message varied from 9 miles to 91 miles, while the average haul per interstate message was 204 miles.[9] These figures reflect data from the late 1940's. In 1959 the average distance per interstate call was 283 miles. At the same time, for example, the Kansas intrastate message-toll calls averaged 54 miles.[10] These comparisons point up the fact that most intrastate messages are short-haul, whereas most interstate messages are long-haul. Advancements in the art of telephony have made for greater economies in the use of long-haul facilities than of short-haul facilities.

Volume of traffic, or traffic-density characteristics, also differentiate intrastate and interstate message-toll traffic. Interstate traffic is concentrated between and among the major population centers, whereas intrastate toll lines are built into all communities in a state, regardless of how small the volume of long-distance traffic may be to and from such communities. The Toll Rate Subcommittee study, for example, found that a factor leading to cost differences between the two types of toll service was the "Greater average density of traffic on interstate toll routes than on intrastate routes, making possible lower cost toll circuits and more efficient utilization of such circuits with resulting economies."[11]

Differences in length of haul and traffic density, as between the two types of toll service, result in the use of significantly different facilities in each case. The high cost per circuit-mile facilities serve the short-haul and less dense intrastate traffic. Most interstate traffic is concentrated in high-volume channels between major cities, which makes economically feasible the use of low-cost-per-circuit-mile coaxial cable and microwave radio relays. On the other hand, much of the intrastate toll network in each state consists of open wire and cable.

The construction and maintenance costs of these two different systems of transmitting long-distance messages differ considerably. The Toll Rate Subcommittee has stated, for example, that ". . . the developments in carrier techniques have been chiefly applicable to the longer haul circuits on heavy routes. Such developments have reduced Long Lines investment per circuit mile from about $109 in 1943 to less than $60 in 1950 (45 per cent) despite large additions of high cost plant, whereas the average circuit mile cost of the Associated Companies has been reduced from $134 to $120 (10 per cent) during this period."[12] A 1959 example of the average cost difference, again citing Kansas as an example, was $155 per circuit mile for Kansas intrastate plant, as compared with $40 for the high-volume interstate circuits of the Long Lines Department.

Construction labor and expense are the same to bury a coaxial cable to carry 3,600 circuits or an ordinary cable to carry 20 circuits. Although the total construction cost per mile of the large-volume circuits is, of course, greater than for smaller-volume cable or open wire, the important economic factor is that the construction cost per circuit mile is less. For example, the 1959 construction cost per circuit mile for three-circuit-capacity open wire was $867, whereas for 1,100-circuit TD-2 microwave it was $23 per circuit mile. Maintenance expenses are less for much of the long-haul toll facilities because they are not exposed to weather hazards. The foregoing points up the fact that the low-cost facilities can only be used to provide long-haul, high-volume traffic; this is principally interstate service.

[9] *Ibid.*, p. 122.

[10] Data for this and other comparisons supplied upon request by Southwestern Bell Telephone Co.

[11] NARUC, 1951 *Proceedings, op. cit.*, p. 132.

[12] *Ibid.*

Interstate calls produce more revenue per call than intrastate calls, owing to their: (a) greater average distance; (b) greater average duration—for example, 5.5 minutes for interstate calls as against 4.33 minutes for Kansas intrastate; and (c) greater proportion of person calls as against the preponderance of station calls in intrastate toll service. In Kansas in 1959, the average revenue per interstate call was $1.78 as against 63¢ for the average Kansas intrastate call. These differences between intrastate and interstate communications provide a basis for understanding why interstate rates on a mileage basis tend to be less than intrastate long-distance rates.

Further, the prospect is that new scientific developments will tend to make interstate service even less costly in the future. First, microwave and other high-volume message carriers are being put to increasing use. Because of the relatively high cost of providing drop-offs, these carriers are utilized primarily between major communications centers. Thus, where a microwave system connects two principal points, it is necessary to provide a cable along the same route to serve points between those cities. Second, the Bell System is increasing its installation of automatic alternate-routing mechanisms, which select idle circuits in order to send message over whatever route may be available. For example, an eastbound message to Baltimore from Wichita, Kansas, may be routed via St. Louis, Pittsburgh, or Washington, D.C., depending upon the most direct idle route available. This permits utilization of long-haul channels to maximum capacity, and there is far less unused circuit time than on a toll cable connecting smaller communities. Third, and related to the two developments above, the Bell System has developed the National Switching Plan, by which the land area of the United States and Canada is divided into eleven regional zones, each of which is served by a regional communications center. Below the regional centers are sectional centers, and below them, primary centers. The National Switching Plan is devised to permit the routing of calls from originating points through primary, sectional, and regional communications centers. The principal economies of this plan lie in the maximum utilization of high-volume communications facilities between regional centers and between sectional and regional centers. In view of these new developments in telephony and the division of toll-rate regulatory authority between the federal and state governments, it seems likely that the toll-rate disparity will continue into the future.

To an important extent, the toll-rate disparity is due to the division of regulatory authority between federal and state commissions. First, interstate toll rates are quoted under one basic rate schedule for the entire United States. This rate schedule reflects an averaging of service characteristics throughout the country. The result is a highly simplified pricing system, for under equal circumstances (distance, time of day, and so forth) interstate calls are generally priced alike, regardless of the particular two communities that may be involved. On the other hand, the intrastate toll rates under the jurisdiction of each state inevitably reflect the differing circumstances found from state to state. The costs of furnishing telephone service differ substantially in different states, owing to differences in physical development of the territory, terrain, density and continuity of telephone development, volumes of traffic and degree of concentration on heavy routes, type and age of plant, prevailing wage levels, taxation, the prevalence of extended-area service, the destructiveness of the weather, and other factors. Therefore, uniform interstate and intrastate rate schedules would yield different results in each state and would very likely produce varying rates of return in the different states.

Second, part of the toll-rate disparity is due to differences from state to state in apportioning the approved state-wide revenue requirement between exchange service and intrastate toll service. If, for example, less of the state-wide revenue requirement is to be recovered from intrastate toll service, then more will have to be recovered from exchange service—and vice versa. This points up the fact that intrastate toll rates are directly related to exchange rates, both of which are under the respective state commissions. Interstate toll rates, on the other hand, do not have this same relation to exchange rates.

Let us look at the effect of the division of toll-rate regulation between state and federal commissions from another standpoint. Assume there were no toll-rate disparity, and that all long-distance calls were priced under the present interstate toll-rate schedule. What would be some of the consequences? First of all, intrastate toll rates and revenues would be reduced, and revenues from local exchange rates would have to be increased by a like amount—assuming no change in the state-wide revenue requirement or in the volume of business. Second, a policy of conforming intrastate toll rates to interstate rates would, in effect, delegate to the FCC the regulatory authority over intrastate toll rates. Such would be the case because, in order to maintain the same toll rates, the state commissions would have to change intrastate rates each time the FCC ordered a change in interstate toll rates. However, this would also mean that the state commissions would lose a measure of control over exchange rates, for any change in intrastate toll rates would have to be offset by compensating changes in exchange rates. Thus, if the FCC reduced interstate toll rates, as it has in many instances, intrastate toll rates would have to be reduced by the state commissions, and local exchange rates would have to be increased by a corresponding amount. On the face of it, such does not seem desirable. However, a further effect would be a shift in the burden of the state-wide revenue requirement from business to residence customers, because the latter mainly require exchange service while business customers primarily provide the demand for message-toll service. From the above, it appears that the prospect of narrowing the toll-rate disparity, or eliminating it, does not lie in a simple reduction of toll rates at the state level.

Accordingly, the state commissions that are concerned with the toll-rate disparity have approached this matter by seeking changes in the allocation of joint plant and expenses—as between interstate and intrastate operations—so as to increase the amounts allocated to interstate operations. The purpose of such efforts has been to reduce the state-wide revenue requirement by shifting a portion of the state-wide expenses and plant to interstate operations. This brings us to a consideration of "separations," or the allocations of joint expenses and plant cost between interstate and intrastate telephone service.

F. The Separations of Interstate and Intrastate Plant and Expenses. Up to this point in the discussion of telephone rates, little has been said about joint-cost allocations. This does not mean that telephone rate making is not concerned with that matter, for the allocation of telephone joint costs involves a basic matter meriting special consideration. However, the point to note at the outset is that the principal allocation problem in telephone rate making arises in distinguishing between the interstate and intrastate cost of service, respectively, and not in the distribution of an approved cost of service to customer classes or to classes of service.

Before going further, let us establish some basic terms that will be relied on in the following discussion. (a) The allocations of joint telephone plant and expenses are referred to as "separations"; instead of speaking of allocation methods, the term "separations procedures" is used in this context. (b) Separations procedures are set forth in a volume called the *Separations Manual,* of which more will be said presently. (c) The procedures contained in the *Manual* are designed primarily to allocate plant, revenues, expenses, taxes, and reserves between state and interstate jurisdictions so as to enable each commission to determine the cost-of-service and revenue requirement for the telephone service rendered within its area of authority. (d) Where the Bell System is concerned, the principal individual suppliers of telephone service are the Long Lines Department and the respective operating companies, which are referred to as the "Associated Companies." (e) The organization that has been most prominent in developing and amending telephone separations procedures is the National Association of Railroad and Utilities Commissioners (NARUC), working through its expert committees. In matters concerning telephone separations, the NARUC committees generally have represented the point of view of the state commissions.

The *Separations Manual* is the product of cooperative effort extending through a period of over twenty years. The *Manual* has been developed by the efforts of staff experts from the state commissions (acting through committees of the NARUC), the Federal Communications Commission, the Bell System, and the United States Independent Telephone Assocation. The *Manual* does not, of itself, have the force of law. However, its adoption and subsequent amendments generally have taken place after compromise and in a spirit of cooperation. Hence, the *Manual* has been put into practice in almost every jurisdiction in the country.

Departures from uniformity in the application of *Manual* procedures are a constant cause of concern. They have occurred periodically in the decisions of some of the state commissions. Concern over departures from uniform application of *Manual* procedures is explainable in terms of their undesirable results. Either of two results is inherent in any departure: (a) some plant and expenses will not be allocated to either interstate or intrastate service; or (b) some of the same plant and expenses will be allocated to both services. In (a) the telephone company would not be compensated adequately. In (b) the consuming public would be required to pay twice the amount necessary to provide for the plant and operations involved. Neither situation is reasonable. If a state commission chooses to reduce the intrastate allocation below the amount resulting under *Manual* procedures, the record shows that in some but not all cases it will be upheld in the state courts. One has to agree with the NARUC: "That it is essential that a single, proper uniform method of separation be used by the State and Federal jurisdictions. . . ."[13]

(1) *Actual Use—The Basis of Separations.* The Supreme Court has held that separations must be based upon actual use. In 1930, Chief Justice Hughes, speaking for a unanimous Court, held that the principle of relative actual use as between the two services was applicable in telephone rate making. This was decided in *Smith* v. *Illinois Bell Telephone Co.* There, the Court ruled: "The separation of the intrastate and inter-

[13] National Association of Railroad and Utilities Commissioners, 1954 *Proceedings,* p. 336.

state property, revenues and expenses of the company is important not simply as a theoretical allocation to two branches of the business. It is essential to the appropriate recognition of the competent governmental authority in each field of regulation."[14]

In the *Separations Manual* that was ultimately developed in 1947 to meet the requirements of the *Smith* case, separations are made on the "actual use" basis, which gives consideration to relative occupancy and relative time measurements. The actual measurements of use are: (a) determined for telephone plant or for work performed by operating forces on a unit basis (such as "conversation-minute-miles" per message and "traffic units" per call) in studies of traffic handled or work performed during a representative period; and (b) applied to over-all traffic volumes, that is, 24-hour rather than busy-hour volumes.

The definitions of these measurements of use are as follows. (1) "Conversation-minute-miles," also called "message-minute-miles," or MMM for short, is defined as the product of (a) the number of messages, (b) the average minutes of conversation per message, and (c) the average route miles of circuits involved. (2) "Minutes of use" is a unit of measurement expressed as either holding time or conversation time, with holding time defined as the time in which an item of telephone plant is in actual use either by a customer or an operator. (3) A "traffic unit" is a unit of measurement of traffic operating work, which is used as a common denominator to express the relative time required for handling the various kinds of calls or work functions.

Major revisions in the *Separations Manual* occurred in 1951 and 1954. The first of these involved simplifications and amendments of the separations procedures relating to exchange plant costs. These changes in the *Separations Manual* were adopted at the 1951 annual NARUC convention which met in Charleston, S.C. Hence, this is referred to as the Charleston Plan. Second, the 1954 convention approved a revision of the procedures applicable to the separations of message telephone interexchange toll-lines plant and related expenses of the Associated Companies and the Bell System. This is called the Modified Phoenix Plan, because it represented a compromise form of a plan adopted by the NARUC some years earlier in Phoenix, Arizona, but not approved by other interested parties. Thereafter, through and including the 1957 *Separations Manual,* the further changes have been intended to conform the *Manual* with current operating conditions and regulatory requirements.

(2) *The 1957 "Separations Manual."* The 1957 *Separations Manual* brings together all the amendments and simplifications developed over the previous years and also includes changes reflecting current operating conditions and regulatory requirements. The *Manual* sets forth an outline of separations procedures for telephone companies on a "station-to-station" basis. This requires some explanation. First, a "station" is a telephone instrument, such as that found in the average home or business. It is the property of the telephone company. Second, the station-to-station basis of the *Separations Manual* is a term describing the extent of the telephone facilities subject to separations. Specifically, "station-to-station" is the term applied to the basis of toll rate making, which contemplates that the toll charge shall cover the use made of all facilities between the originating station and the terminating station, including the stations, and the services rendered in connection therewith. The station-to-station basis attributes a por-

[14] 282 U.S. 133, 148.

tion of exchange plant and expenses to interstate toll operations.

Separations Manual procedures are applicable to either property costs or values and revenues, expenses, taxes, and reserves as recorded on the books of the company or to estimated amounts. The first step in the separation procedures involves the assignment of plant to categories, in most instances by identification from records, and the determination of the cost of the plant so identified. The second step requires the separation or apportionment of the cost of the plant in each category to the various operations by the application of appropriate use factors or by direct assignment.

The various measures of actual use, which serve as the primary basis for the separations, have been defined previously. We shall now relate these measurements to the separations of plant costs. Telephone plant, in general, may be divided into two broad classifications: (a) interexchange plant, which is plant used primarily to furnish toll services, and (b) exchange plant, which is plant used primarily to furnish local services. Within these two classifications, there are three broad types of plant: (a) manual switching plant; (b) dial switching plant; and (c) circuit plant. For each of these types of plant used jointly for state and interstate operations, the bases for the separations of such plant among these operations are: (a) operator work time expressed in traffic units is the basis for measuring the use of manual switching plant; (b) holding-time minutes is the basis for measuring the use of toll and local dial switching plant; (c) conversation-minute-miles is the basis for measuring the use of interexchange-circuit plant; and (d) minutes of use is the basis for measuring the use of exchange-circuit plant.

Some principal expense items, as well as depreciation expense, and property and miscellaneous taxes are apportioned among the operations on the basis of the cost of related plant. In the apportionment of revenues, local service revenues and message-toll service revenues are assigned directly to those services rather than allocated.

In implementing the separations procedures, an adjustment is necessary in applying the minutes-of-use basis of measurement to exchange-circuit plant. For the apportionment of such plant between state and interstate operations, the *Manual* provides that the basis shall be "the relative number of minutes of use" of exchange-circuit plant, and that "the minutes of use are the minutes of holding time for the area under study for all telephone connections established within the various exchanges in providing the operations involved."[15] An adjustment is necessary here because of the nature of the timing process employed. If A calls B within a local exchange area and talks for five minutes, there is but one "connection" and the holding time is five minutes. However, the counting devices used for this purpose count both originating and terminating minutes of use, and thus count five minutes for the use of A's telephone and five minutes for the use of B's telephone—giving a total of ten minutes. For this reason, the originating and terminating local minutes of use are divided by two in order to get the "connection" minutes of use as required by the *Manual*.

(3) *The Separation of Toll-Circuit Plant.* The basic measurement of actual use applied to the interexchange message-toll telephone-circuit plant of the Associated Companies of the Bell System is conversation-minute-miles, sometimes referred to as message-minute-miles or MMM's. The implementation of this basic measurement of use was amended in 1954 by the adoption of the Modified Phoenix Plan.

[15] *Separations Manual,* October 1957, Par. 23.4331.

(A) *The Bell System Toll Lines Plant.* The Associated Companies provide the plant required to furnish the local and intrastate toll services within their respective territories and interstate service in certain cases. The Long Lines Department of the American Company provides facilities which interconnect the various Associated Companies; these facilities form a network generally restricted to the main arteries of communications—the "backbone" routes. The Associated Companies normally provide all facilities on the side or "feeder" routes and some main-route facilities. Along these main routes the plant facilities in some instances are provided on a joint basis and owned in varying degrees by the Long Lines Department and the Associated Companies. The Associated Company toll network provides facilities which may be connected to those of Long Lines in order to furnish through service on the most economical basis.

Long Lines' interstate circuits are predominantly of greater length than the jointly used circuits of the Associated Companies; further, Long Lines' circuits have greater traffic density per circuit and more circuits per route. Accordingly, the average cost per mile or per unit of use of Long Lines' circuits is less than the average cost of the jointly used circuits of the Associated Companies. Toll-line book investment as of June 1953, for example, averaged about $120 per circuit mile of all Associated Company jointly used plant, while that for Long Lines was $48. A comparison on a usage basis indicated that all jointly used Associated Company toll plant averaged annually about 42,000 MMM's (messages × minutes × miles) per circuit mile, as compared with 54,300 MMM's for Long Lines' plant.[16]

(B) *The Modified Phoenix Plan.* The 1957 *Manual* provides for the separation of interexchange message toll-circuit plant by a procedure called the Modified Phoenix Plan, adopted as an amendment to the *Manual* in 1954. Briefly stated, the Modified Phoenix Plan provides that the book costs of the toll lines plant in a given state shall be segregated between: (a) terminating facilities, that is, facilities of which one or both terminals are within the state; and (b) transiting facilities, that is, facilities of which neither terminal is within the state, and which therefore provide no service within the state. The book costs of the terminating facilities, including those of the Long Lines Department located within the state, are allocated to intrastate and interstate service on the basis of the relative MMM's of use. The book costs of the transiting facilities are assigned directly to interstate service in accordance with their single use. Expenses follow plant. Thus, the Modified Phoenix Plan provides that the book costs of Long Lines Department toll-lines plant within a state (excluding "transiting" plant which crosses but does not serve customers in that state) would be combined with book costs of Associated Company toll-lines plant terminating in the state. The combined total of Long Lines and Associated Company terminating plant then would be apportioned between the state and interstate categories on the MMM basis, and transiting plant would be directly assigned to interstate operations. Based on June 1954 operations, the Modified Phoenix Plan was estimated to have the effect of transferring to interstate operations an estimated $152 million in plant investment and $20 million in expenses. Together, it was estimated that intrastate toll costs would be reduced by 21 per cent and that annual intrastate revenue requirements would be reduced by about $35 million.[17] Most of the other amendments to the *Manual* also have had the effect of trans-

[16] NARUC, 1954 *Proceedings, op. cit.*, p. 273.

[17] *Ibid.*, pp. 268, 275.

ferring plant and expenses to the interstate system.

The Modified Phoenix Plan effects an averaging of the lower cost per circuit-mile plant of the Long Lines Department with the relatively higher cost per circuit-mile plant of the Associated Companies. The result of the averaging process is to attribute an equal amount of plant cost to each MMM of use, regardless of the book costs or traffic-density characteristics of different portions of the plant involved. Thus, the Modified Phoenix Plan resulted in a shift of plant to interstate operations owing to (a) the averaging of the cost of terminating-circuit plant used exclusively in producing interstate toll service of about $48 per mile, with the cost of Associated Company jointly used circuit plant at an average book cost of about $120 per mile; and (b) the averaging of the relatively greater use of circuits used exclusively in interstate toll service of 54,300 MMM's per circuit mile with that of the jointly used Associated Company circuit plant of 42,000 MMM's. One FCC Commissioner has opposed the allocation of plant otherwise directly assignable to interstate operations.[18]

2. WATER SUPPLY AND RATES

The water supply system in each community provides the public with a safe and potable supply of water under pressure. In addition, the water supply organization makes possible the operation of a network of sewers; a water-carrying system is the most economical method of collecting and disposing of community sewage. Further, with respect to public fire protection, the community water supply is as important as the fire department itself. Accordingly, the community water supply system is vitally important to urban living. The following survey is not intended to be a full discussion of all the significant economic problems bearing on water supply; rather, its purpose is limited to a development of the public utility and rate aspects of water supply in the United States.

Public utilities provide a relatively small proportion of the total water supply of the United States—about nine per cent of the total. The largest single use of water is the industrial self-supply, which compromises about half the total. About two-thirds of the self-supplied industrial water is used by electric power plants for condenser cooling, which normally does not contaminate the water but does raise its temperature before returning it to the source. The principal uses of water are compared in Table 11.6.

A. Development of Water Service. Before water supply systems were developed in urban areas, water was furnished by backyard wells and cisterns. The first water supply system in this country was established in Boston in 1652. It provided both domestic water supply and fire protection to a single street. However, the development of water supply systems was slow, in no small part owing to the superiority, in many cases, of the backyard well in furnishing a safe and palatable supply. There were 17 water works in the United States in 1800, and 83 in 1850. A great boom in the construction of water supply systems occurred in the last two decades of the nineteenth century and thereafter. By 1900 there were about 4,000 water supply systems; this total was practically doubled by 1924. In 1959 there were about 18,000 water supply organizations. For 1958, it was reliably estimated that the gross investment in United States water works facilities aggregated $12 billion, making this one of the largest industries in the

[18] *Ibid., Proceedings,* p. 266.

Table 11.6

United States Water Use Pattern
1955
(billion gallons per day)

Use	*Volume*	*% Distribution*
Rural	2.5	1%
Public supply	17	9
Industrial self-supply . . .	110	52
Irrigation	81	38
Total	210.5	100%

Source: Mineral Facts and Problems, 1960 ed., Bureau of Mines Bulletin 585, p. 959.

country.[19] More than half this amount was attributed to the period following World War II.

A water supply system serves to acquire, collect, process, and deliver water of proper quality to its customers' premises. Water supplies are derived from surface-water or ground-water sources. Surface-water sources, which provide about 75 per cent of the public water supply, include collecting and impounding reservoirs, lakes, and rivers. Ground-water sources are tapped by wells. Conducting water from its source to the processing plant, in some cases, can be accomplished by means of gravity; more often, however, pumping is necessary to transmit the water to the treatment plant and from there to the distribution system. The treatment required varies widely from place to place. Some water requires little or no treatment other than chlorination. Other water requires complex processing that may include softening. Treatment costs, accordingly, will vary considerably among different systems. Surface water ordinarily requires more treatment than ground water. Distribution takes place through a network of mains and service connections, with the water driven by pressure created as the result of sufficient elevation on the system. Water systems make use of storage facilities, which are often located in the areas where it is consumed. Storage facilities assist in meeting peak demands—which would otherwise fall on the facilities serving to supply, treat, pump, and distribute water.

Early in the development of water supply, a strong tendency toward government ownership emerged that characterizes this sector of the economy to the present time. "Government ownership" in this case refers to ownership and operation of water supply systems by city and village governments and other political subdivisions of the states and entities such as districts and authorities. Government ownership was an economic necessity for many communities. The unusually high capital investment required to establish a water supply system, even by comparison with other utilities, caused many communities to rely upon the public credit for financing in the absence of sufficient or timely private capital investment. Another factor leading to government ownership of water supply systems is the particularly close relation between water supply and public health, sanitation, and fire protection.

At present about 75 per cent of the water supply systems in the United

[19] Louis R. Howson, "Fifty Years' Experience with Water Utility Costs and Revenues," 51 *American Water Works Association Journal* 693, 697 (1959).

States are government-owned. These systems include those in practically all of the major cities. In Washington, D.C., water is supplied to the water department of the local government by the Army Corps of Engineers.

Most state regulatory commissions do not have jurisdiction to regulate the rates, accounts, financing, or service of government-owned water utilities. In fact, government-owned water utilities are subject to state-commission regulation in only six states—Maine, Montana, Nevada, West Virginia, Wisconsin, and Wyoming. Accordingly, the rates of most government-owned water supply systems are fixed by the communities they serve. Conventionally, this authority to set rates rests with the city council. The exemption from state-commission regulation does not necessarily hold, however, when government-owned water systems extend service beyond the limits of the municipal corporation. The courts have not ruled uniformly on whether the exemption from state regulation applies in such cases. The investor-owned water utilities, on the other hand, are generally subject to state-commission regulation on the same basis as other utilities. In Ohio, where city councils have the initial authority to set all but telephone rates and the state commission serves as an appellate body, an investor-owned water company may file a rate increase application with the state commission if the city council fails to take action on such a proposal within a specified period of time.

B. ***Economic Characteristics.*** Water supply systems furnish a service to the public that is uniquely without competition from substitutes. The local water utility is ordinarily a pure monopoly, except to the extent that industrial consumers of water establish their own supplies. Unlike other utilities, the demand for metered water service is restricted to people's needs almost irrespective of price. Thus, although relatively high rates for water service may serve to restrain its use somewhat, low rates ordinarily constitute small incentive to increase consumption. Exceptions to this may arise in arid and semi-arid areas and with respect to the use of water in non-conserving air-conditioning units; the latter will be discussed shortly. Promotional water rates and other load-building efforts are practically unheard of. For example, the 344 Wisconsin water utilities in 1958 incurred an aggregate operating expense of $38 for sales promotion. In summary, it may be said that the market demand for water supplied by municipal systems is essentially inelastic for metered service.

The investment required in water supply systems is comparatively great in relation to revenues. The investment commonly is $4 to $5 per dollar of annual revenue, which is high even by comparison with other public utilities. This slow rate of capital turnover is related to a comparatively low operating ratio, as might be expected, because of the greater requirements for debt service.

Water utility costs are dominated by items which are of a fixed nature, because they are related to size of plant and the number of permanent personnel. Accordingly, the annual cost of operation is not much affected by fluctuations in the volume of water sold. The principal expense items that relate to volume, and hence are variable rather than fixed, are fuel and electricity (which are consumed for pumping) and chemicals (which are used in purification). Customer costs are comparatively low because: (a) little is ordinarily provided by way of services other than the delivery of water; and (b) the practice of many water utilities of billing at quarterly or longer intervals. Commodity or production costs (corresponding to the energy costs of electric utilities) can vary widely from place to place, depending upon the amount of pumping required and the type of treatment necessary to render the water safe, potable, and reasonably clear.

The peak demand period for water works systems extends over a four-month period, June through September, when the sources of water supply are usually low. The summer peak-day demand is generally at least 1.5 times the average daily demand. The provision of storage capacity aids in normalizing hourly pumping rates during ordinary peak days and, if elevated, assists in maintaining water pressure. Properly located storage capacity reduces the size of distribution mains required.

The summer peak period traditionally has been caused by residential lawn sprinkling and, to a lesser degree, by golf course sprinkling and swimming pool use. In recent years, the summer peak in some communities has increased greatly, owing to the growth in demand for service to non-conserving air-conditioning units, which use water to remove heat from the air in non-residential buildings. The warmed water, once used, is not recirculated for reuse but is discharged into the sewer system. Where this type of air-conditioning unit has increased in use, the summer peaks have shot up alarmingly. Each ton unit of non-conserving air-conditioning capacity uses about 1,200 gallons of water on a hot day, assuming 10 hours of operation. This daily water consumption may be placed in perspective by noting that a residential customer, without this type of air conditioning, will consume around 3,000 to 4,000 gallons per month. Although the peak demand of the non-conserving air-conditioning load is high, the average annual load factor is low. In Kansas City in 1954, for example, 23 per cent of the peak-day demand on the system resulted from the non-conserving air-conditioning demand. However, the annual water usage by this equipment was only 7.3 per cent of the total. The powerful peak-causing effect of this type of air conditioning has required remedies in terms of restrictions on water use or rate adjustments or both.

About half of the water distributed by the government-owned water systems is consumed by residential customers, who contribute over half the total revenues collected from residential, commercial, and industrial customers. This is due to the operation of the minimum bill provision in the single-rate schedule used by most water utilities. On the other hand, industrial customers account for a lesser percentage of revenues than sales volume. This reflects not only the economies of serving the larger-volume customers but also the value-of-service factor which arises from the alternative of industrial self-supply in some cases. The comparison in Table 11.7, of sales volumes and revenues by class of customer, does not include data on public, miscellaneous, or fire-protection water use or revenues.

Table 11.7

Government-Owned Water Utilities
Sales and Revenues
1955

Customer Class	*Sales Volume*	*Revenues*
Residential	48%	63%
Commercial	19	18
Industrial	33	19

Source: H. F. Seidel, "How Municipal Water Rates Operate," 73 *The American City* 167, 168 (August, 1958).

The financing of government-owned water utilities differs in important ways from conventional public utility financing. Government-owned water utilities finance their capital requirements by borrowing, except to the extent that additions and improvements can be financed from revenues. Investor-owned water utilities, on the other hand, generally have about one-third of their capitalization in the form of equity securities. An extremely important characteristic of government-owned water utility financing is that provision must be made, on a current basis, for the liquidation and retirement of outstanding debt. This differs considerably from the debt-management practices of many private corporations, which refund their maturing debt obligations by issuing new debt. The debt of government-owned water utilities may be issued in the form of serial bonds; where such is the case, a specified portion of the debt matures each year. On the other hand, where an outstanding debt issue will fall due all at one time, it is necessary to accumulate funds over the life of the bonds. This is done by periodic payments into a debt-retirement reserve, which may be established on a sinking fund basis. Government-owned water utilities generally have a lower over-all cost of capital than investor-owned utilities, largely owing to two factors: (a) they issue no equity securities, which normally cost the issuer more than debt capital; and (b) lenders will accept a lower rate of interest, because interest on the debt of government-owned utilities is not subject to federal income taxation.

In the past, and less so at present, government-owned water utilities have been financed by general-obligation bonds, which pledge the general credit and tax revenues of the issuing community. During the 1930's, a number of states changed their laws so as to authorize revenue-bond financing. Revenue bonds are payable only from the income derived from operation of the water utility, and they constitute a lien on the water works property and revenue. The issuance of this form of debt ordinarily does not come under the debt limitation imposed upon cities by the laws or constitutions of many states. A second type of debt, the special-assessment mortgage bond, is payable only from the receipts from special-benefit assessments levied on property owners adjacent to new water mains, and not from general taxes. A third type, the general-obligation assessment bond, is quite similar to the second type above, except that taxes will be levied to meet the obligation if the special assessments are not collected. Fourth, general-obligation revenue bonds assure the lender that if utility revenues are not sufficient to meet debt-service requirements, property taxes will be levied to meet the obligation. Combinations of two or more types of these bonds are used to finance water supply systems and extensions. For example, special-assessment bonds may be issued to finance extensions of service, with general-obligation or revenue bonds used to finance the central water works. This approach distinguishes properly between benefits received by specific property and by the entire community.

Another economic characteristic of water utilities is the joint nature of their supply function, arising from the fact that they provide both water service to utility customers and fire-protection service to the general public. This is sometimes referred to as service to "users" and "nonusers," respectively. The users of water service, of course, are the conventional and special classes of utility customers. The nonusers are the beneficiaries of the capacity installed by water utilities for the purpose of supplying water to the fire departments in their communities. Stated more specifically, the beneficiaries of public fire-protection water service are the owners of property in the community. The importance of such service relates far more to the value of the property protected than to the amount of water consumed.

Private fire-protection service, in the form of service to interior sprinkler systems and additional hydrants, is provided to commercial and industrial customers. This is a service different from public fire protection and amounts to a special class of service. Water supply and distribution systems are designed with due regard for the needs of both users and nonusers. Therefore, in order to provide public fire-protection service, water utilities must invest in more plant capacity than would be required to supply service solely to water users. This takes the form of larger supply capacity and mains, hydrants, extra valves, larger pumps, and additional storage capacity. Accordingly, the costs of providing public fire-protection service are almost entirely composed of readiness-to-serve costs, or fixed costs, largely associated with the plant capacity required. The amount of water used for this purpose is comparatively unimportant.

Although water utility charges for fire-protection service will be the subject of specific examination at a later point, some general aspects of public fire-protection service should be discussed here. Where water service is provided by investor-owned utilities, these companies are generally compensated for their contribution to public fire protection by a direct payment from the local government. Since the property tax is the principal source of revenues to local governments, the fire-protection payment to the investor-owned water utility is essentially supported by the property which received the benefit of the fire protection. Although investor-owned water utilities usually charge the local government for public fire-protection service, such charges sometimes are in nominal amounts only. Where government-owned water utilities are concerned, there is no uniform practice with respect to payments to the utility for public fire-protection service. However, in many instances, the fire-protection payment is relatively low or omitted entirely. There is a wide range of public fire-protection charges, as the above would indicate. For example, in 1955 the investor-owned water utility in Indianapolis received $12 per hydrant per year plus $58.61 per inch-mile (a common denominator, in diameter and distance terms) of main system for fire-protection service. In the same year, the government-owned water utility in Minneapolis made no charge.[20] Table 11.8, drawn from a study of the water utility

[20] American Water Works Association Staff Report, "A Survey of Operating Data for Water Works in 1955," 49 *American Water Works Association Journal* 553, 627, 631 (1957).

Table 11.8

Public Fire-Protection Charges

1955

Annual Charge per Hydrant ($)	*Government-Owned Utilities*	*Investor-Owned Utilities*
None	128	1
less than 10. . .	9	1
10-29	46	15
30-49	40	10
50 or more . . .	20	15
Total	243	42

Source: H. F. Seidel and E. R. Baumann, "A Statistical Analysis of Water Works Data for 1955," 49 *American Water Works Association Journal* 1531, 1547 (1957).

industry in 1955, indicates the diversity of public fire-protection charges by water utilities.

The government-owned water utilities, as a group, either go uncompensated or are undercompensated for public fire-protection service for reasons which merit explanation. First, these utilities usually pay no taxes or tax equivalents to the local government or school districts. In some cases, it is regarded as a fair trade to exchange this exemption from local taxes for the lack of compensation for public fire-protection service. Second, where the taxing powers of municipalities have been limited by their state legislatures, or where there is effective opposition to local tax increases, the local governments have reduced or eliminated their public fire-protection payments in order to use available revenues to sustain other projects and programs. In the interest of equity to the users of water service and the nonusers alike, it seems necessary: (a) for the utility to pay a tax equivalent to the local government, in an amount comparable to what an investor-owned utility would pay; and (b) for the local government to pay the utility a reasonable amount for the public fire-protection service rendered. Unless this is done, there is a haphazard mixing of the respective burdens that should be borne by water users and property owners, and it is only a matter of chance that these burdens will be fairly distributed and borne. Further, the conduct of water utility business on the present basis makes extremely difficult any determination of the economic validity of the rates charged for water service.

As a consequence of their government-ownership status, where such is the case, some water utilities provide free service for use in public buildings, public water fountains, schools, and street and sewer flushing. When this occurs, the situation is much like that wherein public fire-protection service is provided by the utility without reimbursement and defended in part on the grounds that no taxes are paid to the city by the utility. Second, there is the reverse situation where free services, such as billing water customers, are provided to the water utility by other departments of the local government. As a result, there is a tendency in some communities to allow a commingling of utility costs with those of other public business. It would be preferable if government-owned water utilities paid for all the services they receive and were compensated for all the services they provide.

An important economic problem in government ownership is the diversion of utility funds to the use of other departments in the local government. Although some states have laws preventing the diversion of water or sewerage income to other activities, the practice of fund diversion is widespread. In fact, municipal governing bodies have been known to divert water works funds without consulting the management of the utility. The effect of fund diversion is to weaken the protection of the utility function and the lenders alike. Diversion serves, in effect, as a substitute for general taxation. This can and does occur because a government-owned water utility is ordinarily under the authority of the city council, which may be under pressures opposing increased taxes and demanding increased municipal services at the same time. Thus, diversion offers an attractive avenue for escaping a dilemma. However, once diversion of water utility funds begins, the likelihood is that such assistance to other departments may become increasingly required, and that further claims rather than fewer claims will be encountered. The Committee on Rates of the American Water Works Association reports that fund diversions in some cases have been serious to the point of injury to the water service. On this subject, the Committee has stated: "Striking illustrations of the inadequacy of existing water facilities due to fund diversion are common knowledge."[21]

With this background in mind, it becomes possible to approach with understanding the matter of rate of return in publicly owned water supply systems. As the foregoing would suggest, rates of return vary widely. The Committee on Water Rates of the American Water Works Association reports a range in rates of return from zero to 20 per cent. It explains this as due to a number of causes, among them: (a) variations in the amount of debt outstanding; (b) inaccurate records of book value; (c) appropriations in a given year for major improvements; and (d) diversions of funds to meet deficiencies in other departments.[22] Perhaps a more important factor with respect to rate of return is that municipal water utilities usually are not operated for a profit in the ordinary sense of the term; instead, they are generally operated to serve on a cost basis. Costs, in this sense, generally include the required cash outlays and amounts reserved for anticipated cash outlays. In addition, it should be noted that a government-owned utility may earn less than an over-all fair return and still not jeopardize its ability to borrow at favorable rates of interest, because lenders and prospective lenders are concerned largely with a water utility's past, current, and prospective performance in meeting interest and amortization installment requirements, and not enterprise return. In addition, there are no stockholders, and there may be little or no equity, depending upon the way the utility is financed.

C. *Revenue Requirements.* Where regulated public utilities are concerned, the annual revenue requirement is generally determined by reference to the conventional factors: operating expenses, depreciation expense, taxes, and return on rate base. However, this conventional public utility approach to the determination of revenue requirements is not generally applicable where water utilities are concerned. In fact, it is limited to: (a) investor-owned water utilities; and (b) government-owned water utilities in the six states which regulate such utilities. Accordingly, the conventional public utility method of determining revenue requirements is not relevant to the greater part of the water utility industry.

Revenue requirements for most government-owned water utilities are ordinarily determined on a "cash," or "budget," basis. This approach is similar to that used by other departments of the city government, and is therefore much more readily explained to the city administration and council. The budget method is primarily designed to bring sufficient cash into the enterprise to cover estimated cash obligations falling due during the accounting period. Thus, the total revenue requirement presented to the local government for approval is a forecast of estimated cash requirements, supported by data as to the expenditures that must be made plus whatever additional amounts the utility's management may recommend. The Committee on Water Rates of the American Water Works Association states that ". . . the revenue requirements of most municipally controlled water works are not premised on any rate base or rate of return, but on the cash requirements of the system, as determined by local conditions and pol-

[21] Report of the Committee on Water Rates, American Water Works Association, "Determination of Water Rate Schedules," 46 *American Water Works Association Journal* 187, 191 (1954).

[22] *Ibid.*, p. 190.

icies."[23] Further, the Committee takes the position that the cash basis provides a more realistic approach to the revenue-requirement problem of most government-owned water utilities.

This emphasis on cash needs is explained primarily by the fact that government-owned water utilities are largely financed by bonds, whose retirement must be provided for through the generation of cash during the time period they are outstanding. It has been noted previously that water utility bonds are not ordinarily refunded, as is so often the case where corporate debt is concerned. Another factor leading to the use of the cash basis is that government-owned water utilities, as noted earlier, generally are not operated for a profit but only to cover costs.

The items included in the cash budget prepared for a government-owned water utility are not necessarily the same in each instance. As a minimum, the cash budget includes operating and maintenance expenses, debt interest, and amortization. The budget may also include amounts for replacements, normal extensions, and improvements. Other budget items may include an amount for local taxes or tax equivalents, appropriations for major improvements (or reserves therefor), and contributions to other departments of the city government. Depreciation expense, as such, is not necessarily included in the revenue-requirement total. The Committee on Water Rates, for example, regards the amounts budgeted for replacements, normal extensions, and improvements as the equivalent of depreciation expense. A related consideration in this respect is the fact that the budget includes an amount for debt amortization. Nonetheless, sound accounting requires some provision for depreciation expense, even though the funds arising therefrom may be applied to debt amortization. In conclusion, it should be noted that the revenue requirement of any individual government-owned water utility is subject to wide variation depending upon local policy decisions on the above matters.

D. *Water Rates.* The rates charged for general water service are discussed in this section, as well as those for air-conditioning, private fire protection, and sales to suburban communities. General water service, in most cases, is provided under a block meter-rate schedule which includes a minimum charge. However, other types of rate schedules also are in use. Flat rates for unmetered service may be based on the number of water-using fixtures installed in the customer's premises or the number of feet of street frontage or similar criteria. Such rate schedules, which charge a fixed cash amount per billing unit for the billing period, are largely unrelated to the quantity of water used. As a result, unmetered rates encourage waste, as will be shown shortly. In a few places in Canada and in this country, flat rates are based upon property valuation or a percentage of the rental value.

Metered water service predominates. The consumption of water for billing purposes may be stated in either gallons or cubic feet. The straight-line meter rate schedule, which provides for a constant cash charge per metered unit of service, is very little used. Practically all water utilities use a block meter-rate schedule, which includes a graduated minimum charge that increases as the size of the meter increases. (The customer's meter size is determined by the size of the service connection, or pipe, leading into his premises. Most residential customers have a ⅝-inch meter.) The introduction of metered service was found to have a substantial effect in reducing the amount of water consumed. Owing to the necessity nature of water, it is generally believed that the curtail-

[23] *Ibid.*

ment in use brought about by metering served only to prevent its being wasted. So great is the effect of metering upon consumption that it often has been adopted as a substitute for system expansion. Cleveland, for example, was approximately six per cent metered in 1900, and the average per capita consumption was 169 gallons; however, in 1911, when the city was 97.5 per cent metered, the per capita consumption was reduced to 104 gallons.

Water rates vary widely from place to place. A study of the 14 largest cities in the United States showed that annual bills for 30,000 gallons of metered water service varied from $18.54 (including service charge) in San Francisco to $2.40 (less 8 per cent discount if paid in 10 days) in Chicago. Bills on this same basis for 45,000 gallons were $23.08 in San Francisco and $3.60 in Chicago.[24] A number of factors explain this wide range in water rates. (1) According to the latest water industry data available at the time of this writing, the minimum monthly charge per 1,000 cubic feet (Mcf) for government-owned water utilities averaged $2.62, as against $3.70 for investor-owned companies. This difference is explainable by the inclusion of return and taxes in the rates charged by investor-owned utilities, as well as the fact that the government-owned utilities, for the most part, are located in the larger cities and have a comparatively greater production volume.[25] (2) This leads to another factor which influences rates—the size of the utility. The economies of large-scale production appear to be reflected by the fact that the minimum monthly rate per Mcf, as among government-owned water utilities, varies from over $3 for those producing less than 2 million gallons per day (mgd) to about $2 for those producing 50 mgd. (3) Another factor affecting rates is the type of treatment required to produce safe, clear, odorless, potable water. The amount of treatment required is related to the type of water source, for surface water ordinarily requires more treatment than ground water. (4) Another factor which merits noting is the distance from the source of supply to the city. Chicago, for example, is located on the shore of Lake Michigan, while other cities commonly require long-distance transmission of their water supply. The difference in transmission costs thus becomes a further factor explaining the wide range of water rates.

Practically all water utilities have one block meter-rate schedule of three to seven blocks which is applicable to all general water users. If a private fire-protection charge is made, it will be covered by separate provisions of the rate schedule. Demand-rate schedules are rare. Special rate provisions may be applicable to non-conserving air-conditioning service. A feature of some government-owned water utility rate schedules is the rate distinction made between service rendered inside the city and that supplied outside the city. The higher "outside" rates are justifiable in terms of the greater pumping and transportation distance involved in such service, which is ordinarily provided to outlying suburban communities, and the fact that the supplying city merits some compensation for establishing the system which benefits others. The Committee on Water Rates of the American Water Works Association recommends that rates to suburban customers be determined on a public utility basis, rather than on the cash-budget basis used by

---

[24] Philadelphia Bureau of Municipal Affairs, "Metered Water and Sewer Charges in Fourteen Largest Cities of the United States," (1950), as cited in 12 *Ohio State Law Journal* 149, 214 (1951).

[25] H. F. Seidel and E. R. Baumann, "A Statistical Analysis of Water Works Data for 1955," 49 *American Water Works Association Journal* 1531, 1533 (1957).

government-owned utilities for the determination of their revenue requirements.[26]

As noted previously, the block meter-rate schedule used by most water utilities includes minimum charges which vary with the size of the customer's meter. Service charges are relatively little used. The primary purpose of the minimum charge is to assure the solvency of the utility. In an industry where fixed costs predominate to so large a degree, the necessity for firm revenues is all the greater. Basing the minimum charge on the size of the customer's service connection or meter is intended to reflect differences in the utility's readiness-to-serve as among customers of different sizes.

The features of water utility general-service rate schedules, surveyed above, are illustrated in the following examples. The first of these is the rate schedule of the investor-owned and 100 per cent-metered Baton Rouge Water Works Co.

Monthly Rates:

Cubic Feet	*Per 100 Cubic Feet*
First 20,000	33¢
Next 380,000	12.5
Next 400,000	10
Excess	7.5

Minimum Monthly Charges:

Meter Size (in inches)	*Charge*
⅝	$ 1.39
¾	2.78
1	4.86
1½	12.50
2	18.75
3	31.25
4	37.50
6	50.00

Under this rate schedule, the customer with the conventional residential ⅝-inch meter pays a monthly minimum charge of $1.39, for which he may consume up to 3,000 gallons or about 400 cubic feet. This is a representative amount as compared with the rate schedules of other water utilities; few utilities allow more than 4,000 gallons under the minimum charge. Most allow less. In light of the fact that 40 to 50 per cent of all residential consumers use less than 3,000 gallons per month, the allowance of any greater amount under the minimum charge would, in effect, make it a flat rate for a large proportion of residential customers and thus encourage waste. The Baton Rouge utility would charge $2.20 for 5,000 gallons or 667 cubic feet ($6.67 \times .33 = \$2.20$). The above rate schedule also includes separate rates for private fire protection.

A second illustrative rate schedule is that of the Water and Sewer Division of the Department of Public Works of the City of Battle Creek, Michigan. Service is 100 per cent metered. This rate schedule provides for higher rates for sales outside the city; the latter are 50 per cent higher. The rate schedule includes separate charges for private fire-protection service.

Rates per Month:

	Per 100 Cubic Feet	
Cubic Feet	*In City*	*Outside*
First 100	Minimum	Minimum
Next 3,900	20¢	30.0¢
Next 296,000	15	22.5
Next 700,000	9	13.5
Excess	Special Rate by Contract	

Minimum Monthly Charges:

Meter Size	*Charge*	
(in inches)	*In City*	*Outside*
⅝	$ 0.56	$ 0.84
¾	.70	1.05
1	1.03	1.55
1½	2.00	3.00
2	3.36	5.04
3	7.26	10.89
4	12.66	18.99
6	28.26	42.39
8	50.27	75.41
12	113.20	169.80
16	201.06	301.59

There is no uniform practice in establishing the charges for public fire-protection service. The charge may take the

[26] Report of the Committee on Water Rates, *op. cit.*, p. 192.

form of a lump sum, or it may consist of a hydrant charge (a fixed cash charge per hydrant per year), or it may be related on a lineal basis to the water main system providing fire-protection service. It is relatively seldom that a hydrant charge and a water main charge are both collected, although they relate to different facilities.

Private fire-protection service is provided to commercial and industrial customers requiring special facilities, such as automatic sprinkler systems and additional or specially placed hydrants. The charges for such service are in the nature of a demand charge, because readiness-to-serve rather than volume of water consumed is the primary characteristic of such service. The Battle Creek, Michigan utility, mentioned above, charges $40 per year per private fire hydrant and a monthly sprinkler-service charge based upon the size of the service line, as follows:

Size of Line (inches)	*Monthly Charge*
2	$ 1.00
3	2.50
4	4.50
6	10.00
8	17.50
10	27.50

Non-conserving air-conditioning units can cause a serious peak-capacity problem, as noted earlier. It is equitable to charge such customers a surcharge, in the nature of a demand charge, in addition to the regular rates. This additional charge should be sufficient to cover the capital charges on the investment necessary to provide such service. If a charge of this type is not imposed, the costs must be borne by water users generally, which amounts to a subsidy to the owners of non-conserving air-conditioning systems. Surcharges also provide such air-conditioning customers an incentive to install water-conserving facilities. Surcharges have been imposed in an increasing number of communities, as they began to encounter this problem. Annual surcharges are ordinarily based upon the rated capacity (in tons) of non-conserving air-conditioning facilities. The Champaign, Illinois water utility makes an annual charge of $45 per ton, and the Omaha Metropolitan Utilities District imposes a surcharge of $36 per ton.

Other than in the cases mentioned above, demand charges are rarely used in water rates. Milwaukee and Kansas City employ demand charges in billing for water service provided to other communities. The Kansas City demand charge is based upon the maximum daily demand in the peak period, June through September, and the maximum hourly demand during this period between the hours of 4:30 and 8:30 P.M. This demand charge is intended to cover fixed charges and operating expenses relating to an allocation of production and pumping plant and trunk and feeder mains.

E. *A Costing Method to Aid in Making Rates.* Water rates and rate structures are not determined through the use of principles and procedures that are largely standardized in setting rates for electric and gas distribution utilities. A searching examination of water utility rate making resulted in the following conclusion:

> It can be said at once that there is, at the present time, no uniform practice in determining rates and rate structures. Scant consideration has been given to fundamental principles. Too often it has been a matter of adopting any plan which would produce sufficient revenue with the fewest complaints.[27]

[27] Committees of the American Society of Civil Engineers and the Section of Municipal Law of the American Bar Association and representatives of other professional associations, "Fundamental Considerations in Rates and Rate Structures for Water and Sewage Works," 12 *Ohio State Law Journal* 149, 210 (1951).

Water rates are made with little or no reference to the cost analyses which are sometimes employed as an aid in making rates for electric and gas distribution utilities, even though reliance upon cost analyses in setting water rates may be more useful than in the case of these other utilities. Cost data can appropriately occupy a more significant role in the setting of water rates, because water is supplied under conditions that are significantly different from those found in the marketing of electricity and natural gas: (a) water utilities are not competitive with suppliers of a substitute product or service, except where an industrial self-supply may be relied upon; (b) there is little if any need to consider market-demand characteristics in pricing water, for such is unlikely to promote sales or to make use of idle capacity; and (c) the use of storage facilities reduces the capacity required to meet peak requirements and therefore lessens the problem of unused capacity in off-peak periods. In view of the reduced importance of value-of-service factors, cost analyses can assume a more important function in pricing water service.

A procedure for analyzing the costs of water utilities as a basis for establishing water rates has been recommended, on the basis of a detailed study, by a group of professional associations concerned with municipal problems.[28] The Joint Group, as it was known, was composed of committees of the American Society of Civil Engineers and the Municipal Law Section of the American Bar Association and representatives of six other professional organizations.[29] An important difference of opinion between the Joint Group and the Committee on Water Rates of the American Water Works Association subsequently developed on the important matter of allocating joint-capacity costs to public fire-protection service, as noted below.

The approach to the analysis of costs by the Joint Group was much like that discussed earlier in connection with electric utilities. The objectives of the costing methods recommended by the Joint Group were; (a) to set forth principles which would make possible a determination of the shares of a water utility's costs that should be borne by water users and the beneficiaries of public fire-protection service; and (b) to recommend principles for use in translating costs into rate schedules. Little distinction was made between costing and pricing. For these purposes, costs were classified into the capacity, commodity (production), and customer categories previously discussed. In capacity costs were placed all fixed charges, including depreciation expense, taxes and return, and all operating and maintenance expenses not designated specifically as customer or commodity costs. In production or commodity costs were included the costs which vary with volume, that is, the fuel and power costs related to pumping and the chemicals required for purification. The customer costs, of course, are those relating largely to meter reading, accounting, billing, and collecting. It was recommended that administrative and general expenses be distributed to classes on the basis of all other expenses in each class, not including fixed charges.

A principal feature of the costing procedure recommended by the Joint Group was a method for allocating joint-capacity costs between public fire-protection service and general service to water users. After considering and rejecting various allocation methods, the Joint

[28] *Ibid.*

[29] American Water Works Association, National Association of Railroad and Utilities Commissioners, Municipal Finance Officers Association, Federation of Sewage Works Associations, American Public Works Association, and Investment Bankers Association of America.

Group recommended use of the Maximum Demand Method (discussed in connection with electric utility rates) as adapted to water utility circumstances. By this approach, joint-capacity costs would be allocated to public fire protection on the basis of the ratio of: (a) an imputed maximum demand upon the system for fire protection; to (b) the sum of the maximum demands for general water service and fire-protection service. Maximum demand for this purpose would be measured as follows: (a) for general water service, the peak hourly demand upon the system during the year; and (b) for public fire protection, an amount set by the fire insurance industry through the National Board of Fire Underwriters, called the "required fire flows" for cities of varying population groups. To illustrate: for a city of 100,000 population, the required fire flow would be 9,000 gallons per minute for 10 hours, or a peak hourly demand of 540,000 gallons (9,000 × 60). The measurement of fire-protection maximum demand by reference to the required fire flows would not be free of problems, however, because some cities do not have water supply systems capable of furnishing the required fire flow. An adjustment to the basic allocation ratio for such communities was suggested by the Joint Group.

To explain this adjustment, it is necessary first to summarize the standards used by the fire insurance industry in rating a city for the purpose of establishing fire insurance rates on property. The fire insurance industry employs a rating system which totals a maximum score of 5,000 points for all fire-defense criteria. A first-class city by these standards is one which has no more than 500 points of deficiency from the maximum standards. Of the 5,000-point total for all criteria, a maximum of 1,700 points is assignable to the water supply system, on the basis of its adequacy in providing the required fire flow of water for public fire protection. For cities rated below the maximum of 1,700 points, the Joint Group would reduce its proposed allocation to fire protection in proportion to the rated deficiency. This would be done by multiplying the fire-protection allocation percentage by a factor found by dividing 1,700 into 1,700 less any deficiency points.

Disagreement with this recommended allocation method has been expressed by the Committee on Water Rates of the American Water Works Association. First, the Committee has taken the position that the prime function of a water supply system is to provide a commodity to water users, and that public fire-protection service, while important, is a supplementary service. Accordingly, in the Committee's view, the costs allocated to fire protection should not exceed the demonstrable additional costs involved in rendering such service.[30] This point of view, in effect, regards the cost of fire-protection service as an incremental cost. That is, the cost of public fire-protection service is regarded as the cost that would be incurred if a single-purpose general-service water supply system were adapted to provide public fire-protection service in addition. The Joint Group had considered and rejected this approach on the ground that it would allocate an insufficient amount to public fire protection in light of the fact that fire-protection requirements are ordinarily given independent consideration in the design of a water supply system.

3. URBAN TRANSIT FARES AND PROBLEMS[31]

The growth of our large cities in population and area was made possible, in

[30] Report of the Committee on Water Rates, *op. cit.*, p. 200.

[31] Unless otherwise noted, the principal

large part, by the development of urban transit systems, which now serve primarily to transport passengers to and from their jobs. Urban transit systems are organized as common carriers of passengers within cities and suburbs. They operate over fixed routes at regular intervals and charge a standard rate or fare that is ordinarily subject to regulation. Urban transit systems utilize electric street railways, trolley coaches, and motor buses. In some of the largest cities, rapid transit service is provided by subway, elevated electric railway, and private rights-of-way at surface levels. Not included here are taxis, electric railways serving beyond the principal metropolitan area, and intercity motor buses. In 1960 there were about 1,250 urban transit systems in the United States, of which 57 were owned by local governments. These 57 systems accounted for about 43 per cent of the industry's revenues. Government-owned transit systems included part of the New York City system and those in Detroit, Chicago, Boston, Los Angeles, Cleveland, Memphis, Oakland, San Francisco, Seattle, and San Antonio. All the other government-owned and -operated transit systems are in the smaller communities, ranging in size from Sacramento (population of 192,000) to Radford, Virginia (population of 9,400). Generally speaking, the local governments have purchased and operated urban transit systems when the private owners could no longer sustain losses and had no incentive to invest in the modernization of transit enterprises whose futures were regarded as unpromising.

This is tangible evidence of the fact that the urban transit industry is not so profitable as it was in past decades. In a number of communities, urban transit is fighting what appears to be a losing battle for patronage against the competition of private automobiles. This competitive problem has been faced by the urban transit industry since about 1922, when automobile ownership first began to be large enough to restrain the annual growth the industry had been experiencing. In the industry's largest traffic-volume year prior to World War II, 1927, it carried a total of 17,257 million passengers. With the coming of the great depression, this total declined to 11,327 million passengers in 1933. During World War II, and immediately following, the necessary wartime restrictions on automobile use and shortages of gasoline and tires sent city-dwellers back to urban transit in record-breaking numbers. The peak for that period, in 1946, was a total of 23,372 million passengers. However, full employment after the war and the general availability of automobiles have led to a continuation in the long-term decline of urban transit traffic. In 1960 the passenger total was down to 9,395 million, which was about 20 per cent less than in the worst year of the depression of the 1930's.

Much more is involved here than the long-run decline of a once thriving industry, for the other side of the coin shows a collection of problems which menace the very cities that urban transit helped to make possible. Everyone is aware of the problems accompanying the regular increases in annual automobile registrations. They include severe

---

sources of this section are: *The Mass Transportation Problem in Illinois* (Chicago: State Mass Transportation Commission, 1959), which includes the pertinent findings of the *Chicago Area Transportation Study* and the *Cook County Transportation Usage Study; Moody's Transportation Manual,* 1961 ed.; American Transit Association, *Transit Fact Book,* 1960 ed.; Frank H. Mossman, ed. (in Cooperation with the American Transit Association), *Principles of Urban Transportation* (Cleveland: Western Reserve University Press, 1951); unpublished manuscript, "Economic Aspects of Rapid Rail Operation," by Herbert Pence, Jr.; annual reports of the Cleveland Transit System; and *Hearings* on S.345, 87th Cong., 1st sess., 1961.

shortages of peak-hour street space in central business districts and on main traffic arteries, which lead to extreme traffic congestion and a slowing down of all street transportation. There is usually a lack of adequate parking facilities. The combined effect is to make the central business district less attractive to shoppers, among others, a fact which tends to hurt business, to depress real property valuations there, and to reduce property tax yields. In addition, there is an increasing dedication of strategically situated land surface to accommodate the needs of automobiles. Much of this land, and the buildings upon it, are being lost to the local real property tax base. For example, about 68 per cent of the land space of downtown Los Angeles is devoted to streets, highways, access roads, loading areas, and parking facilities. In Cleveland, the 3.5-mile inner belt freeway cost $75 million and took about $30 million worth of taxable property off the total assessed valuation.

The construction of super road systems does not solve these problems, but instead seems only to increase their severity. Super road systems serve to increase the number of automobiles competing to use the already crowded metropolitan street and parking facilities. In addition, the super road systems serving our cities quickly become inadequate. For example, in June of 1959 the Illinois Mass Transportation Commission reported that Chicago's Congress Street Expressway, designed for an estimated maximum vehicular load of 96,000 per day in 1960, was then carrying nearly 115,000 vehicles daily—despite the fact that it had not been completed. In Los Angeles, the Hollywood Freeway, designed to carry 100,000 vehicles per day, achieved a load of nearly 170,000 vehicles daily within a year after it was opened to traffic. This has been the experience in practically all metropolitan centers. As a nation, we have become concerned with transporting automobiles instead of transporting people.

A. *The Development and Decline of Urban Transit.* Horse-drawn vehicles for hire provided the first urban transportation in this country. However, in the 1820's omnibus companies were formed which provided regular service to the public, along specific routes, by horse-drawn vehicles designed to carry a relatively large number of people. The idea of putting cars on steel rails, in order to offer a smoother ride than that of the omnibus, led to the horse car—a horse-drawn street car that gained wide adoption. The first commercially important street railway employing horse cars was established in New York in 1832. The greatest development of this mode of urban transportation came after 1850; by about 1870, it was used in most of the principal cities. The horse-car railway reached its peak in about 1890 and had all but disappeared by 1900, owing to the invention of the electric street railway. The horse car was never entirely satisfactory, because of its slowness and its difficulty in negotiating steep grades.

The first electric street railway companies in this country were organized in the 1880's. However, the electric street railway industry is generally thought to have begun in 1888 in Richmond, Virginia, with the development of a commercially successful overhead trolley which contacted the power supply by a small trolley wheel under-running the power line. This problem had not been solved so successfully in previous models. Once developed, the overhead trolley became standard throughout the country. The electric street railway remained the most important vehicle used by transit companies until the years of peak transit demand during World War II, when the growing need for service was met by the addition of large numbers of motor buses.

Motor buses were introduced as early as 1905 in New York City, but their development did not begin to be important until 1922, when buses designed for urban transit purposes appeared on the market. Before that time, bus bodies had been put on truck chassis, which resulted in an uncomfortable ride. As noted, during World War II the motor bus became the most important urban transit vehicle; this trend was accelerated after the war, when the industry largely abandoned the electric street railway.

Trolley coaches are vehicles that look much like motor buses, but they are operated by electric power supplied from overhead wires. Their trolley contacts are designed to permit maneuverability comparable to that of a motor bus. The trolley coach has been attractive to those transit managements which either own power-generation facilities or can purchase electric energy on favorable terms. Further, the use of electricity avoids motor fuel taxes.

Rapid transit has been developed in some of the largest cities. The predominant form of rapid transit is the subway, an underground electric railway. Second in importance is the elevated electric railway. In both cases large numbers of passengers can be transported at great speed, because fewer stops are made, in comparison with surface lines, and operation is over rights-of-way that are unrestricted by other traffic. The first urban subway system was developed in London in 1863; trains were pulled by steam locomotives. A Boston subway using surface street cars was opened in 1897 and converted to multiple-unit electric cars in 1899. New York City, which now has the world's largest subway system, had subway service as of 1904. New York also had the first elevated railway in this country, which began in 1868 with cable-drawn cars. Cable railways, which operate by attaching the car to a moving, endless cable powered by a stationary engine or motor, were also developed about this time for surface use. They were particularly successful in hilly cities, but very costly to construct. The use of cable cars in elevated service soon gave way to small steam engines which pulled trains of passenger cars. By 1902, electricity had supplanted the steam engines, which were objectionable in the midst of cities and therefore harmful to property values. With the expansion of subway lines in New York City, the elevated railways have been dismantled. Other principal cities, such as Chicago, continue to rely on "El" service.

The early horse car and electric street railway lines did not operate as coordinated systems under a single management, as is the case with urban transit systems today. Instead, the early lines operated individually on specified routes under their own franchises. Dating from horse-car days to about 1917, the fare charged the riding public was five cents. This fare was not related to the cost of service, but was convenient and became a matter of custom. The industry as a whole profited under the five-cent fare, and companies were willing to have it written into their franchises.

Two developments led to the initial financial crises encountered by the electric street railway industry. First, there were numerous consolidations of the individual lines within each city. In many cases the consolidated companies issued bonds in payment for the properties that were absorbed. This led to some top-heavy capital structures among the consolidated electric railway systems and high fixed-interest charges. This was a risky policy, considering that fares were often pegged by franchise terms at five cents. In addition, more than a few lines were overbuilt into areas that could not support them. On the other hand, there was a growing demand for electric railway service, as indicated by the gains registered in the total of passengers carried during each year of this period and into the 1920's.

A second and related development produced a crisis of national significance. With the coming of World War I, prices, and therefore costs, commenced to rise significantly. This spelled ruin for many high debt-ratio electric railway companies whose fares were fixed by franchise terms at five cents. During the war the industry's financial position deteriorated owing to rapidly mounting operating expenses. The combination of inflexible fares and rising expenses forced more than one-third of the industry into bankruptcy by 1919. President Wilson appointed a commission to study the problem. The resulting report did much to inform the public and the regulatory authorities. Subsequently, financial reorganizations, fare increases, and conversion of equipment to permit the less-expensive one-man operation of street cars all had their effects in bringing stability to the industry. This time of trial also stimulated interest in motor buses and trolley coaches as lower-cost substitutes for electric street railways. Starting in 1922, motor buses began to be added to transit fleets in great numbers; the first trolley coaches were put in service in 1928. This trend was to culminate in a basic change in the industry's equipment and economics, as street railway cars were abandoned in favor of rubber-borne vehicles.

The decline of the urban transit industry began in the 1920's with the mass production and sale of automobiles and the vigorous street- and highway-building program which accompanied it. It has been noted previously that, during the 1920's, the industry reached a pre-depression peak in total passengers of 17,257 million, which fell to 11,327 million in the depression and rose to a war-period peak of 23,372 million total passengers. By 1960 this national total had declined to 9,395 million. The transit system in Moline, Illinois, for example, carried 14 million passengers in 1947—but only 2.4 million in 1957, a decline of 82 per cent. In the 15 years following World War II, about 300 small cities, towns, and boroughs lost all forms of urban transit. In addition to private automobile competition, other causes for the decline in the demand for transit service have been longer vacations, shorter work weeks, the decentralization of shopping facilities, and the slowness of urban transit service as a result of traffic congestion.

Although operating economies have been achieved through conversion to rubber-borne vehicles, this has been offset by continuous increases in expenses. Contributing to the latter is the important fact that our metropolitan areas are considerably larger now than during the successful transit years of the 1920's, and this has meant longer routes without necessarily proportionate increases in revenues. In the interest of cost reduction and improvement in the quality of service, the urban transit industry has all but abandoned surface electric railway equipment in favor of trolley coaches and motor buses. In 1960 about two-thirds of the total passengers were carried by motor buses. The breakdown of total passengers by types of service for 1960 is shown in Table 11.9.

The decline of the urban transit industry is particularly apparent when viewed in terms of index numbers comparing the growth of urban population and the use of urban transit service. The following are the relevant 1959 index numbers, with the year 1924 taken as equal to 100: (a) urban population, 156.6; (b) total urban transit rides, 58.6; and (c) rides per capita, 37.6. These index numbers show that in the period 1924 to 1959, the urban population of the United States increased 56.6

Table 11.9

Total Passengers by Types of Service, 1960
(in millions)

Type of Service	*Total Passengers*	*Percentage of Total*
Electric railway:		
Surface	463	4.9%
Elevated and subway.	1,850	19.7
Trolley coach	657	7.0
Motor bus	6,425	68.4
Total	9,395	100.0%

Source: American Transit Association, *Transit Fact Book,* 1961 ed., p. 6.

per cent. However, while the potential market for transit service was growing, the actual amount of service was declining. Thus, the total rides furnished by the industry in 1959 was only 58.6 per cent of the total number in 1924. More indicative of the decline in transit use is the fact that total rides per capita in 1959 was only 37.6 per cent of the corresponding figure for 1924.

To suggest that the decline of the urban transit industry is due primarily to automobile competition is to advance almost too simple an explanation. The reasons for the decline certainly do involve the automobile, but related factors also have major significance. These interrelated factors include: (1) the enormous increase in automobile ownership in the postwar period; (2) the federal housing and housing-finance programs, which are oriented much more toward new and suburban construction than toward revitalization and reconstruction of the existing cities; (3) the federal highway-aid program, which made outlying suburban areas accessible to the increasing number of automobile owners; and (4) the fragmentation of the community into a large number of local governments, which made practically impossible any metropolitan area-wide planning and coordination of urban mass transportation.

The increase in automobile ownership signified increasing average disposable income, which placed many people in a position to choose to use automobiles instead of transit, even where that is more costly, in order to achieve such objectives as comfort, convenience, independence, or psychic gratification. Before automobile ownership became so widespread, the city was a relatively compact unit, and an urban transit system could be developed to serve the entire urban area. With the increase in automobiles, suburban development, and highway facilities, cities spread out geographically, and the result was the metropolitan area, comprised of a complex of local governments. The first consequence of this in many instances was to extend the community beyond the limits of economical urban transit service, owing both to the greater distance factor and to the reduced population density. Second, since the typical metropolitan area is now comprised of many political subdivisions, local governing authority is fragmented to such an extent that either unusual effort or some compelling incentive is required to achieve agreement throughout a metropolitan area on a plan to coordinate the various methods of transporting passengers. This problem is of substantial proportions; the 174 metropolitan areas of the United States include over 15,000 individual local-government units. Before the automobile age came fully into its own, urban mass transportation operated under a unified plan in each community which was often the product of cooperation between officials of the transit company and the city government. After the coming of mass automobile ownership and related developments, the fragmentation of local governing authority has meant that no one governmental unit had jurisdiction over the matter. This has constituted a more formidable obstacle to area-wide mass transportation planning and coordination than the problem of focusing upon methods to accomplish the total transportation task at the least possible cost. In large part, this situation has been aggravated by the generation of large sums of money for street, bridge, and highway construction by motor fuel and related taxes. In the expenditure of such funds, the guiding consideration has been, in effect, the best way to spend the highway funds. This is laudable in itself but insufficient; the more basic consideration should be the best and cheapest way to discharge the total urban transportation function. While it is obvious that the urban transit industry has been the net loser in the course of these developments, it is not at all clear that it is the only one.

B. *Economic Characteristics.* As might be expected from the foregoing account of the decline in urban transit patronage, the industry as a whole has not been financially successful in recent years. The industry's 1959 operations, for example, resulted in an operating ratio (operating expenses, including depreciation, as a percentage of operating revenue) of 91.99 per cent before taxes. The 1959 all-expense (including taxes) operating ratio was 98.14 per cent. Previous years also failed to yield a reasonable return for the operations of the industry as a whole. It was noted previously in the discussion of the rate base (Chapter 6) that urban transit industry earnings are regulated in many jurisdictions on the basis of the operating ratio standard. It has been pointed out that the Interstate Commerce Commission, after an investigation of over 200 intercity and urban transit carriers of passengers, concluded that a reasonable earnings standard would be an operating ratio of 85 per cent before federal income taxes or about 93 per cent after inclusion of such taxes in expenses.[32] As shown in Table 11.10, the urban transit industry for some years has experienced operating ratios well above those found to be reasonable by the ICC; hence, by these standards, earnings have been below a reasonable level. In the accompanying table, the first column of data represents the industry's operating ratio before taxes, and the second column shows the all-expense operating ratio, which includes taxes among expenses. These data indicate that the ICC earnings standards of 85 and 93 per cent, respectively, have not been attained since about 1950, when the World War II automobile shortage was substantially remedied.

The transition from electric street railway to buses and trolley coaches has changed the economic character of the urban transit industry. An electric street railway has the standard public utility characteristic of relatively large fixed investment and slow annual rate of capital turnover. This is due to the required investment in rails, paving, electric distribution system, and long-lived high-cost street cars. In addition, the electric street railway system may include electric generating facilities. The investment cost per passenger of capacity is greater for street cars than for rubber-borne vehicles. On the other hand, an urban transit system that has converted to motor buses and trolley coaches does not have the typical public utility characteristics, for it has a relatively high rate

[32] *Investigation of Bus Fares,* 52 MCC 332, 336 (1950).

Table 11.10

Urban Transit Industry Operating Expenses, Taxes, and Operating Income as Percentages of Operating Revenue (1935–1960)

Year	*Percentages of Operating Revenue*		
	Operating Expenses (Incl. Depr.)	*All Expenses (Incl. Taxes)*	*Operating Income*
1935	78.50%	85.91%	14.09%
1940	81.14	89.65	10.35
1945	77.31	89.23	10.77
1950	89.30	95.43	4.57
1951	90.40	96.87	3.13
1952	91.23	98.02	1.98
1953	90.59	97.02	2.98
1954	90.86	96.95	3.05
1955	89.55	96.09	3.91
1956	89.79	96.07	3.93
1957	91.09	97.36	2.64
1958	93.85	99.51	0.49
1959	91.99	98.14	1.86
1960	91.66	97.82	2.18

Source: American Transit Association, *Transit Fact Book,* 1961 ed., p. 4.

of capital turnover, and annual revenues may be several times the capital investment. In such circumstances, enterprise risk is a function of the level of expenses and not of the investment sunk in the enterprise. Accordingly, it is economically sound to use the operating ratio standard in the rate regulation of a rubber-borne urban transit system, whereas use of the rate-base standard is not. Further support for this conclusion is found in the fact that the total investment in some urban transit companies is prone to fluctuate from year to year—as the form of equipment changes and as service in various areas is abandoned or added. Another factor sometimes considered in regulation is that the operating-ratio method of regulation is more sensitive to the needs of a declining industry.

Weekday operations of urban transit systems are characterized by sharp morning and evening peaks, corresponding to the daily travel to and from work. Thus, equipment and operators must be sufficient in quantity to serve the daily inbound and outbound peak flows of traffic. Depending on the city, much of this peak-period transportation capacity may be largely unused on half or part of each round trip. Moreover, during off-peak hours much of the equipment will be idle. The existence of the twice-daily peaks also raises problems in the scheduling of operators' time in the most productive manner possible. Off-peak transportation service is a convenience offered the public, which the Chicago Area Transportation Study found to be generally unprofitable. The twice-daily transit peaks in Chicago, for example, total about five hours per 24 hours—7:00 A.M. to 9:00 A.M. and 4:00 P.M. to 7:00 P.M. In these five hours, 55.6 per cent of the daily passenger total will be transported. Within the morning peak period, 15.1 per cent of the total daily transit usage occurs in the hour from 8:00 A.M. to 9:00 A.M. In the evening hour from 5:00 P.M. to 6:00 P.M., 13.4 per cent of the total transit usage was found to occur.

As long ago as 1892, Dr. John Hopkinson suggested that it would be appropriate to charge a higher fare during peak periods than during off-peak hours. His reasoning was quite cogent: it costs more to carry the peak-period riders, since it is they who require the substantial peak-period transit capacity and the necessary operators. Much of that peak-period capacity will be unused in off-peak hours. Even where vehicle operators work on split shifts corresponding to the peak periods, it is often difficult to schedule their time so as to derive the maximum benefit from the hours for which they are paid. It might be added that Dr. Hopkinson's suggested higher rate in peak periods also would be justified on the basis of value-of-service factors. Traditionally, however, transit fare structures have given little or no recognition to time of use. Charging a higher fare during peak hours would be sound economics but unquestionably would raise a problem in public relations.

The decline in urban transit passengers since the war has been much more serious than the passenger totals indicate, because generally the peak demands have not been much affected. The passenger losses have been largely in the off-peak periods. Thus, the decline in patronage has not been accompanied by a corresponding cost reduction. The perverse combination of sustained peaks and declining off-peak transit travel seems due to the difficulties of automobile use on congested streets, inadequate and high cost all-day parking facilities, and the fact that there are relatively direct transit routes from city residential neighborhoods to the employment center or centers. These factors do not have the same impact on off-peak riders, who find the streets relatively open to automobile use and low-cost or free parking often available at the places they may wish to visit. Merchants in the central core area of cities have attempted to attract shoppers by offering parking facilities at low cost or no cost. This has provided effective off-peak competition to transit.

Another economic characteristic of some importance is the general tendency of the volume of transit patronage to decline as a consequence of a fare increase. This is sometimes referred to in the transit industry as the "shrinkage factor" or the "resistance factor." This factor is ordinarily expressed in terms of the percentage of passenger loss resulting from each one per cent increase in the fare. The national average shrinkage factor in cities of over 500,000 population is 0.25 per cent, with a range of 0.15 to 0.31 per cent. In one case, where a cash fare increase from 20 cents to 25 cents was under consideration, it was concluded that a 0.20 per cent shrinkage factor was representative of the market response to the fare increase. Thus, it was anticipated that the proposed fare increase would be followed by a five per cent loss in patronage (25, the percentage increase in fare, times 0.20 equals 5).[33]

What explains the apparent preference of an important segment of the riding public for automobiles over urban transit? A study by the Highway Department of Cook County, Illinois showed that, for both automobile users and transit users in the Chicago metropolitan area, the most important single factor was that of time. There, transit facilities have a time advantage for trips into the Chicago business district, while automobiles have a time advantage for trips to points in outlying areas. However, for a second group of automobile users, the primary reason for their choice was the factor of comfort. In addition, about one-third of the automobile trips studied were made by persons who either needed their automobiles in their work

[33] *Re D.C. Transit System, Inc.,* 33 PUR 3d 137, 166–167 (1960).

or had no reasonable access to other transportation.

The study also showed that, when the time by transit is one-half that of the time by automobile, almost all trips are made by transit. When travel time is equal, about 40 per cent of the trips are made by transit. When transit time is twice that required for automobile transportation, only about 10 per cent of the trips are made by transit. The Cook County study also brought out the relative indifference of automobile riders to the fact that it usually costs less to travel by transit. The study indicated that when transit costs are one-tenth the cost of automobile transportation, about 60 per cent of the trips are by transit. When the transit cost is one-half that of automobile travel, 15 per cent of the trips are by transit. When the cost of each is the same, only about 5 per cent of the trips are by transit. The fact that the comparatively greater cost of automobile travel is disregarded by many riders is further pointed up by the fact that automobile occupancy was found to average only 1.49 persons during the Chicago rush hour—indicating that the economies of car pools are obtained by relatively few.

In many cities, increased street congestion during rush hours has had an adverse economic impact on transit in a number of ways. First, the resulting slowdown in traffic has required a greater number of transit vehicles and operators to serve a peak of a given size, which increases both the investment in equipment and the operating payroll without increasing revenues. Second, as transit service is slowed by the increasing street congestion, greater numbers of people are led to consider using their cars instead of transit facilities. The ever greater strangulation of our cities by street congestion may be illustrated by the fact that in 1947 a morning rush-hour trip into downtown Cincinnati by electric street railway from the outlying College Hill area required 22 minutes; in 1956, this same trip by motor bus—a faster vehicle—required 34 minutes. Thus, within the postwar decade the time required to make this trip increased 55 per cent.

C. Urban Transit Fares. From the horse-car era to shortly after 1917 the five-cent fare, which generally included city-wide transfer privileges at no additional charge, was standard almost everywhere in the United States. This fare level did not survive the price inflation during World War I and the following years. During the period 1917–1923, fares rose as a consequence of higher costs of labor, materials, and equipment. This fare-level increase came about with great difficulty because of custom, franchise terms, state laws, and the fact that the five-cent fare became a political football in some communities. Applications to increase fares often involved slow regulatory proceedings and extended litigation. Caught between fixed or slowly changing fares and rapidly rising costs, the urban transit industry was in financial trouble, even though the annual passenger total continued to grow. In particular difficulty were those systems whose lines were overextended into marginal areas or whose debt ratios were excessive as a result of previous consolidations, or both. The outcome, as noted previously, was to involve over one-third the industry in bankruptcy proceedings by 1919.

During the period 1923–1930, automobile competition began to assert itself. Initially, the most serious loss in transit traffic was noted in the evening hours and on weekends. Fare increases continued during this period, and for the first time passenger traffic began to decline. In addition, many fare increases failed to yield increased total revenues and in almost all cases resulted in a loss in passenger traffic. The fare increases in the period 1917–1930 followed no pattern or formula. By 1930 approximately 100 different combinations of fares were being charged by various transit companies. During the 1930–1940 depression decade, cash fares remained largely unchanged. To counteract the great loss of passengers and low load factors caused by the widespread unemployment during that period, transit systems developed a variety of promotional or "merchandising" fares, which included various forms of reduced-rate tokens, shoppers' passes, weekly passes, lower off-peak rates, and others. During the rearmament program of the pre-Pearl Harbor years, passenger totals began to rise as employment increased.

During the war and afterward, until the automobile shortage was overcome, the urban transit industry had some of its largest annual passenger volumes of all time, while going forward with the transition to rubber-borne vehicles. Fare-level increases were numerous after wartime wage and price stabilization controls were lifted. With the conversion to buses and trolley coaches, operating payroll became the largest item of expense, amounting to 60 to 70 per cent of operating revenues. Accordingly, each round of wage increases granted to employees may necessitate an application for a fare increase. It might be noted at this point that some transit systems have found themselves in a "vicious cycle," where fare increases are concerned. Greatly simplified, it may run something like this: wage and other cost increases lead to fare increases, which cause some riders to stop using urban transit and to drive their automobiles instead; this may result in greater traffic congestion and slower transit service, thereby causing still other passengers to abandon urban transit; if about the same quantity of scheduled service is to continue to be provided, the loss in riders and revenue may have to be offset by a further fare increase—thus possibly initiating the cycle all over again. On the other hand, if expenses are reduced by cutting the amount of service provided, other riders may give up using urban transit, which also may start the cycle in operation once more.

The urban transit fare structure ordinarily provides for a standard cash fare plus one or more wholesale or promotional fare options and sometimes a zone fare. These are discussed below.

(1) *Cash Fares.* The standard cash fare for a single ride ordinarily is unrelated to either the length of the ride or the time of day. However, the use of this form of flat rate is simple, understandable, and easy to administer and collect. Exceptions are made in the form of lower fares for school children and for children below a certain age or height. Commonly, uniformed people in public service, such as firemen or policemen, are allowed to ride free. Cash patrons in most cities are entitled to a transfer, issued at time of payment, which permits the rider to use two or more vehicles for a continuing ride in one general direction. Ordinarily transfers are limited in time of duration and may be used only at intersections of different lines or "transfer points."

Moody's 1961 *Transportation Manual* reported that there were only two United States cities where the standard cash fare was less than 10 cents. In the other cities, fares ranged up to 30 cents, distributed as follows:

2 per cent of cities	25 cents or more
36 per cent of cities	20 to 24 cents
48 per cent of cities	15 to 19 cents
14 per cent of cities	10 to 14 cents

(2) *Wholesale and Promotional Fares.* Urban transit systems have devised a variety of fares which may be described as wholesale or promotional. Some of these fare types lend themselves more to one of these features than the other.

Wholesale fares enable the rider to purchase a number of rides at one time. Often, but not necessarily always, the wholesale fare allows the patron a discount from the standard cash fare. An example of a wholesale fare, involving tokens exchangeable for one ride each, would be five tokens for 95 cents—when the cash fare is 20 cents a ride. This amounts to a five per cent discount at the wholesale rate. This form of wholesale rate is thought by some to be promotional in stimulating business. It is more likely that its principal advantage lies in the convenience it provides in reducing the number of transactions and speeding collecting and loading. This form of wholesale fare also imposes a small penalty on the occasional rider who might use the transit system only in bad weather. Transfer privileges accompany payment by token as in the cash fare. In some transit systems, strips of tickets are used instead of tokens.

The most widely used form of wholesale fare is the unlimited weekly pass. Under this fare, the rider pays a lump sum at the beginning of the week for a pass that is good for any quantity of rides. Its appeal is mainly to the regular rider whose expected outlay for transportation on a cash-fare basis is as great or greater than the price of the weekly pass; this price is usually set slightly above the total cost of two rides per working day for the week. The pass is the quickest and simplest method of dealing with large numbers of people. In addition, it is attractive to many because it makes available bargain-fare transportation to those who travel by transit in the evening and on weekends. At the same time it frees the vehicle operator from a lot of work and speeds loading time at principal and transfer points, thus making faster service possible during peak hours. The promotional effect of the weekly pass in increasing revenues is doubtful, unless the community has recreation centers that people are likely to patronize in the evenings.

Another form of wholesale fare is the permit card, for which the rider pays a lump sum each week. When the rider shows the permit card, he is allowed a reduced cash fare. Where a transit system charges a cash fare of 20 cents, for example, the permit card might be sold for a dollar, with the rider required to pay 10 cents for each ride. As in the case of the weekly pass, the permit card enables the rider, or members of his family, a lower average fare per ride as use increases.

Numerous and varied promotional fare plans have been attempted without particular success. These include Sunday, holiday, and weekend passes, off-peak passes, and family evening passes.

(3) *Zone Fares.* As metropolitan areas expanded in size, fare structures began to include zone fares in an effort to relate the fare charged to distance and, hence, to costs. Zone fares require the passenger to pay an additional charge per ride for each additional geographic zone entered. The practice of charging more for a longer ride than for a shorter one is widespread in European transit systems, which use a large number of zones. This is possible because European systems maintain two-man operation, which solves the fare collection problem arising with the use of multi-zone fares. There has been reluctance to adopt zone fares in this country, where one-man operation predominates, largely because of the difficulty of collection in large metropolitan areas where there might be three or more zones. In medium-size communities, where the area served would require only two zones, the collection problem is solved by collecting on a pay-enter basis in the first zone and pay-leave basis in the second zone. Some companies have coupled the zone fare for longer rides with ex-

press service in an effort to attract business and to maintain the goodwill of those who resent zone fares because they exceed the standard fare.

The prevailing form of zone fare used by the urban transit industry in this country is the two-zone system. Use of a greater number of small zones, as in European transit systems, is largely limited in this country to intercity lines. Under the two-zone system, the city is divided into central and outer zones. The fare for the second zone is ordinarily less than the standard fare charged for the first zone. As might be expected, the exact location of the zone boundaries can be a matter of local controversy and the subject of pressure from a number of sources whose purpose usually is to enlarge the size of the inner zone.

In some cases the two-zone fare system has been adopted in an effort to increase system revenues without increasing the standard-fare level. The effect of maintaining a low standard fare is to encourage short-haul riding, for these are the passengers who are so often lost to the system as a result of an increase in the standard fare applicable throughout a metropolitan area. A second approach to the short-haul passenger traffic is through the use of a modification of the two-zone system, in the form of a basically flat-fare system which incorporates a downtown zone. Under this fare system, rides of about a mile are made available at a fare well below the standard fare. Special downtown loop lines providing this service have produced greater revenues per mile than standard-fare traffic because the distance involved is so short.

D. Policies During the Decline of Urban Transit. During the decline of urban transit, a variety of policies and experiments have been suggested and employed to deal with the problem. One of the direct approaches to the problem has been the purchase and operation of urban transit systems by local governments. Although this does not solve the problem of a declining industry that is characterized by low earnings or losses, it is a method of assuring continuity of a public service that is important to many citizens individually and to the community as a whole. When urban transit service is supplied by the local government, the deficits incurred, if any, presumably will be offset by public funds. Transit systems operated by local governments are exempt from federal income taxation and may be exempt from some or all the state and local taxes. Their cost of debt capital is ordinarily lower than that of a stockholder-owned corporation because the interest on such securities is not subject to federal income taxation.

Since World War II, the state and local governments have attempted to assist urban transit by relieving them of tax burdens. In the period 1947–1960 there were over 300 instances where such taxes were either reduced or eliminated. The Congress of the United States in 1956 also adopted this policy in issuing a new franchise to the transit system which serves in the Washington, D.C., metropolitan area. The franchise provided for outright exemption from the corporate gross receipts tax, and that neither the motor fuel nor real estate taxes would be payable in a given year unless the company earned a 6.5 per cent rate of return or had an operating ratio of 93.5 per cent. Despite the numerous instances of tax relief, there are still some transit systems that are very heavily taxed owing to historic circumstances. In the early days of the industry, when it was a virtual monopoly, franchises were sometimes awarded to the company offering to pay the highest percentage of its gross receipts in the form of a tax. Some of those taxes are still in effect. A 1956 report on the urban transit problem, by the New England Governors' Committee on Public Transportation, recommended: (1) a general overhaul and reduction of transit taxes; (2) complete elimination of the gross receipts tax; (3) wider managerial discretion in establishing promotional fares; (4) continued use of the operating-ratio method of regulation; (5) staggered working hours, in order to spread and lower the twice-daily peaks; and (6) various measures for the regulation of automobile traffic so as to speed transit service. The study concluded that the continued existence of privately operated transit systems should be given the fullest support and assistance.[34] In a study completed in 1959, the Illinois Mass Transportation Commission recommended to the state legislature that it enact measures authorizing the officials of one or more municipal corporations or counties to enter into agreements with transportation companies under which the local government(s) involved: (1) would acquire title to the operating equipment of the company; and then (2) hire the transportation company to operate the lines on specified terms, such as a per-mile basis or an established annual operating fee. It was proposed to the legislature that the local and county governments be allowed to levy a limited property tax, subject to referendum, to pay all or part of the cost of acquisition and operation. The legislature was also requested to authorize local and county governments to combine in the creation of mass transit districts or authorities. In other principal respects, the Illinois study agreed with the recommendations of the New England Governors' Committee, above.

Transit companies have experimented with promotional fares and various forms of service designed to win patrons away from the use of automobiles. A promising idea is the "park and ride" plan. Under this approach to the rebuilding of transit loads, automobile owners are encouraged to park their automobiles before they reach the central part of the city and complete their trips by transit. Public parks have been used for such parking, as have outlying filling stations and other sites. In addition, express service and air-conditioned vehicles have proved to be attractive to transit patrons, even where premium fares have been charged.

Convincing evidence of a good market for high-speed transit service is shown by the experience in Cleveland. The Cleveland Transit System is successful. The principal reason is the excellent service provided by its rapid transit line, which operates on its own right-of-way through the length of the metropolitan area. The System's motor bus and trolley coach lines are coordinated to serve rapid transit stations. Transfer privileges are included in the fare. In addition, outlying rapid transit stations provide free automobile parking facilities. Largely because "riding the rapid" has been so widely accepted, the System's 1956 annual report was able to state that "Recent studies show that more than 70 per cent of the people who come to the downtown area to shop and work do so by public transit."

The Cleveland Transit System is owned by the City of Cleveland and governed by a five-member Transit Board appointed by the mayor with the approval of the city council. The System is operated by a general manager. Cleveland purchased the property of the Cleveland Railway Co. in 1942. The rapid transit line opened in 1954, financed by bonds issued with the approval of the voters. It extends approximately 13.3 miles, running east and west parallel to the lakefront. Running

---

[34] Paul J. Garfield, "Municipal Utilities, Developments in 1956," in *The Municipal Yearbook 1957* (Chicago: The International City Managers' Association, 1957), pp. 343–344.

time over the length of the rapid transit line is about 28 minutes. Two factors not to be overlooked here are: (a) general public awareness of the benefits of rapid transit, based on several decades of successful service by the rapid transit system owned by the suburban Cleveland community of Shaker Heights; and (b) the farsighted planning that provided a rapid transit right-of-way when the Cleveland Terminal railroad yards were constructed in the 1920's. Admittedly, Cleveland had advantages not necessarily available to other communities. However, the fact that rapid transit can be successful, nonetheless, also has been demonstrated in Toronto, which opened a combination subway-surface level rapid transit line at about the same time that the Cleveland line went into service. Similar systems operate in New York, Chicago, Philadelphia, and Boston.

The advantage of rapid transit, in comparison with automotive expressways, is that rapid transit is designed to transport people while expressways primarily serve to transport automobiles. A rapid transit right-of-way at surface level requires at most about 75 per cent of a 66-foot expressway right-of-way. Transit stations require far less land than expressway interchanges, and the use of rapid transit causes less land to be needed for parking facilities in the central core area. Above all, rapid transit has an extraordinary capacity for transporting people. One lane of rapid transit can carry as many people in one direction as seven six-lane expressways. Moreover, rapid transit costs less than expressways. Rapid transit was expected to cost, at the time of this writing, $5 million per mile in San Francisco (excluding only the underwater Bay tube) and $3.5 million per mile in Atlanta. Expressways of equal capacity would cost about $42 million per mile. If the street congestion which presently immobilizes the principal cities is to be relieved, rapid transit appears to be the best means available.

E. *Federal Assistance.* In 1961 the federal government initiated a program of loan and grant assistance to state and local governments for the purpose of promoting coordinated mass transportation in metropolitan areas.[35] Senator Harrison A. Williams, Jr., of New Jersey, was the principal sponsor of the legislation. The federal aid program consists of three parts: loans to public agencies for the improvement of transit plant and related purposes; grants to finance urban transportation planning and coordination; and grants for pilot demonstration projects, or experiments, which are intended to test the effects upon transit demand and costs of such factors as service frequency, fare levels, and speed of service. The program is administered by the Housing and Home Finance Agency. Initial appropriations for the above purposes were relatively small and far less than the amounts authorized. (Authorizations are not the same as appropriations.) However, this is of little importance, because the significant element here is federal acceptance of responsibility in the field of mass transportation. Once a responsibility of this kind is accepted, the appropriations ordinarily follow in due course.

The first experiment announced under the pilot demonstration program was designed to find out what the role of urban transit is and can be in a small city of less than 50,000 population. Ithaca, New York was selected for study. The Housing and Home Finance Agency was planning to make a cash grant of $100,000, and Ithaca would add $50,000. The funds would be used to provide free bus service in Ithaca for about one year. This planned experiment in "no-fare transportation" was intended to find out whether the benefits to the city of ex-

[35] 75 Stat. 149.

pected greater transit patronage would exceed the cost of the free transportation. The experiment also was intended to provide information on: (1) the advantages, if any, of eliminating fares, fare collecting, accounting, and bonding all those who handle money; (2) whether schedules could be improved through the elimination of fare collecting, change making, and the issuance of transfers; (3) whether the demand for downtown parking space would decrease as a result of better bus service; and (4) the possible reductions in the cost of traffic policemen and street maintenance in the downtown area.

The lending program comprises the largest single portion of the federal aid plan. It provides for long-term loans to local, state, and multi-state public agencies for: (1) the acquisition, construction, reconstruction, and improvement of mass transportation facilities and equipment, excluding highways; and (2) the coordination of highway, bus, surface rail, and underground transportation facilities, including parking facilities. Stockholder-owned transit companies are not eligible to receive loans under this program, either directly or through loan guarantees. The rate of interest is tied to the cost of loan money to the Treasury. The approval of loans is contingent upon a showing that a comprehensive mass transportation plan is being developed or has been developed for the particular area where the loan funds are to be applied.

As noted above, only public agencies may qualify for loans under the federal transit aid program. Investor-owned companies are not eligible to receive loans; however, such companies may lease and operate the equipment or facilities purchased or constructed by public agencies with funds borrowed from the federal government. Where investor-owned companies are presently serving, it is comtemplated that this leasing arrangement will be adopted.

The federal loan program raises some serious questions. Why are only public agencies eligible to borrow? The question is pertinent, because in the cases of the air carrier and railroad industries the federal government guarantees similiar loans made directly to the investor-owned companies. The answer to this question is that loans are contingent upon the development of comprehensive, area-wide mass transportation plans, and this requires action on the part of the local governments comprising a metropolitan area. If loans were made directly to the transit companies, it was thought in Congress that the planning phase might be bypassed. Accordingly, loans are tied to transportation planning, and only those entities that are in a position to undertake this function can qualify for loans. A second question arising here is whether the use of federal loan funds by local governments to acquire transit property will ultimately mean the extinction of private ownership in the transit industry. Legislative history indicates that the opposite is intended, and that the local governments may lease acquired property to the existing companies for operation.[36]

[36] *Hearings* on S. 345, 87th Cong., 1st sess., 1961, p. 167.

12 The Application of Rate-Making Essentials—A Case Study

The essential aspects of public utility rate making have been covered in the foregoing chapters. To tie these elements together, a case decided by the Federal Power Commission will be examined, and the many issues that can arise in a single case will be noted. The particular case studied in this chapter, involving the investigation of an interstate wholesale electric rate charged by South Carolina Generating Company, was selected because its many facets seem to provide an unusually wide basis for group discussion by beginning readers. At the same time, however, the selection of this particular case for study does not necessarily indicate endorsement or criticism of the regulatory policies adopted.

1. BACKGROUND FACTS

In 1954 the Federal Power Commission instituted an investigation of the wholesale rate charged by South Carolina Generating Company to Georgia Power Company for the sale of electric energy for resale. The case concluded in 1959 and resulted in a small rate reduction. The purpose of the investigation was to determined under Sections 205 and 206 of the Federal Power Act if the contract rate established between the companies was "unjust, unreasonable, or unduly discriminatory." After hearings were held during 1955, the presiding examiner issued his initial decision, subject to Commission review, in March, 1956, finding the rate to be just, reasonable, and not unduly discriminatory. Exceptions to the initial decision were filed, and oral argument was held before the full Commission in May. In October, 1956, the FPC issued its opinion and order in the case and found that the examiner was in error and that the contract rate between the companies was "unjust and unreasonable, and contrary to the public interest."[1] The reasoning behind this judgment will be discussed below.

This case involved the sale of a block of 75,000 Kw of power annually by South Carolina Generating Company to the Georgia Power Company. Originally, the Generating Company's parent, South Carolina Electric & Gas Company, considered the construction of the steam electric generating plant producing this service with the intention of selling the entire planned output of 250,000 Kw to E. I. du Pont de Nemours & Company, acting as a prime contractor for the Atomic Energy Commission. The parent company's initial rate offer was rejected by du Pont as too high. In order to meet the latter's objections, it was necessary to finance construction at a lower cost than was possible under the restrictions in the indentures securing the bonds of the parent company. (Its bonded debt was restricted to 60 per cent of the total amount of any prop-

[1] *Re South Carolina Generating Company*, 16 FPC 52 (1956); rehearing denied, 16 FPC 1365 (1956).

erty additions.) Accordingly, South Carolina Electric & Gas formed South Carolina Generating Company as a wholly owned subsidiary, with the latter to finance the new capacity, using a 90 per cent debt ratio (75 per cent in mortgage bonds and 15 per cent in 10-year notes). The 10 per cent common stock equity in Generating Company was taken up by the parent company. As a consequence of the relatively lower cost of debt capital, in contrast with the cost of equity financing, a contract rate was offered to du Pont which was acceptable. However, in the interim, du Pont found that it needed only 30,-000 rather than 250,000 Kw per year. At this time the plant had an installed capacity of 150,000 Kw and had not reached the planned capacity of 250,000 Kw.

During this time, the parent company informed the nearby Georgia Power Company of the low-cost financing that had been arranged to construct the new facilities. Georgia Power, instead of building additional capacity of its own, entered into a 25-year contract with Generating Company to purchase the annual output of 75,000 Kw of capacity. The output not taken by du Pont and Georgia Power was sold to the parent company for distribution within South Carolina. Of the three sales by Generating Company, only that to Georgia Power was a sale in interstate commerce of electric energy (at wholesale) for resale to the public and therefore subject to the jurisdiction of the FPC over rates.

The wholesale rate under review by the Commission in this case was the product of tough bargaining at arm's length between buyer and seller. In the more usual situation involving retail utility rates, the seller alone initially formulates schedules of rates. In either instance, however, the basic situation is the same, for the rate-making process originates with the seller. The resulting schedule or schedules of rates, however arrived at, are then subject to regulatory review and possible modification. The specific situation in the case under discussion is somewhat simpler than most, because it involves a single wholesale rate for service to one customer. In the more usual utility pricing situation, retail rates for sales to classes of customers would be designed by the utility and presented for commission review.

2. THE QUESTIONED RATE

The rate in question in this case was established by the long-term contract between the Generating Company and Georgia Power, and was filed with the FPC as a rate schedule. The contract called for a two-part rate consisting of an energy charge and a capacity charge. The former charge, over which there was no dispute, was based on fuel and operating maintenance expenses plus minor taxes not related to income. The annual capacity charge was more involved and was split into a "basic capacity charge," which was based upon the fixed costs, and a supplemental capacity charge based upon value of service.

As discussed in Chapter 10, energy costs are output costs and are exclusively variable. The total of such costs fluctuates only if the output of the plant varies. Total-demand or capacity costs, on the other hand, are largely fixed in nature and include such costs as annual depreciation, return on rate base, income and property taxes, and operating supervision and labor.

A. *The Capacity Charge.* The capacity charge per Kw per year, as estimated when the contract was negotiated in 1951, would total $22.50. It was to be comprised of a "basic capacity charge" of $15.30 per Kw plus a supplemental capacity charge of $7.20 per Kw. The basic capacity charge alone was calculated to reflect the fixed capacity costs referred to above, as they were estimated in 1951. However, the contract provided for automatic adjustment of the basic capacity charge to reflect any differences between the estimated and the actually experienced investment and fixed operating expenses of plant. By 1956 the basic capacity charge had escalated from $15.30 to $18.11 per Kw, thus increasing the total capacity charge to Georgia Power from $22.50 to $25.31 per Kw annually. The supplemental capacity charge of $7.20 per Kw originally represented one-half the total savings realized by Georgia Power as a result of purchasing electricity from Generating Company instead of constructing facilities of its own to provide an additional supply.

The Commission disapproved the form and level of the capacity charge as provided in the original contract. Its disapproval was directed particularly to the supplemental capacity charge, which was based on value-of-service considerations. The only acceptable rate was found to be one based upon the traditional public utility cost-of-service formula. In so ruling, the Commission noted the well-established principle that it is free to select and to apply any rate-making method, provided the end result is reasonable.

B. *The Automatic Rate Adjustments.* The contract provided for automatic adjustment (increase or decrease) in both the energy charge and the basic capacity charge to reflect future changes in costs. The adjustment of the energy charge would depend upon changes in fuel costs. The adjustment of the basic capacity charge, as noted previously, would depend upon any difference between estimated and actual fixed costs. The Commission had no objection to the automatic adjustment of the energy charge, but it disallowed the automatic adjustment of the basic capacity charge and ordered it deleted from the company's rate schedule. A further rate-schedule change was ordered which would require an automatic downward adjustment of the capacity charge in the event of a reduction in federal income taxes.

The required elimination of the rate-schedule clauses providing for the automatic adjustment of the capacity charge was appealed to the United States Court of Appeals for the Fourth Circuit, which remanded this issue, among others, to the FPC, requesting a fuller explanation of the Commission's reasoning.[2] The Commission in a second opinion explained "Our reason . . . in eliminating these clauses was that they failed to take into account a factor that tends to decrease the cost of service and apply only to those other factors whose effect, particularly in a period of rising prices, will tend to increase."[3] This factor was the decline in the rate base which would result as the reserve for depreciation accrued through time. The Commission noted that the depreciation reserve was increasing by $372,985 per year. Thus, if the rate of return allowed was 5.55 per cent, the fair return would decrease by 5.55 per cent of $372,985, or $20,700, each year. In addition, the Commission said there would be an additional tax saving of $22,300, apparently reflecting the declining total return on the declining rate base. Thus, the Commission was able to point to factors tending to decrease the cost of service which were not provided for, while factors which tended to increase the cost of service were included. The Commission emphasized that it did not ob-

[2] *South Carolina Generating Company* v. *FPC*, 249 F. 2d 755 (1957); *cert.* denied, 356 U.S. 912 (1958).

[3] *Re South Carolina Generating Co.*, 19 FPC 855 (1958).

ject to rate-making formulas reflecting changes in the entire cost of service. Finally, a distinction was made between the disallowed automatic adjustment of the capacity charge and the approved automatic adjustment of the energy charge. The latter was held to be proper because it involved no declining-rate-base problem and could be precisely evaluated for rate-making purposes. The Fourth Circuit found the Commission's explanation to be satisfactory.[4]

3. COST OF SERVICE

The basic aspects of the company's cost of service, as passed upon by the FPC, include the following: (a) the proper test period; (b) the rate of return; (c) the allowance for income taxes; (d) the working capital allowance; (e) annual and accrued depreciation; (f) interest during construction; and (g) determination of cost of service and approved rate.

A. *The Test Period.* Whenever a cost-of-service study is made, it is necessary to adopt a test period, ordinarily one year, in which costs are considered representative of the future. In selecting 1956 as the test period, the Commission sought to avoid a period which would involve undue conjecture as to costs. The Generating Company and the presiding examiner had used for some purposes a much longer period of time than one year. The FPC found that to be unacceptable, holding that a determination of rates on the basis of estimates of costs 10 to 25 years hence ". . . would be to enter into a realm of conjecture and destroy the purpose of a cost-of-service formula." The Commission pointed out that its jurisdiction is of a continuing nature and that future adjustments in the cost of service could be made when necessary to assure reasonable rates.

B. *Rate of Return.* The Commission next considered the proper rate of return to be allowed. The company maintained that a 6.0 per cent rate of return was necessary. The staff of the Commission, although it took no position during the hearing, recommended 5.55 per cent in its brief. The Commission approved the latter rate of return. Both the company and the staff based their positions upon a weighted-average cost of capital calculated for the South Carolina Electric & Gas system as a whole. This is ordinarily the procedure followed where, as here, corporate subsidiaries are involved, because system-wide credit and earnings are the basis for the financing of individual subsidiaries. In the present case, the parent company guaranteed the debt issued by the subsidiary and issued more of its own common stock to finance its investment in the common stock of the subsidiary.

The first matter which the Commission was required to decide was the appropriate corporate capital structure to use in determining a cost of capital. It rejected the hypothetical capital structure favored by the company and adopted the actual system-wide capital structure as recommended by the staff. The company had proposed adoption of a hypothetical and more or less ideal electric utility capital structure of 50 per cent debt, 15 per cent preferred stock, and 35 per cent common equity, on the grounds, among others, that "system credit was essential to the financing" of the operating facilities and that the hypothetical capitalization should be used ". . . to encourage achievement of that ratio at some future date." The FPC held that, although it was perhaps beneficial to strive for a different debt-equity ratio, such predictions of future capitalization ratios could not be approved as the basis for prescribing cur-

---

[4] *South Carolina Generating Co.* v. *FPC*, 261 F. 2d 915 (1958).

rent rates. The actual system-wide capital structure of 62.8 per cent debt, 9.4 per cent preferred stock, and 27.8 per cent common equity was held to be more truly representative of the facts in the case, and the Commission proceeded to use these figures. A hypothetical capital structure is sometimes adopted by regulatory bodies, particularly in cases where the debt ratio is deemed relatively low. In these hypothetical computations, the debt ratio is sometimes raised so as to give a lower over-all cost of capital. In the case under discussion, a somewhat different situation was presented, for the company, in urging adoption of a hypothetical debt ratio, in effect was seeking a higher over-all cost of capital than would result from use of the actual capital structure.

The problem of the specific cost of capital was dealt with in some detail. First, in determining the cost of debt capital, the Commission rejected the current, or replacement, cost-of-debt approach recommended by the company; this method would have resulted in a cost of debt of 3.5 to 3.75 per cent. Instead, the Commission adopted the actual, or historic, cost method. It found the weighted-average cost of debt to be 3.46 per cent. Second, the Commission also adopted the actual-cost approach to the determination of a cost of preferred stock capital. It found the actual system-wide cost to be 4.9 per cent. In so doing, it rejected the 4.75 per cent figure recommended by the company witness, who had stated that preferred stock should receive 1.0 per cent to 1.25 per cent more than debt money. Since the company's method of determining the return on debt capital was rejected, it was also found necessary to reject the cost figure proposed for the preferred stock.

As is the situation in most rate cases, determining the cost of equity capital presented the most difficult problems in arriving at an approved rate of return. The company contended that a 10.0 per cent return on equity capital was necessary to allow the parent firm to attract money of this type. The Commission initially viewed the market for the parent company's stock in terms of an earnings-price ratio approach. It noted that the earnings-price ratio averaged 7.9 per cent during the period 1950 through 1954, and that on the four public offerings of common stock during this period, the earnings-offering price ratios ranged between 6.37 and 8.1 per cent. The Commission allowed 10.5 per cent, or an amount 33 per cent greater than the average earnings-price ratio.

It is interesting to note here some of of the factors that the FPC found appropriate to consider in determining the cost of equity capital. To the 7.9 per cent average earnings-price ratio the Commission decided it should add 0.5 per cent to cover financing costs. It then considered other factors which are "necessarily a matter of judgment." The FPC stated that "Further allowance should be made for such other factors considered by investors as the relative thinness of equity, competition from public power, . . . adverse weather conditions affecting a system with a relatively high percentage of hydro capacity, [and] . . . the present upward trend in the money market." Thus, about two percentage points were added to the total of average earnings-price ratios and cost of financing for factors that could not be calculated precisely by the Commission.

By using the South Carolina Electric & Gas Company's actual capital structure and the costs noted above for each of the three types of capital, the FPC arrived at an over-all rate of return of 5.55 per cent. Table 12.1 shows these calculations, as well as those of the company. It shows that, although the

Table 12.1

Rate-of-Return Computation

South Carolina Generating Company

Part I: Commission Calculations

Type of Capital	Per Cent of Capitalization	Capital Cost	Rate of Return
Debt.	62.8%	3.46%	2.17%
Preferred stock.	9.4	4.90	0.46
Common equity	27.8	10.50	2.92
Total	100.0%		5.55%

Part II: Company Calculations

Type of Capital	Per Cent of Capitalization	Capital Cost	Rate of Return
Debt.	50.0%	3.60%	1.80%
Preferred stock.	15.0	4.75	0.71
Common equity	35.0	10.00	3.50
Total	100.0%		6.01%

Source: Re South Carolina Generating Company, 16 FPC 52, 62–64 (1956).

company proposed lower costs of preferred and common stock capital than the FPC ultimately adopted, the over-all rate of return allowed was less than what the company sought. The difference arises from the higher debt ratio and lower cost of debt capital adopted by the Commission, which more than offset its higher allowances on preferred and common stock.

Aside from the specific cost-of-capital methods employed, this case illustrates in fairly typical fashion the manner in which commissions reason in arriving at a rate of return. The general approach is one which utilizes a chosen capital structure and gives consideration to various measures of the cost of each type of capital, together with judgment, in order to arrive at a rate of return which will satisfy the standards laid down by the Supreme Court—comparable earnings, capital attraction, and maintenance of financial integrity. The importance of the judgment element in this process cannot be minimized. In this case, for example, the determination of the cost of equity capital included a judgment-based allowance of about two percentage points which: (1) amounted to almost 0.6 per cent in terms of the over-all rate of return allowed; and (2) accounted for about $70,000 or 10 per cent of the total-return amount of $708,064. This is illustrative of the subjective factors bearing upon the rate-making process and points up the importance of having capable, conscientious commissioners who have insight into the problems of the industry they regulate.

C. The Allowance for Income Taxes. The third problem encountered by the Commission in its cost-of-service analysis dealt with the income tax allowance. On this issue the Commission and the United States Court of Appeals disagreed, and the Commission ultimately modified its findings in accordance with the ruling of the Court. The factors involved in this issue are set forth below.

The company had urged that a hypothetical 50 per cent debt ratio and a three per cent annual depreciation rate be used in computing the taxable income and thus the tax allowance for rate-making purposes. (Depreciation will be covered shortly.) It will be recalled that the debt ratio of the subsidiary Generating Company alone was 90 per cent, while that of the entire South Carolina Electric & Gas Company system was 62.8 per cent. The use of the hypothetical debt ratio would have resulted in a comparatively lower tax deduction for interest expense, and thus higher taxable income and a higher tax allowance. On the ground that such a tax allowance would differ from the actual taxes paid in the 1956 test year, the Commission rejected this method as unreasonable and restated its established policy: "We have consistently held that the allowance for taxes should not exceed taxes paid."

The FPC calculated a relatively smaller income tax allowance by using the interest deduction arising from the company's 90 per cent debt ratio, on the grounds that the company would pay taxes on that basis. The effect of this was a comparatively high interest deduction, and hence a lesser taxable-income total and a lesser tax allowance. The company appealed for judicial review of this part of the FPC order, among others. The United States Court of Appeals for the Fourth Circuit remanded this question to the Commission for a fuller explanation of its calculation of the allowance for income taxes.[5]

In arguing before the Court that the Commission's tax allowance was insufficient, the company maintained: (1) that the parent South Carolina Electric & Gas Company had been forced to issue substantial additional amounts of its own common stock to offset, on a consolidated basis, the unusually high debt ratio of the subsidiary Generating Company; and (2) that as a result it did not have so large an interest deduction as it otherwise would and hence paid higher taxes. It was argued that part, but not all, of this extra tax cost to the parent company should be charged to the subsidiary company for rate-making purposes, since the cause of the higher taxes of the system as a whole was the high debt ratio of the subsidiary. To accomplish this, it was suggested that the FPC at least use the system-wide debt ratio of 62.8 per cent to calculate the tax allowance. It will be recalled that the FPC had used the system-wide capitalization as a basis for arriving at a cost of capital for the Generating Company. In remanding the case to the Commission, the Court specifically asked for an explanation of the differing treatment of capital structure in the matters of rate of return and income tax allowance.

The Commission, in attempting to satisfy the Court's objections, raised the following question: "Was cost incurred for income taxes to render the service for which a rate is being determined, and if so, how much? . . . The question here is . . . whether those extra taxes are a cost of Generating Company's service rendered to Georgia Power Company."[6] The Commission held that the extra taxes were not a proper component of the cost of serving Georgia Power Company, because the benefits of the separate subsidiary arrangement accrued solely to the parent. It stated that the parent company purposely adopted the high-debt-ratio method of financing with the expectation that the subsidiary would be able to charge low rates for its power because of low costs of money and low income taxes due to high interest deductions. The FPC maintained that the parent company would benefit: by an improved financial rating resulting from its contract with du Pont; by strengthening its position in a growing market area; and by protecting its service area

[5] *Op. cit.*, Note 2.

[6] *Op. cit.*, Note 3.

from incursion by another utility. The Commission argued that these were the benefits for which the parent company was willing to incur higher tax liability. On this basis the Commission concluded that none of the benefits accruing to the parent company were passed on to the customers of the Georgia Power Company and, therefore, they should not be required to bear the expense.

The Court of Appeals, in a second decision, reversed the Commission on this issue and ruled that the additional taxes incurred were to be included in the cost of service.[7] The Court agreed that the parent company had undertaken new risks and assumed new burdens in order to improve its financial standing and broaden its markets. However, the Court held these facts do not relieve Georgia Power from the obligation to pay a fair and reasonable price for what it gets, based on the costs of the product, which include taxes on income. The Court pointed out that Georgia Power also received "substantial benefits" in the form of lower-cost power than if it had built its own plant. Thus, the Court found that the Commission's conclusion could not be sustained, if the benefit to the consumer rather than cost of service were the governing factor.

The Court considered that the parent-subsidiary relationship of the two utilities "for practical purposes" was such that they constituted a single entity. Noting that the Commission, in fixing a rate of return, had looked to the entire system rather than the subsidiary alone, the Court found it inconsistent for the Commission to look only to the subsidiary when calculating the proper tax allowance. "If the Commission looks at the cost of service alone as the standard of reasonableness of the contract rate, then actual costs should not be disregarded simply because the selling utility chooses to incur them in one place rather than another." Further, the Court called attention to the fact that Georgia Power would not bear all of the increased tax costs resulting from the creation of the subsidiary, but only a proportional share. The utilities had proposed spreading the increased taxes over the entire system. Thus, Georgia Power's share would be a portion of the increased tax cost allocated to Generating Company, with that share proportionally related to the installed capacity dedicated to the service of Georgia Power. The Court once again remanded the case to the Commission, this time for recomputation of the income tax allowance based on the system-wide debt ratio of 62.8 per cent. The Commission did not seek to appeal the Court's decision to the Supreme Court.

In August, 1959, the Commission issued a supplemental order complying with the Court's judgment.[8] The revisions resulted in a capacity charge of $24.344 per Kw per year, an increase of $2.396 per Kw above the charge set previously at $21.948 per Kw per year. Although the cost of service was increased by the additional tax allowance, the net effect was reduced somewhat because the Commission at the same time completely eliminated from its previous rate-base computation the allowance for net working capital. The Commission ruled that the additional cash accruals resulting from the larger tax allowance, pending actual payment of taxes, were sufficient to offset the company's cash and other working capital requirements. This was in accord with the Commission's traditional policy of crediting against the gross working capital requirement the amount "computed to be available on the average" to the company. In this case 68 per cent of the tax allowance was used. The credit exceeded

[7] *Op. cit.*, Note 4.

[8] *Re South Carolina Generating Company*, 22 FPC 188 (1959).

the previous net working capital allowance; hence, this allowance was eliminated. The revised capacity charge of $24.344 per Kw per year approaches the $25.31 initially charged by the company. It is interesting to note, however, that the company and the Commission used different routes to reach their somewhat similar conclusions.

D. *Working Capital.* Generating Company had proposed a working capital allowance of $386,600 for the 1956 test year, based on $195,400 for average materials and supplies inventories plus $191,200 for cash working capital representing 12.5 per cent (or 45 days) of its annual cash operating expenses. The amount allowed was initially reduced to $93,270 by making two adjustments. Since the Generating Company received payment from Georgia Power before the former paid for natural gas used as fuel, the amount included in operating expenses for gas purchases was disallowed. Second, since the Generating Company accrued federal income taxes before such taxes had to be paid, working capital was reduced by the average amount of tax accruals available to the company during the year. It was noted above that in the final judgment by the Court on the question of the allowance for income taxes, a larger tax allowance was prescribed, which the Commission found to be sufficient to completely absorb the net working capital initially allowed. Commissioner Arthur Kline dissented to this policy, pointing out that it was inconsistent to determine credits to the working capital account on the basis of the company as a single entity while determining the debits to working capital on the basis of tax accruals computed on a system-wide basis. In his opinion, both debits and credits to the working capital requirement should have been computed on the same basis.

E. *Depreciation.* The Generating Company urged that a 3.0 per cent rate be used in computing annual depreciation expense. The Commission, however, noted that the parent company had used a rate of 2.75 per cent for many years. The Commission could find no reason for raising the depreciation rate other than the company's argument that close proximity to atomic energy installations increased the risk of the business. This argument was rejected by the FPC, which noted that risks of this type should be compensated for in the rate of return and not depreciation. Consistent with the Commission's longstanding policy that the annual depreciation expense and the accrued depreciation should be consistently related, the 2.75 per cent rate also was applied in the computation of the accrued depreciation deducted in determining the rate base. Thus, the adoption of the lower depreciation rate had the effect of: (a) reducing the annual depreciation expense as against that proposed; (b) increasing taxable income for rate-making purposes; and (c) reducing the accrued depreciation below that calculated under the proposed three per cent rate, which had the further effect of increasing the rate base in the amount of the difference.

F. *Interest During Construction.* The Commission's uniform system of accounts for public utilities and licensees allows a utility to include in its electric plant account as a component of construction costs "the net cost of borrowed funds used for construction purposes and a reasonable rate upon the utility's own funds when so used." The Generating Company had capitalized "interest" of eight per cent per annum on the equity portion of the funds tied up during construction. The presiding examiner had pointed out that equity funds used by the parent company during construction cost 10 per cent. The Commission rejected the eight per cent rate and allowed six per cent. It reasoned that: (a) equity capital is not legally entitled to any return until the plant has been completed and operations begun; (b) the return to equity capital comes from earnings, and no earnings are possible before construction is completed and operations begun; and (c) investment in equity capital is made on the basis of expected future earnings. The six per cent figure was allowed on the grounds that this was the alternative rate which could be earned on the money if it were not invested in construction. Accordingly, the Commission ordered a reduction in the company's average net plant account (used as the property component of the rate base) to reflect the capitalization of an allowance of six per cent per annum on equity funds tied up during construction.

G. Cost and Rate Determination. Taking all the foregoing factors into account, the Commission ultimately concluded that a 1956 jurisdictional cost of service of $3,175,233 was just and reasonable. This was $72,467 less than the revenues that would have resulted from the rate as originally agreed to by the buyer and seller, and represented a test-year revenue reduction of 2.2 per cent. The final cost of service and the two-part rate ultimately approved for the company's jurisdictional business are summarized in Table 12.2. First, each component of the total cost of jurisdictional service is classified to the energy and capacity (demand) cost categories on the basis of whether they are variable or fixed costs. Second, the total energy costs are divided by the annual Kwh total to determine the energy charge under the two-part rate, and the total demand costs are divided by the total Kw of capacity to determine the demand charge under the two-part rate.

While this pricing situation provides the beginning reader with a simple ex-

Table 12.2

South Carolina Generating Company

Revised Cost of Service and Rates

1956

		Cost Classification	
	Total Costs	*Energy Costs*	*Capacity Costs*
Operation and maintenance:			
Fuel	$1,309,000	$1,309,000	$ —
Maintenance	33,400	32,900	500
Other	187,200	—	187,200
Total operation and maintenance	$1,529,600	$1,341,900	$ 187,700
Depreciation	372,985	—	372,985
Taxes, other than income	119,500	7,500	112,000
Income taxes:			
Federal	394,243	—	394,243
State	51,941	—	51,941
Return at 5.55 per cent	708,064	—	708,064
Credit for rents	(1,100)	—	(1,100)
Total cost of service	$3,175,233	$1,349,400	$1,825,833
Kilowatt-hours (000)	—	466,500	—
Energy cost per kilowatt-hour	—	$0.0028926	—
Contract demand–kilowatts	—	—	$75,000
Cost per kilowatt of contract demand	—	—	$24.344

Source: *Re South Carolina Generating Company,* 22 FPC 188, Appendix A (1959).

ample for review purposes, it does so only because this particular rate applies to wholesale sales to an individual customer. The more usual utility pricing situation, of course, involves retail sales to more than one class of customer. There, no less than in many wholesale sales, costing and pricing are not considered to be the same thing. Supply costs at most serve as a guide to the design of retail rates, not as an exclusive determinant, because market-demand factors also must be accorded important weight. In the case under discussion, it was established that the value of service—as measured by the alternative supply costs to the buyer—substantially exceeded the rate being investigated. As a practical matter, that rate could not have exceeded the value of service, regardless of costs.

4. SUMMARY

This brief review of an actual case decided by the Federal Power Commission is intended to highlight the variety, complexity, and nature of problems encountered in day-to-day regulation. It must be emphasized that the problems encountered in this case are "average" in the sense that they are no more or less numerous or complex than those found in many cases. This case also illustrates the pragmatic, step-by-step, company-by-company type of regulation found in the public utility field. There are principles and precedents which serve as guideposts, but a commission must maintain considerable flexibility to be able to handle each individual situation. Finally, this case emphasizes the highly significant role of the expertise of regulatory agencies. Expert judgment is present in every commission decision and order, and, while questioned by the courts in some instances, this judgment is most often allowed to stand as the best that is available. Thus, while we are basically a nation living under a government of laws, in fields such as public utility regulation we must depend heavily on a government of men also.

PART III

THE REGULATORY AGENCIES

13 The Regulatory Agencies

This chapter concerns the state and federal regulatory agencies insofar as they have jurisdiction over the public utilities under consideration here. This survey of the regulatory agencies is intended to complement the earlier discussions of the development and scope of public utility regulation (Chapter 3) and administrative procedure and review (Chapter 4).

The essential nature of commission regulation of public utilities was discerned by Professor John R. Commons, whose many contributions to the study of economics included an illumination of the function and importance of collective action in the economic affairs of our society. In this respect, Professor Commons also looked searchingly into the instrumentalities of government in order to examine the economic impact of their policies and decisions. The result of his work was to broaden the scope of formal economic analysis, which previously had been essentially concerned with the economics of individual action in a context that assumed government to be a neutral factor.

The focus of Professor Commons' studies of the economics of collective action was the "institution," and from this followed the name of his type of economics—institutional economics. He defined an *institution* as collective action in control of individual action.[1] In the institution of public utility regulation, the state and federal commissions are instruments of collective action, created by government, for the purpose of controlling the individual action of the respective suppliers of public utility services. Professor Commons' studies in this area enabled him to make important contributions to the drafting of the pioneering Wisconsin regulatory statute enacted in 1907. He also organized and taught at the University of Wisconsin the first course work in the economics of public utilities under regulation.

1. THE STATE COMMISSIONS

There are state governmental agencies with authority to regulate public utilities in all fifty states, the District of Columbia, and Puerto Rico. The Canadian provincial governments also have agencies of this type. The state commissions differ somewhat from one another in the nature of their statutory juris-

[1] John R. Commons, *Institutional Economics* (New York: The Macmillan Company, 1934), pp. 69, 73.

diction and powers. This is to be expected. However, insofar as most of them are concerned, the areas of similarity are substantially greater than the areas of dissimilarity. In a few states, as discussed in Chapter 3, local franchise regulation is of predominant importance. In those states, the commissions have jurisdiction over the transportation utilities, and some have jurisdiction over the public utilities under discussion here—insofar as utility operations outside the limits of municipal corporations are concerned. All but two of the local-franchise-regulation states have vested jurisdiction over telephone utilities in their state commissions. Finally, some of these commissions act in an appellate capacity with respect to locally determined utility rates. At the time of writing, the Alaska commission was not as yet active.

The state commissions devote a considerable portion of their resources to the regulation of the motor carrier industry. In some states, the regulation of this industry comprises the most important single area of their jurisdiction—as measured in terms of the relative number of motor carrier cases decided each year. On the other hand, the state commissions now have relatively little regulatory jurisdiction over railroads. Acts of Congress and court decisions have tended to broaden the scope of federal regulatory authority over that industry, in part by narrowing the scope of effective state commission jurisdiction.

A. *Jurisdiction of State Commissions.* Most state commissions have regulatory jurisdiction over the principal types of public utilities operating under stockholder ownership. In addition, some commissions also have jurisdiction over docks, wharves, warehouses, toll roads, toll bridges, canals, cotton gins, sewers, tunnels, and stockyards, among others. In some states in the Southwest, the regulation of oil and gas conservation comprises an important part of the commissions' jurisdiction. The extent of state commission jurisdiction over the rates of the principal stockholder-owned public utilities is summarized in Table 13.1.

The state commissions have relatively little regulatory jurisdiction over the rates of the municipally owned public utilities. The commissions in seven states have relatively comprehensive

Table 13.1

Rate Jurisdiction, 1960

Fifty State Utility Commissions*

(Privately Owned Public Utilities)

Utility Service	*Commissions With Rate Jurisdiction*	*Utility Service*	*Commissions With Rate Jurisdiction*
Electric light and power. .	44	Water	42
Manufactured gas	40	Telephone	48
Natural gas	42	Telegraph	46
Street railways	32	Oil pipeline	25
Motor buses	47	Gas pipeline	33

* The District of Columbia Public Utilities Commission has rate jurisdiction over electric, gas and telephone utilities; the local transit utility is regulated by the Washington Metropolitan Area Transit Commission.

Source: The Book of the States 1960–1961 (Chicago: Council of State Governments, 1960), p. 501.

jurisdiction over the rates charged by the different types of municipal utilities. Six other state commissions have rate jurisdiction over some but not all of the different types of municipally owned utilities.[2]

B. *The Commissioners.* The respective state commissions are composed of differing numbers of commissioners, ranging from one to seven. Rhode Island and Oregon each have a single commissioner, while South Carolina and Massachusetts each have seven. Thirty-eight states and the District of Columbia have three commissioners, and eight states have five-man commissions. The larger commissions appear to have an advantage in that they are better able to assign a commissioner to preside over the hearings in the more important cases or to assign a commissioner to be present during such hearings.

The selection of commissioners in most states is by gubernatorial appointment. Of the states which provide for selection by appointment, about two-thirds require the appointee to be approved by the state legislature. In fourteen states, the commissioners are elected, and in two states they are selected by the legislature.

The length of term of the state commissioners in the great majority of instances is six years. Twelve states provide for terms of four years. The shortest fixed term is three years and the longest is ten years. One state, Rhode Island, provides for an indefinite term of office.

The annual salaries of the state commissioners vary within a wide range. In general, they are low relative to the substantial responsibility placed upon the commissioners and by comparison with the salary level of federal commissioners. Fourteen states in 1960 paid annual salaries of less than $9,000, while 22 states paid salaries in the $9,000 to $12,000 range. Only five states provided salaries in a range above $12,000 and up to $15,000. Salaries in seven states exceeded $15,000 per year. Members of the federal commissions are paid $20,000 annually. In many states, the chairman of the commission is paid a somewhat higher salary than that of the other members of the same commission. This additional amount, where provided for, ranges from $500 to $3,000 per year.[3]

The qualifications of the commissioners in some states are set forth by statute. In most such instances, state residence for a specific number of years is usually required. Only a few states have statutes which require the commissioners to be members of certain professions, such as law or accounting, or to have specified types of experience. Studies of the occupational backgrounds of the state commissioners were made in 1929 by editor and legal scholar Francis X. Welch and in 1954 by Professor Lincoln Smith. The 1929 study showed a preference in the states for laymen, or generalists, as commissioners and noted some signs of a trend away from the placement of lawyers in such positions. The 1954 study, a quarter of a century later, indicated that this trend toward laymen as commissioners had advanced moderately in the states. Over half the state commissioners in 1954 were found to be generalists from many walks of life. Somewhat fewer than half the commissioners had professional and administrative occupational backgrounds. However, out of the total of 182 commissioners studied, 72 had previous government service.[4]

---

2 *The Book of the States 1960–1961* (Chicago: Council of State Governments, 1960), p. 501; *Moody's Public Utility Manual 1960,* pp. a 152–153.

3 *Ibid.*

4 Lincoln Smith, "Laymen as Regulatory Commissioners," 63 *Public Utilities Fortnightly* 673 (1959).

C. Organization and Staff. The regulatory commissions employ various types of technical specialists as well as administrative and clerical personnel—referred to collectively as the "staff" of the commission. The size and detail of organization of the respective commission staffs vary considerably from state to state.

The staffs of most of the state commissions are organized on a *functional basis*. That is, individual departments are responsible for the different types of work, such as engineering, accounting, finance, rates and research, law, and administration. Under this functional form of organization, each department is responsible for the work in its area insofar as all types of utilities are concerned. A second form of staff organization, termed the *utility basis,* calls for separate departments, such as public utilities, motor carriers, and railroads. Each of these departments is then staffed to perform its own work in the respective functional area. In practice, many commission staffs represent some combination of the functional and utility types of organization. The most usual form of departure from the functional basis of organization arises with respect to the separate departments for motor carrier regulation.

The size of the staff varies considerably from state to state, depending upon a number of factors. Not the least of these is the number of utilities under jurisdiction, for in the less populous states and small states there are not many utilities to regulate. Then again, in some states, the regulatory commission also has substantial responsibility for types of business regulation other than public utility regulation. Another factor affecting the size of commission staffs is the adequacy of legislative appropriations and the availability of funds arising from charges collected from regulated companies to defray regulatory expenses. Still another factor determining staff size is the extent to which commission jurisdiction is shared with local governments. In addition, in some states the responsibility for regulating different utilities is divided among more than one commission. Accordingly, simple comparison of the total number of staff personnel in the respective commissions would not be particularly meaningful without further qualitative analysis. For example, as of July 1, 1959 the Texas Railroad Commission had 368 employees, including commissioners and staff, while the Kentucky Public Service Commission had 39. The Texas Commission has very little jurisdiction over public utilities, in that Texas is primarily a local-regulation state. However, the Texas Commission has substantial regulatory jurisdiction in the non-public utility area of oil and gas conservation. It also exercises jurisdiction over railroads, motor buses, common and contract motor carriers of property, and petroleum pipelines. On the other hand, the relatively smaller Kentucky PCS has comprehensive regulatory authority over public utilities while two other Kentucky state agencies have jurisdiction over railroads and motor carriers, respectively.

With the foregoing in mind, the size of some of the state commission staffs may be surveyed. As of January 1, 1959 the New York and California commissions had 654 and 650 employees, respectively, including commissioners. On the other hand, the Nevada and Delaware commissions had total employees of eight each. Between these extremes there is considerable variation in staff size, with about half the state commissions comprised of 55 or fewer total employees. Some random examples are: Florida, 87; New Hampshire, 26; Michigan, 101; Wisconsin, 142; Utah, 23; Pennsylvania, 313; New Jersey,

114; Mississippi, 42; and Wyoming, 17.[5]

The annual salary level of the key staff personnel in the state commissions generally is below that for the principal staff members of federal commissions. Many state commissions pay their key staff personnel $8,000 to $10,000 per year (with others paying more and a few less). To the extent that such positions as chief accountant, general counsel, and others are comparable as between the state and federal commissions, it appears that the federal salary level is about one-third higher than that in representative state commissions.[6] The fact that the over-all range of state salaries is relatively wide, and also generally below the federal salary level, doubtless explains Professor Cushman's observation, "The state commissions lose their good men to the federal government and to other states perhaps more often than to private business."[7] In this respect, he also notes that in some cases public utilities have entered into gentlemen's agreements not to raid the staffs of the state commissions. As a final comment on the relative salary levels of the state and federal commission staff members, it should be pointed out that generally different approaches are taken in establishing salary levels in the state and federal governments. In many states there is a basic attitude that the state employees should not be paid more than the amount earned by representative heads of families in the state. On the other hand, the federal government has made considerable effort to be a model employer.

A program to improve the skills of state commission staff members has been organized by the National Association of Railroad and Utilities Commissioners. Since 1959, the Association has operated two-week training courses at the university level for the benefit of state commission staff personnel. In addition, the Association organizes workshops and seminars as part of its annual convention, for the purpose of developing informal discussions of matters too specialized to be considered in the general convention sessions. Finally, it should be recognized that a substantial amount of work has been done, in an effort to resolve general regulatory problems, by the various committees of the Association. The membership of these committees is comprised, at least in part, of state commission staff members. The committee reports are made generally available so that each of the commissions and their staffs may benefit from the detailed studies of the committees.

D. *Financing of Commissions.* The state commissions are financed by funds derived from three sources: (a) legislative appropriations of general tax funds; (b) general assessments upon all utility companies for general regulatory purposes; and (c) special assessments upon particular public utilities involved in specific regulatory actions. A study by the Federal Power Commission indicates that general assessments in many states are the sole or major source of commission financing.[8] However, most states impose statutory limitations upon the amount that may be assessed. In some states this amount is limited to some stated percentage of the valuation of utility property.[9]

Assessing at least some of the costs

5 *Proceedings,* 1959 Convention (Washington, D.C.: National Association of Railroad and Utilities Commissioners, 1960), p. 307.

6 *Ibid.,* pp. 301–308.

7 Robert E. Cushman, *The Independent Regulatory Commission* (New York: Oxford University Press, 1941), p. 497.

8 *State Commission Jurisdiction and Regulation of Electric and Gas Utilities* (Washington, D.C.: Federal Power Commission, 1954), pp. 32–33.

9 *Moody's Public Utility Manual 1960,* pp. a 151–152.

of regulation against utility companies is a long-established practice in the states. In 1882, for example, a South Carolina law provided for assessments upon railroads in an amount sufficient to cover the costs of operating the state railroad commission. This assessment—prorated among railroads on the basis of track mileage in the state—ultimately was upheld.[10] The same practice is seldom used in the federal commissions.

A principal reason for the assessment of regulatory expenses against utilities is found in the conventional legislative problem of raising adequate tax funds with the least public resistance. In charging the utilities with at least some of the costs of regulation, the state legislature is able to avoid making those governmental costs a part of the general tax burden directly. A second reason for such assessments is to give the regulatory commission some degree of freedom from dependence upon legislative appropriations. That is, where the commission may assess some or all of the costs of regulation against the utility companies, it can undertake regulatory action that might not be possible if it were entirely dependent upon legislative appropriations. It may be noted that certain of the special assessments that are levied have little to do with regulation directly. In some states it has been found efficient to collect certain highway-use taxes from motor carriers through the state regulatory commissions, because they have jurisdiction over motor carrier-operating authority. The revenue thus produced is all or largely devoted to the state highway program rather than to regulation.

State commission expenditures have increased through time, reflecting in no small part the effects of inflation and an increased attention to utility regulation. A general indication of the expenditure trend may be suggested by the following annual totals for the state commissions on a combined basis.[11]

1920	$ 4,387,435
1929	$ 7,201,947
1947	$15,408,433
1958	$41,969,357

E. ***Statutory Provisions Affecting Rate Changes.*** The statutory provisions governing rate changes differ somewhat from state to state, but in general they have similar characteristics. First, the state laws governing changes in rates almost always provide for a specified waiting period between: (a) the filing of a notice of, or application for, a change in rate, and (b) the proposed effective date of that rate change. In most states this period is 30 days, although in one state it is 60 days, and in a few others it is less than 30 days. Some states have no provision of this kind.[12]

After a rate-change application is filed, the commissions in many of the states have available two alternative courses of action: (1) the commission may examine the data filed in support of the proposed rate change, conclude that the proposed change is justified, and permit it to go into effect; or, (2) suspend the proposed rate change, which is to defer its becoming effective for a stated period of time. If the commission orders a suspension, then the suspension period may provide time for the staff of the commission to make an investigation and for the commission to hold a hearing on the proposed rate change and

10 *Charlotte, Col. and Aug. Ry.* v. *Gibbes*, 142 U.S. 386 (1892).

11 For 1920, William E. Mosher and Finla G. Crawford, *Public Utility Regulation* (New York: Harper & Row, 1933), p. 70; for 1929 and 1947, Eli W. Clemens, *Economics and Public Utilities* (New York: Appleton-Century-Crofts, Inc., 1950), p. 413; for 1958, *Proceedings,* 1958 Annual Convention (Washington, D.C.: National Association of Railroad and Utilities Commissioners, 1959), pp. 305–306.

12 American Gas Association, "Report of Rate Committee, 1956–1957," Table V, p. 28.

to reach a decision. If a decision is not reached during the suspension period, various procedures may be followed, as discussed shortly. The suspension power is available to most but not all state commissions; however, the duration of the suspension period varies from state to state. Further, many state laws provide for an additional suspension period if the commission has begun to hold hearings. The total specified suspension periods vary from 60 days to one year, depending on the state law, but in a few states there is no time limit. In some states, where there is a specified total suspension period, the commission and the utility company may arrange for still further suspension by agreement, if a decision has not been reached.

At the expiration of the suspension period in a number of states, if there has been no decision, the proposed new rates may be made effective "under bond." That is, the new rates may be charged and collected subject to the refunding or repayment of amounts later found to be unjustified. In other states, if there has been no decision by the end of the suspension period, the commission must allow the proposed new rates to become effective. Certainly some, and perhaps many, utilities decline to exercise their rights under this feature of their state laws. In still other states, if the case is not decided by the end of the suspension period, the commission has the alternative of either allowing the proposed rates to become effective or promulgating other rates.[13]

F. *Processing Time of Rate Cases.* The amount of time required to process a public utility rate case can be a factor of substantial economic significance. This is particularly true during a period marked by both an inflationary tendency and generally vigorous plant expansion, such as that experienced during the period following 1940. When these conditions prevail, they exercise a rather continuous downward pressure upon the rate of return actually earned by many public utilities. This presents two closely similar and related problems: (1) "attrition," or the erosion of the rate of return authorized to be earned, because of rising trends of costs experienced through a period of time; and (2) "regulatory lag," or the loss in revenue experienced by a utility when it earns an inadequate rate of return during the time period between the filing of a rate increase application and the date of an order granting rate relief.

In the case of attrition, the state public utility commissions in some cases have made forward adjustments intended to offset anticipated cost increases. Some of the measures that have been adopted for this purpose are: (a) allowance of an additional increment in the rate of return authorized; (b) adoption of a year-end rate base rather than an average test-year rate base; and (c) approval of rate-schedule provisions (for electric and gas distribution utilities) which permit automatic rate increases to reflect actual increases in such items as the cost of fuel or purchased gas and, sometimes, taxes and wages. An example of an adjustment to rate of return to offset an expected declining trend of future earnings may be noted in a California commission case. There, the commission concluded that a 6.5 per cent rate of return was fair and reasonable at the time the case was decided; however, owing to the anticipation that there would be a declining tendency in the rate-of-return percentage actually earned, the commission approved a 6.9 per cent rate of return.[14]

The second problem, regulatory lag, arises from the loss in revenues experienced by a utility, whose rates are in need of upward adjustment, during the

---

[13] *Ibid.*

[14] *Re Pacific Lighting Gas Supply Co.,* 18 PUR 3d 128 (1957).

period between filing an application for a rate increase and the date when rate relief is granted. The longer the period of time required to process the rate-increase application, the greater the revenue loss arising from the regulatory lag. Accordingly, the time required to process a rate case assumes economic significance.

A comprehensive study of the time required to process rate cases decided by the state commissions in a six-year period provides some uniquely helpful information. This study, by a committee of the American Gas Association, covered a total of 193 gas, electric, and telephone cases decided by the state commissions during the period 1948 to 1953 inclusive.[15] An effort was made to include all reported cases in the study.

First, with respect to the time elapsing between the filing dates of rate increases and the first hearing dates: (a) 109 of the 193 cases, or 56 per cent, had first hearing dates within 60 days of filing; (b) 146 cases, or 75 per cent, reached hearing within 90 days; (c) 94 per cent had begun hearings within six months; and (d) only one case was not heard within a year. Analysis of the data showed no particular difference in this respect as among different types of utility services or different years in the period studied. Study of these data in conjunction with state laws relating to permissible suspension periods, after which rates could be placed into effect without commission approval, showed that such laws are effective in speeding the processing of rate cases. That is, companies operating in states having statutory provisions permitting rates to go into effect in seven months or less had 82 per cent of their first hearing dates within 90 days after filing. Where state laws either made no provision for putting new rates into effect without commission approval or allowed suspension periods of as long as 11 months, 70 and 74 per cent, respectively, of the cases had their first hearings within 90 days. Thus, hearings tended to be held somewhat more quickly in states where rates may become effective in seven months or less as compared with those states in which there is a longer period before new rates may become effective.

Second, the time between the filing of rate increases and the effective date of final rates was analyzed. Of the 193 cases studied, rate increases were denied in 22 cases after time intervals ranging up to a year or more. Of the 171 increases granted: (a) 17 were processed within 90 days; (b) 62, within six months; and (c) 139, within one year. The data showed that in those states having statutory provisions which permitted rates to be placed into effect after a short suspension period without commission approval, rate relief was granted in a shorter period of time than in states with long suspension periods or no provisions for placing rates into effect without commission approval. This analysis, by states, covered 167 of the 171 rate increases allowed. It showed that, of the 55 cases in states where the maximum suspension period was seven months or less, 51 per cent of the cases resulted in new rates being placed into effect within 180 days. In the remaining 112 cases, arising in states where suspension periods exceeded seven months or where no provision was made for placing rates into effect without commission approval, less than 30 per cent of the cases produced new rates within 180 days. This serves to indicate that accelerated processing of state commission rate cases results much more often when the statutory suspension period is short. However, among other variables meriting consideration here are the differences among commissions in size of staff, workload, and the disposition of the commissioners to decide cases promptly

---

[15] *Op. cit.*, Note 12, p. 10.

or to consider them for longer periods of time. It is likely, but not known, that in some instances commissions would have decided cases relatively quickly regardless of the duration of the statutory suspension period. Nevertheless, the study whose results are referred to above must be credited with a most useful contribution.

G. Compensating for Regulatory Lag. A plan for compensating a utility for the revenues lost owing to a regulatory lag was developed in 1949 by the Board of Public Utility Commissioners of the province of Alberta, Canada, and it has been applied in subsequent cases.[16] The Alberta procedure, in short, compensates the utility for the revenues lost owing to regulatory lag by: (a) adding to the rate base the amount of revenue loss; and (b) amortizing that amount over a relatively short period of time. The policy of the Board has been stated with clarity:

> A criticism directed against rate making is the lag which occurs between an application for revision of utility rates and the announcement of the new rates. If an increase is warranted and if put into effect only at the time of decision, then the utility suffers a loss due to the lag between the two dates. To avoid loss, the Board has decided that any deficiency of earning (transitional loss) should be computed and added to the rate base to be written off over a period of years.[17]

In the decision initiating this policy, the Alberta Board considered these facts: (a) the application to increase rates was filed on September 15, 1948; (b) the company was authorized to charge higher rates on an "interim" basis on July 1, 1949; and (c) the final rate order, authorizing rates substantially the same as the interim rates, was issued in December of 1949. Thus, the revenue loss meriting compensation was that occurring in the period September 1948 to July 1949. First, it was determined that 18,015,458 Mcf of gas had been sold by the utility during that period. Second, the Board calculated that the company had lost revenues equal to the difference between the average rate charged during the period (20.89¢/Mcf) and the average rate that should have been charged, as ultimately determined (22.96¢/Mcf). Third, the difference between the two average rates, 2.07¢/Mcf, was multiplied by the sales volume during the revenue-lag period to determine that the loss in revenues amounted to $372,920. Fourth, this amount was added to the rate base and the utility was authorized to write it off over a five-and-one-half-year period. The rate schedules filed by the utility were allowed to reflect this authorization.

The Alberta method has not been adopted by commissions in the United States, although in one instance the District of Columbia commission allowed a utility a 6.25 per cent rate of return, instead of the 6.1 per cent it considered adequate, in consideration of the revenue loss due to regulatory lag, the expectation that costs would continue to rise, value of service, and other intangible factors.[18] In this respect it may be noted that the impact and seriousness of attrition and regulatory lag, in large part, are determined by how rapidly inflation progresses during a given period of time. Rapid inflation has been relatively rare, at least by comparison with either the familiar gradual inflation or price stability, and the most serious inequities arise only during fairly rapid inflation.

---

[16] *Ibid.*, p. 21; *Re Canadian Western Natural Gas Co., Ltd.*, not reported (1949); *Re Northwestern Utilities Limited,* 95 PUR (NS) 201 (1952).

[17] 95 PUR (NS) 201, 202.

[18] *Re Chesapeake and Potomac Telephone Co.*, 6 PUR 3d 222 (1954).

2. FEDERAL POWER COMMISSION

Through the years, the range of authority exercised by the Federal Power Commission has grown continuously, so that it has become one of the most important regulatory agencies in the federal government. In one sense, it is misnamed, for in light of its jurisdiction and work load it might be called with greater accuracy the "Federal Natural Gas Commission." On the other hand, if the term "power" is taken literally rather than in the sense of electric power, the name is highly appropriate, for few agencies of government exceed it in power.

A. *History and Development.* The original Federal Power Commission was created in 1920 to administer the Federal Water Power Act of that year. The Commission at that time consisted of the Secretaries of War, Agriculture, and Interior and was responsible for the licensing of hydroelectric projects on navigable waters or government lands. The purpose of the Act was to encourage the development and effective utilization of our water power resources. The cabinet members who comprised the original Commission were not able to give adequate time to its affairs; moreover, the Commission was dependent upon "borrowed" staff members from other agencies. On the whole, a more effective form of organization appeared to be required. Accordingly, President Hoover in 1929 recommended to the Congress that the Commission be reorganized and administered by five full-time Commissioners with the assistance of its own technical staff.

This was done in 1930, when the present Commission was created as a five-member, quasi-judicial, independent regulatory agency. The members are appointed by the President, with the advice and consent of the Senate. No more than three members of the Commission may belong to the same political party. The term of office is five years. At present, the Chairman is designated by the President.

At the same time that President Hoover recommended to Congress that it reorganize the Commission, he also proposed the enactment of legislation for federal regulatory control of the charges for electricity moving in interstate commerce, since the state commissions had no jurisdiction to regulate such transactions. This recommendation, which was ultimately enacted into law in the Federal Power Act of 1935, followed from the Supreme Court's 1927 decision in the *Attleboro* case, which held that a state commission could not regulate the wholesale rate of electricity sold at a state line to a utility in an adjoining state for the purpose of resale to consumers.[19] The Court held, in effect, that this transaction involved interstate commerce and was therefore beyond state jurisdiction. Thus, the *Attleboro* decision pointed up the existence of a "regulatory gap"—an area in which the states could not regulate and in which the federal government had not undertaken regulation.

The Federal Power Act of 1935: (a) revised and extended the Commission's authority over hydroelectric power generation facilities; and (b) vested in the Commission a comprehensive authority to regulate the rates and services of the electric utility industry with respect to both wholesale sales in interstate commerce for resale to the public and interstate transmission of electricity. In its regulation of the interstate electric power industry, the Commission has authority over: (a) the disposition, merger, or consolidation of facilities and the acquisition of the securities of another public utility; (b) the issuance of securities; (c) the exportation of electric

[19] *PUC of R.I.* v. *Attleboro Steam and Elec. Co.*, 273 U.S. 83 (1927).

energy to a foreign country; (d) the rates, charges, and services of the companies under its jurisdiction; (e) accounting and depreciation practices; and (f) the holding of certain interlocking positions in different companies.

In 1938 Congress passed the Natural Gas Act, and thereby conferred substantial regulatory authority upon the Commission with respect to interstate transmission and sales for resale by the natural gas pipeline industry. This Act is closely similar in scope and authority to the Federal Power Act as it relates to the interstate electric utility industry. The Natural Gas Act was in part a consequence of a 1924 Supreme Court decision which held that a state could not regulate the rates charged for natural gas produced in one state and transported across a state line for sale at wholesale to local gas distributing companies.[20]

The Natural Gas Act and the Federal Power Act, insofar as the latter relates to electric utilities, differ from one another in only a few respects: (1) The Commission has no authority to review or approve the issuance of securities under the Natural Gas Act, whereas it has substantial but not unlimited authority to regulate the issuance of securities by jurisdictional electric utilities. (2) The Natural Gas Act gives the Commission authority over: (a) the construction and extension of facilities for the interstate transportation and sale of natural gas, for which a certificate of public convenience and necessity is a prerequisite; and (b) the abandonment of interstate facilities or service, for which Commission approval also is necessary. Neither of these powers exists under the Federal Power Act; however, jurisdictional electric utilities may not dispose of facilities of a value exceeding $50,000 without securing authority from the Commission. (3) Section 5(b) of the Natural Gas Act authorizes the Commission to determine the cost of production or transportation of natural gas in cases where the Commission has no rate jurisdiction—a provision enacted at the insistence of the Ohio cities which administer local-franchise regulation of gas distribution utilities among others. There is no exactly similar provision in the Federal Power Act. (4) The Federal Power Act gives the Commission authority over consolidations and the acquisition of the securities of another public utility. The Natural Gas Act in this respect covers acquisitions of facilities.

In 1954 the Supreme Court decided in the momentous *Phillips Petroleum Co.* case that under the Natural Gas Act the Commission had jurisdiction over the sales of natural gas made by independent producers to interstate pipeline companies.[21] The Commission had held previously that these sales were not covered by the Natural Gas Act. As a result of this decision, thousands of oil companies and individual oil operators —which are the principal producers of natural gas—were brought under Commission jurisdiction insofar as their sales to interstate natural gas pipelines are concerned.

The Commission also has several other important responsibilities: (1) Under the Flood Control and River and Harbor Acts, beginning with 1938, the Commission is charged with the responsibility of making recommendations to the Secretary of the Army with regard to the installation of penstocks or similar facilities adapted to the possible future power use in flood control and navigation projects to be constructed by the Army Corps of Engineers. (2) The statutes establishing certain federal multipurpose hydroelectric projects provide

[20] *Missouri* v. *Kansas Natural Gas Co.,* 265 U.S. 298 (1924).

[21] *Phillips Petroleum Co.* v. *State of Wisconsin,* 347 U.S. 672 (1954).

that the rate schedules covering their sales of surplus electric power must be confirmed and approved by the Commission before they may become effective. These projects include those constructed under the Bonneville Project Act, the Fort Peck Project Act, the Flood Control Act of 1944, and the Eklutna Project Act. (3) Under Executive Order No. 10485, issued in 1953, the Commission is authorized to issue permits for the construction, operation, maintenance, or connection of facilities at the borders of the United States for the exportation or importation of electric energy or natural gas from or to the United States. (4) An expert employee of the Commission participates in the work of the International Joint Commission, which supervises problems relating to the waters which cross the international boundary with Canada.

Table 13.2 shows the size of the industries under Commission jurisdiction, as of 1959, in terms of the number of companies, plant investment, and operating revenues.

During fiscal year 1959, the Commission staff averaged 792 employees. Approximately one-half of the Commission's employees and budget (totaling $6,806,603) were required for its regulation of the natural gas industry; about 20 per cent was required for the regulation of non-federal hydroelectric projects; and about 15 per cent, for regulation of the interstate electric power industry. Other activities required substantially lesser amounts.[22]

The economic and regulatory policies of the Federal Power Commission are the subject of discussion at numerous points in this book. However, special attention is given to its policies with respect to electric utilities, natural gas pipelines, and natural gas producers in Chapters 12, 14, and 15. The remainder of this section is concerned with the Commission's activities in the hydroelectric power area of its jurisdiction.

B. *Hydroelectric Power Regulation.*

[22] Special Subcommittee on Legislative Oversight, House Committee on Interstate and Foreign Commerce, *Independent Regulatory Commissions,* Subcommittee Print, 86th Cong. 2d sess., 1960 (Washington, D.C.: Government Printing Office, 1960), p. 75.

Table 13.2

Federal Power Commission
Size of Regulated Industries
1959

	Electric	Natural Gas	
		Pipelines	*Producers*
Total companies	183	96	18,807[1]
Plant investment[4]	$31,932	$11,032	NA[2]
Operating revenues[4]	$ 6,988	$ 4,054	$891[3]

[1] Total number of individuals or companies included in rate schedules filed with Commission.

[2] Not available as such because much of the investment is in the nature of a joint cost, in that both gas and petroleum liquids may result from that part of the investment which is productive.

[3] 1958 data; revenues from sales to interstate pipeline companies.

[4] Millions of dollars.

Source: Special Subcommittee on Legislative Oversight of the House Committee on Interstate and Foreign Commerce, *Independent Regulatory Commissions,* Subcommittee Print, 86th Congress, 2d Session, 1960, p. 76.

The Federal Water Power Act of 1920, as amended in 1935, comprises Part I of the Federal Power Act. It empowers the Commission to issue licenses for the construction and operation of water-power facilities on jurisdictional waters. The following discussion presents a brief historical survey of the development of water-power regulation and a summary of the Commission's authority and activities in this area of its jurisdiction.

(1) *Development of Regulation.* In the early days of the republic, the interest of the government in river development was directed primarily toward the needs of navigation. Beginning in 1884, Congress passed numerous acts authorizing the construction of individual hydroelectric power dams.[23] Some thirty such acts were passed between 1884 and 1906. Where power projects were on the public domain, the Secretary of the Interior was authorized to issue permits for the use of public lands for the generation or distribution of electric power.

These early acts, referred to above, often differed from one another in their terms and provisions. They differed particularly in the term or time period over which the right to operate the dam would endure. That is, some were perpetual, while others had a specified term; of the latter, relatively few provided for the disposition of the property at the expiration of the term. In addition, there was an element of uncertainty in such grants of authority, because they could be altered or repealed at any time without recourse by the grantee or liability of the government.

The General Dam Act of 1906 established conditions governing the authorization of power projects on navigable waters of the United States. It provided that plans for hydroelectric developments on navigable waters would require not only Congressional authorization but also the approval of the Chief of Army Engineers and the Secretary of War, who could impose special conditions in the interest of navigation. In 1910 an amendment was added which limited authorizations to 50 years.

Taken together, these laws did not provide a generally satisfactory system, as evidenced by the fact that only about 1,000,000 kilowatts had been developed under federal authorization prior to the Federal Water Power Act of 1920. One reason for the relatively slow development of these resources was that the uncertainty engendered by the early acts did not encourage investment of capital. This condition was alleviated by the Act of 1920, which established uniform rules for the orderly development of hydroelectric resources. More important, perhaps, is the fact that the licenses issued under it, authorizing the development of hydroelectric sites, are contracts which make clear and enforceable the rights of the licensees.

Immediately after the passage of the Act of 1920, there was a substantial increase in the number of applications for licenses. During the first three years of the administration of the Act of 1920, twice as much generating capacity was built or being built under licenses than had been installed under permits from various departments during the preceding 20 years. By the end of 1958, the total hydro capacity in operation in the United States was 30.1 million kilowatts, of which 13.7 million were in federal plants and 16.4 million in non-federal plants (privately owned, state, and local). Of the non-federal capacity, 9.9 million kilowatts were under license. By the end of 1960, 267 major licenses were outstanding, covering the operation of 12.7 million kilowatts; 6.5 mil-

[23] An important source relied upon is an address entitled "Licensing Requirements and Procedures Under the Federal Power Act," presented by Francis L. Adams, Chief, Bureau of Power, Federal Power Commission, at the American Power Conference annual meeting of April 1, 1959, in Chicago.

lion kilowatts were being constructed under licenses and 4.6 million kilowatts were involved in planned future units already licensed. In addition, capacity totaling 9.8 million kilowatts was involved in pending applications for licenses.[24]

(2) *Commission Authority.* The Commission is authorized to grant licenses for the construction and operation of non-federal hydroelectric power[25] facilities: (a) on the navigable waters of the United States and the waters in the public lands, reservations, and Territories of the United States; or (b) in any of the streams or other bodies of water over which Congress has jurisdiction under its authority to regulate interstate and foreign commerce; or (c) for the purpose of using the surplus water or water power from any government dam. The Constitutional basis for this authority is the Commerce Clause, which delegates to Congress an unlimited power to regulate interstate and foreign commerce.

Licenses are issued for a definite period but not in excess of 50 years. As a general rule, licenses are issued for the full 50-year term. Upon the expiration of a license: (a) the government may take over the property (this does not apply to any projects owned by state or local governments, except the St. Lawrence project of New York State); or (b) a new license may be issued to the original licensee; or (c) a new licensee may be permitted to take over the property. In the event that the property is taken over, the original licensee must be paid his net investment in the property, but not more than its fair value, plus reasonable severance damages. Net investment includes the actual original cost, plus the cost of additions and betterments, less the cost of property retired, accrued depreciation, and a portion of excess project earnings (see below). The right is also reserved to the United States or any state or municipality to take over a licensed project at any time by condemnation upon the payment of just compensation. A system of accounts is provided for, which was intended to aid the Commission in a determination of the actual legitimate cost of licensed projects.

The Commission has only a limited authority to regulate the rates, services, and securities of licensees. If the states in which the power is sold do not regulate the rates, services, and securities of a licensee, or if the states are unable to agree, the Federal Commission may undertake such regulation until the state governments proceed to do so. The licensees are required to pay annual charges to the United States to cover the costs of administering the water-power provisions of the Act and to compensate the government for the use, if any, of its lands or other property. The Act also provides that licensees shall make payments to the United States "for the expropriation to the government of excessive profits."[26] The latter provision is intended to apply only when the states have not undertaken regulation and during the first 20 years of a license. The Commission has assumed that it cannot expropriate where the states have regulatory agencies; such agencies exist in practically all states in which there is water power.

After the first 20 years of operation, the licensee must establish an amortization reserve for the accumulation of excess project earnings, that is, the earn-

[24] FPC Release No. 11,415, April 10, 1961.

[25] The Commission's former General Counsel, Willard W. Gatchell, has written that ". . . there is no express limitation of the licensing authority to hydroelectric plants as distinguished from steam-electric plants." However, the Commission has construed its licensing authority to be limited to water power facilities. 14 *George Washington L. R.* 42, 44 (1945).

[26] Federal Power Act, 49 Stat. 838, Section 10 (e).

ings which exceed the rate of return on net investment as specified in the license. This reserve, in the discretion of the Commission, is to be held until the termination of the license or to be applied from time to time in reduction of the net investment. The amortization reserve existing when the license expires serves to reduce the sum payable by the United States if it chooses to take over the project. As a general policy, the Commission has specified a six per cent annual rate of return as reasonable for this purpose. The Commission also has provided that one-half of any excess earnings above six per cent are to be transferred to the amortization reserve. If, after the first 20 years, there is a deficiency in project earnings below six per cent, the deficiency is deducted from any future excess earnings until the deficiency has been recovered.[27]

This provision for an amortization reserve, unlike the provision for the expropriation of excess earnings referred to above, is not contingent upon the absence of state rate regulation. Accordingly, it is possible that the Commission could prevent a licensee from earning the full amount of the return authorized by a state commission where the latter exceeds the amount specified in the license.

(3) *Licensing Provisions.* The Commission is authorized to license a project that is found to be the best adapted to a comprehensive plan for improving or developing a waterway for the benefit of interstate or foreign commerce, for the improvement and utilization of water-power resources, and for other beneficial public uses, including recreation. In this respect, the Commission considers: (a) the development of the water resources of a river basin as a whole; and (b) the realization of the multiple benefits which may be available at each site. To this end, the staff of the Commission investigates and collects data concerning developed and undeveloped water resources on a general and river-basin basis, and makes surveys and studies, including power-market surveys, of the requirements for comprehensive development of river-basin water resources for hydroelectric power and other purposes.

In order to qualify for a license, a project does not necessarily have to include all units of a comprehensive plan. However, such units as are included in the license application must fit into such a plan. In cases where equally well-adapted plans are submitted to the Commission by public (state or municipal) and private applicants, the law requires that "preference" be given to the public applicant. Whenever the Commission decides that the development of any water resources should be undertaken by the United States itself, the Commission is required to submit detailed recommendations to Congress and to refrain from approving any project that would affect the recommended development.

A licensee whose facilities provide benefits (for example, water storage and regulation of stream flow) to downstream non-federal projects receives an annual compensation therefor. A licensee receiving benefits from the project facilities of another licensee or the United States must pay compensation therefor. The amount of the annual payments is determined by the Commission and is based upon a proportion of the annual charges for interest, maintenance, and depreciation on the project facilities providing the benefits.

The Act declares it unlawful for any non-federal entity to construct or operate a power project on government lands or on waters under the jurisdiction of Congress except under the terms of: (1) a valid federal permit issued before

[27] *Terms and Conditions of License,* 16 FPC 1121 (1953).

1920; or (2) a license issued by the Commission. Accordingly, the law requires that a "declaration of intention" be filed with the FPC for *any* project proposed for construction on waters *other than* those defined as navigable and over which Congress has jurisdiction. If upon investigation the Commission should find that the interests of interstate or foreign commerce would be affected by the proposed construction, those facilities may not be constructed until a license is obtained from the Commission. If the Commission finds that the above interests would not be affected, and if no public lands or reservations are affected, construction may proceed upon compliance with state laws. From 1920 to mid-1958, 211 declarations of intention were filed. Of these, 76 projects were held to require a license.

When a non-federal entity wants to develop a water-power site on jurisdictional waters but has not formulated project plans to the extent required for the issuance of a license, an application may be filed for a preliminary permit. The purpose of procuring a preliminary permit is to establish and hold a priority for a future license application as against possible competitors. The maximum period for a preliminary permit is three years. During its term, the holder thereof presumably will prepare the necessary material to support an application for a license.

An applicant for a license must file with the Commission the maps, plans, specifications, cost estimates, and financing information which may be required for a full understanding of the proposed project, as well as evidence of compliance with state laws and whatever other information may be requested. If the application is not contested, there will be no need of a hearing, and a license may be obtained in a relatively short time. However, if the application is contested, a formal hearing will be necessary, and the ultimate decision can require quite some time. In addition to the standard or "major" licenses of the kind discussed above, the Commission also issues "minor part" licenses, which cover a minor part of a completed project or very small new projects. In the case of a minor part license, the Commission may waive its exacting requirements applicable to major licenses.

In the process of issuing licenses, the Commission notifies the federal, state, and local governmental departments whose interests may be affected. The statute provides that no license affecting the navigable waters of the United States may be issued until the plans of the proposed dam or other structures have been approved by the Secretary of the Army and the Chief of Engineers.

(4) *Definition of a Navigable Stream.* Under the Federal Water Power Act of 1920, the Commission was authorized to issue licenses for water-power facilities on "navigable waters" of the United States. Hence, the question of the navigability of a stream was basic to a determination of whether the Commission had jurisdiction over a particular power facility. However, the Federal Power Act of 1935 amended and broadened the Commission's licensing authority to include water-power facilities located on "streams or other bodies of water over which Congress has jurisdiction" under the Commerce Clause of the Constitution. Accordingly, navigability is not the sole test of Commission jurisdiction; an equally important test is whether particular facilities affect the interests of interstate or foreign commerce. If either of these standards is found to be applicable to particular water-power facilities, the jurisdiction of the Commission is established.

The definition of navigable waters of the United States is very broad. This results from both statutory language and judicial interpretation. The Act defines as navigable waters those parts of streams and other bodies of water: (a) which come under the Congressional authority to regulate commerce; (b) which in their natural or improved condition—notwithstanding interruptions between the navigable parts by falls, rapids, the need to portage, and so forth—are suitable for use in interstate and foreign commerce; or (c) which have been authorized by Congress for improvement or which have been recommended to Congress for improvement after investigation under its authority.

The *Appalachian Electric Power Co.* case, decided by the Supreme Court in 1940, is the leading judicial ruling on the question of navigability.[28] There, the company planned to construct a dam, without a license from the Commission, on the New River in Virginia. The United States sought to block this project, claiming that the New River is a navigable water of the United States and that the Commission had properly found that the interests of commerce would be affected by the proposed construction. The Court ruled only on the question of navigability.

The New River was navigated by only a few ferry boats after the coming of railroads. It ultimately flows into the Kanawha, which is clearly navigable. The Government had spent small amounts on river improvements.

Attorneys for 41 of the then 48 states filed briefs opposing federal jurisdiction.

The Supreme Court found that the Commission had jurisdiction on the ground that the river is navigable. It held, among other things, that the absence of commercial navigation did not prevent a finding of navigability, and that, in determining the navigable character of a river, it is proper to consider its possibility for interstate commerce after reasonable improvements. Further, it was held that navigability may be established by the past floating of logs or by use of boats of various sizes, and that use by personal or private boats demonstrates the availability of the stream for the simpler types of commercial navigation.

(5) *Illustrative Case.* An illustration of basic Commission policies in this area is provided by the *Citizens Utilities Co.* case,[29] which involved a question of Commission jurisdiction as tested by the criteria of: (a) navigability; or (b) affecting the interests of interstate or foreign commerce.

This case arose when Citizens proceeded to construct a dam on the Clyde River, at a point near Newport, Vermont. Citizens then was operating two other dams on the Clyde and two at the outlets of streams emptying into it. The construction of the new dam had been authorized by the State. No federal permits or licenses had been procured for any of these facilities.

The Clyde River flows for some 28 miles in northeastern Vermont, from the vicinity of Island Pond and Spectacle Pond through some other ponds and into Lake Memphremagog, which lies partly in Canada. The lake ultimately connects with the St. Lawrence River and the Atlantic Ocean. Atlantic salmon spawn in the last mile of the Clyde. Throughout the entire length of the Clyde, but particularly in the upper half, there are fallen trees, sand bars, and debris which constitute impediments to navigation. In much of the lower half of the Clyde, the stream bed is quite rocky and is strewn with huge boulders which show above the surface of the water.

The Commission, upon learning of the construction of the new dam on the Clyde, required Citizens to file a declara-

---

[28] *U.S.* v. *Appalachian Electric Power Co.*, 311 U.S. 377 (1940).

[29] *Re Citizens Utilities Company*, 27 PUR 3d 183 (1959).

tion of intention and instituted an investigation to determine whether the company was required to apply for a license. Thereafter, the Commission ruled that the Clyde is a "navigable water of the United States," and that the operation of the company's facilities (by impounding and releasing water) affected the interests of interstate or foreign commerce. Accordingly, the company was ordered to apply for a license covering all of its hydroelectric facilities. In the proceedings before the Commission, the company was supported by the State and the Vermont State Water Conservation Board; it was opposed by the staff of the Commission and certain fish and game clubs and wildlife conservation groups.

The evidence upon which the Commission's finding of navigability rested included these elements: (a) motor boats, rowboats, and canoes have been used on the river for fishing, hunting, and trapping; (b) logs were floated on the river as late as 1918, and the lumber therefrom was marketed in southern New England; (c) colonial settlers as well as Indians transporting captives used the river for travel to and from Canada and the English settlements to the south; and (d) in 1825 Congress received, but never acted upon, a recommendation for improvements on the Clyde.

The Commission concluded that the river is suitable for the simpler forms of navigation; that pleasure boating could be continued into Canada; that it could be improved for light-draft navigation by removal of fallen trees and debris and by providing portaging facilities; and that, should the need develop, Congress could improve the river for deeper-draft navigation according to the 1825 survey.

Second, insofar as Citizens' facilties affected the interests of interstate or foreign commerce, the Commission held that the operation of those facilities affected the navigable capacity of the lower Clyde, interfered with boating, and caused damage to fish at their spawning grounds owing to insufficient water during the times when the company was impounding it for future use. Accordingly, it was held necessary to require Citizens to apply for a license for all of its hydroelectric facilities so that relief could be afforded to the recreational and commercial interests involved in boating and fishing. The Commission was upheld upon appeal. There, it was ruled that the last mile of the Clyde is navigable and that company dams affected downstream navigable capacity. The Court found it unnecessary to rule on the question of how much of the Clyde is navigable.[30]

The effect of federal jurisdiction over Citizens' hydroelectric facilities may be judged in terms of the statutory requirements summarized previously. For example, it would appear necessary for a determination to be made of the original cost of Citizens' facilities, some of which were about 40 years old at the time of the decision.

In conclusion, it is necessary to point out that numerous licenses, issued under the Act of 1920, will expire beginning in 1970. In 1970 alone there will be 27 expirations. At that time the Commission will begin a new phase in its regulation of licensed projects. If the federal government does not choose to exercise its right to take over properties covered by expired licenses, then the state and municipal governments will be in a position to submit license applications to the FPC along with the present licensees and any other interested person. As noted previously, state and municipal applicants are accorded "preference" by law, if their plans are equally as well adapted to proper river development as

[30] *Citizens Utilities Company* v. *FPC*, 297 F 2d. 1; 34 PUR 3d 481 (1960).

those of other applicants. The prospect is that efforts by a governmental unit, at any level, to gain control of presently licensed facilities would precipitate a renewed private-versus-public power controversy.

3. FEDERAL COMMUNICATIONS COMMISSION

The Communications Act of 1934 created the Federal Communications Commission. It is composed of seven members. The term of office is seven years. Appointments to the Commission are made by the President with the advice and consent of the Senate. Not more than four Commissioners may be members of the same political party. The President designates one of the Commissioners as Chairman. As of June 30, 1959, the Commission had 1,190 staff members engaged in its regular work and 91 engaged in reimbursable work for other agencies.

The Commission's Common Carrier Bureau is directly concerned with the public utility regulation of communications "common carriers." The Bureau in 1959 accounted for only about 11 per cent of the Commission's work load as measured in man-years. This serves to emphasize that, for the most part, the work of the Commission lies outside the area of public utility regulation. By far the major part of its total regulatory effort is directed toward the radio and television broadcasting industry, which exemplifies the regulation of business affected with a public interest rather than public utility regulation. This is explained further below.

The Commission was established for the purpose of coordinating through one agency the various programs for the regulation of communications, which before 1934 had been located in a number of different governmental agencies. The Communications Act placed under the authority of the Commission: (a) the regulation of broadcasting, formerly under the Federal Radio Commission; (b) the jurisdiction over telegraph and telephone rates, formerly vested in the Interstate Commerce Commission; (c) the jurisdiction over government telegraph rates, which had been under the Post Office Department; and (d) some powers of the Department of State with respect to the Cable Landing License Act of 1921. In addition, the 1934 Act conferred increased authority upon the Commission with respect to the rate regulation of the interstate and international message communications carriers.

Within the area of public utility regulation, the Commission regulates the rates and services of interstate and international communications common carriers by telephone and telegraph, whether by wire, cable, or radio. (The term "radio" in this sense does not refer to radio broadcasting stations; rather it is used in the sense of "wireless," or radiotelegraph, communications wherein radio waves are substituted for wire or cable as a means of message transmission.) The Act specifically declares that broadcasting stations are not common carriers. Hence, the Commission does not have authority to regulate the prices charged by broadcasters for the use of air time, nor can it regulate their profits. In brief, a communications common carrier under the Act is one whose service is open to public hire for the purpose of handling written or vocal "correspondence." Communication which is purely intrastate in character is not, in general, subject to Commission jurisdiction. In one important sense, every domestic telephone company that has an interstate toll-line connection operates in interstate commerce. However, the Act recognizes two types of carriers: (a) those subject to the Act; and (b) "connecting carriers."

The latter do not operate facilities crossing state or national boundaries but engage in interstate or foreign communication solely through physical connection with other non-affiliated carriers. They are exempted from certain principal provisions of the Act, which apply to fully subject carriers.

Under its primary public utility-regulatory authority, the Commission regulates rates for: (a) interstate telephone and telegraph services; (b) communication service between the United States and foreign points, including communication by ocean cable and radiotelegraph carriers; and (c) communication service between the United States and ships at sea. At the same time, the Commission reviews the adequacy and quality of these services.

The common-carrier communication industries under Commission jurisdiction are shown in Table 13.3 in terms of the number of companies in each industry, their net investment, and their operating revenues in 1959.

Federal regulation of interstate electrical communication may be said to date from passage of the Post Roads Act in 1866. This legislation was intended to foster the construction of telegraph lines by granting, among other things, rights-of-way over public lands. In 1888 the Congress vested in the Interstate Commerce Commission limited regulatory authority over telegraph companies to which the United States had granted subsidies. Under this authority the Commission could require the companies to interconnect their lines where required by the public interest.

Federal regulation of the rates and practices of interstate and international communications carriers by telephone, telegraph, and cable was vested in the Interstate Commerce Commission (ICC) by the Mann-Elkins Act of 1910. This authority did not apply to message transmission "wholly within one state"; the jurisdiction over intrastate commerce, of course, rests with the state governments. At the time the Mann-Elkins Act was passed, most of the telephone service and about 25 per cent of the telegraph traffic was intrastate and beyond federal jurisdiction. The Mann-Elkins Act gave the ICC authority to maintain the communication rates under its jurisdiction at a just and reasonable level. Further, the ICC was authorized to eliminate discriminatory or unduly preferential rates, to undertake property valuations, to prescribe uniform systems of accounts and to require the filing of

Table 13.3

Federal Communications Commission

Regulated Common Carrier Industries

1959

Carrier Industry	*Companies*	*Net Plant ($000)*	*Total Operating Revenues ($000)*
Telephone[1]	53	$18,453,004	$7,798,579
Telegraph, domestic	1	222,834	260,849
Telegraph, international:			
Radiotelegraph	6	34,916	47,778
Ocean cable	3	38,962	36,599

[1] Telephone carriers whose annual operating revenues exceed $250,000.

Source: Federal Communications Commission, *Annual Report for Fiscal 1960,* pp. 111–113.

reports concerning matters within its jurisdiction. The Mann-Elkins Act did not require the communication carriers to file their tariffs with the ICC, nor did it give the Commission authority to suspend changes in rates pending an investigation to determine their reasonableness.

During the 24 years that the ICC exercised this authority, it established uniform systems of accounts, undertook valuation studies, and required monthly and annual reports of financial and operating statistics. Among other rate matters, the ICC brought about interstate telephone rate reductions in 1926, 1927, 1929, and 1930. It also exercised authority over telephone consolidations under the Willis-Graham Act.

The ICC was not a vigorous regulator in the communications field. Writers in this field almost always charge it with neglect of its responsibility to regulate the communication companies. Yet, there is ample reason to question this judgment, for an absence of vigorous regulation cannot be deemed an administrative sin unless it can be shown that vigorous regulation was required at that stage of the industry's development. The exhaustive investigation of the telephone industry, initiated in 1935 by the Communications Commission, demonstrated that the Bell System had discharged most creditably its responsibilities to serve. Above all, the financial and accounting practices of the Bell System were found to be entirely exemplary. It merits noting that, although the telephone investigation was conducted during a period marked by a general hostility toward business, no legislation followed from that investigation.

The Communications Act of 1934 conferred greater regulatory authority upon the Communications Commission than had been vested in the ICC. Section 1 of the Act provides for the regulation of:

> . . . interstate and foreign commerce in communication by wire and radio so as to make available, so far as possible to all the people of the United States a rapid, efficient, nationwide, and worldwide wire and radio communication service with adequate facilities at reasonable charges, for the purpose of national defense, for the purpose of promoting safety of life and property through the use of wire and radio communication. . . .

Among the statutory provisions of the Act is the requirement that every common carrier of communications furnish service at reasonable charges upon reasonable request. No carrier may construct or acquire interstate or foreign facilities without Commission approval. Likewise, it cannot discontinue or curtail interstate or foreign service without Commission approval. All charges, practices, classifications, and regulations in connection with interstate and foreign communication service must be just and reasonable. To implement this requirement, the common carriers concerned are required to file tariff schedules of rates, which are subject to review and regulation by the Commission. These schedules are open to public inspection in the carriers' offices and at the Commission's Washington office.

To aid its regulation of rates and services, the Commission prescribes the forms of records and accounts kept by the carriers. Under this authority, it has established uniform systems of accounts for them to follow. Commission regulation in this respect includes the establishment and maintenance of original cost accounting, continuing property records, pension cost records, and depreciation records.

Carriers file monthly and annual reports with the Commission, giving specified financial and operating information; they also file copies of contracts with other carriers relating to traffic subject to the Act. It is unlawful for any person to hold office in more than one carrier unless specifically authorized by the Commission. The applications of domestic telephone and telegraph carriers for authority to merge or to consolidate are ruled upon by the Commission. After obtaining the approval of the Secretary of State, the Commission can issue, withhold, or revoke licenses to land or operate submarine cables in the United States.

The regulation of broadcasting falls into two principal phases. The first phase deals with the allocation of spectrum space to the different types of broadcast services. The second phase is concerned with individual broadcasting stations and involves: consideration of applications to build and to operate; the assignment of specific frequencies, powers, time of operation, and call letters; the periodic inspection of equipment and the engineering aspects of operation; passing upon transfers and assignments of broadcasting facilities and changes in existing authorizations; modifying and renewing construction permits and licenses; reviewing the general service of each station to determine whether it has been operating in the public interest; and licensing radio operators.

4. SECURITIES AND EXCHANGE COMMISSION

The Securities and Exchange Commission was organized in 1934 as an independent bipartisan quasi-judicial agency. It is composed of five members, not more than three of whom may be members of the same political party. The members of the Commission are appointed for five-year terms by the President with the advice and consent of the Senate; the Chairman is designated by the President. The technical staff of the Commission averaged over 900 employees in 1959.

The Commission administers the Securities Act of 1933, the Securities Exchange Act of 1934, the Public Utility Holding Company Act of 1935, the Trust Indenture Act of 1939, the Investment Company Act of 1940, and the Investment Advisers Act of 1940. In addition, the Commission is assigned certain functions under Chapter X of the Bankruptcy Act, the Internal Revenue Code of 1954, the Bretton Woods Agreement Act, and the Inter-American Development Bank Act.

The functions of the Commission relating to public utility financial regulation and holding company regulation are discussed in Chapters 19 and 20. However, it may be noted here that, although the Commission in the past has had a substantial work load under the Public Utility Holding Company Act, its work in this area has diminished continuously as it has succeeded in accomplishing the objective of that Act. In short, the Public Utility Holding Company Act provides for the regulation of electric and gas holding company systems so as: (a) to limit system operations to physically integrated and co-ordinated properties; (b) to simplify complex corporate and capital structures and eliminate any unfair distribution of voting power; and (c) to require that the issuance and sale of securities by holding companies and their subsidiaries (unless exempt as an issue authorized by the state of incorporation of the issuer) shall be reasonably adapted to the security structure and earning power of the issuer and necessary to the efficient operation of the issuer's business; further, the consideration received and fees paid shall be fair and the terms and conditions of the sale shall not be detrimental to investors, consumers, and the public.

As of June 15, 1938, the 53 public utility holding company systems registered with the Commission comprised 137 holding companies and 1,483 operating companies. They accounted for over 80 per cent of the electric utility, gas utility, and gas pipeline assets in the United States. As the Commission proceeded to administer the corporate integration and simplification provisions of Section 11(b) of the Act, the number of registered holding company systems declined. By June 30, 1959, the number of registered holding company systems had been reduced to 18, which comprised 19 holding companies and 141 active operating companies. These companies accounted for less than 20 per cent of the assets of the entire electric utility, gas utility, and gas pipeline industries in the United States. As the number of companies subject to direct regulation under the Holding Company Act declined, the average annual personnel employment of the Commission assigned to this work also declined—from an annual maximum of over 234 man-years to 26.6 man-years in 1959.[31]

5. APPRAISALS OF REGULATORY AGENCIES

Dean James M. Landis, who has served on two federal regulatory commissions as member and chairman, respectively, has commented that the ultimate test of administration is "in the policy that it formulates."[32] This applies particularly to the state and federal regulatory commissions, for the policies they formulate in administering broadly worded regulatory statutes affect the budgets of millions of consumers and the earnings and value of billions of dollars in assets. With this in mind, an effort has been made throughout this book to identify the key areas of regulatory policy making and to analyze the relevant considerations which bear upon the policies formulated.

The purpose of this section is to survey some of the appraisals that have been made of the institution of commission regulation. Any over-all appraisal of the regulatory agencies, to be useful, must concern itself with their policies or the effects of those policies. This is a most formidable task, for it is much more feasible to analyze commission policy in individual areas—say, the rate-of-return effects of the normalization of federal income taxes—than it is to present a broad overview of the institution of commission regulation as a whole. However, efforts have been made to develop broad-scope appraisals of the institution of commission regulation which merit recognition, for their collective impact upon public opinion and legislative bodies has been substantial.

Professor Harry M. Trebing, an economist, has examined commission regulation with some emphasis upon comparative prices and productivity over a half-century for both regulated and nonregulated industries.[33] He concluded, as a result of this study of the effects of regulatory policy, that the long-run record of the regulated industries has been "more than creditable." That is, he found that generally during the period 1899–1953, the prices charged by the regulated industries increased less than those of the mining and manufacturing industries, while the productivity of the regulated industries, over-all, increased at a more rapid rate. He noted the performance of the electric utility industry as particularly outstanding—a 38 per

[31] *Op. cit.,* Note 22, pp. 148–149.

[32] James M. Landis, *The Administrative Process* (New Haven: Yale University Press, 1938), p. 39. See also James M. Landis, *Report on Regulatory Agencies to the President-Elect,* December, 1960, subsequently issued as a Committee Print of the Senate Committee on the Judiciary, 86th Cong., 2d sess., 1960 (Washington, D.C.: Government Printing Office, 1960).

[33] Harry M. Trebing, "What's Wrong with Commission Regulation?" 65 *Public Utilities Fortnightly* 660, 738 (1960).

cent decrease in average prices over the period and a 1664 per cent increase in aggregate productivity per unit of total input. He further concluded that there is no conclusive argument or evidence which would prove that the concept of commission regulation is unworkable.

A decidedly negative appraisal of the federal regulatory commissions has been made by a number of political scientists. Their criticism is not based upon analysis of commission policies in the administration of their statutory responsibilities.[34] Rather, it is based primarily upon the ground that the federal commissions are "independent," that is, outside any department of the Executive branch and not subject to direction by the President. In this respect, the political scientists appear to have overlooked the exercise of authority by the Bureau of the Budget (a part of the Executive branch) over the federal commissions' legislative recommendations and, more important, over their proposed budgets. Agency budgets are translatable in terms of administrative and regulatory programs. Thus, the Bureau of the Budget has substantial authority with respect to the scale and composition of agency operations.

The characteristic of "independence" is seen by the political scientists to be the cause of a host of undesirable results. Among these are included: (1) occupation of important fields of administration beyond the reach of presidential direction, which tends to diminish his constitutional power to see that laws are enforced; (2) insulation of the agency from political forces expressing the will of the people; and (3) agreement with the desires of the regulated industries.

The writings of the political scientists in this area indicate a preoccupation with the Interstate Commerce Commission (but not, for example, with the negligible rate of return earned by the railroad industry), and a tendency to generalize from the particular, using the ICC as a point of departure.[35] Through the years there has been a rather unified position taken in Congress to the effect that the federal commissions are arms of the the Legislative branch, wherein additional direct participation by the Executive branch would be unwelcome.

Louis L. Jaffe, a noted professor of law and a critic of some aspects of the federal commissions, states in an article entitled "The Independent Agency—A New Scapegoat" that the political scientists have attributed to commission "independence" a variety of ills for which it is not responsible.[36] He considers the critics' "greatest weakness" to be a failure to recognize that commissions are required to operate in many important areas under a total lack of meaningful statutory policy, and suggests that the critics' real quarrel is with Congress.

Professor Marver H. Bernstein, perhaps the leading political scientist in the study of the federal regulatory commissions, has concluded that they have failed to fulfill the requirements of effective regulation.[37] In his book, *Regulating Business by Independent Commission,* he was able to reach this conclusion without reference to a single substantive decision of any federal regulatory commission. If Dean Landis is correct in stating that the ultimate

34 An apparent exception is Emmette S. Redford, *National Regulatory Commissions: Need for a New Look* (College Park, Md.: Bureau of Government Research, 1959).

35 Marver H. Bernstein, *Regulating Business by Independent Commission* (Princeton, N.J.: Princeton University Press, 1955); David B. Truman, *The Governmental Process* (New York: Alfred A. Knopf, Inc., 1951), pp. 416–421; Leonard D. White, *Introduction to the Study of Public Administration* (New York: The Macmillan Company, 1948), pp. 103–107.

36 65 *Yale Law Journ.* 1068 (1956).

37 *Op. cit.,* Note 35.

test of administration is in the policy that it formulates, then Professor Bernstein's analysis would appear to be insufficient, for it is unconcerned with the policies formulated by the commissions in the day-to-day administration of their principal statutory responsibilities.

Professor Bernstein's conclusion is based upon some of the following grounds. (1) Commissions tend to rely upon the "presumed" expertness of their staffs, instead of political leadership and popular support for effective regulation. (2) They have not succeeded in building the political support necessary to achieve the enactment of legislation on controversial public policy questions. (3) Their independence from control by the President is a barrier to the integration of their economic policies with those of the government as a whole. (4) The commissions, by their insulation from popular political forces, have subjected themselves to undue influence by the regulated industries, while tending to become "protective spokesmen" for those industries. (5) Attention to the search for the public interest is diminished to the extent that the commissions adopt judicialized procedures.[38]

The evidence upon which Professor Bernstein's position rests consists mainly of quoted statements by other political scientists and secondary sources. For example, a principal basis for his assertions with respect to regulated industries controlling the regulatory commissions appears to be a single sentence quoted from a report by a subcommittee of the Senate Committee on Labor and Public Welfare.[39] All this is hardly convincing —which is not to deny that there is room for improvement in the institution of commission regulation. However, it is difficult to reconcile these assertions of regulatory ineffectiveness with the realities of regulatory policy.

The principal Congressional inquiry into the operation of the federal regulatory commissions was that conducted by the Special Subcommittee on Legislative Oversight of the House Committee on Interstate and Foreign Commerce. Under the leadership of Chairman Oren Harris of Arkansas, the Subcommittee conducted a thorough inquiry during the period 1957–1960.[40] A major cause of this inquiry was the charge—later verified—of "improper influence and off-the-record communications" in the awarding of television station operating licenses by the Communications Commission.[41] Although a truly bad situation was brought out on the record with respect to these television matters, it would be erroneous to draw a generalization from this that would encompass accurately the federal regulatory commissions as a group. The Subcommittee, for example, inquired into alleged improper off-the-record communications in a Federal Power Commission case, and concluded that the matter in question was sanctioned by the Administrative Procedure Act.[42] Insofar as the public utility regulatory activities of the federal commissions were concerned, the final report of the Subcommittee dealt specifically and at length only with the Federal Power Commission.

In the section of its final report dealing with that Commission, the Subcommittee advanced suggestions intended to be applicable to all the federal commissions having jurisdiction over licenses

38 *Ibid.*, pp. 118, 180, 284–297.

39 *Ibid.*, pp. 93–94. The Committee Print referred to related to S. Con. Res. 21, 82nd Cong., 1st sess., to establish a commission on ethics in the Federal Government; the full Committee substituted and approved S. J. Res. 107, which died on the Senate calendar.

40 Special Subcommittee on Legislative Oversight of the Committee on Interstate and Foreign Commerce, *Independent Regulatory Commissions,* House Report No. 2238, 86th Cong., 2d sess., 1961 (Washington, D.C.: Government Printing Office, 1961).

41 *Ibid.*, p. 7.

42 *Ibid.*, p. 24.

and rates. Most important of these were the recommendations on the subject of off-the-record communications with commissioners, sometimes referred to as "ex parte communications." (The term *ex parte* means "in the interest of one side only.") Not all such communications are unlawful or improper. However, the Subcommittee found a need to establish further ground rules and to solve a particularly vexing problem that had been complained of during its hearings with respect to the Federal Power Commission.

That problem arises from the fact that members of the staff of the Commission, who represent positions taken on the record in the formal hearings on adjudicative matters, also are in constant contact with the Commissioners and thus are in a unique position to advance their own views. On the one hand, this is an obvious "Achilles' Heel" in the regulatory process of any commission where it occurs. On the other hand, the members of commissions clearly are in need of technical assistance from their staffs. With respect to such "off-the-record" communications, the Chairman of the Federal Power Commission testified: "There is no doubt about it, we do that and we have to do it, due to the technical nature of our work."[43]

The Subcommittee recommended a practical solution to this problem. First, it proposed the creation of a panel of technical experts to work for commission members exclusively. Second, it recommended amending the Administrative Procedure Act "so as to prohibit any staff member other than one of the technical panel from communicating with any Commissioner concerning an assigned case pending decision after oral argument. The same prohibition should apply as between staff members and members of the Commissioners' technical panel." Third, members of regulated industries would be barred from communicating with individual Commissioners or panel members concerning any case pending decision. The Subcommittee concluded: "It would seem that a great deal of the regulated industry's complaint would be blunted by an absolute prohibition against extra-record communications by those members of the staff who, unlike the technical panel members, actually participated in the hearings."[44]

Another matter complained of in hearings before the Subcommittee relates to the policy of the FPC staff, when presenting evidence on certain subjects in Commission proceedings, of declining either to take a position or to make a recommendation while on the witness stand. The practice of the FPC staff in these instances is to defer taking a position until it files its brief—some time after the hearing record has been closed. This tactic permits an FPC witness to present (in exhibit form) a collection of basic data without indicating how the data may be used or the conclusions that may be derived from it. Since the staff's brief first reveals the position taken, it is impossible to test the validity of that position on cross-examination or to present meaningful rebuttal evidence. Complaints by regulated industries, alleging that these tactics deprive them of the opportunity of knowing and meeting the opposition case, were duly noted in the published report of the Subcommittee's staff. However, no recommendation was made on this matter in the Subcommittee's final report.

After the election of President Kennedy in 1960, he asked Dean Landis

---

43 Staff Report to the Special Subcommittee on Legislative Oversight of the House Committee on Interstate and Foreign Commerce, *Independent Regulatory Commissions,* Subcommittee Print, 1960 (Washington, D.C.: Government Printing Office, 1960), p. 86.

44 *Op. cit.,* Note 40, p. 25.

(referred to previously) to prepare a report on the operations of the federal regulatory commissions.[45] The Landis Report, as it is called, set forth a number of suggestions for improving the organization and procedures of certain of the commissions. The purpose of these recommendations was to overcome the problem of administrative delay in the disposition of cases pending decision. One recommendation, subsequently enacted in 1961, called for restoring to the President the power to propose to Congress plans for agency reorganization, which plans would become law unless vetoed by Congress within a stated time period. The Landis Report also recommended that reorganization plans be submitted to Congress providing for the delegation of all decision making to panels of Commission members, single Commission members, hearing examiners, or boards of employees—subject to discretionary review by the entire Commission on petition by a party in interest. This general format had been developed previously by the Interstate Commerce Commission, where it has been regarded as successful. In this respect, it may be noted that the problem of administrative delay, or regulatory lag, is not confined to the commissions. This problem also is found in the courts. For example, the Attorney General of the United States, in testifying before the House Judiciary Committee on the need for additional federal judgeships, stated that as of January, 1961, the federal courts had a backlog of 71,992 undecided cases, and that recent legislation had created more litigation.[46]

The Landis Report found in the federal regulatory commissions a serious lack of policy formulation, both intra-agency and inter-agency. "Policy formulation" was defined as "planning measures as how best to dispose of pending problems or how best to forecast and explore solutions to problems still on the horizon."[47] It was pointed out that the commissions can formulate policy by methods other than the formal decision-making process in contested cases; rule-making proceedings and studies in depth were suggested as alternative routes to policy formulation which experience had shown to be practical. Dean Landis observed that, when policy making is undertaken through the decision-making process, issues arise less as the result of deliberate planning and more as the result of "incidence or accidence of cases or controversies." The Report made clear that the general failure to use methods of policy formulation other than the decision-making process is due primarily to the pressure of workload on the adjudicatory side. One of the major objectives of Dean Landis' recommendation with respect to the delegation of decision making was to increase the amount of time available to Commissioners for policy formulation.

In conclusion, as a final view of the institution of commission regulation, it appears fair to say that it has proved to be workable but nevertheless offers room for improvement. In this respect, the legislative bodies which created these agencies stand in the best position to assist. The salary levels of commissioners and staff merit reconsideration from the standpoint of balancing responsibility with compensation. Only in this way can the commissions attract their share of the more able people entering public service and hold them once they have become productive. Second, Congressional reappraisal of the basic federal regulatory statutes would appear to be timely

[45] *Op. cit.*, Note 32.

[46] *The Washington Post*, March 2, 1961, sec. A, p. 20.

[47] *Op. cit.*, Note 32, p. 22.

for the purposes of: (a) determining whether those statutes are still entirely appropriate in light of the changes that have occurred in the regulated industries; and (b) clarifying the policy mandates of these basic statutes so as to provide additional guidance.

At the commission level, improved coordination between the federal and state commissions sharing jurisdiction over the same industries would appear to be useful. This applies perhaps most importantly where the natural gas industry is concerned. The efforts of the NARUC in telephone industry matters provide an example of useful coordination by the commissions concerned with different aspects of the same problem. This example may serve as a basis for coordinating regulatory problems affecting other industries. The commissions might also take steps to reduce further (since some progress already has been made) the administrative burdens upon commissioners, so that more time may be available for policy formulation by routes other than formal case decisions. Some commissions may find it worthwhile to re-examine their internal procedures to clarify the status of their technical staff members to assure that personnel involved in the prosecution of cases are also quite separate from the decision-making function. This is by no means a complete summary, but is intended only to suggest some of the important areas in which improvement can be made as the institution of commission regulation continues its evolution.

6. THE ATOMIC ENERGY COMMISSION

This section is concerned with the regulatory functions of the Atomic Energy Commission, which are primarily directed toward protecting the public health and safety from the hazards associated with nuclear materials and nuclear facilities. Essentially, the AEC regulatory process involves licensing the construction and operation of nuclear facilities and the use of nuclear materials which, in the judgment of the Commission, will provide adequate protection to the health and safety of the public.

The AEC was created by the Atomic Energy Act of 1946, and its operations began in 1947. The Commission consists of five members, appointed by the President and confirmed by the Senate. The term of office is five years. The Chairman of the AEC is designated by the President.

A. *Introduction to Atomic Energy Program.* The United States has multiple national objectives in the atomic energy field, including maintenance of the common defense and security, development of the peaceful uses of atomic energy, and protection of the public health and safety. Congress has placed primary governmental responsibility for the achievement of these objectives in one agency, the AEC.

The Commission discharges functions in three major areas: (1) In its "operational" functions, the Commission procures raw materials, produces fissionable materials, manufactures nuclear weapons, and performs research and development. (2) In its "promotional" functions, the Commission develops—through research and assistance—the peaceful uses of atomic energy, particularly nuclear reactors and radioisotopes. (3) In its "regulatory" functions, the Commission acts to assure the safe possession and use of nuclear facilities and materials and to protect the public from potential radiation and related hazards.

The regulatory jurisdiction of the AEC and its promotional activities are closely related to the development of the Commission's civilian nuclear power program. In short, this relationship arises because compliance with AEC licensing requirements is a prerequisite to the acquisition of nuclear materials and the construction and operation of nuclear power reactors.

The AEC civilian nuclear power program is directed toward technological development which will enable electricity to be produced from nuclear fuels on an economic basis. As such, this program ultimately may have a significant and beneficial effect upon the quantity and cost of the future energy supply in the United States and in friendly nations. The civilian nuclear power program is being developed under two general types of arrangements: (a) cooperative projects involving the AEC, electric utilities, and equipment manufacturers; and (b) privately financed projects in which the AEC does not provide direct assistance. In this respect, it may be noted that public policy in the development of power reactors provides for principal participation by private business, whereas in other countries the national governments have chosen to undertake such development themselves.

The objectives of the civilian nuclear power program were stated by the Commission in 1958: (1) to reduce the cost of nuclear electric power to levels competitive with power from fossil fuels in high energy-cost areas of this country by 1968; (2) to assist friendly nations having high energy costs to achieve competitive levels by about 1963; (3) to support a continuing long-range program to further reduce the cost of nuclear power in order to increase the economic benefits and to extend these benefits to wider areas; (4) to maintain for the United States a position of leadership in the technology of nuclear power for civilian use; and (5) to develop reactors to make full use of the nuclear energy latent in both uranium and thorium, in that uranium 235 alone may not be sufficiently plentiful to meet our needs over the long range.[48]

At the end of 1960 the electrical nuclear power capacity of the United States was 365,000 kilowatts, a net increase of 290,000 kilowatts over the previous year. In June of 1960 the privately financed Dresden Nuclear Power Station of the Commonwealth Edison Company attained full-power operation, sending 180,000 kilowatts over transmission lines into Chicago and northern Illinois. This is considered adequate capacity to serve a city of 200,000 population. Of the 54 civilian reactor projects under design or construction at June 30, 1960, a total of 23 were power prototypes and experiments. All domestic reactor projects as of that date, including military reactors, totaled 66 in all, which were estimated to cost $1.3 billion. Of this amount, it was estimated that the AEC would incur costs of $172 million and that privately owned public utilities, among other participants, would contribute $502 million.[49] A further discussion of the civilian nuclear power program, together with a survey of the economics of nuclear power, will be presented in Chapter 21, in connection with an analysis of the future prospects of technology and each of the principal energy sources.

B. *Regulatory Program.* Although the Atomic Energy Act of 1946 created the AEC, its principal regulatory powers over civilian atomic energy activity derive from substantial amendments to the basic Act in 1954. Prior to 1954, the AEC was authorized to license the use of nuclear materials. The 1954 amendments permitted and encouraged private industry to participate in the construction, ownership, and operation of nuclear reactors but at the same time required

[48] Atomic Energy Commission, *Major Activities in The Atomic Energy Programs, 1960* (Washington, D.C.: Government Printing Office, 1961), p. 20.

[49] *Ibid.*, pp. 13–22.

the Commission to regulate these reactors to protect the health and safety of the public. The 1954 amendments continued the pre-existing responsibilities of the Commission to license the use of nuclear materials. In 1957 the Atomic Energy Act was further amended so as to require a public hearing on applications for construction of major facilities such as power or test reactors. The 1957 amendments also established the Advisory Committee on Reactor Safeguards (ACRS) as a statutory committee and required a public report by the ACRS on all applications for licenses subject to the public hearing requirement.

The Atomic Energy Act of 1954, as amended, provides in Section 2, that: (a) the processing and utilization of nuclear materials affect interstate and foreign commerce and must be regulated in the national interest and in order to protect the health and safety of the public; (b) production and utilization facilities are affected with the public interest and therefore must be regulated to assure the common defense and security and to protect the public health and safety; and (c) the necessity for protection against interstate damage places the operation of production and utilization facilities in interstate commerce.

As presently constituted, the AEC regulatory program is a three-part system which involves: (1) establishing radiation-protection standards; (2) licensing facilities and materials; and (3) inspection and enforcement.

The first part, establishment of radiation-protection standards, recognizes that an increase in total radiation exposure is one of the inevitable consequences of developing atomic energy. These standards therefore prescribe the maximum permissible radiation doses and concentrations of radioactivity to which employees in radiation industries and the general public may be exposed. In the past these standards have been based upon the recommendation of the National Committee on Radiation Protection and Measurement, a semi-private scientific organization. More recently, AEC standards have taken into account the "guides" prescribed by the Federal Radiation Council, established in 1959 as a governmental policy and coordinating body.

As a second part of the process, the AEC licenses nuclear facilities and materials and individual operators of reactors. It is unlawful to possess or to use nuclear materials, as defined in the Act, or to construct and operate nuclear facilities without a license from the AEC. The licensing process will be discussed shortly. However, at this point a somewhat unique aspect of AEC licensing adjudication should be noted. This is the "separated staff." A "separated staff" is established within the Commission for each case that goes to a public hearing, which consists of the Division of Licensing and Regulation, the Division of Compliance, the attorneys for those two divisions, and such other portions of the AEC staff as may be required to assist in the presentation of the staff's position at the hearing. The effect of the separation is to prevent the "separated staff" from discussing the case, except on the record, with the hearing examiner or Commission. In this respect, it will be recalled from the previous section that the Legislative Oversight Subcommittee: (1) heard complaints regarding *ex parte* contacts between the staff and Commissioners elsewhere; and (2) recommended a separate technical staff for the prosecution of cases and another to give needed technical assistance to the Commissioners. In the case of the AEC, the situation is the very opposite of that complained of to the Oversight Subcommittee. The separation of the AEC Staff from the Commission in formal cases appears to be complete, to the extent of leaving the Commissioners without technical assistance in making their decisions. The Congressional Joint Committee on Atomic Energy has stated: "The Commissioners, in reviewing decisions (by hearing examiners), are not assisted by persons having training or experience in reactor safety matters and their regulations preclude them from consulting experts in the Division of Licensing and Regulation who, for purposes of the case, are isolated in the 'separated staff.' "[50]

The third part of the AEC regulatory process consists of periodic inspection of each licensee's activities to assure compliance with the terms of the license, the statute, and regulations. Failure of a licensee to comply may result in modification, suspension, or revocation of the license or criminal prosecution.

Although the AEC clearly has substantial regulatory authority, it is not generally considered to be a regulatory agency as such; for example, it was not included among the "Big Six" federal regulatory agencies studied by the Legislative Oversight Subcommittee referred to in the previous section. In part, this is explained by the fact that the AEC regulatory program is relatively new (but growing) and comprises but a small part of total AEC activity. For example, of the total AEC operating and construction expenditures of $2.66 billion in fiscal 1961, only about $2.5 million (or less than one-tenth of one per cent) was devoted to the regulatory program. The Commissioners have estimated that they individually spend from one-sixth to one-third of their time on regulatory matters.[51] Then, too, the AEC regulatory process is unique in some important respects. The AEC, in the typical case involving the licensing of a power or test reactor, is not called upon to adjudicate between competing interests, public or private, but rather to reach a judgment as to the safety of a proposed activity. This judgment, because of the abstruse scientific data involved, cannot normally be made on the basis of demonstrable facts alone, but instead must rest upon a complex combination of fact, new scientific and technical theories, and the application of policy considerations. Finally, the AEC operations are closely supervised by the Congressional Joint Committee on Atomic Energy, whereas the principal federal regulatory agencies are essentially independent of similar supervision.

The number of regulatory proceedings processed by the AEC is relatively small. The number of active power-reactor cases, for example, increased from none in 1955 to six by the end of 1958, and 13 by the end of 1960. Three private test reactors were under construction or in operation at the end of 1960. The number of research reactor-construction permittees and licensees increased from six in 1955 to 41 by the end of 1958 and to 61 by the end of 1960. In the materials-licensing field, the regulatory work load has increased similarly.

Although the number of research reactors is larger, the power and test reactors present greater potential hazards and require more thorough safety review and AEC staff effort. The task of regulating large power and test reactors is also complicated by the fact that novel technological problems are usually posed by each new reactor, and that a typical reactor costs from $20 million to $100 million and takes several years to design and build. Further, the number of AEC licenses is not large when compared with those of some of the other federal agencies. However, because of the magnitude of the potential hazard,

[50] Joint Committee on Atomic Energy, *Improving the AEC Regulatory Process,* Volume I, Joint Committee Print, 87 Cong., 1st sess., 1961 (Washington, D.C.: Government Printing Office, 1961), p. 2.

[51] *Ibid.,* pp. 10, 15.

a sizable staff relative to the number of licenses is required for effective review of individual applications.

The AEC regulatory responsibility is not concluded when an operating license is issued for a facility. The licensee may, and during the current developmental period probably will, request authority to make changes in design, fuel loadings, or operating procedures, thereby raising safety questions which require decisions to be made.

It may be noted that the AEC has safety responsibilities for materials and facilities used and owned by federal, state, and local governmental units, as well as by private industry. The AEC must review safety aspects of its own operations and concur on safety standards of Defense Department reactors and weapons. Other federal agencies must obtain AEC licenses for use of the materials and facilities covered by the Act. These agencies include the National Aeronautics and Space Administration (nuclear-propelled rockets and satellites) and the Maritime Administration (nuclear-powered ships). State and local agencies also must obtain AEC licenses.

The AEC regulatory process, in the case of major reactor facilities, involves five "phases." Before reviewing these phases, it is important to point out that the AEC does not issue just one "license" as other agencies ordinarily would. First, the applicant must qualify for a "construction permit"; thereafter, upon completion of construction, it must qualify for an "operating license." The same five-phase regulatory process is required for both the construction permit and the operating license. In addition, the same five-phase procedure may be repeated at interim stages in the licensing process as modifications, amendments, or additional information are brought to the attention of the Commission. Further, the AEC may issue "provisional" construction permits and operating licenses, before issuing "final" permits and licenses, as it proceeds on a cautious step-by-step basis to ascertain the possible health and safety hazards that may be present in an applicant's proposal.

Applications to construct and operate major power or test reactors are reviewed through the following five-phase regulatory process. (AEC procedures for licensing the use of nuclear materials are relatively simplified because of the lesser hazards involved.)

(1) Application Submittal. Initially, the applicant is required to submit a detailed description of the proposed reactor facility and a study of every possible risk in its operation, known as a "hazards summary report."

(2) AEC Staff Review. In this phase the application is evaluated by the Division of Licensing and Regulation, with assistance of other interested divisions, after which a "hazards analysis" memorandum is prepared. If the proposed facility is one for which a public hearing is required, the "hazards analysis" is submitted to the Advisory Committee on Reactor Safeguards (ACRS), referred to previously.

(3) ACRS Review. The ACRS, working with the AEC hazards evaluation staff, will undertake an exhaustive study of the proposed project and submit a written report to the AEC Chairman, which is thereafter made public. Although the ACRS makes recommendations rather than formal decisions, its recommendations—especially if adverse—may well determine the final decision.

(4) Hearing Phase. A formal hearing before an examiner provides the applicant, AEC staff members, and intervening interests, if any, an opportunity to present testimony. The examiner will issue an initial decision.

(5) Final Action. The initial decision becomes final unless one of the parties files an exception; however, if no exception is filed, the Commission as a matter

of policy institutes a review of the initial decision on its own motion. In preparing its final decision and order, the Commission has various assistants, but at present none who are trained or experienced in reactor safety matters. It will be recalled that the Commission is precluded from consulting its experts on reactor safety in the Division of Licensing and Regulation, since they are isolated in the "separated staff." It merits noting, however, that Commission membership has included distinguished scientists. Thereafter, if the application is approved, the license is issued for a stated period but not longer than 40 years.

Before a reactor can be licensed for operation, it is necessary for the Commission to find: (1) that it will be operated in conformity with the basic standards for protection against radiation; and (2) that the health and safety of the public will not be endangered.[52] However, while findings to the above effect are required before reactor operation can be licensed, experience in reactor technology is too limited to enable comparable findings to be made at early stages in the development of a reactor project. Accordingly, the AEC makes a less exacting safety determination when it issues a construction permit. Thus, the AEC will issue a construction permit when "satisfied that it has information sufficient to provide reasonable assurance that a facility of the general type proposed can be constructed and operated at the proposed location without undue risk to the health and safety of the public and that omitted information will be supplied."[53]

The standards and requirements with respect to construction permits were at issue in the first contested licensing proceeding decided by the AEC under the 1954 Act. This case ultimately was taken to the Supreme Court, which upheld the Commission in its use of different standards for the issuance of permits and licenses, respectively, as described above. The issue and judgment are summarized in the following section.

C. Power Reactor Development Company Case. The AEC issued a provisional construction permit to the Power Reactor Development Company (PRDC) and established a procedure for periodic reports and continuing review of safety characteristics. The exceptions of several intervening labor unions were considered and rejected. The Commission made clear that the applicant would be required to pass a more severe test when the reactor was completed and before an operating license would be issued. PRDC then commenced construction of a 100,000-electrical-kilowatt developmental power reactor at a site in Michigan, near both Detroit and Toledo.

The interveners had contended that the AEC, in granting the provisional construction permit, was required to make the same definitive findings as to safety and hazards that would be required if it were to issue an operating license. Principally on this issue, the case ultimately reached the Supreme Court and produced the first basic test of the scope of AEC regulatory power under the 1954 Act.

In 1961 a divided Court upheld the AEC action as a proper exercise of authority under terms of the governing statute and its legislative history.[54]

This decision established: (1) that the AEC, when issuing a construction permit, is not required to make the same definitive finding of safety of operation that it would have to make before issu-

[52] 10 CFR, Sec. 50.40 (a) (1959).

[53] 10 CFR, Sec. 50.53 (1959).

[54] *Power Reactor Development Company and United States, et al.* v. *International Union of Electrical, Radio and Machine Workers, AFL-CIO, et al.* (Nos. 315 and 454—October Term, 1960). Decided June 12, 1961.

ing a license to operate; and (2) that the issuance of a construction permit does not at the same time commit the AEC to grant an operating license.

As a result of this decision, the AEC was able to continue the stage-by-stage review and processing of applications to construct and operate major reactor facilities, employing less exacting requirements in the early construction stages than in the later operating stages. (The AEC issues provisional operating licenses at successively higher operating levels, approaching full power.) If the Supreme Court had taken an opposite position, then it would have been most difficult for the AEC to continue its civilian reactor-development program under the existing statute. Reactor technology and experience, in this early phase of their development, would likely be found too limited in many cases to enable the same exacting findings to be made in the construction stages that can be made after the years of effort required to approach an operational stage. Further, this decision gave full notice to the public utility and industrial developers of nuclear power projects that an investment in construction may amount to nothing if a project fails to satisfy the requirements for an operating license. The Commission and the Congressional Joint Committee on Atomic Energy, which closely supervises AEC actions, are entirely aware of the disastrous consequences of error. There is every reason to believe that the regulatory powers sanctioned by the Supreme Court will be utilized with utmost caution.

PART IV

THE EMERGING NATURAL GAS INDUSTRY AND THE ENERGY ECONOMY

14 Natural Gas Pipeline Development and Regulation

One of the most significant developments in the public utility field during the postwar years has been the expansion of the natural gas pipeline network to practically all parts of the United States. This development has permitted a tremendous increase in the use of natural gas throughout the non-producing areas of the country and has brought with it new problems to the utility industry and those who regulate it.

The three chapters that follow take up three aspects of the natural gas industry. The matter of pipeline rates was covered in Chapter 10. The present chapter explores the growth and development of the entire natural gas industry with primary emphasis on the pipeline industry and its regulation. Chapter 15 analyzes the development of natural gas-producer regulation and some of the problems that have been encountered. Chapter 16 surveys the supply of and demand for energy and fuels, competition among fuels, and their future prospects.

1. THE GROWTH OF RESERVES AND PRODUCTION OF NATURAL GAS

Although natural gas is a service at the consumer's burner tip, it is a commodity when it is drilled for, produced, and sold to pipelines. It is a commodity with several unique characteristics, some of which cause economic and regulatory problems, as discussed presently. One characteristic of natural gas is that it is an exhaustible or "wasting" resource of relatively limited supply (relative to current demand at going prices), but one whose supply is constantly being replenished by discoveries of new reserves. Such new reserves come from marginal prospects, deeper formations, and relatively inaccessible locations, such as the tidelands of the Continental Shelf, the bayous of Louisiana, and the Rocky Mountain area of Wyoming. Historically, this scarcity situation has not always been present. The story of the evolution from surplus to scarcity is basic to understanding many of the problems the gas industry faces today.

A. Oil and Gas—Joint Products from One Industry. Broadly speaking, there is a single industry, the petroleum industry, which explores for, drills for, and produces oil and natural gas. Some companies operate in all stages of the oil industry, that is, from exploration through product marketing, but rarely does a company operate in all stages of the gas industry.[1] In general, the trans-

[1] An example of a gas company which does operate in all phases is the Hope Natural Gas Company. It explores and drills for gas, gath-

portation and distribution of natural gas are performed by separate industries.

A petroleum company ordinarily produces both oil and gas, as well as the light liquid hydrocarbons. This is true because oil and gas are found in the same types of geologic structures and are, in fact, of the same chemical hydrocarbon family. Thus, the two products frequently occur together in nature and may be produced from the same well. Some gas will be found with oil in virtually all cases; however, gas in some instances is found alone. At one point in history, oil companies drilled for oil, and the discovery of gas without oil was considered to be only slightly better than a dry hole. Today, oil companies seem to search for "hydrocarbons" rather than primarily for oil. As gas prices have risen, drilling for gas alone, to the extent that this is possible, has become a relatively more attractive prospect than before.

Some oil companies produce, gather, and process natural gas to remove the heavier, liquid components[2] and then sell the residue gas (methane and ethane) to transmission companies or industrial users. In other instances, oil companies sell the gas at the wellhead or in the field, and the transmission company gathers and processes it. Rarely does an oil company transport gas by pipeline and sell it for resale in interstate commerce. Insofar as gas is concerned, petroleum companies are called "independent producers," because they are unaffiliated with pipeline transportation. Thus, while the oil industry searches for and produces oil and gas jointly, once the two products are separated, another entirely different industry takes up the job of transporting the gas to ultimate consumers. This is the gas transmission or pipeline industry.

B. *Natural Gas Reserves and Production.* The basis for any industry producing an exhaustible resource is the quantity of reserves available. In many industries which process exhaustible resources, the total domestic recoverable reserves are known because they lie on or relatively close to the surface of the earth. Thus, we know generally, for example, how much iron ore we have of various qualities. It is unlikely that very much will be added to the known total in the future.[3] Natural gas reserves are quite different, however. Each year a significant portion of new reserves is discovered in the United States. In 1938, proved recoverable gas reserves in the United States were estimated to be about 70.0 trillion cubic feet.[4] During the period from 1938 through 1960, some 165 trillion cubic feet of gas were produced, or more than twice as much gas as was known to exist in 1938. Yet, at the end of 1960, proved recoverable reserves in the United States were estimated at 264 trillion cubic feet.[5] In every single year since statistics began to be kept, additions to reserves have exceeded production of natural gas. On the other hand, the number of years' supply in terms of current rates of production has dropped sharply.

Table 14.1 indicates the reserves, production, and disposition of gas during

---

ers gas and processes it in natural gasoline or cycling plants, transmits it in long-distance lines, sells some gas at wholesale to retailing companies, and itself retails gas to residential, commercial, and industrial consumers in some areas.

[2] "Liquefied petroleum gases," or LPG's, include butane and propane primarily, with small quantities of heavier liquids.

[3] Technology will undoubtedly find ways to produce reserves of ore which lie at considerable depths. This is unlikely to occur in the near future unless major breakthroughs occur in mining technology.

[4] American Gas Association, *Historical Statistics of the Gas Industry* (New York: 1956), Table 7, p. 21. Estimate by Mr. Lyon F. Terry, Chase National Bank.

[5] *World Oil,* April, 1960, p. 121, from the American Gas Association; see Table 14.1.

the postwar years. While reserves and production in recent years have been concentrated more and more in the Southwest, consumption of gas has become more and more dispersed geographically. The states of Texas, Louisiana, Oklahoma, Kansas, and New Mexico accounted for 89.3 per cent of the gas reserves and 87.2 per cent of the net production of gas during 1960.

C. Consumption of Gas. Consumption of natural gas occurred in every state except Vermont, Maine, and Hawaii during 1960, and significant quantities were used in states quite distant from major gas-producing areas. Those regions which were the heaviest net consumers were the Middle Atlantic, East North Central, West North Central, and Pacific regions. The greatest consuming area, as would be expected, was the major producing region. Large quantities of gas are used in the field to furnish power for drilling and pumping units. Also, oil refineries and many power-oriented manufacturing industries are located in this region, and virtually all electricity is generated by gas. The five principal producing states consumed 53 per cent of all gas consumed in the United States during 1939. By 1960 this figure had dropped to 40 per cent of United States consumption. This reflects the development of new markets in nonproducing states.

2. THE DEVELOPMENT OF NATURAL GAS TRANSMISSION SYSTEMS

The reserve, production, and consumption data presented in the preced-

Table 14.1

Reserves, Production, and Disposition of Natural Gas in the United States, 1945–1960[1]
(in billions of cubic feet)

Year	*Reserves as of Dec. 31*[2]	*Marketed Production of Gas*[3]	*Residential Consumption*	*Commercial Consumption*	*Field Use*	*Carbon Black*	*Other Industrial Consumption*[4]
1945. .	147,789	3,919	607	230	917	432	1,714
1946. .	160,576	4,031	661	242	898	478	1,734
1947. .	165,927	4,582	802	285	934	485	1,921
1948. .	173,869	5,148	896	323	1,022	481	2,224
1949. .	180,381	5,420	993	348	1,060	428	2,368
1950. .	185,593	6,282	1,198	388	1,187	411	2,842
1951. .	193,812	7,457	1,475	464	1,442	426	3,295
1952. .	199,716	8,013	1,622	516	1,484	368	3,624
1953. .	211,447	8,397	1,686	531	1,471	301	3,991
1954. .	211,711	8,743	1,894	585	1,457	251	4,216
1955. .	223,697	9,405	2,124	629	1,508	245	4,565
1956. .	237,775	10,064	2,328	717	1,421	243	4,999
1957. .	246,569	10,680	2,500	776	1,480	234	5,290
1958. .	254,142	11,030	2,714	872	1,604	211	5,359
1959. .	262,597	12,046	2,913	975	1,737	215	5,980
1960. .	263,759	12,727	3,103	1,020	1,780	198	6,409

1 At 14.65 psia and 60 degrees F.

2 Proved recoverable reserves after annual production has been deducted each year.

3 Marketed Production comprises gas sold or consumed by producers, including (since 1947) losses in transmission, quantities added to storage, and increases in gas in pipelines. It excludes gas used in repressuring and gas vented or wasted.

4 Includes gas consumed in petroleum refineries and electric generating plants, as well as other industrial uses.

Sources: American Gas Association, *Historical Statistics of the Gas Industry;* U.S. Bureau of Mines, Mineral Industry Surveys.

ing section point up the explosive rate at which the area of gas transmission expanded during these years. In 1927 there was not a single gas-transmission line connecting the Southwest producing areas with the large population centers in the Middle West, North East, and Pacific Coast. By about the mid-1950's, virtually every significant population center in the country was connected directly or indirectly with the prolific Southwestern gas fields. The immense web of transmission lines now in existence is shown on the map in Figure 14-A. While the late 1920's and the early 1930's saw the beginnings of pipeline construction connecting major producing areas with major markets, the phenomenal increase in pipeline construction did not begin until after World War II, in the late 1940's.

A. ***The Gas Supply Situation.*** The 1920's and 1930's were a period of tremendous expansion of gas supply in the Southwest. In 1916 the Monroe field in northern Louisiana was discovered. Two years later in 1918, the Panhandle field in the Texas Panhandle, the world's largest, was brought in. Then in 1922 the Hugoton field was discovered, and it was eventually found to stretch from the northern Texas Panhandle through the Oklahoma Panhandle and deep into southwest Kansas. In the late twenties, several major fields were discovered on the Texas Gulf Coast. Intensive drilling in east Texas after the discovery of the huge East Texas oil field led to the discovery of the Carthage field in 1936, which was destined to be the second largest gas field in the state. Stepped-up oil exploration in the Texas coastal region resulted in a number of significant discoveries in the 1930's. In addition to these major gas fields, this period marks the time when several bonanza oil fields in the Southwest were first being tapped. Since gas in commercial quantities is commonly present with oil, these oil discoveries made available additional supplies of gas. Prior to state conservation regulation of oil production in the mid-1930's, gas was considered a nuisance, and much of it was flared or vented as it was produced with crude oil.

The upshot of the numerous gas finds was oversupply relative to the fairly small local or regional market demand. During the 1930's many new fields were only partially drilled up, and huge quantities of gas were shut-in for lack of a market. Other known fields went untouched but were available when needed. The average price in Texas for gas consumed in the field as fuel for drilling and pumping dropped to 2.4 cents per Mcf during 1940 and was only 3.8 cents per Mcf for the nation as a whole. Gas-using carbon black plants sprang up in the excess-supply areas and were able to purchase gas in the late 1930's for less than one cent per Mcf. (In 1960 the average United States price for field use was 12.4 cents and for carbon black 10.0 cents per Mcf.) In some instances, in those early days, oil producers were willing to give gas away in order to comply with state laws which prohibited gas waste. This was done in order to produce oil. In the 1930's a few long-distance transmission lines began to tap the low-priced gas resources of the Southwest. For the most part, these lines ran east and north from northern Louisiana and the Hugoton-Panhandle area of Texas, Oklahoma, and Kansas. Those early lines were fortunate in that they were in a buyer's market and consequently paid extremely low prices for their gas.[6]

B. ***Technology Creates a Market.*** The transition from manufactured gas to natural gas in the midwestern and the

[6] Discussion of gas conservation is beyond the scope of this book. However, it should be noted that low prices for gas in the late 1930's were justified by the supply-demand conditions. Looking back, it seems wasteful to use gas in carbon black plants. However, such use is better than mere flaring of the gas.

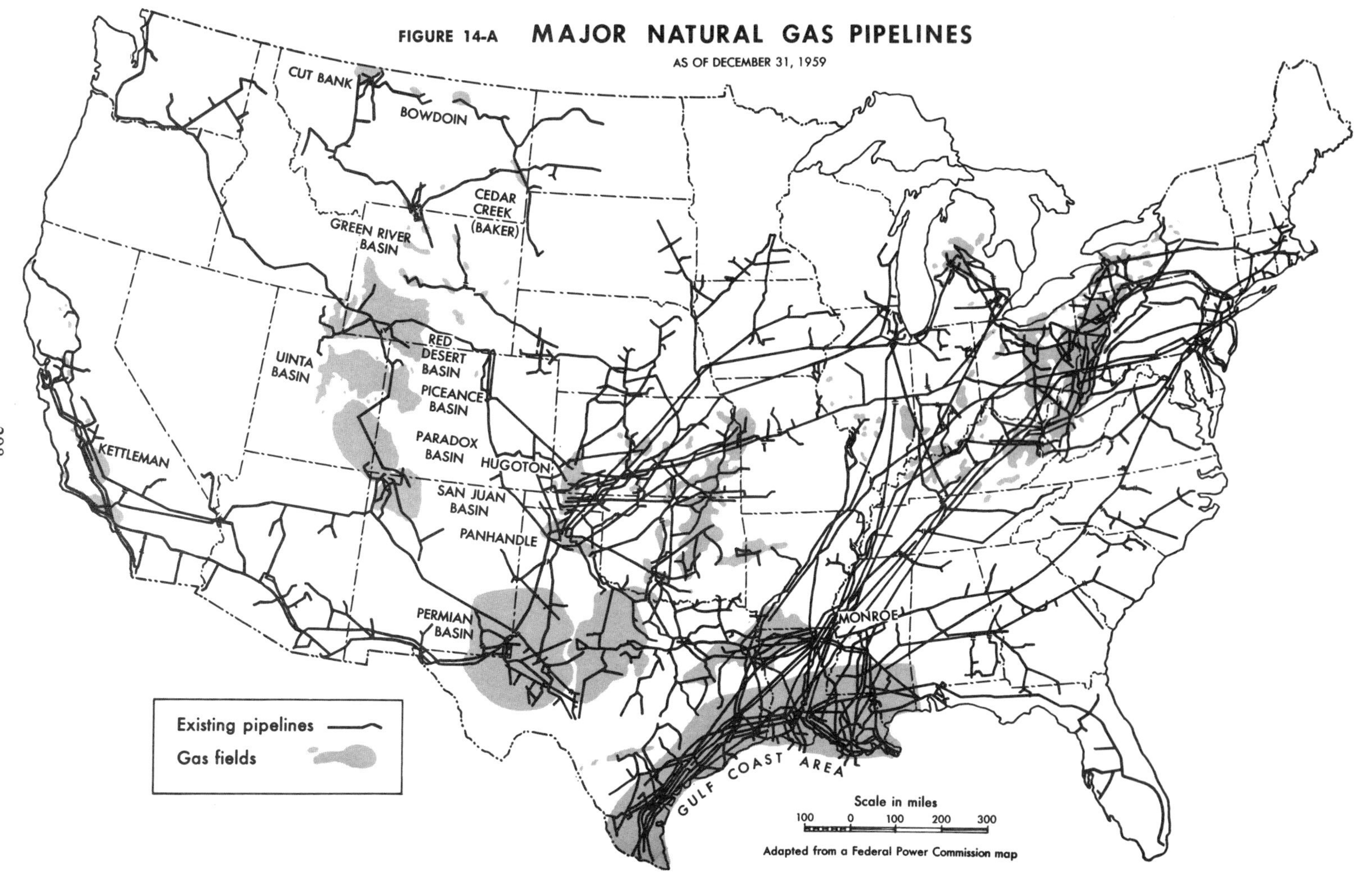

FIGURE 14-A MAJOR NATURAL GAS PIPELINES
AS OF DECEMBER 31, 1959

northeastern markets cannot be explained solely by any one factor, but technology can certainly be given much of the credit. It assisted in a negative manner by not keeping the costs of manufactured gas down. The American Gas Association estimates that the cost per Mcf of 500 Btu content manufactured gas rose from 16.5 cents in 1939 to 48.8 cents in 1948.[7]

Most important, however, were the vast technological innovations in gas-pipeline construction and operation, which brought about cost reductions in a period of generally rising prices. Some of the most prominent improvements in pipeline construction during this period include: (1) development of pressure welding for joining lengths of pipe; (2) development of steel for thin-walled pipe which could withstand extremely high pressures; (3) manufacture of larger and larger-diameter pipe; (4) development of the fusion and continuous electric-welding process in pipe manufacturing; (5) development of large-capacity, high-speed compressors for booster stations along lines; (6) virtually complete mechanization of the pipe-laying process, including pipe cleaning, coating, wrapping, bending, welding, and ditch-digging and refilling; (7) aerial surveying for route selection; (8) novel methods for river, highway, railway, and other troublesome crossings; (9) development of automatic recording, metering, and controlling equipment used in conjunction with radio and telecommunication facilities.[8]

[7] American Gas Association, *Gas Rate Fundamentals* (New York: 1960), p. 11.

[8] See Federal Power Commission, *Natural Gas Investigation, Smith-Wimberly Report,* Docket G–580, 1948, pp. 239 ff.; Frank E. Richardson, "Modern Gas-Pipe-Line Construction," *Oil & Gas Journal,* Vol. 48, No. 1, May 12, 1950, pp. 99 ff.; and "The Pipe Line Industry," *Oil & Gas Journal,* Vol. 48, No. 20, September 21, 1950, pp. 187 ff., for discussions of the technology of long-line gas transmission.

Reductions in pipeline construction costs were accompanied by reduced line-operating costs. At this time, when pipeline costs were falling and gas field prices were stable at low levels, costs of competing fuels to consumers were rising. Indexes of retail fuel prices computed by the United States Bureau of Labor Statistics indicate that between 1935 and 1950 natural gas prices fell 20.6 per cent, anthracite coal rose 94.0 per cent, bituminous coal rose 106.4 per cent, and Number 2 fuel oil rose 96.8 per cent.[9] Much the same situation is found in the industrial-fuel market, although differences were probably smaller. As distance became less and less of a barrier and as costs of competing fuels rose, natural gas consumption began in areas of the country previously served only by manufactured gas.

C. Postwar Pipeline Expansion. World War II delayed gas transmission-line expansion just as it was beginning to boom. Steel was allocated to more essential uses. Home cooking, space-heating, and water-heating equipment manufacture was practically at a standstill because of material shortages. Exploration for and development of oil and gas fields continued, although at a somewhat reduced rate, so that after the war the nation was faced with even larger supplies of gas. As soon as critical materials were made available for pipeline construction, there was a scramble among newly formed companies and existing ones to construct lines to serve the great unsaturated gas markets of the Midwest and Northeast. In addition, some of the war emergency-pipeline capacity, constructed for the transportation of petroleum and petroleum products, was con-

[9] U.S. Bureau of Labor Statistics, "Retail Price Indexes of Fuels and Electricity, January 1935–December 1957," Washington, 1958, mimeo. Gas index based on retail prices for 30.6 therms of natural gas.

verted to gas transportation immediately after World War II to provide the first long-distance gas supply to eastern markets.

Table 14.2 points up the rapid growth in this period. Miles of line in service had more than doubled by the end of 1957 as compared with 1945. Expenditures averaged more than one-half billion dollars per year, and total expenditures were about $9 billion for the period between 1946 and 1960. Such vast systems as El Paso Natural Gas Company, Tennessee Gas Transmission Company, Texas Eastern Transmission Corporation, Texas Illinois Natural Gas Pipeline Company, Transcontinental Gas Pipe Line Corporation, Trunkline Gas Company, Texas Gas Transmission Corporation, Pacific Northwest Pipeline Corporation, Transwestern Pipeline Company, Michigan Wisconsin Pipe Line Company, and American Louisiana Pipe Line Company have been developed since World War II. Prewar companies such as Panhandle Eastern Pipe Line Company, Northern Natural Gas Company, Cities Service Gas Co., Colorado Interstate Gas Company, Natural Gas Pipeline Company of America, Southern Natural Gas Company, and United Gas Pipe Line Company also expanded their systems rapidly or did so through organizing new major pipelines as affiliates. The postwar companies alone had more than $3.8 billion of gas plant in service at the end of 1958.[10] With total assets of more than $10.7 billion at the end of 1960, the natural-gas transmission industry has become one of the major industries in the United States.

[10] Federal Power Commission, *Statistics of Natural Gas Companies, 1958* (Washington: Government Printing Office, 1959), Section V.

Table 14.2

Natural-Gas Transmission-Line Construction Expenditure and Mileage in Postwar Years, 1945–1960

Year	*Expenditures on New Construction*[1] *(million dollars)*	*Cumulative Expenditures (million dollars)*	*Miles of Line in Service*[2] *(December 31)*
1945	N.A.	N.A.	77,280
1946	116.6	116.6	82,480
1947	423.5	540.1	88,020
1948	366.7	906.8	91,970
1949	567.7	1,474.5	98,270
1950	713.3	2,187.8	109,360
1951	867.3	3,055.1	116,590
1952	493.1	3,548.2	119,540
1953	672.9	4,221.1	126,730
1954	389.5	4,610.6	135,370
1955	586.4	5,197.0	142,490
1956	702.2	5,899.2	151,180
1957	751.3	6,650.5	157,540
1958	713.1	7,363.6	162,990
1959	692.2	8,055.8	172,240
1960	848.0	8,903.8	181,770

1 Current dollars. Expenditures are for transmission facilities only.

2 No adjustment is made for line diameter. Generally speaking, line size has increased in recent years. These data exclude gathering and distribution lines.

N. A.—Not available.

Sources: American Gas Association, *Historical Statistics of the Gas Industry; Gas Facts,* 1961.

3. REGULATION OF INTERSTATE GAS-TRANSMISSION LINES

Federal regulation of interstate natural gas transmission came about as part of a program to correct the abuse of power by the public utility holding companies, which reached their zenith during the 1920's. The United States Supreme Court (as discussed in Chapter 13) had made clear that states were powerless to regulate interstate transmission or sale of gas or electricity.

A. *The Federal Trade Commission Report on Utility Corporations.* Discontent with the utility holding companies became so widespread that Congress in 1928 passed a resolution directing the Federal Trade Commission to investigate and report on the matter and to recommend remedial legislation.[11] Although natural gas operations comprised but a small part of the utility holding company properties, they were inextricably woven into the whole. The Federal Trade Commission investigation and reports led, in part at least, to passage of the Federal Power Act of 1935, the Public Utility Holding Company Act of 1935, and the Natural Gas Act of 1938. The part of the FTC report dealing with natural gas was issued late in 1935; it identified the following problems, among others: (1) a high degree of concentration in the purchasing of natural gas and its transportation, with four systems dominating some of the major producing areas and the pipelines leading therefrom to principal markets; (2) discrimination by pipelines, in some instances, in field purchases of natural gas from independent producers, many of whom were found to be at the "mercy" of the pipelines; (3) unregulated competition in building natural gas lines to markets; (4) costly rivalry among natural gas pipelines or holding-company interests to conquer or defend territories of distribution; and (5) excessive and inequitable variation in the wholesale rates for natural gas as among different localities.[12] The FTC report recommended that:

> A Federal regulatory law should be enacted applicable to interstate natural gas pipe lines for ultimate sale to and use by the public, regulating contracts for the purchase of gas to be transported interstate (footnote omitted) or regarding rates for carriage or city gas rates at the end of such transportation, or all of these. Security issues, accounts, beginning and abandonment of operations and intercorporate relations of companies owning or controlling gas pipe lines should also be regulated.[13]

Two months later, in 1936, a bill was introduced in Congress to carry out these recommendations. However, because of the fear of federal invasion of states' rights in the regulation of gas distribution, among other things, modifications were found to be necessary. The Natural Gas Act was finally adopted in June of 1938, and the Federal Power Commission was made responsible for its administration.

B. *The Natural Gas Act of 1938.* The Act, with its relatively few amendments, is short and to the point. It provides for federal regulation of both the interstate transportation of natural gas and the sale for resale of natural gas in interstate commerce. A brief review of the Act at this point will lay the groundwork for discussion of pipeline regulation and independent natural gas producers; the rates and sales of the latter have come under Federal Power Commission jurisdiction since the Supreme Court's *Phil-*

[11] U.S. 70th Cong., 1st sess., Senate Resolution No. 83.

[12] U.S. 70th Cong., 1st sess., *Federal Trade Commission Report on Utility Corporations,* Senate Doc. No. 92, Part 84-A (Washington, D.C.: Government Printing Office, 1935), pp. 615–616.

[13] *Ibid.,* pp. 616–617.

lips decision.[14] This will be discussed in the next chapter.

Section 1 of the Act has three parts. Subsection (a) sets forth the need to regulate the interstate business of transporting and selling natural gas for ultimate distribution to the public. Subsection (b) defines the jurisdiction of the Federal Power Commission to include: the transportation of natural gas in interstate commerce; sales of natural gas in interstate commerce for resale; and natural gas companies engaged in such transportation or sale. This subsection states that the Act shall not apply to local distribution or to the production or gathering of natural gas. The interpretation of the "production or gathering" phrase has been debated more, perhaps, than any other single portion of the Act. Subsection (c) of Section 1 exempts from FPC jurisdiction local gas distributors whose operations, although technically interstate in nature, are of local importance only. Accordingly, a gas distributor which buys gas from an interstate pipeline at or within a state boundary and transmits it to distribution points within its service area is exempt from the provisions of the Act: (1) if all the gas so purchased is consumed within that state; and (2) if the company's rates, service, and facilities are regulated by a state commission.[15]

Section 4 deals with changes in rates and authorizes the Commission to suspend proposed rate changes for periods up to five months. Much of the FPC gas work involves pipeline and producer rate changes filed under this section. Section 5 authorizes the FPC to investigate the existing rates of natural gas companies in order to determine whether they are just and reasonable. Under this Section the Commission cannot approve an increase in existing rates, but it can order them decreased if they are not the "lowest reasonable rates." Section 6 provides for the ascertainment of: (a) the actual cost of the property owned by all natural gas companies subject to the Act; and (b) the facts relating to the fair value of such property.

Section 7 of the Natural Gas Act deals with the extension of facilities, the abandonment of service, and the certification of both new sales and the construction of new facilities. Subsection (a) authorizes the Commission to compel a pipeline to extend service to gas distributors, if such service would not impair the ability of the pipeline to render adequate service to its existing customers. Subsection (b) prohibits the abandonment of facilities or service without authority from the FPC.

Subsection (c) of the original Act was entirely replaced by an amendment passed in 1942.[16] In the original subsection of the Act, the Commission's jurisdiction in granting certificates of public convenience and necessity was limited to the construction or extension of facilities for the transportation of gas to a market already served by another natural gas company. Thus, pipelines planning to serve new markets were not required to obtain certificates of public convenience and necessity. Also, a company serving a given territory could enlarge its facilities within that territory to meet increased market demand without authorization from the Commission. Original subsection (c) was difficult to administer, and little opposition was raised in Congressional hearings on proposed amendments.[17] The amendments to Section 7 included the replacing of

[14] *Phillips Petroleum Co.* v. *Wisconsin, et al.,* 347 U.S. 672 (1954).

[15] U.S. 83rd Cong., 2nd sess., P. L. 323, Chap. 115, approved March 27, 1954.

[16] U.S. 77th Cong., 2nd sess., P. L. 444, Chap. 49, approved February 7, 1942.

[17] U.S. 77th Cong., 1st sess., House of Representatives, House Report No. 2190, p. 3.

subsection (c) with a new provision and the addition of subsections (d) through (g).

The present subsection (c) states that "No natural gas company . . . shall engage in the transportation or sale of natural gas . . . unless there is in force with respect to such natural-gas company a certificate of public convenience and necessity issued by the Commission. . . ." Thus, enactment of this subsection greatly enlarged the scope of Commission jurisdiction over the construction and operation of transmission facilities.

Subsection (e) states: "The Commission shall have the power to attach to the issuance of the certificate and to the exercise of the rights granted thereunder such reasonable terms and conditions as the public convenience and necessity may require." This is important because the Commission can make compliance with its policies on service, initial rates, gas supply, or other such aspects, a condition of obtaining the right to do business or to expand it. It is, perhaps, one of the Commission's strongest regulatory powers, since failure to abide by the Commission's requirements set down in the certificate can mean automatic revocation of the certificate.[18]

Subsection (f) gives the Commission the power to determine a service area for respective pipelines. This power has been used only once, in special circumstances. Subsection (g) states that the Commission retains the right to authorize a company to construct facilities in an area already served by another company, if such facilities are in the public interest. Subsection (h), added in 1947, gives the holder of a certificate of public convenience and necessity the right to exercise the power of eminent domain.[19]

[18] See FPC, *Natural Gas Investigation, Smith-Wimberly Report*. Docket G–580, 1948, Part XI, for a discussion of the problems encountered in the administration of Section 7 of the Act.

4. ASPECTS OF REGULATORY POLICY

Federal regulation in an interstate public utility field is by no means unique, and the Natural Gas Act of 1938 adopted many of the same concepts and procedures found in earlier regulatory legislation, particularly the concept of "just and reasonable" rates. The problems discussed in earlier chapters, of determination of the proper rate base, the proper rate of return, workable accounting procedures, and the design of reasonable rates, are essentially common to the regulation of all utility industries and gas-transmission companies as well. In fact, several landmark court decisions affecting public utility regulation resulted from pipeline cases.

This section will deal with matters which are, for the most part, unique to gas-pipeline regulation. Among those that require discussion are the following: (a) the rate-making treatment of pipeline-produced gas; (b) FPC control over divestments and purchases of gas reserves by pipeline companies; (c) FPC control over non-jurisdictional sales; and (d) requirements and problems in pipeline-certification proceedings. The rate-making treatment of pipe-line-produced gas is related to the problem of selecting an appropriate method for the regulation of independent producers.

A. *Rate-Making Treatment of Pipeline-Produced Gas.* The traditional rate base-rate of return method of regulating public utility rates creates a special problem when applied to an interstate pipeline that produces and gathers some of the gas it transmits. In rate cases involving such pipelines, a question some-

[19] U.S. 80th Cong., 1st sess., P. L. 245, Chap. 333, approved July 25, 1947.

times arises concerning the allowance, or amount, to be included in the pipeline's cost of service for its own gas production. A correlative question goes to a determination of the incentive required by pipeline producers to explore for and develop replacement and additional gas supplies. The same questions do not arise in rate cases involving those pipelines which purchase all the gas they transmit. Their cost of purchased gas is treated as an operating expense for rate-making purposes. The present section surveys the development of the rate-making treatment of pipeline-produced gas and examines some of the economic factors which bear upon regulatory policy in this area.

In determining the pipeline cost of service for rate-making purposes, two general approaches are available to calculate the allowance for pipeline-produced gas. First, under the traditional rate base-rate of return approach: (a) the net original cost of the gas-producing and gas-gathering properties is included in the pipeline rate base; and (b) the operating and other expenses associated with gas production and gathering are included in pipeline expenses. Second, under the "commodity value" or "fair field price" approach: (a) the production and gathering net investment and operating and other expenses are excluded from the pipeline cost of service; and instead, (b) an amount is included in operating expenses which reflects the value of the gas as determined by the weighted-average arm's-length payments for deliveries of virtually identical natural gas in the fields (and sometimes the very same wells) where it is produced.

The first, or rate-base, approach does not distinguish a pipeline's gas-production and gathering functions from its gas-transmission function. The second, or field-price, approach makes this distinction and is intended to recognize that natural gas is not produced under public utility-type circumstances, but is a commodity for which there is a going market price. In this regard, proponents of the field-price approach emphasize: (1) that natural gas is produced under highly competitive and risky conditions, without the protective monopoly rights usually pertaining to public utility status; (2) that, unlike a public utility, the gas-production function is not characterized by any reliable relationship between costs and productivity; and (3) that, under the multiple ownership of individual gas wells and fields, which is characteristic of the industry, it is discriminatory to permit different prices for producers who are similarly situated.

Before continuing, it is necessary to outline some of the background of the problem under discussion. Much of the pipeline-owned gas production is in the Panhandle field (in Texas) and the Hugoton field (in Texas, Oklahoma, and Kansas).[20] These are two of the oldest major fields in the country. The pipelines which produce gas in these fields include some of the oldest long-distance transmission companies in the industry. (Generally speaking, the pipelines organized and constructed since 1943 have depended almost entirely upon purchased gas rather than their own production.) The early pipelines, commencing in the late 1920's and through the 1930's, acquired lands in fee and, more conventionally, leasehold rights in lands owned by others. They explored for and developed their own gas production and sometimes purchased reserves in place. They also constructed field gathering systems.

The historical cost of pipeline-produced gas in the Panhandle and Hugoton

---

[20] Other pipeline-owned production is in the Appalachian area, primarily in West Virginia, in the San Juan Basin of New Mexico, and in Louisiana, among other places. This discussion primarily is concerned with Panhandle and Hugoton gas.

fields is low by comparison with latter-day field prices obtainable by others in the same area and paid by these same pipelines for purchased gas. Before noting some of the reasons for this, it should be pointed out that most of the pipeline-produced gas in the Panhandle and Hugoton fields is produced as a single product, whereas much of the United States natural-gas supply is produced as a joint product together with oil or other petroleum liquids. Thus, the joint-cost allocation problem is not so important here as it is in efforts to apply the cost-of-service approach to independent producers of gas.

An important influence affecting the cost of pipeline-produced gas arises from the fact that much of the now productive lands and leaseholds were acquired before the demand for natural gas had grown to significant size. Natural gas is worthless in the absence of transportation and developed markets. Accordingly, since much of this gas was discovered before the pipelines were built or the markets developed, the early pipelines were able to acquire lands and leaseholds at prices which by present standards were very low. In some cases, landowners conveyed leasehold rights free to the pipelines to induce exploration, in the hope of receiving future royalty income. However, the uncertainty of demand in the beginning years caused the early pipelines to be regarded as quite risky and their investments in property and exploration to be regarded as speculative. Another factor bearing on the cost of this gas is the fact that the price level in the period when most of the discovery and development occurred, particularly in the 1930's, was well below the postwar price level. Accordingly, the costs booked for drilling and construction labor, supplies, services, equipment, and pipe signify a higher real value than their postwar dollar equivalents. At the same time, the exploration for gas turned out to be highly successful, and large-volume reserves were proved up at relatively shallow depths. With this all too brief background, regulatory policy in this area will now be discussed.

Regulatory policy, with respect to pipeline-produced gas, requires the use of the rate base-rate of return method. Except for one decision adopting the field-price method, subsequently reversed by the courts on procedural grounds, this has been the policy of the FPC from the beginning of its administration of the Act. The following discussion traces the development of regulatory policy in this area and brings out some of the economic factors which bear upon that policy.

In the first pipeline rate case under the Natural Gas Act to reach the Supreme Court, the *Natural Gas Pipeline Co.* case, the FPC had included production and gathering properties in the rate base at their cost of reproduction. The company did not object to this policy, although it did object to the exclusion of certain items from the FPC determination of reproduction costs. This case, decided by the Supreme Court in 1942, essentially turned on the constitutionality of the Act and the validity of the Commission's order. It did not directly involve or produce a ruling on the issue under discussion here.[21]

The famous *Hope Natural Gas Co.* case, decided by the Supreme Court in 1944, involved the question of pipeline-produced gas somewhat more directly. There, in proceedings before the Commission, Hope had presented evidence as to the reproduction cost and trended original cost of all of its physical property. The Commission had refused to place any reliance upon this evidence and had used instead a rate base reflecting actual historical cost. Here, as in

[21] *FPC* v. *Natural Gas Pipeline Co.,* 315 U.S. 575 (1942).

the previous case, the company had not objected to the inclusion of its relatively high-cost Appalachian-area production properties in the rate base.

The Court upheld the Commission upon a finding that the end result was reasonable. It also ruled on contentions advanced by the State of West Virginia, an intervener, which claimed that the Commission had not allowed a sufficient return on gas production properties. West Virginia had spelled out the relation of various aspects of its economy to the amount allowed for gas produced by Hope in that state, alleging that the Commission's approach undervalued Hope's properties to the detriment of the property tax base of the State and also jeopardized its conservation policies by discouraging exploration and hastening the abandonment of marginal wells. The Court declined to substitute its judgment for that of the Commission on this matter stating:

> It is suggested that the Commission has failed to perform its duty under the Act in that it has not allowed a return for gas production that will be enough to induce private enterprise to perform completely and efficiently its functions for the public. The Commission, however, was not oblivious of those matters. It considered them. It allowed, for example, delay rentals and exploration and development costs in operating expenses. No serious attempt has been made here to show that they are inadequate. We certainly cannot say that they are, unless we are to substitute our opinions for the expert judgment of the administrators to whom Congress entrusted the decision. Moreover, if in light of experience they turn out to be inadequate for development of new sources of supply, the doors of the Commission are open for increased allowances. This is not an order for all time. The Act contains machinery for obtaining rate adjustments.[22]

[22] *FPC* v. *Hope Natural Gas Co.,* 320 U.S. 591, 615 (1944).

Justice Jackson, dissenting in the *Hope* case, took serious exception to the majority's approval of the rate-base method where producing properties were concerned. He maintained that the transmission and production functions are of "opposite character," and challenged the usefulness of the rate-base method essentially on the grounds: (a) that natural gas has a market price in the field, which permits it to be valued accurately; and (b) that the absence of a consistent relationship between costs expended and the volume of gas produced made the rate-base method unworkable. He stated:

> The prudent investment theory has relative merits in fixing rates for a utility which creates its service merely by its investment. The amount and quality of service rendered by the usual utility will, at least roughly, be measured by the amount of capital it puts into the enterprise. But it has no rational application where there is no such relationship between investment and capacity to serve. There is no such relationship between investment and amount of gas produced. Let us assume that Doe and Roe each produces in West Virginia for delivery to Cleveland the same quantity of natural gas per day. Doe, however, through luck or foresight or whatever it takes, gets his gas from investing $50,000 in leases and drilling. Roe drilled poorer territory, got smaller wells, and has invested $250,000. Does anybody imagine that Roe can get or ought to get for his gas five times as much as Doe because he spent five times as much? The service one renders to society in the gas business is measured by what he gets out of the ground, not by what he puts into it, and there is little more relation between the investment and the results than in a game of poker.[23]

The legal question of the method to be used in pricing pipeline-produced gas was squarely presented to the Supreme Court for the first time in the *Colorado Interstate–Canadian River* cases, de-

[23] 320 U.S. 591, 649.

cided in 1945. There, the company contested the Commission's policy of including its producing properties in its rate base at net original cost. (After the *Hope* case, the Commission no longer accepted evidence on any other basis.) The company contended: (1) that the Commission was without authority to include producing or gathering properties in the rate base or to include production and gathering expenses in the cost of service, because that would constitute regulation of production and gathering, which Section 1(b) of the Act exempted from regulation; and (2) that the correct procedure would be to allow in the operating expenses the "fair field price" or "fair market value, as a commodity, of the gas."

A closely divided Court held against these contentions, ruling that "We do not say the Commission lacks the authority to depart from the rate-base method. We only hold that the Commission is not precluded from using it."[24] Referring to Section 1(b) of the Act, the Court said: "We only decide that it does not preclude the Commission from reflecting production and gathering facilities of a natural gas company in the rate base and determining the expenses incident thereto for the purposes of determining the reasonableness of rates subject to its jurisdiction."[25] Justice Jackson again took serious exception, characterizing the results of applying the rate-base method to producing properties as "delirious." He pointed out that five leases, containing about 47,000 acres, were put in the rate base at an original cost of $4,244.24, while three others were put in at zero, even though their present market value after exploration and development was shown to be over $3,000,000.[26] (As discussed in the next chapter, Justice Jackson's conclusions on the impracticality of the rate-base approach were adopted by the Supreme Court in 1963.)

In 1954, the FPC reversed its policy and approved the use of the field-price approach in a rate case involving Panhandle Eastern Pipe Line Co.[27] This pipeline is a large producer, owning some gas wells completely and partnership interests in over 80 others. This decision, as discussed shortly, was reversed; at the time of this writing, FPC policy had returned to the rate-base method. Although reversed, the 1954 Panhandle decision provides further dimension to the problem of regulating pipeline-produced gas.

When the Commission approved the field-price method for gas produced by Panhandle, it indicated that it did so in light of developments since the *Colorado Interstate–Canadian River* cases in 1945. It referred to the fact that some of the pipelines had disposed of producing properties. It observed that "no new major pipeline which has been certificated since the Commission's pricing practice was first established—including some of the largest systems serving enormous new markets—produces any significant portion of its total supply." It noted that the ratio of pipeline-produced gas to total gas transported in interstate commerce had declined markedly, and that for Panhandle the ratio had declined from 52.4 per cent to 22.6 per cent, 1942 to 1952. The Commission regarded this as an indication that use of the rate-base method had been a factor which discouraged pipelines from finding their own gas; it deemed this an "undesirable result." The Commission also was aware that some of the older pipelines had based their system expansions upon gas purchased

[24] *Colorado Interstate Gas Co.* v. *FPC* and *Canadian River Gas Co.* v. *FPC,* 324 U.S. 581, 601 (1945).

[25] 324 U.S. 581, 603.

[26] 324 U.S. 581, 610–611.

[27] *Re Panhandle Eastern Pipe Line Co.,* 13 FPC 53 (1954).

in higher-priced, more distant producing areas such as the Texas Gulf coast and Permian Basin of West Texas.

In approving the use of the field-price approach, the Commission found that in this case, for the first time, "we have before us . . . a complete record which fully sets forth the results of the two methods of gas pricing now at issue." It considered and rejected the rate-base approach advocated by the FPC staff, which would have resulted in: (1) a maximum net return on the production and gathering rate base of .85 cents per Mcf; or (2) a negative return of 1.24 cents per Mcf, if the cost of service were reduced by eliminating the tax benefits arising from the statutory tax deduction for depletion and by crediting the value of natural-gas liquids extracted.

The field price adopted for application to Panhandle's own gas production was based upon the weighted-average arm's-length payments for virtually identical natural gas in the fields (and sometimes from the very same wells) where it is produced. This amounted to 8.4 cents per Mcf, or 1.3 cents more than an allowance based upon cost of service. The average field price adopted was below the then current prices in new sales contracts of: (a) 9.4 to 15 cents in the Texas Hugoton; (b) 12 to 13 cents in the Kansas Hugoton; and (c) 11.5 to 15 cents in the Texas Panhandle.

The Commission concluded that the field-price method would better serve the public interest for two principal reasons: (1) the use of the rate-base method would not "promote the conservation in both the production and the use of natural gas which is in the public interest," because it would result in "an arbitrarily depressed price" which "would tend to both accelerate the consumption and fail to encourage the discovery and development of this limited and irreplaceable natural resource"; and (2) "the interest of the public definitely lies in the direction of natural-gas production by pipeline systems themselves, as distinguished from their complete dependence for gas supply upon purchases from other producers." The Commission favored pipeline production of natural gas for these reasons: (1) pipeline-owned production strengthens bargaining power in the negotiation of gas purchase contracts with independent producers; (2) pipelines owning production can take uniform quantities of purchased gas and make up for load-factor variations with their own gas, thus resulting in lower field purchase prices; and (3) pipeline control of distant reserves assures consumers of supplies in the future. The Commission concluded, "No policy which, while immediately leading to somewhat lower rates, fails to create an atmosphere favorable to the exploration for natural gas by pipeline systems and the minimization of its flaring in production or waste in its utilization promotes the sound conservation of this irreplaceable natural resource, which is in the long run interest of the Nation."[28]

The effect of this 1954 decision was to cause an immediate spurt in Panhandle's lease-acquisition and exploratory drilling activity. During the years preceding this decision, Panhandle had discontinued exploratory drilling and had engaged only in the drilling of development wells for the purpose of protecting against lease expirations and drainage. Thus, it drilled 17 wells in 1953 and 22 in 1954. After the Commission approved the use of the field-price method, Panhandle drilled 56 wells in 1955 and 46 wells in the first nine months of 1956; about half of these were exploratory. Thereafter, following the reversal of this Commission decision,

[28] 13 FPC 53, 74–75.

Panhandle discontinued its lease-acquisition and exploration program.[29]

In the *City of Detroit* case, decided in 1955, the Commission was reversed by the Court of Appeals for the District of Columbia Circuit, and the Supreme Court denied *certiorari*.[30] The Court agreed with the Commission to the extent of concluding that the allowance of a field price for the company's own produced gas as an element in the ultimate composition of rates is not unlawful merely because it departs from the traditional rate-base method. It did not find acceptable, however, the Commission's justification for shifting to the field-price method, and in particular it found the Commission's proceedings "fatally defective" because they did not show that the increase in rates thus caused was no more than reasonably necessary for the purposes advanced for any increase.

The Court emphasized that the primary aim of the Natural Gas Act had been held by the Supreme Court to be "to protect consumers against exploitation at the hands of natural gas companies." It rejected as outside the Commission's jurisdiction considerations relating to the effect which low prices may have in accelerating the consumption of natural gas. In the case of the objective of encouraging the discovery and development of gas resources, the Court was prepared to have the commission consider this factor at least to the extent of allowing recovery of development and exploration costs. It was also prepared to have the Commission consider encouraging the ownership by pipeline companies of their own production. But it insisted that the Commission relate such factors to the objective of guarding the consumer against excessive rates:

> . . . If the Commission contemplates increasing rates for the purpose of encouraging exploration and development, or the ownership by pipeline companies of their own producing facilities, it must see to it that the increase is in fact needed, and is no more than is needed, for the purpose. Further than this we think the Commission cannot go without additional authority from Congress.

The Court commented, however, that, if "the necessary relationship between means and end" were shown in the case before it, it "would not consider the rates so high as to be unlawful."

Finally the Court observed that, although the rate-base method is not the only method which may be used by the Commission, "it is essential in such a case as this that it be used as a basis of comparison. . . . *Unless it is continued to be used at least as a point of departure,* the whole experience under the Act is discarded and no anchor, as it were, is available by which to hold the terms 'just and reasonable' to some recognizable meaning." (Emphasis supplied.)[31]

Upon remand, the Commission in 1961 reversed its 1954 decision approving the field-price approach. It ordered Panhandle to file revised rates reflecting a six per cent rate of return on the net investment in production and gathering properties. The FPC declined to give weight to evidence, presented upon reopening, of Panhandle's increased exploratory program following approval of the field-price method, the discontinuation of its exploratory program following the denial of *certiorari* in the *City of Detroit* case, and the prospective large-scale exploratory program it would undertake if field price were recognized.

[29] *Re Panhandle Eastern Pipe Line Co.* (FPC Docket No. G-2506), Transcript, pp. 3570–3581.

[30] *City of Detroit* v. *FPC,* 230 F. 2d 810 (1955); *cert.* denied, 352 U.S. 829 (1956).

[31] 230 F. 2d 815, 817–819.

The FPC rejected Panhandle's contention that its customers would benefit by a combination of field price regulation and increased exploration, as compared to purchases of gas supplies from independent producers. The Commission looked instead to the difference in cost to consumers between field price regulation and cost of service regulation.

The Commission said it realized that the test required by the Court in *City of Detroit* is a difficult one in that it contemplates a showing of what is needed above the cost of service in order to encourage exploration and development. Of more than passing interest was the Commission's comment that the cost-of-service allowance for Panhandle's own gas production "will be nowhere near what appears to be required to encourage a vigorous and continuing program of exploration and development."[32]

In the latter respect, the Commission's view would appear to coincide with that of Panhandle, which has maintained that the rate-base method would neither provide revenues sufficient to replenish gas reserves as they are consumed nor permit reserves to be increased. This, of course, results from the difference in level between historical costs and the present costs of replenishing and increasing gas supplies. This position, on behalf of Panhandle, was set forth in the following statement by the late Dr. Leslie T. Fournier.

> . . . When Panhandle produces gas from the ground it must replace that gas in the ground, or gradually go out of the production business. The present date cost of replenishing the gas supply is many times the original cost of the gas withdrawn. Therefore, when the Commission allows Panhandle only the very low original cost of . . . gas as it is produced rather than the much higher present-day cost of finding and developing new gas, the company is faced with the immediate necessity of not only plowing back all funds provided by the production operations but also to raise huge additional sums each year to enable it to replenish the gas supply.
>
> In these times of sharply rising costs of exploration, development and production there is little prospect that a producer such as Panhandle can ever reach the point where the funds provided by the operations will equal the outlay required to maintain production. He is on a treadmill. The more he produces, the more he must spend for new supplies to replenish old supplies for which he receives less than he must spend for the new supplies. The only way he can get off this treadmill is to stop replenishing the gas in the ground and liquidate the business. This is his only way out of the dilemma caused by the imposition of the utility cost rate base method on a wasting asset business such as Panhandle's gas production operation.[33]

In conclusion it should be pointed out that the question of the proper allowance for pipeline-produced gas is one part of the larger problem of regulating the price of gas in the field, whether produced by pipeline or independent producers. Regulation in this area poses a unique problem because the exploration, development, and production of gas are not public utility functions and are not clothed with the same "duty to serve" obligations as the conventional public utility functions. Thus, the finding and development of natural gas reserves cannot be compelled, but can be induced, by public authority. A final resolution of the problem of the proper allowance for pipeline-produced gas very likely will await the further development of regulatory policy in the closely related area of independent-producer rate making. To a large extent,

[32] *Re Panhandle Eastern Pipe Line Co.* (Docket No. G–2506), Opinion No. 344 (mimeo) p. 8, decided with Opinion No. 269–A (Docket No. G–1116), April 7, 1961.

[33] *Re Panhandle Eastern Pipe Line Co.* (FPC Docket No. G–14755 et al.), Transcript, pp. 2435–2436.

the key to this entire problem area lies in determinations of: (a) the supplies of gas that may be required in the future; and (b) the price incentives required to provide such supplies in advance of need. This matter will be discussed in the following chapter.

B. *Divestments and Purchases of Producing Properties.* Divestments and purchases of gas-producing properties by interstate pipelines appear to be beyond FPC jurisdiction. Although there is an active national market in oil and gas-producing properties, interstate pipelines have been involved in relatively few transactions where major gas reserves are concerned.

The relatively few major divestments of gas-producing properties by pipelines resulted from the FPC policy of using the rate base-rate of return method to compensate pipelines for their own gas production.[34] If a pipeline company owns substantial undedicated reserves, which are carried on its books at a relatively low historical cost, it may be advantageous for the pipeline to sell the reserves in the ground rather than to produce them. In this way it enjoys something akin to the commodity value of its gas rather than being restricted to earnings based upon original cost. The difference between cost and value sometimes can be substantial. In one instance, for example, producing properties valued at $8.4 million were included in a company's rate base at a net actual cost of $955,000.[35]

The leading case in this area grew out of the fact that, in 1948, Panhandle Eastern Pipe Line Co. exchanged a large amount of undedicated gas acreage that it owned in Kansas for all the shares of stock of a newly formed subsidiary, Hugoton Production Co. (Hugoton then proceeded to sell gas, on an intrastate basis, primarily to Kansas Power and Light Co.) Panhandle then declared as part of a dividend to its own shareholders a stock dividend of all the Hugoton stock. The FPC ordered that this disposal of stock be discounted until a hearing could be held. Panhandle declined to comply, and the FPC asked for and received an injunction to enforce its order. On appeal to the United States Supreme Court, the injunction was vacated, and the FPC was found to have no jurisdiction over such transactions. The Commission had taken the position that disposition of these properties constituted an abandonment of service, over which it had jurisdiction under Section 7 of the Act. However, the Court held that this transaction fell within the "production or gathering" exemption in Section 1(b).[36]

Since this case in 1949, the Court has decided the *Phillips* case and its several successor cases, all of which have expanded greatly the scope of FPC jurisdiction. It remains to be seen whether another case involving the spinning off of a new production company would be decided in the same way. Beginning in 1951, the FPC has asked Congress each year to amend the Natural Gas Act ". . . to require Commission approval for the transfer by an interstate natural gas pipeline company of natural gas reserves where such reserves have constituted part of the bases for issuance of certificates of public convenience and necessity."[37] This proposal was introduced as proposed legislation, at the request of the Commission, in the 84th

[34] Robert S. Eckley, *Economic Development in Southwestern Kansas, Part III, Mineral Resources and Industries* (Lawrence, Kans.: University of Kansas, 1955), p. 10.

[35] *Panhandle Eastern Pipe Line Co.* v. *FPC*, 324 U.S. 635, 648 (1945).

[36] *FPC* v. *Panhandle Eastern Pipe Line Co. et al.*, 337 U.S. 498 (1949).

[37] Federal Power Commission, *Annual Report for Fiscal Year Ended June 30, 1960* (Washington, D.C.: Government Printing Office, 1961), p. 19.

Congress and the 86th Congress. The bills never came to hearing.

Interstate pipelines have made a relatively few major acquisitions of gas-producing properties from independent producers. In the only case decided to date, the Commission held that it was without jurisdiction with respect to an interstate pipeline's purchase of developed, undedicated producing leases from the independent producers who discovered the field. Upon review by the District of Columbia Circuit, the FPC ruling on the matter of jurisdiction was not disturbed, although the case was remanded on other grounds.[38]

C. Interstate Direct Sales. It has been noted previously that FPC jurisdiction over natural gas companies extends to: (a) interstate transportation; and (b) sales in interstate commerce for resale to the public. The Commission has only limited jurisdiction over interstate sales by pipelines directly to consumers. These sales, generally termed "main line industrial sales," are very important to some pipelines in terms of both volume and revenue. Sales of this kind, when made on an interruptible basis, may be particularly large during the warmer months when the seasonal heating demand is at its lowest. Pipelines with little or no storage on their systems depend heavily upon such sales to maintain their annual load factors at economic levels. In general, the market for direct pipeline sales is characterized by: (a) large-volume buyers, who have substantial bargaining power; and (b) rigorous inter-fuel price competition.

The FPC does not have authority to fix the rates charged by pipelines for direct sales to consumers in interstate commerce. Such authority extends only to sales for resale to the public in interstate commerce. However, the Supreme Court has said *in dictum* that the FPC may take direct industrial rates into consideration when it fixes the rates over which it does have jurisdiction.[39] In addition, the Supreme Court has held that direct industrial rates: (1) must be compensatory to the seller, and must not be discriminatory to the pipeline's jurisdictional customers; and (2) are subject, in all other respects, to regulation by the utility commissions of the states in which such sales are made.[40]

Because the jurisdiction of the FPC extends to transportation in interstate commerce, regardless of whether a direct sale or a sale for resale is involved, pipelines planning to make direct industrial sales must qualify for an FPC certificate of public convenience and necessity before constructing or operating the facilities necessary to make delivery. This is required because the delivery line off the main line is considered to be a part of the pipeline's interstate transportation facilities.[41] In certificate cases involving applications for authority to construct facilities of this kind, the pipeline applicant is required to make substantially the same showing that would be required if it were proposing to expand its facilities to make a sale for resale. These requirements are discussed in the next section.

D. Pipeline Certificates. Interstate natural-gas pipeline companies must obtain authorization from the FPC before either commencing to do business or changing the nature of their jurisdictional business. This authorization is in the form of a "certificate of public convenience and necessity."

In pipeline certificate cases, issues sometimes arise as to whether the appli-

---

[38] *PSC of New York* v. *FPC,* 287 F. 2d 143 (1960).

[39] *Panhandle Eastern Pipe Line Co.* v. *FPC,* 324 U.S. 635, 646 (1945).

[40] *Panhandle Eastern Pipe Line Co.* v. *PSC of Indiana,* 332 U.S. 507 (1947).

[41] *Panhandle Eastern Pipe Line Co.* v. *FPC,* 232 F. 2d 467 (1956), *cert.* denied, 352 U.S. 891 (1956).

cant has satisfied one or more of the Commission's basic requirements. These will be discussed shortly. In addition, pipeline certificate proceedings sometimes involve issues concerning: (a) the form and level of the initial rates for new service, as proposed either by an existing pipeline in connection with a major expansion or by a new company seeking to enter the industry; and (b) the nature of the end-market use to be made of the gas and the competitive effect of the proposed gas service upon the suppliers of coal or oil.

Section 7 of the Natural Gas Act requires interstate pipelines to obtain a certificate before: (a) transporting or selling natural gas, subject to FPC jurisdiction; or (b) constructing, extending, operating, or acquiring pipeline facilities for such purposes. After hearing and decision, a certificate will be issued if the Commission finds: (a) that the applicant is able and willing to perform the proposed service; and (b) that the proposed facilities and services are or will be required by the present or future public convenience and necessity. If more than one pipeline seeks a certificate to provide the same service, the Commission will set the competitive applications for a consolidated hearing wherein each applicant can present evidence in support of its application.[42] In deciding among the competitive applications, the Commission may select one applicant as the best qualified and reject the other applications, or it may divide the market area and issue certificates to more than one applicant. In this respect it may be noted that the Commission generally does not favor giving one pipeline company a monopoly in serving a particular market. This position has been tested and upheld. The reviewing court found that ". . . nothing in the Natural Gas Act suggests that Congress thought monopoly better than competition or one source of supply better than two, or intended for any reason to give an existing supplier of natural gas for distribution in a particular community the privilege of furnishing an increased supply."[43] The Supreme Court declined to review this decision. The Natural Gas Act permits, but does not require, the Commission to establish "service areas" for each pipeline. The Commission has not chosen to use this authority, except in one case involving unusual circumstances.

In the *Kansas Pipe Line & Gas Co.* decision of 1939, the Commission set forth the basic requirements that must be satisfied by an applicant before a certificate can be issued.[44] Under these requirements, a certificate applicant must present evidence establishing the adequacy of each of the following: (a) gas supply; (b) markets; (c) proposed facilities; and (d) financing. An applicant for a certificate is also required to show anticipated construction costs and operating expenses as well as the public need for the proposed project or service. Further, the applicant must present schedules of proposed rates and an estimate of revenues. These requirements have remained essentially unchanged and have been applied in subsequent decisions. If an applicant fails to make a proper showing in one or more of these matters, the Commission may deny the certificate or, more likely, grant the certificate and attach terms and conditions which, when fulfilled, will satisfy the Commission's requirements. The applicant has the alternative of accepting the conditioned certificate in 30 days or rejecting the entire certificate.

The gas supply supporting the appli-

[42] *Ashbacker Radio Co.* v. *FCC,* 326 U.S. 327 (1945).

[43] *Panhandle Eastern Pipe Line Co.* v. *FPC, et al.,* 169 F. 2d 881, 884 (1948), *cert.* denied, 335 U.S. 854 (1948).

[44] *Re Kansas Pipe Line & Gas Co.,* 30 PUR (NS) 321 (1939).

cant's project must be sufficient to enable the proposed service to be rendered for a period of time long enough to justify the project from the standpoint of both consumer and investor. The measure of the adequacy of an applicant's gas supply, formerly used by the FPC, was the "life index," which is defined as the total estimated proven supply of gas divided by the annual supply requirement. The life index, in effect, expresses the gas supply in terms of years of consumption. As a general rule, a 20-year supply has been regarded as adequate. The following life-index figures for a group of major pipelines in 1945 and 1959 indicate the declining trend in pipeline gas reserves, experienced generally during the postwar expansion period.[45]

measures the length of time over which a specified required annual volume can be produced. The deliverability-life concept, unlike the life-index concept, takes into account the important fact that, as gas reserves are depleted, their capacity to produce at high sustained rates declines. Thus, while the life index contains the inherent assumption that a given gas supply can be produced in equal annual quantities, the deliverability-life approach recognizes that, after about 70 per cent or less of a gas reserve has been produced, the remainder will be produced in declining annual amounts over an extended period of time.

The FPC has determined that a 12-year deliverability-life showing is the minimal gas-supply requirement for a pipeline company. However, in a limited

	1945	*1959*
Northern Natural Gas Co.	36.14 years	28.40 years
Tennessee Gas Transmission Co.	27.10 years	20.58 years
El Paso Natural Gas Co.	30.00 years	27.85 years
Panhandle Eastern Pipe Line Co.	35.07 years	25.10 years
Southern Natural Gas Co.	26.10 years	19.15 years
Natural Gas Pipeline Co.	27.10 years	19.10 years

During the period 1946–1960, marketed natural gas production increased 164.8 per cent in the United States, while additions to supply increased only 64.2 per cent. The national life index fell from 32.5 years in 1946 to 20.1 years in 1960.[46] This indicates that the finding of new gas supplies has not kept pace with the expansion of the pipeline industry, and that the postwar expansion was accomplished through the availability of pre-existing reserves of gas.

In recent years, the FPC has relied less upon life-index data, as a measure of the adequacy of pipeline gas reserves, and more upon another measure—deliverability life. This approach, in short,

[45] Olof W. Nelson, "Gas Supply in FPC Certificate Proceedings" (Paper delivered before an N. A. R. U. C. regional conference, 1961), p. 3.

[46] *Ibid.*

number of instances, the Commission has been willing to issue a certificate even though the gas supply shown had fallen below the minimum standard. There, the primary criterion employed is whether the pipeline has shown an over-all increase in its gas-supply situation in a recent period.[47]

Pipeline certificate cases sometimes involve a dispute as to the proposed initial rate. Opposition to the form or level of the pipeline's proposed rates may come from a customer group, the FPC staff, or the coal interveners. The Commission's stated policy is to attempt to reach agreement on such questions prior to or during the certificate hearings. When this cannot be done, the Commission has found it necessary to attach a "rate condition" to the certificates is-

[47] *Texas Illinois Natural Gas Pipeline Co.*, 22 FPC 979, 980, 981 (1959).

sued, requiring the filing of proper rates at some time in the future. Any of four general forms of rate conditions may be attached to a certificate: (a) The applicant may be required to file a specific rate as decided upon by the Commission. (b) The applicant may be required to file rates satisfactory to the Commission shortly before the commencement of the proposed service. This allows the applicant to determine construction costs and estimated expenses more accurately and to propose rates on the basis of such data. (c) The Commission may allow certain rates to become effective for an interim period of operation, with permanent rates to be filed on the basis of actual operating experience during the interim period. (d) A certificate authorizing deliveries to a new resale customer by an established pipeline may be conditioned to require the sale to be initiated under the pipeline's applicable existing rate schedules.[48]

Certificate proceedings before the FPC frequently bring out the fact that natural gas is sold in a competitive fuel market. This is particularly true where industrial and space-heating markets are concerned. Representatives of the coal and coal-hauling railroad industries, both management and labor, frequently intervene in pipeline-certificate cases seeking to have the applications delayed or denied. In essence, the principal objective of the various coal interests is to protect their market for steam coal, that is, boiler fuel. These intervening parties have asserted, among other things, that the use of natural gas as a boiler fuel by industry and electric utilities is an "inferior" use, and that gas should be conserved for "superior" uses such as cooking and other domestic purposes. The FPC policy has been to consider the end use to be made of the gas as one of a number of factors to be weighed in determining the over-all public interest in issuing a certificate. How much weight may be accorded to the factor of end use has not been entirely resolved.

A good example of the issue of competition between natural gas and coal is found in the 1956 "Black Dog" case.[49] This case involved an application by Northern Natural Gas Co. for a certificate to construct and operate facilities to serve the Black Dog power-generating station of Northern States Power Co. with a large volume of natural gas on an interruptible basis for use as boiler fuel. This is a main-line industrial sale, of the type discussed in the previous section. Accordingly, although the Commission would not have authority to fix the rate, the seller would have to qualify for a certificate and show that the rate would be compensatory.

The coal interveners opposed the issuance of the certificate in order to prevent the loss of this market to gas. Their opposition rested primarily on these grounds: (1) there would be an adverse economic impact upon the coal-producing areas in southern Illinois and western Kentucky if the certificate were issued; (2) the rate to be charged would be non-compensatory because it was below the pipeline's allocated full-commodity charge; and (3) natural gas reserves are limited, while coal reserves are large, which necessitates conserving the gas for "superior" uses.

The Commission, in a split decision, issued the certificate. It found that the private interests (coal and railroads) which might be adversely affected by this competitive sale must yield to the public interest requiring the issuance of the certificate. The Commission concluded: (1) that this sale would cause

[48] Federal Power Commission, *Annual Report to Congress for the Fiscal Year Ended June 30, 1952* (Washington, D.C.: Government Printing Office, 1953, pp. 110–111.

[49] *Re Northern Natural Gas Co.,* 15 FPC 1634 (1956).

a material improvement in Northern's load factor and would produce substantial additional revenues which might result in lower rates to Northern's other customers; (2) that the pipeline's gas reserves were sufficient; (3) that Northern States Power Co. would realize significant savings in fuel costs; and (4) that the price for the gas was sufficient to assure Northern of revenues in excess of a proper allocation of cost.

The rate for the Black Dog sale was 24.1 cents/Mcf for the first 600,000 Mcf per month and 23.1 cents for all gas over that amount. This commodity charge (as discussed in Chapter 10) had been determined by the Commission when it ordered Northern to charge zone rates and permitted the zone differential to be reflected in the demand charge. In taking this action, the Commission was fully aware that Northern's commodity charge could go no higher without causing gas to lose industrial sales to coal competition.

In ruling that the Black Dog price was acceptable, the Commission stated that Northern's management had reason to think that a price in excess of the Commission's own determination of the commodity charge would be satisfactory to the Commission. The fact that the Black Dog sale was priced above the approved commodity charge, even as constructed, made it apparent that it would make some contribution to fixed costs and pay all out-of-pocket costs.

In a more recent case, which ultimately reached the Supreme Court, the Commission was upheld in giving consideration to the end-use factor in denying a pipeline application for a certificate. There, a combination gas and electric-distribution utility contracted to purchase gas, produced in Texas, for use exclusively as boiler fuel in the generation of electricity. The utility also contracted with a pipeline to secure transportation of this gas. The pipeline applied for a certificate authorizing the construction and operation of the facilities required to provide this service.

The Commission denied the application, although finding that its conventional requirements had been satisfied. Among other reasons for the denial was the conclusion that consumption of this gas as boiler fuel would be an "inferior" use from the standpoint of conserving a valuable natural resource. This view had been urged by the coal interveners, among others. The Commission, in denying a petition for rehearing, stated that the end-use factor was neither of "decisive" nor of "determinative" importance; rather, it was one among other factors which, taken together, not individually, justified denial of the certificate.[50]

The Supreme Court held that the Commission did not abuse its discretion in considering the end-use factor, among others, in deciding that the public convenience and necessity did not require the issuance of the certificate. The Court also upheld the Commission on this issue on the grounds: (a) that the state commissions could not be expected to regulate end use uniformly; and (b) that Congress intended that there should be no "attractive gap" in regulation.[51] Thus, it appears that the Commission's authority to consider end use as a factor in certificate cases is firmly established.

---

[50] *Transcontinental Gas Pipe Line Corp.*, 21 FPC 399 (1959).

[51] *FPC* v. *Transcontinental Gas Pipe Line Corp.*, 365 U.S. 1 (1961).

15 Regulation of Independent Natural Gas Producers

The Supreme Court held in 1954 that prices paid to "independent" producers of natural gas, selling in interstate commerce, are subject to regulation by the Federal Power Commission under the Natural Gas Act. This was the historic *Phillips Petroleum Company* decision. The term "independent" gas producer is commonly used to denote firms that produce or gather gas but which are not primarily engaged in the operation of an interstate pipeline. This category includes virtually all major integrated oil companies (those which produce, refine, transport, and market oil and its products), as well as the smaller and non-integrated or partially integrated producers.

The independent producer may sell the rights to gas in the ground, or the gas production itself at or near the well-head, at some central point in the field after gathering the production from one or more wells, or at the inlet or outlet of a plant where the gas is purified and/or stripped of its natural gasoline content prior to its transmission to market. Somewhat more than one-half of the output of natural gas is sold to interstate pipelines. In the Southwest and other producing areas, gas producers also sell large amounts directly to local pipelines, to steam electric utilities and various industries for use as fuel, to local gas utilities for distribution to the public, and to the petrochemical industry as raw material as well as fuel. In addition, a relatively important volume of gas is consumed in the producing fields as fuel for power, drilling, pumping, and other equipment. The Federal Power Commission has jurisdiction over the prices charged by gas producers for sales in interstate commerce for resale to the public which, in essence, means sales to interstate pipelines. Thus, FPC jurisdiction applies to one, but not all, of the markets supplied by gas producers.

The purpose of this chapter is (1) to portray in broad terms what the gas-producing industry includes and what it does; (2) to survey briefly how regulation came about and how it has been implemented; (3) to describe the unique economic characteristics of the industry; (4) to examine the principal regulatory methods used or proposed for gas production; and (5) to trace the development of regulatory policies. Since producer regulation is relatively new, many of the problems remain, as yet, unsolved. The problems of producer regulation are afforded a fairly detailed analysis because they involve departures or attempted departures from orthodox public utility regulation.

1. THE STRUCTURE OF THE GAS-PRODUCING INDUSTRY

A. *The Relationship of Gas to Oil.* *Petroleum* is properly defined as a mixture of hydrocarbons which, taken separately, may be gaseous, liquid, or solid at atmospheric temperature and pressure. By varying the temperature and pressure, each of these hydrocarbons may be converted into a gas, a liquid, or a solid. At normal temperatures and pressures, all inflammable natural gas contains some liquefiable hydrocarbons, which may be separated to form natural gasoline or heavier liquids. All crude oil contains natural gas. The volume of gas in oil produced from a well may be too small to have commercial value under existing market and operating conditions. Similarly, the amount of liquefiable hydrocarbons in a natural gas may be too small to repay the cost of extraction. The petroleum industry recognizes a special case, known as *condensate gas* (sometimes improperly called "distillate gas"). All the condensate is gaseous in the reservoir, where the pressure may be high and the temperature may exceed 300 degrees Fahrenheit. On reduction of temperature and pressure at the surface, the cooled gas yields condensate in liquid form, leaving the remaining hydrocarbons as gas suitable for processing. The condensate liquid is a mixture of hydrocarbons which can be separated into liquefied petroleum gases (chiefly propane and butane), natural gasoline, and light oils. After the condensate liquid is separated, the gas that remains may be processed in order to extract natural gasoline and lighter hydrocarbons. The residue is salable as natural gas. In summary, *petroleum* includes natural gas, natural gas products, oil, and solids, such as asphalt and paraffin. These products are miscible in all proportions, are discovered and produced together, and become distinct or separate materials only after processing in the field, in special plants, or in refineries.

At the producing stage, the oil and gas industry is largely a single industry. This is reflected in the fact that about 75 per cent of the costs of exploring for and producing oil and gas are joint costs. The geological and geophysical work which precedes exploratory drilling is the same for both oil and gas, and, with small variation, so is the leasing, drilling, and equipping of wells. If a geophysical report indicates a likely "trap" in which oil and gas may have accumulated, there is no possible way of determining with certainty the actual hydrocarbon contents of the trap (if there is anything at all) without penetrating it with a drilling bit, although in some areas past experience is an indicator of what, if anything, may be found. The hole may be a failure (dry), or it may be productive. If productive, it may not produce "commercial" quantities—enough gas or oil to make the well pay its operating expenses. A well produces a "commercial quantity" of oil and/or gas so long as its production sells for more than operating expenses, even though the well never returns its capital investment. If oil is found, it is always accompanied by natural gas. The volume of gas varies from an amount too small to repay the cost of saving the gas to a volume of gas the value of which may exceed the value of the oil produced. In recent years, deeper drilling has discovered increasing quantities of condensate gas, discussed previously. Natural gas may be found by itself in "wet" or "dry" form. "Wet gas" is that from which some liquids can be profitably removed by processing. The term "dry gas" is used to describe: (a) natural gas which has no commercially extractable liquefiable content; and (b) the residue from natural gas after removal of its liquefiable content.

About one-third of the United States gas reserves are comprised of "associated gas," that is, gas located in the same reservoir with oil. Associated gas may be completely dissolved in the oil, or part of the associated gas may lie in a "gas cap" above but in contact with the oil. When oil production commences through a well, reduced pressure releases gas from solution in the oil. The gas forms a froth or foam and blows the oil out of the well. The high-pressure gas in the gas cap, if there is one, presses down on the oil, forces it to flow to the low-pressure area surrounding the well, and assists the recovery of the oil. Gas promotes oil recovery by providing energy to move the oil and assists its flow by frothing the oil into a lightweight column in the well. Many oil wells flow because water underlying the oil pushes it into the well and up to the surface. Oil recovery is more complete when oil is driven or washed out of the reservoir by a water drive. On the other hand, when oil production commences, the gas that comes out of solution in the oil forms gas bubbles in the pore spaces of the reservoir and retards the flow of oil. Oil recovery by water drive, under very favorable conditions, may exceed 90 per cent of the oil reserve. When oil is produced by gas expansion, ordinarily less than one-third of the oil reserve is recovered. Associated gas is usually produced at low rates to facilitate the oil production. After oil production dwindles to insignificance, a high percentage of the associated gas is produced, but at decreasing rates as the gas pressure declines.

While there are thousands of producers, a list of the twenty or thirty largest gas-producing companies would be all but indistinguishable from a list of the major oil companies. Ranks, of course, vary among firms and by years for different products or other measures of size. Although gross revenues from gas sales are substantial for the major oil and gas producers, gas revenues as a percentages of total revenues from all sales are quite small. Gross revenues from gas sales as a percentage of total revenues range between three and ten per cent for the major integrated oil companies, with the majority of these on the low side of the range. While most of these companies transport and refine crude oil and in many cases market oil products, very few carry natural gas past the liquid-removal and processing stage. Thus, it should be kept in mind that gas producers usually are also oil producers. This is important because, as discussed below, some problems of gas-producer regulation are created by or complicated by the joint production of gas and oil.

For many years and through World War II, the industry was almost entirely concerned with discovering oil. When natural gas was discovered instead, or at the same time, it was not regarded as immediately important. This reflected the fact that much of the gas had no market and hence was worth very little or was valueless. (Even today, in some of the oil fields abroad, vast amounts of high-quality gas are valueless for the same reason.) Accordingly, before the postwar boom in long-distance pipeline construction, the national average field price of natural gas declined to an historic low point of 4.5 cents per Mcf in 1940, which reflected a gradual but continuous decline from a national average of 11.1 cents per Mcf in 1922.[1] Thus, the enormous reserves of gas, which justified the financing and construction of most of the present pipeline network, were discovered as the result of drilling motivated by the quest for oil.

After World War II, improved pipeline technology and the relatively high price of coal provided a basis for a construction boom in long-distance pipelines and an expanding national market for natural gas. As this market developed, natural gas emerged as a "coproduct" of oil and as an important competitor in the supply of some important energy demands. By 1960, natural gas accounted for virtually one-half of

[1] *Re Cities Service Production Company,* FPC Docket No. G–9510 et al., Exhibit No. 55 (1961); price data taken from U.S. Geological Survey and U.S. Bureau of Mines sources.

the energy output of the oil and gas industry. At the same time, however, natural gas sales were responsible for only about 17 per cent of the annual revenues from crude oil and gas. This fact is due to the widely different market prices of natural gas and crude oil equated on a heat-content basis, which results from a complex of historical factors and the fact that the cost per Btu of transportation is far greater for gas than for oil. Thus, in the early 1960's, the price of natural gas at the wellhead averaged about 15 cents per million Btu's, while the same quantity of crude-oil energy at the same point was worth over three times as much. As natural gas grew in importance as a source of energy, one result was a tendency toward declining average revenue per unit of energy produced by the oil and gas industry. This has occurred, of course, because of the relatively greater growth in the product yielding the lesser unit revenues.

B. *Who Looks for and Produces Gas?* Thousands of individuals and companies explore for, drill for, and produce natural gas in one capacity or another. In 1960 the Federal Power Commission reported that 18,807 ownership interests, comprising individuals and companies, sold gas in interstate commerce; their revenues from sales to interstate pipelines were about $900 million annually. By contrast, the interstate pipeline industry was reported as comprising 96 companies with annual revenues of almost $3 billion from sales to gas distributors. The annual revenues of the local gas distributors were about $5 billion for sales of natural gas to ultimate consumers.[2] On the average, less than 15 cents of the residential consumer's dollar spent for natural gas is due to charges by independent producers; this figure would be somewhat higher if all customers, including industrials, were taken into account.

In addition to the ownership interests in gas produced for the interstate market, there are perhaps several thousand more which sell gas in intrastate gas markets. This indicates that the ownership structure in oil and gas properties is very complex. While there are many individuals and business entities owning some portion of production, not all actually seek and drill for oil and gas. One of the problems complicating producer regulation is the large number of sellers involved; technically, each ownership interest is a "natural gas company" under the Act. In the interest of reducing the burden of regulatory paperwork, the Commission authorizes only one co-owner member of a group to make the necessary filings for the entire group. In 1959 the FPC reported that interstate pipelines were supplied by slightly less than 5,600 producers, taken alone or as the first-named party in association with others.

The question of who actually does the exploratory and developmental drilling for oil and gas is one of some interest. In 1959, for example, the 24 large United States companies drilled 21.2 per cent of all new wells, with the smaller operators drilling the remainder. However, the 24 large companies drilled 53.9 per cent of the California wells, 58.8 per cent of the South Louisiana wells, and 33.5 per cent of those in New Mexico.[3] Since the large companies generally have substantial financial and scientific resources at their disposal, it seems likely

[2] U.S. House of Representatives, Committee on Interstate and Foreign Commerce, *Independent Regulatory Commissions,* Subcommittee Print, 86th Cong., 2nd sess. (Washington: Government Printing Office, 1960), p. 76; Federal Power Commission, *Statistics of Natural Gas Companies, 1960* (Washington: Government Printing Office, 1961), p. xvi; *Gas Facts,* 1961 ed., p. 116.

[3] *World Oil,* February 15, 1960, p. 105.

that they would obtain more of the most promising drilling prospects. On the other hand, the smaller operators perform a particularly valuable function by undertaking to drill what very likely are the relatively higher risk prospects, and often receive financial contributions from the larger companies to do so. Data are not available to show which group had more success in drilling, nor are there data which break down oil and gas drilling between the larger and smaller operations.

There has been considerable debate on whether a company can, in fact, explore specifically for gas rather than for hydrocarbons (oil and gas) generally. Much drilling is labeled "developmental," which denotes the "drilling-up" of a known producing field. Here, of course, there is more certainty of whether oil or gas will be found. In exploratory drilling ("wildcatting"), the outcome is much less certain. Geologists generally agree that: (1) gas is more apt to be found in deep tests than oil because of high temperatures, which favor the generation of gas rather than of oil; (2) gas can be produced from reservoirs whose characteristics are unfavorable for oil production; (3) because of its low density, gas will be the last to spill out of certain types of geologic traps and will be saved, while oil is lost; (4) methane, the major component of natural gas, is believed to be the most common form of hydrocarbon; and (5) there are certain types of rock which are more apt to produce gas than oil.[4] Another factor is what Dr. Bruce C. Netschert has called "the accumulation of knowledge." This refers in part to the expectations, based upon experience, of what a successful well in a particular area is apt to produce. In this respect, Dr. Netschert has referred to "the emergence of the ability of the industry to direct at least part of its search for natural gas alone. . . ."[5] These factors are clues indicating where to look for gas which, if a company desires, it can follow in programming its exploratory drilling activity. If the profit incentives are greater in gas than in oil, all but the regional operators should have some flexibility in their exploratory activity. The Phillips Petroleum Company, for example, budgeted 50 per cent of its exploratory expenditures in 1959 for the search for gas.[6]

C. *Competition in the Production of Gas.* In the earlier discussion on the characteristics of public utilities, it was noted that a tendency toward natural monopoly is but one among a number of conditions required to warrant public utility status. Advocates of producer regulation have leaned heavily on the argument that there is monopolistic control over supplies of gas in the field, and that this control is not in the public interest.[7]

The evidence on monopoly has been sifted rather carefully. While it is true that the field market for natural gas is not perfectly competitive in the theoretical sense that economists define that term, it is very doubtful that the market for any goods or services meets that definition. On the other hand, there is substantial evidence indicating that the field market for natural gas is effectively, or workably, competitive. One indication is that there is very low concentration among the producing companies in

[4] See the panel discussion on "What's the Secret of Successful Gas Search," in the *Oil and Gas Journal,* April 24, 1961, p. 92.

[5] *Area Rate Proceeding,* FPC Docket No. AR61-1 et al., Transcript, pp. 6305, 6342 (1962).

[6] *Oil and Gas Journal,* April 24, 1961, p. 103.

[7] For example, see the testimony of Senator Paul H. Douglas on the Harris-Fulbright Bill, *Hearings Before the Senate Committee on Interstate and Foreign Commerce on Amendments to the Natural Gas Act,* 84th Cong., 1st sess. (Washington: Government Printing Office, 1955), pp. 1499 ff.

gas production and interstate gas sales. Table 15.1 shows the results of a Census Bureau tabulation on concentration in gas production in 1954, the year that regulation commenced. It shows that the four largest producers accounted for 21.7 per cent of production. In 1960, the 23 firms having direct sales of gas to interstate pipelines of more than 100 million Mcf accounted for about 57 per cent of total sales to pipelines.[8] However, these data include sales by the 23 producers together with their sales on behalf of co-owners. Thus, the 57 per cent figure is somewhat overstated. Phillips Petroleum Company, the largest seller, accounted for about 8.4 per cent of the total, again on the basis of its sales plus those handled for co-owners.

A comparison can be made with data presented in a congressional study of concentration in American manufacturing industry, using 1954 Census data. It showed the following percentage figures on concentration (based on value of shipments) for the four largest companies in each industry: passenger cars, 98 per cent; steel ingot production, 76 per cent; petroleum refining, 32 per cent; primary aluminum, 99 per cent; cigarettes, 82 per cent; cotton fabrics, 17 per cent; meat packing, 39 per cent; and tires and tubes, 78 per cent.[9] Concentration ratios in many mining industries are also quite high. For the year 1954, the following approximate concentration ratios (of four leading companies) were found: copper, 80 per cent; iron ore, 62 per cent; lead, 56 per cent; and bituminous coal, 17 per cent.[10] While concentration ratios based on national figures cannot be accepted alone as completely reliable indicators of monopolistic tendencies, they do give useful guidance in this area. If interstate gas sellers were ranked among the 1,023 manufactured-product groups studied by Congress with respect to the percentage of control exercised by the four largest firms, they would rank about 875th (in descending order of concentration). Thus, it is difficult to

8 Federal Power Commission, "Direct Sales by Producers of Natural Gas to Interstate Natural Gas Pipeline Companies—1960" (Washington: 1961), Tables 1 and 4, mimeo.

9 United States Senate, Committee on the Judiciary, *Concentration in American Industry,* Subcommittee Report, 85th Cong., 1st sess. (Washington: Government Printing Office, 1957), Table 37.

10 *Re Continental Oil Co.,* FPC Docket No. G–16966 et al., Exhibit No. 45 (1959); based on various government and industry sources.

Table 15.1

Concentration Ratios for Natural Gas Production[1]

United States

1954

Operating Companies Ranked by Volume of Production	*Production (Bil. cu. ft.)*	*Per Cent of Total Production*
First 4 companies	2,199	21.7
First 8 companies	3,178	31.4
First 20 companies	5,493	54.3
First 50 companies	7,458	73.7
First 100 companies	8,481	83.8
All 4,855 companies reporting	10,122	100.0

1 Includes natural gas used for repressuring, pressure maintenance, and cycling, and natural gas vented to air, burned in flares, and other oil and gas field losses.

Source: Special tabulation prepared by the Bureau of the Census, U.S. Department of Commerce, from 1954 *Census of Mineral Industries.*

demonstrate that there is monopoly control in gas production.

Much greater concentration is found on the buying side of the field market for natural gas than on the selling side. For the United States in 1957, for example, the first four sellers accounted for 20.4 per cent of the sales volume taken by interstate pipelines, while the first four buyers purchased 43.9 per cent of the sales volume. For the seven Southwest producing states in 1957, the first four sellers accounted for 21.4 per cent of the sales volume, while the first four interstate pipeline buyers purchased 45.5 per cent of the total.[11] The established tendency of concentration ratios to rise as the market is broken down into constituent parts is illustrated by a study of the South Louisiana producing area. Professor M. A. Adelman found that the four largest pipeline purchasers of interstate gas accounted for about 81 per cent of this market in 1954, while the four largest gas producer-sellers accounted for about 31 per cent of the supply.[12]

In recent years a number of economists have studied this problem, and the consensus appears to be that there is "workable" competition on the seller's side of the field market.[13] These studies have examined the market structure with respect to control of production, sales and revenues, and by fields, regions, states, and the nation. Despite the apparent "workableness" of gas-producer competition, critics of the industry have continually alleged the existence of monopoly and of excess profits. As discussed below, Federal Power Commission proceedings have demonstrated that no excess profits situation exists. However, from the standpoint of theoretical economics, it is conceivable that a type of "excess profit" or "economic rent" can exist in an industry without monopoly being present.

D. *Economic Rent and Institutional Barriers.* It was noted above that studies made of the selling side of the field market for natural gas generally have concluded that it is workably competitive. Thus, those who argue for producer regulation because of monopoly would appear to have little basis for such a claim. However, the evidence is not so clear cut on the question of whether or not public regulation of gas field prices is justified on other grounds. From the standpoint of theoretical economic analysis, excess profits need not arise only from structural monopoly or monopolistic behavior on the part of sellers in a given market. They can also arise as returns to scarcity, in which case they are economic rents or quasi-rents. Also, excess profits may arise in a competitive market in which factor mobility is low or in which institutional rigidities prohibit normal adjustments.

Economists who see a problem of returns to scarcity, or economic rent, in

---

[11] *Ibid.*

[12] *Re Champlin Oil & Refining Company,* et al., FPC Docket No. G–9277 et al., Exhibit Nos. 12 and 13 (1958).

[13] This is the general conclusion in the following studies: Edward J. Neuner, *The Natural Gas Industry: Monopoly and Competition in Field Markets* (Norman: University of Oklahoma Press, 1960); Leslie Cookenboo, Jr., *Competition in the Field Market for Natural Gas,* The Rice Institute Pamphlet, Vol. XLIV, No. 4 (Houston: 1958); Paul W. MacAvoy, "Price Formation in Natural Gas Fields," Unpublished Doctoral Dissertation at Yale University, 1959; Martin L. Lindahl, "Federal Regulation of Natural Gas Producers and Gatherers," *Papers and Proceedings of the American Economic Association,* May 1956, pp. 532 ff. For a partially contrary view, see Joel B. Dirlam, "Natural Gas: Cost, Conservation, and Pricing," *Papers and Proceedings of the American Economic Association,* May 1958, pp. 491 ff. Professor Alfred E. Kahn takes the view that, while there may be competition in gas production, other factors make necessary the controls normally used in a monopoly situation; "Economic Issues in Regulating the Field Price of Natural Gas," *Papers and Proceedings of the American Economic Association,* May 1960, p. 506.

the gas-producing industry suggest that such returns can exist even in a competitive pricing situation. They state that economic rent, or a profit in excess of what is required to call forth the necessary supply, arises under conditions where there is: (1) a relatively fixed supply of a natural resource; and (2) an increasing demand. Within this framework, they suggest a need for public regulation which would serve to prevent the accrual of such earnings to owners of natural gas resources.[14]

The possibility of the accrual of economic rents to gas producers raises a whole new array of economic questions and public policy problems. If economic rent arises, it must result from a relatively inelastic fixed supply of gas in the presence of a relatively inelastic increasing demand.[15] That there has been a rapidly increasing demand for gas in the postwar years is undeniable. The elasticities of gas supply and demand are not at all so obvious. Certainly, the elasticity of demand of *connected* residential consumers would appear to be quite low. However, the *potential* residential customer who is contemplating using gas for cooking, water heating, and space heating and who has not yet invested in the necessary appliances has near-perfect substitutes at his disposal; thus, his demand is apt to be more elastic. Since rate discrimination within a given class of customers is not allowed, the elasticity of demand for residential gas may be greatly influenced by the *potential* customer. The demand for gas by industrial customers is generally conceded to be relatively elastic because many of those users can and do shift from one fuel to another, depending on the relative prices of competitive fuels. Since industrial sales make up a substantial proportion of total gas sales, the evidence is not convincing that the total demand for gas is relatively inelastic.

The question of whether the supply of gas is relatively fixed and inelastic has been the subject of much discussion. It would appear that, in the short run, supply is relatively inelastic. Increases in the field price of gas can do very little in the short run to call forth new gas supplies. However, in the longer time period, the combination of apparently static oil prices and production plus rising gas prices certainly has stimulated to the extent possible the search for and development of gas reserves at greater depths and in gas-likely areas.[16] It is impossible to weigh accurately the relative importance of static oil prices and production versus rising gas prices, but gas is receiving much more attention now than in earlier years—among other things, because of its increasing contribution to oil company revenues. Indications of this in the postwar period are: (a) the increase in estimated proved reserves; (b) the increase in the gas-oil ratio of new discoveries; and (c) the increase in gas discoveries as a proportion of total new hydrocarbon reserves, equated on a Btu basis. Thus, during the 15-year postwar period, estimated proved gas reserves increased by about 78 per cent despite growing annual production. The gas-oil ratio in discoveries of proved reserves increased from 4.5 Mcf per barrel to 8.4 Mcf per barrel

[14] *Ibid.*, Neuner, p. xix; *Re Area Rate Proceeding,* FPC Docket No. AR61–1 et al., prepared testimony of Dr. Alfred E. Kahn, pp. 34–35 (1962).

[15] The same result could come about if supply and demand were both increasing but demand was growing relative to supply.

[16] Dr. Dirlam questions even the long-run response of gas supplies to prices. *Op. cit.* However, he is opposed on this point by Dr. Cookenboo. Leslie Cookenboo, Jr., Discussion of Dr. Dirlam's paper, *Papers and Proceedings of the American Economic Association,* May 1958, pp. 516 ff. See also Theodore H. Levin and Dale Berman, "Measuring Price-Supply Relationship for Natural Gas," 68 *Public Utilities Fortnightly* 1 (1961).

over the decade 1947–1956, and new gas reserves as a proportion of new hydrocarbon reserves (on a Btu basis) increased from about 40 per cent in the late 1940's to about 55 per cent by the late 1950's.[17]

Bridging the gap between the concept and the measurement of returns to scarcity in natural gas production involves formidable problems; while the concept has received much attention, measurement has not. However, if such returns were present during the postwar decade, it is rather paradoxical that they arose from the action of buyers rather than sellers of gas. The great prewar surfeit of gas suddenly found a market because of improved pipeline technology and the rising price of coal, among other factors. Almost overnight the surplus appeared to become a shortage with buyers bidding up prices in order to obtain sufficient reserves to meet FPC certification requirements and to protect their large pipeline investments. Once the initial surge of demand was filled, long-run factors seemed to take hold once again. Producers searched for and found new reserves, pipelines began to encounter distributor and industry price resistance, and the going price for undedicated reserves by the early 1960's apparently had stabilized.

When all these factors are combined, it is difficulty to say with certainty that economic rents have arisen or will arise continually in the field market for gas and be generally widespread in the industry. It is even more difficult to say, if rents do arise, that this should call forth utility-type regulation. In general, direct price regulation which converts producer surplus to consumer surplus is used only rarely in the United States economy, except for traditional public utilities.

The institutional barriers to competitive behavior in the field market fall primarily into two groups. There is some degree of immobility on the part of an established pipeline which may cause the pipeline to pay a somewhat higher price than would be the case if it had mobility. The higher price may be less costly than building more line. If pipelines have more than one source of supply, which is generally the case, and if there is competition among sellers, then excess profits (for these reasons) are not forthcoming.

The second type of barrier is the long-term gas-purchase contract between pipeline buyer and producer. It is conceivable that the rigidities introduced by 20-year contracts and whatever forms of price escalation the FPC will allow, might cause prices to be higher than they would be otherwise. However, there is no certainty in this, for it is in the interest of the pipelines to play off one producing area against another, favoring the lower-priced areas with larger takes of gas. Then, too, any change in institutional arrangements, such as the long-term contract, has its costs, regardless of whether or not some new arrangement is better than the old. Market imperfections which may result from institutional barriers, such as factor immobility and long-term purchase contracts of themselves do not appear to be so disruptive as to call forth utility-type regulation.

2. FEDERAL REGULATORY JURISDICTION OVER GAS PRODUCERS

In 1954, sixteen years after the Natural Gas Act was passed, the Supreme Court held that it applied to interstate sales by independent producers of nat-

---

[17] American Gas Association, *Gas Facts*, 1961 ed., p. 13; Bruce C. Netschert, *The Future Supply of Oil and Gas* (Baltimore: The Johns Hopkins Press, 1958), p. 87; American Gas Association and American Petroleum Institute, *Reports on Proved Reserves of Crude Oil, Natural Gas Liquids, and Natural Gas* (New York: 1957).

ural gas. Needless to say, this decision caused a substantial controversy. Congress twice voted to amend the Act so as to eliminate or narrow the scope of regulatory jurisdiction. Each bill was vetoed.

A. *The Issue of Jurisdiction.* Controversy on the regulatory jurisdiction over producers of natural gas has centered around Section 1(b) of the Natural Gas Act, which provides that the Act "shall not apply . . . to the production or gathering of natural gas." The pertinent section is as follows:

> The provisions of this act shall apply to the transportation of natural gas in interstate commerce, to the sale in interstate commerce of natural gas for resale for ultimate public consumption for domestic, commercial, industrial, or any other use, and to natural-gas companies engaged in such transportation or sale, *but shall not apply* to any other transportation or sale of natural gas or to the local distribution of natural gas or to the facilities used for such distribution or *to the production or gathering of natural gas.* [Emphasis supplied.]

On first reading, it would seem that natural gas producers are exempt from the Act. The Supreme Court, as noted, has held to the contrary. The Court reasoned that Congress had directed the Commission to regulate the price of gas moving in interstate commerce, and that the FPC could not properly regulate this price if it did not also regulate the prices of gas in the field. Therefore, the Court concluded that the exemption quoted applies to the physical acts of production and gathering, but not to the selling of gas in interstate commerce.

Much has been said and written about the "intent" of Congress in this section of the Act. This much, however, appears to be certain with respect to the passage of the Act: (a) Congress was deeply concerned with regulating the wholesale sales of interstate pipelines to gas distributors; (b) the prominent jurisdictional question before Congress arose from the fear of the states that federal authority would absorb state jurisdiction over local gas distributors, as it had in the area of railroad regulation; and (c) there was no protest in Congress from representatives of the gas-producing states. When the question of regulation of field prices arose, it became necessary to interpret the intent of Congress. The evolution of this interpretation by the Commission and the courts is dicussed below.

B. *The Evolution of Regulatory Control.* This section will deal with Federal Power Commission and court decisions which have ultimately placed gas producers under FPC jurisdiction with respect to their prices for interstate sales. It is convenient to divide this group of decisions into three historical periods: (1) decisions leading up to the Phillips case in 1954, (2) the Phillips case at the Commission, appellate court, and Supreme Court levels, and (3) decisions since the Phillips case. In the last period, only decisions dealing specifically with jurisdiction will be discussed. Cases involving methods and problems of producer regulation will be reviewed in the later sections of this chapter.

(1) *Decisions Leading up to the Phillips Case.* The question of FPC jurisdiction over gas producers came before the Federal Power Commission as early as 1940, in the *Columbian Fuel* case. There, the Commission held that ". . . it was not the intention of Congress to subject to regulation under the Natural Gas Act all persons whose only sales of natural gas in interstate commerce, as in this case, are made as an incident to and immediately upon completion of such persons' production and gathering. . . ."[18] However, the FPC left the door open by adding that, should monopoly arise in

[18] *Re Columbian Fuel Corporation,* 2 FPC 200, 208 (1940).

gas production, it would look into the question of field-price regulation again. The dissenting opinion by Commissioner John W. Scott in this case warrants attention, because it was later adopted in the reasoning of the courts. He maintained that Section 1(b) should be read so as to say that production and gathering are exempt from regulation, but that sales of gas in interstate commerce are not. This would mean that only producers *not* selling in interstate commence would be exempt. Commissioner Scott pointed out that there was legal precedent in the *Carter Coal* case supporting the view that a person producing and selling a commodity in interstate commerce does two things. He produces and he sells. If the sale is interstate, whether such destination is intended or not, the seller is engaged in interstate commence.[19]

In 1943 the FPC issued an important decision on the jurisdictional issue in a case arising out of a complaint by the Louisiana Public Service Commission against Interstate Natural Gas Company. The company produced and purchased gas and transported it prior to making sales within Louisiana to three interstate pipeline companies. It also conducted business as an interstate pipeline. Thus, its operations were not confined to production. Interstate opposed FPC jurisdiction over its sales to the three pipelines. It contended that the sales of gas which ultimately crossed state lines were beyond FPC jurisdiction, because they were an integral part of production and gathering. The FPC, in ruling that it had jurisdiction, rejected this contention and referred to the *Carter Coal* case, in which the distinction between production and sale was made.[20]

[19] *Carter* v. *Carter Coal Co.*, 298 U.S. 238, 302 (1936).

[20] *Re Interstate Natural Gas Co., Inc.*, 3 FPC 416, 432 (1943).

The company ultimately took an appeal to the Supreme Court, which held in 1947 that the Commission had jurisdiction over the sales in question. Initially, it ruled that these sales were made in interstate commerce. With respect to the "production or gathering" exemption in Section 1(b) of the Act, the Court held: (1) that Congress thereby intended to give the states full freedom to regulate physical production and gathering in the interest of conservation or other matters of local concern; and (2) that the FPC had authority to regulate all interstate sales made during production and gathering, except those sales that were so closely connected with production and gathering as to render federal regulation a substantial interference with state regulatory functions. The Court found nothing in the record to indicate that FPC regulation of the price of these sales was inconsistent with the regulation of production and gathering by the State of Louisiana. The Court concluded:

> By the time the sales are consummated, nothing further in the gathering process remains to be done. We have held that these sales are in interstate commerce. It cannot be doubted that their regulation is predominantly a matter of national, as contrasted to local, concern. All the gas sold in these transactions is destined for consumption in states other than Louisiana. Unreasonable charges exacted at this stage of the interstate movement become perpetuated in large part in fixed items of costs which must be covered by the rates charged subsequent purchasers of the gas including the ultimate consumer. It was to avoid such situations that the Natural Gas Act was passed.[21]

Independent producers were highly uncertain of their jurisdictional status as a result of the Commission's *Interstate* decision in 1943 and an appellate

[21] *Interstate Natural Gas Company* v. *FPC*, 331 U.S. 682, 692–693 (1947).

court decision in 1946 upholding the Commission. Prior to the Supreme Court decision in that case, the Commission sought to clarify the situation. Thus, in 1947 it revived a number of jurisdictional cases and held in each instance that a producer which did not transport gas in interstate commerce was exempt from regulation.[22] However, at this point the Commission could do very little. After the *Interstate* decision by the Supreme Court in June of 1947, the FPC issued an order in August declaring that it did not have jurisdiction in producer cases.[23] This order could have no lasting impact, since the Commission could not do by administrative action what Congress had failed to do by unambiguous law and what the Supreme Court had held to be, in effect, an incorrect interpretation of the Act.

(2) *The Phillips Case.* The Supreme Court decided the jurisdictional issue in its 1954 opinion in the *Phillips Petroleum Company* case. This case had its beginnings in a 1947 FPC decision granting a certificate of public convenience and necessity to the Michigan Wisconsin Pipe Line Company.[24] The pipeline was solely supplied by Phillips, which made delivery after processing the gas to remove liquids and impurities. The City of Detroit and the State of Wisconsin, intervening in this case, requested that Phillips be made a party to the pipeline proceeding and be declared a natural gas company under the Act. The Commission held that a determination of whether Phillips was or was not a natural gas company could not be made in that proceeding. However, in 1948 the FPC instituted an investigation to determine: (1) whether Phillips was a natural gas company under the Act; and (2) whether its interstate gas prices were unjust or unreasonable. The Commission went ahead with hearings limited to the jurisdictional question. Thus began the great experiment in producer regulation.

In summary, the events of the next 15 years were these: (1) the Commission held it did not have jurisdiction; (2) the courts reversed the Commission, holding that the rates for interstate sales by independent producers were subject to the Act; (3) the Commission investigated Phillips' interstate rates and found in 1960 that its gas costs exceeded its gas revenues by about $9 million in the 1954 test year; and (4) an appellate court and the Supreme Court both upheld the Commission.

In deciding in 1951 that it did not have jurisdiction over Phillips, the Commission held: (1) that the business of producing and gathering was exempt under Section 1(b), and that sales occurring during production and gathering were exempt as a part of that business; and (2) that Phillips' transportation and sale of gas constituted a part of the gathering process or were so closely related thereto as to require exemption.[25]

This decision was appealed by the State of Wisconsin, among others, and an appellate court reversed the Commission. It was held that "Phillips sells gas after the time and beyond the place at which production and gathering are complete and after processing has intervened."[26] Phillips then appealed to the Supreme Court. On June 7, 1954 the

---

[22] *Re Fin-Ker Oil & Gas Production Co.*, 6 FPC 92 (1947); *Re Tennessee Gas & Transmission Co. and the Chicago Corp.*, 6 FPC 98 (1947); *Re Kansas-Nebraska Natural Gas Co. and Kansas Natural Gas, Inc.*, 6 FPC 664 (1947); *Re R. J. and D. E. Whelan*, 6 FPC 672 (1947).

[23] *Re A Rule to Make Clear the Position of the Commission Regarding the Independent Production and Gathering of Natural Gas*, Order No. 139, 18 CFR 2.54 (1947).

[24] *Re Michigan Wisconsin Pipe Line Company*, 6 FPC 1 (1947).

[25] *Re Phillips Petroleum Company*, 10 FPC 246 (1951).

[26] *State of Wisconsin* v. *FPC*, 205 F.2d 706, 708 (1953).

Court handed down its historic decision holding that Phillips was a natural gas company under the Act. The majority concluded that:

> . . . the legislative history indicates a congressional intent to give the Commission jurisdiction over the rates of all wholesales of natural gas in interstate commerce, whether by a pipeline company or not and whether occurring before, during, or after transmission by an interstate pipeline company.
>
> Regulation of the sales in interstate commerce for resale made by a so-called independent natural gas producer is not essentially different from regulation of such sales when made by an affiliate of an interstate pipeline company. . . . Protection of consumers against exploitation at the hands of natural gas companies was the primary aim of the Natural Gas Act.[27]

(3) *Post-Phillips Decisions Extending FPC Jurisdiction.* The decision in the *Phillips* case dealt with sales made after production, gathering, and processing. Subsequent cases have taken the *Phillips* decision back to the wellhead. That is, the courts have held that sales made to interstate pipeline companies at the wellhead, or deliveries made in the vicinity of the well or field, before processing, are within the Commission's jurisdiction. Further, the post-*Phillips* court decisions have held that Congress intended wellhead sales to be regulated whether made during production or made before, during, or after gathering. The FPC has been upheld by the appellate courts in all cases testing its jurisdiction in this respect, and the Supreme Court has denied *certiorari* where efforts were made to take a further appeal.[28]

There has been no occasion to determine whether or not the interstate journey has begun prior to the point of delivery where delivery is above ground at the mouth of the well. Thus, there remains a significant unanswered question as to how far federal jurisdiction could go when and if pressed to its furthest limit. As a Texas court has stated, in a case involving the parallel question of where interstate commerce begins for purposes of taxing natural gas sales:

> The same reasoning (viz., that the gas "moves in a continuous flow from the mouths of wells into interstate commerce") could send the interstate commerce label down the well and into the subterranean chambers, where the movement of gas actually commences. The mouth of the well is merely an arbitrary point along the road traveled by the gas. There is no legal reason known to us for fixing the mouth of the well as the dividing line separating State and Federal jurisdictions in matters of commerce and taxation.[29]

3. BACKGROUND TO REGULATION

This section first summarizes briefly the implementation of regulation by the Federal Power Commission, and then proceeds to outline the principal provisions of producers' gas sales contracts. These contracts constitute the producers' rate schedules on file with the Commission; therefore, regulatory case decisions and policy making in general often are directly concerned with contract provisions.

A. *Implementation of Regulation.* Shortly after the *Phillips* decision, the FPC began to issue a series of orders designed to establish regulatory procedures and control. These orders were in the form of rules and regulations having the effect of law, which the Commission

---

[27] *Phillips Petroleum Company* v. *Wisconsin,* 347 U.S. 672, 682, 685 (1954).

[28] *J. M. Huber Corp.* v. *FPC,* 236 F.2d 550 (1956); *Humble Oil & Refining Co.* v. *FPC,* 247 F.2d 903 (1957); *Deep South Oil Co. of Texas* v. *FPC,* 247 F.2d 882 (1957); *Saturn Oil & Gas Co.* v. *FPC,* 250 F.2d 61 (1957); *Continental Oil Co.* v. *FPC,* 266 F.2d 208 (1959).

[29] *Calvert* v. *Panhandle Eastern Pipe Line Co.,* 255 S. W. 2d 535, 545 (1953).

is authorized to issue for the purpose of making effective the provisions of the Act. Independent producers subject to the Act were defined to include any person engaged in production or gathering who transferred or sold gas in interstate commerce for resale but who was not primarily engaged in operating an interstate pipeline.

Independent producers were required: (1) to submit copies of their existing interstate sales contracts, which would constitute rate schedules; (2) to apply for certificates of public convenience and necessity authorizing existing interstate sales; (3) to apply for and to receive certificates before making any new or additional interstate sales; (4) to submit for Commission review any proposed rate changes provided for by existing or subsequent interstate contracts; and (5) to secure Commission approval before abandoning any interstate sale. This constituted the framework for a comprehensive system of regulation.

Compliance by producers with these requirements created an enormous new work load for the staff and members of the Commission. A comparison of FPC certification activities before and after the *Phillips* decision suggests the magnitude of the increase. Prior to the *Phillips* decision, the FPC received a total of 1,244 certificate applications; this total includes all applications filed in the 12-year period from 1942, when the certificate provisions of the Act became effective, through June of 1954. This is an average of about 100 per year. By contrast, in the first full year following the *Phillips* decision, the FPC received 6,047 certificate applications from producers alone. Much the same occurred with respect to rate filings. Prior to *Phillips,* the Commission had been processing about 700 gas rate filings each year. In the first year after *Phillips,* this normal work load was augmented by about 11,000 producer rate schedules, as well as 2,633 filings, called *supplements,* proposing rate increases or modifications of filed rate schedules.[30] By 1960, the Commission had on file more than 33,000 supplements to existing rate schedules. A substantial backlog of undecided cases accumulated during this period, in part because the size of the staff did not increase by nearly so much as the work load, and in part because the Commission was finding its way toward a workable basis of regulation. Ultimately, the Commission was subjected to public criticism on this score, much of it quite unfair, by critics who at the same time had little to offer by way of solution to the many problems confronting the regulators.[31]

B. *Gas Sales Contracts.* Long-term contracts, negotiated by arm's length bargaining, are the conventional basis for gas sales by independent producers. Contracts of 20 years' duration or longer, dedicating to the buyer the production from specified acreage, are basic in the gas-producing industry primarily because of the financial and regulatory needs of the pipelines. Pipeline bond financing requires the assurance of adequate gas supplies for the life of a loan. Similarly, as discussed in the previous chapter, FPC certification of pipeline facilities also requires a showing of adequate long-term gas supplies. The long-term contract enables pipelines to meet these requirements.

Each contract is tailored to fit the specific circumstances of a sale, but the major points usually covered include: the amounts, prices, and quality of gas to be taken; the delivery, gathering,

[30] 44 *Georgetown L. J.* 555, 559–560 (1956).

[31] R. A. Smith, "The Unnatural Problems of Natural Gas," *Fortune,* September 1959, p. 120; U.S. Senate, Committee on the Judiciary, Subcommittee on Administrative Practice and Procedure, *Report on Regulatory Agencies to the President-Elect,* Committee Print, 86th Cong., 2nd sess. (Washington: Government Printing Office, 1960), pp. 54–58.

processing, and metering conditions; and the method and timing of payments.

Gas sales contracts are unique among commodity sales contracts, since they commonly provide for deliveries over a period of 20 years or longer. Buyers and sellers cannot foresee the possible changes in costs of operation or market values or marketing conditions which may occur during the life of a long-term contract. This causes both buyers and sellers to be concerned with three types of monetary clauses which may change the revenues from gas sales. These are: (a) tax reimbursement clauses, (b) processing payment clauses; and (c) indefinite pricing clauses. Only the last of these will be discussed here, as part of a general survey of pricing provisions.

The pricing clause of every contract provides a specific price per Mcf for gas delivered, which may be unchanged for the life of the contract. More commonly, a schedule of gradually increasing specific prices is established, and each is subject to regulatory review before becoming permanently effective. These contracted increases, commonly known as "fixed price escalations," provide for an increase in price at specified times. Most commonly, the price is increased one or two cents every four or five years. In many contracts, small annual increases (such as two mills per Mcf) are specified instead. The dates of price increases may be definitely stated, as, for example, January 1 of 1965, 1970, 1975, and so forth. Such a program has the advantage for the buyer that all or at least a majority of the prices it pays will increase on the same date; the time of increase can be foreseen; the amount is easily calculated and the buyer's financial program can be adjusted in keeping with its needs. Other buyers prefer to increase prices at four- or five-year intervals after the date of first delivery under the contract. Less commonly, the fixed-price escalations come at fixed intervals after the date of the contract.

The rationale for fixed-price escalations is that, during the early years of the contract, the buyer has high investment and undeveloped markets, and the seller has low operating costs. During later years of the contract life, the buyer's investment is substantially depreciated, and his markets are more fully developed, while the seller's operating costs (in real terms) have risen as his wells become depleted. The seller's equipment has deteriorated; his wells require more work-overs and, because of reduced pressure and increased water production, his expenses increase while his volume of sales and corresponding revenue diminish. Thus, the early lower price benefits the buyer and is acceptable to the seller. The later higher price benefits the seller, keeps the seller's wells on production longer, and thus benefits the buyer by permitting more purchases through the same installed facilities.

Indefinite pricing clauses are intended to protect the seller from unforeseen economic developments during the life of a long-term contract. Their effect is to promote long-term, rather than short-term, contracts. The most commonly found form of the indefinite pricing provision is the "favored nation" clause; the next most frequently used pricing provision of this type is the "redetermination clause." These pricing provisions are described below. Opponents of these pricing clauses maintain that they cause increases in gas prices without regard to changes in the seller's cost of production. Sellers maintain that without such clauses they would have no protection against inflation or rising costs of operation and of replacing their wasting assets, among other contingencies. The FPC has ruled that favored-nation clauses, among other types of indefinite pricing clauses not discussed here, shall be inoperative in contracts executed on or after April 3, 1961, but has authorized a form of redetermination clause in contracts executed on or after that date.

The *favored-nation clause* received its name from its similarity to the "most-favored-nation" type of tariff agreement, in which Nation A agrees to levy a tariff on the goods of Nation B which is no higher than the tariff levied by Nation A on that nation which is best treated, or "most favored." In gas contracts, a favored-nation clause is an agreement that a buyer will pay a seller the highest price which the buyer pays to any seller in a specified area for gas of similar quality, quantity, and delivery conditions. Favored-nation price adjustments become due at any time that the buyer pays a higher price to another seller, within the prescribed area and conditions. The purpose of this type of clause is to pay the going market price for all gas of uniform quality and delivery conditions.

Redetermination clauses, as the term implies, provide that either party at specified times may ask for a redetermination of the price to be paid during a subsequent period. Many variations of the redetermination clause exist. The purpose of all such clauses is to obtain for the seller the price currently being paid in the area. Normally the clause provides that either party may request a redetermination of the price to be paid from the beginning of some period when a fixed-price escalation is due. A typical clause provides that notice shall be given a fixed number of months prior to the date of a fixed-price escalation. If the parties do not agree on the proper price within a specified period, the price is then submitted to arbitration, under the provisions of the arbitration clause of the contract, and the price determined by the arbitrators is usually binding on both parties.

4. ECONOMIC CHARACTERISTICS OF THE GAS-PRODUCING INDUSTRY

Before discussing the specific methods of regulation that have been suggested for the gas-producing industry, it would be helpful to consider some of its unique economic characteristics. The present section first contrasts the general economic characteristics of public utilities and gas producers, and then examines the cost and revenue aspects of the oil and gas-producing industry.

A. General Characteristics. With the advent of regulation, gas producers selling in interstate commerce commenced to share one principal legal characteristic with traditional public utilities—the prices of both industries are required by law to be just, reasonable, and not unduly discriminatory or preferential. However, while regulation obviously affects the way that business is conducted in some phases of the oil and gas-producing industry, it does not alter the basic characteristics of the industry itself. Thus, gas producers sell a commodity, which they first had to discover in nature, while public utilities essentially sell services which are largely the product of capital facilities. In sharp contrast with public utilities, which are generally characterized by natural monopoly and decreasing cost tendencies, oil and gas producers comprise a workably competitive minerals-producing industry. As such, it is one of the "extractive" industries, which include agriculture, mining, and lumbering. Economists traditionally regard extractive industries as characterized by increasing-cost tendencies. This general concept, in large part, is based upon the need of such industries to resort to the less desirable known sites and opportunities provided by nature as production increases and as the basic resource is depleted.

Other differences between utilities and gas producers also merit attention. A brief review of some of the important characteristics of public utilities would be helpful to this end. Public utilities have a legal monopoly in their markets and service areas, although they may compete with sellers of substitute services. Both utilities and their customers benefit from regulatory protection shielding utilities from direct service and price competition. Utilities are required to supply all reasonable requests for service, and they can be compelled to expand or improve their plant and facilities to accommodate growth in market demand or to improve the quality of their service. The grant of public authority to operate a public utility ordinarily includes the right to use the public alleyways and streets, as well as the right of eminent domain, or condemnation. These rights are granted in recognition of the fact that public utilities are responsible for the transportation of their various services, by wires, cables, mains, or vehicles, either above or below ground. As noted in Chapter 1, the courts have regarded performance of a transportation function as one of the most important tests in deciding upon the question of public utility status.

For regulatory purposes, the individual-company cost-of-service, or rate-base, method is appropriately applied to public utilities for two principal reasons: (1) their total cost of service can be ascertained with reasonable accuracy; and (2), other things equal, there is a dependable and consistent relationship between the costs incurred by a utility for productive facilities and the capacity of a utility system to provide service. In most instances, public utilities are able to earn the rates of return allowed under regulation, so that the authorized rate of return is both an upper limit on earnings and a realistic earnings objective. As discussed earlier, public utilities are considered by investors to be comparatively less risky than industrial enterprises, as indicated by their substantial debt ratios, among other factors.

Gas producers, on the other hand, do not have a legal or economic monopoly with respect to their markets. At the same time, however, they do not have a legal obligation to explore for or to develop gas reserves or to produce gas beyond the requirements of existing sales contracts. Since there is no legal compulsion to explore for or to develop supplies of gas, economic incentive must be depended upon to induce the performance of these functions. Most gas producers do not perform any important transportation function. Their sales usually are made at or near the wellhead. Under the conventional industry practice, the pipeline purchaser builds gathering lines to each well or to an adjacent separator, where oil, some petroleum liquids, and water may be removed. As a general rule, gas producers are reluctant to invest in gathering facilities; however, in many areas the producer lays a short line to a central point in the field, where the gas is purchased. Sometimes, too, separate gathering companies purchase at the wellhead and process, purify, and compress the gas before transporting it to the main pipeline, where the gas is resold. The FPC regards gathering companies as pipelines for regulatory purposes, if they perform more than a local transportation function. As in other competitive industries, there is complete freedom to enter and to leave the business of producing oil and gas. However, a producer or his successor cannot terminate gas deliveries to an interstate pipeline before authorization is granted by the Commission. Both new business entities and business failures are a common occurrence in the industry.

Gas producers and public utilities are clearly different with respect to the significance of their respective costs. First, it is impossible to calculate a meaningful cost of service for most individual gas producers, because of the dominance of joint costs that are related to both oil and gas. Joint costs, as noted earlier, comprise about 75 per cent of the total cost of oil and gas exploration and production. Accordingly, a conventional public utility-type cost-of-service analysis of a particular producer requires the allocation of these substantial joint costs between natural gas and petroleum liquids. In a costing situation of this kind, a very wide range of cost results is readily obtainable, depending upon the joint cost-allocation methods selected. The results do not necessarily or reliably reflect the incurrence of costs; rather, they reflect only the differences in the costing techniques employed. It is for this reason that the different studies, presented in evidence before the FPC, quite commonly have shown average unit costs ranging from 10 cents per Mcf (or less) to 50 cents per Mcf (or more) for a single company.

Second, there is no reasonably predictable relationship between dollars spent on exploration and the amount of oil and gas discovered. This characteristic of the industry is explainable only in part by differences among producers in business and scientific efficiency. The principal reason for the erratic relationship between exploratory expenditures and discoveries arises from the high degree of uncertainty as to the results of any given exploratory effort. Where exploratory wells are concerned, the "luck" factor is a more important determinant of productivity than in most other risk situations involving capital outlays by business firms. In this respect the oil and gas industry differs strikingly from public utilities, where the additional productive capacity resulting from capital expenditures can be closely predicted. The nature of the industry-wide risk involved in the exploration for oil and gas is suggested by the experience of the industry as a whole: (1) an average of one exploratory test in 27 has found a small field; and (2) the probability of finding a major reserve has averaged one in about 400 attempts.[32] The economic significance of these probabilities is that the exploration phase of the oil and gas industry is associated with very high risks; this level of risk does not characterize the public utility industry. The risks of exploration are such that financial institutions will not lend money for this purpose on the security of the assets that may be discovered by a proposed exploratory effort. Exploratory wells generally account for about one-fourth of the total wells drilled, and almost all of the remainder are development wells which are characterized by a substantially lesser degree of risk and uncertainty. The representative experience of the industry in developmental drilling has been a dry-hole ratio of about one in four. During the decade of the 1950's, the annual number of dry development wells about equaled the number of dry exploratory wells.

Third, the costs incurred by oil and gas producers cannot be recovered from the sales of their products if to do so would require charging a price in excess of the market price. This results from the fact that they sell competitively and, unlike utilities, do not have an exclusive market wherein proper costs can be recovered from sales to the extent that consumers are able and willing to pay prices covering such costs. On the other hand, if the Commission somehow were to require pipelines to buy from producers at prices reflecting individual company costs, the effect would be to

[32] The fields referred to are: Class D, 6 to 60 million Mcf; and Class A, over 300 million Mcf, or their oil or oil-gas equivalents. Data on discoveries reflect industry experience in a 17-state area, 1943–1952. Frederick H. Lahee, "Statistics on Natural-Gas Discoveries," 42 *Bulletin of the American Association of Petroleum Geologists* 2037, 2044–2047 (1958).

penalize the fortunate and efficient producers and to reward the unfortunate and inefficient.

B. *Cost Characteristics of Gas Supplies in the Field.* Some of the most difficult questions to answer about gas production concern costs—what it costs to find and produce gas; whether costs are generally rising or falling over time; if falling or rising, by how much; and what factors may be causing these movements. This section discusses costs in general terms and is intended to introduce the beginning reader to an increasingly important area of economic research. Any inquiry into gas costs immediately encounters the problem of allocating the joint costs of gas and oil. Because of the dominance of joint costs, it is impossible to determine "accurate" costs of gas production, except in the relatively few instances where an enterprise produces dry gas alone. As a result, much of the work that has been done in this field has been concerned with the costs of the oil and gas industry as a whole.

The cost of supplying gas at the surface of the earth includes the combined costs of: (1) geological, geophysical, and other preliminary exploration activities; (2) lease acquisition and rental payments; (3) well drilling, including necessary site preparation, access roads (or canals), and water and fuel supply; (4) well completion and equipping, including casing, tubing, special contract services, and wellhead fittings (the Christmas tree); (5) producing expenses over the life of the well; and possibly (6) removal of liquids and/or impurities, the separation of oil and gas, or other steps to make the gas suitable for long-distance transmission. The various steps in exploration and drilling are practically the same for oil and gas up to the point of field development.

(1) *The Problem of Measuring Costs.* The costs of finding oil and gas should be based on some unit of what is produced or found. For oil, it could be cost per barrel or per Btu of energy. For gas, it could be cost per Mcf or per Btu. Let us consider gas alone to simplify the problem.[33] Theoretically, a calculation of discovery costs should be based on Mcf's of gas reserves discovered by a given expenditure. Thus, ideally, two figures are needed: (1) the total proven reserves of gas; and (2) the total cost per unit incurred in finding and making these reserves available. Here, computations of the cost per Mcf of reserves break down. For a company that is a going concern, there is a continuous stream of expenditures, and there are continuous changes in estimated proved reserves, either because of new discoveries or because of extensions and revisions (often negative) of estimates of previous discoveries, or both. However, no satisfactory method has been developed to assign specific expenditures to specific quantities of reserves found. The problem is further complicated by the fact that much expenditure will not result in any new reserves, thus making impossible the "accurate" assignment of costs to specific reserves. Moreover, there is a major problem in ascertaining the quantity of reserves actually discovered. Equally expert reservoir engineers sometimes differ widely in their estimates. During producing operations, unpredictable developments may radically increase or decrease the anticipated volume of ultimate production. In addition, many years of development and operation may be required before the reserves in a field are known. Large initial expenditures may yield a discovery well with small reserves. Ultimate reserves of a large pool cannot be ascertained from

[33] For a discussion of the cost-measurement problem, see John E. Hodges and Henry Steele, *An Investigation of the Problems of Cost Determination for the Discovery, Development, and Production of Liquid Hydrocarbon and Natural Gas Resources,* Rice Institute Pamphlet, Vol. XLVI, No. 3 (Houston: 1959).

one or two wells, and later modest expenditures may result in large additions to reserves. After all the gas in a field has been produced and the wells abandoned, it might be possible to ascertain the cost of what had been produced. At that point in time, however, such information would not be particularly valuable, since few fields are enough alike to merit detailed cost comparisons. This discussion has not touched upon the problems created when oil is considered. How, for example, would dry-hole expenses be allocated among specific reserves of oil and gas? It cannot be done except in some arbitrary fashion.

(2) *Factors Influencing Costs.* The most widely quoted cost study in the oil and gas industry is the "Joint Association Survey of Industry Drilling Costs" conducted by the American Petroleum Institute, the Independent Petroleum Association of America, and the Mid-Continent Oil & Gas Association.[34] This study covers the costs of drilling and equipping wells up to the Christmas tree, but does not include leasing, exploration, or producing costs. A second part of the Joint Association Survey covers estimated expenditures and receipts of the United States oil and gas-producing industry.

For 1959 drilling operations and expenditures, the Joint Association Survey showed that wells classified as gas wells were substantially deeper than those classified as oil wells. The representative gas well cost over $100,000 each, or almost twice as much as the representative oil well. The 1959 cost per foot for gas wells averaged $18.45, as compared with $13.63 for oil wells.

Productive wells of all kinds in the 3,751 to 5,000-foot depth range cost an estimated average of $10.61 per foot to drill and complete in 1959, while wells in the 12,501 to 15,000-foot depth range averaged $30.84 per foot. Productive wells over 15,000 feet averaged $42.07 per foot. These averages suggest that the cost per incremental foot increases with greater depth. The Joint Association Survey data, for the three depth ranges noted above, show incremental costs per foot of $11.91, $72.79, and $101.50. These data, taken in conjunction with the fact that average drilling depths are slowly increasing, indicate that greater drilling depth leads to more than proportionate cost increases, unless offset by cost-saving technological innovations.

The situation with respect to the costs of finding and developing oil and gas might be summarized as one in which greater average depth and less accessible and less promising drilling sites tend to push costs upward and in which technology and higher ratios of gas to oil in new discoveries tend to push down the average cost per Btu of new hydrocarbon supplies. While there is no clear-cut answer to the question of which set of forces will be the stronger over the long run, the chances seem better for costs to rise than to fall.[35]

[34] Cited here as "Joint Association Survey." Surveys were made for 1953, 1955–1956, and 1959, as part of a continuing series. The data used here are from the 1959 Survey. Another basic source of information is found in the cost indexes developed by the Cost Study Committee of the Independent Petroleum Association of America. See particularly the committee report released April 30, 1962.

[35] At least two studies conclude that finding and development costs in real terms will be fairly constant over the next 15 to 25 years. See Sam H. Schurr and Bruce C. Netschert, *Energy in the American Economy, 1850–1975* (Baltimore: Johns Hopkins Press for Resources for the Future, Inc., 1960); Walter J. Levy and Milton Lipton, "Some Major Determinants of Future Oil Requirements and Supplies," *Proceedings of the Fifth World Petroleum Congress* (1959), Section IX, p. 6. The problems in applying real-cost concepts are suggested in *Re Area Rate Proceeding,* FPC Docket No. AR61–1 et al., prepared testimony of Celia Star Gody (1962).

C. Revenues and Profits in Gas Production. Earlier chapters have pointed out that regulatory agencies scrutinize closely the rate of return earned by utilities under the rates they are authorized to charge. In the regulation of gas producers, a determination of the experienced rate of return encounters many of the same obstacles noted in the discussion of costs above. This is logical, since net profits are revenues minus costs. Viewed prospectively, a determination of the earnings requirement of gas production alone is ordinarily complicated by the fact that there is revenue coming to the firm from oil and oil product sales, perhaps from condensate or gas liquids sales, perhaps from sulphur, helium, petrochemicals, or nuclear ores and processing, or perhaps from non-jurisdictional gas sales, as well as from jurisdictional gas sales. The market structure for each product and the market behavior of the producer in selling each product will vary greatly. Thus, the first thing that can be said about the revenue and profits situation is that it, too, is extremely complicated and interrelated. Jurisdictional gas sales account for a small portion of the revenues of the major gas producers. Owing to the diverse activities of the larger companies particularly, it is difficult to make judgments in terms of the comparable earnings and capital-attraction standards, or the reasonable over-all return required to maintain the financial integrity of the regulated function.

It can be shown with various statistical series that major oil companies which produce gas do not appear to earn particularly high profits. During the postwar period, the earnings of non-integrated oil and gas producers (whose securities are held by the public) have been comparatively higher but subject to much greater variation. For comparison purposes, the following percentages show average earnings after taxes on common equity for some principal industries in the decade 1950–1959.[36]

Natural gas distributors	10.9%
Interstate natural gas pipelines	12.4%
50 largest United States manufacturers	14.7%
24 integrated petroleum companies	13.0%
17 non-integrated oil and gas companies	16.6%

Oil-industry earnings in recent years from domestic oil operations have been and are apt to continue relatively depressed because of a long-term oversupply of proved crude oil reserves in the world. This market glut is likely to last for a long time, barring a major war or an emergency situation affecting Middle East or African crude suppliers. Revenues normally obtained from the oil part of a firm's business, and which are used for oil and gas explorations, are apt to be smaller in the future than they have been in the past. At the same time, the market for gas is growing with some vigor. Thus, a forecast of natural gas demand, sponsored by a group of major gas distributors, concluded, with some qualifications, that 1970 requirements would be 18.5 trillion cubic feet, as compared with 12.2 trillion in 1959.[37] This all seems to suggest that gas revenues in the future will have to bear a greater responsibility for the exploratory function than they have in the past.

5. METHODS OF REGULATION

Neither the Natural Gas Act nor the courts have specified the regulatory

[36] *Re United Gas Pipe Line Co., et al.,* FPC Docket No. CP–60 et al., Exhibit No. 9 (1961).

[37] *Re Shell Oil Company,* FPC Docket No. G–9446 et al., Exhibit No. 55 (1961). Demand defined as consumption plus lost and wasted gas less shrinkage due to liquids extraction.

methods that are to be used by the Commission in reviewing the rates proposed by gas producers. As a result, the FPC has been concerned with the selection of an appropriate method of determining whether the contract rates of gas producers are "just and reasonable," as required by the Act. During the period 1954 to 1960 the Commission undertook to decide rate cases involving individual gas producers, without adopting any particular regulatory method to the exclusion of others. Late in 1960 the FPC adopted a new approach for the future, under which it would seek to establish fair prices for the gas itself on an industry-wide basis within each principal producing area of the country. Thus, the Commission terminated the policy of deciding rate cases on an individual-company basis (except for those then in process) and commenced a program of determining rate levels on an industry-area basis. This is sometimes referred to as "area pricing." The present section examines briefly the principal regulatory methods proposed in the individual-company rate cases as well as the area pricing of industry sales in interstate commerce.

A. Methods Proposed in Individual-Company Cases. During the period 1954 through 1960, before the adoption of the area-pricing approach to producer regulation, the Commission proceeded with rate cases involving individual producers. In general, two principal methods of regulation and types of evidence were presented for consideration: (1) the traditional public utility-type cost of service; and (2) the competitive market-price standard, supported by evidence of industry cost trends. Each of these is discussed below.

(1) *Public Utility Cost-of-Service Method.* A public utility-type cost of service, as applied to an individual gas producer, is intended to determine a cost of gas sold in interstate commerce during a test year. This type of analysis of a gas producer's costs entails a segregation of costs among three principal functions: exporation and development, production, and gas processing. Thereafter, it is necessary to assign the identifiable costs and to allocate the joint costs to particular products. In this way a cost of all gas produced and sold can be calculated, after which a further allocation of gas costs between jurisdictional and non-jurisdictional sales is required. A total cost of jurisdictional gas sales, once calculated, would be compared with revenues from interstate gas sales during the same period, in order to determine whether the producer had an excess of revenue over costs or a revenue deficiency. The next step would be to reach a conclusion with respect to the propriety of the prices fixed by contract for individual sales.

The nature of the costing process is next described briefly and without detail. Direct production expenses consist principally of operating (or lifting) expenses, depreciation, depletion and amortization, production and property taxes, and gas department expenses. Indirect production expense is an allocated portion of the general corporate overhead expense. The production rate base primarily reflects the net investment in producing leaseholds and in lease and well equipment, as well as capitalized intangible development costs (primarily labor and other services) and production department buildings, facilities, and a share of general assets. For purposes of joint-cost allocation, the oil and gas production expenses and rate base, respectively, ordinarily would be separated on the basis of the various types of producing leases held by the company. These might include: gas-only and oil-only leases (where the direct expenses and investment would be assigned rather than allocated), oil-casinghead gas leases and gas-condensate leases (both of which produce joint products), and combination leases, which produce more than one of the foregoing types of output. The latter is usually, but not necessarily, the result of simultaneous production from more than one producing horizon. In addition, there might be a separate category for cycling leases—those on which the gas is produced, stripped of certain liquefiable hydrocarbons, and then reinjected into the formation. Different costing techniques and allocation methods might be applied to each of the joint-product leases and in costing the gas and the liquids separated on the leases or by plant processing.

The exploration expenses of the test year and the exploration rate base, unlike the production expenses and rate base, are not necessarily associated with the fields from which the test-year production is obtained. That is, the test-year production for a given company might come from Louisiana and East Texas, while the exploration outlays might reflect activity in West Texas and New Mexico. Thus, exploration expenses and rate base ordinarily would be treated separately from production. Exploration expenses consist primarily of such items as dry-hole costs, geological department expense, geophysical department expense, nonproductive leases abandoned and expired, an allocated portion of general overhead expenses, and others. Even for major companies, exploration expenses vary considerably from year to year, reflecting variations in both the amount of exploratory activity and the number and depth of the dry holes drilled. The exploration rate base is comprised primarily of the net investment in nonproducing and untested acreage, exploration equipment, and a portion of the general and administrative net investment. After exploration expenses and investment are determined, it is necessary to allocate each between gas and liquids. In addition, it would be necessary to provide allowances for rate of return on the production and exploration rate bases and for federal income taxes. The general problem of joint-cost allocation was discussed in Chapter 10. Making a cost study of this kind for a major producer with hundreds of producing leases is a substantial undertaking. The accountants and engineers of the FPC staff, when making a cost study based upon the books and records of a major producer, ordinarily have devoted at least three man-years of time to the project before the preparation of exhibits and testimony and before the hearing itself commences.

(2) *The Competitive Market-Price Method.* The competitive market-price, or field-price, method of determining the reasonableness of natural gas prices has been proposed in a number of cases, sometimes in different forms, depending upon the availability of data and the techniques employed by individual analysts. The basic theory underlying this approach holds that society achieves maximum benefits by allowing competitively determined prices to guide available productive resources into their best uses in the most efficient or least-cost combinations. In short, this approach is grounded on the principle that, if prices in the markets where producers sell gas are competitively determined, then the public interest will be best served if those prices are allowed to perform their proper economic functions of allocating scarce resources, calling forth the required supply, and rationing it among buyers in the field markets. An example of one form of the competitive market-price standard was discussed in the previous chapter in connection with the allowance for pipeline-produced gas in calculating a cost of service for rate-making purposes.

Perhaps the most refined form of this method is the competitive market price-cost standard. This approach considers: (a) prices set competitively for comparable supplies of gas; in conjunction with (b) data on various industry cost trends. An initial step requires proof of effective competition in the field markets in which the producer sells gas. Second, it is necessary to test the over-all reasonableness of current producer prices by comparison with industry cost trends in conjunction with supply-demand trends. In this respect, industry cost data provide a check on the results produced by the competitive market. For the purpose of comparing changes in prices and changes in costs, more than one base period might be used, for example, beginning with 1947–1949 and with 1954. Of necessity, because of the predominance of joint costs, many of these comparisons would have to be made for total hydrocarbons, although available data permit some comparisons to be made for gas alone. If it is shown that the over-all level of producer prices is reasonable, on the basis of price trends in line with cost trends and other data, then it would be possible to proceed with the next step. Third, it is necessary to analyze the provisions of existing sales contracts for the purpose of identifying those that are comparable with the particular sales in question. In making this comparative analysis, due consideration would be given to the principal factors which influence contract prices. The major criteria of comparability are: (a) date of contract, or the factors associated with the movement of market-price levels through time; (b) distance of the gas supply from consumer markets; (c) volume of reserves committed; (d) term, or length, of contract; and (e) quality and delivery conditions of the gas. Fourth, on the basis of this analysis, current market prices are determined for the various subareas of the market, largely on the basis of statistical measurement as applied to the prices in comparable contracts. The current market price in each subarea would be expressed in the form of either a single price or a dominant range of prices. Fifth, the contract price of each sale in question would be compared with the competitive market price or price range in order to test its reasonableness by this standard. In conclusion, it may be noted that application of the competitive market price-cost method involves a substantial amount of economic analysis as well as a continuous research program for the development of the required data.

B. *Area Pricing as a Standard for Regulation.* The preceding discussion dealt with methods proposed for the regulation of individual producing companies. This section discusses a third alternative, called *area pricing*. This method of regulating rates departs from the individual-company approach, with the objective of establishing fair prices for the gas itself on an industry-wide basis in each of the principal producing areas of the country. At the time of this writing, the Commission was proceeding as expeditiously as possible to implement the area-pricing concept.

(1) *The Rationale.* The adoption of the area-pricing approach to producer regulation was announced by the Commission on September 28, 1960, as part of its opinion on the investigation of the rates of Phillips Petroleum Company. This opinion, among other things, expressly rejected the individual-company rate-base approach to producer regulation as unworkable. The area-pricing approach was adopted as the alternative for the future. The Commission stated that ". . . the ultimate solution to producer regulation will be in the determination of fair prices for gas, based upon reasonable financial requirements of the industry and not on the particular rate

base and expenses of each natural gas company."[38]

The Commission's ultimate objective in adopting area pricing is to set prices in all producing areas that would be: (1) adequate to maintain the gas supplies needed by the public; but (2) no higher than necessary to achieve that purpose. In order to determine prices that would satisfy this two-part objective, the Commission announced the intention of considering both cost and economic data, adding that costs incurred in the past comprise only a part of the information required for intelligent regulation.[39] In this respect, the Commission explained that it planned to consider cost evidence pertaining to a representative sampling of the industry in each area as part of the basis for fixing prices for all producers in the area. Shortly after the area-pricing approach was adopted, the Commission instituted area-industry rate investigations of the Permian Basin (West Texas and Southeast New Mexico) and South Louisiana producing regions. Consistent with the foregoing, the investigations were designed to proceed on the basis of separate phases involving hearings on economic and cost evidence, respectively. Nevertheless, the Commission was aware from the outset that the development of appropriate natural gas prices for each area would be a time-consuming process. Therefore, simultaneously with the adoption of the area-pricing approach, the Commission also established interim pricing guides to aid in the regulation of producers until the individual-area proceedings were completed.

(2) *Interim Rate Regulation.* Concurrently with the adoption of the area-pricing plan, the Commission issued Statement of General Policy No. 61–1, establishing interim price standards which would serve to aid regulation until decisions were reached in the individual-area proceedings.[40] As a first step, the Commission defined 23 separate pricing areas. These comprised the 11 Texas Railroad Commission districts (established previously for the administration of state conservation regulations), southern and northern Louisiana, Oklahoma (divided into three areas), Kansas, New Mexico (two areas), Mississippi, Colorado, Wyoming, and West Virginia. The Commission stated that these pricing areas, although well known, were not necessarily in complete accord with the geographical and economic factors which may be relevant to gas pricing. Accordingly, it anticipated future changes in area boundaries as may be necessary to eliminate possible inequities.

Second, the Commission established two "rate guidance levels" for gas produced and sold in each area: (a) "initial service rates," which would serve as a regulatory guide with respect to proposed rates for sales under new contracts; and (b) "increased rates," which would serve as a regulatory guide with respect to proposed increases in rates charged under existing contracts. The rate guidance levels were made applicable to "pipeline-quality" gas as that term is generally understood in each area. This "two-price" policy was intended to recognize: (a) that the general level of prices provided for under existing contracts in many cases reflected the relatively low rates of past periods when natural gas was not sold nationally; and (b) that newly executed contracts com-

---

[38] *Re Phillips Petroleum Co.,* 24 FPC 537, 547 (1960).

[39] Economic evidence, as distinguished from cost evidence, concerns, among other things, market analysis and history, competitive market prices, trends in drilling productivity, reserves and deliverability, risk and incentives, and forecasts of market demand.

[40] Federal Power Commission, *Rules of Practice and Procedure,* Part 2, Section 2.56 (1960).

monly reflect the relatively higher prices that have prevailed since natural gas has been distributed nationwide. Accordingly, the initial-service rate levels were set somewhat higher than the levels for increased rates. However, the Commission anticipated that these differences in price levels would be reduced and eventually eliminated.

This system of interim rate regulation was designed to work in two ways. The initial-service rate levels, applicable to rates proposed for sales under new contracts, established the price line above which the Commission would not issue a certificate of public convenience and necessity (authority to sell) without justification of the contract price. The increased rate levels, applicable to proposed increased rates under existing contracts, established the price line above which the Commission would suspend proposed rate increases provided for in the contracts of producers. Suspended rates also would require justification by the producer. In arriving at these rate-guidance levels, the Commission indicated that it had considered all the relevant facts available, including cost information from all decided and pending cases, existing and historical price structures, volumes of production, price trends in the various areas over a number of years, trends in exploration and development, trends in demands, and the available markets for the gas. The Commission made clear that its rate-guidance levels did not constitute a determination of just and reasonable rates, and would not foreclose any person from justifying a particular rate in any area. In addition, as with the area boundaries, it was provided that the rate-guidance levels would be changed from time to time as the facts warranted. In the period following the adoption of interim pricing regulation, the Commission proceeded to make adjustments in its rate-guidance levels, both upward and downward.

(3) *Some Unresolved Problems.* The area-pricing system is not entirely free of problems, as might be expected with any new regulatory method. One of the earliest problems to arise involved a possible question of confiscation of property. While there appears to be general agreement that a producer could not charge or collect a price higher than the contract price, even where the area price exceeds the contract price, there is an unresolved problem in reversed circumstances. Specifically, the problem involves the right of a producer to collect a contract price in excess of an area rate-guidance level when the producer maintains that the contract price is justified on the basis of individual-company costs. A corollary problem relates to the extent of a producer's right to present evidence in support of its own contract rates in proceedings concerned with the economics and costs of industry-wide operations in a given area. The question posed here asks whether there would be an unconstitutional deprivation of property: (a) if a producer were denied a contract rate exceeding an area rate-guidance level where justification could be shown by reference to its own costs; or (b) if an individual producer were denied the right in an area rate proceeding to present evidence as to its own circumstances.

A second problem concerns the exact nature of the evidence that will be accepted as relevant or required by the Commission. In addition to specifying economic and cost evidence as important, the Commission also has indicated that consideration would be given to each of the types of data, noted above, which were relied upon in setting the rate-guidance levels for interim regulation. A more specific translation of these types of evidence into support for any particular price level or levels has been left for the producers, interveners, and staff to develop. In short, the Commission has not defined either its concept of the "reasonable financial requirements of the industry" or the nature of the cost evidence that will be required. Until these matters are resolved, the exact nature of the area pricing standard will remain in question.

A third problem concerns the boundaries of the pricing areas. Oil and gas reservoirs, like so many other things, are not necessarily confined neatly within state boundaries or other man-made geographic regions. As a result, apparent inequities have arisen where, for example, a particular geological formation underlies two adjacent pricing areas, each with different area prices. The Commission, as noted previously, was aware of this potential problem from the beginning of area pricing, and has since reaffirmed its intention of eventually revising area boundaries as the facts and equities require.

A fourth problem area arises out of differences in the provisions of sales contracts for natural gas produced within given pricing areas. The Commission has indicated an interest in achieving greater uniformity in the provisions of gas sales contracts, apparently with the objective of facilitating area pricing. Two notices of proposed rule making have been issued which respectively relate to contract provisions governing: (a) the period of time over which reserves would be depleted by deliveries; and (b) gas quality and deliverability factors.[41] The first of these apparently would have the effect of lengthening the depletion periods provided for in most postwar contracts; such contract provisions commonly represent concessions on other matters in the bargaining over contract provisions. Deferring production reduces the present worth of the sale price. The second proposal listed seven quality and deliverability factors which the producer would be required to meet, including: (1) minimum heating value; (2) maximum water content; (3) maximum liquefiable hydrocarbon content; (4) maximum hydrogen sulphide content; (5) maximum sulphur content; (6) freedom from odors, dust, and solid and liquid materials; and (7) minimum delivery pressure. Failure to meet one or more of these standards would result in an automatic penalty in the form of a reduction in the price payable. Gas of higher quality than the minimum standards, however, would not be sold at a higher price. Perhaps the greatest objection by producers to this proposed rule is their claim that existing contract prices already take into account differences in quality, and that further price adjustments would have the effect of doubling the penalty.

[41] 26 *Fed. Reg.* 4614, 4615 (1961).

6. REGULATORY POLICY AND PROBLEMS

Although regulatory policy with respect to gas producers is in the process of evolving, reference to some of the past decisions would helpful in bringing out the problems which have impeded policy development and the reasons for the ultimate adoption of the area-pricing method. The following sections discuss FPC policy in the areas of both rate and certificate regulation.

A. *Rate-Regulation Policy.* In an early policy decision, the Commission adopted the date of the Supreme Court decision in *Phillips* (June 7, 1954) as the starting date of regulation. The purpose of this was to avoid the problems anticipated in any effort to roll back prices to 1938, when the Natural Gas Act was adopted. Thereafter, the Commission proceeded to hear and decide cases involving suspended rate increases. The cases decided first were relatively few, and the Commission made clear that the resulting decisions were not to be considered as precedents. However, in 1956, the courts decided the *City of Detroit* case, discussed in the previous chapter. This decision exerted an impact upon the direction of rate-regulatory policy almost at once. Although *City of Detroit* involved the rates of a pipeline, not an independent producer, it nevertheless dealt with the regulatory treatment of pipeline-produced gas for rate-making purposes. The court, in setting aside the Commission's use of a field-price method of evaluating pipeline-produced gas, held the conventional rate-base method of determining rates ". . . not to be the only one available under the statute, [but] it is essential in such a case as this that it be used as a basis of comparison. . . . Unless it is continued to be used at least as a point of departure, the whole experience under the Act is discarded and no anchor, as it were, is available by which to hold the terms 'just and reasonable' to some recognizable meaning."[42]

In the leading case of *Union Oil Company of California*, decided in 1956, the FPC took a decisive step and dismissed proposed rate increases for lack of supporting cost-of-service evidence, citing the requirements of *City of Detroit*.[43] This was the first time that the Commission indicated what a producer would be required to show in order to prove a rate to be just and reasonable. While evidence of competitive market prices and other types of data were held to deserve consideration, they were deemed insufficient in the absence of cost-of-service evidence to discharge the producer's burden of proving a proposed rate increase to be just and reasonable. On the basis of *Union Oil*, the Commission then dismissed the rate increases proposed in a number of other producer cases where cost-of-service evidence was lacking. Before discussing further the cases decided under *Union Oil* decision, it is necessary to consider a parallel but opposite policy development.

In the "West Edmond" case, decided in 1958, the FPC approved rate increases proposed by a group of 11 producers, even though no cost-of-service evidence was presented. Each of the rate increases related to gas produced in the West Edmond Field in Oklahoma. The Commission distinguished this case as factually different from those decided under *Union Oil*, but suggested that it was typical of many other proceedings. Ten of the 11 producers involved in this case were involved in extensive production operations throughout the country, so that this case involved only a fragment of the operations of any one of the ten. There were a total of 133 lessees in the the West Edmond Field, who held interests in 754 tracts, each tract having a different percentage participation in the production of the principal formation. (The latter followed from the fact that this producing formation was shaped something like a piece of pie standing on edge, so that each tract represented a differing share of production depending upon its area and the thickness of the underlying formation.) In addition, there were three other producing formations in this field, and not all wells produced from the same strata. Under the facts in this case, the Commission concluded that it was impossible to employ the traditional rate-base method. The Commission also found that "It is impractical and not conducive to effective regulatory results to use the rate base method in a case involving eleven independent producers

[42] *City of Detroit* v. *FPC*, 230 F.2d 810, 818–819 (1956); *certiorari* denied, 352 U.S. 829 (1956).

[43] 16 FPC 100 (1956).

operating in one field where only a small portion of the rates of each company is being investigated." In addition, the Commission concluded that the ultimate result of applying the cost-of-service method to the West Edmond Field producers would be ". . . 133 widely varying prices for gas produced from one formation in one field." Accordingly, the Commission looked instead to evidence of competitive market prices, the relation between revenues and out-of-pocket operating expenses in the field, and general cost trends in the industry and in the economy as a whole. In consideration of the fact that the price proposed was 25 per cent below the current market price and the other evidence, the Commission concluded that the rate increases should be allowed.[44]

The West Edmond case was decided before the courts were ready to rule on the *Union Oil* case and the others decided under it. In general, the courts upheld the FPC decisions but returned the cases to the Commission for the taking of additional evidence.[45] While the courts refrained from taking a position on the appropriate or required methods of regulating the industry, they also seemed willing to permit the Commission to exercise considerable discretion in this matter, as it ultimately was to do in adopting area pricing. The problems brought out in the West Edmond case appeared to have the effect of inducing caution with respect to a rigid insistence upon compliance with *City of Detroit.* Thus, the United States Court of Appeals held in one of these cases:

> We do not think that either the Commission or the petitioner should be baffled or handicapped in this new field of regulation by any formulas by whatever name they are known. Specifically, if there is an accounting or rate-making formula known to the public utilities industry as a "conventional rate-base method of rate-making" which the Commission in its order of dismissal in this case said must be used at least as a basis of comparison or point of departure, we say the Commission need not require it unless such method is the only way by which the Commission can make its required determination. . . .[46]

During the period 1955 to 1960, the Commission was actively engaged in hearing and deciding a relatively large number of producer rate cases. In view of the uncertainties surrounding the evidence required and the regulatory method ultimately to be adopted, the majority of producers involved in these cases presented evidence of all possible kinds. However, some chose to rely entirely or almost entirely on cost-of-service evidence. The latter group included the Phillips Petroleum Company, whose rates were under investigation as a result of the original motions filed in 1947 by the State of Wisconsin and City of Detroit. In the *Phillips* and other cases of this period, the participants included numerous interveners representing consumer interests and the staff of the Commission. The staff and interveners invariably chose to rely solely upon public utility cost-of-service-type evidence.

The records of these cases furnished a reservoir of experience and information. They also appeared to raise rather than to solve policy problems in this area of regulation. For example, the staff of the Commission submitted cost-of-service data in the cases of Sinclair Oil & Gas Company and Western Natural Gas Company showing costs for each of the interstate gas sales involved in those cases. In the case of Sinclair, the staff

---

[44] *Re Pan American Petroleum Corp., et al.,* 19 FPC 463, 467–468 (1958).

[45] *Bel Oil Corp. et al.* v. *FPC,* 255 F.2d 548 (1958); *Forest Oil Corp.* v. *FPC,* 263 F.2d 622 (1959), among others. However, the Commission was upheld without remand in *Episcopal T.S.* v. *FPC,* 269 F.2d 228 (1959).

[46] *Ibid.,* 263 F.2d 622, 626.

showed unit costs for each of 48 sales which ranged from 4.1 cents to $5.47 per Mcf. Western Natural, whose producing operations are comparatively less diverse, was shown to have unit costs for its 18 sales ranging between 4.3 cents and 52.7 cents. If regulated rates had been based upon these costs, several problems would have arisen. First, interstate pipelines would not pay Southwestern gas producers more than about 21 cents per Mcf at the highest and in most instances less. Second, the dispersion of rates would exceed the range of prices in existing contracts and would have a possibly disruptive effect upon the historical pattern of rates in different field markets and end markets. Thus, Sinclair's contract rates ranged from 5.8 cents to 20.0 cents, or an average deviation from the median rate of 19 per cent, as compared to a 290 per cent deviation from the median unit cost of service. The average dispersion of the Western Natural rates was 32 per cent, compared with 88 per cent for unit costs. Third, different prices would result for the gas produced by co-owners from the same field and from the same well. Thus, for the large Carthage Field of East Texas, which is fully developed, the staff of the Commission found unit costs for six producers which ranged from 5.4 cents to 12.3 cents; for a seventh producer, the staff found a unit cost of 25.5 cents.[47]

The rate cases decided by the FPC during this period also provided further experience which aided in the development of policy. Up to the *Phillips* rate decision in September, 1960, there had been 11 producer rate-increase cases heard and decided by the Commission on a cost-of-service basis. In ten of these cases, the costs showed that the proposed prices were more than justified. The eleventh case, for other reasons, could not be resolved on the rate issue. In addition, in the four completed company-wide rate investigations, brought under Section 5(a) of the Natural Gas Act, the producers' prices also were shown to be justified on a cost basis.[48] The decision on Phillips' rates added one more to this list.

The record in the *Phillips* rate investigation was based almost entirely on cost-of-service evidence, and the Commission decided it on that basis while refraining from translating costs into rates. In short, the FPC found that Phillips had a 1954 test-year cost of interstate service of $54.5 million, or 11.1 cents per Mcf, as against jurisdictional revenues of $45.6 million, or 9.3 cents per Mcf. Moreover, the Commission recognized in principle estimated additional costs of $5.2 million, which it did not need to take into account to reach its decision. If this amount were included, the total unit cost would have been 12.35 cents per Mcf. Accordingly, Phillips' interstate gas operations resulted in a revenue deficiency of about 9 to 14 million dollars in the test year. On this basis, the Commission allowed Phillips' pending rate increases and dismissed the rate investigation. However, as noted earlier, the significant aspect of this decision with respect to over-all rate policy was the rejection of the cost-of-service method as unworkable and the adoption of area pricing.

Since the FPC had used a rate-base or cost method to decide so many previous cases, why did it appear to change so abruptly to area pricing in the *Phillips* opinion? An initial answer to that question is that the change to industry-area pricing was not abrupt. As Charles E. McGee pointed out in an address before

[47] *Re United Gas Pipe Line Company, et al.*, FPC Docket No. CP60–36 et al., Transcript, pp. 3077–3081 (1961).

[48] *Re Phillips Petroleum Company*, 24 FPC 537, 546 (1960); notes 8 and 9. The Commission apparently overlooked the decision dismissing one investigation: *Re Western Natural Gas Company*, 23 FPC 235 (1960).

the American Bar Association, the Commission's earlier decisions contained a number of references to the economic feasibility of pricing gas on an industry basis in the light of industry revenue requirements.[49] The specific answers to the question above, as set forth by the Commission in its *Phillips* rate decision, are summarized below:

(1) The experience of five years has indicated that the rate-base method of regulating utilities is "unworkable" when applied to producers' rates.

(2) Independent gas producers are not "by any stretch of the imagination" properly classified as public utilities.

(3) There is no assured relationship between the amount a producer invests and what, if anything, he will have to sell, or whether there will be a market for his product at a price that covers costs.

(4) "Every method of [joint cost] allocation advanced was shown to have at least some element of guesswork or to ignore some facts." Thus, there is no "correct" way to allocate joint costs to gas and to oil.

(5) Prices determined by costs cannot be accepted if they are higher than a buyer will pay or lower than a seller will accept.

(6) There is no accurate way to estimate ultimate recoverable reserves; thus, a cost figure per Mcf of reserves is uncertain.

(7) "Ridiculous results" would arise in unitized or jointly operated properties (as in the West Edmond case). The cost of gas from a single well may differ for each co-owner.

(8) Low-cost gas would be driven into the intrastate market and high-cost gas into the interstate market.

(9) The administrative burden of cost regulation is impossible. There were (as of September 28, 1960) 11,091 rate schedules and 33,231 supplements to these schedules. Many of these supplements proposing rate changes could only be decided after a full hearing.

(10) Cost regulation thus far has resulted in higher, rather than lower, producer rates.

(11) Gas has been underpriced, and current contract prices, for the most part, are more than fair to consumers.

The United States Supreme Court upheld the FPC decision in the *Phillips* rate case in a 5–4 decision, handed down in May of 1963. The appeal was brought by the states of California, New York, and Wisconsin and some of the gas distribution utilities served by pipelines supplied in part by Phillips. No challenge was made to any aspect of the Commission's determination of Phillips' jurisdictional cost of service for the test year. Instead, the Court was asked to rule on three technical questions of law relating to the Commission's disposition of the case after determining Phillips' cost of service. Only one of these questions was pressed vigorously by all the parties seeking judicial review. That question was whether the FPC had erred in dismissing the investigation of Phillips' rates without prescribing rates for the future. The FPC took this course, among other reasons, because the individual company approach was being replaced by the area approach under which rates for the future would be determined for all producers in a given area simultaneously.

The Commission's action was upheld as permissible under the Act. The Court ruled that the FPC had acted within its statutory authority in electing to assign its resources to area investigations instead of reopening the *Phillips* record to make the determination sought by the protesting parties. Expressly reaffirming

[49] Charles E. McGee, "Independent Producers—After Six Years of FPC," an address before the Minerals and Natural Resources Section, American Bar Association, November 10, 1960.

the principles of *Natural Gas Pipeline Co.* and *Hope Natural Gas Co.*, the Court ruled that no single method must be followed by the FPC in regulating rates, and that it is the result reached not the method employed that is controlling. "More specifically, the Court has never held that the individual company cost-of-service method is a *sine qua non* of natural gas regulation." Citing the opinions of Justice Jackson on this subject in *Hope Natural Gas Co.* and *Colorado Interstate Gas Co.* (parts of which were quoted in Chapters 6 and 14), the Court said:

> We recognize the unusual difficulties inherent in regulating the price of a commodity such as natural gas. We respect the Commission's considered judgment, backed by sound and persuasive reasoning, that the individual company cost-of-service method is not a feasible or suitable one for regulating the rates of independent producers. We share the Commission's hopes that the area approach may prove to be the ultimate solution. [Footnote omitted.][50]

The Court thus recognized that the individual company cost approach would not be suitable for regulation of the price of a commodity such as natural gas. This is not to say that the Court gave formal approval to the area method adopted by the FPC. No question of that kind was before the Court for review. However, the area method could not go unnoticed, because its adoption was an integral part of the Commission's rejection of the individual company approach. For the present, at least, the Court was willing to allow the Commission to proceed with its area plan, in part because it saw no indication that the area method will fall short of statutory or constitutional standards. The dissenting opinion, on this point, disagreed on the basis of anticipated problems involving the constitutional rights of individual producers. The minority opinion took the position that area pricing, to be constitutionally sound, must include a showing that the individual producer will recover his costs at the prescribed area rate. This and other problems await solution in the future.

B. Certificate Regulation Policy. A producer must secure a certificate of public convenience and necessity before making a new interstate sale of gas. To qualify for this authority, it is necessary for the producer to demonstrate willingness and ability to deliver the gas. Where particularly large reserves of gas are involved in a new sale, the pipeline buyer ordinarily undertakes to prove the market need for the gas. These elements of proof are commonly discharged in routine fashion. However, one further requirement is not at all routine.

The producer applying for a certificate must prove that the proposed price for the new gas is consistent with the present or future public convenience and necessity. In many instances, where the proposed price of a new sale is at or below the prevailing price level in the producing area, the matter of price is not a contested issue. However, where the contract price for the new sale exceeds the price that has long prevailed in an area, a substantial contest may develop. It is in instances of this kind in which the producer's responsibility for justifying the new sales price takes on particular importance. During the first nine years of producer regulation, neither the Commission nor the courts had come to any conclusion on how this requirement could be satisfied. However, the initial-service rate-guidance levels established under the interim regulatory system provide a basis for Commission action on the prices proposed by certificate applicants, and ultimately the Commission

[50] *Wisconsin et al.* v. *Federal Power Commission et al.*, Slip opinion, p. 16 (1963).

will determine appropriate price levels in the respective area proceedings.

The Commission has three principal alternatives when passing on a certificate application; it may approve or deny the application, or adopt a position somewhere in between. That is, the Commission may grant the certificate subject to the acceptance of such conditions as it may prescribe within the limits of its authority. In this way—by "conditioning" a certificate—the Commission can prescribe the terms under which it will permit a supply of gas to be brought into interstate commerce. Other things equal, a producer need not accept a certificate issued subject to conditions imposed by the Commission. In some cases, producers have rejected conditioned certificates, preferring to sell in the intrastate market. In most instances, however, the producers have accepted conditioned certificates on the terms specified by the Commission.

The Commission has used its authority to issue conditioned certificates primarily for the purpose of reducing the rates contained in producers' contracts. Thus, as early as 1955 the Commission issued a certificate to Signal Oil and Gas Company, conditioned upon the acceptance of a 10-cent price in lieu of the 12-cent price contained in the producer's contract. This decision is of great importance, because it contained all the elements of future Commission policy in this area of producer regulation.

The position adopted in *Signal Oil* was based on the grounds that the 12-cent price, if approved, would tend to raise the 10-cent rate level then prevailing in the South Central Oklahoma producing area. The Commission held that Signal had failed to demonstrate that the price it proposed to charge was required in the public interest. Thus, the Commission adopted a policy of "holding the line" and preserving the *status quo* ". . . at least until experience and time have given us the opportunity to develop more comprehensive criteria governing determination of rates of independent producers." The Commission expressly adopted this course of action in preference to an available alternative course which it was urged to consider. Under the rejected alternative, the Commission could have granted the certificate at the 12-cent price and then instituted a rate investigation to determine whether that price was just and reasonable. The Commission refused to accept this alternative on the ground that an investigation would require a long time to complete, and hence could not produce the desired objective so directly as the issuance of a conditioned certificate. The Commission was upheld upon review.[51]

In the CATC decision of 1957, the FPC issued a certificate authorizing very large sales of gas produced in the Gulf of Mexico, offshore South Louisiana.[52] The price proposed and allowed was 21.4 cents. This ruling was challenged in the courts on the principal grounds that: (1) the 21.4-cent offshore price exceeded the prevailing level of onshore South Louisiana prices, claimed to be no more than about 18 cents; and (2) the applicants had failed to prove that the higher price level was required in the public interest. The Supreme Court reversed the Commission.[53] On the basis of the record before the Commission in the CATC case, the Court held that the Commission had exceeded its authority in issuing an unconditioned

---

[51] *Re Signal Oil and Gas Company,* 14 FPC 134, 149 (1955); *Signal Oil and Gas Company* v. *FPC* 238 F.2d 771 (1956); *certiorari* denied, 353 U.S. 923 (1957).

[52] *Re Continental Oil Company, et al.,* 17 FPC 880 (1957). The CATC producers are Continental, The Atlantic Refining Company, Tidewater Oil Company, and Cities Service Production Company.

[53] *The Atlantic Refining Company* v. *FPC,* 360 U.S. 378 (1959).

certificate. The case was returned to the Commission for further proceedings.

In the subsequent reopened proceedings before the Commission, the record ran to 7,655 pages and included 50 exhibits. The Commission ultimately approved certificates at a conditioned rate of 18.5 cents, and ordered refunds plus interest of all amounts collected above that price.[54] This ruling rested on the determination of an "in line" price for South Louisiana in 1956, the date of the contracts involved in this case. The "in line" price was derived primarily from evidence of market prices as reflected in gas sales contracts negotiated in the South Louisiana area during 1956. Accordingly, the CATC case was ultimately decided as if the Commission in the first instance had followed the policy set forth in its *Signal* opinion. Further developments in this area apparently will depend upon changes in the rate-guidance levels or decisions in the various area-rate proceedings, as the Commission determines prices that are sufficient, but no more than necessary, to maintain the gas supplies required by the public.

[54] *Re Continental Oil Company, et al.*, Opinion No. 351, FPC Docket No. G-11024 et al., January 22, 1962. An additional 1.5 cents per Mcf will be allowed for tax reimbursement if the offshore area involved is ultimately determined to lie within the taxing jurisdiction of Louisiana.

16 Energy Supply and Demand—Past, Present, and Future

The story of natural gas is not complete unless it is placed in the broader context of supply of and demand for all energy. Some of the long-run implications of gas regulation come to the fore in such a discussion. Also, an evaluation of our energy situation has particular relevance in a study of public utility economics, since utilities will be asked to bear much of the burden of transmitting and distributing these energy supplies in the future. This chapter will review the supply of and demand for energy in the past and present and will examine estimates of the future energy situation. Stress will be laid on the impact of technology and government regulation in shaping supply and demand patterns.

1. ENERGY, GROWTH, AND PUBLIC UTILITIES

If a list of essential resources were compiled for a highly mechanized, well-developed economy, energy would certainly rank near the top. Nations have gone to war, at least in part, to secure a more adequate energy supply. Wars have been lost because, among other things, energy supplies were depleted or destroyed. In other words, energy and energy sources are essential to the well-being of any developing or mature nation. This is not to say that a nation must have energy resources in the ground or in its streams. But it must have access to energy and be able to supplement domestic supplies with imports, if the former are inadequate. In a nation with more than about $200 per capita annual income, there seems to be a fairly high correlation between income per capita and energy consumption per capita.[1]

Because energy is so critical, governments throughout the world have made considerable efforts to discover and exploit cheap energy supplies. In the United States there is a long history of federal incentives to encourage private enterprise to search for fossil fuels. Other nations which must import large quantities of fuels have instituted elaborate programs in the attempt to become self-sufficient in energy supplies. In a country such as the United States, which is industrially mature, there is fairly widespread acceptance of the idea that energy requirements will grow somewhat more slowly than real Gross National Product. This is explained by the fact that basic industries, which are heavy fuel users, are already highly developed, and much of the national growth will come from services, trade, and other non-manufacturing or non-mining activities.[2]

Energy supplies in this country originate largely with fossil fuels—oil, gas, and coal—or with falling water. The fuels are converted into heat energy and used directly in this form, or the heat is used to generate electrical energy. Electrical energy can also be generated from falling water. Since two utility industries—(1) gas transmission and distribution, and (2) electric generation, transmission, and distribution—are closely tied to the fuel industries, the supply-and-demand conditions in fuels, the shifts in patterns of fuel use, the technological innovations in production and use of fuels, and the government regulation relating to fuels will all have a significant impact on the posture of the gas and electric industries in the future. In broader terms, these matters concerning fuels are a critical element in the economic growth and development of the United States.

2. PAST AND PRESENT SUPPLIES AND CONSUMPTION OF ENERGY

Energy supply-and-demand patterns in the past point to many of the nation's current problems and also indicate the shifts in supply and demand that may become important in the future. A brief statistical summary of the United States fuel position, with some analysis of the trends evidenced by the data, will set the stage for a discussion of present and future problems.[3]

A. Consumption of Energy by Types. The shifts in energy supplies in the United States since 1900 have been substantial. Coal, in 1900, accounted for 88.9 per cent of the energy produced, while oil accounted for 4.7 per cent, natural gas and gas liquids for 3.2 per cent, and water power for 3.2 per cent. By 1960, coal's contribution had dropped to 27.2 per cent while oil rose to 35.7 per cent, natural gas to 33.0 per

---

[1] Charles P. Kindleberger, *Economic Development* (New York: McGraw-Hill Book Company, Inc., 1958), p. 24.

[2] For an interesting discussion of these ideas, see Edward S. Mason, *Energy Requirements and Economic Growth,* Report on the Productive Uses of Nuclear Energy (National Planning Association, Washington, D.C., 1955), Chapters 1 and 2. For a recent review of energy use and GNP, see Charles A. R. Wardwell, "Energy Output and Use Related to the Gross National Product," *Survey of Current Business,* February, 1961 (Washington: Government Printing Office), pp. 28 ff.

[3] For a comprehensive work on the supply of and demand for energy, see Sam H. Schurr and Bruce C. Netschert, *Energy in the American Economy, 1850-1975* (Baltimore: Johns Hopkins Press for Resources for the Future, Inc., 1960).

cent, and water power to 4.1 per cent. At the same time, total energy production between 1900 and 1960 rose from 7,893 trillion Btu's to 41,844 trillion Btu's, an increase of about 400 per cent.[4] The dramatic increase in total energy production gives ample evidence of the rapid energizing and industrialization of the economy since 1900. Table 16.1 shows the production of energy by types for selected years since 1900. The most startling thing about these data is the obvious shift in use patterns.[5]

There is no simple explanation for these shifts, but a major factor was technology on both the consuming and the producing side. While the trend of coal production has been relatively constant, the production of oil, gas, and hydro-power has increased rapidly since 1900. The rapid increase in oil consumption reflects (1) the advent of the internal-combustion engine and particularly the automobile, truck, tractor, and airplane, (2) the dieselization of railroad locomotives and conversion of ocean vessels from coal to fuel oil, (3) the development of small, efficient oil-fired space-heating equipment, (4) the development of cheap, efficient methods of transportation for oil and oil products, and (5) tremendous cost-saving advances in oil drilling, production, and refining.

The spectacular growth in gas consumption has been due primarily to (1) the development of cheap, efficient means of transmitting gas over long distances, (2) until recently its by-product nature in oil production, and (3) its oversupply, followed by price regulation which resulted in substantial underpricing of gas relative to other fuels. The increased output of hydro-power at about the same rate as energy requirements generally can be attributed to (1) development of federal multipurpose projects, (2) new emphasis on conservation, irrigation, and flood control, (3) economic development of areas in which hydro-power sites are located, and (4) advances in equipment used in hydroelectric generation.

The static nature of coal production has been due largely to the failure to gain or the actual loss of (1) the railroad and maritime markets to oil, (2) the home-heating market to oil and gas, (3) the manufactured-gas market to natural gas, (4) part of the industrial market, including some electric generation, to residual fuel oil and gas. Some of this was inevitable with changes in technology. However, other factors have also had a hand in transforming coal from a prosperous to a declining industry. Slowness to innovate, rising labor costs, and high transportation costs have all hurt coal. Some of these things will be discussed in more detail later.

B. *The Location of Fuel Production and Reserves.* As is true with many natural resources, the location of fossil fuels does not coincide too well with the markets for the fuels. It is necessary, therefore, to transport the fuel, either in a crude or in a refined state or in the form of electrical energy, to where the energy is needed. Twenty states have little or no fuel production. Densely populated areas, such as New England,

---

[4] U.S. Bureau of Mines, *Minerals Yearbook, 1960, Vol. II: Fuels* (Washington: Government Printing Office, 1961), pp. 4–5.

[5] Production rather than consumption data are used here because the data go back to 1900 for production and only to 1920 for consumption. The percentages on the basis of *consumption* for coal, oil, gas and gas liquids, and water power for 1958 were 24.3, 42.0, 29.5, and 4.2, respectively, as compared with *production* figures of 28.9, 36.3, 30.5, and 4.3, respectively. There were significant exports of coal and significant imports of crude oil and residual fuel oil which explain the differences in consumption and production. Over all, the United States in 1959 produced 40,389 trillion Btu's of energy and consumed 42,932 trillion Btu's, leaving this nation 2,543 trillion Btu's of energy to obtain from imports or existing inventories. *Ibid.*, Chapter I.

Table 16.1

Production of Mineral-Energy Fuels and Energy from Water Power in Trillion British Thermal Units and Percentage Contributed by Each in Continental United States[1]

(1900–1960)

Year	Bituminous Coal and Lignite	Anthracite	Crude Petroleum	Natural Gas Wet	Water Power	Total Grand	Percentages: Bituminous Coal and Lignite	Anthracite	Crude Petroleum	Natural Gas Wet	Water Power
1900. . .	5,563	1,457	369	254	250	7,893	70.5	18.4	4.7	3.2	3.2
1905. . .	8,255	1,973	781	377	386	11,772	70.1	16.8	6.6	3.2	3.3
1910. . .	10,928	2,146	1,215	547	539	15,375	71.1	14.0	7.9	3.5	3.5
1915. . .	11,597	2,260	1,630	676	659	16,822	69.0	13.4	9.7	4.0	3.9
1920. . .	14,897	2,276	2,569	883	738	21,365	69.7	10.7	12.0	4.1	3.5
1925. . .	13,623	1,570	4,430	1,314	668	21,607	63.1	7.2	20.5	6.1	3.1
1930. . .	12,246	1,762	5,208	2,148	752	22,119	55.4	8.0	23.5	9.7	3.4
1935. . .	9,753	1,325	5,780	2,136	806	19,803	49.2	6.7	29.2	10.8	4.1
1940. . .	12,068	1,308	7,849	2,979	880	25,088	48.1	5.2	31.3	11.9	3.5
1945. . .	15,126	1,395	9,939	4,423	1,442	32,333	46.8	4.3	30.7	13.7	4.5
1950. . .	13,517	1,120	11,449	6,841	1,573	34,510	39.2	3.2	33.2	19.8	4.6
1955. . .	12,157	665	14,410	10,204	1,447	38,900	31.3	1.7	37.1	26.2	3.7
1958. . .	10,745[3]	538	14,204	11,943	1,693	39,132	27.5	1.4	36.3	30.5	4.3
1959. . .	10,795[3]	524	14,933	13,036	1,645	40,932	26.4	1.3	36.5	31.8	4.0
1960[2,3] .	10,886	478	14,935	13,822	1,723	41,844	26.0	1.2	35.7	33.0	4.1

[1] The unit heat values employed are: Anthracite, 12,700 Btu per pound; bituminous coal and lignite, 13,100 Btu per pound; petroleum, 5,800,000 Btu per barrel; natural gas, total production × 1,075 Btu minus repressuring vent and waste gas × 1,035. "Water Power" includes installations owned by manufacturing plants and mines, as well as government and privately owned public utilities. The fuel equivalent of waterpower is calculated from the kilowatt-hours of power produced wherever available, as is true of all public utility plants since 1919. Otherwise, the fuel equivalent is calculated from the reported horsepower of installed water wheels, assuming a capacity factor of 20 per cent for factories and mines and 40 per cent for public utilities. Data for Alaska excluded.

[2] Preliminary data except for coal.

[3] 50–state basis.

Source: U.S. Bureau of Mines, *Minerals Yearbook, 1960, Vol. II: Fuels* (Washington: Government Printing Office, 1961), pp. 4–5.

New York, New Jersey, and Florida, are virtually devoid of energy except for some limited hydro-power in New England and small quantities of oil and gas in New York and Florida. This calls for heavy movements of fuels from the fuel-surplus areas—the Middle West and Middle South for coal and the Southwest for oil and gas—to these fuel-deficient areas. The pattern of geographic concentration is even more noticeable for proven fuel reserves than for production. Coal resources are fairly widely scattered, but the states in the Rocky Mountain region, which have significant reserves but little or no production, stand out. Five of the top ten states ranked by coal reserves are located in the thinly populated Rocky Mountain or Northern Plains region. These states have about 50 per cent of the recoverable coal in the United States.

The picture for oil and gas is even more concentrated. At the end of 1960, the five southwestern states of Texas, Louisiana, Oklahoma, New Mexico, and Kansas had 77 per cent of the liquid hydrocarbon reserves and about 89 per cent of the natural gas reserves. Since oil and gas can be moved more readily than coal, the divergence of supplies and potential markets is not so critical. Also, this oil and gas-producing area itself furnishes a substantial market. Nevertheless, huge quantities of fuel are moved out of this fuel-surplus region. Table 16.2 shows the movement of gas between major producing and major consuming areas. The heavy net exporting states in the Southwest furnish a large portion of the gas to the heavy net importing states. For example, the five Southwestern states in 1958 supplied New York State with about 78 per cent of its gas imports, Illinois with 99 per cent, and Michigan with almost all her imports.[6] Comparable data are difficult to obtain for petroleum products, but the same general pattern holds. Gasoline consumption, for example, tends to be heaviest where there is dense population. Thus, either crude oil or refined gasoline must be moved from the producing area to the consuming area.

C. Fuel and Water Power Consumption by Use and by Area. The location problems of supply and demand have already been touched on but need to be brought into sharper focus by a discussion of the uses to which these various forms of energy are put in the various regions of the nation. In order to avoid confusion, each type of fuel, as well as water power, will be discussed separately, and then the several types will be considered together.

(1) *Coal.* Bituminous coal and lignite consumption can be broken down into five major categories: (1) electric power utilities, (2) railroads, (3) manufacturing and mining, (4) retail deliveries to other consumers, and (5) exports. The most obvious thing which consumption data reveal is that there has been a large relative gain for electric generation in the total picture of coal consumption. While in 1933 electric generation took 27.1 million tons of the total domestic consumption of 317.7 tons, or 9 per cent, in 1959 it took 165.8 million out of 366.2 million tons, or 45 per cent. Offsetting the substantial gains made in electric generation were the virtual disappearance of railroad consumption, from 23 per cent to less than 1 per cent between 1933 and 1959, and the decline in "retail deliveries" from 56 per cent in 1933 to 8 per cent in 1959. Other uses more or less retained their relative positions in total consumption.[7]

The war and immediate postwar period from 1941 through 1948 recorded

[6] *Minerals Yearbook, 1958, Vol. II: Fuels,* pp. 317–319.

[7] *Minerals Yearbook, 1959, Vol. II: Fuels,* p. 120.

Table 16.2
Interstate Movements of Natural Gas, 1958
(millions of cubic feet)

Large Net Exporting States	*Quantity Shipped*	*Quantity Received*	*Net Import (+) or Export (–)*
Texas	2,700,103	146,244[1]	–2,553,859
Louisiana	1,625,487	118,916[2]	–1,506,571
Oklahoma	355,279	21,336[3]	– 333,943
Kansas	424,547	237,707[4]	– 186,840
New Mexico	572,586	68,857[5]	– 503,729
Large Net Importing States			
New Jersey	-0-	127,784	+ 127,784
New York	2,416	364,424	+ 362,008
Pennsylvania	83,770	481,284	+ 397,514
Illinois	2,483	445,495	+ 443,012
Indiana	1,210	161,287	+ 160,071
Michigan	-0-	283,412	+ 283,412
Ohio	534	618,509	+ 617,975
Iowa	-0-	182,281	+ 182,281
Minnesota	-0-	149,984	+ 149,984
Nebraska	324	104,553	+ 104,229
Missouri	-0-	248,470	+ 248,470
Georgia	-0-	166,304	+ 166,304
Alabama	50	175,022	+ 174,972
Tennessee	833	148,159	+ 147,326
Arkansas	991	186,081	+ 185,090
Arizona	-0-	108,988	+ 108,988
California	-0-	642,026	+ 642,026

1 All but 10,499 MMcf received from neighboring states.

2 All but 2,105 MMcf received from neighboring states.

3 All Oklahoma gas received from neighboring states.

4 233,960 MMcf received from Oklahoma, Texas, and Louisiana, most of the remainder probably from New Mexico, Colorado, and North Dakota.

5 Received primarily from Texas, Utah, Colorado, and Oklahoma.

Source: United States Bureau of Mines, *Minerals Yearbook, 1958, Vol. II: Fuels* (Washington: Government Printing Office, 1959), p. 317.

the peaks in coal consumption. This reflected stepped-up industrial activity and the pressing into service of every piece of railroad equipment that could be found. During the peak year, 593.8 million tons of bituminous coal and lignite were consumed. By 1959, total consumption had dropped to 366.2 million tons. Perhaps more distressing to the coal industry than the loss of the railroad and home-heating markets is the failure of coal to maintain its growth rate with the growth rate of some of its best customers. These losses of potential new markets are primarily economic in nature. Coal has been priced out of these markets in most cases. This problem will be dealt with shortly. There are no recent data available on industrial coal consumption by states, except for coal used in electric generation.[8] However,

8 See, however, a detailed study of fuel consumption by industry based on the *1947 Census of Manufactures* data, Leland W. McCloud, *Comparative Costs of Competitive Fuel,* West Virginia University Business and Economic Studies, Vol. 1, No. 4, June 1951. See also Harold J. Barnett, *Energy Uses and Supplies, 1939, 1947, 1965,* U.S. Bureau of Mines Information Circular 7582, 1950; W. H. Lyon and D. S. Colby, *Production, Consumption, and Use of Fuels and Electric*

because of relatively high transportation costs, coal production and consumption are not usually far removed.[9] The exceptions to this are those areas which have no fuel supply and to which coal can be moved most cheaply. A good example of this is interior New England.

(2) *Oil.* Crude oil is rarely used in its unrefined state.[10] Therefore, it is necessary to get some idea of the range of products that are refined from crude oil. Gasoline is the primary money-maker for the domestic petroleum industry, and the yield of gasoline is, therefore, made quite high. In 1960, 45.2 per cent of a barrel of crude oil came out as gasoline. A refinery can vary its product mix considerably by rerunning or re-processing certain products. For example, during the fall months, gasoline yields from a barrel of oil are reduced and heating oils (distillates, primarily) are increased. The change in output reflects the diminution of automobile driving and the onset of the heating season. The most notable change in recent years is the decreasing yield of residual fuel oil. As recently as 1946, about 25 per cent of a barrel of oil came out as residual fuel oil. By 1960 the yield had dropped to about 11 per cent. The drop reflects the relatively low price for residual fuel oil and the importation of cheap residual to the East Coast consuming areas, chiefly from Venezuela and the Dutch and British West Indies.

A further word needs to be said about the use of petroleum products and the location of consumption. Gasoline consumption is, of course, closely correlated with motor vehicle registration, although per-vehicle consumption tends to be higher in the South and West, where the climate is more moderate and where driving distances are apt to be longer. California, in 1960, led in gasoline consumption with 6.0 billion gallons, Texas followed with 4.5 billion gallons, and New York with 4.3 billion gallons. These three states accounted for more than 24 per cent of total United States consumption. Not all gasoline consumption occurs in motor vehicles. Street and highway use accounted for 90.8 per cent of total consumption in 1960, with other uses accounting for a little more than 9 per cent. Largest non-highway consumers of gasoline are farm vehicles and aircraft.

Sales of distillate and residual heating oils in the United States are concentrated in states having cool climates and/or which are not easily reached by natural gas, but which are reached quite easily by water. In 1960, the Number One state was New York, followed by Massachusetts, Pennsylvania, New Jersey, and Illinois, in that order. These five states consumed 294.2 million barrels of heating oils in 1960, or about 52 per cent of the total United States consumption of 547.9 million barrels. Table 16.3 breaks down distillate and residual fuel oil sales by use for 1959. Distillate sales are heaviest for heating and railroad locomotive fuel, while residual sales are heaviest for industrial use, heating, fuel for vessels, and electric-power generation. In terms of the location of consumption of distillate and residual fuel oils, better than 50 per cent was used in states bordering on the Atlantic Ocean during 1959, with particularly heavy concentration in the Middle Atlantic States. The states bordering on the Great Lakes and California were also heavy consumers.

Gasoline, distillate fuel oil, and resi-

Energy in the United States in 1929, 1939, and 1947, U.S. Bureau of Mines Report of Investigations 4805, (1951); and Perry D. Teitelbaum, *Energy Production and Consumption in the United States,* U.S. Bureau of Mines Report of Investigations 5821, 1961.

[9] Coking coal is sometimes moved long distances to steel mills.

[10] Exceptions to this include crude oil used as fuel for pipeline pumping, for drilling and pumping equipment in the field, and for fuel in oil refineries.

dual fuel oil account for 80 per cent of a refined barrel of oil. The remaining products used as fuel include jet fuel, kerosene, coke, still gas, and liquefied gases. *Still gas,* a refinery by-product, is the largest percentage yield of these, and virtually all of this is consumed in refineries as fuel or used as petrochemical feedstock. Jet fuel, which is a blend of gasoline, kerosene, and light distillate oil, is gaining in importance but is still small. Much of the liquefied gas from refineries, primarily butane and propane, is used as feedstock for petrochemical plants, with the remainder being consumed in space heating and cooking. Kerosene is used primarily as range oil. Coke, as a fuel, is used primarily in the refinery. Much of the remainder goes into non-fuel uses.

(3) *Natural Gas.* The consumption of natural gas is largely restricted to fuel uses, although some gas and some of the liquids from gas are used as feedstock for chemical plants. Table 14.1, in an earlier chapter, shows a breakdown of natural gas consumption. As would be expected, gas consumption is greatest in producing states. However, many non-producing states in recent years have greatly expanded consumption. While the five major producing states in the Southwest (Texas, Louisiana, Oklahoma, Kansas, and New Mexico) consumed 54 per cent of the national total in 1947, they consumed only about 40 per cent in 1960. Residential consumption accounts for a substantial part of the increase because many of the non-producing states have cool climates and thus rather large heating loads. The Gas Appliance Manufacturers Association reported that the number of gas house-heating customers in the nation rose from 7,443,000 in 1949 to 21,836,-000 in 1961. In several areas, market saturation for gas house-heating rose substantially. For example, in the Middle Atlantic States, it increased from 10 per cent in 1949 to 37 per cent in 1961. In the East North Central region, it rose from 20 per cent to 68 per cent; in the West North Central region, from 37 to 85 per cent.[11] Unfortunately, total residential gas consumption cannot be broken down by residential use, that is, cooking, water heat-

[11] American Gas Association, *Historical Statistics of the Gas Industry,* Table 142, from Gas Appliance Manufacturers Association; and *Gas Facts, 1962,* Table 139 (New York: 1956 and 1962).

Table 16.3

United States Consumption of Distillate[1] and Residual Fuel Oils by Use, 1959[2]

Use	*Distillate (Million Barrels)*	*Residual (Million Barrels)*
Railroads	87.8	5.6
Vessels	19.3	102.0
Gas and electric power plants	5.0	82.2
Industry	33.0	167.7
Heating oils	402.6	111.9
Military	11.4	31.4
Oil company use	8.6	46.2
Miscellaneous	77.1	7.3
Range oil	14.2	-0-
Total	659.0	554.4

[1] Includes diesel oil.
[2] Includes Alaska.

Source: U.S. Bureau of Mines, *Minerals Yearbook, 1959, Vol. II: Fuels* (Washington: Government Printing Office, 1960), pp. 425 and 430.

ing, and space heating, and other. The gas is usually sold on a single meter with a stepped-down block rate which applies when large quantities are consumed in the heating season. The same general analysis applies to commercial uses of gas, which are primarily space heating and cooking.

Industrial consumption of gas accounts for about 62 per cent of the increase in gas sales in the United States since 1947. It rose from 3,339 billion cubic feet in 1947 to 8,386 billion cubic feet in 1960. Much of this increase has occurred in the Southwest, where tremendous postwar industrial expansion has brought about record gas consumption in activities other than petroleum. If gas used in petroleum refineries, pipelines, and carbon black plants is excluded, the "other industrial" and electric power categories evidenced rapid growth in many states other than the major producing states. It is in this category—industrial other than petroleum—that gas is a major competitor with coal and oil. This is particularly true in the industrial areas in the Midwest and East. The growth of industrial consumption of gas has been spectacular in some states. In New York, for example, power generation and industry other than refineries and pipelines took 6,060 million cubic feet of gas in 1947. By 1960 the figure had risen to 128,995 million cubic feet. In Illinois the increase was from 93,565 to 215,375 million cubic feet for these years.[12] This same story can be told for several other states in these areas.

(4) *Water Power.* The last of the major energy sources in the United States is water power. Over the years the percentage of total energy supplied by falling water has remained fairly constant, in the range of 3.3 per cent to 5.0 per cent. This indicates that the growth rate in developing hydro-power has been close to the increase in the demand for total energy. Although falling water was used at one time as a direct source of power for turning water wheels in industrial establishments, virtually all water power today is converted into electric energy. Total public and private installed hydroelectric generating capacity at the end of 1959 was 31,700,000 kilowatts, of which 30,977,000 kilowatts was owned by utilities and 723,000 kilowatts was owned by industrial establishments.[13] On January 1, 1959 there was an additional 12.3 million kilowatts under construction, and 23.7 million kilowatts authorized or planned, for a total of 36.0 million kilowatts under development in the immediate future.[14]

The consumption of electricity must, of necessity, occur relatively close to the point of generation. Since hydro-power sites are distributed very unevenly over the nation, the consumption pattern is also uneven. About one-half of the installed capacity is found in the Pacific and Rocky Mountain States, while some of the states on the Great Plains and Gulf Coast have very little. In most areas, hydroelectric generation is tied to steam electric generation so as to smooth out seasonal variations in water flows. Some industries which are heavy users of electricity, such as electrometallurgical and atomic energy industries, locate near power sites or may even develop their own sites. Examples of this are found in the Tennessee, Columbia, and St. Lawrence River Basins.

---

[12] 1947 data from D. S. Colby and B. E. Oppegard, "Natural Gas Statistics, 1936–50," U.S. Bureau of Mines, *Information Circular 7644*, 1952; 1959 data from *Minerals Yearbook, 1960, Vol. II: Fuels,* pp. 332–333.

[13] U.S. Federal Power Commission, Release No. 10,076, August 5, 1960, Table 4.

[14] U.S. 86th Congress, 1st Session, Joint Economic Committee, *Hearings on Energy Resources and Technology,* October 12–16, 1959, pp. 110–111, statement by Francis L. Adams, Chief, Bureau of Power, FPC.

3. COMPETITION AMONG ENERGY SUPPLIES FOR VARIOUS MARKETS

From the preceding discussion three things are clear concerning competition among energy supplies. (1) There are a number of significant markets in which one type or form of energy is clearly superior to all others. This is partially a function of relative costs, but more important are the unique physical characteristics of the particular fuel. (2) There are, on the other hand, a number of markets in which substitution of one or more fuels for another can be done quickly and easily. Physical characteristics are of minor importance here, and use of one fuel instead of another is primarily a function of relative costs. (3) A major determinant of relative fuel costs is location, or the distance between supplies and markets. This section will take up the various major markets for energy and discuss the physical and economic factors that shape each of these.

A. The Importance of Location. It is extremely difficult to come to grips with the problems of fuel competition on a national basis because location of supplies and markets plays such a significant role. In discussing markets in which economic rather than physical factors dominate, it is impossible to make generalizations about consumption which apply to the entire nation. For example, to say that gas is the cheapest fuel means nothing unless some specific location is noted. The best that can be said is that, since transportation costs make up such a large part of total costs to the consumer for all fuels, the dominant fuel in an area will usually be the one produced locally or nearby. Thus, for electric generation in the Southwest, natural gas is used as plant fuel almost exclusively. In West Virginia, coal is used; while in Maine and Florida, fuel oil is a heat source for steam plants because of the cheapness of ocean-tanker transport for oil.

The significance of transportation costs is illustrated in a comparison of retail prices and freight costs for fuel. The Interstate Commerce Commission estimated that the average value of coal f.o.b. at mines in 1960 was $4.69 per ton. In the same year, the average railroad freight charge per net ton was $3.40.[15] In 1960, residual fuel oil (Number 5) had an average price of $2.97 per barrel at New York harbor, and the tanker rate from Gulf Coast ports to New York was about 30½ cents per barrel.[16] Residual oil cannot be transported economically by pipeline or rail for long distances; thus, it is dependent upon markets that can be reached by relatively cheap tanker transportation. Even then, tanker rates are 10 or 11 per cent of the wholesale price at dockside in New York. Natural gas transportation costs are more difficult to estimate. Some idea of this cost can be gotten from a comparison of wellhead prices for gas in Texas and value at point of consumption for industrial uses in a state such as New York. In 1960, the Texas field price for gas averaged 11.3 cents per Mcf, while in New York the average value for industrial uses other than oil-field use and carbon black was 66.3 cents per Mcf; in Illinois it was 40.4 cents per Mcf and in Texas it was 19.0 cents per Mcf.[17] These few examples point up the importance of the costs of moving fuels to points of consumption. In the discussion of specific markets that follows, the location factor bulks large and should be kept in mind at all times. Existing fuel reserves are continually being depleted,

---

15 Based on ICC estimates of average length of haul of about 290 to 300 miles. U.S. Bureau of Mines, *Minerals Yearbook, 1960, Vol. II: Fuels,* p. 45, from the ICC.

16 *Ibid.,* pp. 450 and 454.

17 *Ibid.,* pp. 324 and 332.

and markets for fuels are constantly shifting. As this occurs, the transportation element in fuel costs changes. Thus, transportation is one important factor in analyzing future supplies of and demands for energy.

B. *The Markets for Energy.* At the outset it is important to delineate the area of competitive fuels that is under discussion. A recent estimate by Schurr and Netschert for 1955 of the consumption of energy in the economy by sectors will bring into focus the areas of competition. These estimates show that mining and manufacturing accounted for 39.2 per cent of consumption; commercial uses, 8.5 per cent; households, 18.6 per cent; transportation, 20.2 per cent; and other uses, 13.5 per cent.[18] Estimates developed from the 1954 Census data indicated a similar consumption pattern of fuels by 23 sectors in the economy. This estimate is revealed in the breakdown for 1954, which is shown in Table 16.4.

Among the non-energy-producing fuel-consuming sectors, there are several areas where there is little or no inter-fuel competition. Perhaps the most outstanding of these is the transportation sector, in which liquid fuels are predominant. Motor vehicles, aircraft, railroads, farm vehicles, and water carriers are all consumers of gasoline, kerosene, distillate or residual fuel oil, LPG, or some mixture of these. In most instances there is relatively little inter-fuel competition among these petroleum-based liquids, and virtually none between these fuels and gas, coal, wood, or hydro-power. Thus, this large chunk of the demand for energy can be set aside as relatively noncompetitive. Non-fuel uses can also be considered relatively noncompetitive.

(1) *Residential and Commercial Markets.* One-half of the remaining consumption of energy occurs in the domestic and commercial markets. Competition here may be quite intense. Actually there is some form of competition among energy sources for heating, cooking, clothes drying, water heating, air conditioning, and refrigeration. Cooking is done primarily with gas, electricity, or LPG, although "range oil" (kerosene), coal, and wood are used in some rural and low-income areas. The *1960 Census of Housing* reported that about 51.5 per cent of the living units in the United States used gas for cooking, while 30.8 per cent cooked with

[18] The best collection of energy consumption data is found in Schurr and Netschert, *op. cit.* See especially Chapter 6, "Summary of the Energy Consumption Estimates," and the "Statistical Appendix to Part II."

Table 16.4

Disposition of United States Energy Supply, 1954, by Major Sectors

Primary energy producers	3.6%
Secondary energy producers (energy processing)	12.7
Manufacturing except energy processing	21.4
Mineral industries, except energy producing	0.7
Transportation	20.4
Nonfarm residential and commercial	24.6
Farm	3.9
U. S. government	3.6
Non-fuel uses	4.0
Additions to inventories	3.7
Unallocated	1.4
Total disposition-(39,790.1 × 10^{12} B.t.u.)	100.0%

Source: Perry D. Teitelbaum, *Energy Production and Consumption in the United States,* U.S. Bureau of Mines Report of Investigations 5821, with Resources for the Future, Inc. (Washington: 1961), Table 4.

electricity.[19] The rather vigorous campaign staged by the electric-appliance and electric-distribution industries has resulted in substantial gains for electric cooking in many areas of the country. It is estimated that about 17.2 million, or 34 per cent, of the wired homes in the nation had electric cooking ranges as of January 1, 1960.[20] In gas-producing states, gas cooking far outweighs electric cooking. In the past few years, the gas-appliance manufacturers and distributors have initiated their own sales campaign and have improved the appearance and performance of gas-cooking equipment considerably.

Gas and electricity also compete for the residential water-heating market, although here gas dominates the field more than in home cooking. Sales of gas water heaters for the years 1946–1959 were 26,622,000 units.[21] Electric water heaters were in use in 18.6 per cent of the wired homes, January 1, 1960; however, sales of electric water heaters dropped 10.2 per cent in 1959 while gas water-heater sales rose 12.8 per cent.[22] Clothes drying is the other residential market in which gas and electricity are competitive. Sales of electric dryers in 1959 were 935,000 units, up 10.9 per cent over 1958, while gas-dryer sales were 490,000 units, up 23.4 per cent.[23] Competition between gas and electricity for cooking and clothes drying is frequently non-price competition. Women get used to cooking or drying with gas or electricity and are reluctant to change to the other fuel unless substantial price differentials arise.

A study was sponsored by the American Gas Association in 1955 to explore the comparative costs of cooking and water heating with gas and with electricity in representative cities throughout the nation. While it is true that there are many variables that must be included in such a comparison, the results were certainly conclusive in establishing gas as the most economical fuel for cooking and water heating. Gas not only was cheaper from an operating-cost standpoint, but gas appliances, in general, appeared to be less expensive for comparable equipment, and installation and maintenance costs were frequently less.[24] Perhaps more influential than the price of energy in the decision of whether to use gas or electricity is the cost of the appliance. Also, the energy or fuel used in other appliances or heating equipment is a factor in determining the choice of a cooking or clothes-drying fuel. If a home is heated with oil and has an electric water heater, the chances are remote that gas will be piped to the house just for cooking or clothes-drying purposes. Similarly, if gas is used for space and water heating, it will probably be used for cooking and clothes drying. Since incremental units of gas or electric service can usually be purchased at lower costs than the initial units, it is economical to "bunch" appliances and heating equipment in a single fuel insofar as is possible. The same generalizations apply to water heating, although personal preference is not as strong a factor in selection. Electricity is apt to be used in high gas-cost areas or where gas is not available at all.

The residential heating market presents an entirely different situation. Here gas, oil, and coal compete vigorously through pricing factors and non-

---

19 American Gas Association, *Gas Facts, 1962,* Tables 140 and 141, from *1960 Census of Housing.*

20 *Electrical World,* Vol. 153, No. 9, February 29, 1960, p. 84.

21 A. G. A., *Historical Statistics and Supplements, op. cit.,* Table 142.

22 *Electrical World,* Vol. 153, No. 9, February 29, 1960, p. 84.

23 *Ibid.*

24 C. G. Segeler and E. M. Kafka, "Comparative Total Costs of Gas and Electricity for Cooking and Waterheating in Residences" (New York: American Gas Association, 1955).

price aspects. One of the big shifts in fuel consumption during the postwar years has been out of coal and oil into natural or "mixed" gas.[25] Just how large this shift has been is evidenced by the data in Table 16.5, which show domestic central-heating equipment in use and annual sales since 1947 by type of fuel. The data on equipment in use show that, while oil has more or less maintained its

[25] "Mixed gas" is a mixture of manufactured and natural gas with a Btu content somewhere around 907 per cubic foot. Dry natural gas usually contains about 1,035 Btu's per cubic foot and manufactured gas, about 540 Btu's per cubic foot. National Coal Association, *Bituminous Coal Facts,* 1958, p. 50.

Table 16.5

U.S. Automatic Domestic Central-Heating Equipment in Use, and Sales, 1947–1961*

(Thousands of Units)

Year	*Equipment in Use January 1*				
	Oil Burners	*Coal Stokers*	*Gas-Fired Burners*	*Total*	*Gas as a % of Total*
1961.	9,825	492	12,932	23,247	56
1960.	9,647	552	11,906	22,105	54
1959.	9,325	624	10,798	20,747	52
1958.	9,028	690	9,798	19,516	50
1957.	8,732	739	8,981	18,452	49
1956.	8,255	793	7,999	17,047	47
1955.	7,642	894	6,948	15,483	45
1954.	7,018	991	6,077	14,086	43
1953.	6,346	1,080	5,332	12,758	42
1952.	5,705	1,125	4,677	11,507	41
1951.	5,172	1,176	4,087	10,435	39
1950.	4,491	1,236	3,120	8,846	35
1949.	3,976	1,238	2,539	7,752	33
1948.	3,651	1,186	2,297	7,134	32
1947.	2,821	1,161	2,028	6,009	34

Year	*Equipment Sales*				
	Oil Burners	*Coal Stokers*	*Gas-Fired Burners*	*Total*	*Gas as a % of Total*
1961.	N.A.	N.A.	N.A.	N.A.	N.A.
1960.	517	11	1,171	1,699	69
1959.	636	14	1,320	1,970	67
1958.	568	13	1,159	1,740	67
1957.	580	12	986	1,579	62
1956.	709	13	1,087	1,810	60
1955.	809	13	1,152	1,974	58
1954.	738	13	947	1,698	56
1953.	823	13	800	1,637	49
1952.	778	19	748	1,544	48
1951.	675	19	653	1,347	48
1950.	847	20	991	1,857	53
1949.	615	30	637	1,282	50
1948.	455	76	272	803	34
1947.	888	62	322	1,272	25

* Excludes electrical space heating. It is estimated that in 1960 there were about 100,000 heat pumps in use in homes.

N.A.—not available.

Source: American Petroleum Institute, *Petroleum Facts and Figures, 1959 and 1961 Editions* (New York), authority, *Fueloil and Oilheat.*

position since 1947, gas equipment has risen from 34 to 56 per cent and coal has dropped from 19 to 5 per cent. Equipment-sales figures are even more striking. In 1947 oil, coal, and gas had 70, 5, and 25 per cent of the sales, respectively. By 1960, oil and gas had about 30 and 69 per cent, respectively, and coal had less than one per cent. Oil and gas had about reversed positions during the 14-year period, and coal-equipment sales had almost disappeared. A considerable number of homes in the nation are not equipped with central-heating equipment. This is especially true in the southern third of the nation from coast to coast. The *1950 Census of Housing* reported the breakdown of heating by fuels for each region shown in Table 16.6. About 51 per cent of the heated homes in the nation used central-heating equipment, while 49 per cent were not centrally heated. Climate is the major determinant of whether central heating is used or not, with the cold Northern states having predominantly central heating and the Southern and Western states having non-central heating.

The regional breakdown for 1950 shows wide variations in fuel usage. For central heating, coal ranked first, followed by utility gas and liquid fuel. For non-centrally heated dwelling units, gas ranked first, followed by coal, liquid fuel, and wood. However, for a given region, the order of importance may be quite different. Liquid fuel predominates in New England, gas in the Southwest, Mountain, and Pacific regions, and coal in the East North Central states. It is interesting to note that wood ranked as the Number One fuel for non-centrally heated units in the South Atlantic region and second in the East South Central and West South Central states. The 1960 data will no doubt reveal substantial changes that have occurred in the post-war years. A total of 485,000 gas wall and floor heaters and 1,407,000 direct gas space heaters were sold in 1958.[26] In the same year, 670,000 wall or base-board electric heaters and 1,295,000 portable electric heaters were sold.[27] Recent estimates indicate that in 1960 there were about 819,000 homes using some type of electric resistance heating and about 101,000 homes using heat pumps with central systems.[28] There are still in use numerous small room heaters fired with coal, kerosene, or wood, but these types are dropping rapidly in importance.

Attention in the remainder of this section will be directed to gas, oil, and coal residential heating. Table 16.7 shows the costs of competing residential heating fuels on an equivalent Btu basis for 1946 and 1961, and the percentage change in costs between 1946 and 1961 for selected cities studied by the Bureau of Labor Statistics. In every single city having more than one fuel, gas prices increased the least during this inflationary period. In three of the 19 cities, gas was used exclusively. In 13 of the remaining 16 cities, gas was the lowest-priced heating fuel during 1961, with bituminous coal lowest in Baltimore and anthracite coal lowest in Philadelphia and Scranton. Very little more need be said to explain the rapid shift of house-heating customers from coal and oil to gas. When a consumer can get a superior fuel in terms of cleanliness, even heat, odor, smoke, storage, convenience, and reliability, *and* in addition get this superior fuel at lower cost, there is little incentive to use the other fuels. Gas has further advantages in that, generally speaking, gas-burning equipment has a lower initial cost, it is less costly to maintain, and no fuel storage costs are

---

[26] A. G. A., *Gas Facts, 1959,* p. 148.

[27] *Electrical World,* Vol. 153, No. 9, February 29, 1960, p. 85.

[28] *Ibid.,* Vol. 155, No. 23, June 5, 1961, p. 57.

Table 16.6

Fuels Used for Residential Heating in 1950, by Regions

Use	*Total U.S.*	*New England*	*Middle Atlantic*	*East North Central*	*West North Central*	*South Atlantic*	*East South Central*	*West South Central*	*Moun-tain*	*Pacific*
Total Living Units - 000's.	42,056	2,587	8,500	8,711	4,072	5,424	2,925	3,944	1,412	4,480
Not heated	570	40	116	28	11	211	21	68	15	59
Heated	41,486	2,547	8,384	8,683	4,061	5,213	2,904	3,875	1,397	4,420
Central Heating - 000's . . .	21,191	1,704	6,745	5,714	2,089	1,477	487	492	548	1,934
Percent Using -										
Coal	45.5	38.8	49.6	64.5	44.7	34.4	47.2	2.0	25.7	5.5
Wood	1.2	2.1	0.5	1.2	2.0	1.0	1.6	1.4	1.5	2.4
Utility gas.	27.0	6.3	17.8	19.6	32.2	21.2	41.1	89.4	58.8	70.0
Bottled gas	0.8	0.5	0.4	0.4	1.8	0.9	1.6	4.1	2.0	1.3
Liquid fuel	22.8	49.5	28.9	12.4	16.9	38.6	4.9	1.6	9.1	17.0
Other fuel.	1.9	2.2	1.7	1.3	1.7	3.0	2.7	1.0	2.4	3.3
Not reported	0.8	0.7	1.0	0.6	0.7	0.8	0.6	0.6	0.5	0.6
Non-central Heating - 000's. . . .	20,295	843	1,639	2,969	1,972	3,736	2,417	3,383	849	2,486
Per cent using -										
Coal	23.9	13.3	42.8	40.5	26.0	26.6	38.7	2.5	27.3	2.9
Wood	19.3	12.1	6.2	7.7	16.3	34.2	32.5	19.3	13.2	13.0
Utility gas	26.4	5.9	19.6	14.3	16.6	9.8	15.8	57.0	28.5	54.3
Bottled gas	4.0	0.8	0.7	1.2	3.5	2.4	3.0	10.5	5.8	4.6
Liquid fuel	22.8	65.5	27.8	33.1	39.5	22.9	6.5	8.4	20.7	19.5
Electricity	1.4	0.2	0.4	0.6	0.6	1.7	2.1	0.5	2.2	3.6
Other fuel.	1.8	1.9	1.9	2.2	2.1	2.0	1.0	1.5	2.0	1.8
Not reported	0.3	0.4	0.5	0.3	0.3	0.3	0.3	0.3	0.2	0.3

Source: U.S. Bureau of the Census, *1950 Census of Housing,* Volume 1, Part 1 (Washington: Government Printing Office, 1952), Table 20, pp. 26–27.

incurred. As old coal- and oil-burning equipment wears out, it is being and will be replaced by gas-burning equipment, as long as the total cost of heating with gas remains lower than the cost of competitive methods of heating. However, heating equipment is long-lived, and coal and fuel oil consumption will drop slowly.[29]

How is it that gas prices are so much

[29] Heating-oil sales may remain stable because of new markets and rising gas prices.

Table 16.7

Costs of Residential Heating Fuels for 19 Selected Cities
December 1946 and 1961[1]
(Cents per million Btu)

Cities	*1946*	*1961*	*% Change - 1946-1961*
Atlanta:			
Bituminous coal.	89.6	152.9	70.6
Gas	75.2	106.9	42.2
Baltimore:			
Anthracite	94.2	128.6	36.5
Bituminous coal.	72.5	120.9	66.8
Fuel oil	112.8	199.4	76.8
Gas[2]	125.0	156.2	25.0
Chicago:			
Bituminous coal.	85.6	161.9	89.1
Fuel oil	[3]	202.5	[3]
Gas	87.5	127.5	45.7
Cincinnati:			
Bituminous coal.	77.5	153.1	97.5
Gas	64.5	100.5	55.8
Cleveland:			
Bituminous coal.	89.8	173.0	92.7
Gas	62.5	83.5	33.6
Detroit:			
Bituminous coal.	89.0	155.3	74.5
Fuel oil	[3]	198.3	[3]
Gas	78.4	104.0	32.7
Houston:			
Gas	67.9	93.3	37.4
Kansas City:			
Bituminous coal.	41.5	[3]	[3]
Fuel oil	115.8	204.2	76.3
Gas	61.4	68.1	10.9
Los Angeles:			
Gas	57.9	91.1	57.3
Minneapolis:			
Bituminous coal.	124.0	216.6	74.7
Fuel oil	116.5	192.0	64.8
Gas	78.1	125.9	61.2
New York:			
Anthracite	95.5	164.6	72.3
Fuel Oil.	114.6	202.2	76.4
Gas	120.5	159.6	32.4
Philadelphia:			
Anthracite.	95.5	153.4	60.6
Fuel Oil.	109.3	199.7	82.7
Gas	117.9	157.5	33.6

Table 16.7 (Continued)

Cities	1948	1961	% Change - 1946-1961
Pittsburgh:			
Bituminous coal.	46.7	101.0	116.3
Gas	60.4	99.6	64.9
Portland, Oregon:			
Bituminous coal.	141.0	222.0	57.4
Fuel oil	105.1	188.2	79.1
Gas	108.0	161.7	49.7
St. Louis:			
Bituminous coal.	60.3	132.9	120.4
Fuel oil	[3]	213.2	[3]
Gas	77.0	106.3	38.1
San Francisco:			
Gas	42.1	75.3	78.9
Scranton:			
Anthracite	74.2	106.6	43.7
Gas	150.4	150.0	−0.3
Seattle:			
Bituminous coal.	145.6	220.9	51.7
Fuel oil	113.2	216.7	91.4
Gas	125.8	146.3	16.3
Washington:			
Anthracite	96.1	164.6	71.3
Fuel oil	117.7	201.5	71.2
Gas	129.5	164.0	26.6

[1] Prices shown represent fuel costs with correction for differential efficiencies in heating equipment recommended by the American Gas Association. See source for complete statement.

[2] Gas prices prior to 1949 do not reflect level of fuel adjustment clauses.

[3] Not available.

Source: American Gas Association, *Historical Statistics of the Gas Industry,* and *Supplement;* computed from data published by the U.S. Bureau of Labor Statistics.

less than prices of competitive fuels, if gas is so much superior to competitive fuels for house-heating purposes? This is illogical in an economy in which resources compete through a price system. There are several factors explaining this peculiar and, in some ways, undesirable situation. (1) The nation has experienced considerable inflation during the postwar years, and this has affected coal and fuel oil prices somewhat more than gas prices because of the overabundance of undedicated gas reserves in the late 1940's. The BLS index of retail fuel prices shows that between 1946 and 1958, gas rose 36 per cent, anthracite coal 73 per cent, bituminous coal 78 per cent, and Number 2 fuel oil 79 per cent. The small increase in gas prices is even more significant when it is realized that field prices for gas in 1946 were quite low. The over-all Consumer Price Index during this period rose 48 per cent. (2) Long-term purchase contracts for gas in the field have introduced a great deal of stability to gas field prices during a period when the real as well as the money value of gas has been rising. (3) Regulation has perhaps kept gas prices down somewhat, although such a statement is difficult to prove because no one can say what prices would have been in the absence of regulation. Gas prices in the field are probably lower than they would be without regulation. The average price of gas in the field during 1959 was 15.1 cents per Mcf,[30] while the average value at points of residential consumption was 107.0 cents per Mcf for the nation as a whole and ranged from 61.3 cents per Mcf in Kansas to $2.78 per Mcf in Florida.[31] Thus, most of the cost of gas to the residential buyer results from its transmission and distribution, rather than the initial field price of the commodity.[32] Regulation of gas transmission and distribution is on an original-cost basis for the most part; thus, the price to the consumer bears little or no relationship to the heat value of the fuel or the value of service to the consumer. Thus far, gas has cost less to produce and deliver to the consumer than other heating fuels. Technology and industrial gas consumption play a big role in this.

It should be pointed out that the Atlantic Seaboard formula, used by the FPC to establish pipeline rates,[33] has the undenied effect of favoring the home-heating customer, which causes this market to be stimulated. This favoritism works to the detriment of industrial gas consumers, since they, in effect, must subsidize the residential users.

(4) The residential consumption of gas in the United States is highly seasonal, with the peak coming in the cold winter months. For example, in the first quarter of 1959, residential gas sales were 12,873.9 million therms and in the third quarter of the same year were 2,297.9 million therms—about one-fifth of the winter consumption.[34] Load-factor problems of pipelines have already been discussed,[35] but it should be noted again that these lines are characterized by decreasing average costs. The cost per Mcf of transmitting gas falls as more gas is put through the line, up to its capacity. It is impossible at present in many areas to find a summer residential market that will consume as much gas as the heating market;[36] therefore, pipelines are forced either (a) to reduce throughput of the line and thus increase average costs for the whole year, (b) to move the gas to a spot nearby the ultimate market and store it there during the summer months, or (c) to find a summer market which will pay the variable or out-of-pocket costs of handling the incremental gas and make some contribution to the fixed charges. The most desirable of these three alternatives from a social and pipeline-company viewpoint is storage, provided that this storage can be gotten at a reasonable cost. If storage facilities are not available or are too costly, the pipeline must turn to the "interruptible" industrial market. Pipeline and distribution utilities are taking a long-term look at gas sales and are deciding that storage facilities will provide higher net revenues in the long run. This interest is evidenced by the fact that in 1955, the nation's total underground gas-storage capacity, planned or in existence, was about 1.6 billion Mcf. In 1960 this figure had almost doubled to 3.03 billion Mcf.[37] Most of this storage is located in the Northeastern and Midwestern states, where depleted oil and gas fields are used. In some instances "aquifers"[38] or abandoned coal mines have been adapted to store gas. Ideally, a pipeline should store enough gas near

[30] New reserves in large blocks were selling from about 10 to 20 cents per Mcf.

[31] U.S. Bureau of Mines, Minerals Industry Surveys, *Natural Gas, Annual,* Sept. 1962.

[32] An economist might phrase this in terms of a high degree of "place utility," as well as some "form utility."

[33] See Chapter 10 for a detailed discussion of this formula.

[34] A. G. A., *Gas Facts, 1960,* p. 137.

[35] See Chapter 10.

[36] Although the air-conditioning market holds out great promise, and home electric generation by gas turbine is a possibility.

[37] *Oil and Gas Journal,* Vol. 58, No. 22 (May 30, 1960), pp. 89 ff.

[38] Water formations.

its markets during the slack summer months to augment the maximum throughput of the line in winter months to meet the heavy residential and commercial heating loads. Thus, the pipeline is compelled by economic necessities to sell in the industrial market where one fuel is usually as suitable as another and the decision to use is based primarily on price.[39]

There are those who complain bitterly about the "waste" that occurs when gas is burned for many industrial uses where other fuels would do just as well. The fact is usually overlooked that residential and commercial gas rates would be higher if the industrial load did not bear part of the fixed cost.

(5) A fifth factor in explaining lower gas prices for heating is technology. Tremendous strides have been made in pipeline technology which permits rapid, efficient, long-distance movement of gas. However, this technology is applicable primarily to lines serving urban areas. Small towns and farms cannot be served by a pipeline unless they happen to lie along a transmission-line route to a large-market area. There will, therefore, always be a sizable part of the heating market that will utilize coal, fuel oil, LPG, or wood. The outlook for the heating market will be discussed later in this chapter.

(2) *Industrial Markets.* The industrial market for energy can best be discussed in two parts: (a) the use of energy for the generation of electricity which may then be sold for residential, commercial, or industrial use, and (b) the use of fuels for direct industrial applications, such as process heating. There is obvious overlapping in this arbitrary splitting of the industrial market. However, a clearer picture of use patterns and special problems can be gotten by such handling.

[39] This market will be discussed in more detail in the next section.

(a) The Generation of Electricity. The generation of electricity consumes more fuel in the United States than any other single use. This is merely a reflection of the versatility of electricity and the wide variety of uses to which it can be put. About 18 per cent of our fuel consumption in 1957 went for electric generation. Between 1946 and 1960, coal's share of electric generation declined from 77.12 per cent to 53.59 per cent, fuel oil fell from 9.72 per cent to 6.12 per cent, and gas rose from 13.00 per cent to 20.97 per cent.[40]

What accounted for the relative shift away from coal and oil to gas for electric generation? Several comments are necessary before examining the changing patterns of use. First, with the exception of anthracite coal, there has been an increase in consumption for electric generation for all fuels. Between 1946 and 1958, bituminous coal and lignite rose 122.5 per cent, fuel oil 102.0 per cent, and gas 348.4 per cent. Fuel-burning plants increased their generation from 144.8 billion Kwh in 1946 to 504.8 billion Kwh in 1958, a rise of almost 250 per cent. At the same time, total fuel consumption rose from 92.5 million to 227.7 million coal-equivalent tons for an increase of only 146 per cent. Thus, there was substantially improved efficiency in fuel-burning generating plants and at the same time large increases in fuel consumption in absolute terms.[41] The depressed condition of the bituminous coal industry cannot, therefore, be blamed on falling coal consumption for electric generation. The coal industry has suffered serious inroads in consumption for heating and rail transportation which have not been entirely offset by

[40] National Coal Association, *Trends in Electric Utility Industry Experience, 1946–1958,* 1960, p. vi; and Federal Power Commission, *Annual Report 1961,* p. 28.

[41] *Ibid.,* National Coal Association, pp. v and 75.

increased use for electric power generation.

A second point to be noted is that many state and regional phenomena are hidden by looking only at national data. The coal industry has had more intensive competition from oil and gas in some areas than in others. These factors will be discussed shortly.

Other aspects often overlooked are the relative growth rates of population and industrialization in different regions. The fastest-growing areas have, for the most part, been those which are not served by coal but rather by oil and gas. There are exceptions to this, but these are fairly minor. California, a populous oil and gas-using state, remote from large coal deposits, had a 46.77 per cent increase in population between 1950 and 1960. Florida, in a similar situation, grew by 76.56 per cent. On the other hand, population in West Virginia shrank by 7.76 per cent, while Pennsylvania's and Kentucky's growth rates were a meager 6.86 and 2.28 per cent, respectively.[42] This, no doubt, has had an influence on electricity consumption and indirectly on coal consumption for electric generation.

For steam generation of electricity, coal, oil, and gas are in most cases interchangeable. Many generating plants are equipped to burn at least two and sometimes all three of these fuels. In this way they can take advantage of the lowest price among the alternative fuels. Table 16.8 shows the generation of electricity by each type of fuel, by regions, for 1946 and 1958. During this 12-year period, gas began to be used in the New England and Middle Atlantic states for electric generation. Coal dropped in importance while residual fuel oil increased. In the East North Central, East South Central, and South Atlantic states coal about held its own. In the West North Central and Mountain states, coal and fuel oil both gave way to gas. And in the Pacific states, fuel oil dropped sharply, replaced by gas. Data are not available which show the comparative costs of competitive fuels since 1946, but some of the data do go back as far as 1951 or 1952. Table 16.9 shows the changes in costs of fuels for electric generation by census regions for the earliest year available and 1958. An asterisk beside a figure indicates the most commonly used fuel in that particular region. It is apparent that gas, as recently as 1951, was an extremely low-priced fuel for electric generation in most areas. No doubt much gas consumed for this purpose was interruptible, summer, or off-peak gas which could find no market elsewhere. The picture seems to be changing rather rapidly. In the Middle Atlantic, East North Central, and South Atlantic states, gas prices have risen much more rapidly than coal prices in recent years and now are about equal to coal prices on a Btu basis. If this trend continues, it will probably cause a shift back to coal, thus leaving gas to be used in the so-called "superior" uses of space heating, cooking, and water heating or for high-grade industrial uses in which fine temperature control is of great importance.

In the Mountain States there is an abundance of coal, which may become significant as new strip-mining and mechanical underground mining techniques are applied and as gas prices rise there, also. In much of this region, the fossil fuels must compete with hydroelectric energy, which puts definite ceilings on their prices. California is turning more and more to gas for electric generation and may be tapping fields as far east as the Texas Gulf Coast in the near future. With the plentiful gas supplies being developed in the Rocky Mountain states

[42] U.S. Bureau of the Census, "Preliminary Population Estimates for 1960," Release June 17, 1960.

Table 16.8

Generation of Electricity by Fuel, by Census Region, 1946 and 1958
(Costs per million Btu's—Cents)

Fuels	*Total U.S.*[5]	*New England*	*Middle Atlantic*[1]	*East North Central*	*West North Central*[2]	*South Atlantic*	*East South Central*	*West South Central*	*Mountain*[3]	*Pacific*[4]
Coal:										
1946 - Mil. KWH	111,653	6,540	35,153	46,059	5,446	15,598	1,869	298	688	2
1958 - Mil. KWH	344,365	13,370	69,006	138,093	12,768	55,565	53,211	2	2,350	-0-
1946 - Coal as % of total	77.12	75.72	92.58	98.05	52.73	79.82	67.53	2.56	35.59	0.05
1958 - Coal as % of total	68.21	64.99	79.51	96.10	41.91	75.03	92.56	0.01	17.58	-0-
Fuel Oil:										
1946 - Mil. KWH	14,082	2,100	2,782	657	1,112	2,800	30	4,434	307	3,861
1958 - Mil. KWH	40,391	6,218	9,820	668	677	2,536	68	126	1,140	9,120
1946 - Oil as % of total	9.72	24.30	7.33	1.40	10.76	14.33	1.08	3.73	15.87	77.29
1958 - Oil as % of total	7.99	30.22	11.31	0.47	2.23	16.93	0.12	0.25	8.72	32.42
Gas:										
1946 - Mil. KWH	18,820	-0-	32	257	3,758	1,143	869	10,889	929	942
1958 - Mil. KWH	119,759	984	7,808	4,924	16,934	5,961	4,206	50,447	9,566	18,929
1946 - Gas as % of total	13.00	-0-	0.08	0.55	36.38	5.85	31.38	93.71	48.06	18.77
1958 - Gas as % of total	23.72	4.78	8.99	3.42	55.59	8.05	7.32	99.74	73.17	67.29

[1] During 1958, 147 million Kwh were produced from nuclear energy, making up 0.17 per cent of the total.

[2] During 1946, 14 million Kwh were produced from wood wastes, making up 0.13 per cent of the total; in 1958, the figures were 88 million Kwh and 0.29 per cent.

[3] Wood: 1946—9 million Kwh and 0.48 per cent; 1958—18 million Kwh and 0.13 per cent.

[4] Wood: 1946—189 million Kwh and 3.79 per cent; 1958—62 million Kwh and 0.22 per cent, also; in 1958, 18 million Kwh of nuclear energy, 0.06 per cent.

[5] Wood: 1946—216 million Kwh and 0.15 per cent; 1958—175 million Kwh and 0.03 per cent; also, in 1958, 165 million Kwh of nuclear energy, 0.03 per cent.

Source: National Coal Association, *Trends in Electric Utility Industry Experience, 1946–1958* (Washington: 1960), Tables 2 and 4.

Table 16.9

Comparative Costs of Electric Generation by Fuels, by Census Regions, 1951 and 1958

(Costs per million Btu's—Cents)

Fuels	*New England*	*Middle Atlantic*	*East North Central*	*West North Central*	*South Atlantic*	*East South Central*
Coal:						
1951	36.4*	28.2*	25.9*	28.4*	27.0*[3]	20.1*[3]
1958	40.1*	32.3*	25.8*	28.1	28.6*	19.4*
Fuel Oil:						
1951	35.6	35.8	64.9	44.7	33.4[3]	45.4[4]
1958	40.7	38.5	68.5	51.3	39.7	37.6
Gas:						
1951	N.A.	26.1	19.0	18.1	18.6[3]	19.6[3]
1958	37.8	32.0	24.5	22.0*	27.7	21.6

Fuels	*West South Central*	*Mountain*	*Pacific*[1]	*U.S.*	*Coal Consuming States*[2]
Coal:					
1951	16.3[3]	22.8[3]	N.A.	27.3*[3]	27.0*
1958	15.6	21.9	N.A.	27.4*	27.3*
Fuel Oil:					
1951	43.7[3]	23.9[3]	29.0(1952)*	33.1(1952)	35.9
1958	41.8	25.2	42.0	39.6	39.0
Gas:					
1951	9.3*[3]	16.0*[3]	20.1(1952)	14.5(1952)	19.0
1958	13.8*	22.7*	30.3*	20.7	25.0

* Indicates the fuel accounting for the largest share of Btu consumption for electric generation.

1 Excluded consumption by Pacific Gas and Electric Company.

2 All states Florida, Mississippi, Arizona, and those in the West South Central and Pacific regions.

N.A.—Not available.

Source: National Coal Association, *Trends in Electric Utility Experience, 1946–1958* (Washington: 1960), Table 5.

and in Western Canada, there is little likelihood that this trend will change.

(b) Industrial Fuel Consumption Other Than for Electric Generation. Consumption of fuels by industries other than electric-generating companies has long been an area in which inadequate data have thwarted analysis. The *1958 Census of Manufactures* did collect and publish data on fuels consumed by industry by states.[43] This tabulation had been omitted for the *1954 Census,* and the recent figures now provide a means of analyzing shifts in fuel consumption for different industries in different parts of the country. Table 16.10 shows a comparison of 1947 and 1958 data on a nationwide basis.[44] The figures for coal

43 U.S. Bureau of the Census, *1958 Census of Manufactures,* Document MC 58(1)–6, "Fuels and Electricity Consumed."

44 See U.S. Bureau of the Census, *1947 Census of Manufactures,* Document MC 203, "Fuels and Electric Energy Consumed," for the special 1947 study. These data became the basis for several monographs and studies. Included among these are Leland W. McCloud, *Comparative Costs of Competitive Fuels,* West Virginia University Business and Economic

Table 16.10

Consumption of Fuels by Major Manufacturing Industry Groups, 1947 and 1958

Industry Groups	*Coal*[1]			*Coke*[2]			*Fuel Oils*[3]			*Gas*[4]		
	1947	*1958*	*Per-centage Change*	*1947*	*1958*	*Per-centage Change*	*1947*	*1958*	*Per-centage Change*	*1947*	*1958*	*Per-centage Change*
20-Foods	13,269	8,663	−34.7	195	65	−66.7	15,314	25,225	+64.7	127,177	243,866	+91.8
21-Tobaccos	489	245	−49.9	0	0	--	121	278	+129.8	76	595	+682.9
22-Textiles	6,612	3,066	−53.6	18	0	−100.0	11,320	10,696	−5.5	6,725	22,184	+33.0
23-Apparel	611	0	−100.0	5	0	−100.0	732	212	−71.0	3,245	128	−96.1
24-Lumber	876	256	−70.8	0	0	--	3,251	2,286	−29.7	3,266	6,866	+110.2
25-Furniture	1,017	356	−70.0	6	0	−100.0	436	488	+11.9	3,024	3,204	+6.0
26-Pulp, paper	14,875	14,465	−2.8	12	0	−100.0	11,908	25,285	+112.3	70,742	212,213	+200.0
27-Print.-Publ.	371	0	−100.0	4	0	−100.0	745	0	−100.0	8,091	0	−100.0
28-Chemicals	18,988	19,434	+2.3	2,113	0	−100.0	16,673	15,714	−5.8	174,082	558,801	+221.0
29-Petroleum	2,572	1,200	−53.3	41	0	−100.0	3,630	3,805	+4.8	696,872	794,456	+14.0
30-Rubber	2,842	2,426	−14.6	3	0	−100.0	1,460	3,061	+109.7	7,932	20,700	+161.0
31-Leather	1,220	467	−61.3	3	0	−100.0	753	920	+22.2	732	1,928	+163.4
32-Stone-glass	16,985	11,786	−30.6	370	166	−55.1	14,679	13,651	−7.0	249,785	446,111	+78.6
33-Prim. metals	15,669	11,325	−37.7	61,797	12,999	−79.0	64,372	47,083	−26.9	2,503,464	6,145,100[5]	N.C.[5]
34-Fabr. metals	2,307	1,020	−55.8	405	149	−63.2	5,230	6,151	+17.6	36,516	49,241	+34.8
35-Mach. excl. elec.	4,195	1,616	−61.5	650	121	−81.4	6,260	3,797	−40.0	36,827	25,522	−30.7
36-Elec. mach.	2,101	968	−53.9	188	6	−96.2	2,268	2,347	+3.5	12,885	19,056	+47.9
37-Transp. equip.	4,532	3,840	−15.3	346	78	−77.5	5,258	7,388	+40.5	58,285	55,772	−4.3
38-Instruments	385	432	+12.2	2	0	−100.0	567	152	−73.2	2,351	595	−74.7
39-Miscellaneous	953	147	−84.6	13	0	−100.0	1,970	1,044	−47.0	4,341	5,779	+33.1
Total	110,869	81,716	−26.3	66,171	13,585	−79.5	166,947	166,719	−0.1	4,004,953	7,929,311[5]	N.C.[5]

[1] In 000's of tons. Includes bituminous, lignite, and anthracite coal.

[2] In 000's of tons.

[3] In 000's of barrels (42 gallons to the barrel).

[4] In millions of cubic feet. Includes natural, manufactured, and mixed gas.

[5] For 1958, includes 634,683 MMcf of purchased gas, 671,909 MMcf of still gas, and 4,838,518 MMcf of coke oven and blast furnace gas. The breakdown for 1947 is incomplete, thus some blast furnace and other by-product gasses are omitted from the 1947 data.

N.C.—not comparable data.

Sources: U.S. Bureau of the Census, *Census of Manufactures for 1947* and *for 1958* (Washington: Government Printing Office).

combine bituminous, lignite, and anthracite coal, which have different Btu contents. The 1947 and 1958 patterns of coal consumption among types of coal would have to be proportionately the same for the data to be completely comparable. There has generally been a trend away from anthracite (25.4 million Btu's per ton) toward bituminous coal and lignite (26.2 million Btu's per ton). Therefore, the decline in tonnage consumption between 1947 and 1954 would be slightly greater than the decline in Btu consumption. The same situation holds for gas. In 1947 about one-third the gas consumed was natural gas (1,035 Btu's per cubic foot), one-third manufactured gas (540 Btu's per cubic foot), and one-third mixed gas (907 Btu's per cubic foot). There has been a tendency for the natural-gas share to rise and the manufactured and mixed gas share to fall. Thus, in terms of Btu's, gas consumption has risen substantially more than the 47.7 per cent increase in cubic-foot consumption.

A cursory glance at the consumption figures reveals some very definite trends between 1947 and 1958. Coal consumption has slipped substantially, not only in relative terms but also in absolute terms. The only important coal-consuming industry which increased consumption was the chemical industry. The 2.3 per cent increase in this industry reflects, in part, the sharp drop in coke consumption and, in part, the rapid growth of the chemical industry in the coal-producing upper Ohio River Valley in recent years. Fuel-oil consumption registered virtually no change between 1947 and 1958 despite the 26.9 per cent decline in use by the primary metals industry, the Number One fuel-oil consumer.

Gas consumption rose substantially in the 11-year period. The gas picture is somewhat clouded by the predominance of the primary metals industry. In 1947 this industry accounted for about 63 per cent of industrial gas consumption and in 1958 for about 77 per cent. A large part of the gas used in this industry is a by-product of the coking plants which are located nearby and which produce coke for the steel industry. Coke-oven gas is used for firing coke ovens and for boiler fuel in the steel industry. Only 8 per cent of the coke-oven gas produced during 1958 went into residential, commercial, and other industrial uses.[45] In addition, large quantities of extremely lean blast-furnace gas (100 Btu's per cubic foot) were produced as a by-product of the steel industry. Some of this gas goes back to heat the coking ovens and some is used in steel plants.

If the primary metal group is taken out of the picture, industrial gas consumption rose from 1,501 billion cubic feet in 1947 to 1,784 billion cubic feet in 1958, an increase of about 19 per cent. During the same period the manufacturing component of the Federal Reserve Board Index of Industrial Production

Studies, Vol. 1, No. 4 (June, 1951); William H. Lyon and D. S. Colby, *Production, Consumption, and Use of Fuels and Electric Energy in the United States in 1929, 1939, and 1947,* U.S. Bureau of Mines, Report of Investigations 4805, October, 1951; and Harold J. Barnett, *Energy Uses and Supplies, 1939, 1947, 1965,* U.S. Bureau of Mines Information Circular 7582, October, 1950. The Bureau of Mines and Resources for the Future, Inc., have jointly sponsored the most definitive study yet done on energy production and consumption in the United States. It compares the 1939, 1947, and 1954 Census data, and pushes further than any previous study into the problems of definitions, measurements, comparability, and reliability. The 1954 data are given in considerable detail. This should serve as an excellent pattern for future studies. See Perry D. Teitelbaum, *Energy Production and Consumption in the United States: An Analytical Study Based on 1954 Data,* U.S. Bureau of Mines and Resources for the Future, Inc., Bureau of Mines Report of Investigations 5821 (1961).

[45] U.S. Bureau of Mines, *Minerals Yearbook, 1958, Vol. II: Fuels,* p. 249.

rose 40 per cent. The impact of natural gas on the industrial fuel market is evident from these data. There are about six major fuel-using industry groups. These include (1) food and kindred products, (2) pulp, paper, and allied products, (3) chemicals and allied products, (4) products of petroleum and coal, (5) stone, clay, and glass products, and (6) primary metals. Between 1947 and 1958 coal use registered a decline in all of these but the chemical industry. Fuel-oil consumption increased substantially in the pulp and paper industry and increased moderately in the others, except stone, clay, and glass and primary metals, in which declines were noted. Gas usage increased more than 14 per cent in all six of these industry groups and jumped more than 90 per cent in the cases of foods, paper, chemicals, and probably primary metals.

It is difficult to pinpoint all the reasons for growth or decline in specific fuel uses by various industry groups. Certainly, the growth rate of the industry itself is a major contributing factor. The chemical industry, which increased output by about 120 per cent between 1947 and 1958, is a good example of this. Cyclical conditions also have a large influence on the data, particularly for 1958, a recession year. Some industries feel recessions more than others, and fuel-consumption figures give evidence of this. For longer periods, industrial location influences fuel-consumption patterns. Large-scale industrial migrations to a region with a different fuel orientation may change national figures. No doubt some of the southern and western movement has been responsible for changes in fuel use. Finally, of course, there are price conditions. Some industries are in a position to use almost any type of fuel, and the particular choice depends on relative prices. It is virtually impossible to talk about fuel prices on a national basis for particular industries. Only if state data are available is it possible to draw any meaningful conclusions. A further difficulty is added by the fact that industrial fuel sales are in large quantities at prices closely competitive and arrived at through negotiation. Fuel contract prices are not often revealed, for obvious competitive reasons. The prices charged for direct industrial gas sales by transmission companies are nominally exempt from regulation under the Natural Gas Act, thus FPC data do not reveal the complete picture. Perhaps the best gauge of prices for large industrial fuel users are the costs reported in the same general area for the same fuels by electric generating companies.

4. ENERGY SUPPLIES AND CONSUMPTION IN THE FUTURE

The story of competitive fuels is not complete without some discussion of the outlook for energy supplies and consumption. It has become a very fashionable game to make "forecasts" of energy supply and demand for the next 25 to 50 years. The chances are excellent that such forecasts will be as inaccurate as those made 50 years ago about today's energy picture. Yet, these estimates are absolutely essential for long-run national planning, be it private or public planning. In many respects, an inaccurate forecast is better than none at all. As time passes and a given target date draws closer and closer, forecasts are revised. The very fact that so many people are trying to brush aside the fog that shrouds the future is grim testimony to the essential nature of energy to an industrial nation in a world apparently doomed to decades of cold war. The remainder of this chapter will present a number of estimates of energy supply and demand. Although there is substantial disagreement among these estimates, they are all made by authorities in this area who have access to the best and most complete information available.

A. Estimates of Future Energy Supplies. Estimates of energy supplies are somewhat a function of the demand for energy. Most of the world's usable energy supply today is made up of substances composed of carbon and hydrogen atoms—hydrocarbons—initially a vegetable substance. Vegetable matter is created by the mysterious phenomenon called *photosynthesis,* in which carbon dioxide and water are acted on by solar energy to form a carbohydrate. The conversion of a carbohydrate to energy is merely the reverse process, in which the carbohydrate is burned with oxygen to produce carbon dioxide, water, and heat. Coal, lignite, peat, oil, and natural gas are merely different combinations of carbon and hydrogen, dead and decayed plant substance that has accumulated over millions of years. The supply of carbon and hydrogen atoms is limitless, since the atmosphere as well as the earth's surface contains large quantities of both. It is possible, for example, to make an excellent motor fuel (an alcohol) from potatoes. The Germans did it during the Second World War. Any "starchy" substance can be "refined" into fuel. Whether a usable fuel can be made depends on technological know-how, which is also limitless in quantity but slow and expensive to accumulate.[46]

One author has pointed out that "it is not a question of emptying the bin" of fuel reserves, but rather it is a question of economy—how deep to dig.[47]

[46] For a discussion of this, see Eugene Ayres, "Major Sources of Energy," Paper presented to the Refining Division at the 28th Annual Meeting of the American Petroleum Institute, at Chicago, November 9, 1948.

[47] P. C. Putnam, *Energy in the Future* (New York: D. Van Nostrand Company, Inc., 1953), p. 117.

Estimates of energy supplies, therefore, of necessity imply a cost or a price, or, in other words, reflect a "demand" schedule for the energy which indicates meaningful price ranges.[48] Any forecast of energy supplies is actually a forecast of only those energy supplies which can be produced at costs which exist today or which are at least in the realm of reasonableness relative to today's costs. This is an exceedingly serious limitation on the usefulness of supply forecasts. What in effect this means is that the forecaster is assuming today's cost patterns, which reflect today's technology; or perhaps he will assume a future decline in costs due to improving technology that corresponds to past trends of falling costs. Actually, the analyst has no other alternative than to make some such assumption. Still, it is an exceedingly tenuous assumption that would prove to be true only by chance. It is important to remember that supply forecasts implicitly include a cost factor. Sources of energy are limitless; the problem is largely a technical one of supplying from them at reasonable cost.

The following discussion will deal with only those supplies of energy which make a major contribution to total mechanical-energy consumption at the present time. Huge amounts of energy are consumed as food by human beings. This energy source will not be discussed.[49] The discussion of oil shale, tar sands, nuclear energy, solar energy, and

[48] In the United States, the supply curve for motor fuel produced from potatoes no doubt lies above the demand curve for motor fuel for all ranges of output. Thus, to speak of energy supplies coming from potatoes is meaningless in the United States. But potatoes *could* be used for motor fuel, if the demand curve shifted upward or the supply curve shifted downward.

[49] It might be noted that, if an economy has a choice between using potatoes (or other starches) for fuel or for food, the choice becomes one which basically affects fuel policy.

some of the other types undergoing research will be postponed until the last chapter in the book. All of these sources are significant for the future but not competitive at the present time.

There are numerous books, articles, and speeches on future fuel supplies of the United States and the world. The ones mentioned in this discussion are some of the most recent and generally the most widely read. The omission of a particular study is not intended to reflect on the usefulness or reliability of that study.[50]

(1) *Coal.* Looking first at coal, it is fairly easy to give a summary of estimates of reserves for the United States, since only one major study has been done in this area in recent years. This was done between 1947 and 1953 by the United States Geological Survey with cooperation from the various state agencies concerned with coal. These data have been updated by the National Coal Association in terms of production and mining losses and are shown in Table 16.11. The recoverable-reserve figures shown in the last column include a number of assumptions. The coal represented by these figures is in seams at least 14 inches thick for anthracite and bituminous coal and at least 30 inches thick for sub-bituminous coal and lignite. Also, it includes coal with no more than 33 per cent ash content and having no more than 3,000 feet of overburden. In 1953, approximately 68 per cent of the reserves were "inferred reserves," for which few actual measurements are available and which are based on broad geologic features. Most "inferred reserves" lie more than two miles from the outcrop on the surface.[51]

Despite the shortcomings of reserve figures for coal, it is apparent that the nation's coal supplies are ample to meet fuel needs for the next several decades, although their location is not ideal relative to present industrial location.[52] As technology improves, the percentage of recovered coal should rise, and new reserves which lie completely unexposed will no doubt be discovered. Also, large quantities of coal lying beneath the 3,000-foot level may eventually be recoverable. The major problem facing coal is costs. These costs include not only those incurred in the actual mining, but also those for cleaning, crushing, sizing, and transporting of the coal to market. Tremendous cost-saving potentialities lie on the horizon. One of these is new equipment for strip or open-pit mining. While as recently as 1957 it was stated that 100 feet of overburden was the practical limit for strip mining,[53] machines have now been developed which can remove 125 feet of overburden.[54] Open-pit mining allows recovery of up to 90 per cent or more of the coal in place, while underground operations recover only 40 to 80 per cent. In 1940, only 9.4 per cent of United States coal production came from strip

[50] For a study of energy requirements and supplies projected to 1980, see Coordinating and Planning Department, Texas Eastern Transmission Company, *Energy and Fuels in the United States, 1947–1980* (Houston: 1961). For a longer-range study which forecasts possible energy depletion rates in the United States and the world through the year 2000, see Milton F. Searl, *Fossil Fuels in the Future,* Office of Operations Analysis and Forecasting, U.S. Atomic Energy Commission, TID–8209 (Washington: 1960).

[51] See U.S. Geological Survey, *Coal Resources of the United States,* Circular 293, 1954, for a detailed discussion of the limitations of coal-reserve data.

[52] See Putnam, *op. cit.,* Chapter 6, for a lengthy discussion of how grossly overstated coal-reserve figures for the United States are. He estimated that only 260 billion tons of bituminous coal were available in 1950.

[53] Federal Reserve Bank of Cleveland, *Changing Fortunes of Bituminous Coal,* reprints of a series of articles appearing in the *Monthly Business Review* in 1956, p. 7.

[54] U.S. Bureau of Mines, *Minerals Yearbook, 1958, Vol. II: Fuels,* p. 138.

Table 16.11

Coal Reserves of the United States, by State, January 1, 1959
(Millions of Short Tons)

States	Estimated Original Reserves					Reserves Depleted to 1-1-59		
	Bitu-minous	Sub-Bituminous	Lignite	Anthracite and Semi-Anthracite	Total	Production Plus Loss in Mining, Assuming Past Losses Equal Production	Remaining Reserves 1-1-59	Recoverable Reserves 1-1-59 Assuming 50% Recovery
Alabama	67,570	....	....	....	67,570	1,868	65,702	32,851
Alaska	23,800	82,594	....	1,000	107,394	24	107,370	53,685
Arkansas	1,396	....	90	230	1,716	198	1,518	759
Colorado	63,203	18,492	....	90	81,785	1,006	80,779	40,389
Georgia	100	....	....	....	100	24	76	38
Illinois	137,321[1]	....	....	....	137,321	858[2]	136,463	68,232
Indiana	37,293	....	....	....	37,293	2,264	35,029	17,514
Iowa	29,160	....	....	....	29,160	712	28,448	14,224
Kansas	20,774[1]	....	....	....	20,774	24[2]	20,750	10,375
Kentucky	72,318	....	....	....	72,318	5,158	67,160	33,580
Maryland	1,200[1]	....	....	....	1,200	10[2]	1,190	595
Michigan	297	....	....	....	297	92	205	103
Missouri	79,362	....	....	....	79,362	570	78,792	39,396
Montana	2,363	132,151	87,533	....	222,047	340	221,707	110,853
New Mexico	10,948	50,801	....	6	61,755	250	61,505	30,753
North Carolina	112	....	....	....	112	2	110	55
North Dakota	....	....	350,910	....	350,910	188	350,722	175,361
Ohio	43,844	....	....	....	43,844	4,036	39,808	19,904
Oklahoma	3,673	....	....	....	3,673	356	3,317	1,658
Pennsylvania	75,093	....	....	22,805	97,898	26,836	71,062	35,531
South Dakota	....	....	2,033	....	2,033	2	2,031	1,016
Tennessee	25,665	....	....	....	25,665	766	24,899	12,449
Texas	8,000	....	7,070	....	15,070	186	14,884	7,442
Utah	88,184	5,156	....	....	93,340	508	92,832	46,416
Virginia	11,696	....	....	355	12,051	1,508	10,543	5,272
Washington	11,413	52,442	....	23	63,878	296	63,582	31,791
West Virginia	116,618	....	....	....	116,618	12,496	104,122	52,061
Wyoming	13,235	108,319	....	....	121,554	800	120,754	60,377
Other states	780	15,180	50	....	16,010	18	15,992	7,996
Total	945,418	465,135	447,686	24,509	1,882,748	61,396	1,821,352	910,676

[1] Remaining reserves as of January 1, 1950.
[2] Production since 1948.

Source: National Coal Association, *Bituminous Coal Facts 1960,* Estimates of original reserves from U.S. Geological Survey, Circular 293, 1954.

mines. By 1959, this figure had risen to 29.4 per cent.[55]

Technological developments in underground mining have also cut costs substantially. Mechanical digging, conveying, crushing, cleaning, and handling are being introduced as rapidly as possible. Most of this new equipment is profitable in large mines but not small ones. Thus, there will probably be a tendency for the smaller mines to close and for the larger mines to supply a greater portion of our coal needs. Promising experiments are currently under way to transport coal over long distances by pipeline and conveyor belt.

(2) *Oil and Gas.* Although coal-reserve figures must be carefully qualified and defined, their accuracy is much greater than estimates of ultimate oil and gas reserves in the United States. The reason is quite obvious. Commercial oil and gas deposits are frequently found many thousands of feet below the earth's surface in relatively small traps. While large areas of the nation are covered with one or more types of sedimentary rock in which oil and gas are known to occur, there is no assurance how much, if any, oil and gas exist in these formations. Currently known or proven oil and gas reserves are relatively small in terms of today's rates of consumption—about 13 years' supply for liquid hydrocarbons and about 20 years' supply for natural gas. Proved, recoverable liquid hydrocarbon reserves stood at 38.4 billion barrels at the beginning of 1961. One authority collected estimates of *ultimate* reserves, and found that the figures ranged from 87 billion to 1,945 billion barrels as of January 1957.[56] However, these reserve figures include a recovery factor of about 33 per cent of the oil in place; thus, the actual oil-reserve potential is three times these figures, or from 261 billion to almost 6 trillion barrels. How much of the currently unrecoverable oil will be recovered in the future depends largely on technological advances in drilling and primary, secondary, and tertiary recovery techniques. The oil industry is rapidly coming to realize the significance of its secondary reserves.

Estimates of total future supply of gas are subject to many of the same reservations as are oil reserves, although estimates cover a smaller range. As of January, 1957, a group of estimates of future gas reserves ranged from less than 300 trillion cubic feet to almost 1,000 trillion cubic feet.[57] Later estimates have pushed this up to 1,200 trillion cubic feet. This compares to known recoverable reserves at the beginning of 1961 of 263.8 trillion cubic feet. The lower ranges of these estimates of ultimate gas reserves seem much too low. The recovery factor for gas is about 75 to 90 per cent; thus, technology cannot play as important a role here as with oil. However, it can increase ultimate recovery somewhat.

The wide ranges in reserve estimates are ample indication that such forecasting is subject to large errors. If these estimates follow true to form, they will prove to be conservative. What good, then, are such estimates? They are worthwhile, when considered in conjunction with consumption forecasts, to give some idea of what pressures will exist on fuel supplies in the future and what price effects and consequent consumption shifts these pressures will have.

B. *Estimates of Future Energy Consumption.* Estimating the use of fuels in the future is almost as hazardous as esti-

[55] *Minerals Yearbook, 1959, Vol. II: Fuels,* p. 71.

[56] Bruce C. Netschert, *The Future Supply of Oil and Gas* (Baltimore: Johns Hopkins Press for Resources for the Future, Inc., 1958), Chapter 1. See this study for an excellent bibliography of reserve studies.

[57] *Ibid.,* Chapter 2.

mating supplies. Who would have suspected 40 years ago that oil would replace coal on the railroads, and that gas would replace coal in home heating? Who would have guessed 20 years ago that atomic energy would be harnessed for industrial uses? Thus, when someone predicts the demands for various energy supplies 50 years hence, he is making certain assumptions about the growth of total energy requirements and about the technology which dictates consumption patterns among fuels. The pitfalls concerning the validity of forecasting technological change have already been mentioned.

(1) *Short-Run Demand Forecast.* The shorter one makes his forecast, the more likely it is that he will come close to being correct. Every industry must estimate the demands for its products for a few months or years into the future. The coal, oil, and gas industries all have heavy capital costs which must be amortized over a number of years. Some forecasting of demand, more accurately called *consumption,* must be done to justify investments. Various companies, trade organizations, and government agencies make short-run estimates of consumption. In these forecasts, such potential variables as price and technology are usually implicitly assumed to be constant.[58] For purposes of discussion in this chapter, short-run forecasts of consumption are not particularly pertinent. Actually, many of the same forces at work in the long run are also operating in the short run, but the effects are so small as to go undetected. For the day-to-day, bread-and-butter business of running a company, these short-run projections are far more important than the long-term estimates.

(2) *Long-Run Demand Forecasts.* Energy requirements are closely tied to the level of economic well-being and the rate of economic development. Any long-run estimates, therefore, must assume (a) some rate of growth, perhaps increasing or decreasing from the present state of the economy, and (b) some relationship between energy requirements and economic development, usually stated in terms of something like Btu's required per dollar of real Gross National Product per capita.[59] The President's Materials Policy Commission (often referred to as the Paley Commission) for the period 1950 to 1975 projected a 100 per cent increase for the United States in real GNP, a 27 per cent increase in population, and a 40 per cent growth in real gross private domestic investment.[60] On the basis of these predictions, the Commission estimated for the period 1950 to 1975 a 260 per cent growth in electric energy requirements, a 110 per cent increase in the demand for petroleum, a 56 per cent increase in coal demand, and a 138 per cent increase in the demand for natural gas.[61] By 1959 petroleum consumption had increased 45 per cent over the 1950 level and by 1958 natural gas had risen 76 per cent and electricity consumption by 87 per cent. Since 1958 was a recession year in which gas and electricity consumption was less than normal, the

---

58 Examples of such regular forecasts are the annual and quarterly forecasts of petroleum demand by the Independent Petroleum Association of America, the FPC forecasts of fuel consumption for electric generation, Bureau of Mines monthly and annual forecasts of demand for crude oil, American Gas Association forecasts of gas consumption, and forecasts—usually for internal use—made by companies in each industry. In addition, there are numerous short-run forecasts made in speeches, articles, and books by industry representatives and outsiders who study the industries.

59 See Mason, *Energy Requirements and Economic Growth, op. cit.,* for discussion of energy requirements in nations at various stages of economic development.

60 U.S. President's Materials Policy Commission, *Resources for Freedom,* Vol. II, "The Outlook for Key Commodities" (Washington: Government Printing Office, 1952), p. 116.

61 *Ibid.,* pp. 127–130.

Paley Commission estimates would appear to be quite low.[62]

A more recent estimate of energy consumption by source for 1957 made by Resources for the Future is compared with the Paley Commission figures in Table 16.12. There is a five- to seven-year period between dates of the forecasts, and the result is a raising of the estimates in all categories except anthracite coal, which declined by 30 per cent. Particularly startling are the 33 per cent and 40 per cent increases in estimates of gas and electricity consumption, respectively.[63] Given this general range of demands by source of energy, how will each be divided up among uses?

I. Coal. One recent, authoritative coal industry estimate of bituminous coal consumption by use is shown in Table 16.13. Thus, while electric utilities accounted for 42 per cent of United States coal consumption in 1958, by 1975 they are expected to consume 67 per cent, and by 1980, 72 per cent of the total. Railroads, space-heating, and other uses (largely, other industrial fuel consumption) are all expected to drop correspondingly. The forecast by this industry representative for total domestic bituminous coal consumption in 1975 is only 598 million tons. This is far below the 731 million tons forecast for 1975 by the Paley Commission in 1950, or the 758 million tons forecast by Resources for the Future in 1957–1958. The estimates of coal to be used in electric generation seem somewhat low also. The President of the American Electric Power Company in the same congressional hearing forecast that, by 1975, 475 million tons of coal would be consumed by the electric-generating industry alone,[64] compared with the coal industry's estimate of 400 million tons. The Paley Commission came up with a completely different pattern of use for coal in 1975, as is indicated in the last column of the preceding table. Electric utilities are expected to consume only 41 per cent of total coal consumption in 1975, while industrial uses will account for 31 per cent. The differences among the experts are great. From today's vantage point it appears that the Paley Commission's estimates for coal use in space heating and railroads by 1975 are too high, while its estimates for coal consumption in electric generation are too low.[65] At the same time, the coal industry representative's estimates for "other industrial uses" by 1975 seem to be quite conservative. Such estimates imply that natural gas and/or residual oil will largely take over these markets. This seems likely to occur only if coal prices rise relative to those of other fuels; the prospect is that coal prices will not do so.

II. Oil. The breakdown of the expected demand for crude oil and natural gas liquids is given in the Paley Commission report by class of refined prod-

[62] Department of Commerce figures indicate that between 1950 and 1960, real GNP in the United States rose 38 per cent, while total consumption of energy from mineral fuels and water power rose only 28 per cent. Wardwell, *op. cit.*, p. 29.

[63] A forecast for 1975 made recently for the Atomic Energy Commission reveals substantially different consumption patterns. They are as follows: (1) coal—560 million tons; (2) oil and NGL—6.7 billion barrels; (3) natural gas—26 trillion cubic feet; and (4) hydroelectric—244 billion Kwh. W. C. Schroeder, "Fuels—Consumption and Availability for 1975 and 2000," Joint Committee on Atomic Energy, *Background Material for the Review of the International Atomic Policies and Programs of the U.S.*, Vol. 4, Committee Print, 86th Congress, 2nd Session (Washington: Government Printing Office, 1960), p. 1456.

[64] *Hearings on Energy Resources and Technology, op. cit.*, Testimony of Philip Sporn, President, American Electric Power Company, p. 77.

[65] The PMPC was projecting a 1950 figure for coal used in electric generation of 88 million tons. By 1958, partially a recession year, this figure had already reached 153 million tons.

Table 16.12

Forecasts of Energy Consumption by Source, for 1975

Source	*PMPC*[1]	*RFF*[2]	*% Increase Estimate by RFF*
Bituminous coal[3]	731	754	3
Anthracite coal[3]	20	14	−30
Oil and NGL[4]	5,000	5,923	18
Natural gas[5]	15,000	19,881	33
Hydropower[6]	261	265	2
Consumed as electricity[6] . . .	1,400	1,966	40

1 President's Materials Policy Commission, *Resources for Freedom,* Vol. II, "The Outlook for Key Commodities," pp. 127–130, and Vol. III, "The Outlook for Energy Sources," pp. 37–38 (Washington: Government Printing Office, 1952).

2 U.S. 86th Congress, 1st Session, Joint Economic Committee, *Hearings on Energy Resources and Technology,* Testimony of Sam H. Schurr, Director of Energy and Mineral Resources Program, Resources for the Future, October 12, 1959 (Washington: Government Printing Office, 1959), p. 20.

3 Millions of tons.

4 Millions of barrels.

5 Billions of cubic feet.

6 Billions of Kwh.

uct. Motor fuel was expected to rise by 110 per cent between 1950 and 1975, and kerosene and distillates by 130 per cent. Thus, gasoline by 1975 will account for 42 per cent of total oil demand, as compared with 45 per cent in 1958. Kerosene and distillates will make up 24 per cent of the total in 1975, which was their approximate share in 1958.[66]

An estimate of total petroleum demand for 1975 made in 1956 by Wallace

66 See PMPC, *op. cit.,* Vol. II, p. 129, for 1975 estimates.

Table 16.13

Forecasts of Coal Consumption by Use

(Millions of Tons)

Disposition	*Actual*	*Lamb Forecast*				*PMPC Forecast*
		Projected				
	1958	*1965*	*1970*	*1975*	*1980*	*1975*
U.S.:						
Electric utilities	153	236	315	400	510	300
Coke	77	110	117	123	130	157
Railroads and space heating	39	25	20	15	10	45
Other	98	80	70	60	50	229
Total	367	451	522	598	700	731
Exports:						
Total	50	30	30	30	30	64
Grand total	417	481	552	628	730	795

Source: Joint Economic Committee, *Hearings on Energy Resources and Technology* (Washington: Government Printing Office, 1959), Testimony of G. A. Lamb, Manager, Business Surveys, Consolidation Coal Company, p. 219; and PMPC, Vol. II, p. 130.

E. Pratt was 4.9 billion barrels, slightly below the Paley Commission estimate of 5.0 billion barrels and considerably below the 5.9 billion-barrel estimate by Resources for the Future. Despite his apparent conservative bias, it is interesting to note the breakdown which Mr. Pratt gives of this total demand forecast. This is shown in Table 16.14.

The percentage of total consumption going to each use changes very little over the 20-year period covered in the forecast. This is somewhat in conflict with the Paley Commission expectation that oil consumption for house-heating uses would rise 150 per cent between 1950 and 1975.[67] If imports of cheap residual oil reach major proportions in the next few years, it is entirely possible that oil's share of the utility and industrial markets may increase. The transportation market seems secure for petroleum in the foreseeable future.

III. Gas. The breakdown of natural gas consumption in the future presents a difficult problem. A great deal hinges on the price of gas relative to coal and oil. It seems quite evident that gas will be the favored home-heating fuel even at premium prices. How much the price of gas can be maintained above oil and still be favored is yet to be tested. Mr. Pratt in his testimony also gave some estimates of gas use in 1965 and 1975. These data are shown in Table 16.15 along with the Paley Commission estimates.

While both of these total estimates seem low in light of current consumption, they are surprisingly close in their breakdown. Both seem to indicate that space heating will take an increasing proportion of the total, while the shares of electric-generation and industrial uses will decline. Federal regulation will no doubt greatly influence the consumption pattern of gas in the future.

IV. Electricity. Electricity is produced both from fuels and from hydropower. At the end of 1958, the United States had 160,219,000 kilowatts of installed generating capacity, of which 30,098,000 kilowatts, or 18.8 per cent, was hydro capacity and the remainder steam and internal combustion capacity. By 1965, the Federal Power Commission expects total capacity to rise to 244,800,000 kilowatts, with 16.6 per cent hydro, and by 1975 total capacity will reach 376,200,000 kilowatts with only 13.7 per cent hydro.[68] Thus, by 1975, while total

[67] PMPC, *op. cit.*, Vol. II, p. 129.

[68] U.S. Federal Power Commission, Release No. 10,480, June 17, 1959, Table 4.

Table 16.14

Forecasts of Oil Consumption by Use

(Millions of Barrels)

Uses	*Actual 1955*	*Projected by Pratt*	
		1965	*1975*
Transportation	1,533	2,044	2,446
Space heating	548	803	986
Electric utilities	73	110	183
Industrial and other	876	1,095	1,314
Total	3,030	4,052	4,928

Source: Joint Committee on Atomic Energy, *Peaceful Uses of Atomic Energy* Vol. 2, U.S. 84th Congress, 2nd Session (Washington: Government Printing Office, 1956), p. 92.

capacity is going up 135 per cent, hydro capacity will rise only 72 per cent. Fossil and nuclear fuels must make up the difference, rising almost 150 per cent. Another authority estimates that by 1975 hydro-power will account for only 11 per cent of electric generation, with coal contributing 68 per cent, gas 9 per cent, oil 4 per cent, and nuclear fuels 7 per cent.[69]

Virtually everyone is in agreement that, although hydroelectric generation will increase, it will not rise as fast as the demand for electricity. Coal accounted for 68 per cent of the electricity generated in 1958, while oil's share was about 8 per cent and that of gas 24 per cent.[70] If, as perhaps may happen, the Southwestern, Mountain, and Western states grow faster in population and industry than the Northeastern and Midwestern states, what fuel will supply the needed electricity? The implications of such a question are quite interesting. There are very limited coal resources in the Southwestern and Pacific Coast states. Perhaps the interregional shifts in fuel consumption will be quite great, with the West North Central, East North Central, Middle Atlantic, South Atlantic, and East South Central regions heavily concentrated in coal except along the immediate coast, while the rest of the nation utilizes gas, oil, and nuclear energy. Such possible shifts need to be carefully studied.

5. A NATIONAL FUELS POLICY

This chapter, in a very cursory fashion, has presented the extremely complex picture of competitive fuels. One further word needs to be said on fuels policy. Perhaps the first question to be answered is whether the federal government should specifically spell out in legislation or by presidential proclamation a fuels policy for the United States. At the present time, there is a national fuels policy in existence, made up of the numerous state and federal laws dealing with energy exploration, production, processing, transportation, and utilization. This present policy has grown up, bit by bit, with little or no thought within the federal government or among state governments whether or not specific laws are consistent and com-

[69] Joint Economic Committee, *Hearings on Energy Resources and Technology, op. cit.*, Sporn, p. 79.

[70] National Coal Association, *Trends in Electric Utility Industry Experience, 1946–58, op. cit.*, p. vi.

Table 16.15

Forecasts of Gas Consumption by Use

(Billions of Cubic Feet)

Uses	*PMPC*	*Projected by Pratt*	
	1975	*1965*	*1975*
Residential heating	4,200	3,500	4,900
Residential non-heating	300		
Commercial	1,000		
Industrial	8,800	7,700	7,700
Electric utilities		2,300	2,400
Pipeline fuel and losses	700		
Total	15,000	13,500	15,000

Sources: President's Materials Policy Commission, *Resources for Freedom,* Vol. II (Washington, D.C.: 1952), p. 130; Hearings, Joint Committee on Atomic Energy, *Peaceful Uses of Atomic Energy,* Vol. II (Washington, D.C., 1956), p. 92.

plementary.[71] Virtually everyone is agreed that fuel is necessary to the economic well-being of the nation. However, how important is the health of *each* domestic fuel-producing industry? Should there be restrictions on the imports of crude oil or on imports of residual fuel oil? Should there be regulation of the prices charged by gas producers? Should coal be carried by rail at less than its full cost? Should the "end use" of fuels be regulated in some way other than through the workings of the free pricing system? Should industrial sales by gas pipelines be regulated by the FPC? Should uranium production be federally subsidized, and should research on electric-power generation from nuclear energy have federal support? And so the questions go. The answers are not simple ones, nor are they solved entirely by economics. Politics, foreign relations, regional development, and national defense all weigh heavily in decisions relating to a fuels policy.

Recommendations have been made by official and private groups for the adoption of some workable fuels policy.[72] It would certainly appear that some sort of consistent national policy is needed. For example, it is illogical for the federal government to restrict the entry of foreign crude oil into United States markets to protect this market for domestic oil and at the same time force the underpricing of gas and stimulate gas consumption, which in turn reduces both oil and coal consumption. There is a definite need to "conserve" all our energy resources. *Conservation* does not mean non-use; it means maximizing the usefulness of the total available resources in such a way as to minimize the long-run costs to society. A fuels policy program might call for less government control in some areas and more in others. First and foremost, there is a vital need to know what the existing laws and regulations actually are. Second, an attempt should be made to achieve consistency here.

[71] A very worthwhile document has been published by the Joint Economic Committee which spells out in some detail the laws governing and functions performed by various state and federal agencies in the energy field. Joint Economic Committee, *Energy Resources and Government,* Committee Print, 86th Congress, 2nd Session (Washington: Government Printing Office, 1960).

[72] See, for example, the recommendations of the Paley Commission dealing with the specific energy sources. The coal industry case is well stated in: National Coal Policy Conference, Inc., *The Case for a National Fuels Policy Study,* Washington, December, 1959, revised March 1960. The oil industry's position was voiced by Mr. Ralph M. Porter, President, American Petroleum Institute, in an address delivered to the 39th Annual Meeting of the American Petroleum Institute, at Chicago on November 9, 1959; and the gas industry's views by the Independent Natural Gas Association of America in the Joint Economic Committee's *Hearings on Energy Resources and Technology, op. cit.,* 1959, p. 322. The most recent effort at stating a fuels policy is found in: 87th Congress, 2nd Session, Senate Committee on Interior and Insular Affairs, *Report of the National Fuels and Energy Study Group,* Committee Print (Washington: Government Printing Office, 1962).

PART V

SPECIAL MANAGERIAL PROBLEMS

17 The Economics of Taxation

This chapter is concerned with the economics of the taxation of public utilities. Relatively little attention will be given to the various taxes imposed upon public utilities. Instead, the principal matters considered here are the following: (1) the comparative money burden of taxation upon public utilities and other industries; (2) the "incidence," or ultimate money burden, of public utility taxation, when and if that burden is shifted to others through price changes; and (3) the "effects," or economic consequences, of the taxation of public utilities as reflected primarily in areas other than prices.

The term "public utilities" will be used in this chapter to refer to stockholder-owned utility companies only, unless otherwise indicated. The purpose of this is to distinguish these utilities from the government-owned public utilities, whose tax liabilities are significantly less. Government-owned utilities include those which are the property of municipalities, states, the federal government, and other levels and units of public authority. As a matter of law, all government-owned public utilities are exempt from federal income taxation; in addition, the interest which the states and their political subdivisions pay upon their indebtedness is similarly exempt. In general, government-owned utilities are also exempt from all or most state and local taxation. Thus, for purposes of the present chapter, it is necessary to distinguish clearly between government-owned and stockholder-owned public utilities.

At the federal level, public utilities are subject to corporate income taxes and Social Security taxes—in the same manner as other business corporations.

At the state and local levels, public utilities are subject to a wide variety of taxes, not all of which are imposed in each state. The principal state and local taxes include: (a) general property taxes; (b) gross receipts taxes (measured as a fixed percentage of gross revenues), which may be imposed in addition to or in lieu of property taxes; (c) net income taxes; and (d) franchise, license, and occupation taxes, which may be based upon gross receipts, net income, capital stock, or other bases, or which may be set at a lump sum. For any particular tax, the rates of taxation vary over a relatively wide range as among different jurisdictions. In addition, it is not unusual to find different taxes or combinations of taxes applicable to the respective utility industries within a particular state.[1]

A significant aspect of the state and local taxation of public utilities is that they have been singled out for special taxation. That is, utilities are required to pay one or more taxes that are not levied upon other industries. This special taxation of public utilities originated in the anti-corporation attitudes of the Granger, Populist, and other such movements of the late nineteenth century. Professor Glaeser has observed that

> So many special forms of taxations were devised that state tax systems became a confused mass of unrelated tax measures, enacted without any basis of principle except that of securing increased revenues out of corporations in general, and out of public utilities in particular.[2]

Thereafter, and particularly during the economic depression decade of the 1930's, the special taxation of public utilities assumed greater proportions. The principal cause of this lies in the fact that public utilities serve as very effective tax collectors for various units of government. During World War II, public utilities experienced heavier tax burdens than ever before in their history. Present-day utility tax burdens are almost equally great.

1. THE BURDEN OF UTILITY TAXATION

This section is concerned with the measurement of the public utility tax burden and comparisons of that burden with those of other basic industries and government-owned utilities. The money burden of taxation is the total tax liability of a taxpayer. Conventionally, the tax burden is measured—for purposes of comparison—as the percentage relation of taxes to gross operating revenues within the annual accounting period.[3] In the following discussion, references to the tax burden are in terms of this measurement.

The burden of taxation upon public utilities is a matter of considerable importance to consumers, and not just to the taxpaying public utilities and the taxing authorities that collect the revenue for various governmental units. The reason that the public utility tax burden is a matter of importance to consumers is that public utilities, in effect, are collectors of taxes rather than bearers of taxes. This is explained by the fact that the Supreme Court has held that all public utility taxes which would be payable if a fair return were earned are properly included in the cost of service determined for rate-making purposes. Accordingly, the money burden of taxation upon public utilities is reflected in the rates they charge to consumers. This will be discussed more fully at a later point.

Four basic propositions may be stated with respect to the tax burden of public utilities.

(a) Historically, the money burden of public utility taxation has increased considerably.

(b) The burden of taxation is relatively greater for some public utility industries than for others.

(c) The burden of public utility taxa-

[1] For a thorough discussion of the taxes imposed on public utilities, see: Harold M. Groves, *Financing Government,* 5th ed. (New York: Holt, Rinehart & Winston, Inc., 1958), pp. 335–350. For a listing of the various taxes and their rates, as imposed by the respective states upon each utility industry, see: *Tax Systems* (New York: Commerce Clearing House, Inc., 1952), pp. 262–269.

[2] Martin G. Glaeser, *Outlines of Public Utility Economics* (New York: The Macmillan Company, 1927), p. 582.

[3] Eli W. Clemens, *Economics and Public Utilities* (New York: Appleton-Century-Crofts, Inc., 1950), pp. 523–525, 566–570; J. Rhoads Foster and Bernard S. Rodey, Jr., *Public Utility Accounting* (Englewood Cliffs, N.J.: Prentice-Hall, Inc., 1951), pp. 450–452.

tion is relatively much greater than that borne by other major industries.

(d) The burden of taxation on stockholder-owned public utilities is substantially greater than the tax burden upon government-owned utilities.

A. *The First Proposition.* The first of these propositions, that the public utility tax burden has increased considerably through time, may be illustrated by reference to the following electric-utility ratios of taxes to gross operating revenues, shown in Table 17.1. The tax burden of 3.4 per cent in 1902 increased to 9.4 per cent by 1927. Wartime taxes caused the tax burden to increase to 24.1 per cent in 1943. Continued high revenue needs by government at all levels have caused the tax burden to be maintained at nearly the same level as that of the war years. Thus, in 1959, the electric-utility tax burden amounted to 23.2 per cent of gross revenues.

B. *The Second and Third Propositions.* The second and third propositions advanced with respect to the relative burden of public utility taxation stated: that this burden is relatively greater for some utilities than for others; and that the burden of public-utility taxation is relatively much greater than that borne by other major industries. These propositions are illustrated in Table 17.2, which shows, among other things, that the comparative tax burden of electric utilities is almost four times the size of that borne by the manufacturing segment of the economy, or about a dozen times greater than that of wholesale and retail trade. The relatively low tax burden shown for the urban transit industry reflects the following facts: (a) some of the stockholder-owned companies have received tax concessions, because of the public interest in maintaining a basic but declining utility industry; and (b) local governments have come to own an increasing number of urban transit systems, and these government-owned utilities are totally or substantially tax-exempt.

Why do public utilities sustain a relatively greater tax burden than other principal industry groups? First, as noted previously, utilities are subject to special business taxes that are not imposed upon other industries. Second, public utilities bear relatively higher tax burdens than other industries because utilities are characterized by a comparatively greater investment in plant and equipment per dollar of gross revenues. Accordingly, taxes based upon the assessed valuation of property result in comparatively greater tax burdens for public utilities than for other industries. This becomes apparent when consideration is given to the great difference in the annual rates of capital turnover which characterize utility and other industries. The comparatively slow rate of capital turnover in the utility industries indicates that the burden of property taxation will be comparatively high because

Table 17.1

Tax Burden—Electric Utilities

Year	*Taxes as a Percentage of Gross Revenues*	*Year*	*Taxes as a Percentage of Gross Revenues*
1902.	3.4%	1937.	15.2%
1912.	5.0	1943.	24.1
1917.	6.5	1951.	23.0
1927.	9.4	1959.	23.2

Sources: Herbert D. Simpson, "Taxation of Public Service Industries," 1 *Journal Land & Public Utility Econ.* 44 (1925); *Moody's Public Utility Manual,* 1960.

Table 17.2

Tax Burdens—Selected Industries, 1958

Industry Group	*Taxes as a Percentage of Gross Revenues*
Non-public utilities	
Agriculture, forestry and fishery	4.1%
Mining and quarrying	7.5
Construction	2.5
Manufacturing	6.0
Wholesale and retail trade	1.9
Services (hotels, laundries, etc.)	4.9
Public utilities	
Urban transit (including government-owned)	5.7%
Natural gas pipelines	9.9
Natural gas distributing utilities	15.0
Electric utilities	23.2
Independent telephone companies	19.4
Bell system	21.8
Water utilities (stockholder-owned)	24.4

Sources: Non-Public Utilities: U.S. Treasury Department, *Statistics of Income, 1957–1958,* Internal Revenue Publication No. 16, 1960. Public Utilities: American Transit Association, *Transit Fact Book,* 1959; American Gas Association, *Gas Facts,* 1959; United States Independent Telephone Association, *Annual Statistical Volume,* 1960; *Moody's Public Utility Manual,* 1960.

the basis of the tax—property valuation—is relatively large, while the related revenue from which the tax is paid is relatively small. By the same analysis, the burden of property taxation tends to decline as the annual rate of capital turnover increases. As a general rule, the relative burden of property taxation is inversely related to the annual rate of capital turnover. Third, the public utility industry has a relatively heavy income tax burden. This results from the fact that corporate income taxes are capital-productivity taxes. (Since interest is a deduction for tax purposes, such taxes can be looked at as levies upon the productivity of equity capital.) Public utility services, to a large extent, represent the productivity of capital and, unlike the products of other industries, are to a lesser extent the product of labor. Accordingly, taxation based upon capital productivity constitutes a relatively greater burden for utilities than for other industries.

C. The Fourth Proposition. The fourth proposition stated that the tax burden of stockholder-owned public utilities is much greater than that borne by government-owned public utilities. This is a result of the tax exemptions accorded the latter utilities. Government ownership of public utilities, as noted in the discussion of rates (Chapters 10 and 11), is particularly widespread in the urban transit and water utility industries. Government-owned electric utilities, on the other hand, account for about one-fourth of the total public utility production of electricity.

Government-owned electric utilities (exclusive of federal projects and co-operatives) for the most part are the property of municipalities and public utility districts. (The latter serve a stated area rather than a municipality and its immediate environs.) The tax burden upon these government-owned electric utilities has risen somewhat through time, but it remains quite small by comparison with that borne by stockholder-owned electric utilities. In 1958, for example, the tax burden of stockholder-owned electric companies was 23.2 per cent of gross revenues, while that of the government-owned (non-federal) electric utilities was 3.1 per cent. Table 17.3 illustrates the relative tax burden of the publicly owned electric utilities, 1922–1958.

Table 17.3

Tax Burden—Government-Owned Electric Utilities*

Year	*Taxes as a Percentage of Gross Revenues*
1922.	0.8%
1927.	1.1
1937.	1.5
1947.	2.4
1958.	3.1

* Exclusive of federal projects and co-operatives.

Sources: Moody's Public Utility Manual, 1947, 1955, 1960.

The largest government-owned producer of electricity is the Tennessee Valley Authority, which is a corporation owned by the federal government. Its system of multipurpose dams, on the Tennessee and its tributaries, provides flood control and assists navigation. The TVA dams also generate a substantial amount of hydroelectric power. In addition, TVA generates an increasing amount of electricity from conventional steam-powered electric-generating plants. The TVA markets firm power at wholesale to municipally owned and co-operatively owned electric distribution systems. The Atomic Energy Commission also is a customer. Excess hydroelectric power is sold to public utilities and industrial customers.

The TVA is exempt from federal taxation. However, it makes payments in lieu of taxes to the state and county governments in its operating area. Its wholesale power contracts with the local distributors require them to make payment in lieu of taxes to their respective local governments.

The financial reports covering the TVA electric-power operations in recent fiscal years show that its payments in lieu of taxes amount to a tax burden of about 2.5 per cent of gross electric operating revenues.[4] In addition, it is indicated that the municipally owned electric-distribution systems, which market TVA power at retail, bear a tax burden of about 5.0 per cent of gross electric operating revenues.[5]

Turning next to the relative actual tax burden of government-owned water utilities, it appears that they bear a lesser average burden than the government-owned electric utilities. The most recent study of the water utility industry by the American Water Works Association shows that, for a representative group of 225 government-owned water utilities, the total of "taxes and miscellaneous expenses," taken together as one item, amounted to 2.0 per cent of gross revenues, with taxes comprising a lesser proportion of this item than miscellaneous expenses.[6]

It appears from the foregoing that the tax burden upon government-owned utilities is minimal by comparison with that borne by stockholder-owned utilities. However, in assessing the relative tax burden of government-owned utilities, it should be recognized that in

---

[4] In fiscal 1959, for example, tax equivalents in the amount of $5,900,391 were paid; gross revenues from electricity sales totaled $237,-540,179. *Moody's Public Utility Manual,* 1960, pp. a67–68.

[5] Based upon the average relation of tax equivalents to gross electric operating revenues, as reported to the Federal Power Commission by the municipally owned electric utilities in Memphis, Nashville, Chattanooga, and Knoxville. Federal Power Commission, *Statistics of Electric Utilities in the United States, Publicly Owned, 1957* (Washington, D.C.: Government Printing Office, 1958), pp. 26–28.

[6] H. F. Seidel and E. R. Baumann, "A Statistical Analysis of Water Works Data for 1955," 49 *Journal of the American Water Works Association* 1531, 1554–1556 (1957). Wisconsin utilities were excluded by the analysts; relatively high state requirements with respect to the payment of tax equivalents render those utilities non-comparable.

some instances they: (a) provide free services to the governmental unit; (b) receive free services from the governmental unit; and (c) make cash payments to the general fund of the governmental unit. Free services provided to a city government, for example, by a municipally owned electric utility may take the form of lighting service for streets, municipal buildings, schools, and public hospitals. Such free services may be regarded as being in the nature of a tax payment. On the other hand, free services, received by the government-owned utility from the governmental unit of which it is a part, are in the nature of a subsidy and serve to reduce the net burden of taxation. Examples of this include rent-free space in public buildings and the benefit of services without charge from other departments of the unit of government. There are no aggregate data that would quantify such contributions by government. Finally, government-owned utilities sometimes make cash contributions to the general fund of the governmental unit of which they are a part. These payments are in the nature of a return on capital and are not properly regarded as the equivalent of tax payments. The Wisconsin commission, for example, in its periodic analysis of the returns earned on various classes of investment in privately owned and municipally owned Wisconsin utilities, treats cash contributions by municipal utilities as return on investment. Such payments by Wisconsin municipal utilities in 1958 amounted to: (a) 2.76 per cent on capital paid in by municipalities; and (b) 0.48 per cent on paid-in capital plus surplus. Professor Clemens also indicates some acceptance of the view that cash payments constitute a return on investment.[7]

[7] Public Service Commission of Wisconsin, *Statistics of Wisconsin Public Utilities,* Bulletin No. 8, 1959, p. 13; Clemens, *op. cit.*, p. 569.

What is the nature of the tax burden sustained by government-owned utilities through the provision of services without charge? In a survey of the value of free services as a percentage of revenue, as provided by 234 government-owned water utilities, the following distribution of results was obtained:[8]

Number of Water Utilities	*Value of Free Services as a Percentage of Revenue*
98	None
48	4% or less
40	4% to 8%
29	8% to 16%
19	Over 16%

The publicly owned electric utilities, excluding federal projects and co-operatives, in 1958 furnished 53,960,000 kilowatt-hours without charge. At their average 1958 rate of 1.22¢/Kwh, such free services provided by government-owned electric utilities would have a value of $658,212, or an average equivalent tax burden of about one-tenth of one per cent of revenues. In the previous year, 1957, a total of 37,793,000 kilowatt-hours were distributed without charge. Valued at their average 1957 rate of 1.19¢/Kwh, the tax-burden equivalent of the free services amounted to less than one-tenth of one per cent of revenues.[9]

D. *The Tax Burden of Investors.* The cost of capital to stockholder-owned utilities is greater than that of government-owned utilities. An important reason for this is that the interest earned on bonds issued by government-owned utilities is exempt from federal income taxation.[10] Owing to this "tax shelter" feature, investors are almost always will-

[8] Seidel and Baumann, *op. cit.*, p. 1553.

[9] Federal Power Commission, *op. cit.*, 1957 and 1958.

[10] The interest earned on TVA revenue bonds, first sold to investors in November of 1960, is not exempt from the federal income tax. However, because the TVA is a federal instrumentality, the interest on its bonds is

ing to accept a lower return on investments in bonds issued by government-owned utilities than on the securities whose interest or dividend income is not tax-exempt. The result of this is a comparatively lower cost of capital to government-owned utilities. Some measure of the differential tax burden on investors is suggested by the fact that, for the year 1943, one study estimated that 32.1 per cent of the interest and dividends distributed by public utilities was paid out in income taxes by the recipients.[11] The average cost of capital to government-owned water utilities has been placed at 60 per cent of the average cost to stockholder-owned water utilities.[12] The American Public Power Association, which represents many government-owned electric utilities, has estimated that there would be "an increase of 30 to 40 per cent in current interest rates if the tax exemption of interest on municipal bonds is removed," while in another estimate the increase was placed at a minimum of 40 per cent.[13]

E. *Tax Burdens and Utility Rates.* The rates charged by stockholder-owned utilities are generally higher than those of government-owned utilities. The principal causes for this are their differential tax burdens and costs of capital, as discussed above. The difference in average rate levels is sometimes used as the basis for invidious and misleading comparisons of the rates charged by stockholder-owned utilities and government-owned utilities. This is particularly apt to occur with respect to electric utilities. Any such comparison of rates is invalid, because the tax burdens and costs of capital of the two categories of utilities are not comparable.

An illustration of this type of rate comparison, for example, was reported in *The New York Times* of October 9, 1960. There, an article on the 1960 fiscal-year electric operations of the Tennessee Valley Authority reported a TVA announcement which stated that the consumers of TVA electricity had "saved" $120 million during the year.[14] This was calculated by a comparison with the amount that would have been paid for the same quantity of electricity priced at the average of rates in effect throughout the nation, as charged by stockholder-owned electric utilities. No reference was made to the fact that TVA and the local electric-distribution systems it supplies at wholesale (municipally owned utilities and co-operatives) sustain a substantially lower tax burden than stockholder-owned utilities, nor was reference made to the fact that TVA and its local electric distributors were financed at lower capital costs than the tax-paying utilities with which comparision was made.

2. THE INCIDENCE OF PUBLIC UTILITY TAXATION

In analyzing the taxation of public utility enterprises, it is necessary to dis-

not subject to state and local income taxation, nor are its bonds subject to personal intangible property taxes. Federal appropriations have been the principal source of TVA investment capital. TVA pays interest to the United States Treasury on the unamortized balance of such federal investments in its electric facilities. The annual rate of interest paid by TVA is determined by the Secretary of the Treasury on the basis of the composite rate of interest on the federal debt. By statutory limitation, the federal government may not pay more than 4.25 per cent interest on its securities of five years or longer maturities.

[11] Foster and Rodey, *op. cit.*, p. 479.

[12] C. Fore, "Procedure for Establishing Water Rates," 51 *Journal of the American Water Works Association* 1011, 1012 (1959).

[13] As quoted in Edison Electric Institute Bulletin, December, 1960, p. 379; and statement by Northcutt Ely, *Tax Revision Compendium,* submitted to House Committee on Ways and Means (Washington, D.C.: Government Printing Office, 1959), p. 784.

[14] Section One, p. 9.

tinguish between the "impact" of the tax burden and its "incidence." The impact of the tax burden is the place where the tax first comes to rest. Thus, the impact of public utility taxation is upon the utilities themselves, because they sustain the tax burden initially. The incidence of the tax burden is the place where it ultimately comes to rest. The process of transferring the tax burden from the point of impact to the point or points of incidence is called "shifting."

A. The General Incidence. Where public utilities are concerned, whether privately or publicly owned, the tax burden is shifted to consumers through the rates charged for service. This results from the fact that regulatory law and commission practice require taxes payable to be recognized as proper costs of service. Expressed differently, public utilities are entitled to the opportunity to earn a fair return after taxes. Accordingly, taxes are treated as operating revenue deductions in determining: (a) the actual return which the utility is earning at any particular time; and (b) the rate of return that would result from a specified level of revenues. In determining the cost of service for public utility rate making, it is proper to include as costs the taxes that would be paid if a fair return were earned. Therefore, the incidence of public utility taxation is a "regulated incidence" and is not determined by the operation of competitive factors. There are only a few exceptions to the general principle that the incidence of public utility taxation is upon consumers. Those exceptions will be noted shortly.

From the beginning of permanent commission regulation, public utility taxes have been recognized as costs of operation. (An exception to this, in the early years of regulation, was the federal income tax. The reasons for the exception are no longer relevant.) As early as 1909 the United States Supreme Court held that public utility franchise taxes were to be regarded as operating expenses, ". . . to be paid out of its earnings before the net amount could be arrived at applicable to dividends, and if such latter were not sufficient to permit the proper return on the property used by the company for the public, then the rate would be inadequate."[15] However, it was not until 1922 that the Supreme Court made clear for all time that public utility taxes, including the federal income tax, were to be regarded as proper costs of supplying public utility services. This was decided in the *Galveston* case, which was reaffirmed the following year. In the *Galveston* decision, Justice Brandeis, speaking for the Court, stated:

> In calculating . . . a proper return it is necessary to deduct from gross revenue the expenses and charges; and all taxes which would be payable if a fair return were earned are appropriate deductions. There is no difference in this respect between state and federal taxes, or between income taxes and others.[16]

The *Galveston* decision resulted in a "regulated incidence" of public utility taxation which would appear to be a necessary auxiliary to the regulation of public utility rates and profits.

The *Galveston* rule, as implemented in the determination of the cost of service for rate-making purposes, does not necessarily require the use of the actual test-year taxes paid. Rate making for the future on the basis of test-year data assumes that such data are representative of probable future conditions. Each test-year cost item, including taxes, is

[15] *Willcox* v. *Consolidated Gas Co.,* 212 U.S. 19, 51 (1909).

[16] *Galveston Electric Co.* v. *Galveston,* 258 U.S. 388, 399–400 (1922). See also *Georgia Railway and Power Co.* v. *Railroad Commission of Georgia,* 262 U.S. 625 (1923).

subject to reasonable adjustment so that it is made to reflect probable future conditions. Thus, for example, a non-recurring test-year item ordinarily would not be recognized. In addition, commissions recognize the effects upon tax liabilities of rate adjustments and the estimated change in revenues resulting therefrom.

Exceptions to the general rule that the incidence of public utility taxation is placed upon consumers may be considered at this point. First, an increase in the public utility tax burden may not be shifted to consumers to the extent that the "regulatory lag" requires time for the processing of a commission order authorizing the utility to raise its rates to recoup its increased taxes. Second, a new or increased tax on public utilities cannot be shifted in the event that the utility is earning a rate of return above the percentage approved in its last rate case. Third, the utility will not be able to shift the burden of new or increased taxes if all classes of customers are already being charged at the level of the full value of service, or maximum reservation price. In such cases, increased rates would lead to overpricing and loss of some part of the market. Hence, the incidence would very likely fall upon the stockholders, unless the utility could shift it to employees or suppliers by paying them less. A prominent example of this is the urban transit utility industry. Finally, it should be noted that numerous commissions did not permit wartime excess profits taxes to be shifted.

B. *The Specific Incidence.* The process of shifting the burden of taxation occurs through price changes. The economic entity that sustains initially the impact of the tax burden will shift it, if possible, either: (a) by paying suppliers of goods and services less; (b) by charging customers more; or (c) by achieving some combination of the two. Public utilities generally follow the second of these alternatives. Thus, the specific incidence of public utility taxation depends upon the pricing policy of each utility company, as reviewed and approved by the commission that has jurisdiction over its rates.

Shifting the public utility tax burden occurs as part of the process of pricing public utility services. In this respect, all or most of the tax burden is generally regarded as one of a number of the joint and constant costs of rendering service. It has been brought out previously (Chapter 10) that, in the process of pricing, such costs are distributed differentially among the respective classes of service by reference, to some degree at least, to the demand or value of service characteristics of each class of service. Accordingly, if the specific incidence of public utility taxation is viewed in this light, it becomes apparent that there is no necessarily equal or proportionate shifting of the public utility tax burden to the respective customer classes. Rather, the logical conclusion is that the incidence of the tax burden: (a) falls more heavily, or completely, upon customer classes or types of services whose demand is relatively high or inelastic; and (b) falls less heavily, if at all, upon customer classes or types of service whose demand is relatively low or elastic. Thus, it seems reasonable to conclude further that public utility taxation, in terms of its specific incidence, is in effect a sales tax upon the consumption of public utility services in those sectors of the market that are characterized by the greatest intensity of demand. Stated another way, the specific incidence is upon the smallest consumers, or those who have little bargaining power, and whose alternatives are the most limited or nonexistent. These consumers bear more than their "fair" share of the shifted tax burden.

3. THE EFFECTS OF UTILITY TAXATION

The effects of taxation are the economic consequences resulting from its imposition, as reflected primarily in areas other than prices. Some of the principal effects are discussed in this section.

Perhaps the most important economic effect of public utility taxation is that the economic costs of such taxes to consumers are apt to exceed the tax revenues that are produced for government. Stated differently, the total consumer burden resulting from public utility taxation tends to exceed the amount of the taxes shifted to consumers. The explanation for this may be found in the fact that public utilities operate, to a large extent, under conditions of decreasing average unit costs with increasing quantities of service produced. In short, a tax upon such industries tends to impede or reverse the process of achieving decreasing average unit costs, so that the resulting burden is comprised of the tax plus the loss of economies that otherwise would have been achieved. Stated in more detail, the taxation of public utilities tends to cause: (a) increased rates; (b) a curtailment in the volume of service that would be demanded in the absence of such taxation; and (c) a loss of the additional economies that would otherwise result from the greater utilization of plant capacity. When the relatively lower unit costs that might have been achieved are not realized, consumers bear a burden in addition to the shifted taxes. This effect of taxation was recognized originally by Alfred Marshall in his *Principles of Economics*, published in 1890.[17]

In almost all instances, taxation that restrains or reduces consumption (of socially useful goods and services) must be regarded as having a social cost, which should be weighed against the social benefits accruing from the public spending of tax revenues. In this respect, it merits noting that the effect of taxation discussed above is very largely confined to the stockholder-owned public utilities. Government-owned utilities, by contrast, enjoy a relative freedom from this effect of taxation. This factor appears to explain, at least in part, the greater-than-average consumption of electricity in the TVA service area.

A second effect of public utility taxation, or a group of related effects, grows out of the cost advantages that government-owned utilities achieve by virtue of the tax exemptions that they and the investors in their securities have been accorded by law. These effects are summarized in the following discussion. (1) Because the incidence of public utility taxation is upon ultimate consumers, the effect of the differential in tax burdens is to require some consumers of utility service to contribute more toward the financial requirements of government than others, solely on the basis of the nature of ownership of the utilities serving the cities where they happen to live. The fact that some citizens thus avoid bearing a part of the tax burden means that those who are not able to do so must contribute relatively more toward the costs of government. (2) The relatively greater tax burden imposed on consumers served by stockholder-owned utilities bears no relation to the "ability to pay" principle of apportioning the financial burden of the costs of government, and seems to be contrary to the "benefits received" principle of apportionment.[18] (3) The cost advantages that the tax exemptions provide government-owned utilities constitute a positive inducement to further government ownership. Professor Clemens has noted that, in some instances, the ad-

---

[17] Alfred Marshall, *Principles of Economics*, 8th ed. (London: The Macmillan Company, 1930), p. 469.

[18] These principles are discussed in Groves, *op. cit.*, pp. 15–25.

vantages of differential taxation have been traded upon by promoters of government ownership, and that tax avoidance appeared to be "a very material factor" influencing the change from private to public ownership in Omaha, Nebraska.[19] (4) Where tax-favored and tax-paying utilities compete directly with one another, as, for example, in seeking to render services in a newly developed area, the privately owned utility is handicapped.

A third effect of public utility taxation relates to the size of rate-increase applications submitted by utilities for commission review. Because of the tax factor, a utility applying for a rate increase must request authority to collect more in additional revenues than it needs in additional net income. This factor can be a cause of misunderstanding on the part of those who do not appreciate the role of public utilities as tax collectors. For example, in 1949 the Wisconsin commission was told by the state legislature to give an explanation for the $11.5 million in rate increases it had allowed the Wisconsin Telephone Company in the four postwar years. In the commission's reply, it was pointed out, among other things, that $3.9 million (or 34 per cent) of the rate increase total was necessary to meet the requirements of the federal income tax, the state income tax, and the state gross revenue tax. In addition, the commission noted that telephone subscribers were also required to pay over $1.9 million in federal excise taxes on telephone service.

The commission summarized the effect of taxation by showing that the telephone subscriber was required to pay: (1) a total of $2.09 in order for Wisconsin Telephone Company to receive $1.00 of additional net income from local operations; and (2) a total of $2.33 for the company to receive an additional dollar of net income from toll operations.[20]

A fourth effect of public utility taxation is to deter the replacement of existing plant and equipment by the installation of more efficient units as well as the expansion of existing facilities. In the balancing of prospective costs and revenues that necessarily precedes any managerial decision to invest, taxes must be regarded as part of costs. Because the tax burden of public utilities is relatively greater than that of other industries, a prospective gain in efficiency or expansion of capacity that might be achieved by a substitution or addition of facilities is also relatively harder to justify on a cost-and-revenue-projection basis. Thus, the employment of capital is adversely affected by the relatively greater tax burden borne by utilities, and the achievement of possible economies and expanded output is thereby delayed or prevented.[21]

---

[19] Clemens, *op. cit.*, p. 568.

[20] Public Service Commission of Wisconsin, "Report to Legislative Council Re Telephone Rate Increases," November 17, 1949, pp. 1–2.

[21] The preceding discussion does not purport to delve into the question of whether government-owned or privately owned utilities are "best." The statement here is merely that privately owned utilities bear some burdens that government-owned utilities do not bear. The arguments for and against public ownership go far beyond the limited discussion presented here.

18 The Labor Force and Labor Relations

Much of the discussion in this book has dealt with the "public" nature of utility-type activities. Because they are constantly in the public eye and are performing a necessary public service, utilities encounter somewhat unique problems in the area of employee relations. This chapter will describe the characteristics of the public utility work force and point out some of the special problems that arise and solutions that have been tried.

1. THE NATURE OF THE UTILITY WORK FORCE

Employment in public utility industries during 1959 was about 1.4 million employees, of which over half were in communications, about 40 per cent in gas and electric utilities, and the remainder in urban railway and bus transportation, water, and sewage disposal. Employment data for the period 1947–1959, by type of utility, are shown in Table 18.1. While utility sales and investment have risen rapidly during the postwar period, total employment rose only slightly, from 1,323,000 in 1947 to 1,435,000 in 1959. Closer examination reveals that employment in telegraph communications dropped 37 per cent and in urban transit, 50 per cent. The number of workers in the telephone, gas, and electric industries has increased slowly during the postwar years but has nowhere kept pace with the vast expansion in investment and output. Much of the explanation for this apparent paradox lies in the fact that utilities are intensive capital-using industries, and they have enjoyed a number of major technological innovations which have been of a "labor-saving" nature.

Table 18.2 shows a comparison of the work force in utilities with those in manufacturing, construction, wholesale and retail trade, and finance, insurance, and real estate. The first part of the table shows a percentage breakdown of the employees by occupation or skills. Utilities rank first among the groups in the portion of their work force made up by professional and technical employees. Utilities are second only to construction in the proportion of craftsmen and foremen in their work force, and second only to finance, insurance, and real estate in clerical workers. On the other hand, public utilities employ very few sales or service workers, and they have a relatively small proportion of employees in managerial positions. Within specific utility industries, the breakdown of employees by occupation varies greatly. Of the 631,501 employees of Class A telephone carriers in 1958, 206,038 or 33 per cent were operators, 175,851 or 28 per cent were construction, installation, or maintenance workers, and 133,-583 or 21 per cent were clerical employees.[1]

A study of gas and electric utilities

[1] Federal Communications Commission, *Statistics of Communications Common Carriers, December 31, 1958,* Washington: Government Printing Office, 1960, p. 22.

Table 18.1

Employment in Utility Industries 1947–1959

(000's)

Year	Total All Utilities	Communications			Total Gas and Electric	Electric Light & Power	Gas	Electric and Gas Combined[1]	Local Railways and Bus Lines	Other Utilities[2]
		Combined Total	Telephone	Telegraph						
1959.	1435	743	705.5	37.2	576.6	255.9	153.3	167.4	92.3	23.2
1958.	1468	771	732.4	38.3	578.5	258.3	151.5	168.7	96.4	22.9
1957.	1514	810	768.2	41.4	577.2	258.7	149.0	169.5	103.6	23.0
1956.	1498	795	751.2	42.6	569.1	250.2	145.3	173.6	109.5	23.6
1955.	1451	750	706.7	42.3	562.1	248.7	140.8	172.6	116.1	23.0
1954.	1447	741	698.8	41.4	557.1	249.0	139.1	169.0	126.4	22.4
1953.	1452	747	702.2	43.7	552.4	248.2	133.2	171.1	129.1	23.2
1952.	1419	720	678.4	40.4	543.3	244.0	128.4	171.0	133.1	22.6
1951.	1384	690	644.0	45.3	533.3	240.4	123.8	169.1	139.0	22.0
1950.	1358	664	619.5	44.0	526.0	238.9	117.6	169.4	145	22.5
1949.	1380	686	636.7	48.6	514.9	236.4	N.A.	N.A.	156	23.0
1948.	1380	696	638.9	56.1	498.0	N.A.	N.A.	N.A.	163	23.2
1947.	1323	646	586	59	469.5	N.A.	N.A.	N.A.	185	22.6

[1] Companies which provide both electric and gas service.

[2] Primarily water and sewage-disposal utilities.

N.A.—Not available.

Source: U.S. Bureau of Labor Statistics, *Employment and Earnings,* Annual Supplements.

Table 18.2

Employed Persons, by Major Occupation Group—1959

Groups	*Manufacturing* %	*Construction* %	*Wholesale & Retail* %	*Financial, Insurance, & Real Estate* %	*Communications & Other Public Utility*[1] %
All occupations	100.0	100.0	100.0	100.0	100.0
Professional, technical and kindred workers	8.4	4.4	1.9	3.1	9.1
Managers, officials, and proprietors	6.0	11.9	24.3	20.3	5.9
Clerical and kindred workers	12.6	4.5	12.9	42.7	35.2
Sales	3.1	0.4	23.8	22.5	0.6
Craftsmen, foremen, and kindred workers	19.2	50.3	5.9	2.3	29.9
Operatives and kindred workers	41.9	8.7	13.9	0.5	9.3
Service workers	1.8	0.4	13.1	7.2	1.5
Laborers	7.0	19.4	4.1	1.3	8.5
By sex:					
Male	74.7	96.3	63.4	54.7	70.3
Female	25.3	3.7	36.6	45.3	19.7
% Unemployed in category	6.0	12.9	5.8	2.6	2.2

[1] Includes telephone, telegraph, electric, gas, and other local utilities not elsewhere classified. Excludes transportation.

Source: U.S. Bureau of Labor Statistics, *Employment and Earnings,* Annual Supplement, May 1960.

made in late 1957 showed that 72 per cent of the nonsupervisory workers were "physical" workers and 28 per cent were office workers. Among the "physical" workers in electric utilities, linemen journeymen, a highly skilled group, were the most numerous and were among the best-paid. Groundmen and meter readers, two other large groups, received considerably lower pay, reflecting the lower level of skills required.[2] The gas utility work force is dominated by (1) gas main-installation and service laborers, (2) gas appliance servicemen, (3) gas main fitters, (4) meter readers, and (5) fitter's helpers. Appliance servicemen and fitters were the most highly skilled and received the highest hourly wages.[3]

The second part of Table 18.2 shows a breakdown between men and women employees. Contrary to what might be expected, women make up less than 20 per cent of the work force of communications and other non-transportation utilities. Only the construction industry has a smaller proportion of women in its work force. If only Class A telephone utilities are considered, some 371,153 out of 631,501 employees, or about 59 per cent, are women.[4] The number of women in utilities other than telephone is quite small, since virtually none of the physical workers are women. Well over half the office workers in gas and electric utilities are women, but they make up only about 17 per cent of the total work force.[5]

The last part of Table 18.2 shows the percentage of the work force in each of the specified categories that was unemployed during 1959. The figure for utilities is the lowest among the industry groups shown. This might be expected, since utility operations are relatively stable, and cuts in labor force are not very large even when operations are curtailed. There is, of course, some "technological" unemployment among telephone and telegraph operators as their job functions are automated. However, a considerable effort has been made on the part of the Bell System, at least, to find suitable jobs for displaced workers.

Stable employment is in part an indication that workers are reasonably well satisfied with wages, hours, and other working conditions. With the possible exception of local railways and bus lines, this generalization seems to hold for the utility industries. Table 18.3 shows a comparison of weekly earnings, weekly hours, and hourly earnings for individual utility activities and other major industry groups, including manufacturing, mining, contract construction, retail trade, and banking. The highest hourly wage rates are found in the building trades, in which highly skilled, seasonal work is done and in which strong union forces exist. These characteristics show up in the rather high hourly wage and the shortest average work week.

Closely behind the building-trade workers are telephone installers, linemen, and maintenance workers. Here again, skills are extremely important. In terms of weekly wages, this part of the telephone industry work force is paid relatively more than workers in the construction industry. This is due to the considerably longer average work week. The low wages paid in such industries as retail trade and banking are not approached in the utility field except in the telephone industry, where operators' wage levels are about comparable. This reflects, in part, the fact that women who have very little in the way of special or scarce skills are hired for this func-

[2] U.S. Bureau of Labor Statistics, *Wage Structure: Electric and Gas Utilities, September, 1957,* BLS Report No. 135, June, 1958, Table 14.

[3] *Ibid.*

[4] FCC, *Communication Statistics, 1958,* p. 21.

[5] BLS, *Wage Structure: Electric and Gas Utilities, September, 1957.*

Table 18.3

Hours and Earnings of Workers in Utility and Other Industries, 1959

Occupations	*Average Weekly Earnings*	*Average Weekly Hours*	*Average Hourly Earnings*
Local railways and bus lines	$ 94.59	42.8	$2.21
Telephone	68.44[1]	37.4	1.83
	115.87[2]	42.6	2.72
Telegraph	95.99	42.1	2.28
Electric light and power utilities	106.34	40.9	2.60
Gas utilities	99.39	40.9	2.43
Electric light and gas utilities combined	110.56	41.1	2.69
All manufacturing	89.47	40.3	2.22
Mining	107.73	40.5	2.66
Contract construction	114.82	36.8	3.12
Retail trade	67.06	38.1	1.76
Banking	68.07	37.4	1.82

1 Switchboard operating employees.
2 Line construction employees.
Source: U.S. Bureau of Labor Statistics, *Employment and Earnings,* Annual Supplement, May 1960, Table C–6.

tion. Also, the substantial number of part-time employees in this category tends to lower the averages. Other than that, the utility industries compare quite favorably with other American industries. At the low end of the wage range among utilities is the declining urban transit industry. But even here, weekly earnings exceed those in manufacturing. With employment in the transit industry shrinking, the employees have a relatively weaker bargaining position.

Although it is difficult to generalize about fringe benefits, and even more difficult to quantify and compare benefits among industries, it is probably safe to say that utility workers do as well as, if not better than, workers in the average manufacturing or mining establishment.[6] Good and bad examples can be found in any industry. The large utilities certainly are on a par with large manufacturing concerns. The Bell System is often referred to as "Ma Bell" by its employees, evidence of the beneficent maternalism practiced by these companies. Some of the large electric and gas utilities do much the same thing. This is not to say that these companies have no labor problems. However, fringe benefits are rarely a major issue in labor-management disputes.

Only a brief sketch of unionization in the utility field can be given here. Table 18.4 shows a partial picture of unionization among utilities. The first part of the table indicates the number of unions and the number of union members in the telecommunications industry, the electric and gas utility industry, and the local street railway and bus industry. These data are somewhat difficult to interpret because there are many unions which have some workers in the utility industry but whose membership includes non-utility workers. Excluded from the data are employees of local utilities other than gas, electric, and communications.

Part two of Table 18.4 indicates the extent of unionization in two utility industries compared with all manufacturing and with all non-manufacturing industries, including utilities. In com-

6 See the discussion in BLS, *Wage Structure: Electric and Gas Utilities, September, 1957.*

Table 18.4

Unionization in the Utility Industry—1958

Utility	All Unions		AFL-CIO Affiliates		Independent	
	No. of Unions	No. of Members[2]	No. of Unions	No. of Members[2]	No. of Unions	No. of Members[2]
Telephone and telegraph	6	409	3	310	3	99
Electricity and gas	13	259	10	234	3	25
Urban transit[1]	1	125	1	125	0	0
Total	20	793	14	669	6	124

Percentage Distribution of Membership of National and International Unions in Industry Groups—1958

Percentage	Telephone and Telegraph		Gas and Electricity		Manufacturing		Non-Manufacturing	
	No. of Unions	No. of Members[2]	No. of Unions	No. of Members[2]	No. of Unions	No. of Members[2]	No. of Unions	No. of Members[2]
0-19	2	64	11	188	13	677	9	1312
20-39	0	0	0	0	5	1720	5	164
40-59	0	0	0	0	8	571	6	1078
60-79	0	0	0	0	7	1084	6	1735
80-100	4	344	2	71	75	4307	74	4285
Total	6	408	13	259	108	8359	100	8574

[1] Includes only the major street railway and bus employees' union. Data are not available on the other unions in this industry.

[2] 000's of union members.

Source: U.S. Bureau of Labor Statistics, *Directory of National and International Labor Unions in the U.S., 1959,* BLS Bulletin No. 1267, Dec., 1959, pp. 12 and 13.

munications it would appear that unionization his been quite complete, while in gas and electric utilities the unionization has been only partial. This is quite logical, since there is not the same degree of atomization and fragmentation in telephone and telegraph that there is in the gas and electric utility industry. Bargaining with a state-wide or region-wide company has fostered the growth of unions of comparable scope. Labor in the telephone industry is organized primarily by the Communication Workers of America, an AFL-CIO affiliate which had 735 locals and 255,365 members in 1959.[7] Two smaller unions, the Alliance of Independent Telephone Unions, with 12 locals and 90,000 members, and the American Communications Association, with five locals and 8,000 members, are not affiliated with the AFL-CIO but are important in certain localities.[8] These three unions account for a large part of the non-managerial work force in the telephone industry.

Another strongly unionized industry is the local transit industry, whose labor force is represented by the Street, Electric Railway and Motor Coach Employees of America. This union had 412 locals and 124,637 members in 1959.[9] Membership was greater than total reported employment for this industry in 1959.[10] In addition, there are probably some transit employees that belong to government employees' unions, the teamsters' union, the transport workers' union, and some craft unions.

The workers in the telegraph industry are organized by the Commercial Telegraphers' Union, an AFL-CIO affiliate that had 134 locals and 29,262 members in 1959. This union has been shrinking in size as employment in this industry has declined.

The largest union in the gas and electric utility field is the Utility Workers Union of America, another AFL-CIO affiliate, with 255 locals and 66,000 members. In addition, there is an independent union, the Brotherhood of Utility Workers of New England, with 20 locals and 4,600 members. Some of the large industrial unions, such as the International Brotherhood of Electrical Workers (AFL-CIO), have substantial membership in the utility field also. Some employees of gas utilities are members of the Oil, Chemical and Atomic Workers union. Finally, there are quite a few employees of municipally owned urban transit, water, sewage, and electric utilities that belong to unions of government employees.

2. LABOR-MANAGEMENT RELATIONS IN PUBLIC UTILITIES

Labor-management relations in utility industries are generally good. The foregoing description of the characteristics, wages, hours, and composition of the utility work force leaves the impression that employees in this industry are about as well off as the average worker in manufacturing, better off than most workers in trade, finance, and service industries, and have a very high degree of employment security. Despite the generally favorable climate for employer-employee relations, the utility industry does have some disputes and does have work stoppages of varying degrees of severity. Table 18.5 compares work stoppages in (1) the public utility group, including transportation, communications, electric and gas utilities, and sanitary services, with (2) all manufacturing and (3) all non-manufacturing

[7] U.S. Bureau of Labor Statistics, *Directory of National and International Labor Unions in the United States, 1959,* BLS Bulletin No. 1267, December 1959.

[8] *Ibid.*

[9] *Ibid.*

[10] See Table 18.1.

Table 18.5

Work Stoppages in Utilities, Manufacturing, and Non-Manufacturing Industries, 1946–1958

Year	Public Utilities[1]			% of Estimated Work Time of All Employees		
	No. of Strikes	Workers Involved[2]	Man Days Idle[2]	Utilities	Mfg.	Non-Mfg.[3]
1958.	242	132	2,270	0.23	0.39	0.12
1957.	209	169	2,010	0.19	0.22	0.10
1956.	243	130	1,170	0.11	0.63	0.11
1955.	275	253	4,860	0.47	0.45	0.14
1954.	282	146	1,410	0.14	0.33	0.14
1953.	372	256	2,380	0.22	0.36	0.19
1952.	406	372	4,170	0.39	1.03	0.27
1951.	387	231	1,790	0.17	0.43	0.11
1950.	386	405	2,380	0.25	0.66	0.30
1949.	347	154	2,320	0.25	0.73	0.30
1948.	293	160	3,290	0.34	0.46	0.31
1947.	282	468	11,500	1.19	0.43	0.39
1946.	479	1,020	9,020	0.94	2.42	0.72

[1] Includes transportation, communications, electric, gas, and sanitary services.

[2] In 000's.

[3] Includes utilities.

Sources: U.S. Bureau of Labor Statistics, Bulletins 918 (1947), 935 (1948), 963 (1949), 1003 (1950), 1035 (1951), 1090 (1952), 1136 (1953), 1163 (1954), 1184 (1955), 1196 (1956), 1218 (1957), 1234 (1958), 1258 (1959).

industries, including public utilities. Data are not available which separate the several industries in the utility group. Despite this shortcoming, the picture is quite clear. In almost every postwar year, the percentage of estimated work time consumed in work stoppages in the utility group falls somewhere between the figures for the manufacturing and non-manufacturing groups. No doubt the non-local transportation industry accounts for some of the utility total. The remainder of this section will take up the problem of labor disputes in utility industries and some of the proposed solutions.

A. *The Public-Interest Concept as Applied to Labor Relations.* It has been amply demonstrated in earlier chapters that public utilities are among those industries "peculiarly affected with the public interest."[11] This characteristic, along with the fact that most utility companies enjoy a natural monopoly, is the basis for regulation of rates, profits, and service. The courts on numerous occasions have held that a utility has a duty to serve and cannot refuse any reasonable request for service.[12] At the same time, the right of workers to strike is their most powerful weapon, and the United States Supreme Court has held that a state cannot deprive employees of this right.[13] This creates a dilemma. How can a utility fulfill its obligation to render adequate service when its employees are guaranteed the right to strike? Clearly, it is impossible to have service if workers will not work. What can be done to reconcile this conflict?

B. *Mediation and Arbitration.* The

[11] See particularly Chapters 1 and 2.

[12] See the discussion and citations in 43 *American Jurisprudence* 586, 588.

[13] *United Automobile Workers of America v. O'Brien,* 339 U.S. 454 (1950).

best way to settle any labor-management dispute is through collective bargaining, which normally ends in some kind of compromise that is agreed to by employees and management. Most of the many thousands of labor contracts in force today are made in just such a way. As contracts, they are enforceable, and once signed must be fulfilled over the life of the contract. The employer agrees to a number of things, including: (1) payment of a certain wage or schedule of wages plus "fringe" benefits; (2) requiring no more than a stipulated number of hours of work at standard wages; (3) recognition of certain grievance machinery and procedures; (4) discharge and discipline only for "just cause"; (5) maintenance of certain standards of working conditions. The employees, on the other hand, agree to work for the agreed-upon wage and not to strike, picket, or boycott the employer nor to disrupt work in any way. Either a lockout or a strike violates the contract.

In situations in which agreement cannot be reached by the two parties in normal bargaining procedures, it is customary to seek mediation. The mediator is a disinterested third party whose participation is approved by both sides. This individual acts as a go-between and tries to bring the two parties to an agreement. He does not hand down an opinion of what he feels the solution should be, nor are his services in any way binding on either of the contesting parties. It is often easier to give some ground to a mediator than to your opponent. Today, there exists at the federal level the Federal Mediation and Conciliation Service, which holds itself out to provide mediators in labor disputes coming under its jurisdiction. In addition as of December, 1958, some 38 states and Puerto Rico had statutes under which mediation is carried on by some state agency. Seven other states mediate without explicit statutory authority.[14] Two of the remaining five states have provisions for state mediation or arbitration of public utility disputes. The Labor-Management Relations Act of 1947 (Taft-Hartley) provides that the Federal Service will make itself available whenever there is a "substantial" interruption of interstate commerce. In other instances, it is authorized to assist states in any way to mediate disputes but is enjoined from interfering if state agencies are willing and able to handle the matter.

Arbitration differs from mediation in that a mutually agreed-upon third party or arbitrator actually makes an arbitration "award," which is essentially his best judgment, after he has reviewed the case, as to what the solution should be. Arbitration may be "voluntary," in which case the opposing sides voluntarily agree to arbitrate and to be bound by the arbitrator's award. Arbitration may also be "compulsory," in which case the parties to the dispute are compelled by government to arbitrate their dispute. Under compulsory arbitration, the services are not optional; it is mandatory that they be used. Likewise, the award is binding by law and not dependent upon voluntary agreement to arbitrate. Under both voluntary and compulsory arbitration, failure to comply with the award usually constitutes contempt of court, for which fines and other penalties may be assessed.

In public utility labor disputes, mediation and voluntary arbitration are used quite successfully. Arbitration, in most labor disputes, is used to interpret the terms of a contract already in force. However, in some arbitration cases, this method is used to determine the *terms*

---

[14] U.S. Bureau of Labor Statistics, *State Mediation Laws and Agencies,* Bulletin 176 (Revised), 1958, p. 3.

of the contract.[15] Arbitration of wage terms crops up more frequently among utilities than in other industries. Between 1945 and 1950, it is estimated that, out of 209 reported awards in wage arbitration cases, 37 were in the urban transit industry, 19 in heat, light, power, and water, and 8 in communications, or a total of almost 26 per cent of all such awards.[16]

There are several reasons why wages are more frequently arbitrated in utility industries than in other industries. (1) Both union and management feel that wage arbitration is preferable to a work stoppage, because of their realization of the major impact of a work stoppage upon the public. (2) Unions hesitate to invoke a strike for fear of losing public sympathy. (3) Both sides know that government (at any level) within its power will not tolerate stoppages in what are considered essential services. (4) Utility unions frequently feel that they can get more from arbitration than from collective bargaining. (5) Utility management is more apt to agree to arbitration because any wage-cost increase resulting from the arbitration can be more easily justified before a regulatory commission than can an increase made from collective bargaining. And (6) management does not wish to incur public disfavor either, especially since regulatory commissions are often sensitive to public opinion.[17] Wage arbitration, while not widespread, has a tendency to set standards for other utilities in the area. When contract terms are arbitrated before collective bargaining has been exhausted, both union and management are abdicating a responsibility they have to the people they represent as well as to the public. The responsibility for a wage increase which eventually is reflected in a rate or fare increase is passed from labor and management to an arbitrator. Such a situation should be avoided in all but those extreme cases in which all other means of reaching agreement have been tried and have failed.

C. Attempts to Prevent or Halt Work Stoppages in Public Utilities. During World War II a combination of factors worked to keep industrial peace in the United States. Most important were the patriotism of both labor and management, federal wage and price controls, and extreme public displeasure at work stoppage that hurt the war effort. After the war, the precipitous lifting of wartime controls and the resulting "galloping" inflation, plus a series of maladjustments that developed during the labor-management truce period, loosed upon the nation a series of work stoppages in virtually every industry. In 1946, an estimated 2.42 per cent of the working time was lost in manufacturing. Table 18.5 indicates that, for the transportation and utility group, the percentage of work time lost was 0.94 per cent in 1946 and 1.19 per cent in 1947.

Public reaction to this situation was immediate and dramatic. At the federal level, the Labor Management Relations Act (Taft-Hartley) was passed in 1947, giving the President the power to declare that a work stoppage has resulted in a "national emergency." He may empanel a fact-finding board and ask for a court order enjoining the stoppage for an 80-day "cooling-off period," if he feels the facts warrant such action.[18] The findings of the President's board of inquiry are made public, and the contesting parties are offered the assistance

---

[15] See Irving Bernstein, *Arbitration of Wages* (Berkeley: University of California Press, 1954), for a discussion of arbitration of wage provisions in labor contracts.

[16] *Ibid.*, p. 15.

[17] *Ibid.*, p. 17.

[18] 29 *USCA*, Sec. 176–178.

of the Federal Mediation and Conciliation Service. The Taft-Hartley Act does not make the work stoppage illegal or prevent it from continuing after the 80 days have elapsed. Neither does the Act require compulsory arbitration or authorize government seizure of the property.[19]

Since most utilities are local, statewide, or, at most, regional in character, the likelihood of the Taft-Hartley emergency provisions being used is quite remote. While great public pressure can be brought to bear on the opposing sides during the "cooling-off" period, the Act stops short of permanently prohibiting a work stoppage. The Taft-Hartley Act has an interesting history with regard to public utilities. In 1946 there was introduced in Congress the Case bill, which, among other things, would have denied temporarily the right to strike to public utility employees. The bill passed both houses of the 79th Congress but was vetoed by President Truman on the grounds that it unfairly singled out utility employees for special restriction.[20] The substitute bill that finally passed omitted the sections dealing with utilities.

The flurry of work stoppages in 1946–1947 had a greater impact on state labor utility legislation. Fourteen states have passed special legislation relating to public utility labor disputes; most of the laws were passed between 1946 and 1948. Kansas passed a statute as early as 1920 which, among other things, provided for compulsory arbitration through a State Industrial Relations Court. The act stayed on the books until 1951, but was not administered after 1923. Today five states[21] have laws requiring compulsory arbitration.[22] In five other states[23] the governor is authorized to seize and operate any utility in which a strike or lockout occurs or is threatened. In Hawaii, Illinois, and Minnesota, there are laws which require that fact-finding panels be set up to investigate utility disputes, but such laws do not require compulsory arbitration or permit seizure.[24]

The Massachusetts law has perhaps been the most original statute passed to deal with emergency disputes, including those in most public utility fields. It provides a "choice-of-procedures" approach and gives the Governor the power to use any or all of the following alternatives: (1) require both parties to appear before a moderator to show

[19] The federal seizure of the struck steel mills in 1952, ordered by President Truman, was done on the basis of his power as commander-in-chief during periods of national emergency and actually had no statutory warrant. Such action is not authorized by the Taft-Hartley Act. In this particular instance, the United States Supreme Court held that such presidential action *at that time* was unconstitutional. *Youngstown Sheet and Tube Co.* v. *Sawyer,* 343 U.S. 579 (1952).

[20] United States 79th Congress, 2d Sess., H.R. 4908, 1946. See also Edward Sussna, "State Intervention in Public Utility Labor Management Relations," 9 *Labor Law Journal* 35 (January 1958). The Congress finally rejected the inclusion in the Taft-Hartley Act of a compulsory-arbitration provision and an anti-strike provision. See the statement of Senator Taft arguing against such inclusion at 93 *Congressional Record* 3835–3836 (1947).

[21] Florida, Indiana, Nebraska, Pennsylvania, and Wisconsin.

[22] Michigan had a compulsory arbitration law, but it was declared unconstitutional. *United Automobile Workers of America* v. *O'Brien,* 339 U.S. 454 (1950). Voluntary arbitration was substituted for compulsory arbitration.

[23] Maryland, Massachusetts, Missouri, New Jersey, and Virginia.

[24] U.S. Bureau of Labor Statistics, Bulletins 176 and 176 (revised) *op. cit.,* 1954 and 1958. See also an interesting study done by the Section of Public Utility Law, American Bar Association, *Report of the Special Committee on Labor Legislation in the Public Utility Field, 1946–1947,* Cleveland, Sept. 1947. This study contains some of the legal background leading up to the passage of state laws and includes an analysis of the Virginia, New Jersey, and other state laws.

cause why the dispute should not be submitted to arbitration; (2) request the parties to submit their dispute to a three-man board for a recommended settlement; (3) declare an emergency and arrange with the disputing parties to continue production; (4) seize and operate the facilities involved.[25] The law has been invoked several times, and it appears to have worked fairly satisfactorily. The key to its success appears to have been the restraint used by the Governor in applying the law. Under less judicious application, it could become as ineffective as emergency-dispute statutes in other states.[26]

After this initial spurt of "anti-strike" laws at the state level, labor disputes declined, and passage of such laws in other states ceased. However, should conditions dictate, it is likely that some other states would see fit to pass such legislation in the future.[27]

Several questions arise from "anti-strike" laws. First, are they constitutional, or do they cause involuntary servitude and place substantial limitations on individual freedom? Second, what has been the experience of the states that have had such laws? Have utility labor disputes been reduced in number or in significance? Third, what, if any, are the conflicts between federal and state law in this matter? Fourth, what would be the economic impact of universal "anti-strike" laws for public utilities? These are important questions, the answers to which may alter not only labor relations for utility industries, but labor relations for the entire nation.

The first question, while certainly basic, need not detain us here. The constitutional right of a state to prevent labor disputes and to impose compulsory arbitration was upheld by the United States Supreme Court in 1926.[28] The Court pointed out that neither the common law nor the Fourteenth Amendment confers an absolute power to strike. The American Bar Association has pointed out that, in fact, the right and power to strike are largely dependent upon existing federal legislation. That Congress has the power to regulate working conditions and "prevent the interruption of interstate commerce by strikes" was decided during World War I.[29] If Congress has this power in interstate commerce, it follows that the state legislature has the same power in intrastate commerce.[30] Specific state statutes have foundered on a state constitutional question, but it has been primarily because of an improper statutory delegation of the administrative function to the judiciary[31] or because the legislation failed to establish adequate standards for arbitration.[32] On the constitutional question of federal supremacy, the state laws have been held to be violative of the federal constitution.

The second and third questions raised above can perhaps be best answered together, since the experience of the states has been one of frustration in the face of the federal Taft-Hartley Act. In 1950 the constitutionality of the Public

---

25 Lloyd G. Reynolds, *Labor Economics and Labor Relations,* 3d ed. (Englewood Cliffs, N.J.: Prentice-Hall, Inc., 1959), pp. 306–307.

26 See Geo. P. Shultz, "The Massachusetts Choice-of-Procedures Approach to Emergency Disputes," *Industrial and Labor Relations Review,* April, 1957.

27 Maryland did, in fact, pass a seizure law in 1956 specifically for the purpose of quelling a work stoppage on the Baltimore transit system. *Annotated Code of Maryland* (1957), Article 89, Secs. 14–24.

28 *Dorchy* v. *Kansas,* 272 U.S. 306 (1926).

29 *Wilson* v. *New,* 243 U.S. 332 (1917).

30 For a discussion of the constitutionality question, see: "Constitutionality of Compulsory Arbitration Statutes in the Public Utility Field," 44 *Illinois Law Review* 546 (1949).

31 *Local 170* v. *Gadola,* 34 N.W. (2d) 71 (1948).

32 *State* v. *Traffic Telephone Workers Federation,* 66 A. (2d) 616 (1949).

Utility Anti-Strike Law of Wisconsin[33] was challenged by the union representing the employees of the Milwaukee Electric Railway and Transport Company after the Wisconsin Employment Relations Board secured a court order prohibiting a strike. The Wisconsin Supreme Court upheld the validity of the order,[34] and the case was appealed to the United States Supreme Court. The statute specifically made a strike by utility employees unlawful. The United States Supreme Court held[35] that the Wisconsin statute conflicted with a provision included in the Taft-Hartley Act which states that "Nothing in this subchapter, except as specifically provided for herein, shall be construed so as either to interfere with or impede or diminish in any way the right to strike, or to affect the limitations or qualifications on that right."[36] The Court pointed out that it had held previously that "Congress had occupied this field and closed it to state regulation."[37] The effect of this decision was to limit the application of the state anti-strike laws to situations which were exclusively intrastate. It is rather interesting to note that organized labor frequently has referred to the Taft-Hartley Act as the "slave labor act," although it has been used in utility labor disputes to uphold the right to strike. Since the Court's interpretation of what constitutes interstate commerce and thus of what comes under federal jurisdiction has been extremely broad, it is impossible to see how the state laws of the Wisconsin type have much application.[38]

The effect of the Wisconsin decision was immediate. In Florida and Indiana, state courts declared the laws in these respective states unconstitutional. In Hawaii the Attorney-General made a similar ruling with respect to the statute in that jurisdiction. In Missouri, the Attorney-General ruled the state law unconstitutional, but the Missouri Supreme Court reversed this ruling on the grounds that the Missouri law is clearly intended for emergencies, does not forbid strikes until the state takes over the utility, and does not include compulsory arbitration.[39] The constitutionality of the other state statutes remained untested as of 1960, or in some instances the laws had been amended to bring them into accord with controlling court decisions. Maryland in 1956 passed a seizure law which has yet to be tested.[40] There is considerable disagreement about this law which can only be settled by court decision.[41] Most of the state laws still on the books are seldom invoked because of the constitutional uncertainties involved.

How effective have state laws been which limit the right to strike in public utility disputes? Authorities on this subject find difficulty in agreeing. One detailed study of utility work stoppages in states which had some form of anti-strike law operative between 1947 and

[33] *Wis. Stat,* 1949, Sections 111.50 *et seq.*

[34] *Amalgamated Association of Street, Electric Railway and Motor Coach Employees* v. *Wisconsin Employment Relations Board,* 42 N.W. (2d) 471 (1950).

[35] *Amalgamated Association of Street, Electric Railway and Motor Coach Employees* v. *Wisconsin Employment Relations Board,* 340 U.S. 383 (1951).

[36] 29 *USCA* Sec. 163.

[37] 339 U.S. 454, 457 (1950), citing 338 U.S. 953 (1950), 336 U.S. 18 (1949), 330 U.S. 767 (1947), and 325 U.S. 538 (1945).

[38] See *Consolidated Edison Co.* v. *Labor Board,* 305 U.S. 601 (1939) for a lengthy discussion of the application of federal labor laws to purely local utility activities.

[39] *State Board of Mediation* v. *Pigg,* 244 S. Co. (2d) 75 (1951).

[40] *Annotated Code of Maryland,* Article 89, Secs. 14–24 (1957).

[41] For views upholding the constitutionality of the Maryland Act, see S. H. Lehrer, "The Maryland Public Utilities Disputes Act," 7 *Labor Law Journal* 607 (1956); for the opposing views, see B. J. Seff, "Legality of the Maryland Public Utilities Disputes Act," 16 *Maryland Law Review* 304 (1956).

and 1952 concludes that the states can do little to promote labor-management harmony in public utilities.[42] Irving Bernstein, a recognized authority on labor-management relations, concluded in 1956 that the various anti-strike law experiments had worked badly and were falling into disuse.[43] The effectiveness of the Virginia law, which does not ban strikes or require compulsory arbitration, but which does authorize state seizure of struck utilities, has received favorable comment.[44] This law provides for government operation and bans strikes against the government.

D. *Labor Problems in Government-Owned Utilities.* Labor problems in government-owned utilities arise in two situations. First, there are a number of government entities at the federal, state, and local levels which hire workers and operate as a private business does. Such governmental functions are included in what are known as "proprietary" activities. Labor problems between employer and employee can arise here just as easily as if the employer were a private individual or company. Second, there are occasions in which the government takes over or "seizes" a private company and thus in effect becomes an employer in any existing or imminent labor dispute. Under both situations, the employees' rights to strike against the government are severely circumscribed, if not prohibited.

At the federal level, the right to strike included in the Taft-Hartley Act is specifically denied to government employees, and, in fact, such employees cannot make use of the defenses in Taft-Hartley. Under the National Labor Relations Act, "The term 'employer' . . . shall not include the United States or any wholly owned Government corporation, . . . or any State or political subdivision thereof. . . ."[45] Thus, the NLRA cannot apply to government employees at any level. Several states have passed similar laws,[46] while courts in other states, not having specific statutory language, have held that strikes against the government are against public policy.[47] In some instances, employees have struck despite such prohibitions, but extremely adverse public opinion as well as contempt of court proceedings make such action rather unfeasible. Should government ownership spread, the right to strike will be denied to more and more workers.[48] In some cases, where the governmental function is clearly proprietory, the right to strike has still been denied.[49] It seems appropriate to raise the question, if a strike is allowed against a privately owned utility company, why should a similar strike be denied if the company is municipally owned? Such a distinction is highly artificial and discriminatory.[50]

The solution to labor problems between employees and government em-

---

42 Edward Sussna, "State Intervention in Public Utility Labor-Management Relations," 9 *Labor Law Journal* 35, 42 (1958). For a very detailed state-by-state analysis of utility work stoppage in the nine states, see Edward Sussna, "Public Policy Towards Labor-Management Relations in Local Public Utilities in Selected States, 1947–1952," unpublished doctoral dissertation, University of Illinois, 1954.

43 Irving Bernstein, "State Public Utility Laws and Mediation," 7 *Labor Law Journal* 496, 499 (1956).

44 Francis V. Lowden, Jr., "Public Utility Seizure in Virginia," 41 *Virginia Law Review* 397 (1955).

45 29 *USCA* Sec. 152 (2).

46 Cf. N.Y. Labor Relations Act, N.Y. Labor Laws, Sec. 715.

47 Cf. *City of Manchester* v. *Manchester Teachers Guild,* 131 A. (2d) 59 (1957).

48 See Ada Klaus, "Labor Relations in the Public Service: Exploration and Experiment," *Syracuse Law Review* 183 (1959), for a discussion of this problem.

49 *Port of Seattle* v. *International Longshoremen's and Warehousemen's Union,* 324 P. (2d) 1009 (1958).

50 See 34 *Washington Law Review* 216 (1959) for an elaboration of this point.

ployers has not been found. The welfare of the worker is presumably a concern of all the people as embodied in government; therefore, the government worker is presumed to receive equitable treatment. In theory this sounds satisfactory. In practice, it is very unsatisfactory. This is not to say that unionization and collective bargaining would solve all problems. However, the chances are good that labor relations in government work would improve if the basic rights were given to government employees in this area of employment.

Government seizure as a solution to labor-management disputes in privately owned public utilities takes somewhat of a different tack. Clearly, the purpose of the seizure is to prevent a work stoppage and the consequent disruption of service to the public. Some seizure laws do not require compulsory arbitration but merely exert pressure on the opposing sides to reach an agreement. Employees are penalized to the extent that any wage demands they have are suspended until agreement is reached. If the employer is denied the profits from his operation during the time of seizure, the relative weights of the penalties will depend on the specific circumstances surrounding the dispute. The legality of the state seizure laws is now in question as a result of a Supreme Court decision which held the Missouri seizure law to be void, because—as in the Wisconsin case discussed earlier—it conflicted with federal guarantees of the right to strike.[51]

E. Proposed Solutions to Utility Labor Disputes. There are numerous proposed remedies for the strike problem in the public utility field. None of them appears to be perfect. Each has certain advantages and disadvantages. The following discussion generalizes the major proposals and points out their strengths and weaknesses.

(1) *Required Mediation.* One proposal advocates state-supervised mediation coupled with a 60-day cooling-off period.[52] Publicity would be given to the positions of both parties after the cooling-off period. The advantages of such a procedure are that it encourages free collective bargaining, puts unimpaired economic and public pressure on both parties, and allows for face-saving to be accomplished through a third party. The biggest disadvantage is that the work stoppage may resume after the cooling-off period, and thus the public convenience is disturbed. Also, some critics maintain that a cooling-off period intensifies the antagonisms on both sides and makes settlement more difficult. A waiting period puts all the penalty on labor. Each side would no doubt work to impress the public with its arguments.

(2) *Compulsory Arbitration.* This obviously cannot be done effectively at the state level because of the federal guarantee of the right to strike in the Taft-Hartley Act. Federal action would be required in this area, and such proposals have been made. Some thoughtful spokesmen for both labor and management are reluctant to see such a procedure adopted. Compulsory arbitration shifts the responsibility of determining wages, hours, and working conditions from the bargaining table to some man or board. The question becomes: Is continuous utility service worth the price of the freedom forgone under compulsory arbitration? Will compulsory arbitration in the utility area ultimately result in a system of labor courts which decide all major labor-management issues in all areas of the economy?

(3) *Seizure.* Seizure by the state ac-

[51] *Division 1287 of Amalgamated Association of Street, Electric Railway and Motor Coach Employees of America, et al.* v. *State of Missouri* (No. 640), June 10, 1963.

[52] Richard F. Heiges, "State Labor Legislation for Public Utilities' Disputes," 61 *Public Utilities Fortnightly* 587 (April 24, 1958).

complishes the aim of continuous service. It is not always successful, however; and unless accompanied by mediation efforts, it might aggravate rather than salve the situation. Seizure does not get to the heart of the dispute.

(4) *Government nonintervention.* Some authorities advocate handling public utility disputes just like any other labor dispute. They state that government should not interfere except to offer the services of the best mediators available. Professor Bernstein has concluded that the public is best served if the bargaining process is allowed to function unfettered.[53] The best solution seems to be the use of the government as an umpire in labor disputes rather than as a sovereign.

[53] Bernstein, *op. cit.*, p. 500.

PART VI

SPECIAL REGULATORY PROBLEMS

19 Utility Financing and Financial Regulation

The financing of American business is a matter of great importance no matter what industry is discussed, because the ever-increasing pace of innovation and mechanization has pushed capital needs much faster than the economy, as a whole, has grown. The application of machines to new processes, plus the relatively high cost of labor, have resulted in capital goods intensification in United States industry. Public utilities warrant special attention in the general area of financing capital needs because (1) as an industry group, they require huge investments relative to sales or employment, and (2) as an industry group characterized by natural monopoly, they are subject to detailed regulation. This chapter will first take up the methods of financing utilities and will then discuss the financial regulation of the industry. Some attention will also be given to the problem of financing government-owned utilities.

A cursory look at expenditures for plant and equipment by this industry since 1947 shows the relatively heavy financing requirements of utilities. These data are compared with employment figures in Table 19.1. In 1961, public utilities accounted for about 16.1 per cent of the capital expenditures in American industry but for only 2.3 per cent of non-farm employment. Data for sales and net revenues tell much the same story. This section briefly reviews the nature of the industry that makes it so capital-intensive; it then takes up the methods which utilities use to raise these huge quantities of capital; and finally, some mention is made of the types of investors who purchase and hold utility securities.

1. THE NEEDS FOR CAPITAL

Very little need be said here about the reasons why utility industries require so much capital. The discussion in Chapter 2 points up the physical and economic characteristics of these types of activities. A basic characteristic of a utility is that it is a heavy capital-using industry.[1] This fact contributes to the "natural monopoly" aspect of the industry. It is wasteful to duplicate large investments in plant and equipment if one set can get the job done. Hence, competition is discouraged and monop-

[1] See M. J. Ulmer, *Capital in Transportation, Communications, and Public Utilities*, National Bureau of Economic Research (Princeton: Princeton University Press, 1960), for an exhaustive study of capital formation in utility industries.

Table 19.1

Comparison of Capital Expenditures and Employment for Utility Industries[1] and Other Industries, 1947–1961

Year	*Utility Capital Spending*[2]	*Total Capital Spending*[2]	*Utility as a % of Total*	*Utility Employment*[3] *000's*	*Non-Farm Employment 000's*	*Utility as a % of Total*
1947.	1.54	20.61	7.5	1,323	49,761	2.7
1948.	2.54	22.06	11.5	1,380	51,405	2.7
1949.	3.12	19.28	16.2	1,380	50,684	2.7
1950.	3.31	20.60	16.1	1,358	52,450	2.6
1951.	3.66	25.64	14.3	1,384	53,951	2.6
1952.	3.89	26.49	14.7	1,419	54,488	2.6
1953.	4.55	28.32	16.1	1,452	55,651	2.6
1954.	4.22	26.83	15.7	1,447	54,734	2.6
1955.	4.31	28.70	15.0	1,451	56,464	2.6
1956.	4.90	35.08	14.0	1,498	58,394	2.6
1957.	6.20	36.96	16.8	1,514	58,789	2.6
1958.	6.09	30.53	19.9	1,468	58,122	2.5
1959.	5.68	32.56	17.4	1,455	59,745	2.4
1960.	5.68	35.68	15.9	1,452	60,958	2.4
1961.	5.52	34.36	16.1	1,434	61,333	2.3

[1] Excludes transportation utilities, other than urban transit.

[2] Billions of dollars, unadjusted for price changes.

[3] Employment in local railway and bus lines, communications, gas, electric, and other local utilities.

Source: U.S. Dept. of Commerce-SEC, "Statistical Series"; periodic releases, U.S. Bureau of Labor Statistics, *Employment and Earnings, Annual Supplements,* 1948–1962.

oly promoted with the consequent regulations. Another aspect of utilities is their creation of a service rather than a commodity. Readily available, dependable, 24-hour-a-day service is what utilities sell. While in most service industries labor plays a dominant role, in utility industries labor is combined with large amounts of capital equipment.

Coupled with the capital-intensive aspects of utilities is the extraordinary growth rate experienced by these industries in the recent past and the projected growth rates for the future. Since 1946, Gross National Product for the United States in 1959 prices has risen from $316.9 billions to about $500 billion, a total of about 58 per cent. At the same time, generation of electricity rose from 223.2 billion Kwh to 709.7 billion Kwh, a total of 218 per cent. Marketed production of natural gas rose from 4,153 billion cubic feet in 1946 to 12,046 billion cubic feet in 1959, a 190 per cent increase. Local telephone messages jumped from 48,125 million annually in 1946 to 96,543 million annually in 1959, a 101 per cent increase. Water from public water supplies consumed for nonagricultural purposes has risen 42 per cent from 12.0 billion gallons per day in 1946 to 17.0 billion gallons in 1958.

Although these growth figures are amazing, the forecasts for the future are even more impressive. As the economy becomes more mechanized and more urbanized, the demand for utility services is accelerated. For example, Ebasco Services, Incorporated, estimates that the United States will generate between 1640 and 1850 billion Kwh of electricity annually by 1975, up 154 to 187 per cent over the 645 billion Kwh generated in 1958.[2] The American Gas Association forecasts an increase in gas-utility construction expenditures from $1.6 billion in 1958 to $4.3 billion in 1970, and an increase in consumption from 80.3 billion to 162.0 billion therms.[3] The U.S. Department of Commerce has estimated that the water use from public supplies will rise from 17.0 billion gallons per day in 1958 to 29.8 billion gallons per day in 1975.[4] The U.S. Department of Commerce expects the number of telephones to increase from 70.5 million in 1959 to about 121 million by 1970.

If previous forecasts are any indication, future expansion has been significantly underestimated in these figures. Thus, capital needs in utility industries will be a pressing problem. One of the most difficult aspects of utility management will be raising investment funds to meet these capital needs. Some of the discussion in previous chapters has touched upon the financing problems created or intensified by rate-of-return and rate-base regulation. This will be brought out again below, since the entire aspect of financing hinges on this regulation.

2. METHODS OF FINANCING CAPITAL NEEDS

Raising hundreds of millions of dollars of capital each year is no simple task. A utility has a commission-supervised obligation to its consumers to raise its capital at the lowest possible cost consistent with financial safety and adequate service. This requires a detailed knowledge of the capital markets as well as superior judgment in tailoring and timing the various security issues to potential utility investors. Since capital is such an important factor of production to most utilities, they utilize every possible means to raise it. Generally speaking, there are six major sources of funds—four external and two internal. The four external sources are (1) long-term debt, (2) short-term debt, (3) preferred stock, and (4) common stock. The two internal sources of funds are (1) depreciation accruals and (2) retained earnings.

A. *Types of Securities.* Table 19.2 shows the types of securities sold by various utility industries and the purposes for which the money was raised, during 1960. Data for manufacturers are included for comparison. The table shows that utility financing was predominantly debt financing, and that by far the most important use of proceeds was for new plant and equipment. Table 19.3 shows historically the amounts of money raised through public sales by corporations and also shows what part of the money raised was used for new investment rather than for refunding outstanding securities. Although refunding was substantial immediately after the war, most capital raised in recent years has gone into expansion of new plant and equipment.

It is not appropriate to go into any great detail describing the specific features of each type of security used for external financing. Such information is readily available in any corporation finance textbook. A very short description will be given with some comments on the extent to which each type of security is used or not used in utility financing.

Table 19.4 presents a picture of the capital structures of privately owned electric utilities and gas utilities and of the American Telephone and Telegraph Company. In each case, long-term debt

[2] Ebasco Services, Incorporated, *Business and Economics Charts,* New York, 1959, p. 34.

[3] A. G. A., *Projected Gas Industry Statistics 1959–1970,* 1959.

[4] U.S. Department of Commerce, Business and Defense Services Administration, *Water Use in the United States, 1900–1975,* BSB–136, 1956, p. 4.

Table 19.2

Offerings of Securities, 1960[1] by Type of Issue and Use of Proceeds

($000)

Type of Security	Utilities		Manufacturing
	Electric, Gas and Water	Communication	
Bonds	$2,282,556	$ 975,664	$1,519,205
Preferred stock	254,803	16,367	47,143
Common stock	313,856	57,779	586,072
Total	2,851,215	1,049,810	2,152,419
Use of Proceeds:			
New money	2,655,559	1,031,659	1,710,743
Plant & equipment	2,624,059	1.022,870	944,632
Working capital	31,500	8,790	766,111
Retirement of securities	51,170	682	79,327
Other	98,587	4,119	286,196
Total	2,805,315	1,036,460	2,076,267

1 New corporate securities offered for cash in the United States, in amounts over $100,000 and with terms to maturity of more than one year. Totals under the respective headings are not identical, because the "security" data reflect gross proceeds while the "proceeds" data reflect net proceeds. Totals may not add due to rounding.

Source: SEC, 22 *Statistical Bulletin* 16–19 (1963).

is a larger proportion than is ordinarily found among industrial firms. This is especially true in the gas and electric utility industries.

The reasons for the emphasis on senior capital have been discussed but should be summarized here. Foremost, of course, is the sheer magnitude of the amounts of capital needed. To raise all of a utility's capital through the issuance of common stock would be extremely expensive, unnecessary, and impractical, if not impossible. To finance expansion solely through retained earnings would encounter some of the same problems and would be extremely unpalatable to regulatory commissions and consumers. This point is made even stronger by the fact that interest on long-term debt is a deductible expense when computing federal income taxes. Thus, even if a utility had to pay the same *yield* to investors to raise either debt or equity money, it would cost the utility customer about twice as much to raise equity money as to raise debt money, assuming a corporate income tax rate of about 50 per cent. This, of course, is true in nonregulated industries also.

In addition to the large quantities of capital required, which dictates the flotation of bonds, there is generally felt to be a lower risk for most utility enterprises than for industrial firms. The demand for utility services is comparatively stable, some of the rigors of competition have been supplanted by regulation, and earnings, while not by any means guaranteed, are given some degree of stability by regulation. Bonds are also attractive to utilities because with bonds it is possible to tap huge reserves of loanable funds in the hands of "institutional" investors.[5] These investors are conservative either by nature or because of legal limitations. Stocks do not appeal to this group in very great amounts.[6]

5 "Institutional investors" are such institutions as insurance companies, banks, trust funds, pension funds, philanthropic and educational institutions, and so forth.

6 "Variable annuities," if allowed to grow, may add substantial quantities of stock to insurance company portfolios.

Table 19.3

Net Proceeds and New Money from Sale of New Corporate Securities Offered for Cash in the United States, 1945–1959[1]

(Millions of dollars)

Year	*Electric, Gas and Water*		*Communications*[2]		*Total Utilities*[2]	
	Total Net Proceeds[3]	*Total New Money*[4]	*Total Net Proceeds*[3]	*Total New Money*[4]	*Total Net Proceeds*[3]	*Total New Money*[4]
1959. . . .	3,204	3,057	707	703	3,911	3,760
1958. . . .	3,743	3,441	1,412	1,265	5,155	4,706
1957. . . .	3,872	3,659	1,444	1,428	5,316	5,087
1956. . . .	2,487	2,410	1,405	1,371	3,892	3,781
1955. . . .	2,428	2,218	1,121	1,040	3,549	3,258
1954. . . .	3,665	2,598	711	641	4,376	3,239
1953. . . .	2,972	2,756	874	861	3,846	3,617
1952. . . .	2,626	2,458	753	739	3,379	3,197
1951. . . .	2,412	2,186	605	594	3,017	2,780
1950. . . .	2,608	1,728	395	304	3,003	2,032
1949. . . .	2,276	1,838	567	505	2,843	2,343
1948. . . .	2,150	1,872	891	870	3,041	2,742
1948[2] . . .					3,039	2,744
1947. . . .	N.A.	N.A.	N.A.	N.A.	3,212	2,188
1946. . . .	N.A.	N.A.	N.A.	N.A.	2,129	785
1945. . . .	N.A.	N.A.	N.A.	N.A.	2,291	69

[1] Includes only public sales of corporations. No adjustments are made for price changes.

[2] "Communications" includes radio from 1948 through 1958, as do figures for "Total Utilities." The figures for "Total Utilities" for 1945 through 1948 exclude radio.

[3] Represents amount received by issuer after payment of compensation to distributors and other costs of flotation.

[4] Represents new external financing not used for refunding or retirement of securities.

N.A.—Not available.

Source: Securities and Exchange Commission, *26th Annual Report* (1960), pp. 239 and 241, and *18th Annual Report* (1952), p. 215.

The most common type of long-term debt instrument used in utility financing is the open-end, first-mortgage bond.[7] Such a bond has specific plant and equipment items pledged as security for the loan. The open-end feature enables a company to continue to issue first-mortgage bonds as additional plant and equipment comes into existence. It is customary, and the SEC has used its influence in this regard, to limit additional mortgage bonds to some percentage of the value of the mortgaged property. This figure is usually about 60 per cent.[8]

Some utilities also issue debenture bonds. These are bonds which have no specific pledge of property behind them. They are most prevalent in the telephone and gas industries, although a number of electric companies with high credit ratings have also issued debentures. Actually debenture bonds are backed to the extent that there is any unpledged property owned by the corpo-

[7] In the telephone industry, the debenture type is much more common.

[8] H. G. Guthmann and H. E. Dougall, *Corporate Financial Policy,* 3rd ed. (Englewood Cliffs, N.J.: Prentice-Hall, Inc., 1955), p. 240.

Table 19.4

Capitalization Ratios of Gas, Electric, and Telephone Utilities, 1958

% of Total Capital Represented by:	*Gas Distributing Companies*[1]	*Gas Transmission Companies*[2]	*Electric Cos.*[3]	*The Bell System*[4]
Long-term debt . . .	46.5	61.1	52.7	35.0
Preferred stock. . .	4.5	9.6	11.4	-0-
Common stock and surplus	49.0	29.3	32.5	52.7
Premium on capital stock.	[5]	[5]	3.4	12.2
Total.	100.0	100.0	100.0	100.0

[1] Straight natural gas-distributing utilities, that is, those deriving at least 95 per cent of their operating revenues from gas distribution operations.

[2] Straight natural gas-transmission utilities, that is, those deriving at least 95 per cent of their operating revenues from gas transmission operations.

[3] Class A and B privately owned electric utilities reporting to the Federal Power Commission.

[4] Consolidated figures for all the companies in the Bell System. Data for Dec. 31, 1959.

[5] Included in figures for preferred and common stock.

Sources: Gas-company data from American Gas Association, *Gas Facts, 1959,* pp. 185 and 186; electric-company data from Edison Electric Institute, *Electric Utility Industry Statistics in the United States, 1959,* Table 52, from Federal Power Commission; Bell System data from the A.T. & T. *Annual Report, 1959,* p. 25.

ration. If no mortgage bonds are outstanding, then the debenture is, in effect, the equivalent of a mortgage bond. If a corporation fails or is liquidated, a debenture-holder's claim comes after that of a pledged security-holder but before preferred or common stockholders. The indenture for debenture bonds frequently contains provisions which protect the investor from future additional financing. Mercantile and manufacturing firms are more apt to issue debentures than are public utilities because in such lines of business, fixed assets may be relatively small and needed for support in obtaining short-term credit.

Convertible bonds are used by some utilities. As the term implies, this feature gives the bondholder the right to convert his debt interest into an ownership interest under stipulated conditions. The conversion is usually at the option of the bondholder within certain time limits at a specific price or ratio. He will make the conversion: (1) when the anticipated dividend income from the common stock more than compensates for the lost interest income and the added risk of stock ownership; or (2) if the market price of the stock relative to the market price of the bond is advantageous; or (3) if rights to new proposed stock issues appear attractive; or (4) if the conversion ratio is about to be diminished or is about to expire and market prices dictate conversion.[9]

The convertible feature has advantages to both the issuing company and the holder. Normally such a bond carries a lower rate of interest than a nonconvertible bond because of the prospects of dividends and growth in common stock. Also, this feature may make

[9] See *ibid.*, pp. 229–233, 250–252, for an elaboration of conversion features.

a bond issue salable that would not be otherwise. Another advantage is that a company pays a low cost for capital initially, and later, when conversion takes place, enjoys a reduction in its fixed charges and a consequent rise in its credit standing. This pattern may fit nicely into the revenue pattern of a firm. A utility is apt to build for the future, thus creating some temporarily unused capacity. It is advantageous to pay as little as possible for capital used to build this, as yet, unused capacity. As demand for the service grows, a utility can better afford to pay the higher cost of equity capital, and conversions will occur because of this ability. As this happens, long-term indebtedness and fixed charges shrink, thus raising the credit standing of the company and permitting the issuance of more bonds if further expansion is necessary. One of the most successful users of convertible bonds is the American Telephone and Telegraph Company.

Table 19.4 indicates that preferred stock is not the major type of security issued by utilities, but it is certainly significant. As a group, utilities have used preferred stock more than industrial corporations have. It has some of the characteristics of common stock and some of those of bonds. It has a preferential claim on dividends and assets of a corporation over the claims of the common stock. The preferred dividend is usually a fixed percentage, and frequently the stock is redeemable at the option of the company. In most instances, dividends are "cumulative," which means that all previously unpaid dividends on preferred stock must be paid before common stock dividends are paid. Voting rights are usually restricted or eliminated on preferred stock, since it is felt that the common stockholder will act in a way so as to benefit all stockholders. Thus, for the investors, preferred stock in a given company is less risky than common stock but riskier than bonds. The dividends are greater than interest on bonds but are usually less than common stock dividends, if business has been reasonably good. It is an intermediate-risk type of security which appeals to a group of investors who want more income than could be earned from bonds but who do not want to or legally cannot assume the risks of common stock ownership. In public utility economics, preferred stock so closely resembles perpetual long-term debt that it is treated as such in determining reasonable rates of return.

Common stock requires little comment. It is here that the ownership or equity rights and obligations are found. The common stockholder is an owner of the corporation and as an owner has, in theory at least, the final voice in management decisions. He elects the board of directors, which in turn decides policy and selects the managers of the company. For most large corporations, the proxy machinery is in the hands of the existing management, thus making this management self-perpetuating. There are, of course, examples of bad management turned out of power in proxy battles. The common stockholder has the legal right to residual earnings that remain after bond and preferred stockholders are paid. These residual earnings may be quite large or completely absent; thus, the common stockholder bears considerably more risk than do holders of senior securities. One of the most difficult tasks for a regulatory commission is to decide what returns common stock should receive. This question was discussed at length in Chapter 9 on the rate of return.

The issuance of new common stock occurs infrequently in most companies, although in rapid-growth periods it is often necessary. Dilution of the equity may occur to the existing stock unless this is offset by prior "rights" granted to existing stockholders to purchase new issues. Stock dividends or stock splits occur, at times, which increase the number of shares of stock outstanding. Finally, common stock held in the company treasury may be issued by the conversion of preferred stock or bonds with convertible provisions, if such exist. This transforms temporary or semi-permanent capital into permanent capital.

One final outside source of funds is short-term debt. Since it is short-term in nature, it cannot properly be called capital. However, it is highly significant in utility financing for two reasons. (1) It is expensive to make frequent trips to the capital market for small issues. Financing costs per dollar of capital raised diminish as the size of the issue increases. Thus, it may be more practical for a utility to borrow on a short-term basis for several years until a considerable debt accumulates, and then refinance the short-term debt with bonds. (2) The problems of timing frequently dictate the use of short-term debt. Long-term interest rates may fluctuate quite widely, and a one-half of one per cent differential on a $40 million, 30-year bond issue is quite significant. It would mean paying $6 million more in interest over 30 years. Thus, the time at which an issue is floated is critical. If the market is judged to be unfavorable for a new long-term issue, a company may borrow on a short-term basis and still carry on the necessary or planned investment. This is true if there is an expectation for market conditions to improve.

The organization which has used short-term, interim financing most successfully is the Bell Telephone System. Each of the Bell operating companies has some long-term debt outstanding and increases this debt occasionally. However, being a member of the A.T. & T. holding company system enables each operating company to use a great of deal discretion when issuing new long-term securities. The parent, A.T. & T., gives advances to its subsidiaries to fill their capital needs. No doubt there are economies of scale in large capital issues. A.T. & T. can thus control the flow of new Bell securities into the market, thereby avoiding to some extent high-cost periods and possible "bunching" of new issues which might depress the prices of Bell System securities. However, Bell's pressing money needs force it to the market every month. As of December 31, 1959, A.T. & T. had advances outstanding to its principal telephone subsidiaries in an amount of $541,550,000.[10]

B. *Internal Financing.* Retained earnings contribute a rather small share of new capital for utilities compared with unregulated enterprises. This is due, in part, to the large capital needs of utilities, to the relatively low rate of return allowed utilities, and to what might be termed a "customary" payout ratio in the utility field which is quite high.[11]

A much more important internal source of funds is the accruals from depreciation deductions that are made regularly and charged against current income. The concept of depreciation has already been explained in Chapter 8 and need not be repeated here. It is obvious that, in a physical sense, plant and equipment do not wear out and are not replaced at the rate at which depreciation reserves accumulate. The funds that are constantly becoming available are normally put back into new plant and equipment. Given little or no inflation, it is quite likely that, because of technological advances, a dollar put into plant and equipment today will be considerably more productive than a dollar invested ten years ago. In light of the tremendous amounts of capital used by utilities, the stream of cash coming

---

[10] A.T. & T. *Annual Report, 1959,* p. 29.

[11] See Chapter 9 for a discussion of the payout ratio and its role in profit regulation.

from depreciation makes a significant contribution to capital spending.

For Bell, between 1946 and 1958 external sources accounted for 70 per cent of the new funds while internal sources accounted for 30 per cent. For investor-owned electric utilities between 1949 and 1958, an annual average of 34 per cent of new funds were raised internally and 66 per cent externally. Professor Ulmer has estimated the sources of new funds for several utility groups during the 1940's.[12] For electric light and power utilities, the most important sources of funds in the 1940's were depreciation, 38 per cent; bonds, 25 per cent; stocks, 18 per cent; and profits, 13 per cent. For the period 1949–1958, these sources contributed 24 per cent, 45 per cent, 22 per cent, and 10 per cent, respectively. The extremely rapid postwar growth necessitated the use of external sources when funds from depreciation were insufficient. No doubt the inflation in the postwar years has contributed to the emphasis on external sources also.

The picture for the telephone industry is quite different. In the 1940's, depreciation took care of 38 per cent of the needed funds, while in the postwar years this source has contributed only 15 per cent. Bonds have also diminished in relative importance as a source of funds, dropping from 46 per cent to 36 per cent. On the other hand, stock has greatly increased in importance, from a mere 9 per cent to over 40 per cent. The decline of depreciation charges as a source of funds reflects the same forces operating on electric utilities, namely, very rapid growth plus inflation. The decline in bonds reflects a complex set of factors. A.T. & T. no doubt took advantage of low interest rates in the 1940's, which were pegged by the Federal Reserve System and the Treasury. Also, A.T. & T. probably felt forced to turn to the bond market in the late 1940's, when capital for expansion was essential but difficult to get in the stock market. Relatively high interest rates, plus a desire to maintain its traditional debt-to-equity ratio, dictated A.T. & T.'s raising new money through stock issues in the 1950's.

3. CAPITAL STRUCTURE

Because of the large amount of capital required by utilities and because the cost of capital bulks large as an expense, regulatory authorities are interested in the capital structure of a company. Management feels strongly that decisions concerning capitalization should be left out of the regulatory purview, but most commissions feel that they must exercise some power here because of the critical nature of the costs involved.

There have developed over the years "conventional" debt limits, for the various types of utility industries which are tied roughly to bond ratings. However, such ratings frequently are set as much by custom as by specific factors. For electric companies, 60 per cent of the capitalization seems to be the general rule, although the SEC has encouraged operating subsidiaries of holding companies to reduce debt to 50 per cent.[13] The ratio of debt, including bonds, debentures, and notes, to total capital for electric companies in Table 19.4 was 53 per cent. Debt ratios for gas-distributing companies are close to those of electric companies, with debt accounting for about 47 per cent of the total capitalization. The figures for gas-transmission companies are quite different. Debt for these companies accounts for about 62 per cent of capitalization and in some instances is as high as 75 per cent. A.T. & T. is the major exception to

[12] Ulmer, *op. cit.*, pp. 151 and 152.

[13] *Re El Paso Electric Company,* 8 SEC 366 (1940).

high debt ratios among utilities. At the end of 1959, A.T. & T. held about 33 per cent of its capital in the form of debt. This unusually low figure for a large utility is fought over vigorously before regulatory commissions.[14]

Some mention must be made of debt-retirement problems for utilities, since debt plays such a large part in utility financing. Although there is still some argument over whether long-term debt is temporary or permanent capital, it seems to be pretty well accepted that it usually plays the role of permanent capital. What this means is that, rather than retiring debt in any large quantities, utilities refinance it, issuing a new debt issue to replace an old one. In some instances debt is converted into stock.

Stripped of the extremely difficult and delicate problems of judging the market, timing, and the like, refinancing operations work in the following way for a company experiencing long-term growth. Cash from depreciation accruals is used to buy new plant and equipment rather than to retire outstanding debt. When a debt issue comes due, the money that might have been used to retire the debt is in the form of plant and equipment; thus, a new debt issue is floated to replace the maturing issue, but, in effect, the new issue has been used to buy the new plant and equipment. Sinking fund-retirement procedures are not widely used any more because of the inefficient use of funds. Exceptions to this are found among gas pipelines. In cases where the market for the utility service is shrinking or where something like a natural gas reserve is being depleted, sinking fund retirement is appropriate. An alternative to this would be to have serialized bonds with given amounts callable on certain dates. In this way the debt is gradually reduced over its life. Over the years, inability to refund has been the major cause of corporate bankruptcy in the United States.

4. THE PROBLEM OF BIGNESS

The enormous size of the utility industry in terms of capital investment has been amply illustrated in the preceding discussion. Size itself raises financing problems for companies in this field. The problem is really that the investors have too much of a good thing, which in this case is the securities of utility companies. At any given point in time and for any structure of interest rates and yields, there is a given supply of and demand for investment funds. This is by no means a homogeneous market, since some suppliers of funds want long-term debt, others want short-term debt, and still others want equity. There are, of course, all sorts of variations in between these types. On the demand side, some corporations wish to borrow for the long term, others for a short term, and still others wish to sell ownership shares.[15]

Although utilities in most instances enjoy a substantial degree of natural monopoly as sellers of utility services, they must compete in the factor market for labor, land, and capital. This competition in capital markets is not only with other utilities, but also with industrial firms, financial institutions, and governmental bodies—local, state, and federal. For example, a sizable issue of long-term U.S. Treasury bonds has two major effects on any utility attempting to issue new long-term debt: (1) the supply of funds available in the long-term debt market may be largely absorbed by the

[14] See Chapter 9 for a discussion of debt ratios.

[15] See the panel discussion before the Edison Electric Institute Annual Convention, "Financing the Sixties' Expansion Program," Atlantic City, 1960, for arguments supporting the heterogeneity of the capital market.

Treasury issue, and (2) the cost of floating long-term debt may rise significantly.

Another factor affecting the salability of a stock or bond issue is the amount of securities of that particular company held by potential investors and the amount of similar securities held. It is here that some utilities encounter difficulties. It is quite logical for investors to want to diversify among companies and industries to reduce the risk of their portfolios. A large utility may, therefore, have some difficulty persuading investors to add to an already substantial investment. Such a situation can easily arise despite a company's high credit standing, sound financial policies, and favorable outlook for future growth. This peculiarity calls for extreme caution and skill on the part of financial managers of major utilities.

The best example of this phenomenon is, of course, the Bell System. As of December 31, 1961, A.T. & T. and its affiliated companies had a capital stock equity of $14.5 billion and a funded debt of about $7.3 billion.[16] Between 1970 and 1996, the Bell System will have to retire or refinance annually over $100 million of debt in 23 of the 27 years. In 13 of the 27 years, over $200 million will mature; while in 9 of the 27 years, over $300 million in debt will fall due.[17] If new debt money needed for expansion is added to these figures, the amounts become staggering. How much more in telephone bonds are investors willing to buy? What would happen if a major telephone bond issue failed to sell? These are indeed serious if not critical questions facing the Bell System. The problems are compounded by the likelihood of continued rapid growth.

This picture of Bell financing is of long-term debt only and does not consider the issuance of stock or short-term borrowing. The huge amounts of money which must be raised annually by Bell probably go far in explaining the seemingly low debt ratio of about 35 per cent for the system as a whole. This low debt ratio facilitates fund raising in several ways: (1) The credit rating of Bell System securities, both stocks and bonds, is high. (2) A low debt ratio gives the system a margin of protection for raising new funds. If equity money is not available, this cushion can be used by issuing debt. (3) Finally, the low debt ratio minimizes the chances of failure of any refinancing operation.

Thus, size, rapid growth, or a combination of the two create some problems for a utility. Some firms other than Bell, such as Pacific Gas and Electric and Commonwealth Edison, have some of the same problems, although on a smaller scale. Small utilities with very rapid growth encounter some of the same difficulties. This problem will probably intensify, since the telephone, electric, and gas industries in general are all growing faster than the economy as a whole.

5. WHO HOLDS UTILITY SECURITIES?

Before turning to financial regulation, it is appropriate to inquire into the question of who buys and owns utility securities. About all that can be done is to hypothecate from what limited data are available. The question of who owns utility bonds is not too difficult. These securities are of relatively low risk, for the most part,[18] and have great appeal to those investor groups who want to minimize their risk factor. This group includes insurance companies, trust, pension, and endowment funds, some investment and mutual funds, and other similarly situated investors. Life insur-

[16] A.T. & T., *Annual Report, 1961*, p. 27.

[17] A.T. & T., Company Records, data of September 30, 1959.

[18] Bonds of some privately owned urban transit companies are the major exception.

ance companies alone, at the end of 1959, held $16.6 billion in utility bonds, representing about two-fifths of the outstanding debt of utilities in the United States. The dollar figure has almost quadrupled since 1940, and in 1959 it accounted for about 14.5 per cent of the assets of life insurance companies.[19] A study in 1955 indicated that these utility holdings were broken down as follows: 55 per cent in electric companies, 23 per cent in communications, and 4 per cent in water companies, urban transit companies, and other utilities.[20]

The specific figures on the bondholdings of other groups are not available. However, it is reasonable to assume that other institutional investors bulk large among the owners of such securities. The bondholder looks for a high degree of safety for both his principal and his interest. Most utility-type activities afford him this safety, or at least more of it than can be had from most other corporate bonds. On the other hand, government securities at the local, state, or federal level usually carry less risk than do utility bonds, since the taxing power is frequently behind such debt. Interest rates on bonds reflect these varying degrees of risk.[21]

The problem of determining who owns utility stocks is somewhat more difficult. Data reported for life insurance companies reveal that in 1959 about $1,005 million in utility preferred stock and $661 million in utility common stock, or a total of $1,666 million, was held by life insurance institutions.[22] This is a relatively small amount compared with life insurance companies' holdings of utility bonds of some $16.6 billion. Although, again, the data are not available, it must be assumed that individuals hold by far the largest chunk of utility stocks.[23] In light of the dividend and growth characteristics of utility companies, it would appear that most of these investors are interested in relatively stable and relatively high-dividend income and are not so interested in speculative price fluctuations or in spectacular growth. Many utility stocks fill this need admirably and appeal to a group of investors which otherwise might turn to a debt form of asset.[24]

Data reported by A.T. & T. on the characteristics of its common stock distribution can be taken as representative of the large utility companies. These data are shown in Table 19.5 in percentage terms as of the spring of 1960. The figures indicate a rather widespread distribution of stock by type of person, with perhaps a larger than usual number of shares held by institutions. Sizes of holdings are also widely dispersed. Almost 45 per cent of the shares are in holdings of less than 300 shares. As would be expected, there is a large geographic concentration of holders and of holdings of A.T. & T. stock. This has little to do with the location of A.T. & T., but rather reflects the fact that the financial center of the United States is New York City. Much the same distribution would probably occur for other large utilities except where the location of a company might strongly influence the geographic holdings.

[19] Institute of Life Insurance, *Life Insurance Fact Book, 1960,* New York, 1959, pp. 64, 65.

[20] *Ibid.,* pp. 74–75. See also H. J. Johnson, "The Life Insurance Investment in Public Utilities," 52 *Public Utilities Fortnightly* 341 (September 10, 1953).

[21] The fact that interest income from local bonds is not subject to federal income taxation distorts this interest-risk relationship somewhat.

[22] Institute of Life Insurance, *op. cit.,* p. 79.

[23] Owen Ely, "Who Is the Utility Stockholder?" 53 *Public Utilities Fortnightly* 14, January 6, 1955.

[24] Charles Tatham, Manager Public Utilities Department, Bache & Company, "The Place of Utility Common Stocks in Your Investment Portfolio," Address before The New School, April 12, 1960.

Table 19.5

Characteristics of A.T. & T. Company Stock Distribution
(As of March, 1960)

	% of Stockholders	*% of Shares*
By Class of Person:		
Men	20.4	21.0
Women	43.0	35.4
Joint accounts	30.2	20.5
Deceased & estates	0.8	1.0
Fiduciary accounts	4.4	3.7
Institutions, etc.	1.2	14.6
Brokers & security dealers	*	3.8
Total	100.0	100.0
By Shareholding:		
1 - 10	16.3	0.8
11 - 30	25.0	4.2
31 - 49	11.9	3.8
50 - 99	18.9	10.9
100 - 299	19.4	25.7
300 - 999	7.7	28.5
1,000 - 2,999	0.7	8.3
3,000 - 9,999	0.1	3.4
10,000 and over	*	14.4
Total	100.0	100.0
By Area:		
New England	12.4	11.6
Eastern	42.7	47.5
Southern	7.8	7.9
Central	16.9	13.8
Northwestern	2.6	2.0
Southwestern	5.3	5.1
Mountain	2.3	2.0
Pacific	9.7	9.0
U.S. Possessions	*	*
Foreign	0.3	1.1
Total	100.0	100.0

* Less than 0.05 of 1 per cent.
Source: A.T. & T., Company Records.

6. THE EVOLUTION OF FINANCIAL REGULATION

In order to grasp the significance of security regulation, it is necessary to glance briefly at the events that occurred before such regulation was established. Briefly, financial abuses by public utility holding companies and others involved in securities and security markets brought on regulatory controls. Part of this story will be told in the following chapter.

Although most emphasis in public utility economics is given to the regulation of the rate base and the rate of return, most people closely associated with regulation maintain that financial and accounting regulations are, in truth, the most critical areas. To illustrate this point, one might ask how meaningful rate-base regulation is if the accounts are not kept in a proper and orderly manner, and what good a rate increase does if money raised with long-term debt is used for poorly planned, unusable plant and equipment or, worse still, is used to pay dividends. More directly, the manner in which a utility raises its capital has a substantial impact on the cost of capital, which in itself is a large expense item of the capital-using utility industry. Thus, utility management and regulators have in recent years been more and more aware of the far-reaching effects of financing and financial regulation. Other aspects of regulation are successful only to the extent that financial regulation is successful.

Federal investigation into holding-company practices (discussed in the following chapter) pointed up the need for security regulation in the 1920's and 1930's.[25] Unsuccessful attempts at such regulation were made before this at the state level. Finally, state regulation was supplemented with an extensive system of federal regulation, and the combination has proved very effective in correcting abuses in this field. The following section describes this evolution of financial regulation and places special emphasis on the federal requirements currently in effect which apply to public utilities.

A. *State Regulation.* State public utility regulation did not, in most instances, include security regulation at the outset. There was a general feeling that such regulation was unnecessary, if rate regulation was imposed. Utility management actively opposed any commission intervention in financial matters. This was felt to be an area of management prerogative. In some states, these arguments were heeded by legislators, and security regulation was kept out of the hands of commissions. In other states, regulation in varying degrees has been applied.

(1) *Types of Regulation.* Early state security regulation was similar to other aspects of utility regulation in that the financial limitations on the corporations were spelled out in the charters granted to a utility by special acts of the legislatures. The ineffectiveness of such measures is obvious. Such regulation was unenforceable, inflexible, and generally unsatisfactory to all concerned. Massachusetts was probably the first state to have anything like an effective law dealing with securities when in 1852 it established regulations concerning railroad financing. Before 1900 several states had passed laws of a general nature which regulated security issues, and the Interstate Commerce Commission was given some authority over railroad securities. New York in 1907 passed the first effective law for utility security regulation. Security issues had to be authorized by the state commission, and it was authorized to publicize the facts about a particular issue. It was illegal to use the funds raised for any purpose other than what was authorized.[26] Other states followed New York's example. One of the most recent studies of state commission jurisdiction was made in 1960 by the Federal Power Commission in cooperation with the NARUC.[27] Some 42 states and the District of Columbia and Puerto Rico had some sort of regulation of security issuance in 1960, while 8 states either had no commission or had a commission but specifically did not authorize this type of regulation. Regulatory powers over securities and related matters apply only to privately owned public utilities. There are virtually no controls over securities of publicly owned utilities.

(2) *An Evaluation of State Regulation.* Space does not permit a close

[25] See I. R. Barnes, *The Economics of Public Utility Regulation* (New York: Appleton-Century-Crofts, Inc., 1942), Chapters 19 and 20, for a detailed discussion of security abuses in the 1920's and 1930's.

[26] See M. G. Glaeser, *Outlines of Public Utility Economics* (New York: The Macmillan Company, 1927), pp. 393 ff., for a good discussion of early state security laws.

[27] U.S. Federal Power Commission, *State Commission Jurisdiction and Regulation of Gas and Electric Utilities, 1960* (Washington: Government Printing Office, 1960).

analysis of state laws dealing with public utility security regulation. These laws are generally quite similar to the federal laws in terms of what is required of the company involved. It is important to note that, over the years, more and more states have adopted such laws, and state enforcement has become stronger.[28]

However, the best thing that can be said of state regulation is that it supplements federal regulation and reaches those companies not otherwise covered by the rather stringent rules of the SEC, FPC, or FCC. It is a small part of total security regulation albeit an important one. The failure of state regulation needs no more proof than the enumeration of the evils and abuses in the utility industry that was given in the early 1930's by the FTC.

The major reasons for failure of state regulation were inherent in the nature of the industry to be regulated as it existed in the 1920's and 1930's. The holding-company movement made the utility industries interstate in nature and thus outside the jurisdiction of any single state commission. Since holding companies are not utilities themselves, utility regulation is not applicable to them anyway. Many operating companies, particularly in areas where states are small, are large enough to be interstate in nature and thus outside of state regulation, even without being part of a holding-company system. In addition to these problems which are inherent from the structure of the industry, there existed in the 1920's and 1930's, and to some extent today, the problem of inadequate staff and funds for regulation. Only well-trained and well-supported commission staffs are capable of dealing adequately with the extremely complex aspects of security regulation. Special skills and thorough investigation are essential to the success of security policing. On top of this deficiency are some poorly written state statutes and lack of commission experience. Finally, the corporate abuses and the involved problems of dissolution and general untangling of corporate relationships present a formidable task for any agency. For a body not specializing in such work, the job is virtually impossible.

B. *Federal Regulation.* Whether better state regulation of securities could have prevented federal regulation is doubtful. The holding-company movement had reached such large proportions that only federal regulation could tackle the task of breaking up the affected firms. Also, interstate gas and electric transmission lines were growing rapidly, and the United States Supreme Court had held that they could be regulated only by the federal government.[29]

The result was the passage of six federal laws which dealt, in part, directly or indirectly with the issuance of utility securities. These are the Securities Act of 1933, the Securities Exchange Act of 1934, the Public Utility Holding Company Act of 1935, the Federal Power Act of 1935, the Communications Act of 1934, and the Natural Gas Act of 1938.

(1) *Security Regulation Under the Securities and Exchange Commission.* The Securities Act of 1933 is perhaps the best one to discuss first. It is a general statute which applies to all corporations selling securities in interstate commerce. It ". . . is designed to provide disclosure to investors of material facts concerning securities publicly offered for sale by use of the mails or instrumentalities of interstate commerce, and to prevent misrepresentation, deceit, or other

[28] See The Twentieth Century Fund, *Electric Power and Government Policy* (New York: 1948), pp. 250–276, for a good discussion of state security regulation.

[29] *Missouri* v. *Kansas Natural Gas Company,* 265 U.S. 298 (1924); and *Public Service Commission* v. *Attleboro Steam and Electric Company,* 273 U.S. 83 (1927).

fraudulent practices in the sale of securities."[30] It is sometimes known as the "truth in securities" act. The Act was initially administered by the Federal Trade Commission but was transferred to the Securities and Exchange Commission in 1934 when the Securities Exchange Act was passed. The Act does not require that the SEC pass on the merits of the securities offered or on the enterprise or activities to be conducted with the funds raised. It merely requires that all pertinent information be laid before the prospective investor so that he can make a choice. Approval of an issue by the SEC is in no way an indorsement of it by the SEC.

To obtain this goal of complete and accurate information, the Securities Act provides for the following things:

1. A registration statement and prospectus must be filed with the SEC. The Act spells out in considerable detail what information must be contained in such a statement, and the Commission itself has the power to require additional facts if the situation warrants it.

2. Examination by the SEC Division of Corporation Finance of the registration statement is required to assure compliance with the standards set forth in the Act.

3. Administrative procedures are set forth to handle situations in which full compliance is not achieved. The SEC can issue a "stop order" which prevents a security from being issued until an investigation of the possible irregularities can be completed and the difficulties straightened out. Wilful noncompliance is rare and can be fairly readily detected.

4. A waiting period of about three weeks is required between the filing of the registration statement and the actual offering for sale of the securities. This is to provide time for potential investors to become acquainted with the information furnished in the statement.

5. Legal remedies are provided for violation of the Act. Criminal liability and penalties are provided for wilful violation of the Act, including such things as making wilful omissions or untrue statements of fact in the registration statement. In addition, any person suffering damages as a result of wilful omission or misstatement of facts can claim such damages in court from the issuing company, its officers, directors, underwriters, accountants, and so forth.

It should be re-emphasized that the Securities Act is a broad one which covers all securities except the following: (1) those issued for private sale and not offered publicly; (2) those issued by the federal, state, or local governments; (3) those issued by common carriers regulated by the Interstate Commerce Commission; (4) those issued by banks, insurance companies, savings and loan associations, and nonprofit institutions; and (5) issues in amounts less than $300,000. The utility industries certainly loom large in the annual figures on new registrations. Table 19.6 shows data for the fiscal years 1958, 1959, and 1960. In light of the large part of total new financing done by utilities, it is appropriate to consider the Securities Act in the discussion of utility financing.

The companion piece to the Securities Act is the Securities Exchange Act which established the SEC in 1934. The latter Act is only indirectly related to utility financing. It requires securities exchanges to register with the SEC and to comply with the laws, rules, and regulations of the Commission. It also provides for exchanges to police their own memberships. The Act requires the registration of securities listed on each of the exchanges. Dealers and brokers doing "over-the-counter" business are regulated. Such regulation is beneficial to all security issuers in that the people who

---

[30] U.S. Securities and Exchange Commission, *25th Annual Report* (1959), p. 26.

Table 19.6

Securities Registered with the SEC and Sold for Cash
For the Account of Issuer, Fiscal Years 1958–1960

Industry	*1960* Mil. $'s	*1960* % of Total $ Issued	*1959* Mil. $'s	*1959* % of Total $ Issued	*1958* Mil. $'s	*1958* % of Total $ Issued
Electric, gas, and water	2,313	21.2	2,726	22.5	3,373	25.4
Communication	1,000	9.2	591	4.9	2,978	22.4
Total utility.	3,313	30.4	3,317	27.4	6,351	47.8

Source: Securities and Exchange Commission, *26 Annual Report* (1960), p. 34.

buy, sell, or trade in securities cannot readily damage the credit standing of a company or industry.

The Public Utility Holding Company Act is discussed at length in the following chapter.

(2) *Security Regulation Under the Federal Power Commission.* Interstate electric utilities have rather stringent security regulations under the Federal Power Act. The Act provides that:

> No public utility shall issue any security . . . unless and until, and then only to the extent that, upon application by the public utility, the Commission by order authorizes such issue or assumption of liability. The Commission shall make such order only if it finds that such issue or assumption (a) is for some lawful object, within the corporate purposes of the applicant and compatible with the public interest, which is necessary or appropriate for or consistent with the proper performance by the applicant of service as a public utility and which will not impair its ability to perform that service, and (b) is reasonably necessary or appropriate for such purposes.[31]

The Act further states that the proceeds of an issue can be used only for purposes approved by the FPC. If there are state laws that cover security regulation, the federal law is not applicable. If an electric utility comes under the security regulation of both the Federal Power Act and the Public Utility Holding Company Act, the latter takes precedence unless the Securities and Exchange Commission has exempted the utility from the Holding Company Act.[32] These statutory provisions dealing with securities are further spelled out in the Regulations of the FPC.[33] This rather complete control over the financing of electric utilities has resulted in very orderly and sound development of the capital structures in this industry.

The Natural Gas Act does not specifically provide for security regulation of interstate natural gas pipelines or of producers selling in interstate commerce. However, in the case of pipelines, considerable control is exercised. As noted in Chapter 14, a pipeline applicant for a certificate of public convenience and necessity must demonstrate, among other things, that adequate financing has been arranged to back its proposal. This enables the Commission to pass upon the financing plans of both proposed new pipelines and the major expansions proposed by existing pipelines. In the event that the Commission disapproves of some aspect of a proposed financial plan, it is authorized by the Act to attach to the certificate "such reasonable terms and conditions as the public convenience and necessity may require."[34] The Com-

31 Federal Power Act of 1935, 16 USC 324c.

32 *Ibid.*, 16 USC 825g.

33 See particularly 18 CFR 34.1–34.10.

34 Natural Gas Act of 1938 as amended, 15 USC 717.

mission's Regulations spell out the financial requirements which a pipeline applicant must satisfy in order to qualify for a certificate.[35]

The FPC, in gas pipeline certificate cases, has held as a general policy that at least 15 per cent of the capitalization of a new pipeline must be in common equity and that no more than 75 per cent can be in debt securities.[36] In one certificate case, the FPC allowed an 81.6 per cent debt ratio, in view of the fact that some 10-year unsecured notes would be retired by a cash payment or converted into preferred stock. However, the Commission conditioned its approval by restricting ". . . dividends on common stock until the interim notes are converted into preferred stock or the total long-term debt, including the notes, is reduced to 75 per cent or less of the total capitalization."[37] In a similar case, the FPC agreed to an 85 per cent debt ratio, including 10 per cent in interim notes, on the ground that tight money conditions dictated such a policy.[38] This ruling, too, was conditioned by a restriction on dividend payments pending a reduction of the debt ratio.

The Public Utility Holding Company Act covers gas as well as electric utilities, although not nearly as many gas companies are involved.[39]

(3) *Security Regulation Under the Federal Communications Commission.* The telecommunications industry has not been subject to the same type of control over its security issues as has the electric utility industry. Of course, the provisions of the Securities Act of 1933 and the relevant state statutes are applicable to its financing activities. The Communications Act of 1934, like the Natural Gas Act, is silent on the matter of security regulation. However, the Communications Act contains a section requiring certification of expansions, which authorizes the Federal Communications Commission to ". . . attach to the issuance of the certificate such terms and conditions as in its judgment the public convenience and necessity may require."[40] As in the case of the powers granted to the FPC under the Natural Gas Act, the FCC may condition a certificate with one or more requirements concerning securities. The fact that the telephone and telegraph industries have had very little special security regulation seems to indicate a lack of necessity for these types of controls.

(4) *An Evaluation of Federal Regulation.* Federal regulation of the financial aspects of utilities has been, for the most part, successful. Certainly, the work of the SEC in obtaining truthful statements concerning new security issues has been a success. Administration of the security provisions of the Holding Company Act has also been successful. This judgment is based on the over-all objectives of the Act. In this instance, the *use* to which funds are put is passed on by the SEC. FPC regulation of securities issuance by electric utilities under the Federal Power Act also seems to have been effective. The apparent conflict between SEC and FPC regulatory jurisdictions has rarely, if ever, come to the surface. There appears to be an informal understanding between these two agencies.[41]

---

35 18 CFR 157.1–157.4.

36 *Re San Juan Pipe Line Company, et al.* 9 FPC 170, 187 (1950); *Re Midwestern Gas Transmission Company,* Opinion No. 320, May 12, 1959 mimeo. ed.

37 *Ibid.,* mimeo. ed., p. 4.

38 *Re Transwestern Pipeline Company, et al.,* FPC Opinion No. 328, August 10, 1959 mimeo. ed.

39 See R. H. Huitt, "Natural Gas Regulation Under the Holding Company Act," 19 *Law and Contemporary Problems* 455 (1954).

40 15 USC Sec. 214c.

41 See Francis X. Welch, "Functions of the Federal Power Commission in Relation to the Securities and Exchange Commission," 14 *George Washington Law Review* 81 (1945), for a good discussion of the possible conflict and the way in which this has been handled.

It has been noted that the FPC and the FCC do not have direct jurisdiction over the securities issued by the gas pipelines and interstate communications utilities, respectively. As yet, this has caused no serious problems, and until it does, perhaps regulation can be done without. The question of jurisdictional conflicts between state and federal agencies in security regulation exists but primarily at the hypothetical level.[42] State regulation has been greatly shored up by the various federal acts, and, in fact, states have taken the accomplishments at the federal level in this field as an example of what can be done and have strengthened their own securities laws.

7. FINANCING PUBLICLY OWNED UTILITIES

To round out the picture of utility financing and financial regulation, it is essential that some consideration be given to publicly owned utilities. "Public ownership" is a broad term used here to cover ownership by federal, state, municipal, and other local governmental units as well as cooperative ownership.[43]

A. *Municipal Ownership.* By far the most important type of public ownership is at the local level, in the form of municipal ownership of water, sewage, electric, transit, and gas utility functions. Table 19.7 indicates the number of cities of 5,000 population or more having municipally owned utilities in 1958. Outstanding among these are water utilities. Next in importance is the sewage utility function, which is closely related to water supply and distribution.[44]

The data in Table 19.7 are broken down by size of city and by utility function. Approximate percentage figures are included to indicate generally how significant municipal ownership is in these cities for different categories of utility services.[45] It is interesting to note several relationships between size of city and degree of public ownership. For water supply and distribution, there appears to be a direct relationship between the two; the larger the city, the more apt it is to have a publicly owned water system. There is a substantial difference, 18.7 percentage points, between the largest and smallest size classifications.

For electric utilities, the reverse seems to be true. A smaller percentage of the large communities have publicly owned electric systems than do the small communities. This reflects the large number of small communities which cannot be tied efficiently into an integrated major electric system. It also reflects the relatively low profits which can be made from local electric distribution. In an important number of instances, it is far easier and less costly to set up a Diesel, gasoline, or gas-driven generator to furnish a small town's electricity needs, which are largely nonindustrial, than to tie it into a large grid by putting up miles of transmission line to serve the relatively small load. In addition, federally generated power usually is sold first to "preference" customers, which are municipal or cooperative distribution systems, and second to privately owned systems. In some areas this has stimu-

[42] John E. Benton, "Jurisdiction of the Federal Power Commission and of State Agencies in the Regulation of the Electric Power and Natural Gas Industries," 14 *George Washington Law Review* 53 (1945).

[43] The reader interested in this specific area should consult Martin G. Glaeser, *Public Utilities in American Capitalism* (New York: The Macmillan Company, 1957), Part 3, for a comprehensive treatment of the subject.

[44] See Chapter 11 for a discussion of water-utility characteristics and rate procedures.

[45] Accurate population data are difficult to obtain; thus there may be some small errors in the percentage figures for the three smallest size-groups of cities. For larger cities, the data are fairly reliable. The significance of the figures lies in their magnitude rather than in their precise amounts.

Table 19.7

Municipal Ownership of Utility Services by Size of City, 1958[1]

(Population in Thousands)

Type of Utility	All Cities 5 or more		(17) Cities over 500		(23) Cities 250-500		(68) Cities 100-250	
	No.	% Own. Util.	No.	% Own. Util.	No.	% Own. Util.	No.	% Own. Util.
Water distribution only	155	6.2	-0-	-0-	-0-	-0-	2	2.9
Water supply and distribution	1,677	67.3	15	88.2	19	82.6	56	82.4
Sewage treatment	1,286	51.6	12	70.6	16	69.6	37	54.4
Electric generation and distribution	279	11.2	2	11.8	3	13.0	4	5.9
Elec. distribution only	223	8.9	-0-	-0-	1	4.3	3	4.4
Gas distribution only. .	86	3.5	-0-	-0-	1	4.3	1	1.5
Gas mfg. & distribution	41	1.6	2	11.8	3	13.0	3	4.4
Bus, trolley or street railway	40	1.6	7	41.2	2	8.7	1	1.5

Type of Utility	(133) Cities 50-100		(291) Cities 25-50		(846) Cities 10-25		(1184) Cities 5-10	
	No.	% Own. Util.	No.	% Own. Util.	No.	% Own. Util.	No.	% Own. Util.
Water distribution only	9	6.8	20	6.9	51	6.0	73	6.0
Water supply and distribution.	94	70.7	185	63.6	542	63.9	766	62.9
Sewage treatment. . . .	56	42.1	142	58.8	425	50.1	598	49.1
Electric generation and distribution. . . .	11	8.3	31	10.7	88	10.4	140	11.5
Elec. distribution only	3	2.3	15	5.2	68	8.0	133	10.9
Gas distribution only. .	2	1.5	6	2.1	23	2.7	53	4.4
Gas mfg. & distribution	2	1.5	6	2.1	17	2.0	8	0.7
Bus, trolley or street railway	4	3.0	8	2.7	14	1.7	4	0.3

[1] Population data from 1950 Census or later special censuses. Some error inherent in the percentages because of different population figures.

Source: Basic data from *The Municipal Yearbook, 1958* (Chicago: International City Managers' Association, 1959), p. 87. Percentages computed.

lated growth in municipal ownership of electric systems. In 1958, stockholder-owned electric utilities served 79 per cent of the ultimate customers, compared with 12 per cent for municipally owned utilities, and sold 77 per cent of the Kwh, compared with 8 per cent for the municipal systems. Cooperatives, power districts, and state and federal government projects accounted for the remainder.[46]

The financing of municipally owned utilities is primarily by long-term borrowing, complemented by capital contributions by the city and by the reinvestment of earnings. "Revenue bonds" rather than "general obligation bonds" are generally issued. A revenue bond depends on the revenues from the utility service for payment of interest and the amortization of principal. They are used for a number of reasons, including: (1) a city's inability to issue general-obligation bonds because of legal debt limitations placed on municipalities in particular states; (2) a city's desire to avoid increasing its own debt liability which must be paid from taxes, thus

[46] Edison Electric Institute, *The Electric Industry*, 1959 ed. (New York: 1960), p. 29.

protecting its property taxpayers; (3) a desire to assure that the utility venture will be self-supporting; (4) a belief that utility service should be paid for by its users and not by taxpayers generally; (5) in some states, revenue bonds can be issued without a special bond election, which is not ordinarily true for general-obligation bonds; and (6) revenue bonds are relatively remote from local politics and therefore sometimes can be sold on more favorable terms than general-obligation bonds.[47] Needless to say, there are all kinds of variations in bonds issued by municipalities. Each situation is a little different, and the financing is tailored to fit the needs of the particular case.[48] Some of the varieties of this type of financing were discussed in Chapter 11. One final point should be noted about municipal bonds: the federal income tax does not apply to interest income that is earned on bonds issued by a municipality. The tax advantage accorded to holders of such bonds is reflected in comparatively lower interest costs to municipal-utility borrowers.

B. ***State and Federal Ownership.*** State and federal ownership of utilities is significant only in the electric field. Out of a total of about 156 million kilowatts of installed generating capacity in the United States at the end of 1959, investor-owned utilities accounted for 75.9 per cent, co-operatives for 0.7 per cent, municipal utilities for 7.0 per cent, federal projects for 14.0 per cent, and power districts and state projects for 2.5 per cent.[49] State projects are most important in Nebraska, where they account for all the electric generating capacity and where all electricity is marketed through public utility districts.[50] Other states with significant amounts of state owned-operating capacity include Texas, Oklahoma, New York, and South Carolina. Financing of state projects is quite similar to municipal financing in some respects. The financing of the Nebraska, Oklahoma, and South Carolina hydroelectric projects was done through Public Works Administration loans and grants. The loans carry a low rate of interest and are payable from the revenues earned by the projects. The hydroelectric projects of these three states also perform functions other than power generation. Especially important are flood control, irrigation, and conservation. Of lesser importance are navigation and recreation.

The Power Authority of the State of New York in conjunction with the Hydroelectric Power Commission of Ontario has undertaken the development of power on the St. Lawrence River. This has been done together with the navigation improvements constructed by the federally owned Saint Lawrence Seaway Development Corporation and the Canadian counterpart, the Saint Lawrence Seaway Authority of Canada. The Power Authority has financed its share of dam-construction costs and transmission lines by issuing revenue bonds. The Power Authority is also developing some of the power potential of Niagara Falls. This work is also being financed with revenue bonds.

Federally owned power projects fall into several categories. Table 19.8 lists the major federal power-generating agencies and their electric-generating capacity. In all cases except the Tennessee Valley Authority, the capacity is hydroelectric. In the case of TVA, only

---

[47] *Moody's Manual on Public Utilities, 1957,* p. a22.

[48] See Chapter 11 for a discussion of municipal securities and their relation to rates charged.

[49] Computed from data found in Edison Electric Institute, *Electric Utility Industry in the United States, 1959,* Table 2, mimeo.

[50] See Judson King, "Nebraska the Public Power State," 39 *Public Utilities Fortnightly* 357, 419, 483, March 13 and 27, and April 10, 1947.

Table 19.8

Federally Owned Electric Generating Capacity Installed and Under Construction, June 30, 1959

Agency	*Installed Capacity (KW)*	*Capacity Under Construction (KW)*
Tennessee Valley Authority	10,997,210	1,720,000
Hydro (34%)	3,727,460	295,000
Steam (66%)	7,269,750	1,452,000
Bureau of Reclamation	5,902,050[1]	1,680,000[4]
Bonneville Power Administration	3,469,000[2,3]	2,097,000
Southeastern Power Administration. . . .	1,259,600[2]	548,000
Southwestern Power Administration. . . .	601,000[2]	190,000
Total.	22,228,860	6,235,000

[1] Includes 745,000 Kw in Corps of Engineers and 31,500 Kw in International Boundary and Water Commission.

[2] Includes capacity in Corps of Engineers Projects.

[3] Excludes Reclamation dams.

[4] Includes 595,000 of capacity under construction by the Corps of Engineers.

Sources: Tennessee Valley Authority, *Annual Report for 1959,* and Department of the Interior, *Annual Report of the Secretary for 1959.*

about 34 per cent of the total is comprised of hydro capacity, and the remaining 66 per cent is steam-generating facilities. Virtually all the federal hydroelectric projects are multipurpose to some extent. Flood control is, of course, paramount in virtually all cases, although Bureau of Reclamation dams are primarily intended to provide irrigation water and power for pumping it.

The financing of federally owned projects is extremely complex owing primarily to the multipurpose nature of the projects. The funds for construction of the facilities have come from the general fund of the United States Treasury and thus can be said to come from federal tax revenues or borrowing. Except in the case of TVA, no federal power agency can issue its own bonds. Repayment of the portion of project costs allocated to power is made over a long period, usually 40 to 50 years, and the agency must pay interest on the capital funds "borrowed" from the Treasury. Virtually all federal power agencies are ahead of schedule in their repayments to the Treasury.

In August, 1959, Congress amended the TVA Act in two important respects. Beginning in the fiscal year 1961, TVA must pay to the Treasury not less than $10 million in each of the first five years, $15 million in each of the next five years, and $20 million each year thereafter until a total of $1 billion has been repaid. This would pay back a major portion of the $1.2 billion that Congress has appropriated to date. In addition, TVA must pay a return on the government investment in power facilities at a rate equal to the average interest on the Treasury's marketable debt for that year. The amendment further provided that the TVA could issue bonds or notes in an amount up to $750 million to assist in financing its power program. The servicing of this debt has precedence over repayments to the Treasury. These new obligations are not guaranteed by the federal government. They are revenue bonds payable solely from TVA power proceeds.[51] This type of federal financing has never been used before in undertakings of this kind. It accomplishes at least two things. It frees TVA from having to go to Congress for appropriations to finance its power facilities. It also gives the TVA considerably more latitude in its decision making in the power field, although it by no means gives TVA autonomy from congressional control.[52]

Ownership of utilities by co-operatives is found primarily in the electric and telephone fields.[53] Co-operative ownership is a cross between public and private ownership. It is public in the sense that co-operative associations are exempt from federal taxation, financed by federal loans at very low interest, and provided with technical and managerial services by a federal agency. It is private in the sense that it is owned by its customer-members.

[51] Public Law 86–137, August 6, 1959, amending Section 15d of the TVA Act.

[52] See U.S. 86th Congress, 1st Session, House of Representatives, Report No. 271, April 14, 1959, for a discussion of both sides of the question of "TVA Self-Financing." For an interesting description of the proposed TVA financing, see Brig. General Herbert D. Vogel, Chairman, TVA, "TVA Power Revenue Bonds to Finance Unprecedented Power Needs," 16 *Analysts Journal* 47 (March–April 1960).

[53] Co-ops are also found operating irrigation systems, but this will not be discussed.

The Rural Electrification Administration was established in 1935 for the purpose of promoting the use of electricity in rural areas. It was authorized to assist in the extension and improvement of rural telephone service in 1949. Congress supplies funds to the REA, which the latter lends, for the most part, to co-operative associations of customers. The REA is also authorized to lend to other borrowers for the above purposes, and in some instances it has done so. Rural electric systems financed by the Rural Electrification Administration sold 23.6 billion Kwh of electricity during the year ended June 30, 1959 to 4,654,000 customers.[54] Rural telephone systems financed by REA were serving 875,000 subscribers.[55] Some 95 per cent of the 954 REA electric borrowers were co-operatives.

The loan financing of REA borrowers is ordinarily on a 35-year basis. Interest of only two per cent per annum is charged. As of June 30, 1959 there had been $3.9 billion loaned to electric borrowers and $575 million to telephone borrowers. Current annual payments of interest and repayments of principal were about $143 million in 1960.[56]

[54] Rural Electrification Administration, *Annual Report for 1959,* p. 1.

[55] *Ibid.*

[56] *Ibid.,* pp. 31 and 34.

20 The Structure and Organization of Utility Industries

The structure and organization of American industry accounts, in part, for the success of our economic system. This industrial organization has been a complex mixture of monopoly, partial monopoly, price and non-price competition, and various forms of government regulation. At different times in history, public utilities have had strong elements of all these. A brief sketching of this industrial growth process in the utility fields will create a better understanding of why our present-day utility industries are organized the way they are.

This chapter will first take up the public utility holding company movement of the 1900–1930 period. A brief description of the holding-company abuses primarily in the electric and gas industries and the legislation passed to correct these abuses will be followed by an evaluation of the current status of utility holding companies. The fact that very large coal and atomic fuel-powered steam-generating plants are the most efficient and useful makes this holding company discussion quite current. The second part of the chapter evaluates the Bell Telephone system, pointing out how the holding-company device can be effectively used to achieve high-quality, low-cost, efficient service and maintain financial strength and integrity. Finally, this chapter will raise some perplexing and as yet unanswered questions concerning the broad public policy issues encountered in regulating business. It appears that there are some basic inconsistencies or conflicts between the ultimate goals of utility regulation and the ultimate goals of antitrust regulation which need to be explored.

1. THE EVOLUTION OF GAS AND ELECTRIC HOLDING COMPANIES AND THEIR REGULATION[1]

Before considering the historical development of holding companies, it is necessary to define several terms and concepts. A *holding company* is a form of business organization which owns or in some way controls another business organization. The holding company itself is usually a corporation, but it does not have to be. It exercises control in its "subsidiary" companies through ownership of voting stock or by any one of a number of other formal or informal ways. Stock ownership need not be complete and, in fact, for practical control can frequently be far less than one-half. This, of course, varies with any given situation. It should be remembered that the emphasis in a holding-company structure is control rather than ownership. It should also be added that a holding company may or may not perform functions other than just controlling "subsidiary" companies. In other words, it may be an "operating company" as well as a holding company.

A subsidiary company may be another holding company, an operating company, or a company performing non-utility functions. Regardless of its functions, its policies can be controlled by the parent holding company.

The term *operating company* usually refers to a firm which actually renders some *utility* service, such as the generation, transmission, and distribution of electricity or the transmission and distribution of gas. An operating company may serve only in this capacity or may also control other companies, thus constituting both an operating company and a holding company. In the early public utility holding-company structures, it was common to find subsidiary companies which performed an auxiliary

[1] The development, abuses, investigation, and ultimate regulation of gas and electric holding companies has been dealt with in great detail in a number of studies. See particularly *Report of the FTC on Utility Corporations,* Senate Doc. 92, Part 72–A, 70th Congress, 1st Session (1935); I. R. Barnes, *The Economics of Public Utility Regulation* (New York: Appleton-Century-Crofts, Inc., 1942), Chapters 4 and 19; and Eli W. Clemens, *Economics and Public Utilities* (New York: Appleton-Century-Crofts, Inc., 1950), Chapter 21. Particular attention should be given to the bibliographies in these books which refer to the numerous cases, documents, and studies which have accumulated in the holding-company area.

service for the operating companies. Such things as engineering, legal, financial, accounting, and economic services were frequently handled through one or more non-utility subsidiaries.

A. *Early Public Utility Holding-Company Development.* The holding-company movement was slow to get started among gas and electric utilities partly because of technological factors. Suitable methods of gas manufacture, transmission, and distribution, as well as electric generation and distribution, had not been perfected. By 1882 some of the technical hurdles had been crossed, and the first central electric-generating plant was completed in New York City. In the same year, the manufacture of water gas was introduced by the United Gas Improvement Company in Pennsylvania. The stated purpose of this company was to make improvements in the gas industry, which it did by acquiring patent licenses on water gas-manufacturing processes and inducing gas companies to switch from coal gas to water gas. After meeting with little success in selling water gas-manufacturing equipment, United Gas leased gas works throughout the country and put the new equipment in the plants. Finally, in order to gain better control, United Gas purchased majority stock interests in some gas works. Thus, there began in the 1880's one of the major utility holding companies. It is important to note that the impetus for control of operating companies was a completely legitimate and, in fact, a desirable one. It was a case of a manufacturer and holder of process patents trying to broaden the market for its products and processes.

A similar story is found in the electric industry. Beginning in the 1890's, both Westinghouse and General Electric took steps to assure a market for their electrical equipment by owning or controlling electric distributing companies. This action was dictated by the skepticism of independent distributing companies about the new generating equipment. Several techniques of control were used, but most successful was the holding-company arrangement set up by General Electric. It proceeded to establish separate holding companies to hold primarily bonds but also some stocks of local electric distributing companies. In some instances, the holding companies promoted the development of new operating companies. Control of the holding companies was retained by General Electric.

Such an arrangement had advantages for GE, the operating companies, and the investing and consuming public. The advantage to the equipment manufacturer was the development of a market with the least possible outlay on the part of GE. By holding only a controlling interest in the stock of the holding companies, which, in turn, invested in the securities of operating companies, General Electric avoided tying up as much capital as would have been necessary had it loaned to or invested in the operating companies directly. The operating companies benefited by having sufficient capital and having their credit ratings, in effect, underwritten by General Electric. Would-be investors in operating-company securities could invest in holding-company securities and have not only the assurance that General Electric was safeguarding their interest, but also the protection of diversified risk. This diversification arose because of the geographical scattering of operating utilities controlled by the holding company. Consumers benefited, at least in the early years, from improved service with better equipment relative to what had been used previously, and from the general financial stability enjoyed by an operating company through being a satellite to a holding-company organization. Probably not only was the quality of service higher, but also rates were lower. This was likely the result of more efficient equipment and lower financing costs. Thus, the two early General Electric holding companies[2] were directed primarily at giving financial assistance to operating utilities. The greatest shortcoming was that the reins of managerial control usually remained in the hands of the local utility, and the result was frequently poor planning, unbalanced capital structure, and poor management generally. In 1905, General Electric decided that it needed a larger voice in the control of operating utilities. Poor financial management had resulted in bond-heavy capital structures, with the consequent vulnerability to cyclical fluctuations which was a deterrent to growth. The solution was the formation of the Electric Bond and Share Company (Ebasco) under the skilled leadership of S. Z. Mitchell, a well-known and successful utility manager. Ebasco proceeded to buy large blocks of stock in utilities and to revamp their management when control was secured.

A third utility empire that developed from different roots than United Gas or Ebasco was that of Stone and Webster. While the two systems dicussed above originated under the impetus of equipment manufacturers' desires for a market, the Stone and Webster system evolved out of the need by local utilities for advice and consultation on a variety of technical, financial, and legal problems. Stone and Webster originated as an engineering consulting firm serving primarily the electric distribution industry. Since cash was often hard to come by for operating companies, Stone and Webster sometimes received payment in the form of stock or bonds of the utility. Joined by a banking group, Stone and Webster engaged in purchasing control in unprofitable companies and streamlining the management and operations to make the companies profitable. Thus, securities could be purchased at low prices and sold at considerably higher ones. It should be noted, again, that all parties benefited from such action. Stone and Webster profited, other stockholders benefited as stock prices rose, the utility was completely renovated and modernized by experts, and the consumers received better service at what was probably lower cost because of the elimination of inefficiencies.

Another group of holding companies got its start because of the financing problems faced by operating utilities. Investment banking groups were vitally interested in the success and continuing expansion of the utility industry because of the large quantities of capital that had to be raised. These banking interests frequently performed the underwriting function for utility security issues. In some instances, these bankers were left with large blocks of unsold securities. The establishment of holding companies was a convenient way in which to dispose of the unsold issues. In this way, the holding companies began to gain control of some operating utilities.

A few generalizations can be made from this sketchy description of the types of early holding companies. (1) The use of the holding-company device was beneficial to investor and consumer, for the most part. Obviously, there were examples of abuse and "milking" of subsidiary companies, but these were the exception rather than the rule. (2) The holding company was not set up primarily as a profit-making operation in and of itself. Many of them were established to promote profits in services or goods sold to the operating utilities. (3) The holding company was a logical step in the evolution of the gas and electric industries. Industrialization and urbanization were occurring with startling rapidity. The embryo utility industry

[2] United Electric Securities Company and Electrical Securities Corporation.

was fragmented, competitive, and inefficient—completely unsuited to serve the new economy. Holding companies pulled isolated operating companies together, furnished capital and professional advice, and cut duplication and inefficiency. Up to about 1910, the scales seemed to weigh heavily in favor of using utility holding companies.

B. *The Appearance of Holding-Company Abuses.* As the pace of industrial activity quickened in the first three decades of the twentieth century, the complexion of the public utility holding company changed—slowly at first and then more rapidly. The profit motive had been basic to the establishment of the first holding companies, and properly so. But the profits sought were generally of long-term, nonspeculative nature and were frequently consistent with the public interest and a by-product of better service. It soon became apparent to financial manipulators that the holding-company device was perfect for reaping huge short-run, speculative profits while affording almost complete legal protection to those controlling the holding company. To be sure, some good accompanied the evils of the holding companies of the 1920's, but the abuses were so great and public sentiment so adverse that the holding company still remains under a pall of suspicion in some people's eyes. It is possible here only to outline the major types of abuses that resulted from utility holding-company practices.[3]

[3] The utility industry of the 1920's was perhaps the most thoroughly investigated industry in American history. The Federal Trade Commission spent seven years and issued more than eighty volumes of hearings and reports on various aspects of the industry. This series is entitled *Report on Utility Corporations,* 70th Congress, 1st Session, Senate Document 92. Part 72–A of the Report contains the summary and conclusions concerning the electric industry, and Parts 84A, B, and C do the same for the gas industry.

(1) *Pyramiding.* The most general abuse by holding companies, and the one which ultimately brought the downfall of many utility empires, was known as "pyramiding." This involved the creation of layer after layer of holding and sub-holding companies on top of operating companies. Intercorporate relationships could become infinitely complex and interwoven because of loans, exchanges of securities, selling and buying back of properties, interlocking directorates, and similar practices. It was possible for a relatively small investment at the top to control huge aggregations of assets.

The greatest danger from such a pyramid was that if the fixed charges on the bonds of the operating utilities were just barely paid or not paid at all, no dividends were paid to the holding company directly above the operating utilities. Since such dividends were essential for the holding company to pay its fixed charges, particularly its own bond interest obligations, this company collapsed unless it could in some other way get the necessary money. It is quite obvious that all holding companies above would also collapse, since there were no funds for fixed charges or dividends. The whole structure resembled a house of cards which collapsed if one card was removed.

The holding company structures were so intricate that some aspects were never unwound. In the Standard Gas and Electric Company, the pyramid was such that an investment of less than $1 million controlled $370 million.[4] In prosperous times a pyramid could bring the investors in the top holding company returns as high as 200 per cent. In bad years the investor faced disaster. Thus it was in 1929 and 1930 that one after

[4] Barnes, *op. cit.,* p. 78, citing Federal Trade Commission, *Report on Control of Power Companies,* 69th Congress, 2nd Session, Senate Doc. 213, 1927, p. 192.

another of the pyramids collapsed as a result of relatively small decreases in earnings of the operating companies. While pyramiding was not the sole cause of abuses by holding companies, it did have a tendency to contribute to all the other problems.

(2) *Financial Abuses.* Many of the utility holding company promoters were not particularly interested in waiting for dividends to be paid. Money could be made in other ways. An individual might occupy a seat on the boards of directors of a number of holding and operating companies and receive exorbitant directors' fees. Also, he might be a well-paid officer in numerous companies. A frequent abuse in holding company structures was the writing up of assets of operating companies as they were transferred from one holding company to another in the same pyramid. This, coupled with stock-watering, combined to inflate to excessively high levels both the assets and capitalization of the companies involved. Since it was essential that the operating companies pay dividends if the holding company was to survive, a fairly common abuse was for operating companies to pay dividends by making inadequate provision for depreciation. This bleeding of operating companies was slow to show up but eventually caused some of the most serious problems in refinancing and reorganization in later years. In some instances these financial abuses were made worse by the falsification of accounts and stock-price manipulation by some unscrupulous promoters.

(3) *Service Company Fees.* It has already been mentioned that one reason for the establishment of some holding companies was the need for specialized professional services. The role of these service companies was essential to the success of their client utility companies. The promoters of holding companies soon realized that it was extremely profitable to attach several of the service companies to the holding company and have them render the necessary services to the operating utilities. The fees charged could be regarded as "expenses" for the operating companies and would accrue directly to the holding company. In some instances the "milking" of operating companies through excessive fees was all that was needed to drain off profits to the benefit of the top-level holding company. In this way, independent investors in middle-layer holding companies were bypassed. Service contract fees had a claim on income prior to senior securities.

C. Advantages of Holding Company Structures. The advantages of using the holding-company device might be broken down into two groups, the first applying to the early holding companies and the second applying to later holding companies. There is, of course, considerable overlap.

The distinguishing feature of the early period was the innovating stimulus contributed by holding companies controlled by manufacturers of equipment used by utilities or by holders of patents on processes which utilities used. Technology had still not developed to the point where cities and towns could be joined together in "service areas." In addition, urbanization was only beginning in many sections of the country. The early holding companies did, however, hasten utility development in specific communities, with the consequent improvements noted earlier.

The later holding companies hastened the pulling together of relatively inefficient operating units into more efficient, rational systems. Whether this could have been done as effectively under some other arrangement is questionable but impossible to prove one way or the other. Larger size and the establishment of service companies probably were factors in providing better management and professional services such as centralized engineering and purchasing, as well as advice in financing, law, construction, accounting, advertising, and merchandising. Whether the costs of these special services were offset by increased revenues resulting from the advice is impossible to know.

A distinct advantage that a holding company structure enjoyed was its ability to raise capital more quickly and cheaply than small operating units could. At least, this was true until a general distrust of utility securities was generated in the public's mind in the period immediately following the stock market crash in 1929. Finally, the holding company did provide strength through regional diversification. Weak units could be supported by stronger ones by mere association with them. This was of benefit to both consumers and investors.

D. The Public Utility Holding Company Act of 1935. The foregoing discussion of the possible advantages and disadvantages of public utility holding companies is couched in very general terms in an attempt to leave an impression that such structures could be beneficial or destructive depending on their behavior. This section describes the attempt that was made to eliminate the bad features while retaining the good aspects of public utility holding companies.

(1) *The Need for Federal Legislation.* By the mid-1920's, many states, as well as the federal government, were becoming restive over what was occurring in the public utility industry. The abuses in the industry were increasing while the benefits were diminishing. State attempts to regulate the holding companies either directly by special legislation or indirectly through commission regulation of operating utilities failed. In the first case, the holding companies were not public utilities, charged no rates, had no rate base, and were not "affected with the public interest," as that phrase was usually interpreted by the courts. They were, in every other sense, affected with the public interest. Also, holding companies generally operated in more than one state with their home offices invariably located where operating subsidiaries were not found. State attempts to regulate holding companies through the operating units of the system also failed. Regulation of rates for service had little or no effect on the proliferation of holding companies. Attempts at stringent regulation frequently hastened the collapse of the operating company involved, although not necessarily of the parent holding company. This frequently harmed consumers and innocent investors the most.

By 1927 Congress had felt sufficient public pressure to call for an investigation of the gas and electric utility industries by the Federal Trade Commission. From 1929 to 1935 was a period of stock market crash followed by prolonged depression, and the situation in the industry deteriorated badly.

Since utility regulation clearly failed to correct the situation, why were not the antitrust laws applied? The Sherman, Clayton, and Federal Trade Commission Acts stressed the illegality of combinations or conspiracies in restraint of trade, monopolies or attempts to monopolize, and various practices which tended to lessen competition substantially or create monopoly. But it has already been demonstrated that monopoly and suppression of competition among utilities is frequently beneficial and desirable. The remedy to this dilemma was the passage of a federal law which was, in effect, a type of antitrust law specifically designed for and applied to gas and electric public utility holding companies. The aim of this law was (1) to retain the benefits to the public generally of having public utilities serve as natural monopolies but (2) at the same time to make sure that concentration of economic power not consistent with greater public benefit was avoided.

(2) *Provisions of the Holding Company Act.* The Public Utility Holding Company Act[5] was one of six pieces of related federal legislation passed or proposed in the period from 1933 through 1935; it is in many ways a compromise. It provides for: (1) the dissolution of holding companies in excess of two layers; (2) the selling off of pieces of holding companies which are not put together into efficient units; and (3) rather rigorous regulations for accounting, financing, acquisitions, and parent-subsidiary relationships. Yet it does not require complete dissolution by any means, and it tries to foster the good aspects of holding companies. The administering body is designated as the Securities and Exchange Commission. A *holding company* is defined as "any company which directly or indirectly owns, controls, or holds with power to vote, 10 per centum or more of the outstanding voting securities of a public utility company or of a company which is a holding company. . . ."[6] Although certain exceptions are noted, this stringent 10 per cent definition generally applies. The Act goes into detail on registration procedure, sale of securities, rights of stockholders, adherence to state laws, conditions under which acquisitions can be made, regulation of dividend payments, proxy solicitation, intercompany loans and transactions, and political contributions. In addition, the Act gives the SEC control over service and construction contracts and empowers the Commission to establish uniform accounting procedures and to require periodic reports.

The heart of the Act is found in Section 11, which contains the famous "death sentence clause," a label given to it by the critics of the dissolution mandate. This section requires that each holding company ". . . shall limit the operations of the holding company system . . . to a single integrated public-utility system, and to such other businesses as are reasonably incidental, or economically necessary or appropriate to the operations of such integrated utility system. . . ."[7] However, the Act provides three exceptions or conditions under which a holding company can hold one or more additional integrated systems. These are: (1) if there would be "losses of substantial economies" unless operated by the holding company; (2) if all additional systems are located in one state or adjoining states; and (3) if the system is not so large ". . . as to impair the advantages of local management, efficient operation, or the effectiveness of regulation."

Section 11 further requires that steps be taken to conform to the standards set out above, that is, reorganization plans be filed as soon as possible with the Commission. Actually, a deadline of January 1, 1936 was set for the submission of reorganization plans, but the constitutionality of the Act was tested and registrations were few until this legal hurdle was cleared. The SEC promptly filed suit against Electric Bond and Share Company for failure to comply with the registration requirements found in Sections 4 and 5 of the Act. The United States Supreme Court upheld the Commission in 1938, and most of the holding companies quickly registered with the SEC.[8] Section 11b (1), which requires physical disintegration of holding companies was unsuccessfully challenged, but the Supreme Court decision in this case was not forthcoming

---

[5] 15 USC 79a–79z.

[6] 15 USC 79b, par. a (7).

[7] 15 USC 79k, par. b (1).

[8] *Electric Bond and Share Company* v. *SEC*, 303 U.S. 419 (1938).

until 1946.[9] Section 11b (2), which deals with simplification of corporate structure, was also challenged and upheld.[10]

The SEC moved at what seemed to be a snail's pace in carrying out reorganization plans. It preferred to have a plan submitted voluntarily by a company, and once a plan was submitted, it worked slowly and carefully to see that all interests were treated equitably. The Commission has earned the respect of the utility industry and the public alike for its effective and judicious handling of what appeared to be an impossible task. The soothsayers of doom that predicted the Act would wreck the utility industry were far from right. On the other extreme, there are critics of the SEC who claim that it has not moved as fast as it could or should. This judgment is difficult to evaluate, but perhaps the cautious conservatism of the SEC has been responsible, in part at least, for the healthy electric and gas utility industry in the United States today.

E. Evaluation of the Public Utility Holding Company Act. An evaluation of the Act and of SEC performance under the Act must be broken into at least two questions: first, Has Congressional intent, as expressed in the Act, been fulfilled? and second, Is there now a need for Congress to repeal or substantially alter the Holding Company Act of 1935?

(1) *Work of the SEC Under the Act.* Section 1 of the Public Utility Holding Company Act states, in part, that ". . . it is hereby declared to be the policy of this title . . . to meet the problems and eliminate the evils as enumerated in this section, connected with public-utility holding companies . . .; and for the purpose of effectuating such policy to compel the simplification of public-utility holding-company systems and the elimination therefrom of properties detrimental to the proper functioning of such systems, and to provide as soon as practicable for the elimination of public-utility holding companies except as otherwise expressly provided in this title."[11]

This is, to say the least, an awesome mandate to a newly created agency, relatively inexperienced in the matters of corporate simplification and reorganization. Congress also had virtually no experience in handling such problems and as a result "passed the buck," so to speak, and allowed to SEC wide discretion in promulgating rules and regulations to enforce the Holding Company Act. This was indeed fortunate. The Act as it was written was extremely flexible and adaptable to varying circumstances. The SEC was not bound in every direction by the enabling statute, and, in fact, to implement the statute required substantial rule making by the SEC.[12]

The SEC has been eminently successful in carrying out the mandate of Congress, while at the same time maintaining the respect and cooperation of the utility industry generally. The critical area of regulation for the SEC is Section 11 of the Act, which provides for dissolution, simplification, and reorganization. By 1952 the SEC was able to say ". . . that the task of bringing about compliance with Section 11 which had its real beginning in 1940 is rapidly nearing completion."[13] On June 30, 1952, electric and gas utility plants owned by registered holding company systems were about 30 per cent of total

[9] *North American Company* v. *SEC,* 327 U.S. 686 (1946).

[10] *American Power and Light Company* v. *SEC,* 329 U.S. 90 (1946).

[11] 15 USC 79a, par. C.

[12] D. C. Cook and H. B. Cohn, "Capital Structures of Electric Utilities Under the Public Utility Holding Company Act," 45 *Virginia Law Review* 981 (1959).

[13] Securities and Exchange Commission, *18th Annual Report* (Washington: Government Printing Office, 1952), p. 82.

private electric utility investment and 28 per cent of total private gas utility investment. Estimates of conditions in the early 1930's indicate that 15 holding company systems controlled 80 per cent of all electric energy generation, 20 systems controlled 98.5 per cent of all interstate transmission of electric energy, and 11 systems controlled 80 per cent of all natural gas pipeline mileage.[14] This shrinkage is a rather creditable performance on behalf of the SEC. Although compliance was bitterly fought in many cases, rarely did the consumer suffer from poor-quality service.

There have been a total of 2,412 companies subject to the Act as registered holding companies or subsidiaries over the period from June 15, 1938 to June 30, 1960. Some 2,070 of the 2,412 have been released from the Act or have ceased to exist. During this period, 924 (of the 2,070) companies with assets of about $13 billion were divested by their respective parents and thus are no longer covered by the Act. Of the remaining 1,146 companies, 783 disappeared through dissolution, merger, or consolidation, and 363 were exempt by SEC action.[15]

There has been a tremendous shrinkage in both number of companies and amount of assets under SEC jurisdiction. This is a phenomenon welcomed by the regulators as well as the regulated. As one SEC official put it, the SEC has been "working hard to do itself out of jurisdiction to the tune . . . of well over $1 billion a year."[16]

Virtually all major Section 11 cases have been completed, and in the Commission's report for 1958 it was noted that "while there were net decreases during fiscal 1956 and 1957 of 32 and 11, respectively, in the number of companies comprising the active systems, certain systems are carrying out realignment programs, and it is too early to state whether a leveling off has occurred in the total number of companies subject to regulation under the Act."[17] The number of companies still subject to the Act dropped from 176 to 172 between June 30, 1958 and June 30, 1960, while assets from December 31, 1957 to December 31, 1959 increased from $9,948 million to $11,530 million.[18] It would appear, therefore, that the reduction in companies subject to the Act has all but ceased, and the future is apt to see a growth in assets that at least parallels the growth of the electric and gas industries generally in the economy. The impact of atomic energy for electric generation may conceivably be an important factor in reversing the process and may cause a growth in the holding company systems. This aspect will be discussed below.

It is proper to ask at this point what the effects of the shrinkage described above have been on investors, consumers, the efficiency of the industry, and the public generally. It is impossible to measure the effects of such things as balanced capital structures and independent management in dollar terms. Nor is it possible to compare in a meaningful way the interest rates on senior securities before and after holding company regulation. However, there are some indications of improved industry conditions. One authority, after examining SEC and FPC records, concluded that public utility capitalizations and asset values now accord more reasonably.[19] In 1937 the capital structure of electric utilities was 58 per cent debt, 18.4 per cent preferred stock, and 23.6

---

14 *Ibid.*, p. 83.

15 SEC, *26th Annual Report* (1960), p. 132.

16 N. D. Lobell, "Fifteen Years of the Holding Company Act," 47 *Public Utilities Fortnightly* 292, 297 (March 1, 1951).

17 SEC, *24th Annual Report* (1958), p. 109.

18 *Ibid.*, p. 108, and *26th Annual Report*, p. 131.

19 Cook and Cohn, *op. cit.*, p. 993.

per cent common equity. By the end of 1957, these figures were 51.7 per cent, 12 per cent, and 36.3 per cent, respectively.[20] This shift to sounder capital structures reflects, in part, SEC urging.

Improved investor appraisal of utility securities is evidenced in a number of ways. In 1958 it took only 6.3 cents of each dollar of operating revenues to pay interest charges, whereas in 1937 the cost was 13.1 cents.[21] This reflects both a reduced debt ratio and lower costs of debt capital. Holding company common stock prices have risen substantially, as have revenues and earnings per share of equity. A study in 1952 of the market value of senior securities of 12 major holding company systems in late 1951 as compared with the date of registration revealed that $723 million of senior securities had appreciated to $1,614 million. This was an increase of more than $890 million.[22]

Not only has the investor benefited from the Utility Holding Company Act, but so too has the consumer in the form of lower rates (particularly in "real" terms) and higher-quality service. Some of these benefits have been due to technological improvement, while others have merely been due to correction of inefficiencies existent under unregulated conditions. In addition, such things as the imposition of mandatory competitive bidding for new security issues has assured consumers of reasonable financing costs, which, in turn, are reflected in ultimate rates.

(2) *Proposed Changes in the Public Utility Holding Company Act.* Although much of the emphasis in the discussion of the Holding Company Act has been on compliance with Section 11, which provides for simplification, dissolution, and reorganization, it should be remembered that there are a number of sections which provide "a health program" for companies operating under the Act.[23] Many of the one-time utility holding companies have divested themselves of utility properties to the extent that they fall now under the Investment Company Act of 1940.[24] Yet, as the SEC's reorganization program draws to a close, there are a number of holding companies that appear to be permanently under the jurisdiction of the Holding Company Act. To the extent that this is true, wise national policy seems to dictate against complete repeal of the Act.

There are still those critics of the utility industry who want to see the Act applied more forcefully so that all holding companies are broken up. This suggestion is as extreme as the advocacy of complete repeal. In the words of President Roosevelt when he transmitted the report of the National Power Policy Committee to Congress in 1935:

> . . . for practical reasons we should offer a chance of survival to those holding companies which can prove to the Securities and Exchange Commission that their existence is necessary for the achievement of the public ends which private utility companies are supposed to serve.[25]

Whether major changes should be made in the Act or not presents another problem. Two major areas seem likely to receive considerable attention. The first is the problem of future integration.[26] It seems inevitable that there

[20] *Ibid.*, p. 995.

[21] *Ibid.*, p. 996.

[22] U.S. Senate, Select Committee on Small Business, *The Public Utility Holding Company Act of 1935*, Subcommittee Print No. 4, 82nd Cong., 2nd Session (Washington: Government Printing Office, 1952), p. 23.

[23] Lobell, *op. cit.*

[24] 15 USC 80a.

[25] U.S. House of Representatives, House Document No. 137, 74th Congress, 1st Session, Letter of transmittal (1935).

[26] For a discussion of this, see R. F. Ritchie, *Integration of Public Utility Holding Companies* (Ann Arbor: University of Michigan Law School, 1954).

will be economic and technological pressures dictating larger systems in the electric industry. Accompanying these pressures will be demands for a loosening of SEC holding company controls. This brings attention to the second major problem area, which is in many ways a cause of the first. The technology of conventional steam generation and the technology of atomic energy will have an impact on the structure of the electric utility industry and will tend to promote larger units.

In 1955, bills were introduced in Congress by Senators Potter and Pastore ". . . to encourage maximum development of low-cost electric energy by amending certain provisions of the [Public Utility Holding Company] Act. . . ."[27] The bills would have exempted from the Act, under certain circumstances, companies pooling their resources: (a) to build large-scale electric generating facilities; and (b) to develop low-cost electric energy from all sources of power, including nuclear energy (which became a matter of central interest as hearings progressed). In many respects, these two types of utility cooperation are different and may require different treatment.

The SEC has the power to create specific exemptions from the Act within the rather broad provisions of Section 2 (a). In the case of companies cooperating in atomic energy development, the SEC amended its Rule U-7 to read as follows: "Any company whose only connection with the generation, transmission, or distribution of electric energy is the ownership or operation of facilities used for the production of heat or steam from special nuclear material . . . shall not be deemed an electric utility company within the meaning of Section 2 (a) (3) of the Act, *if such company is organized not for profit and is engaged primarily in research and development activities.*" [Emphasis supplied.][28] Thus, the SEC has set up provisions for passing on the status of cooperative ventures in atomic energy in the developmental stage and has, in fact, approved several such projects.[29] However, the Commission implies in its rule that it considers the risk and technological problems of atomic energy electric generation to be no different than those of conventional generation after the research and development stages have been completed. Insofar as this is true, the SEC wished not to grant permanent exemptions by amending the Holding Company Act, and the Atomic Energy Commission concurred strongly with this view.[30] Generally speaking, the SEC has been willing to allow atomic energy cooperation and has proved to most people that it can be done under the present Act without amendment.[31] Perhaps a more severe test will come when the SEC has to decide when the development stage for various projects has ended and how then to bring under regulation companies which were formerly exempt.

The other aspect of the proposed

[27] U.S. 84th Cong., 1st sess., S. 2643 and H. R. 6294, Sec. 2 (1955).

[28] SEC, Holding Company Release No. 13221 (July 13, 1956).

[29] See, for example, *Yankee Atomic Electric Company et al.,* SEC, Holding Company Release No. 13048 (November 25, 1955), and *Power Reactor Development Company,* SEC, Holding Company Release No. 13364 (January 17, 1957).

[30] See U.S. Senate, Committee on Interstate and Foreign Commerce, *Hearings on Amendments to Public Utility Holding Company Act, 1935 on S. 2643,* 84th Cong., 2nd sess. (1956), p. 4. These hearings contain the views of the FPC, SEC, AEC, and other government agencies on the propriety of the proposed amendments.

[31] See J. S. Armstrong, Chairman of the SEC, "Nuclear Power Projects and the Holding Company Act." 59 *Public Utilities Fortnightly* 721 (May 23, 1957), for the SEC's views on atomic energy developments.

amendment, that of allowing cooperation on large-scale power development, is more significant perhaps. One official argues that "To solve the problem of finding the huge blocks of power needed in the future there is a growing demand for joint generating cooperation between two or more electric utility operating companies."[32] He points to the following advantages:

1. Large steam generating plants (100,000 kw and larger) are more efficient than smaller ones, but it usually takes more than one system to absorb the output from such a plant.
2. Large plants have lower relative costs of financing.
3. Suitable sites for steam plants are getting scarce, and those available should be utilized by large plants.
4. Many of the remaining hydroelectric sites are too big for one company to develop or use.
5. Efficient atomic-energy plants are also too large for one company.[33]

There are some groups which would take issue with the assumptions underlying and conclusions derived from such statements. A Subcommittee of the Senate Judiciary Committee chaired by Senator Kefauver held hearings on monopoly in the electric power industry and concluded that the merger or cooperation of power companies to set up another company to wholesale power constituted a threat to the nation and had, in fact, ". . . many of the holding company evils which Congress sought by legislation to suppress. . . ."[34] This view was by no means unanimous in Congress, and the question became deeply embroiled in partisan politics. The most spectacular public display of the battle was the famous "Dixon-Yates Controversy." A similarly sticky problem revolves around permitting public development of giant electric projects but prohibiting private development, if it is to be done jointly by several companies. Time, technology, and economic necessity will force a solution to these problems.

[32] E. S. Loughlin, Chairman, Connecticut PUC, "Is the Holding Company Act Retarding Progress?", 59 *Public Utilities Fortnightly* 819 (June 6, 1957).

[33] *Ibid.*, pp. 825–826.

[34] U.S. Senate, Antitrust and Monopoly Subcommittee of the Committee on the Judiciary, *Monopoly in the Power Industry,* Interim Report, 83d Cong., 2nd sess. (Washington: Government Printing Office, 1955), p. 4.

2. THE BELL SYSTEM

A. The Development of the Bell System. Although the American Telephone & Telegraph Company and its affiliated companies comprise one of the largest business enterprises in the world, the story of how this company grew has never been authoritatively told in an unbiased fashion. This is strange because the Bell System is primarily a public utility and thus subject to public scrutiny at the state and federal levels. This section will explore the evolution of this holding company system, using what data are available.[35] The brief sketch of A.T. & T. that follows points out clearly that the holding-company

[35] Several studies and reports have been written on the history and development of the Bell System. Included among these are: U.S. Federal Communications Commission, *Investigation of the Telephone Industry in the U.S.,* 76th Cong., 1st sess., House Doc. No. 340 (Washington: Government Printing Office, 1939); comments of A.T. & T. on the FCC Investigation, which were filed with the Commission but never published by the FCC; A. W. Page, *The Bell Telephone System* (New York: Harper & Row, Publishers, 1941); Horace Coon, *American Tel and Tel* (New York: Longmans, Green & Company, 1939); N. R. Danielian, *A.T. & T.* (New York: Vanguard Press, 1939); J. W. Stehman, *The Financial History of the American Telephone & Telegraph Company* (New York: Houghton Mifflin Company, 1925). The following discussion is taken largely from these sources.

device can be used constructively and effectively in the development of a public utility system. This is not to say that this company has never been the subject of criticism; however, the record indicates that it has rendered high-quality, efficient service at reasonable rates and has exercised considerable self-restraint in areas of potential abuse that emerge when one firm achieves as much economic power as A.T. & T. has.

(1) *The Birth of the Bell System.* The telephone was invented in 1875 by Alexander Graham Bell, a speech and hearing therapist. With Thomas A. Watson, an engineer to build an instrument, and Thomas Sanders and G. G. Hubbard to supply the necessary money, the telephone industry was launched. These four men first formed the Bell Patent Association to license patents and to manufacture and lease telephone equipment. This leasing technique, espoused by Hubbard, proved to be one of the keys to later success in the industry. It enabled the company to stay informed on what equipment was in use and to maintain standard transmission quality.

In 1878 the New England Bell Company and the Bell Telephone Corporation were organized to develop the New England market with Bell patents. In 1879 these companies were joined into the National Telephone Company by William H. Forbes, who, with Theodore N. Vail, was to be the great builder of A.T. & T. Western Union, which in 1877 had turned down a chance to buy the Bell patents for $100,000.00, realized in 1878 that the telephone industry was real competition for telegraphy. Western Union poured money and effort into research and came forth with patents of its own which enabled it to enter the telephone industry. Bell at this time was extremely small, compared with its competitor, Western Union. However, the improvement in Bell equipment plus the hard bargaining of Theodore Vail resulted in survival for what was to become the Bell System. In 1879 an agreement was reached between Bell and Western Union in which Bell agreed to stay out of telegraphy and Western Union agreed to stay out of telephony. No one realized the significance of this agreement at the time.

With this major potential competition out of the way, the Bell System proceeded to expand. Vail used control over patents and over long-distance lines to gain control of many "independent" companies, that is, companies not associated with Bell. In 1880 the American Bell Telephone Company was formed to absorb National Telephone. In the same year a "long lines" department was started. The year before, a research department had been set up. As early as 1881, the Bell System began looking for ways to exist after basic patents would run out in 1893 and 1894. One solution was to build, buy, or control long-distance networks, which Bell did. Another was to control local exchanges. The latter technique was done as much as possible through provisions in licensing agreements so as to avoid committing a great deal of capital. The granting of a permanent license to an operating company carried the following stipulations:

1. The licensor (Bell) was to receive 30 to 50 per cent (usually, 35 per cent) of the capital stock of the licensee.

2. The licensee was generally prohibited from borrowing money without the consent of the licensor.

3. The costs of extension and development of the licensee's business were to be met by the issue of capital stock and not by the use of the profits of the business.

4. The licensor was expressly granted representation on the licensee's board of directors and usually also on its executive committee.

5. The licensee was required to make

such reports and to give such information regarding the operations of its exchanges and prices charged as the licensor might from time to time request.[36] The licensee received the right to use Bell licenses and equipment and the privilege of tying in with Bell's long-distance facilities when available.

There seemed to be a conscious policy on the part of Bell to gain local support in these early years from some local ownership. In 1882 Bell purchased a 40 per cent interest in the Western Electric Manufacturing Company, a manufacturer of telephone equipment. In 1883 a program was launched to consolidate local exchanges into statewide networks. In 1885 the American Telephone & Telegraph Company was organized in New York with broad charter provisions which allowed it to own stock in other companies; American Bell retained control of A.T. & T. In 1887, partly because of ill health and partly because of internal friction in the company, Vail left the Bell System.

(2) *Growth and Consolidation, 1887–1913.* In 1893 and 1894 the basic Bell patents expired, and there was a flurry of activity among independents. However, the careful planning by Bell under the leadership of Vail reaped handsome rewards. The nation's long-distance lines were in the hands of the Bell Company, as was much of the telephone equipment-manufacturing capacity. License agreements had placed many operating companies under Bell control. Many of the independent companies that were established after 1894 were located in the West and not in areas directly competive with Bell. The Bell System expanded rapidly both by internal growth and through acquisition. The 1890's were extremely prosperous years for the burgeoning telephone industry. In 1894 the Bell System had 582,506 instruments rented, and it operated 396,674 miles of wire. By 1900 there were 1,580,101 instruments and 1,016,770 miles of wire.[37]

Efforts were made by independents to penetrate Bell-dominated areas. In most places these efforts failed because (1) unprofitable rate provisions were included in the charter provisions, and (2) the capital necessary for expansion and improvement was lacking. Starting in 1889, one last effort was made by independents to break the Bell "monopoly." A company was organized with the backing of several wealthy New York and Boston financiers. A group of independent companies in the Midwest, operating under Bell-patent licenses, came under the domination of the Erie Telephone and Telegraph Company, a holding company. A.T. & T. could not compete directly with these firms because of the terms of its licensing agreement. A fight arose between Bell and the independent group over control of the Erie Company. The independents gained this control but exhausted their capital in doing so. Funds had to be borrowed, and stock of the independent companies was pledged as collateral. Bell quietly bought up stock in the independent companies and ultimately gained control of the Erie Company and its subsidiaries. This ended the last major threat to Bell dominance in the telephone industry.

The period 1900 to 1907 was the period of greatest independent growth. However, this growth was stunted by several problems: (1) lack of capital; (2) lack of manufacturing subsidiaries or sources of specialized equipment; (3) diseconomies of smallness; (4) lack of technical and financial know-how; and (5) unwise or ill-informed action on the part of management. These problems were compounded by the manner in which the Bell System competed. One

[36] FCC, *Investigation of the Telephone Industry in the U.S., op. cit.*, p. 19.

[37] Coon, *op. cit.*, p. 77.

critic has listed the following Bell practices: (1) control of patents; (2) patent fencing; (3) threatened or real patent-infringement suits; (4) propaganda aimed at undermining the position of independents with the public and legislatures; (5) refusal to sell independents telephone equipment; and (6) exertion of pressure on the financial community to dry up the supply of capital for independent companies.[38]

It should be noted that rarely, if ever, have charges brought against the Bell System for such alleged misdeeds been upheld in court. Also, there is absolutely nothing wrong with controlling patents or with launching patent-infringement suits. Nor is it illegal to refuse to buy from or to sell to certain companies which are competitors. The critic seems to forget that "natural monoply" was not an accepted concept at that time, and that competition was quite fierce at times among telephone companies. Over all, the competitive practices of the Bell System seem appropriate, given the times and the accepted business practices of the times.[39]

By 1902, the Bell System was encountering difficulties in its public relations. In addition, complaints of high rates and poor service were becoming more frequent. On top of this, the financial management of the company left much to be desired. The financial interests on the Bell board of directors brought back Theodore N. Vail as president to rejuvenate the company. A struggle among investment banking interests ensued for control of Bell, with the George F. Baker–J. P. Morgan interests emerging victorious. This group was happy to have Vail in power, and he immediately set about putting the Bell house in order. His accomplishments were nothing short of miraculous. They can only be outlined here. (1) Standardization of equipment and supplies was pushed to reduce inventories and take advantages of large-scale manufacturing. (2) Public relations became of central concern, with the "service" concept as the basis. (3) Vail developed a philosophy which espoused a single monopolistic telephone and telegraph system in the nation under government regulation. (4) A logical corollary to this was absorption of independents. (5) Another consequence was a dislike and distrust of government ownership, since Vail felt that private industry could do the best job possible. (6) Independents were allowed the use of Bell's long lines and were able to buy from Western Electric. This was not entirely altruistic on Bell's part. Profits were made from long-lines rentals and equipment sales. More important, however, was Vail's idea to forestall independent entry into either long-distance lines or equipment manufacturing. Such a policy forced out of business some independent manufacturers, standardized at a higher quality telephone equipment among independents, and made future acquisition by and integration into Bell easier.

For the most part, Vail's policies were successful. After the Panic of 1907, independents ceased to grow very much, and until 1913 Bell followed a conscious policy of acquisition. Bell was never able to gain control of all local exchanges, nor was it completely successful in driving competing manufacturers out of business; however, it did completely dominate long-distance telephone service. In 1907 Bell gained control of Western Union, and Vail's dream of a single communications system came close to fruition. During the first decade of Vail's presidency, the Bell System operating companies began to be con-

---

38 *Ibid.*, Chapter 7.

39 See FCC, *Investigation of the Telephone Industry in the U.S.*, Comments Submitted to FCC by A.T. & T. Company on Exhibits 1989, 2110, and 2112, September and October, 1937, for a lengthy denial by the Bell System of charges of misuse of patents.

solidated, and the System as it is known today began to take shape.

(3) *Maturity and Regulation, 1913–1959.* The year 1913 was an important one in the telephone industry. Up until this time the Bell System had followed a conscious policy of absorbing independent companies and had gained control over Western Union. In 1913 the famous "Kingsbury Commitment" (named for N. C. Kingsbury, Vice-President of A.T. & T.) was made by A.T. & T. to the United States Department of Justice, in which the company agreed: (1) not to acquire competing companies; (2) to connect its long lines with other telephone companies; and (3) to divorce itself from Western Union. The System did not agree to forgo acquisition of noncompeting companies. This "commitment" was the outcome of a threatened antitrust suit by the Department of Justice. Vail, wishing to avoid the public notoriety such a case would draw, decided to concede various points to forestall antitrust action.

State regulation of telephone utilities began as early as 1907 in Wisconsin and was quickly adopted by other states. State regulation was successful in varying degrees. In 1910, the Mann-Elkins Act was passed placing interstate telephone service under the jurisdiction of the Interstate Commerce Commission.[40] Federal regulation under this Act consisted primarily of establishing a uniform system of accounts and a system of telephone depreciation accounting. More complete and more stringent federal regulation was imposed in 1934 by the Federal Communications Act.[41]

By 1959 A.T. & T. was one of the largest corporations in the United States, with assets in excess of $20 billion, net profits of more than $1.1 billion, almost 60 million telephones in use, 729,000 employees, and 1.7 million stockholders.[42]

B. Intercorporate Relations Within the Bell System. The Bell System is composed of American Telephone & Telegraph Company, a holding-operating company; 23 subsidiary or affiliated operating companies rendering telephone service to the public; plus Bell Telephone Laboratories, Inc., a research and development subsidiary; Western Electric Company, Inc., a manufacturing and purchasing subsidiary; and several miscellaneous subsidiaries holding real estate. Some of the A.T. & T. subsidiaries or affiliates have subsidaries of their own. Table 20.1 shows the amount of capital stock and the percentage of total stock owned by A.T. & T. in its affiliates and subsidiaries. Compared with the electric and gas holding companies of the 1920's, this mammoth system has been greatly streamlined and operates along fairly simple lines. A sketching of the relationships among the various parts of this system will point up both the advantages and the disadvantages of such arrangements.

(1) *A.T. & T. and the Associated Companies.* A.T. & T., the parent holding company of the Bell System, acts in several capacities. It is, for the most part, the money-raiser and over-all financial overseer of the System. It was pointed out in Chapter 19 that this is an awesome task for this large a system. A.T. & T. also maintains legal, rates and revenues, engineering, traffic, statistics, long-range planning, public relations, employee relations, marketing, and related departments which cooperate with and assist the associated companies. A.T. & T. also keeps detailed records on service performance of each office and exchange throughout the System. It

40 36 Stat. 539, Chapter 309.

41 See Chapter 13 for a detailed discussion of FCC regulation. See Chapter 11 for a description of the pricing of telephone service.

42 A.T. & T., *Annual Report, 1959.*

maintains, through its ownership of Western Electric and Bell Labs, a source of equipment, service, supplies, and technical know-how for the entire System. Finally, it operates the "Long Lines Department," which maintains the interstate long-distance service.

As early as 1885, the Bell System recognized the practicalities of having the long-distance telephone or toll oper-

Table 20.1

Subsidiaries and Affiliates of American Telephone & Telegraph Company, 1961

Affiliates	*Capital Stocks Owned by A.T. & T. Co.*		*Advances from A.T. & T. Co.*[a]
	% Owned	*Equity*[a]	
Principal Telephone Subsidiaries:			
New England Tel. & Tel. Co.	69.32	$ 447,018	$ 49,600
New York Tel. Co.	100.00	1,663,474	. . . . .
New Jersey Bell Tel. Co.	100.00	621,637	18,800
Bell Tel. Co. of Pennsylvania.	100.00	771,884	10,000
Diamond State Tel. Co..	100.00	50,497	1,300
Chesapeake & Potomac Tel. Co.	100.00	112,211	9,600
Chesapeake & Potomac Tel. Co. of Maryland	100.00	287,173	16,200
Chesapeake & Potomac Tel. Co. of Virginia. .	100.00	273,593	49,700
Chesapeake & Potomac Tel. Co. of W. Virginia	100.00	107,449	12,600
Southern Bell Tel. & Tel. Co.	100.00	1,548,600	39,500
Ohio Bell Tel. Co.	100.00	607,775	23,500
Michigan Bell Tel. Co.	100.00	490,521	22,000
Indiana Bell Tel. Co., Inc.	100.00	248,405	6,950
Wisconsin Tel. Co..	100.00	255,869	13,400
Illinois Bell Tel. Co.	99.32	914,949	25,500
Northwestern Bell Tel. Co.	100.00	522,701	22,000
Southwestern Bell Tel. Co.	100.00	1,548,493	113,800
Mountain States Tel. & Tel. Co.	86.75	511,176	81,900
Pacific Northwest Bell Tel. Co.	[b] 51.04	193,090	6,400
Pacific Tel. & Tel. Co.	89.62	1,667,634	. . . . .
Bell Tel. Co. of Nevada	[c]	. . . . .	. . . . .
Total		$12,844,149	$522,750
Subsidiaries Not Consolidated:			
Bell Telephone Laboratories, Inc.	[d] 50.00	$ 27,500	. . . . .
Western Electric Co., Inc.	99.82	1,142,310	40,000
195 Broadway Corporation	100.00	29,051	7,800
Other [e]	. . . . .	33,615	12,694
Total		$ 1,232,476	$ 60,494
		Cost [a]	
Other Companies:			
Southern New England Tel. Co.	18.91	$ 36,990	16,400
Cincinnati & Suburban Bell Tel. Co..	29.80	21,065	5,000
Bell Tel. Co. of Canada.	3.16	18,855	. . . . .
Miscellaneous investments [e]	. . . . .	32,473	. . . . .
Total		$ 109,383	$ 21,400

[a] Thousands of dollars.

[b] 42.72% owned by Pacific Tel. & Tel. Co.; equity in capital stock, $161,623.000. Also held demand note of $150,025,000.

[c] Wholly owned subsidiary of Pacific Tel. & Tel. Co.; equity in capital stock, $48,453,000.

[d] Remaining shares owned by Western Electric Company.

[e] Includes investments of principal telephone subsidiaries.

Source: A.T. & T., *Annual Report, 1961,* p. 32.

ations in a single organization. Early growth was slow because of the technical difficulties of transmitting messages over long distance. With the invention around 1900 of the "loading coil," which provided for the transmission of speech in a clear, efficient manner, long lines grew fairly rapidly. Further improvements in relay equipment pushed lines to the West and South. By 1914, the vacuum-tube repeater was in use, and the first transcontinental line was completed. In 1913, there were only 2,334 miles of toll wire in use. This figure had risen to 11,008 in 1929 and 15,396 in 1936.[43]

The "Long Lines Department" of A.T. & T. operates almost as a separate subsidiary. It is strictly an operating division which oversees most of the interstate toll business of the System in excess of 40 miles. Some operating companies operate their own interstate long-distance lines, while others handle only intrastate messages. In 1958, for example, the Long Lines Department of A.T. & T. handled only about 17 per cent of the total long-distance messages in the system but accounted for about 55 per cent of total toll revenues for the system.[44] There are actually two categories of long-distance calls. The interstate calls generally are for longer distance, use different equipment in many instances, and often have a better load factor than the short-haul intrastate calls. The allocation of costs between associated companies and the Long Lines Department has been a continuing problem for regulators. These problems of cost "separations" are discussed elsewhere.[45]

The division of toll revenues between an associated company and A.T. & T. is specifically set forth in a "license agreement" between the two companies.[46] This agreement stipulates the payment by A.T. & T. for toll calls originating at stations of associated companies, and also provides for a payment by the associated companies to A.T. & T. for the use of certain facilities and services.[47] There is relatively little controversy over this division of toll revenues.

A.T. & T., as a holding company, maintains relationships with its subsidiaries in addition to the long-lines connection, and these relationships have come in for considerable criticism over the history of the System.[48] In addition

[43] FCC, *Investigation of the Telephone Industry, op. cit.,* p. 359.

[44] A.T. & T. Company Records.

[45] See Chapter 11.

[46] Such license agreements contain provisions covering other important matters.

[47] The license agreement provides that the licensee (the associated operating company) shall receive compensation based ". . . upon communications originating at an exchange or toll station of the Licensee . . . and passing over the lines of the Licensor . . . , [with] compensation based upon the average revenue per originating message in accordance with the schedule of commissions set forth in Appendix A. . . ."

In addition, the license agreement provides that: "In consideration of the premises and for all benefits accruing to the Licensee hereunder, the Licensee shall pay the Licensor a sum equal to two and one-half percent (2½%) of the total gross earnings of the Licensee. . . ." This latter payment is discussed further below. American Telephone and Telegraph Company, *Agreement Between American Telephone and Telegraph Company and the Diamond State Telephone Company Covering Services, Licenses and Privileges,* May 26, 1931, and amended September 30, 1948, pp. 4–5. This license contract is merely used as an example of what is typical in the System.

[48] See House Committee on the Judiciary, *Hearings on the Consent Decree Program of the Department of Justice,* 85th Cong., 2d Sess., Part II, Vol. II, pp. 2508–2520 (Washington: Government Printing Office, 1958), for a Company Memorandum on these criticisms. There was, of course, a great deal of criticism of the acquisition, ownership, and control policies of A.T. & T. in the FCC, *Investigation of the Telephone Industry in the U.S.* See Chapters 4 through 6. In addition, the FCC–NARUC has had special committees from time to time which have made reports on corporate relationships within the System.

to providing long-distance connections, A.T. & T. agrees to provide the following services to its associated companies: (1) advice and assistance in general engineering, plant, traffic, operating, commercial, accounting, patent, legal, administrative, and other matters; (2) advice and assistance in any required financing; (3) cooperation in employee relations; and (4) maintenance of needed technical specialists and information to assure the smooth running of the business.[49]

The price that A.T. & T. charged for these services originally was 2½ per cent of the total gross earnings of the associated company. Because of criticism of this figure, and because of the difficulty of proving that the costs of the services to A.T. & T. were this amount, the figure was reduced first to 1½ per cent and ultimately to one per cent effective October 1, 1948.[50] In addition, A.T. & T. submits cost statements to associated companies. It should be noted that implicit in the license contract is the assurance to the associated company that it will enjoy the benefits of research and development work done by Bell Laboratories. Since precise cost allocations are virtually impossible to make for the services rendered by A.T. & T., the System is still questioned about the validity of the one per cent figure. The answer A.T. & T. gives is usually something like the following:

> I believe that this basis (1 percent of gross earnings) of determining the license payments is fair and reasonable as long as the amounts received are reasonable in relation to the costs incurred and the capital employed by the American Company in furnishing the services. . . . the American Company has realized little or no return on the capital employed in rendering these services.[51]

The Bell System generally does introduce cost-of-service studies to justify the one per cent. The state regulatory commissions who have considered the question of the license contract fees have found the one per cent fee to be reasonable. In all likelihood, one per cent does not cover the costs to A.T. & T. of rendering the services and is generally conceded to be far less than it would cost each associated company.[52]

(2) *A.T. & T. and Bell Labs.* There has been a great deal of emphasis on research ever since the beginnings of the Bell System. This research function was initially performed within both A.T. & T. and Western Electric. In 1924, Bell Telephone Laboratories, Inc. was established to take over the engineering and some of the patent aspects of Western Electric. In 1934 A.T. & T. transferred its research and development activities to the Labs. This organization carries on research in a wide variety of fields, some closely related to common-carrier communication, others seemingly quite unrelated to or far removed from the communication business but which actually play an important role in Bell System work. The Labs do basic research as well as product research.[53] The benefits from this research accrue to consumers of communications services through the operating subsidiaries of A.T. & T., either directly in the form of new methods or materials to use, or indirectly in the form of research done for Western Electric in the development of new equipment and supplies. The cost of research

[49] *Agreement Between A.T. & T. Co. and Diamond State Telephone, op. cit.*, pp. 4–5.

[50] *Ibid.*, attachment.

[51] Proposed testimony of Donald A. Dobbie before the Arkansas Public Service Commission, Docket U–1423 (1959).

[52] *Consent Decree Program, op. cit.*, pp. 2508–2520.

[53] Some "development" expense (as contrasted with research expense) is borne by Western Electric.

leading to direct benefits is paid for in the license contract fees paid to A.T. & T. by the associated companies, since A.T. & T. contributes to the budget of Bell Labs. The cost of research leading to the indirect benefits are paid for by the associated companies in the prices that Western Electric charges for the equipment and materials it supplies these operating companies. It seems highly probable that the "costs" of research result in savings for the System far in excess of the research costs themselves.

Table 20.2 shows the research and development expenditures by the Bell System from 1956 through 1959 and the relationship of these expenditures to product sales. Since the Bell Labs do a great deal of work for the federal government's defense program, the information is broken down between the Bell System and military accounts. The amounts involved are large and appear to be growing larger. However, in relation to the research accomplishments achieved, the amounts are very small.[54]

Some critics of the Bell System have argued that the Labs should be divorced from A.T. & T. and/or from Western Electric.[55] The benefits from such divorcement seem highly questionable. Consideration of this point will be taken up in the discussion of the Western Electric Company and the arguments for divorcing certain parts of the Bell System. Since all patents obtained by Bell Labs must be turned over to A.T. & T., Western Electric, or the federal government, discussion of this aspect of the System is best considered in the discussion of Western Electric also.

(3) *A.T. & T., Western Electric, and the Associated Companies.* Western

[54] See Chapter 21 for a discussion of new products and ideas on the horizon in the communications field.

[55] See, for example, *U.S.* v. *Western Electric Company, Inc. and American Telephone & Telegraph Company, Inc.*, Civil Action No. 17–49, U.S. District Court for New Jersey, Complaint, January 14, 1949, p. 71.

Table 20.2

Bell System Research and Development Expenditure

(Thousands)

	1956	*1957*	*1958*	*1959*
Expense:				
Bell	$ 88,125	$ 93,992	$ 100,506	$ 114,555
Military	55,400	69,358	76,224	115,200
Total	143,525	163,350	176,730	229,755
Product Sales:				
Bell [1,2]	1,788,895	1,964,597	1,650,600	1,680,000
Military[2]	625,000	561,000	568,000	670,000
Total	2,413,895	2,525,597	2,218,600	2,350,000
Expense/Sales:				
Bell	4.9%	4.8%	6.1%	6.8%
Military	8.9	12.4	13.4	17.2
Total	5.9	6.5	8.0	9.8

[1] Includes sales of standard telephone products to non-Bell companies and U.S. Government.

[2] Estimated.

Note: This information is based on reports to National Science Foundation, following the instructions accompanying its report form.

Source: A.T. & T., Company Records, 1960.

Electric is the manufacturing, purchasing, and warehousing subsidiary of the Bell System. It has been described in the following way:

> Generally, its function is twofold: First, it is the manufacturing branch of the Bell System; and second, it is the purchasing and supply department of the Bell System. In connection with its latter function, Western is also a developer, storekeeper, installer, repairer, salvager, and junker of the Bell System.[56]

As a purchaser it ranks second only to the federal government. It spent over one billion dollars in 1959 alone and maintains a large organization to handle this aspect of its business.[57]

Western Electric, taken by itself, is a large manufacturing corporation and, in fact, ranked tenth among United States manufacturing corporations in 1959, measured by sales.[58] At the end of 1959 its gross plant amounted to more than $912 million, and during that year sales were $2,278 million, off slightly from a peak of almost $2,448 million in 1957. Sales to Bell companies accounted for 69 per cent of the total in 1959, while 29 per cent went to the federal government and the remainder to other customers, some of whom were Western's subsidiaries.[59] At the end of 1959 there were about 130,000 employees scattered in hundreds of manufacturing and service jobs throughout the nation. The company owned or leased 56 manufacturing or related plants and maintained "distributing houses" in 32 major cities to supply materials to the System. These distribution centers also have facilities for inspecting, repairing, salvaging, and junking materials flowing to or from the associated companies.[60]

Western's relationships with associated Bell companies are largely governed by what is known as a "Standard Supply Contract." This contract covers all the various functions that Western performs for an associated company and generally sets the terms on which business will be done between the two companies. The contract is quite general in nature and appears to bind only one of the parties, Western, to deal with the operating company, and not vice versa. This nominally leaves the operating companies free to purchase from anyone. As a practical matter, Western's prices are usually the lowest (although there are a few exceptions). This, plus the need for standardization within the System, makes extensive outside purchasing impractical.

The Standard Supply Contract is more a working agreement arrived at over years of close working relationships within the System than a competitively negotiated, arm's-length contract.[61] The contract is quite general with regard to prices and terms. It merely states that: "The Electric Company's prices and terms shall be as low as to its most favored customers for like materials and services under comparable conditions."[62] Price lists are published by

---

56 FCC, *Investigation of the Telephone Industry, op. cit.*, p. 35. See also the annual reports of the FCC–NARUC.

57 See the September 29, 1959 issue of *Purchasing* magazine for an excellent discussion of purchasing done by Western Electric.

58 *Fortune*, Directory of 500 largest United States industrial corporations, August, 1960.

59 FCC–NARUC, *Subcommittee Report on Western Electric*, 1960, pp. 7 and 10.

60 A.T. & T., Company Records.

61 The supply contract reads as follows: "The Electric Company (Western) will manufacture or purchase materials which the Telephone Company may reasonably require for its business and which it may order from the Electric Company; provided, however, that nothing contained herein obligates the Telephone Company to purchase any materials from the Electric Company." Western Electric Company, Inc., *Standard Supply Contract*, June 2, 1930 and supplements, Article I, Section 1.

62 *Ibid.*, Article II, Section 1.

Western insofar as is practicable, and it is these price lists which establish price levels for Western's equipment rather than the supply contract itself. The NARUC–FCC committee reporting on Western Electric came to the following conclusion about supply contracts:

> But, in view of the intercorporate relationship between the Bell companies and Western, the reasonableness of those business practices cannot be taken as supported or established by the fact that they are provided for in the Standard Supply Contract. For the same reason, the reasonableness of the level of Western's prices cannot be taken as supported or established by the fact that the procedures for the setting of such prices, and the general terms and conditions relating thereto, are provided for in the Standard Supply Contract.[63]

As is true for any large industrial firm, it is difficult if not impossible to determine whether specific prices of Western are and have been reasonable or not. Clearly, Congress was aware of the potential problem area when it passed the Communications Act of 1934. Section 215a reads, in part, as follows:

> The Commission shall examine into transactions entered into by any common carrier which relate to the furnishing of equipment, supplies, research, services, finances, credit, or personnel to such carrier . . . and shall report to Congress whether any such transactions . . . may result in any undue or unreasonable increase in charges . . . , and the Commission shall have the access to and the right of inspection and examination of all accounts, records and memoranda . . . of persons furnishing such equipment. . . .[64]

The FCC in administering the Act has not asked for more powers in this area, except the power to set up a system of accounts for Western Electric.[65] This power has not been granted, or, if it can be implied from other specific powers, the FCC has not undertaken the task as yet. The FCC in 1948 did undertake jointly with the National Association of Railroad and Utility Commissioners (NARUC) a study of Western Electric's prices, accounting procedures, and profits. This study was updated in 1958 and is under continuous review by a committee of the NARUC.[66] It contains the most complete analysis of Western's pricing methods, as well as of its profit status, that has ever been made.

Prices for individual products manufactured by Western are built upon the "shop costs" of the product. A standard cost system is used wherein the labor, materials, and manufacturing overhead are predetermined, assuming efficient operating conditions. Variations from the predetermined costs are recorded and adjustments made periodically to compensate for these variations. To the standard shop cost are added:

1. Average expected variations during the period the price will be in effect;
2. Development and special engineering expense;
3. Merchandising and general expenses;
4. Federal income taxes, and
5. A margin of profit.[67]

One measure of "reasonable" prices is the profits that accrue from these prices. Another measure is a comparison with

---

63 NARUC–FCC, *Report on Western Electric,* original report, p. 30.

64 47 USC 215a.

65 FCC, *Investigation of the Telephone Industry,* pp. 585–586 and 601.

66 NARUC–FCC Staff Committee on Telephone Regulatory Problems, *Report on Preliminary Survey and Investigation of Western Electric Company, Inc.* (New York: July 15, 1948), mimeo.; and *Report on Operating Results of Western Electric Company, Incorporated, Years 1947 to 1957 Inclusive* (New York: September 1958), mimeo.

67 *Ibid.,* p. 126.

competitors' prices. By both these measures, Western comes off quite well. During 1958, the Antitrust Subcommittee of the House Committee on the Judiciary looked into the question of price comparisons, and the evidence was overwhelmingly in favor of Western.

Western Electric's return on investment also appears to be low relative to other major manufacturing companies. Between 1947 and 1959, Western's rate of return exceeded the average for the 50 major companies in only three years. Compared with General Electric and Westinghouse, Western was consistently lower.

Some critics of Western Electric have not always accepted price and profit comparisons as proof of reasonableness. For example, the Wisconsin Public Service Commission stated that:

> With respect to price comparisons, the Commission is satisfied both from this record and its experiences in the regulation of independent companies in this state that for the most part Western's prices are lower than those of other manufacturing companies and in some instances the differentials are substantial. However, such a result is reasonably to be expected because of its relationship to the Bell System. Western for all practical purposes has a budgeted market. It incurs practically no selling expense and because of the certainty and stability of its market, it is able to conform its manufacturing equipment and labor force to the requirements of its assured customers. Also its size in relation to other manufacturers of similar equipment is a dominant factor. . . . A still further advantage in favor of Western is that a part of the cost of fundamental research and development in connection with new telephone products is borne directly by the . . . operating companies through . . . American Telephone and Telegraph Company.
>
> * * * * *
>
> The reasonableness of Western's profits from sales to Bell companies properly should be considered from the standpoint of a manufacturing company which enjoys a greater freedom from risk than most if not all other manufacturing companies. . . . As a general proposition, the Commission believes that Western's return on investment from sales to Bell customers should not deviate substantially from the returns earned by regulated public utilities.[68]

Despite the comments by the Wisconsin Commission, it has never disallowed part of a rate base because the prices of Western Electric were found to be too high.[69]

Generally speaking, Western Electric's pricing policies have had tacit or formal approval from regulatory bodies.[70] An example of the type of approving statement of Western's policies is found in a North Dakota telephone rate case:

> The evidence shows that Western Electric prices are, in general lower than those obtained by other manufactures of comparable equipment, and that its average return on investment from 1916 to 1950 was 7.6 per cent. Because of Western's dominant size in relation to other manufacturers of similar equipment, the certainty of its market, and the fact that normally ninety per cent of its sales are made to affiliated companies, this Commission feels that the reasonableness of Western prices cannot be determined by price comparison alone. However, it does not appear from the evidence introduced that Western's earnings over the years have been excessive, particularly, when compared to those of other companies in the manufacturing industry. We are not, therefore, making any

---

68 *Re Wisconsin Telephone Company,* 80 PUR (NS) 482 (1949).

69 See also FCC, *Investigation of the Telephone Industry,* pp. 586–589, for a discussion of price comparisons. See *op. cit., Consent Decree Program,* pp. 2313–2343, for a series of excerpts from state rate-case decisions generally approving Western Electric's pricing practices and profits.

70 California is a major exception. It has disallowed some of Western's prices for rate-base computations. See *Re Pacific Telephone & Telegraph Company,* 5 PUR 3d 396 (1954).

adjustments in the equipment costs of the applicant.[71]

A big stumbling block to finding an answer to this question is the standard shop cost accounting procedures, which some critics claim do not give the best cost picture. Such accounting practices are not unique to Western; several large multi-product manufacturing firms use this technique. In the recent consent judgment agreed to by Western and A.T. & T., this problem was recognized and an attempt at a solution was made by the inclusion of the following statement:

> Western is ordered and directed to maintain cost accounting methods that conform with such accounting principles as may be generally accepted and that afford a valid basis . . . for determining the cost to Western of equipment sold to A.T. & T. and Bell Operating Companies. . . .[72]

It is too soon to tell what impact this mandate will have on Western's prices, or just what changes, if any, will be made in Western's cost accounting procedures.

Generally speaking, the Bell System is the only major public utility that maintains its own manufacturing subsidiary to furnish equipment and supplies to the operating end of the business. (General Telephone and Electronics Company also has a manufacturing arm.) This unique aspect of the Bell System has brought forth criticism over the years and in 1949 resulted in an antitrust complaint with was settled by a consent judgment in 1956.[73]

Some of the allegations made against the A.T. & T.–Western relationship are as follows:

1. The rate bases of the associated Bell companies and of the Long Lines Department of A.T. & T. are in large part a function of the prices charged by Western Electric for equipment, materials, and labor. Yet Western Electric, being a manufacturing company, is not regulated as a public utility, hence the prices it charges are not subject to regulatory scrutiny.

2. Western Electric and A.T. & T. have been accused of monopolizing the production, manufacture, distribution, sale, and installation of telephones and related apparatus and supplies, and thus being inimical to the public interest.[74]

3. A.T. & T. and Western Electric have been charged, also, with "bigness," and the alleged evils that accompany bigness.

None of these issues have ever been brought to trial, and some are, on the surface, quite desirable and appropriate, depending on what philosophy of regulation is chosen. This question of regulatory philosophy appears to be at the heart of the matter. To accuse A.T. & T. and Western Electric of bigness raises the question of whether, in public utility regulation, the nation wishes to have monopoly or competition. This question will be discussed below. If the decision is for monopoly, then bigness is ideal. The questions of acquisitions, control over long lines, non-entry by competitors, and patent control also revolve around the issue of monopoly versus competition.

The 1956 consent decree left the intercorporate relationships within the Bell System virtually unchanged,[75] al-

[71] *Re Northwestern Bell Telephone Company, Finding of Fact, Conclusions of Law, and Order,* North Dakota Public Service Commission, February 15, 1952.

[72] *U.S.* v. *Western Electric Company, Inc., and A.T. & T. Company,* Final Judgment, Article IX, January 24, 1956.

[73] *U.S.* v. *Western Electric Company, Inc., and A.T. & T. Company, op. cit.,* Final Judgment, January 24, 1956.

[74] *Ibid.* See "Complaint," pp. 20 ff., for offenses charged the companies.

[75] A.T. & T. and Western must get out of all business not directly related to communications, and they must license all patents, present and future, to any American concern. The latter requirement they are already fulfilling.

though Western's regulatory status seems uncertain. There has been some criticism of the government in not pressing for divorcement of A.T. & T. and Western instead of merely bringing Western closer to public utility status.[76]

If Western Electric is to be, in fact, made or left a public utility, should it be regulated as such (at least, that part of Western's business done with the rest of the Bell System)? This would involve much more stringent price and profit regulation, a task which the FCC is probably not able to undertake without clarifying legislation and which it is probably not willing to undertake even if allowed to do so. Western itself has done much to forestall such regulation by maintaining relatively low prices and low profits while furnishing continuingly improved equipment.

The real impact of the consent decree on the Bell System was one which apparently was not felt to be important at the time but which may turn out to be extremely burdensome. A.T. & T. is prohibited from engaging in the private communications business and Western is prohibited from manufacturing equipment for such business. If, as appears likely in the future, private radio and wire service become widely used, the Bell System will find that it has agreed not to enter this business.

One final comment is necessary to round out the picture of Western Electric and A.T. & T., namely the relationship of the System to major manufacturers of electrical equipment. Bell has maintained for many years patent cross-licensing agreements with General Electric, Westinghouse Electric, RCA, and other companies. Under these agreements there was some exclusive patent licensing in both directions to the benefit of those concerned. In recent years the Bell System has adopted in almost all cases a policy of nonexclusive licensing and is quite explicit in pointing out that

> The major objective of this policy is to obtain non-exclusive licenses under the patents of our licensees in order that we may be free to design and manufacture the best possible equipment. . . . In addition to freedom of design, other important consequences follow from our licensing policy: The amount of patent search to determine whether we are infringing the patents of others is greatly reduced, the existence of a cross-license agreement permits freedom of scientific liaison with our Licensees. These mutual privileges are regarded by BTL [Bell Labs] as the most important result of cross-licensing.[77]

C. Acquisition Policies of A.T. & T. Much of the early history of the growth of the Bell System was discussed earlier and need not be repeated here. However, it is important to note the general policies for expansion that A.T. & T. has followed in recent years. It will be recalled that A.T. & T. obtained from many of its operating licensees a substantial share of stock in the particular operating company. This was in exchange for the exclusive use of Bell equipment in a given geographic area. Many small independents willingly joined the Bell System in order to enjoy the benefits of Bell patents, know-how, and credit rating. In 1907 the Bell System and independent companies each owned about half of the telephones in the nation. However, between 1907 and 1912 Bell had increased its share from 51 per cent to 58 per cent of the total number of telephones.

In early 1913, the United States Attorney General expressed the opinion that some proposed acquisitions by Bell companies would be in violation of the Sherman Antitrust Law. At this point

[76] John Sheahan, "Integration and Exclusion in the Telephone Equipment Industry," 70 *Quarterly Journal of Economics* 249, 267 (1956).

[77] *Consent Decree Program, op. cit.*, pp. 2626–2627.

the Bell System formulated in a letter to the Attorney General what has come to be known as "The Kingsbury Commitment." This letter reads, in part, as follows:

> Neither the American Telephone & Telegraph Company nor any other company in the Bell System will hereafter acquire, directly or indirectly, through purchase of its physical property or of its securities or otherwise, dominion or control over any other telephone company owning, controlling or operating any exchange or line which is or may be operated in competition with any exchange or line included in the Bell System or which constitute or may constitute a link or portion of any system so operated or which may be so operated in competition with any exchange or line included in the Bell System.[78]

Thus the Bell System agreed not to acquire any competing company. In the letter A.T. & T. also agreed to make toll-line connections with independent companies and to dispose of Western Union. It is important to note that there was no restriction on Bell System acquisitions of noncompeting independents. By 1917, Bell had increased its dominance in the industry so that it controlled 63 per cent of the telephones. Presumably this growth was from internal expansion of existing companies plus the acquisition of some noncompeting companies.

In 1917 a modification was made in the Kingsbury Commitment in which Bell informally agreed to acquire competing companies only if it gave up an equal number of telephones to an independent company. Such an arrangement was exceedingly difficult to manage, since there might be two or more independent companies involved. The FCC reported that between 1914 and 1921 the Bell System gained 303,378 stations through purchase.[79] The problems of the Bell System during this period in abiding by the Kingsbury Commitment are often overlooked. Bell was obviously the most attractive potential purchaser to anyone who had an independent to sell. This was true not just because of financial strength, but also because the acquired property would probably be more valuable as part of the Bell System than as an independent. The Justice Department, in view of the then prevalent "rule of reason," was in no position to prosecute A.T. & T. for violation of the Sherman Act. By 1921 it was clear that the independents were losing ground rapidly and would never be a serious threat to the Bell System.

Also in 1921, the Willis-Graham Act was passed,[80] which amended the Transportation Act of 1920 to allow competitive companies to consolidate without fear of antitrust prosecution if they first obtained approval of the appropriate state authorities and the Interstate Commerce Commission.[81] The Bell System asked the Justice Department to clarify the status of the Kingsbury Commitment and was informed that it could consider the Commitment terminated.[82] Bell acquisitions increased markedly, so that by 1922 about 66 per cent of the telephones of the nation were in the Bell System.

By mid-1922, there was considerable apprehension in the independent segment of the industry over Bell acquisitions. A.T. & T., after considerable nego-

---

[78] Letter from Mr. N. C. Kingsbury, Vice-President of A.T. & T., to the Attorney General of the United States, December 19, 1913.

[79] *FCC, Investigation of the Telephone Industry, op. cit.*, p. 140.

[80] 42 Stat. 27, Chap. 20.

[81] The Willis-Graham Act later became part of Section 221(a) of the Communications Act of 1934.

[82] "You may therefore consider as terminated and no longer effective the agreements contained in . . . the letter of your company to the Attorney General . . . usually referred to as the 'Kingsbury Commitment.' " Letter from Attorney General to E. K. Hall, Vice-President of A.T. & T., September 19, 1921.

tiation, sent to the United States Independent Telephone Association (USITA) a statement of Bell acquisition policy. This became known as the "Hall Memorandum." It reads, in part, as follows:

> . . . the general policy of this Company and its associated companies is today, and so far as we can foresee will continue to be, not to purchase or consolidate with connecting or duplicating companies except in special cases.
>
> * * * * *
>
> We should consider that such an exception was proved only in cases where it seemed to be demanded either:
>
> (1) For the convenience of the public as evidenced by the wishes of States authorities or by local public sentiment in or adjoining the territory served; or
>
> (2) By special reason which made the transaction seem desirable and essential from the point of view of the protection of our own property or the general public service.
>
> * * * * *
>
> Types of cases which might be expected to come up for consideration under the second general classification would be:
>
> 1. Companies in which we now have a disproportionately large investment without actual control.
>
> 2. *Cases where connecting company or other telephone property is pressed for sale, and where it seems that the general public service will be improved by its operation as a integral part of our service.* [Emphasis supplied.][83]

The Memorandum further stated that the USITA would be given notice 30 days before any formal acquisition agreement was consummated, and 30 days before A.T. & T. or a Bell company filed with a regulatory commission for approval of an application to acquire another company.

The Hall Memorandum stood as Company policy, although several small modifications were made and considerable discussion ensued over the problem of Bell "relinquishments." Considerable pressure was put on Bell to adopt a "balancing purchases agreement" in which Bell would agree to sell stations to independents in a number equal to the number acquired by Bell. A.T. & T. refused to adopt this plan, and stated that ". . . we feel that for us to agree with your Association that in case of a purchase of . . . telephone stations by some Bell Company, we would at some time, somewhere and for some unknown consideration, sell a substantially similar number of stations, would be unbusinesslike, imprudent and absolutely unjustifiable from any point of view. It is too much like drawing a blank check."[84]

Over the years, the Bell System has practiced a policy of disposing of minority stock interests in independent companies and to some extent has made offsetting sales to independents when acquisitions were made by Bell. However, A.T. & T. steadfastly refused to make any formal agreement with regard to balancing purchases. In late 1943, two Bell operating companies applied to the FCC for approval of acquisition of the Keystone Telephone Company of Philadelphia. The USITA filed no objections and the application was approved. This removed the last major city in which competition existed between Bell and independent companies. The USITA was advised by legal counsel shortly after this acquisition that there were no legal grounds for demanding balancing purchases from Bell, but that Bell acquisitions could conceivably be construed as violations of the Sherman Act. It was felt that this was true despite the Communi-

---

[83] Letter from E. K. Hall, Vice-President of A.T. & T., to F. B. MacKinnon, President, USITA, June 14, 1922.

[84] Letter from E. K. Hall, Vice-President of A.T. & T., to F. B. MacKinnon, President of USITA, April 14, 1926.

cations Act Section 221 mandate that acquisitions be approved.[85]

In 1954 another problem arose involving a proposed Bell acquisition of the Tomball, Texas exchange. The USITA complained bitterly that two independents were willing and able to acquire this exchange and urged that Southwestern Bell recede from its commitment to acquire. Bell replied that "Mr. Hall's letter of June 14, 1922, which was discussed thoroughly with you and other members of your Committee in February, covers quite clearly that there will be from time to time special cases under which the Bell System companies would want to purchase Independent company property. . . . We consider the Tomball case to be such a special case."[86] A.T. & T. further stated that "Southwestern Bell proposes to buy the property for the protection of its own property and in the interest of the general public service and to this end has taken an option upon its purchase."[87] The Tomball situation brought about a request from the USITA that the 30-day notice procedure carried on by Bell be discontinued. This, no doubt, was meant to be a criticism of Bell policy and an indication that Bell was acting in bad faith. This action did not seem to influence the Bell System's policies in any way.

Critics of the Bell System claim that the Hall Memorandum is open-ended and can be interpreted as broadly as Bell wishes. Actually, what has happened is that the "exceptions" noted in the memorandum have become the rule, and acquisitions have resulted because of distress situations or because an independent or its users have approached Bell. Under these circumstances, charges by the USITA that Bell's policy is unfair are hard to substantiate.

A recent acquisition case points up some of these problems. Section 221a of the Communications Act of 1934 states, in part ". . . that if the Commission finds that the proposed consolidation, acquisition, or control will be of advantage to the persons to whom service is to be rendered *and in the public interest,* it shall certify to that effect; and thereupon any Act or Acts of Congress [that is, antitrust laws] making the proposed transactions unlawful shall not apply." [Emphasis supplied.][88] Under this provision the Wisconsin Telephone Company filed for a certificate approving its application to acquire the properties of the Menomonee Falls Telephone Company and the Lisbon Telephone Corporation.[89] The USITA requested a public hearing, at which time it protested the acquisition on the grounds that "Application of the public interest standard of Section 221(a) requires consideration of competitive factors and of the national policy set forth in the anti-trust laws."[90] The Wisconsin Public Service Commission supported Wisconsin Bell's application for a certificate.

To achieve the desired competitive conditions in this and other cases, the independents have urged upon Bell the following four proposals:

(a) The Bell System should make offsetting sales to equalize net station gains resulting from Bell System acquisitions of Independent telephone properties; (b) the

[85] *Memorandum Opinion Rendered to the USITA,* by Winthrop, Stimson, Putnam & Roberts, February 7, 1944.

[86] Letter from G. L. Best, Vice-President of A.T. & T., to H. A. Barnhart, Chairman of the Bell Acquisitions Committee of the USITA, August 6, 1954.

[87] Letter from J. T. Quisenberry, General Solicitor of A.T. & T., to C. S. Bailey, Executive Vice-President of the USITA, August 6, 1954.

[88] 47 USC 221a.

[89] FCC, *Re Wisconsin Telephone Company,* Docket No. 12308, decision July 6, 1959.

[90] *Ibid.,* "Proposed Findings of Fact and Conclusions by USITA," July 1, 1958, p. 59, mimeo.

Bell System should dispose of its minority stock interests in Independent telephone properties; (c) the Bell System should give the Independent industry notice of its intention to negotiate for the acquisition of an Independent property before an option or agreement to buy is secured; and (d) the Bell System should withdraw from a proposed acquisition of an Independent property when another Independent is ready, willing, and able to purchase the property involved and provide adequate telephone service.[91]

A realistic appraisal of these proposals clearly indicates that they are unworkable and would not in most cases benefit the public in any direct fashion. The proposal to make offsetting sales has as its rationale that it is desirable to keep some sort of balance between Bell and the independents, apparently with no regard to the social cost that might be involved. Bell has been and is disposing of its minority stock interests in independent companies. The third proposal, that of advance notice, would benefit no one except the seller of the independent property, who would profit if competitive bidding ensued. The last proposal is also unfeasible and rests on the assumption that independent ownership is socially better and more desirable than Bell ownership. Certainly here is a situation in which public interest as enunciated in the antitrust laws is at variance with the public-interest concept in public utility regulation. In this particular case, the independents involved offered substantially less than the Bell Company. Also, Wisconsin Bell had attempted to work out a trade of a like number of stations and had been rejected. Lastly, Wisconsin Bell had been approached by the independent, and not vice versa. The FCC granted the certificate to the Bell Company for the acquisition.

The details in this case are presented to point up the problems that a regulatory commission has in deciding telephone acquisition cases. The Bell System has been quite careful not to acquire independents in an aggressive fashion. It has urged a policy of integration of both the Bell and independent systems. It has frequently upgraded service while not changing rates. In such cases as this, should competition be perpetuated? Some suggestions are given in the last section of this chapter.

91 *Ibid.*, p. 40.

3. ANTITRUST PROBLEMS IN PUBLIC UTILITY INDUSTRIES

In Chapter 2 it was pointed out that natural monopoly is an essential characteristic of a public utility because utility activities are such that one firm brings better service at lower cost to the public than several competing firms. Public utility regulation recognizes and approves monopoly and regulates the monopolistic firm in a manner calculated to promote the public interest.

In this chapter we have examined what has happened when several noncompeting natural monopolies are combined under the control of a single holding company. In the case of the gas and electric holding companies of the 1920's, the net effect on the public interest was detrimental. The upshot of this was the passage of a special "antitrust" law for gas and electric utilities—the Public Utility Holding Company Act. Under this Act the chains of natural monopolies in gas and electricity were broken apart, not so as to achieve competition among the pieces, but so as to reduce the concentration of economic power under the control of one person or group. This action has been partly responsible for the healthy gas and electric industry we have today. In the case of the natural monopolies in the telephone industry, there has been a giant holding-company system created whose history has been quite different. Thus far no similar "antitrust" law has been necessary in the telephone industry to curb practices which are not in the public interest.

An important question in public utility regulation, which has largely gone unanswered, concerns this aspect of industrial organization and structure. Is it possible for the general public to enjoy the benefits accruing from regulated public utilities and at the same time to be protected by "antitrust" laws against the potential dangers generated by allowing natural monopolies to grow larger than is necessary? This is not a question of restoring, maintaining, or creating competition so much as it is a question of suppressing size and the potential dangers that this nation has always felt go along with bigness. The remainder of this section will take up several aspects of the problem of applying the antitrust laws to public utilities which are legally sanctioned monopolies.

A good place to begin is in an examination of the attitudes of experts in the antitrust field toward regulated industry. For example, the Attorney General's National Committee to Study the Antitrust Laws stated in 1955 that:

> This Committee, we repeat, endorses competition as the major rule in our private enterprise economy. We recognize that competition can be impaired either by conduct transgressing the antitrust laws or by government regulation fixing prices or rates or restricting freedom of entry. The Committee notes an apparent trend toward such government control. We call attention to the fact that such regulation tends to beget further regulation.
>
> * * * * *
>
> Even in the areas where Congress has adopted the policy that " 'competition' may [not] have full play," we feel that unless Congress has expressly provided to the contrary, the regulatory guide consistent with the "public interest" as applied to mergers must "include the principles of free enterprise which have long distinguished our economy." It is no longer subject to challenge that "competition is a relevant factor in weighing the public interest." [Footnotes omitted; brackets in the original.]
>
> * * * * *
>
> Where Congress has been silent, the basic policy of our antitrust laws requires the Court's conclusion that competition, at least where all other considerations involved are equal, is in the "public interest." In all instances, the courts, in reviewing agency discretion, should recognize that "administrative authority to grant exemptions from the antitrust laws should be closely confined to those (instances) where the . . . (regulatory) need is clear." [Footnotes omitted; parentheses in the original.][92]

A recent Staff Report of the House Committee on the Judiciary stated that:

> In administering a potential exemption, the agency is guided by the public interest. Although the precise statutory language invoking the public interest, as well as agency interpretations thereunder, differ from industry to industry, the public interest has been authoritatively held to include not only the specific protective policy of the regulatory act, but also the general national policy to encourage competition as embodied in the antitrust laws. [Footnote omitted.] In short, the existence of regulation does not of itself repeal the antitrust laws or exempt the regulated industries; the agency is required to accommodate the sometimes conflicting policies of the two enactments.[93]

A. *The Doctrine of Primary Jurisdiction.* It is important that the procedural ques-

[92] *Report of the Attorney General's National Committee to Study the Antitrust Laws* (Washington: Government Printing Office, 1955), pp. 269–270.

[93] Staff Report to the Antitrust Subcommittee of the Committee on the Judiciary, House of Representatives, *Judicial Doctrine of Primary Jurisdiction as Applied in Antitrust Suits,* 84th Cong., 2nd sess. (Washington: Government Printing Office, 1956), pp. 1–2.

tion of "primary jurisdiction" be resolved before the more basic question of public interest is explored. This doctrine, as clearly stated by the United States Supreme Court, is

> [A] principle, now firmly established, that in cases raising issues of fact not within the conventional experience of judges or cases requiring the exercise of administrative discretion, agencies created by Congress for regulating the subject matter should not be passed over. . . . Uniformity and consistency in the regulation of business entrusted to a particular agency are secured, and the limited functions of review by the Judiciary are more rationally exercised, by preliminary resort for ascertaining and interpreting the circumstances underlying legal issues to agencies that are better equipped than courts by specialization, by insight gained through experience, and by more flexible procedure.[94]

In other words, an industry cannot simultaneously have two masters in regulatory matters; one body must consistently be recognized as having primary jurisdiction. Questions subject to judicial review must be significantly narrowed, but some degree of judicial review must be maintained.[95] Critics of the application of the doctrine maintain that the courts have gone too far in allowing commissions to displace the competitive antitrust-law standards with their expert judgment.[96]

As early as 1907, the United States Supreme Court held that to permit court action for the recovery of unreasonable rates by a rail shipper, when the rates had the approval of the ICC, would thwart the intent of Congress to establish uniform rate regulation through this agency.[97] Under such an interpretation, access to the court was denied in many instances where the expertise of a commission was needed to decide a question. By 1922, this rather strict interpretation was altered by the Supreme Court when it held that there is some line of demarcation beyond which the expert body steps aside and a court takes over.[98] Just where that line lies in regard to the application of the antitrust laws to public utilities has not been firmly established, although a number of cases have been decided which concern regulated industries. For some industries, the statutory exemptions from the antitrust laws are expressly stated, while for others such express exemption is missing. A decision involving the air-carrier industry succinctly sets down the policy in situations where the exemption is specific.

> [In] Each case brought against a regulated company under the antitrust laws, the subject matter and remedy afforded by the regulatory statute are compared with that of the antitrust laws. If the latter either covers subject matter outside the scope of the Commission's power or provides a remedy which the Commission may not give, then they remain in effect to that limited extent. This sort of approach gives the greatest possible effect to Congressional intent. It subjects problems tended to be dealt with in a uniform manner within the framework of a particular industry to the agency empowered to regulate that industry. At the same time it gives effect to the antitrust laws in those areas not carved out

---

94 *United States* v. *Far East Conference,* 342 U.S. 570, 574–575 (1952).

95 For arguments advocating a doctrine of primary jurisdication in regulatory matters, see Robert von Mehren, "The Antitrust Laws and Regulated Industries: The Doctrine of Primary Jurisdiction," 67 *Harvard Law Review* 929 (1954).

96 See, for example, Louis B. Schwartz, "Legal Restriction of Competition in the Regulated Industries: An Abdication of Judicial Responsibility," 67 *Harvard Law Review* 436 (1954), for approval of the doctrine but criticism of its application by the courts.

97 *Abilene Cotton Oil Co.* v. *Texas Pacific Railway Company,* 204 U.S. 426 (1907).

98 *Great Northern Railway Company* v. *Merchants Elevator Company,* 259 U.S. 285 (1922).

from them by more specific economic regulations.[99]

Such a policy seems appropriate for specific exemptions, and to do otherwise would be contrary to congressional intent. In cases where there is no statutory language denying antitrust applications, the problems are compounded. What if a commission in administering a regulatory statute in what it considers to be the best possible way approves some action by a company under its jurisdiction which action later becomes the basis for an antitrust charge? One view is that commission approval is sufficient grounds for dropping antitrust charges. The other view is

> . . . in the absence of express antitrust exemption, Congress did not intend that administrative agencies should, in all cases, be the sole forum for determination of antitrust questions stemming from conduct subject to their jurisdiction. This is especially so . . . since *it is by no means clear that the courts will closely scrutinize agency determinations of the weight given to factors in evaluating public interest.* [Emphasis supplied.][100]

B. *Public Interest.* It would appear then, that the ultimate question lies in a definition of "public interest."[101] The courts have assiduously maintained the responsibility to themselves to decide ". . . whether the Commission has been guided by proper consideration in bringing the deposit of its . . . experience . . . to bear . . . in [determining] the public interest."[102] Is it possible that the "public interest" concept may have a different meaning in public utility regulation from what it has in antitrust regulation? Ideally and ultimately, "public interest" must mean the same thing in both sets of regulations. However, the standards by which an action or situation is judged to be or not to be in the public interest appear to diverge in some instances. The divergence of standards stems, in part, from the aims of utility regulation and the aims of antitrust regulation. Utility regulation gives legal sanction to monopoly, while antitrust regulation is designed to promote, restore, or maintain competition and prohibit monopoly.

A recent Federal Power Commission case illustrates the dilemma of the situation. El Paso Natural Gas Company, which obtains gas primarily in west Texas and New Mexico, is the major wholesaler of gas in California, Nevada, and Arizona, and until recently the only out-of-state line serving California. In early 1957, El Paso acquired control of the stock of the Pacific Northwest Pipeline Corporation, a relatively new company marketing gas in the Pacific Northwest and obtaining gas supplies in New Mexico, the Rocky Mountain region, and Canada.

On July 22, 1957, the United States Department of Justice brought a civil suit against El Paso and Pacific Northwest charging them with violation of Section 7 of the Clayton Act.[103] Section 7 of the Clayton Act states that

> . . . no corporation engaged in commerce shall acquire, directly or indirectly, the whole or any part of the stock . . . and no corporation . . . shall acquire the whole

---

[99] *S.S.W. Inc.*, v. *Air Transport Association,* 191 F. 2d 658, 661–662 (1951).

[100] Both of these views are found in the *Report of Committee to Study Antitrust Laws, op. cit.*, p. 283.

[101] For a discussion of the problem of the "public interest" in conservation and utility regulation, see Wallace F. Lovejoy, "Gas Conservation and Public Utility Regulation in Our National Fuels Policy," 1 *Natural Resources Journal* 257 (November 1961).

[102] *FCC* v. *R.C.A. Communications, Inc.*, 346 U.S. 86, 91 (1953).

[103] *U.S.* v. *El Paso Natural Gas Company and Pacific Northwest Pipeline Corp.,* U.S. District Court for Utah, Civil Action No. 143–57, July 22, 1957.

or any part of the assets of another corporation engaged also in commerce, where in any line of commerce in any section of the country, the effect of such acquisition may be substantially to lessen competition, or to tend to create a monopoly.[104]

This action was taken by the Justice Department despite a further provision in the Clayton Act which states that "Nothing contained in this section shall apply to transactions duly consummated pursuant to authority given by the . . . Federal Power Commission . . . under any statutory provision vesting such power in such Commission. . . ."[105] At the time the suit was brought, El Paso had not applied to the FPC for a certificate of public convenience and necessity authorizing its acquisition of the facilities of Pacific Northwest. However, in less than three weeks such an application was filed with the FPC, and the District Court postponed hearing the antitrust case awaiting FPC determination. After a hearing, the FPC presiding examiner provisionally granted the certificate,[106] and the full Commission approved the examiner's recommendation with slight modifications.[107] The examiner pointed out that the Clayton Act ". . . placed Congressional reliance upon the Commission, acting under the Natural Gas Act, not to approve an acquisition of assets the effect of which would be 'substantially to lessen competition, or to tend to create a monopoly,' *unless in the carefully exercised judgment of the Commission the acquisition would nevertheless be in the public interest.*" [Empahsis supplied.][108] The decision was that " . . . we find that any lessening of competition . . . does not prevent our approving the merger because there are other factors which outweigh the elimination of Pacific as a competitor."[109] But in the discussion of the case, the examiner pointed out that ". . . even in presence of the frank admission by El Paso's President of the 'high probability' of an adverse decision in civil action, if its application here is denied, El Paso still has the right as a regulated natural gas company to come before this Commission and request a determination of the issue of whether . . . its acquisition of the facilities of Pacific is in the public interest."[110]

The State of California appealed the Commission's ruling to the federal courts on the grounds, among other things, that the FPC did not give proper attention to the policies and terms of the antitrust laws. The United States Department of Justice joined in this appeal. Judge Prettyman, an eminent authority on the law concerning administrative agencies, upheld the position of the FPC. He stated:

To approve a transaction the Commission must find it to be in the public interest. Clearly the public interest includes the solution of problems in so important an area of economics and law as the so-called antitrust area. . . . We are here dealing with the interweaving of free competition, regulated monopoly, and public interest. Free competition is a basic postulate of our free enterprise system, but it is not always —in all conditions—in the public interest. The policy of the antitrust laws is to foster free competition. The policy of regulatory measures such as the Natural Gas Act is public regulation of controlled monopoly, or partial monopoly. . . . The antitrust laws and the regulatory laws are not in

104 15 USC Sec. 18.

105 *Ibid.*

106 *Re: Pacific Northwest Pipeline Corporation and El Paso Natural Gas Company,* Docket Nos. G-13018 and G-13019, Examiner's Decision November 20, 1959 (mimeo.).

107 *Ibid.*, FPC Order Issuing Certificate, December 23, 1959 (mimeo.).

108 Examiner's Decision, *op. cit.,* p. 22 (mimeo.).

109 FPC Order Issuing Certificate, *op. cit.,* p. 4 (mimeo.).

110 Examiner's Decision, *op. cit.,* p. 24 (mimeo.).

conflict; they are complementary. Both have as their objective the public interest.[111]

Judge Prettyman also held that the FPC had, in fact, properly taken into consideration the antitrust aspects in the case.

The United States Supreme Court reversed the appellate court on the ground that the Federal Power Commission should have postponed its decision on the merits of the merger application when there was a suit pending in the courts, challenging the merger action under the antitrust law. The Supreme Court ordered the appellate court to vacate the FPC order approving the merger.[112] Subsequently, the Federal District Court in which the original antitrust suit was filed dismissed the case for lack of evidence.[113] Final resolution of this case was pending at the time of this writing.

The seemingly basic question in this controversy revolves around differences of opinion concerning the concentration of economic power. In the case described above, the critics of the merger seem to be saying that there should be limits on corporate size and on economic and political power flowing from size even in the public utility field. The potential dangers created by "bigness" are claimed to outweigh the possible benefits to the public from greater efficiency. These critics also seem to maintain that Commission interpretation of the "public interest" under its antitrust-law mandate neglects this question of bigness. The proponents of the merger, on the other hand, seem to feel that the FPC *is* capable of weighing all the factors involved in the public interest and, in fact, did so in the *El Paso* case. They maintain that commissions deal in detail with these regulated industries and are best equipped to resolve the public interest questions in each case. Congress thus far has taken the latter view, as is reflected in the federal law in this area. However, Congress appears to be not entirely satisfied in the area of agency regulation and has undertaken several studies on agency activities.[114]

The case discussed above of a gas pipeline merger is merely intended to be illustrative of the problems that do and may arise in communications, electricity, transportation, and other utilities.[115] In the *Menomonee Falls* case, discussed earlier, the Independent Telephone Association argued that "Application of the public interest standard of Section 211 (a) [of the Federal Communications Act of 1934] requires consideration of competitive factors and of the national policy set forth in the anti-trust laws."[116] In a recent case, an electric utility sought relief from what it considered an unreasonable rate by resort to the antitrust laws rather than by resort to the FPC. The Supreme Court pointed out that orderly procedure dictated that the utility proceed first to the Commission. However, the Court left unsettled the question how far a commission could go in establishing relationships that might violate the antitrust laws.[117]

One solution to the conflict between utility and antitrust regulation might be

111 *State of California* v. *FPC* (No. 15687 CADC), March 30, 1961.

112 *People of the State of California* v. *FPC*, 368 U.S. 810 (1961).

113 *U.S.* v. *El Paso Natural Gas Co. and Pacific Northwest Pipeline Corp.*, U.S. District Court for the District of Utah, Civil No. 143–57 (1961).

114 See Chapter 13.

115 See the interesting discussion of FPC antitrust problems in J. K. Kuykendall, "Antitrust Laws and Regulated Companies under the FPC," 65 *Public Utilities Fortnightly* 373 (March 17, 1960).

116 *Re Wisconsin Telephone Company, op. cit.*, FCC Docket No. 12308, Brief of the U. S. I. T. A., p. 50.

117 *Pennsylvania Water Company* v. *FPC*, 343 U.S. 414 (1952).

for the Justice Department to present its views in a proceeding before a particular regulatory body. But here the Justice Department might be presuming to advise a commission whose expertise is unsurpassed. Probably the greatest concern in this area is that regulatory agencies and the industries they regulate may develop a single-mindedness about how a particular industry should develop and function. In some respects, this is highly desirable. But at times a regulatory body seems unable to gain the proper perspective of the well-being of the total economy and just where the regulated industry fits into it.[118] The transportation regulatory agencies have been accused of this more often than has the FPC or the FCC.

---

[118] See, for example, *Mergers and Concentration in the Trucking Industry,* Senate Report No. 1441, 85th Cong., 2nd sess. (Washington: Government Printing Office, 1958), p. 4.

PART VII

ENERGY, TECHNOLOGY, AND THE FUTURE

21 Technology and Public Utilities

No discussion of public utilities is complete without at least a glance at what the future seems to hold for these industries with respect to technological innovations. While space limitations prohibit a detailed discussion of technological thresholds, at least a cataloguing of some of the more important breakthroughs is in order. Electronic data processing (EDP) and automation have become practically household terms in the postwar years. In some form and to some extent, these phenomena have penetrated almost every business activity. EDP has certainly been a boon to any business which has large payrolls and inventory control problems. Public utilities have taken advantage of such techniques in all these respects, but especially in their billing and collection activities.

Automation, which includes some types of EDP, has also played an important general role among utilities. Automatic counting, measuring, gauging, recording, and switching equipment is found in various forms throughout the public utility field. Specific mention of these advances will not be made except in cases where they are especially important. In the discussion below, some of the possible or actual technological advances in each utility industry will be discussed briefly.

1. ELECTRIC UTILITIES

A. Improvements in Conventional Methods and Equipment. While the most dramatic advances in the electric utility field are being made in the area of new methods of electric generation and the development of new sources of energy, there has been steady progress in improving the conventional equipment that forms the backbone of the electric industry. Perhaps two of the most troublesome problems are : (1) finding ways to transmit electricity over longer distances without experiencing heavy losses of energy; and (2) finding ways to utilize conventional fuels more efficiently in the electric generating process. Great strides have been made in both these areas.

The desire and need to tie the major electric transmission networks together into what eventually may be a nationwide grid have stimulated research in EHV (extra high-voltage) transmission. Generating capacity and technology have, to some extent, outrun transmission capacity during the postwar years, but this deficiency is being remedied. In the early 1950's, the maximum voltage carried on transmission lines was about 287,000 volts. This is now up to 375,000 volts, and firm plans have been made for 500,000-volt lines. Electrical equipment manufacturers are even experimenting with 750,000-volt and one million-volt lines. Such tremendous strides raise serious energy-loss, insulation, and handling problems which require radically new methods and materials.[1] Further advances in this area can mean a great deal. For example, there are large coal deposits in the eastern Rocky Mountain states, but little is used because of the lack of a market. If transmission efficiency could be improved, this coal could be used to generate electricity to be sold in distant markets.

The efficiency of generating equipment has also improved greatly. As recently as 1947, about 1.28 pounds of coal were required to generate one kilowatt-hour of electricity. By 1961, this figure had fallen to 0.863 of a pound.[2] Steam generating equipment has been developed to the point at which 600-megawatt units can be efficiently constructed. Heavy demands for electricity are making large units possible in some areas. During the 1960's, the industry expects to put into operation 1,000-megawatt units.

These advances, along with such things as synthetic insulation, fully automated generating stations, new designs and materials for towers, underground cable for residential service, and many other improvements, will do a great deal to keep electricity costs from rising greatly.[3]

B. New Methods of Power Generation. One of the most fascinating areas of technological advance in electricity is the development of generating techniques which do not require the use of a turbine-generator, which is customary in today's methods. There are five general areas of experimentation today, each quite different and each aimed at filling particular needs. There are, of course, many variations within each area. It is usually true that the longer the conversion path from the stored energy to electricity, the more inefficient the process. Thus, attempts to shorten the path by eliminating the intermediate stage in the conventional conversion of the original stored energy into mechanical energy and then into electricity, are, in part, attempts to become more efficient. As yet, in only a few special circumstances have these efforts proved to be economical.

(1) *Fuel Cells.* This is a generic term loosely applied to processes which convert the "free energy" of a chemical reaction directly into electrical energy. In one sense, a battery is a type of fuel cell which depends on a chemical reaction to generate electrical energy. The major difference between batteries and fuel cells is that a battery is "fueled" only once and goes "dead" when the fuel has been consumed. A fuel cell is either continuously or periodically refueled with some low-cost fuel.

Since most chemical reactions are speeded up by heat, high-temperature fuel cells are more flexible as to fuels

[1] *Electrical World,* Vol. 152, No. 26, December 28, 1959, pp. 69 ff.

[2] National Coal Assn., *Trends in Electric Utility Industry Experience, 1946–1958* (Washington: 1960), p. 44; and *Ibid., Steam Electric Plant Factors, 1961* (Washington: 1962), p. 34. Similar data appear for oil and gas: 1947, 0.116 gallons of fuel oil per kilowatt-hour; 1961, 0.076 gallons; 1947, 16.2 cu. ft. per kilowatt-hour; 1961, 10.8 cu. ft.

[3] For a good discussion of the research possibilities in the electrical utility field, see L. M. Olmsted, "Research and Development Spark Industry Breakthroughs," *Electrical World,* Vol. 153, No. 15, April 11, 1960, pp. 49–68.

and materials used for electrodes in the cell. If long-run corrosion and conductivity problems can be solved, it is conceivable that large, high-temperature cells using cheap fossil fuels can be utilized to generate industrial and municipal loads of electricity. Low-temperature fuel cells are also feasible but are, at this time, limited primarily to hydrogen for fuel. This element is expensive to produce, thus making the low-temperature cell expensive to operate. Fuel cells have some unique advantages for electric generation. They contain no moving parts, operate silently, produce low-voltage direct current, are efficient regardless of size, and are theoretically about twice as efficient in utilizing the energy in fossil fuels as a conventional steam turbine (70 to 90 per cent for fuel cells, as compared with a maximum 42 per cent for steam turbines). One estimate indicates that high-temperature fuel cells are likely to become competitive with conventional large-scale power sources in from ten to twenty years, if certain critical research problems can be solved.[4] Small low-temperature cells may find some special applications in the near future where capital and fuel costs are not major determining factors.

(2) *Thermoelectricity.* For almost a century and a half, science has been aware that electricity could be generated by creating a temperature differential between two surfaces or portions of a piece of metal. The voltage and output derived from this method have been so low that commercial application has not been feasible. However, in recent years the capabilities of thermoelectric generators have been greatly increased by "stacking" the electric-generating thermocouple devices. Generators in the 500- to 1,000 watt-range with operating efficiency of about 6 per cent are under construction. Small, rugged generators of this type are adaptable to military needs in the field or at places where fuel but not water or machinery parts are available. Commercial application is feasible at remote points along oil and gas pipelines and for cathodic protection against corrosion of steel pipelines.[5] Increased efficiencies to the 20 to 30 per cent range are in the offing, and success along this line would make this type of generation competitive with large diesel and coal generating equipment.[6]

(3) *Thermionic Generation.* Thermionic generation of electricity is similar to thermoelectric generation except that, in the former, the heated electrons, instead of moving through a solid piece of metal to generate electricity, are emitted into a vacuum. As these free electrons are picked up by an anode, they generate an electric current. Such devices must be operated at extremely high temperatures, for which fossil fuels are unsuited. The most likely application will be in conjunction with an atomic pile from which large amounts of heat are generated. The most serious problem in thermionic generation is finding suitable materials which have the necessary properties under high-temperature conditions. Commercial applicability is still a long way off.

(4) *Magnetohydrodynamic Generation.* It has been known for many years that an electric current can be generated by passing a conductor, such as a piece of copper, through a magnetic field. Magnetohydrodynamic (MHD) generation utilizes this principle, but substi-

[4] R. Ruka, "High Temperature Fuel Cells—A Potential Large Scale Power Source," Paper Delivered at a Seminar on New Methods of Power Generation, Research Laboratories, Westinghouse Electric Corporation, March 16, 1960, p. 6.

[5] Sales of small thermoelectric generators for pipeline protection have been reported by the Westinghouse Electric Corporation. *Business Week,* January 21, 1961.

[6] S. J. Angello, "Thermoelectricity: Applying the Seebeck Effect to Power Generation," Paper Delivered at a Seminar on New Methods of Power Generation, *op. cit.*

tutes a flowing liquid metal such as mercury for the solid copper. Current experiments are centered on finding an ionized conductor gas which, when moving through a magnetic field, will generate an electric current. Thus far, the extremely high temperatures needed to heat and ionize the gas have limited the usable materials. While high hopes are held for this process, commercial development awaits a painstaking research program for better materials and methods.

(5) *Solar Generation.* The last and, in some ways, the most promising method of electric generation is with solar energy. This is a perpetual source of energy and occurs in tremendous quantities. In a sunny climate, the average radiation intensities are the equivalent of about 2,000 Btu per square foot per day. However, the hourly transfer of heat is relatively low, only about 350 Btu per square foot per hour. This contrasts with conventional energy-exchange surfaces such as boiler tubes, which transfer heat at a rate of 100,000 Btu per square foot per hour. Thus, to utilize the sun's energy, (1) the energy requirements must be extremely small, or (2) the surfaces used to collect the energy must be large. In addition to these problems are those caused by the intermittent nature of the energy due to darkness, seasonal variations, and cloud variations. To overcome these last three problems, it is necessary to be satisfied with an intermittent supply, or to supplement the solar energy with another energy supply, or to provide some form of solar-energy storage.

The commercial application of solar energy has taken two forms.[7] The first is known as the *solar battery,* which is being used in communications equipment, radios, clocks, toys, and hearing aids, and also in space exploration. In all these cases, the amount of energy needed is small and the cost relatively unimportant. A solar battery utilizes sunlight passed over certain chemical surfaces to generate small quantities of electricity.

The other most promising commercial use is water-heating with solar energy. About 25,000 homes in southern Florida utilize this method. This can only be done in sunny, warm climates. Space-heating has been tried, but thus far has not been too successful. Cooking, refrigeration, and water distillation with solar energy are in various stages of experimentation. Power-plant generation from this source awaits further major technological breakthroughs.[8]

C. *New Uses for Electricity.* A discussion of technology in the electric industry is incomplete without some mention of new uses for electricity. Between 1955 and 1975, electricity consumption is expected to increase by 211 per cent.[9] This tremendous increase will come from both industrial and residential markets. As more and more industrial operations are automated, more and more electricity will be consumed. Also, as the emphasis in manufacturing in the United States shifts from heavy, basic industry to light, high-stage manufacture, electricity will play a more important role. New electro-metallurgical industries, such as aluminum and magnesium reduction, as well as many chemical processes will take huge amounts of electricity.

In the residential or consumer market for electricity, the outlook is very opti-

[7] This discussion is taken largely from the discussion and paper of George O. G. Lof found in the *Hearings before the Subcommittee on Automation and Energy Resources and Technology,* Joint Economic Committee, U.S. 86th Congress, 1st sess., October 16, 1959, pp. 305 ff.

[8] Atomic energy will be discussed with fuels for the future.

[9] Statement of Sam H. Schurr, of Resources for the Future, Inc., in *Hearings on Energy Resources and Technology, supra.*

mistic. In addition to the ever-increasing numbers and kinds of small electrical appliances being used in the home, electricity can look forward to a rapid growth in residential, commercial, and industrial air-conditioning, and to a huge potential market in residential space heating. It was estimated that at the end of 1960 there were 867,000 homes heated with some type of electrical-resistance type equipment and 155,000 heated with heat pumps. By 1970 it is expected that the resistance-type heating will be used in about 4,000,000 homes and the heat pumps in about 1,600,000 homes. The heat pump's share of the electric space-heating market will thus rise from about 15 per cent in 1960 to about 28 per cent in 1970.[10]

While many techniques of heating with electricity have been tried, the most promising seems to be the "heat pump." The heat pump is, in effect, a refrigeration unit which can both heat and cool. It utilizes the heat from the air, or a nearby water source, to heat the house and utilizes the heat in a house to cool the air in the house. All that is needed is electricity to energize a compressor. Today's refrigerator illustrates the principle involved. The refrigeration process gives off heat outside the box and gives off cold inside the box. A heat pump can be reversed in such a way so as to heat in the winter and cool in the summer. This makes it particularly appealing in areas having relatively moderate summer and winter temperatures.

2. GAS UTILITIES

A. Improvements in Transmission and Distribution. Nothing spectacular is happening to or is in the offing for gas transmission and distribution. However, numerous improvements are being made and will continue to be made which will reduce costs and improve service. Since transmission and distribution costs make up the major portion of gas costs at the burner tip, any improvements will be welcomed by consumers.

A number of things can be noted in each of these areas to point up the type of improvement being made. Transmission lines are being laid in larger and larger diameters, with a resulting decrease in pipe and laying costs per Mcf of throughput. New types of coatings and wrappings are being developed to give longer life and lower maintenance costs on the pipe. Improved efficiencies are constantly being realized in pipeline digging, laying, wrapping, bending, cleaning, coating, and filling techniques and equipment. Equipment has been developed to lay pipe on the ocean floor, making accessible the vast gas resources of the Continental Shelf. Experiments are being conducted using jet engines in pipeline compressor stations. Microwave has taken over as the automatic communication system which measures, gauges, records, regulates, and directs the flow of gas through the line without interruption. These are but a few of the developments occurring in transmission.

Gas distribution has enjoyed some of the same improvements. With growth of suburbanization and the consequent diminution in the number of customers per square mile, distribution costs have risen substantially in some areas. Careful forward planning as to location and size of mains is essential if costly enlargement or relocation is to be avoided. The "technology" of city planning and projecting metropolitan growth becomes a critical factor in gas distribution costs.

In the area of gas utilization, the industry has become increasingly aware that promotional effort is necessary if gas is expected to hold its own against competing energy sources. Gas appliances have been improved in appearance

[10] *Electrical World,* Vol. 155, No. 23, June 5, 1961, pp. 57 ff.

and efficiency and, in the case of cooking equipment, have been automated to the same extent as electrical equipment. Gas water-heating and space-heating equipment has also been modernized to meet the demands of modern living. New uses for gas are being explored, with gas lighting and gas air-conditioning being the most successful thus far, but with gas percolators and toasters coming in for their share of research. Gas lighting for outdoor decorative purposes is booming in areas where outdoor living is popular. Air-conditioning is emerging from the trial stage to commercial development. Its importance cannot be overemphasized. Air-conditioning provides some salvation to the industry from its extremely severe problem of a highly seasonal load. With gas consumption about twice or more as great in the winter peak months as in the summer trough months, gas air-conditioning holds the promise of a valuable firm load at a time of year when sales and revenues are at a low point. Gas utilities could probably benefit by subsidizing consumer purchases of air-conditioning equipment to gain a foothold in this market.

Finally, technology is being asked to alleviate the seasonal-load problem in another way. This problem could be greatly relieved if gas storage facilities could be maintained near large consuming centers. Unfortunately, gas cannot be stored above ground economically. Some transmission companies and a few distributors are storing gas underground in depleted oil or gas reservoirs. Where such reservoirs do not exist, attempts are being made to find other underground formations or cavities that will be suitable. Liquefaction of gas also has promise, since storage is relatively inexpensive and compact. Success in these ventures will greatly reduce gas costs in cool climates where the seasonal problem is the greatest.

B. *Gas Manufacturing and Processing.* While known gas reserves are ample to meet current requirements, the gas distribution industry is anticipating some shortages in the future by working on methods of changing solid and liquid fuels to gas. For many years the chief source of gas in nonproducing regions was coal, which was burned to yield a "manufactured" gas. If techniques could be developed which allowed gas manufacture at the coal mine or oil shale or tar sand site, such fuels might very well prove to be competitive with natural gas. Should field prices for gas continue to rise, the incentive to develop substitutes will increase.

One problem that has baffled the gas industry for many years is how to transport gas across large bodies of water. Pipelines are prohibitively expensive (although there has been talk of laying a line under the Mediterranean Sea from Algeria to France in order to utilize North African gas). Since World War I, experimental work has been done off and on to liquefy methane, the lightest and principal component of natural gas. Technology has developed to a point where it is economically feasible to "freeze" methane at −258 degrees(F.) into a liquid and to transport it by special ocean tanker to areas which have only expensive gas alternatives. In 1959, a dry-cargo vessel converted into a low temperature tanker carried 32,000 barrels of liquid methane from Louisiana to England. When vaporized and put into gas mains, this liquid expanded about 600 times.[11] Several successful trips have proven this shipping technique economical. Storage of liquefied methane involves digging an earthen pit and using the liquid to freeze the walls to make a leak-proof container. A simple, insulated roof completes the storage facility.

The significance of this development is apparent in at least two situations.

[11] *Wall Street Journal,* October 5, 1960, p. 1.

Vast quantities of gas are produced today in areas where there is virtually no market for the gas. Such places as Venezuela, Arabia, Iraq, Iran, Kuwait, Algeria, and Libya stand out as nations with gas that can be used only as a drilling or pumping fuel or as a lifting agent for oil. Most of the gas is vented or flared unless it is injected back into the oil-producing formation. If this gas, much of which is accessible to water transportation, could be liquefied and moved to Great Britain, Western Europe, and Japan, the market potential would be large. A liquefaction plant has been constructed to utilize some of the recently discovered North African gas.

The second situation in which liquid methane holds promise is in peak-shaving for distributing utilities in the United States. Some utility companies must maintain gas manufacturing facilities for peak-shaving needs or must contract for transmission line capacity that is needed only for short periods during the coldest winter weather. Liquid methane could relieve this peaking problem if suitable, inexpensive storage could be developed. This would be of particular benefit to areas which have no underground storage for natural gas in its conventional state.

3. COMMUNICATIONS UTILITIES

The technology of the communications utilities is changing so rapidly, that no matter what is said, it is in danger of being obsolete in a relatively short time. The following discussion can only list the highlights of currently promising innovations and take a brief look at what the future may hold. There seems to be a logical break in this analysis. The first part will deal with new developments in equipment and techniques used for commercial methods of communication. The second part will point out some new markets that communications utilities have tapped by developing new services. This discussion will not cover the radio broadcasting industry except insofar as it touches on telephone or telegraph communication.

A. New and Improved Communication Equipment. The communications industry is blessed with having a number of companies which spend substantial amounts of money on research and development. Foremost among these is the Bell Telephone Laboratories, which do work in both civilian and military communications research. In addition, however, there are such companies as General Electric, Westinghouse Electric, General Telephone and Electronics, RCA, and several others. Since rapid, reliable communications are an essential element in an adequate national defense establishment, much money for research has come from the federal government, with a consequent substantial overlap into civilian application.

Probably the greatest single innovation in recent years in communications is the discovery and development of semi-conductors. Best-known among the semi-conductors is the rapidly expanding family of transistors. The first transistor was a product of Bell Labs research in 1948. These tiny devices are used to amplify and control electrical impulses and can do many things a vacuum tube can do, as well as some things this tube cannot do. In addition, transistors cost much less than comparable vacuum tubes. Telecommunication is using transistors in transmission, amplification, switching, routing, and telemetering. Improvements and new applications are forthcoming with amazing rapidity. The transistor has many applications outside the telephone and telegraph industry. It is used in tiny hearing aids, space satellites, and giant computers. In a little over a decade, it has become an essential ingredient in modern technology.

Two major innovations in the telephone industry that will become more important in the near future are "direct distance dialing" (D.D.D.) and electronic switching. D.D.D. is, in effect, the application of local service dialing techniques to long-distance service. It is possible from many telephones today to dial any other telephone in the nation. This is done by first dialing a code number for a particular geographic zone and then dialing the local exchange number desired.

Electronic switching with pulse code modulation (P.C.M.) is perhaps the most exciting development on the technology horizon for the telephone industry. Today a pair of wires is required for each conversation, and a conversation completely ties up any given circuit. Electronic switching with P.C.M. will permit as many as 21 conversations on a given pair of wires at a given time. The conversations are first converted into electrical pulses. Then a rapidly rotating selector will join the several distinct conversations in successive instants so that several streams of pulses are moving over the same wire at the same time. Another rotating selector will separate the streams on the receiving end and convert the pulses back to sound. Application of this new device will cut cable and wire costs and should help to stabilize local service rates as metropolitan areas grow.

Other new equipment includes transoceanic cable with submerged electron-tube repeaters. This gives infinitely better transmission qualities than radio. The use of special, two-inch hollow tubes for waveguide transmission will provide expanded overland carrying capacity for both voice and television circuits and keep interference to a minimum. A large-frequency spectrum is provided that is not vulnerable to fading, atmospheric effects, interference, or other troubles that beset radio. In addition, it is not necessary to seek government approval to use particular bands of the already crowded radio and television frequencies. These are but a few of the exciting new developments for the future in communications.[12]

B. *New Markets for Communication Utilities.* As our society becomes more automated, much of the clerical work, such as recording, tabulating, and storing information, can be done by machines. Electronic data processing has been pushed to a point where it is now feasible for nationwide or regionwide companies to set up data collection communications systems. This is a significant new market for telephone and telegraph which the common carriers would like to reserve for themselves, but which the Federal Communications Commission seems to feel should be open to private as well as common carriers.[13] Microwave provides a relatively cheap and efficient way to transmit data and is also adaptable to voice transmission. Conceivably a group of large communication-service users could jointly set up a microwave system and share the 24-hour daily transmitting period so as to utilize the communication equipment at near capacity. Much information can be transmitted at night for use the next day. Certainly the potential private line business is large. Whether the common carriers will serve it or not remains to be seen.

---

[12] For expanded comments on many of these ideas, see the statement of Paul A. Gorman, Exec. Vice Pres., A.T. & T. Co., before the Joint Economic Committee, in its Committee Print, *New Views on Automation,* 86th Congress, 2d sess. (Washington: Government Printing Office, 1960), pp. 255 ff.

[13] Federal Communications Commission, *In the Matter of Allocation of Frequencies in the Bands Above 890 Mc.,* Docket No. 11866, Memorandum Opinion and Order, October 5, 1960.

Space communication presents another new area which is just beginning to develop. During the summer of 1960, Bell Labs, in cooperation with the National Aeronautics and Space Administration, launched a balloon satellite named Project Echo. This satellite was used for experiments in bouncing sound off an object in space.

On July 10, 1962 a more ambitious space communications project was undertaken by Bell Labs with the launching of an "active" satellite, "Telstar I." Unlike the "passive" Echo type satellites which can merely bounce signals back to the earth, the Telstar I picks up signals, amplifies them and sends them back to earth. The startling success in voice, T.V., data, and facsimile transmission was unexpected. Congress had received a message from President Kennedy the previous summer urging federal support of privately sponsored space communications projects. Congress complied by authorizing the establishment of a privately owned, publicly regulated corporation to develop further the commercial applications of communications satellites.[14] Ownership of the corporation will be 50 per cent in the hands of the communications common carriers and 50 per cent in the hands of the public, and directors will be divided among the owner groups and those presidentially appointed to represent the general national interest. The corporation will be subject to FCC regulation, will work with NASA on research and technical problems, and will work with the State Department in settling international problems that might arise in space communications.[15] Some objection to the establishment of a private corporation was voiced in Congress on the grounds that this activity should be performed by a public corporation.[16] However, the private ownership concept prevailed.

Plans to launch other "passive" and "active" communications satellites are being laid by NASA, the new corporation, and the Defense Department. While the military significance of these technological breakthroughs is important, the commercial applications for voice, telegraph, data, T.V., and facsimile transmission hold out the greatest promise in a rapidly shrinking world whose appetite for more and faster communications is never satisfied.[17]

The demands put on the communications industry by government defense requirements in addition to space research has created a whole separate market for these services. SAGE, DEW Line, White Alice, and BMEWS are a few of the projects which make the news headlines and for which the communications industry has provided the necessary communications systems.

4. TECHNOLOGY IN WATER UTILITIES

Technological advances in the field of water supply and demand are exceedingly important for the general well-being of the United States economy but go far beyond the scope of this book.[18]

---

[14] Public Law 87–624, Aug. 31, 1962.

[15] See U.S. 87th Congress, 2d sess., Senate Report No. 1584; and Senate Committee on Foreign Relations, *Hearings on the Communications Satellite Act of 1962* (Washington: Government Printing Office, 1962), for a discussion of the various provisions of the Act.

[16] U.S. Senate Committee on the Judiciary, *Hearings on Antitrust Problems of the Space Satellite Communications System,* 87th Congress, 2d sess. (Washington: Government Printing Office, 1962).

[17] For summary of what has happened to date and what the future may hold, see *Business Week,* October 27, 1962, p. 86.

[18] See Edw. A. Ackerman and Geo. O. G. Lof, *Technology in American Water Development* (Baltimore: Johns Hopkins Press for Resources for the Future, Inc., 1959), for an exhaustive discussion of the technological problems of water.

However, one aspect of water technology promises to have a direct and major impact on municipal water supplies in the future and thus warrants mentioning. This development is the conversion of saline water into fresh, sweet water. This "manufacturing" of fresh water has implications not only for municipal systems but also for the large water-using industries which must have it to grow.

Parts of the United States have arid or semi-arid climates. Other areas have concentrations of water-using activities, such as irrigation, oil refining, steel, paper, and chemical manufacturing. By 1980, unless supply and demand trends change significantly, many regions will be faced with a shortage of water which is potable and which can be used for industrial purposes. A partial answer to this problem, at least for high-value uses, is conversion of sea water or underground brackish water into fresh water.

In 1952, at the urging of diverse interests in the economy, Congress passed the Saline Water Act,[19] which authorized the Secretary of the Interior to direct research in saline water conversion. From this authority there evolved the Office of Saline Water, which was given $2,000,000 to supervise the research for a five-year period. In 1958, another law was passed which appropriated $10,000,000 for a seven-year period for the construction of five different types of demonstration plants.[20] By mid-1962, the five types of plants had been chosen, the sites for them had been selected, contracts had been let for construction of four of them, and three plants had been completed. The Freeport plant began serving the city of Freeport, Texas in May, 1961; the Webster, North Dakota plant went on stream in October, 1961; and the San Diego plant in November, 1961. Information on the five demonstration plants is found in Table 21.1.

These plants are definitely demonstration plants and will be used for experimentation. It is likely that they will be obsolete in a relatively short time. Under present technology, it is felt that the optimum-size, long-tube, vertical distillation-type plant and necessary auxiliary equipment (15 to 20 million gallons per day) can produce fresh water for less than 60 cents per 1,000 gallons. The optimum-size, multi-stage, flash distillation plant and auxiliary equipment (about 50 million gallons per day) is expected to produce water for 42 cents per 1,000 gallons.[21] The current costs of municipal water supply for large metropolitan areas range from 10 to 13 cents per 1,000 gallons in Chicago, New York, St. Louis, and Spokane, to 30 to 39 cents per 1,000 gallons in Indianapolis, Oklahoma City, Dallas, and San Francisco.[22]

As water shortages develop in specific areas, it is quite likely that saline water conversion will be one alternative of seeking additional supplies. For a long time it will remain an expensive source of fresh water and will supplement rather than replace the most conventional methods of water supply for municipal systems. Fuel is the major operating expense of desalanization, and fuel prices will have an influence on the adoption of desalanization processes. The use of publicly or privately supplied demineralized water for irrigation or large industrial plants is highly unlikely, since current costs of water for these purposes range from 1 to 5 cents per 1,000 gallons.

---

19 2 USC, secs. 1951 ff.

20 Public Law 85–883, September 2, 1958.

21 U.S. Dept. of the Interior, Information Service Releases, May 25, 1959 and December 19, 1960.

22 U.S. Senate Select Committee on National Water Resources, *Water Resources Activities in the United States:* Committee Print No. 7, *Future Water Requirements for Municipal Use,* 86th Congress, 2d sess., January 1960, p. 14.

Table 21.1

Federal Demonstration Plants for Saline Water Conversion—1961

Type of Plant	*Fresh Water Output Capacity (gallons/day)*	*Location*	*Total Cost*	*Estimated Cost/1000 gals.*
Long-tube vertical distillation, sea water	1,000,000	Freeport, Tex.	$1,255,712	$1.00
Multi-stage flash distillation, sea water	1,000,000	San Diego, Calif.	$1,640,000	1.00
Electrodialysis membrane, brackish water	250,000	Webster, S. Dak.	$482,000	0.75
Forced circulation vapor compression distillation, brackish water	1,000,000	Roswell, N. Mex.	$1,794,000	N.A.
Freezing, sea water	1,000,000	Wrightsville Beach, N. C.	N.A.	N.A.

N.A.—Not available at time of writing.

Source: Annual Reports and Press Releases of the Office of Saline Water, U.S. Department of the Interior, 1958–1962.

Table 21.2

Atomic Reactor Activity: Actual Costs and Estimates by Source of Funds

Projects Active as of June 30, 1960

(in millions of dollars)

Funds	*Total Estimated Cost of Projects*	*Cumulative Costs Incurred through June 30, 1960*	*Estimated Costs to be Incurred after June 30, 1960*
All Projects	$1,328.3	$612.1	$716.2
1. From Federal Government	$ 769.2	$323.0	$446.2
(a) Atomic Energy Commission	$ 711.7	$281.0	$430.7
(b) Department of Defense	41.9	28.4	13.5
(c) Other Agencies	15.6	13.6	2.0
2. From Industry and Others	$ 559.1	$289.1	$270.0
(a) Privately Owned Utilities	$ 502.2	$251.8	$250.4
(b) Publicly Owned Utilities	29.2	18.6	10.6
(c) Manufacturers and Universities	27.2	18.7	9.0

Source: Atomic Energy Commission, ***Major Activities In The Atomic Energy Programs*** (Washington, D.C.: Government Printing Office, 1961), p. 14.

5. FUELS IN THE FUTURE

Some of the problems involving competitive fuels were discussed in Chapter 16. However, this earlier discussion dealt, for the most part, with conventional energy sources—petroleum, natural gas, coal, and hydroelectric power. No discussion of fuels is complete without some mention of "unconventional" energy supplies which may be used in the future. These new supplies are largely a function of technology, and the timing of their introduction into major markets hinges, among other things, on cost reductions brought about through technical advances. This discussion logically breaks down into three parts: (1) atomic energy; (2) hydrocarbon fuel from oil shale and tar sands; and (3) "Cinderella" energy sources, such as the sun, the tides, and the wind.[23]

A. *Atomic Energy.* The role of atomic energy as a future peacetime fuel is not, at this time, clearly evident. Many billions of dollars have been poured into atomic research and development in the United States, but much of this expenditure has been for weapons. Peaceful developments have, of course, benefited greatly from this research. Development of atomic energy for the generation of electricity for civilian uses has been relatively slow in this country despite the tremendous headstart that the United States had at the close of World War II. This slowness has been caused in part by (1) the availability of low-cost conventional fuels, (2) the nearly complete refusal of the federal government to engage directly in civilian power development by the construction and operation of reactors for this purpose, and (3) the understandable hesitancy of private business to make the necessary huge investments in equipment that may be obsolete before it is put into operation.

Table 21.2 indicates the expenditures made on the atomic energy reactor program by sources of funds. The federal government is scheduled to pay about 58 per cent of the estimated costs of projects, while privately owned utilities will contribute about 38 per cent. About one-half of the Atomic Energy Commission's expenditures for civilian power reactor prototypes and experiments are for research and development. On the other hand, 80 per cent of private utility costs are for plant and equipment.[24]

Of the $1,328.3 million estimated reactor project expenditures planned or existing in 1960, $1,013.8 million was for civilian reactor projects. The remainder was for military reactors and materials production. By far the biggest part of the money spent or planned is for plant and equipment, as is shown in Table 21.3. Research and development accounts for almost a fourth, however. The AEC estimates that by the end of 1963 that there will be about one million kilowatts of atomic-powered generating capacity in operation (a city of 200,000 population requires about 180,000 kilowatts of capacity today). The short-range objective of the atomic energy program is to have private utilities build large nuclear plants rather than conventional plants, where fossil fuel costs are 35 cents per million Btu's or higher.[25] Other nations, with long-term fuel shortages looming large, have devoted nearly all of their research and development in this field to atomic power generation. A recent statement by Robert McKinney in a report to the Joint Committee on Atomic Energy of

[23] See also the preceding discussion on the generation of electricity without the use of a turbine-generator.

[24] Atomic Energy Commission, *Major Activities in the Atomic Energy Programs* (Washington: Government Printing Office, 1961), p. 13.

[25] *Ibid.*, pp. 17 and 20.

the Congress gives food for thought. In speaking of international research activities in atomic energy, he stated:

> To the extent, however, that civilian atomic power is no longer a major near-term objective, it may be neither likely nor desirable to take up the full capacity of national laboratories with research in this field. . . . In practically all national atomic laboratories abroad—perhaps even more so than in the United States—a period of program reappraisal is now underway, brought on by current re-evaluation of energy supply and demand outlook and delay in the advent of economically attractive atomic power.

Table 21.3

Atomic Reactor Costs by Types of Expense Projects Active as of June 30, 1960

(in millions of dollars)

Total estimated costs of projec. . .	$1,328.3
Types of expense:	
Plant and equipment.	$ 907.5
Research and development.	314.9
Fuel fabrication.	59.9
Land and land rights.	4.6
Training.	14.0
Use charges waived	17.4

Source: Atomic Energy Commission, *Major Activities In The Atomic Energy Programs* (Washington, D.C.: Government Printing Office, 1961), p. 15.

Atomic power is not commercially competitive today in the United States or in any other country. Government and private experts agree that no atomic power plant has yet been purchased by any utility organization on a straight commercial basis in competition with the most economically attractive conventional plant of comparable size which could be built at the same location. In all cases, substantial excess capital or research and development costs not recoverable through the sale of electricity produced have had to be met either by governments, utilities, or manufacturers.[26]

Development and application of atomic energy for civilian power hinge on several things: comparative costs of competitive fuels; future supply and demand outlook for total energy; whether public or private interests will dominate the development; and social acceptance of such problems as risk of radiation exposure and waste disposal. The substantial new discoveries of oil and gas reserves in the world, plus large known coal reserves, indicate relatively stable if not falling real costs of conventional fuel in the short run. Added to this are the very large quantities of hydrocarbon fuels in oil shales and tar sands, both of which are very close to being competitive today.

In the longer run, the outlook for atomic energy is much brighter. Continued advances in technology will no doubt reduce costs of atomic energy, while at the same time the costs of conventional fuels may remain stable or possibly rise. The best summary of estimated atomic power costs for 1970 is shown in Table 21.4.

These figures are certainly within competitive ranges in the United States, and the estimates for Western Europe are comparable. The European Atomic Energy Community (Euratom) estimates that, up to 1965, conventional plants will have an advantage over nuclear plants, while from 1965 to 1970 this advantage will diminish greatly, and from 1970 to 1980 it will disappear.[27] A major difficulty arises because the bright long-range outlook hinges in part on con-

[26] Joint Committee on Atomic Energy, *Review of the International Atomic Policies and Programs of the United States,* Vol. 1, Report of Robert McKinney, October 1960, 86th Congress, 2d sess. (Washington: Government Printing Office, 1960), pp. 27 and 29.

[27] *Ibid.,* Vol. 4, Background Materials, p. 1215, from a report by the European Atomic Energy Community, "Outlook for the Development of Nuclear Energy," May 1960. Conventional plants: to 1965, 8.74 mills; 1965–70,

Table 21.4

Comparative Costs of Electricity Generated from Atomic Energy and Conventional Fuels 1970

Type of Reactor or Fuel	80% Plant Factor Costs of Electricity - Mills per KWH	
	Private Development 14% Annual Capital Charge	*Public Development 6.4% Annual Capital Charge*
Atomic Energy:		
Light water.	7.5	5.0
Organic	7.1	5.1
Gas graphite	7.5-8.1	5.0-5.6
Heavy water	7.9-8.3	4.7-5.1
Conventional Fuels:		
Coal	5.9-7.7	4.4-5.8
Oil	5.0-6.6	4.0-5.2
Gas	5.0-6.6	4.0-5.3

Source: Joint Committee on Atomic Energy, *Review of the International Atomic Policies and Programs of the United States,* Vol. 1, Report of Robert McKinney, October 1960, 86th Congress, 2d session (Washington: Government Printing Office, 1960), pp. 32 and 46.

tinued research and development. If this is left to private industry, the risk burdens are extremely heavy in light of the low short-run profit expectations. One authority estimates that, by 1975, atomic energy might account for 10 to 15 per cent of total electricity production, and that electricity will account for about 25 per cent of total energy requirements. Atomic sources would thus contribute about 2.50 to 3.75 per cent of our total energy by 1975.[28] Within 15 years atomic energy will probably be competitive in some locations and not in others. With government subsidy, it will assume a place in the energy-supply picture of the nation. It may be as important as hydroelectric power. On the other hand, conventional fuels will not be displaced by atomic power. This is anticipated even in longer-range forecasts.

Exploration for uranium and thorium has been intense in only a few areas. However, in 1959, free world reserves of uranium oxide (U_3O_8) recoverable at $10 a pound were estimated at about 1,100,000 short tons and of thorium, about 500,000 short tons. Free-world low-cost reserves are concentrated in Canada, South Africa, and the United States. High-cost U_3O_8 reserves (recoverable at $50 per pound) amount to about 6 million tons in the United States and one million tons in Sweden.[29] Assuming the inefficient fuel utilization of today's plants, these reserves are equal to 200 billion tons of coal equivalent for electric generation. Assuming efficient breeder type plants, these reserves are equal to about 14 trillion tons of coal equivalent—about triple the known free world conventional energy reserves. Certainly atomic energy has a place in the world picture. For the many areas to

7.34 mills; 1970–80, 7.34 mills. Nuclear plants: to 1965, 11 mills; 1965–70, 7.48 mills; 1970–80, less than 7.34 mills.

[28] S. H. Schurr and B. C. Netschert, *Energy in the American Economy, 1850–1975* (Baltimore: The Johns Hopkins Press for Resources for the Future, Inc., 1960), p. 25.

[29] McKinney Report, *op. cit.*, Vol. 1, pp. 37–38.

which conventional fuels are inaccessible, atomic energy will mean a stable and relatively inexpensive source of electricity. Technology holds the key to whether atomic power can compete with conventional fuels where the latter are easily accessible.[30]

B. *Oil Shale and Tar Sands.* For many years two sources of hydrocarbon fuels have held out the promise of great reward to the person who could produce the fuels at prices competitive with conventionally produced crude oil, natural gas, and coal. The first of these is "oil shale," which is, in fact, a laminated marlstone saturated with a solid organic substance called ***kerogen.*** When heated to about 800 degrees (F.), kerogen yields a vapor, which, when condensed, closely resembles crude oil both physically and chemically. Large parts of Colorado, Wyoming, and Utah are underlain with an oil shale deposit known as the Green River formation, which contains an estimated 1.5 trillion barrels of oil.[31] This is many times the estimated *ultimate* recovery of liquid hydrocarbons in this country. Shale-oil production requires mining, crushing, retorting, and semi-refining before it is comparable to crude oil. The economics of such an operation thus far have prohibited large commercial development in this country, although technology is constantly narrowing the cost gap between shale oil and conventional fuels. Unofficial reports from companies working with shales indicate that kerogen of a quality comparable to crude oil can be produced and carried to the Pacific Coast for about $3.00 per barrel. If this is true, then shale oil is on the threshold of being produced, since conventional crude oil prices are in this same general range ($2.60–$3.10 per barrel). If crude oil prices should rise, this would give great incentive to the development of shale reserves; if crude oil prices fall, then shale-oil exploitation will be deferred. It is unlikely in the next decade or so that shale oil will contribute much to our total energy supply. Shale oil will have one very important effect, however: it will keep a ceiling on crude oil prices in this country and in the world for a long, long time.

Tar sands are oil-saturated sands which exist in several parts of the world. The largest known deposits are located in northern Alberta along the Athabasca River. The Athabasca sands cover from 17,000 to 30,000 square miles and contain about 300 billion barrels of recoverable reserves, an amount equal to the known world oil reserves from conventional sources. While the oil or tar is solid at atmospheric conditions, it can be washed out of the sand with warm water or some diluent. Pilot-plant operations are in progress, and applications have recently been approved by the Provincial Government to extract oil from the Athabasca Sands. Until recently the Provincial Government has discouraged development for fear of the adverse impact on the overburdened crude oil market. Initial production, when it comes, will be relatively small, but ultimate recovery could have a major impact on world oil markets.

In other parts of the world where coal, oil, and gas are not so plentiful, oil shale, and to some extent oil sands, will play a more important role. The big unpredictable factor is technology and how it will affect the relative costs of competitive fuels. A summary of a recent survey of world hydrocarbons is

---

30 See particularly *Progress in Atomic Energy,* Vol. 1 of the Proceedings of the Second United Nations International Conference on the Peaceful Uses of Atomic Energy, 1958, for extended discussion of the outlook for atomic energy.

31 Russell J. Cameron, Statement before the Joint Economic Committee, *Energy Resources and Technology,* U.S. 86th Congress, 1st sess. (Washington: Government Printing Office, 1957), pp. 173 ff.

Table 21.5

Resources of Coal, Liquid Hydrocarbons, Natural Gas, Oil Shale, and Tar Sands

Energy Resource[2]	*North America*	*Carib-bean*	*South America*	*Western Europe*	*North Africa*	*Other Africa*	*Middle East*	*Far East*	*Australia*	*Total Free World*
Coal Resources:										
Proved recoverable reserves[3]	6,200	58	14	3,980	[6]	548	[6]	150	182	11,132
In place in recoverable deposits[4]	12,445	119	27	7,973	[6]	1,096	[6]	300	366	22,327
In place in all deposits[5]	46,000	560	110	14,441	1	2,017	[6]	2,221	1,695	67,043
Liquid Hydrocarbon Resources:										
Proved recoverable reserves[3]	238	122	12	9	46	1	1,160	62	[6]	1,650
In place in recoverable deposits[4]	1,740	367	35	28	138	2	3,480	186	[6]	5,975
In place in all deposits[5]	8,700	2,088	1,392	313	1,392	209	9,744	1,218	[6]	25,056
Natural Gas Resources:										
Proved recoverable reserves[3]	308	44	11	6	6	[6]	11	11	[6]	396
In place in recoverable deposits[4]	385	44	11	6	6	[6]	220	11	[6]	682
In place in all deposits[5]	3,300	330	275	55	220	55	2,200	165	[6]	6,600
Oil Shale Resources:										
Proved recoverable reserves[3]	290	[6]	290	[6]	[6]	[6]	[6]	[6]	[6]	638[7]
In place in recoverable deposits[4]	3,086	[6]	1,740	[6]	[6]	[6]	[6]	[6]	[6]	4,942[8]
In place in all deposits[5]	5,800	[6]	3,480	[6]	[6]	[6]	[6]	[6]	[6]	11,600[9]
Tar Sands Resources:										
Proved recoverable reserves[3]	302	[6]	[6]	[6]	[6]	[6]	[6]	[6]	[6]	302
In place in recoverable deposits[4]	1,798	[6]	[6]	[6]	[6]	[6]	[6]	[6]	[6]	1,798
In place in all deposits[5]	1,798	[6]	[6]	[6]	[6]	[6]	[6]	[6]	[6]	5,800[10]
Total Resources:										
Proved recoverable resources[3]	7,337	224	327	3,995	51	549	1,171	223	182	14,117[7]
In place in recoverable deposits[4]	19,454	531	1,813	8,006	143	1,098	3,700	498	366	35,724[8]
In place in all deposits[5]	67,723	3,389	5,303	14,842	1,756	2,282	15,644	3,801	1,695	122,756[9,10]

1 Data for 1957–1959 period. Not specifically dated by source. Data represent availability but not production forecasts.

2 Figures in quadrillion Btu equivalents with no consideration given to conversion efficiencies. Conversion factors are as follows: bituminous coal, 26,200,000 Btu per short ton; crude petroleum, shale oil, and tar sand oil, 5,800,000 Btu per barrel; natural gas liquids, 4,620,000 Btu per barrel; and natural gas, 1,100 Btu per cu. ft.

3 Reserves recoverable with 1960 technology.

4 Reserves recoverable with technological advances between 1960 and 2000.

5 Reserves known or inferred. Information incomplete for many areas.

6 Less than 500 trillion Btu equivalent; in some cases no reserves known.

7 Includes 58 quadrillion Btu equivalent not shown in breakdown of shale oil.

8 Includes 116 quadrillion Btu equivalent not shown in breakdown of shale oil.

9 Includes 2,320 quadrillion Btu equivalent not shown in breakdown of shale oil.

10 Includes 4,002 quadrillion Btu equivalent not shown in breakdown of tar sand oil.

Source: U.S. Dept. of the Interior, "Resources of Coal, Petroleum, Natural Gas, Oil Shale, and Tar Sand in the United States and Allied and Neutral Countries," in Background Material for the Review of the International Atomic Policies and Programs of the United States, Joint Committee on Atomic Energy, Vol. 4, March 1960, 86th Cong., 2nd sess. (Washington: Government Printing Office, 1960).

presented in Table 21.5. These data have been compiled with various cost, price, and technological factors in mind. They do give some idea of what currently recoverable supplies are and what we can expect with certain technical advances.

C. Energy Sources on the Horizon. There are a number of energy sources which are still in the experimental stage or in the dream stage. Whether any of these will become competitive with conventional sources as they are known today is questionable. Again, technology looms large as the major determining factor.

Energy from the sun's rays has always fascinated those who search for energy sources. Large quantities of energy fall on the earth's surface every day. Plants convert the sun's rays into usable energy with the chemical process called "photosynthesis." Since, over geologic time, the sun has played an important role in manufacturing organic matter which is now consumed as fossil fuel, in an indirect sense this has given us our greatest energy supplies.

Today, attempts are being made to catch the sun's rays and convert them directly into usable energy, usually electricity. Thus far only limited success has been achieved. Perhaps the greatest success is the development of the solar battery for use in the communications industry. In such uses, the amount of electricity needed is small and the cost virtually a matter of indifference. Recent experiments which focus the sun's rays on a thermocouple made of some semi-conductors have achieved 10 per cent efficiency. Solar water heating is being done in southern Florida; solar cooking is undergoing tests in Africa and Asia; solar saline-water distillation is in the pilot-plant stage in the desert countries of the Near East and Africa and on islands in some parts of the world; and solar space heating has been attempted with partial success in the Southwestern United States. Further development must await cost-reducing innovations. At this stage, this source is still virtually a dream.

Thermal energy of the sun that is stored in sea water has been utilized near Abidjan on the Ivory Coast of Africa. Here the temperature differential between cold deep waters and warm surface waters is utilized to produce electricity. A maximum cost of 50 mills per Kwh is estimated at this time but could be substantially reduced. If plant sizes were expanded and better sites chosen, the cost could be as low as 3 to 6 mills per Kwh.[32]

Tidal power has been another source of energy which man, as yet, has not been able to capture successfully. The harnessing of the tides in Passamaquody Bay, between New Brunswick and Maine, was a lifelong dream of President Franklin Roosevelt. Construction was begun but never completed. In the mid-1950's, France began construction of a tidal power plant at La Ronce, which, when completed, will have cost about $91 million (1954 prices) and have an annual output of 800 Kwh. Electricity costs are estimated at about 10 mills per Kwh.[33]

These energy supplies have the great attraction of being inexhaustible. At the same time, they present serious if not insurmountable problems. Despite these problems, it is conceivable that such plants could be economically integrated into conventional electric grids. In addition, they can be called on to meet hard-to-reach communities which have pressing but fairly small power needs.

[32] See United Nations, *New Sources of Energy and Economic Development,* Chapter 2, "Characteristic Features of the New Energy Sources," 1957.

[33] *Ibid.*

TABLE OF CASES

A

Abilene Cotton Oil Co. v. Texas Pacific Railway Co., 204 U.S. 426 (1907) 465

Acker v. U.S., 298 U.S. 426, 430–431 (1936) 47

Ajax Pipe Line Corp. (Appendix 4), 50 Val. Rep. 1 (1949) 79

Alabama Gas Corp., Re, 25 PUR 3d 257 (1958) 77

Amalgamated Association of Street, Electric Railway and Motor Coach Employees v. Wisconsin Employment Relations Board, 340 U.S. 383 (1951) 408

American Power & Light Co. v. SEC, 329 U.S. 90 (1946) 442

American Telephone & Telegraph Co. v. United States, 299 U.S. 232 (1936) 91

Area Rate Proceeding, Re, FPC Docket No. AR61–1 et al. (1962) 336

Arkansas Power & Light Co., Re, 13 PUR 3d 1 (1956) 53

Ashbacker Radio Co. v. FCC, 326 U.S. 327 (1945) 313

Atlantic Refining Co., The, v. FPC, 360 U.S. 378 (1959) 349

Atlantic Seaboard Corp., Re, 11 FPC 43; 94 PUR (NS) 235 (1952) 182, 183–185

B

Baltimore Gas & Electric Co. v. People's Counsel, 152 A.2d 825 (1959) 74

Banton v. Belt Line Railway, 268 U.S. 413, 421 (1925) 144

Battle Creek Gas Co. v. FPC, 281 F.2d 42 (1960) 188

Bel Oil Corp., et al. v. FPC, 255 F.2d 548 (1958) 345

Bluefield Waterworks & Improvement Co. v. Public Service Commission of West Virginia, 262 U.S. 679, 692 (1923) 64, 68, 118–119

Boston Edison Co., Re, 24 PUR 3d 153, 159 (1958) 138

Brass v. North Dakota ex rel. Stoesser, 153 U.S. 391 9

Bus Fares, Investigation of, 52 MCC 332, 336 (1950) 82

C

California, People of the State of, v. FPC, 368 U.S. 810 (1961) 468

California, State of, v. FPC (No. 15687CADC), Mar. 30, 1961 468

Calvert v. Panhandle Eastern Pipe Line Co., 255 S.W. 2d 535, 545 (1953) 329

Canadian River Gas Co., et al., Re, 3 FPC 32, 48 (1942) 105

Canadian River Gas Co. v. FPC (and Colorado Interstate Gas Co. v. FPC), 324 U.S. 581, 601 (1945) 307

Canadian Western Natural Gas Co., Ltd., Re (1949) 268

Capital Transit Co. v. Public Utilities Commission, 213 F.2d 176, 187 (1953) 40

Carter v. Carter Coal Co., 298 U.S. 238, 302 (1936) 327

Central Maine Power Co. v. Maine Public Utilities Commission, 136 A.2d 726 (1957) 50

Central Wisconsin Gas Co., Re, 3 PUR 3d 65 (1954) 55

Champlin Oil & Refining Co., et al., Re, FPC Docket No. G-9277 et al., Ex. Nos. 12 & 13 (1958) 323

Charles Wolff Packing Co. v. Court of Industrial Relations, 262 U.S. 522 (1923) 9, 12

Charlotte, Col. & Aug. Railway v. Gibbes, 142 U.S. 386 (1892) 265

Chesapeake & Potomac Telephone Co., Re, 6 PUR 3d 322 (1954) 268
Chesapeake & Potomac Telephone Co., Re, 22 PUR 3d 321, 329 (1958) 73
Chesapeake & Potomac Telephone Co., of Virginia, Re, 85 PUR (NS) 435, 494 (1950) 116
Chicago & Grand Trunk Railway v. Wellman, 143 U.S. 339, 345–346 47
Chicago, Milwaukee & St. Paul Railway v. Minnesota, 134 U.S. 418 (1890) 58, 118
Cities Service Production Co., Re, FPC Docket No. G-9510 et al., Ex. No. 55 (1961) 319
Citizens Utilities Co. of California, Re, 4 PUR 3d 97 (1954) 54
Citizens Utilities Co., Re, 27 PUR 3d 183 (1959) 276
Citizens Utilities Co. v. FPC, 297 F.2d; 34 PUR 3d 481 (1960) 277
Cleveland, City of, Re, v. Hope Natural Gas Co., 3 FPC 150, 190 (1942) 185
Cleveland, City of, v. Ohio Public Utilities Commission, 164 Ohio St. 442 (1956) 75
Cleveland Electric Illuminating Co. v. City of Cleveland, 67 PUR (NS) 65 (1947) 54
Colorado Interstate Gas Co., in re, 10 FPC 105, 106 (1951) 39, 348
Colorado Interstate Gas Co. v. FPC and Canadian River Gas Co. v. FPC, 324 U.S. 581, 601 (1945) 70, 182, 307
Colorado–Wyoming Gas Co. v. FPC, 324 U.S. 626, 634 (1945) 81
Columbian Fuel Corp., Re, 2 FPC 200, 208 (1940) 326
Commonwealth Telephone Co. v. PSCW, 32 N.W.2d 247 (1948) 81
Consolidated Edison Co. v. Labor Board, 305 U.S. 601 (1939) 408
Consolidated Gas, Electric Light & Power Co. of Baltimore, Re, 67 PUR (NS) 144 (1946) 55
Consumers Power Co., Re, 15 PUR 3d 471 (1956) 50
Consumers Power Co., Re, 29 PUR 3d 36 (1959) 54
Consumers Power Co., Re, 38 PUR 3d 355 (1961) 55
Continental Oil Co., et al., Re, 17 FPC 880 (1957) 349
Continental Oil Co. v. FPC, 266 F.2d 208 (1959) 329
Continental Oil Co., et al., Re, Opinion No. 351, FPC Docket No. G-11024 et al., Jan. 22, 1962 350
Continental Oil Co., Re, FPC Docket No. G-16966 et al., Ex. No. 45 (1959) 322–323

D

Davies Warehouse Co. v. Bowles, 321 U.S. 144 (1944) 10
Davies Warehouse Co. v. Brown, 137 F.2d 201 (1943) 10
Deep South Oil Co. of Texas v. FPC, 247 F.2d 882 (1957) 329
Detroit, City of, v. FPC, 230 F.2d 810 (1955) 82, 309, 344
D. C. Transit System, Inc., Re, 33 PUR 3d 137, 166–167 (1960) 241
Division 1287 of Amalgamated Association of Street, Electric Railway and Motor Coach Employees of America, et al., v. State of Missouri (No. 640), June 10, 1963 410
Dorchy v. Kansas, 272 U.S. 306 (1926) 407

E

Eastern Massachusetts Street Railway Co., 95 PUR (NS) 33 (1952) 83
El Paso Electric Co., Re, 8 SEC 366 (1940) 420
El Paso Natural Gas Co., Re, 19 FPC 154; 21 PUR 3d 453 (1958) 179
Electric Bond and Share Co., v. SEC, 303 U.S. 419 (1938) 441
Episcopal T. S. v. FPC, 269 F.2d 228 (1959) 345
Exeter & Hampton Electric Co., Re, 94 PUR (NS) 124 (1952) 56

F

Farmers' Educ. & Coop. Union v. Circuit Court, 85 PUR (NS) 362, 364 (1950) 75
FCC, Re, Wisconsin Telephone Co., Docket No. 12308, decision July 6, 1959 462
FCC v. R.C.A. Communications, Inc., 346 U.S. 86, 91 (1953) 466
FPC v. Hope Natural Gas Co., 320 U.S. 591, 643–644 (1944) 61–62, 66, 69, 70, 73–77, 97, 117, 119, 305–306, 348
FPC v. Natural Gas Pipeline Co., 315 U.S. 575 (1942) 42, 66, 69–70, 117, 305
FPC v. Panhandle Eastern Pipe Line Co. et al., 337 U.S. 498 (1949) 311
FPC v. Transcontinental Gas Pipe Line Corp., 365 U.S. 1 (1961) 316
Fin-Ker Oil & Gas Production Co., Re, 6 FPC 92 (1947) 328
Florida Power & Light Co., 19 PUR 3d 417 (1957) 81
Forest Oil Corp. v. FPC, 263 F.2d 622 (1959) 345
Frost v. Corp. Commission, 278 U.S. 515 (1929) 9

G

Gainesville v. Gainesville Gas and Electric Power Co., 62 So. 919 (1913) 8

Galveston Electric Co. v. Galveston, 258 U.S. 388 (1922) 67, 392

General Order No. 38-A, Re, 62 PUR (NS) 129 (1945) 103

General Passenger Fare Investigation, Docket No. 8008, Nov. 25, 1960 78

Georgia Railway and Power Co. v. Railroad Commission of Georgia, 262 U.S. 625 (1923) 392

German Alliance Insurance Co. v. Lewis, 233 U.S. 389 (1914) 9

Gibbs v. Consolidated Gas Co., 130 U.S. 396 (1889) 8

Great Northern Railway Co. v. Merchants Elevator Co., 259 U.S. 285 (1922) 465

Groesbeck v. Duluth, S. S. & A. Railway Co., 250 U.S. 607, 614–615 (1919) 142

H

Hope Natural Gas Co., Re, 44 PUR (NS) 1, 24 (1942) 105

Huber, J. M., Corp. v. FPC, 236 F.2d 550 (1956) 329

Humble Oil & Refining Co. v. FPC, 247 F.2d 903 (1957) 329

I

Illinois Bell Telephone Co. v. Illinois Commerce Commission, 98 PUR (NS) 379 (1953) 75

Illinois Commerce Commission v. Peoples Gas Light & Coke Co., 99 PUR (NS) 361 (1953) 53

Indiana Natural and Illuminating Gas Co. v. State, 63 N.E. 220 (1902) 8

Interstate Commerce Commission v. Illinois Central Railroad Co., 215 U.S. 452, 470 (1910) 42

Interstate Commerce Commission v. Union Pacific Railroad Co., 222 U.S. 541 (1912) 42

Interstate Natural Gas Co. v. FPC, 331 U.S. 682 (1947) 327

Interstate Natural Gas Co., Inc., Re, 3 FPC 416, 432 (1943) 327

Interstate Power Co. of Wisconsin, Re, 93 PUR (NS) 33 (1952) 52

Iowa-Illinois Gas & Electric Co. v. City of Fort Dodge, 85 N.W.2d 20 (1957) 77, 108

K

Kansas-Nebraska Natural Gas Co. and Kansas Natural Gas, Inc., Re, 6 FPC 664 (1947) 328

Kansas Pipe Line & Gas Co., Re, 30 PUR (NS) 321 (1939) 313

Kentucky Utilities Co., Re, 22 PUR 3d 113 (1958) 74

Knoxville v. Knoxville Water Co., 212 U.S. 1 (1909) 66, 96

L

Lindheimer v. Illinois Bell Telephone Co., 292 U.S. 151 (1934) 95

Local 170 v. Gadola, 34 N.W.2d 71 (1948) 407

Long Acre Electric Light and Power Co., 1 PSCR (1st Dist-N.Y.) 226 (1908) 18–19

Los Angeles Gas & Electric Corp. v. Railroad Commission of California, 289 U.S. 287 (1933) 69

M

Manchester, City of, v. Manchester Teachers Guild, 131 A.2d 59 (1957) 409

Marietta, City of, v. Public Utilities Commission, 74 N.E.2d 74 (1948) 64

Marietta, City of, v. Public Utilities Commission of Ohio, 148 Ohio St. 173 (1947) 75

McCardle v. Indianapolis Water Co., 272 U.S. 400 (1926) 68

Michigan Bell Telephone Co., Re, 32 PUR 3d 395 (1960) 53

Michigan Bell Telephone Co. v. Odell, et al., 45 F.2d 180 (1930) 201

Michigan Wisconsin Pipe Line Co., Re, 6 FPC 1 (1947) 328

Middlesex & Boston Rate Case (1914) 74

Midwestern Gas Transmission Co., Re, Opinion No. 320, May 12, 1959 429

Milwaukee Gas Light Co., et al., Re, 51 PUR (NS) 299, 310 (1943) 137, 140

Minneapolis Gas Co. v. FPC, 278 F.2d 870 (1960) 82

Minneapolis Street Railway Co. v. Minneapolis, 86 N.W.2d 657, 22 PUR 3d 223, 243 (1957) 76

Minnesota Rate Case, 230 U.S. 352, 454 (1913) 66, 67, 69

Missouri ex rel. Missouri Water Co. v. Missouri Public Service Commission, et al., 308 S.W.2d 704 (1957) 77

Missouri v. Kansas Natural Gas Co., 265 U.S. 298 (1924) 35, 270, 426

Mountain States Telephone & Telegraph Co., Re, 8 PUR 3d 176 (1954) 54

Munn v. Illinois, 94 U.S. 113 (1877) 4, 5–9, 16, 33, 58

N

Nebbia v. New York, 291 U.S. 502 9–10

New England Telephone & Telegraph Co., Re, 2 PUR 3d 464 (1953) 52

New England Telephone & Telegraph Co., Re, 83 PUR (NS) 414 (1950) 131
New England Telephone & Telegraph Co. v. State, 64 A.2d 9 (1949) 81
New Jersey Bell Telephone Co., Re, 31 PUR 3d 453 (1959) 77
New Jersey Natural Gas Co., Re, 6 PUR 3d 249 (1954) 53
New Jersey, State of, v. New Jersey Bell Telephone Co., 152 A.2d 35 (1959) 77
New State Ice Co. v. Liebmann, 285 U.S. 262 (1932) 9
New York State Electric & Gas Corp., et al., Re, 20 PUR (NS) 388 (1937) 52
New York State Natural Gas Corp., 5 FPC 184, 191 (1946) 106
New York Telephone Co., Re, PUR 1923B, 545 73
New York Telephone Co., Re, PUR 1930C, 325, 367 140
New York Telephone Co., Re, 20 PUR 3d 129 (1957) 76
New York Telephone Co. v. New York Public Service Commission, 8 PUR 3d 299 (1955) 76
New York Telephone Co. v. New York Public Service Commission, 12 PUR 3d 399 (1956) 76
New York Tel. Co. v. Prendergast, et al., 36 F.2d 54 (1929) 201
North American Co. v. SEC, 327 U.S. 686 (1946) 442
North Carolina, State of, ex rel. Utilities Commission v. State of North Carolina, et al., 3 PUR 3d 307 (1954) 77
Northern Natural Gas Co., 15 FPC 1634 (1956) 315
Northern Natural Gas Co., et al., Re, Docket No. G-19040, et al., Mar. 7, 1961 113
Northern Natural Gas Co., Re, 9 PUR 3d 8 (1955) 186
Northern Pacific Railway Co. v. North Dakota, 236 U.S. 585, 598–599 (1915) 144
Northwestern Bell Telephone Co., Re, Finding of Fact, Conclusions of Law, and Order, North Dakota PSC, Feb. 15, 1952 458
Northwestern Bell Telephone Co., Re, 23 PUR 3d 267 (1958) 76
Northwestern Bell Tel. Co., Re, 66 PUR (NS) 148–150 (1946) 201
Northwestern Bell Telephone Co., Re, 92 PUR (NS) 65, 68 (1952) 75
Northwestern Utilities, Ltd., Re, 95 PUR (NS) 201 (1952) 268

O

Ohio Bell Telephone Co., Re, 82 PUR (NS) 341 (1949) 53
Ohio Valley Water Co. v. Ben Avon Borough, 253 U.S. 287 (1920) 42–43
Omaha Water Co. v. Omaha, 162 F. 225 (1908) 9
Owensboro v. Cumberland Telephone and Telegraph Co., 230 U.S. 58 (1913) 29

P

Pacific Electric Railway Co., et al., Re, 96 PUR (NS) 105 (1952) 53
Pacific Gas & Electric Co., Re, 21 PUR 3d 48, 58 (1957) 50
Pacific Lighting Gas Supply Co., Re, 18 PUR 3d 128 (1957) 266–268
Pacific Northwest Pipeline Corp. and El Paso Natural Gas Co., Re, Docket Nos. G-13018 and G-13019, Examiner's Decision Nov. 20, 1959 467
Pacific Power & Light Co., 3 FPC 329 (1942) 92
Pacific Power & Light Co., Re, 34 PUR 3d 36 (1960) 54
Pacific Telephone & Telegraph Co., Re, 5 PUR 3d 396 (1954) 53, 457
Pan American Petroleum Corp., et al., Re, 19 FPC 463 (1958) 345
Panhandle Eastern Pipe Line Co., Re, (FPC Docket No. G-2506) 309–310
Panhandle Eastern Pipe Line Co., (FPC Docket No. G-14755 et al.) 310
Panhandle Eastern Pipe Line Co., Re, 13 FPC 53 (1954) 307
Panhandle Eastern Pipe Line Co. v. FPC, et al., 169 F.2d 881, 884 (1948) 313
Panhandle Eastern Pipe Line Co. v. FPC, 232 F.2d 467 (1956) 312
Panhandle Eastern Pipe Line Co. v. FPC, 324 U.S. 635, 648 (1945) 311, 312
Panhandle Eastern Pipe Line Co. v. PSC of Indiana, 322 U.S. 507 (1947) 312
Pennsylvania Public Utility Commission v. General Telephone Co., 28 PUR 3d 413 (1959) 55
Pennsylvania Public Utility Commission v. Pennsylvania Power & Light Co., 14 PUR 3d 438 (1956) 53
Pennsylvania Water Co. v. FPC, 343 U.S. 414 (1952) 468
Phillips Petroleum Co., Re, 10 FPC 246 (1951) 328
Phillips Petroleum Co., Re, 24 FPC 537, 546 (1960) 142, 341, 346
Phillips Petroleum Co. v. Wisconsin, et al., 347 U.S. 672 (1954) 12, 270, 302, 317, 329–330
Platt v. San Francisco, 110 P. 304 (1910) 9
Potomac Electric Power Co., Re, 55 PUR (NS) 65, 85 (1944) 105
PSC of New York v. FPC, 287 F.2d 143 (1960) 312

R

Railroad Commission v. Rowan and Nichols Oil Co., 310 U.S. 573, 581–582 (1940) 43

Rates and Rate Schedules of Corporations Supplying Electricity, Re, PUR 1931C, 337, 347 142, 156

Reno Power, Light & Water Co. v. Nevada Public Service Commission, 298 F. 790 (1923) 47

Rhode Island, PUC of, v. Attleboro Steam & Electric Co., 273 U.S. 83 (1927) 35, 269, 426

S

Safe Harbor Water Power Corp., Re, 66 PUR (NS) 212, 244 (1946) 105

Salt Lake City Lines, Inc., Re, 78 PUR (NS) 1, 6 (1949) 83

San Diego, City of, v. San Diego Consolidated Gas & Electric Co., 7 PUR (NS) 443 (1935) 54

San Diego Land & Town Co. v. National City, 174 U.S. 739, 757 (1899) 66

San Jose City Lines, Inc., Re, 7 PUR 3d 80 (1954) 53

San Juan Pipe Line Co., et al., Re, 9 FPC 170, 187 (1950) 429

Saturn Oil & Gas Co. v. FPC, 250 F.2d 61 (1957) 329

Seattle, Port of, v. International Longshoremen's and Warehousemen's Union, 324 P.2d 1009 (1958) 409

Service Pipe Line Co., 56 Val. Rep. 369 (1958) 79

Shell Oil Co., Re, FPC Docket No. G-9446, et al., Exhibit No. 55 (1961) 337

Signal Oil & Gas Co., Re, 14 FPC 134, 149 (1955) 349

Signal Oil & Gas Co. v. FPC 238 F.2d 771 (1956) 349

Smith v. Illinois Bell Telephone Co., 282 U.S. 133, 157 (1930) 52, 216–217

Smyth v. Ames, 169 U.S. 466 (1898) 57, 59, 65, 68, 77, 96, 117, 139

South Carolina Generating Co., Re, 16 FPC 52 (1956) 78, 249, 254(T), 255–256

South Carolina Generating Co., 19 FPC 855 (1958) 251

South Carolina Generating Co., Re, 22 FPC 188 (1959) 256, 257(T)

South Carolina Generating Co. v. FPC, 249 F.2d 755 (1957) 251

South Carolina Generating Co. v. FPC, 261 F.2d 915 (1958) 252

Southern Bell Telephone & Telegraph Co., 7 PUR 3d 43 (1954) 77

Southern Bell Telephone & Telegraph Co., Re, 31 PUR 3d 254 (1959) 77

Southern Bell Telephone & Telegraph Co., Re, 52 PUR (NS) 200–201 (1944) 201

Southwestern Bell Telephone Co. v. PSC of Missouri, 262 U.S. 276, 289 (1923) 47

Southwestern Bell Telephone Co., Re, 2 PUR 3d 1 (1953) 54

Southern California Gas Co., Re, 35 PUR 3d 300, 318 (1960) 55, 141

S.S.W. Inc., v. Air Transport Association, 191 F.2d 658 (1951) 466

St. Croix Falls Minnesota Improvement Co., et al., Re, 3 FPC 148 (1942) 93

St. Joseph Stock Yards Co. v. U.S., 298 U.S. 38 (1936) 42–43

State Board of Mediation v. Pigg, 244 S. Co.2d 75 (1951) 408

State ex rel. Edwards v. Millar, 96 P. 747 (1908) 9

State ex rel. Pacific Telephone & Telegraph Co. v. Dept. of Public Service, 142 P.2d 498, 520 (1943) 74

State ex rel. Southwestern Bell Telephone Co. v. Public Service Commission of Missouri, 262 U.S. 276, 287–288 (1923) 67, 68–69

State v. Traffic Telephone Workers Federation, 66 A.2d 616 (1949) 407

T

Tennessee Gas & Transmission Co. and the Chicago Corp., Re, 6 FPC 98 (1947) 328

Texas Illinois Natural Gas Pipeline Co., 22 FPC 979, 980, 981 (1959) 314

Texas R. Commission v. Houston Natural Gas Corp., 289 S.W.2d 559 (1956) 77, 108

Transcontinental Gas Pipe Line Corp., 21 FPC 399 (1959) 316

Transwestern Pipeline Co., et al., Re, FPC Opinion No. 328, Aug. 10, 1959 429

Trunkline Gas Co. v. FPC, 247 F.2d 159 (1957) 71

Two Rivers, City of, v. Commonwealth Telephone Co., 32 PSCW 120, 70 PUR (NS) 5 (1947) 81

Tyson & Brother v. Banton, 273 U.S. 418 (1927) 9

U

Uniform Systems of Accounts for Electric Corporations, et al., Re, 82 PUR (NS) 161 (1950) 51

Union Oil Co. of California, 16 FPC 100 (1956) 344

United Automobile Workers of America v. O'Brien, 339 U.S. 454 (1950) 406

United Gas Corp. v. Mississippi PSC, 38 PUR 3d 252 (1961) 55

United Gas Pipe Line Co., et al., Re, FPC Docket No. CP60–36, et al. (1961) 337, 346

United Gas Pipe Line Co., et al. v. Memphis Light, Gas & Water Division, 358 U.S. 103 (1958) 180

United Railways & Electric Co. of Baltimore v. West, 280 U.S. 234 (1930) 97, 118

U.S. v. Appalachian Electric Power Co., 311 U.S. 377 (1940) 276

U.S. v. El Paso Natural Gas Co. and Pacific Northwest Pipeline Corp., U.S. District Court for the District of Utah, Civil Action No. 143-57 (1961) 468

U.S. v. El Paso Natural Gas Co. and Pacific Northwest Pipeline Corp., U.S. District Court for Utah, Civil Action No. 143–57, July 22, 1957 466

United States v. Far East Conference, 342 U.S. 570 (1952) 465

U.S. v. Western Electric Co., Inc. and American Telephone & Telegraph Co., Inc., Civil Action No. 17–49, U.S. District Court for New Jersey, Complaint, Jan. 14, 1949 454

U.S. v. Western Electric Co., Inc., and A.T. & T. Co., Final Judgment, Art. IX, Jan. 24, 1956 458

Universal Camera Co. v. NLRB, 340 U.S. 474, 487–488 (1951) 40

V

Virginia Electric & Power Co., 9 PUR 3d 225, 239 (1953) 145

W

Waukesha Gas & Electric Co., v. Railroad Commission, 194 N.W. 846, 854 (1923) 74

Waukesha Gas & Electric Co. v. Railroad Commission, 211 N.W. 760 (1927) 74

West Virginia Chesapeake & Potomac Telephone Co., 295 U.S. 662 (1935) 63, 69

West Ohio Gas Co. v. Public Utilities Commission of Ohio, 294 U.S. 63 (1935) 55

Western Natural Gas Co., Re, 23 FPC 235 (1960) 346–348

Western Union Telegraph Co., Re, 25 FCC 532 (1958) 78, 80

Whelan, R. J. and D. E., Re, 6 FPC 672 (1947) 328

Willapoint Oysters, Inc. v. Ewing, 174 F.2d 676, 693 (1949) 37

Willcox v. Consolidated Gas Co., 212 U.S. 19, 48 (1909) 66, 67, 118, 392

Williams v. Standard Oil Co., 278 U.S. 235 (1929) 9

Wilson v. New, 243 U.S. 332 (1917) 407

Wisconsin, et al. v. FPC, et al. (1963) 348

Wisconsin, State of, v. FPC, 205 F.2d 706, 708 (1953) 328

Wisconsin Telephone Co., Re, FCC Docket No. 12308, Brief of the U.S.I.T.A. 408

Wisconsin Telephone Co., Re, 80 PUR (NS) 482 (1949) 457

Wisconsin Telephone Co. v. PSCW, 323 Wis. 274, 329 (1939) 118

Wolverton v. Mountain States Telephone and Telegraph Co., 142 P. 165 (1914) 9

Y

Youngstown Sheet and Tube Co. v. Sawyer, 343 U.S. 579 (1952) 406

INDEX

A

Accelerated depreciation
economic effects, 111–112
effect on rate-making, 112–114
effect on tax rates, 111–114
"flow-through," 113–114
See also, Depreciation
Accounting, 89–93
depreciation, 98
effect on rate-making, 112–114
tax deductions, 110–114
retroactive, 87
See also, Depreciation, Rate of Return
Accrued depreciation
equities involved, 102–103
source of funds, 419–420
See also, Depreciation
Adjudication, 39–43
appeals, 39
Atomic Energy Commission, 285
costs of, 53
evidence, 342–345
Federal Power Commission, 285
notice, 38–39
See also Judicial review
Advertising expenses, 53
Advisory Committee on Reactor Safeguards, 291–292
Affiliates, 51–53
transactions between, 88
Air conditioning, 474–475
water use, 223–231
American Telephone and Telegraph Company
acquisition policies, 459–463
functions, 189–190, 450–451
Hall Memorandum, 461–462
service charges, 453
services, 453
American Telephone and Telegraph Company (*Cont.*)
size, 448–450
stockholders, 423–424
toll revenue division, 252
See also, Bell System
Amortization, 93
Antitrust policy, 464–465
Antitrust problems, 463–468
Antitrust regulation
Bell System, 458–459
primary jurisdiction, 464–466
public interest, 466–469
Area pricing
Phillips rate case, 346–347
reasons for change to, 346–347
Atlantic Seaboard formula, 181–185, 367
Atomic energy
development, 445
not competitive price-wise, 482
plant costs, 481
present and future costs, 482
Atomic Energy Act
amendments, 288–289

B

Bauer, John, 62, 144
Bell, Alexander Graham, 447–450
policy, 448–449
Bell Patent Association, 447
Bell System, 72
consent degree, 458–459
consolidation, 448–450
cost-of-service, 453
early competition, 448
early development, 446–448, 452
growth, 448–450, 452, 459–460
Kingsbury Commitment, 450, 460

Bell System (*Cont.*)
leasing system, 447
licensing agreements, 447–450, 452–454
Long-Lines Department, 452
monopoly, 458
policy toward independents, 448–449
public relations, 449
Standard Supply Contract, 455–456
structure, 450
subsidiaries, 452–454
and Western Union, 447, 449–450
Willis-Graham Act, 460
Bell Telephone Laboratories, 189–190
research, 453–454
space communications, 478
Ben Avon rule, 42–43
Bernstein, Marver H., 283–284
Bigham, Truman C., 62
Bonbright, James C., 147
Bondholders, 417, 422–424
Bonds
convertible, 417–418
debenture, 416–417
mortgage, 416–417
open-end first-mortgage, 416
revenue, 431–432
See also, Stocks
Book reserves, *See* Depreciation
Brandeis, Justice, 68; q., 142, 392
Broadcasting, 2
Bryan, William Jennings, 59

C

Capacity costs, 141
Capital
customers' contributions, 71–72
effect of taxes, 395
methods of financing, 414–420
needs, 412–415
turnover ratio, 23–24
working, 71, 257
See also Cost of capital, Rate of return
Capital structure, 252–254, 414–415
determination, 129–131
pipeline companies, 429
regulation, 420–421
shift in, 443–444
Charters, 28
Civil Aeronautics Board, 78
Clayton Act, 466–467
Clemens, Eli W., 62
Coal
consumption, 354–356
future estimates, 380
miscellaneous industrial uses, 372–374
decreased use of, 368–369
mining techniques, 376, 378
reserves, 376–377
Coal (*Cont.*)
shift to gas, 368–369
See also, Fuels, Energy Sources, Residential Heating, Petroleum
Commissioners, *See* Federal, State Commissions, Regulatory Commissions
Common carriers, 2
Common law, 4
Common stock
A.T.&T. holders, 423–424
dividends, 26
See also, Stocks, Bonds
Commons, John R. q., 8, 260
Communications Act of 1934, 280–281
Communications utilities, *See* Telephone utilities
Competition, 79–80
antitrust policy, 464–465
gas industry, 339–340
intra-industry, 44, 80
undesirability, 15–16
Competitive risk, 122
Competitive standards, 120
Confiscation, 118
Cooperation, for development of power, 446
Cost allocation
"rolled-in" principle, 188
telephone utilities, 219–220
Cost amortization, *See* Amortization, Depreciation
Cost analysis, 140–142
in rate cases, 141
joint cost allocation, 140–142
pipelines, 183
water utilities, 232–233
Cost basis
water supply systems, 227
Cost depreciation, 108–109
See also Depreciation
Cost factors
energy sources, 375
See also Pricing
Cost methods, 57–65
Cost of capital, 123–133, 253–254
determination, 129–131
dividend-payout ratio, 131
effect of taxes, 390–391
efficiency, 133
retained earnings, 131
Cost of service, 56–57, 113, 145
allocation of demand costs, 159–166
as evidence, 344–345
concept of, 44, 47
debt ratio, 255
depreciation, 257
effect of taxes, 392–395
gas pipelines, 182–183
interest during construction, 257–258
Phillips case, 346–347

Cost of service (*Cont.*)
principles, 143
rate of return, 252–254, 258
tax allowance, 254–257
test period, 252
working capital, 257
Cost reclassification, 89
Costs, 17–18
constant, 139
of construction, 68, 85
See also Plants, reproduction costs
economic basis for computing, 333–335
gas production, 335–337
operating, 20
taxes, 392–393, 394
out-of-pocket, 138–139
telephone utilities
toll calls, 213–214
urban transit, 243
water utilities, 222
See also, Rate-making, Unit costs
Crawford, Finla G., 62
Customer classes, 135–137, 153–154

D

de novo review, 41
Debt, *See* Financing
Debt ratio, 25
Demand, *See* Value of service
Demand-cost allocation, 141, 144, 163–164
Depreciation, 57, 85, 94–114
accelerated, 109–114
purpose, 109–110
accounting, 106
accrued, 102–106
reserve, 104–106
source of funds, 419–420
base, 97–98
causes, 95, 96
concept, 94–95
declining-balance method, 110
in determining rate-base, 66
economic, 106–109
calculation, 106
defined, 107
expenses, annual, 100–102
calculating, 101–102
Great Britain, 108
group base of cost amortization, 101
methods compared, 110
practices, 107
price-level, 107–109
rate-base, 102–106
remaining-life method, 101–102
reserve, 95, 104–106
retirement reserve accounting, 99–100
salvage value, 95
service life, 100–101

Depreciation (*Cont.*)
service value, 95
sinking-fund method, 99
straight-line method, 98–99, 109, 110, 114
sum-of-the-years'-digits method, 110
tax deductions, 110–114
Differential pricing, 22, 144
economic foundation, 143
Douglas, Justice, q., 142

E

Earnings-price ratio, 125–127
Ebasco, 437
Economic depreciation, *See* Depreciation, economic
Economics, 14
concentration of power, 468–469
institutional, defined, 260
theoretical, 147–148
See also Taxation
Edison, Thomas A., 148
Eisenmenger, H. E., 144
Electric Bond and Share Company, 437
Electric plants
adjustments, 94
capacity trends, 150
valuation, 89–90
See also Electric service, Electric utilities, Energy sources
Electric service, 18–19
power measurement, 152
transmission efficiency, 470–471
Electric utilities, 35, 148–164
bonds, 416
characteristics, 151–152
Great Britain, 151
cooperation, 446
cost classification, 158–159
cost factors, 152–154
defined, 154
costing methods, 158–159
Complete Peak, 161–162
Consumption and Demand, 162
E.R.A., 162–163
Maximum Demand, 160–162
Peak Responsibility, 159–160
Phantom Customer, 161
customer classes, 136
customer costs, 158, 159
debt ratios, 420
demand costs, 158–159
allocation, 159–166
equations, 162
diversity factors, 153–154
economics of ownership, 430–431
energy costs, 158, 159
fixed costs, 151
fuel sources, 150

Electric utilities (*Cont.*)
future energy sources, 471–473
Great Britain, 108, 151
history, 148–152
holding companies, 149
development, 436–437
regulation, 281–282
See also, Holding companies
income, 420
investment costs, 151
load curve, 151
load factors, 153, 156–157
operating expenses, 48, 49
peak demand, 152, 160–162
rate changes, 146
rate trends, 149–150
rate-making, case study, 249–259
rate schedules, 154–158
regulation, jurisdiction, 269–271
state and Federal ownership, 432–434
tax share, 391
Electricity, generation, 368–370
future uses, 473–474
Electronic data collection, 477
Electronic data processing, 470
Emergency Price Control Act, 10
Eminent domain, 1
Employee relations, 396
Energy conversion, 471–474
Energy sources
atomic energy, 481–484
cost forecast, 482–483
research, 483
coal production, 352
future, 471–473
magnetohydrodynamic generation, 472–473
oil shale, 484–485
solar, 486
generation, 473
tar sands, 484–485
thermal, 486
thermionic generation, 472
tidal, 486
unconventional, 481
See also Coal, Petroleum, Natural Gas
Energy supplies, 350–360
competition, 359–374
gas-electric, 360
consumption
by area, 354–358
future, 378–383
long-term forecast, 379–383
short-term forecast, 379
See also Production
demand, 375
See also Consumption
development by cooperation
gas-electric appliances
competition, 360–361
Energy supplies (*Cont.*)
markets, 359–374
commercial, 360–363
location, 359–360
residential, 363–368
industrial, 368–374
new sources, 375
production, 352
location, 353–354
statistical summary, 351–352
table, 353
Equity, 129–130
capital, 125–127
Expense ratios, 44, 48
Expenses, *See* Operating Expenses, and under different utilities

F

Fair return, *See* Rate of return
Fair value, 7, 57, 59, 65, 73–78, 108
Federal commissions
criticized, 283–284
independence, 283–284
organization, Landis Report, 286
policy, lack of, 286
procedures, 286
See also Federal Communications Commission, Federal Power Commission, Regulatory commissions, etc.
Federal Communications Commission, 278–281
broadcasting, 281
data collection, stand on, 477
jurisdiction, 278
purpose, 278
security regulation, 429
study of Western Union prices, 456
Federal Maritime Board, 78, 80
Federal Power Act, 269–270, 272
navigable waters, 274–278
Federal Power Commission, 34, 35, 60
antitrust regulation, 467–469
authority, 273–274
Clayton Act, 466–467
Columbian Fuel case, 326
decisions, 39–40
"ex parte" communications, 285
gas pipelines
authorization, 312–316
favored-nation clauses, 331–332
interstate ruling, 327–329
hearings, complaints on, 285
history, 269–271
investigated, 284–285
jurisdiction, 269–272, 274–275, 277
gas industry, 301–303
pipelines, 311–312
producers, 317, 325–329
at law, 39

Federal Power Commission (*Cont.*)
  Phillips case, 326, 328–329
  purpose, 269
  rates, 278
    determination, gas, 338–340
    policy, gas, 305–311, 343–348
  regulation
    certification policy, 348–350
    criticism, 284–285
    implementation, 329–330
    securities, 428–429
  regulatory policy, effect, 308–309
  work-load, 330
  working capital, determination, 71
Federal Radiation Council, 289
Federal Register, 38
Federal Trade Commission, 301
Federal Water Power Act, 269, 272
Ferry-boat service, 4
Financial regulation, 424–430
  See also Security regulation
Financing, 14
  debt-ratios, 420–422
  debt retirement, 421
  from depreciation accruals, 419–420
  holding companies, development, 437–438
  interest rates, 419
  long-term debt, 414, 421–422
  municipally owned utilities, 431–432
  problem of investment size, 421–422
  short-term debt, 419
  TVA, 433–434
Fire insurance rates, 233
Franchises, 28–32
  duration, 29
  perpetual, 29
  states presently using, 31–32
  terms, 30
  urban transit, 236–237, 245
  value, 85–86
Fuels
  miscellaneous industrial uses, 371–374
  national policy, 383–384
  petroleum products, 356–357
  price comparison, 299
  price increases, 363–365
  reserves (table), 485
  residential heating, 361–368
  transportation costs, 359
  uses
    future trends, 369–371
    to generate electricity, 368–370
  See also Energy sources, Gas, Oil, Petroleum, etc.

G

Gas (natural), 35
  associated gas, 318–319
Gas (natural) (*Cont.*)
  characteristics, 165
  competition with coal and other fuels, 315–316
  consumption, 296, 357–358
    future estimates, 382–383
    industrial, 358
      miscellaneous, 372–374
  costs of exploration, 310, 334–336, 339
  demand, 21–22, 324–325
  interruptible, use to generate electricity, 369
  peak-shaving
    future use of liquid methane, 476
  prices, 299, 305–308, 319, 320, 365–368
    history, 305
  production, 295–296
  reserves, 295–296, 311, 318, 324–325, 354, 378, 475
    development, 335–336
    (table), 485
  sales
    interstate commerce, 326–329
  seasonal load, 475
  sources, 294–295
  storage, 367–368, 475
  supplies, 297, 304
  transmission, 297, 298 (table)
    See also Gas pipelines
  use to generate electricity, 368–369
  use in residential heating, 363–368
  See also Fuels, Natural Gas Act
Gas pipelines, 167
  abandonment of service, 311
  Atlantic Seaboard Formula, 181–185
  Black Dog case, 315–316
  capacity, 299–300
  certificates, 312–316
  characteristics, 174–178
  Clayton Act test case, 466–468
  competition, 313, 315
  construction, 299
  contract demand, 181
  costs, 175
    of service, 304–305, 310
  demand charge, 188
  demand-commodity rate, 180, 181
  demands, 175
    sustained peak, 184
  development, 299–300
  divestments, 311–321
  economic factors, 174–178, 304–305
  field-price approach, 307–310
  gathering companies, 333
  Hope Natural Gas Company case, 305–306
  interstate movements of gas (table), 355
  interstate sales, direct, 312–315
  locations, 174
  Natural Gas Pipeline Company, case, 305
  Panhandle Eastern case, 311

Gas pipelines (*Cont.*)
  purchases of producing properties, 311–312
  rates, 173–189
    base load-excess rate, 180–181
    billing basis, 181
    changes, 179–180
    regulation policy, 344
    schedules, 180–181, 186–188
  regulation, 302–311
    certificates, 429
    Federal, 428–429
  seasonal peaks, 367–368
  service areas, 313
  systems, 300
  volumetric rate, 180
  zone rates, 186, 188
Gas transmission, *See* Gas pipelines
Gas utilities and gas producers
  area pricing, 340–343
  certificates, 330
  characteristics, 301
  City of Detroit case, 309–310
  compared to other public utilities, 332–335
  competition, 321–323, 325
  costs of exploration, 339
  cost trends, 168–169
  debt ratios, 420, 421
  debt retirement, 421
  depreciation, 95
  development, 325
  economic characteristics, 321–324, 332–337
    cost, 335–336
    general, 332–335
    profit, 337
  economic problems, 324–325
  economic rent, 323–325
  expenses
    for adjusting appliances, 54
    operating, 48
  history, 166, 168
  holding-companies
    development, 436–437
    regulation, 281–282
  Hope Natural Gas Company, 294–295
  indefinite pricing clauses, 331–332
  interruptible gas sales, 171–172, 173, 176–177, 183–184
  Joint Association Survey, 336
  joint costs, 334–335, 338–339
  life-index, 314–315
  load factors, 171, 175, 178
  manufactured gas, 165–167
  market characteristics, 170–172
  monopolies, 15
  peak demand, 171, 175, 177
  peak-shaving, 170
  potential customers, 324
  price trends, 166
  pricing methods, 338–343
Gas utilities (*Cont.*)
  producers
    certificate regulation, 348–350
    company types, 320–321
    defined, 317
    history, 319–320
    regulation, 317–350
  profits, 323
  rates
    Atlantic Seaboard Formula, 181–185
    changes, 146, 170, 330
      to natural gas, 167–171
    regulation
      FPC policy, 343–348
    schedules, 172–173, 178, 329–330
    space-heating, 172
    value of service, 139–140
  regulation
    FPC control, 301–303, 317, 328–329
    jurisdiction, 270–271
    West Edmond case, 344–345
  revenue, 337
  risks, 334
  sales contracts, 330–332
    area pricing, 343
    favored-nation clauses, 331–332
    redetermination clauses, 331–332
  service, 302
    agreements, 179
    characteristics, 170–171
    costs, 333–335
    firm, 170, 175–176, 178
    interruptible service, 170, 178
  storage, 177–178
    See also Methane
  tariffs, 178–180
  technological advances, 321, 474–475
  transmission future, 474–475
  types, 164–165
  Union Oil Company case, 344–345
  use trends, 168–169
General Dam Act of 1906, 272
General Electric Company, 436–437
General Telephone and Electronics Corporation, 191–193
Glaeser, Martin G., 62, q., 141, 143, 386
Going-concern value, 86
Good-will, 86
Grain elevators, 5–7, 9
Granger commissions, 33
Granges, 6
Greene, W. J., 162

H

Hale, Sir Matthew, 4, 6–7
Harris, Oren, 284
Heat pumps, 474
Heating, future, 473–474

Herz, Henry, 163
Hills, H. W., 161
Holding companies, 35, 301
  abuses, 438–439
  advantages, 436–437, 439–440
  American Telephone and Telegraph Company, 452–453
  antitrust laws, 440
  defined, 435–441
  disadvantages, 437
  Electric Bond and Share Company, 437
  exemptions, 445
  General Electric Company, 436–437
  historical development, 435–438
  investments, 438–439
    effect of shrinkage, 443–444
  need for legislation, 440–441
  operating companies, 435
  pyramiding, 438–439
  regulation, 281–282, 426, 428–429
    failure of state, 440
    under SEC, 442–444
  SEC, 441
  service company fees, 439
  Stone and Webster, 437
  subsidiaries, 435–436
  See also Public Utility Holding Company Act
Hoover, Herbert, 269
Hopkinson, John, 160, 240–241
Hughes, Chief Justice, q., 42–43, 69, 144
Hydroelectric power plants, 269, 270
  amortization reserve, 273–274
  capacities, 272–273
  consumption, 358
    future estimates, 383
  licensing provisions, 273–278
    length of time, 273
  regulation, 271–278
    development, 272
  state and Federal ownership, 432–434

I

Idleness, 20
Index numbers, 69
Inflation, 50, 117, 122–123, 226, 268
  depreciation allowance, 106–109
  effect on financing, 419–420
  fuel prices, 366
  market value, 126
  price, 57–58
  rate of return approach, 132–133
  urban transit costs, 242
Inflation allowance, 77
Interstate Commerce Commission, 35, 78–79
  authority, 279–281
  criticized, 283
Interruptible gas, *See* under Gas, natural, and Gas utilities

J

Jackson, Justice, q., 61–62, 70, 306, 307
Jaffe, Louis L., 283
Johnson Act of 1934, 41
Joint Association Survey, 336
Jones, Eliot, 62
Judicial regulation, 10–11, 12, 27
Judicial review, 36–43, 81, 285
  cost of appeal, 54
  See also Adjudication
"Just price," 3

K

Kerogen, 484

L

Labor-management, *See* under Public utilities
Landis, James M., 282
Landis Report, 286
Legislative Oversight Subcommittee, 285–286, 289–390
Life insurance companies, 422–423
Lilienthal, David E., 89
Lippitt, Henry F., II, 106
Lobbying expenses, 54

M

McGee, Charles E., 346–347
McKinney, Robert, q., 481–482
Maltbie, Milo R., 18–19, 142
Mann-Elkins Act, 279–280, 450
Marginal-cost pricing, 115, 147–148
Mercantilism, 3–4
Merchandising expenses, 55–56
Methane, 476
  "freezing," 475
Milk industry, 9, 10
Milk producers, 2
Mill, John Stuart, 15
Monopolies, 1, 3–4, 5, 7
  Bell System, 448–449, 458
  Clayton Act, 440–441, 466–467
  gas utilities, 313, 321–323, 326–327
  natural, 15–19, 412–413
    antitrust regulation, 463–464
Mosher, William E., 62
Municipal water systems
  saline conversion, 479

N

NARUC–FCC report on Western Electric, 456
NASA, 478

Natural gas, *See* Gas, natural
Natural Gas Act, 270, 311–312
  certificates, 313–315
  provisions, 301–303
  purpose, 326
  regulation, 326, 428–429
Navigable waters, 275–278
  Appalachian Electric Power case, 276
  Clyde River case, 276–277
  defined, 275–276
Necessity, 6
Netschert, Bruce C., 321
Normalization, 112–114
Nuclear plants
  capacity, 288

O

Oil
  companies, 294–295
  consumption, future, 380–382
  reserves, 378, 485 (table)
Oil-gas producers, 318–319, 321
Oil shale, 484–485
Operating expenses
  actual cost, 60–62
  adjusting customers' gas appliances, 54
  advertising, 53
  affiliates, 51–53
  charitable contributions, 55
  disallowances, 47
  increases, 50
  merchandising, 55–56
  pensions, 51
  political, 54
  rate case, 53–54
  reasonable, 48
  regulation, 44–56
  uncollectible bills, 54–55
  wage costs, 50–51
Operating ratio, 24–25
Oram, John, 161
Original costs, 60–62, 73–75, 77, 86–94
  defined, 86
  net, 90
  "write-ups," 87–88, 90

P

Paley Commission, 379–380
Peak demand, 18, 20, 143
  seasonal, 20–21
  See also, Electric utilities, Gas utilities, etc.
Pensions, 51
Petroleum
  defined, 317–318
Petroleum industry, 294–295
  See also Gas, natural, and Oil-gas producers
Petroleum products (other than gas)
  consumption, 356–357
Photosynthesis, 375
Plants
  construction, 72
  replacement costs, 83
  reproduction costs, 62, 68, 83
  size, 23
Prettyman, Judge, q., 467–468
Price control, 3
Price elasticity, 21–22
  of demand, 136
  value of service, 139
Price index number, 107
Price-level depreciation
  See Depreciation, economic
Price-setting policy (gas utilities), 334–335
Price rises, 67
Price wars, 15–16
Pricing
  Bell inter-system prices, 455–456
  differential, 135–137
  gas utilities, 181
    area pricing, 338, 340–343
    fixed-price escalations, 331–332
    indefinite pricing clauses, 331–332
  joint cost allocation, 144
  objectives, 137–138
  telephone utilities, 189–220
Pricing methods
  area pricing, 338, 340–343
  competitive market price, 339–340
  cost of service, 338–339
Pricing policies, 134–248
  Western Union, 456–458
Profit-risk relationship, 120
Profits, 26
  maximization, 115–116
  See also Rate of Return
Public interest, 2, 11, 440, 466–469
Public utilities
  antitrust problems, 463–468
  bankruptcy causes, 421
  capital raised by holding companies, 440
  characteristics, 1
  competition in capital markets, 421–422
  concept, 1, 10–11
  construction costs, 57–58
  contrasted and compared, 332–335
  cooperatives, 434
  defined, 2
  development, 439
  duties, 13
  economic characteristics, 15–27, 79
    capital investments, 23
    demand, 19–22
    investment, 22–24
    natural monopoly, 15–19

Public utilities (*Cont.*)
economic characteristics (*Cont.*)
pricing policies, 22
of supply, 16–19
efficiency, effect of holding companies, 439–440
employees, 398–440
employment, 396–399
financial regulation, 424–430
See also Security regulation
financial risks, 415
financing methods, 414–420
municipally owned, 431–432
needs, 412–415
support of state commissions, 264–265
government-owned, 432–434
labor problems, 409–411
taxation, 385–386, 388–390
growth, 413–414
importance, 13–14
intra-competition, 136
investment size, 421–422
as investments, 25
labor-management relations, 402–411
anti-strike laws, 406–409
arbitration, 403–405, 407, 410
in government-owned utilities, 409–411
mediation, 403–405, 407, 410
work stoppages, 405–406
municipal ownership, 430–432
as operating companies, 435
origin, 3
public-interest concept, 6, 403
See also Public interest
research companies, 445
rights, 12–13, 36–37
risk, 121–123
security holders, 422–424
taxation, 385–395
burden, 388–390
See also Taxation
Unionization, 400–402
Public Utility Holding Company Act, 281–282, 301, 440–446, 463
evaluation, 442–444
proposed changes, 444–446
provisions, 441–442

R

Railroad utilities, 59
rates, 5
security regulation, 425
Rate-adjustment clauses, 146
Rate base, 56–83
accrued depreciation, 102–106
actual cost, 60–62, 74
based on value, 69
Bell System, 458

Rate base (*Cont.*)
depreciation deductions, 104–106
determination, 68–69, 98
electric utilities, 81
end-result doctrine, 70
exceptions, 82–83
exclusions, 71–73
fair value, 73–78
gas utilities, 304, 309
principles, 333–335
rate-of-return, 305–306
individual-company, 79–80
policies, 65–66, 78–79, 106
RCND, 63–67
reproduction cost new, 62
valuation, 73–78
water utilities, 81
Rate cases, 266–268
See also, Adjudication, Judicial review
Rate making
accelerated depreciation, 109–114
Atlantic Seaboard formula, 184–185
capacity charges, 250–251
case study, 249–259
effect of taxes, 112–114
electric utilities, 151
exchange rates, 203–206
fair return, 66–67
formulas, 345
gas utilities, 176–177, 302, 303–311
field-price approach, 304
pipelines, 181–182, 186–188, 303–311
inventories, 84
limits of legislation, 69
normalization, 112
objectives, 135, 137–138, 147
policies
depreciation, 113
gas utilities, 181–182, 343–348
principles, 44–46, 143
rate of return, 253, 258
"rolled-in" principle, 188
telephone utilities
actual use basis, 217
Modified Phoenix Plan, 219–220
separations, 216–218
size of exchange areas, 199–200
state-wide, 200–203
toll calls, 206–215
zone rates, 186–188
See also Pricing, Rate structure, Rates, etc.
Rate of return, 45, 76, 114–134
constitutional basis, 117–118
defined, 116
Hope Natural Gas case, 116, 119
reasonable, 117–119, 120
risk, 120–123
standards, 119
summarized, 133–134

Rate of return (*Cont.*)
  water utilities, 227
  zone of reasonableness, 118
Rate regulation, 44, 83
  administration, 66
  common carriers, 280–281
  depreciation deductions, 104–106, 110–114
  economics, theoretical, 147–148
  end-result doctrine, 116–117
  gas utilities, 181–182
    interim, 341–343
  group basis, 80
  history, 28
  hydroelectric power, 273
  jurisdiction, primary, 465
  methods, 79–83
  operating-ratio method, 82–83
  principles, 79–80
  problems, 346–348
  rate-base principles, 333–335
  rate of interest, 72–73
  schedules, 145–146
    block meter rate, 155–156
    case study, 250–259
    Doherty three-part, 158
    electric power surpluses, 270–271
    flat-rate, 154–155
    gas, 178–179, 180–181
    Hopkinson demand rate, 156–157
    minimum charges, 155–156
    service charges, 155–156
    step meter-rate, 156
    straight-line meter-rate, 155
  telephone utilities, 195–196, 204–206
    toll-rate disparity, 214–215
    tolls, 208–209
  water utilities, 228–231
    Wright demand rate, 157–158
Rates, 5
  adjustments, 146
    automatic, 251–252
  appeal, 41
  changes, 50, 145–146
    automatic, 251–252
    effect of taxes, 395
    gas utilities, 179–180, 302
    statutory provisions, 265–266
    suspension period, 265–266
  compensatory, 138
  cost of service, 53–55, 251–259
  costing vs. pricing, 144–145
  costs methods, 57–65
  determination, 45
  differential pricing, 135–137
  effect of taxes, 391–395
    tax incidence, 392
  maximum and minimum, 139
  milk industry, 10
  policy, 22
Rates (*Cont.*)
  range, 138–140
  reasonable, 58–60, 303
  telephone utilities, 198–200
    rate differentials, 207–210
    service, 196–197, 199–200
  value of service, 139–140
  water utilities, 231–233
RCND, 63–67
REA, 434
Regulation, 27–35
  administration, 69
  broadcasting industry, 281
  communications
    common carriers, 278–281
  Federal, 34–35
    See also Regulatory commissions
  financial
    importance, 424–425
  fuels
    policy, 383–384
  hydroelectric power, 273–278
  jurisdiction
    FCC, 278–279
    primary, 464–466
  monopolies, stand on, 466
  need, 35
  operating expenses, 46–56
  procedures, 36–37
  public interest, 466–469
  risks, 122–123
  state, 32–34
  states rights, 16
  taxes, 392–393
    Galveston rule, 392
  See also Franchises, Judicial review, Holding companies, Security regulation
Regulatory commissions, 45, 260–263
  administration, 37
  appraisal of, 282–287
  capital structure, 130–131
  coordination, 287
  decisions, 39–40
    appeals from, 40–41
  establishment, 32–33
  legislation, 11–12
  policies, 251
    effect, 282, 284, 308–309
    gas utilities, 305, 308–311, 314–315, 326–329, 348–350
    valuation, 73–78, 251
  powers, 37–38
  pricing, 135
  profit levels, 116
  responsibilities, 134
  See also Federal commissions, State commissions
Research, 14–15, 50, *See also* Energy sources
Research companies, 445, 476

Residential heating, 361–368
Resources, *See* Energy
Revenue requirements, 44–45
Road systems, 235
Robison, H. H., 161
Rules, 37–43

S

Salaries, 50–51
Sales promotion expenses, 53
Saline conversion, 479
Saline Water Act, 479
Scott, John W., 327
Securities, 14
  effect on financing, 422
  holders, 422–424
  revenue bonds, 431–432
  risks, 422–423
  types, 414–419
  See also Holding companies
Securities and Exchange Commission, 35, 281–282
  powers, 441–444, 445
  regulation, 426–427, 429
Securities Exchange Act, 426–428
Security regulation, 424–430
  evolution, 424–425
  Federal, 426–430
  gas pipelines, 428–430
  state, 425–426
Semiconductors, 476
Separations, 216–218
Service life, 100–101
Smith, Adam, 4
Smith, Charles W., q., 105
Solar energy, 486
South Carolina Generating Company case study, 249–259
Space communication, 478
St. Lawrence Seaway, 432
State commissions, 262–268
  financing, 264–265
  jurisdiction, 261–262
  organization, 263
  problems of 1920's and 1930's, 426
  processing time, 266–268
  size, 263
  staff, 263–264
States rights, 8
Stockholders, 423–424
Stocks, 26, 123–127, 253–254, 281
  common, 125–126, 418–419
  dividends, 125–126, 418–419
    payout ratios, 26–27, 131
  flotation cost, 128
  holding companies, 435
  preferred, 418
  risk, 418
  See also Holding companies
Stone and Webster, 437
Straight-line depreciation, 109, 110
  See also Depreciation
Super-highways, 235
Supreme Court, 6–11

T

Taft-Hartley Act, 405–409
Tar sands, 484–485
Tariff, 145, 178–180
Taxation, 385–395
  burden of, 388–390, 394
    impact, 392
    incidence, 392–393
    increase with time, 387
    inequalities, 394
    shifting, 392–393
  economic effects, 394–395
  municipally-owned securities, 432
  policies, 110–114
Taxes
  deductions, 110–114
  income, 110–114
  state-imposed, 385–386
Technology, 122–123, 379
Telegraph utilities, regulation, 35, 476
Telephone utilities
  affiliates, 52–53
  American Telephone and Telegraph Co., 419–421
  See also American Telephone and Telegraph Co.
  Bell Telephone System, 419–420
    financing bond issues, 422
    toll lines, 219
  bonds, 416, 418
  cost of service, 199–200
  direct distance dialing, 477
  dual regulation, 189, 194
  electronic switching, 477
  employment, 396–400
  equipment, new and future, 476–477
  exchange service, 193, 195–206
  factors peculiar to, 199–200
  FCC jurisdiction, 278–279
  future trends, 214
  General Telephone and Electronics Corporation, 191–193
  independent companies, 190–191
  interstate-intrastate service, 215–216
  joint cost allocations, *See* Separations
  length of calls, 209–210
  license contract, 190
  Long Lines Department, 219–220
  markets, new and future, 477
  message-minute-miles, 217, 218
  Modified Phoenix Plan, 219–220
  National Switching Plan, 214
  operating expenses, 48

Telephone utilities (*Cont.*)
  plants
    costs, 218
    facilities, 219
    types, 218
  rate base, 67, 193–196
  rate making, 200–203
    business rate design, 204–205
    exchange rates, 203–206
    residence rates, 205–206
    schedule rate design, 195–196
  rates
    actual use basis, 216–217
    exchange areas, 197–198
    exchange service, 196–198
    value of service, 140
    wage factors, 199–200
  regulation, 35, 194–195
    ICC, 278–280
    state, 450
  revenue, 195, 214
  Rural Electrification Act, 191, 434
  rural service, 191
  separations, 216–218
  Separations Manual, 217–218
  service
    areas, 197–200
    classifications, 193, 196–197
    delays, 208
  station defined, 217–218
  structure, 189–191
  toll rates, 206–215
    centers, 197
    distance, 206–207
    interstate-intrastate disparity, 210–215
    person calls, 207–208
    station calls, 207–208
  toll service, 193–194
  unionization, 402
  value of service, 195, 202
  See also American Telephone and Telegraph Company, Bell System
Television stations, 284
Telstar I, 478
Tennessee Valley Authority
  financing, 433–434
  taxation, 389, 391, 394
Thermal energy, 486
Thorium, 483
Tidal energy, 486
Transistors, 14, 476
Transit, *See* Urban transit utilities
Trebing, Harry M., 282–283
Trunkline Gas Company, 71

U

Uncertainty, 121
Unions, 400–402
Unit cost, 17
Uranium, 483
Urban transit utilities, 82–83, 233–248
  advantages, 247
  analysis, 247–248
  Cleveland Transit System, 246–247
  competition from automobiles, 241–242
  decline, 237–238, 241, 245
  defined, 234
  economic characteristics, 239–242
  fares, 242–245
  Federal assistance, 247–248
  financial crises, 236–237
  history, 234–239
  investment costs, 239–240
  loans, 248
  operating ratio, 239
  ownership, 245–246
  passes, 243
  patronage, 234
  problems, 234–237
  peak loads, 240–241, 242
  rate-making, 80
    See also Rate making, Rates
  shrinkage factor, 241
  taxes, 245–246
  transfers, 244
  travel time, 241–242
USITA, 461–462

V

Vail, Theodore N., 447–450
  policies, 449
Valuation, 56–65, 83–94
  accounting, 89–90, 92–93
  acquisition adjustments, 92–93
  appraisal, 83–86
  cost reclassification, 89
  depreciation, 94–114
  original cost, 87–88
    defined, 86
    net, 90
  reclassification, 90–91
  uniform basis, 89
  See also Rate Base
Value of service, 142–145
Vinson, Judge, q., 10–11

W

Water gas, 436
Water rates, variation, 229
Water supply, 220–225
  sources, 221
  treatment, 221, 229
Water supply systems, 220–223
  air-conditioning use, 223–231
  background, 220

Water supply systems (*Cont.*)
block meter rates, 228–230
costs, 222, 225, 227
analysis, 232–233
methods, 231–233
economic characteristics, 222–227
financing, 223–224, 228
fire-protection service, 224–226, 230–231, 233
function, 233
joint-supply, 224–225
fund diversion, 226–227
investments, 222, 225
joint-capacity cost allocation, 232–233
ownership, 221–222, 223–224, 226–228
peak demand, 223
rates, 231–233
determination, 229–231
of return, 227
regulation, 222
revenue requirements, 227–228
Water supply systems (*Cont.*)
saline conversion, 479
service types, 228–229
tax status, 226
taxation, 389
technological advances, 478–479
Watkins, G. P., q., 143, 144
Western Electric Company, 189
function, 455
regulation, future, 459
service costs, 453–454
size, 455
Standard Supply Contract, 455–456
Western Union
accounting practices, 458
agreement with Bell, 447
pricing policies, 456–457
Willis-Graham Act, 280, 460
Working capital, *See* Capital
Wright, Arthur, 160